Tolkien's Faith

Tolkien's Faith

A Spiritual Biography

HOLLY ORDWAY

WORD on FIRE
ACADEMIC

Published by Word on Fire Academic, an imprint of
Word on Fire, Elk Grove Village, IL 60007

Printed in the United States of America

Cover design, typesetting, and interior art direction by Rozann Lee and Cassie Bielak.

Cover, © Pamela Chandler / The Tolkien Society / ArenaPAL; Fig. 1 and 2, public domain; Fig. 3, © Chronicle / Alamy Stock Photo; Fig. 4a, © David Tabb; Fig. 4b, © Ryszard Derdziński; Fig. 5, © Birmingham Archdiocesan Archives; Fig. 6, public domain; Fig. 7, GentryGraves, Creative Commons Attribution-Share Alike 4.0 International; Fig. 8 and 9, Used by permission of the Fathers of the Birmingham Oratory; Fig. 10, © Fr. James Bradley; Fig. 11, © John Aron; Fig. 12, © Fr. James Bradley; Fig. 13, 14, and 15, public domain; Fig. 16 and 17, published with permission of the Rector and Scholars of Exeter College, Oxford; Fig. 18, © Oxfordshire History Centre; Fig. 19, © Olga Watkin; Fig. 20, © Greg Hartman / The Catholic Telegraph; Fig. 21, © St. Mary Immaculate, Warwick; Fig. 22, public domain; Fig. 23, © Staffordshire Arts & Museum Service; Fig. 24 and 25, public domain; Fig. 26, Wernervc, CCAttribution-Share Alike 3.0 Unported; Fig. 27, public domain; Fig. 28, © Olga Watkin; Fig. 29, public domain; Fig. 30, © Steven Beebe; Fig. 31, Used by permission of The Warden and Fellows of Merton College Oxford; Fig. 32 and 33, public domain; Fig. 34, © *The Advocate*, Newspaper for the Catholic Archdiocese of Melbourne 1868–1990; Fig. 35, © Amen House; Fig. 36a, © National Portrait Gallery, London; Fig. 36b. Catalogue number UNIVERSITY 591/1/2/33 Arts Class, 1911-1915 in the University of Aberdeen Museums and Special Collections, licenced under CC By 4.0; Fig. 36c, Reproduced by permission of the President and Fellows of Magdalen College Oxford; Fig. 37, © Fathers of the Oxford Oratory; Fig. 38, © Michael Ward; Fig. 39, © Our Lady of Abingdon; Fig. 40, © Haywood Magee / Picture Post; Fig. 41, © Brandon Vogt; Fig. 42, © The Tolkien Estate Limited 1937. The Bodleian Libraries, University of Oxford, MS. Tolkien Drawings 26; Fig. 43, © Michael Ward; Fig. 44, © Longmans, Green; Fig. 45, © Logos International; Fig. 46, 47, 48, and 49, public domain; Fig. 50, Used by permission of the Marion E. Wade Center, Wheaton College, Wheaton, IL; Fig. 51, © The English Dominican Province; Fig. 52, Used by permission of the Marion E. Wade Center, Wheaton College, Wheaton, IL; Fig. 53, © National Portrait Gallery, London; Fig. 54, © *The Dublin Review*; Fig. 55, Used by permission of The Warden and Fellows of Merton College Oxford; Fig. 56, © 2004 J.R.R. Tolkien. Reprinted by permission of HarperCollins Publishers Ltd.; Fig. 57, Sailko, CC 3.0; Fig. 58, public domain; Fig. 59, Sailko, CC 3.0; Fig. 60, public domain; Fig. 61, © Doubleday; Fig. 62, Sheed and Ward; Fig. 63, Reproduced with permission of The Principal and Chapter of Pusey House; Fig. 64, © Church of Corpus Christi, Headington; Fig. 65, public domain; Fig. 66, author; Fig. 67, © Katarzyna Mroczkowska-Brand; Fig. 68, unknown; Fig. 69, Used by permission of the Marion E. Wade Center, Wheaton College, Wheaton, IL; Fig. 70, © Pamela Chandler / ArenaPal; Fig. 71, © Jason Lepojärvi; Fig. 72, © The Tolkien Trust 1977. The Bodleian Libraries, University of Oxford, MS. Tolkien photogr. 8, fol. 121; final image, © Pamela Chandler / The Tolkien Society / ArenaPAL.

First printing, September 2023.

ISBN: 978-1-68578-991-6

Library of Congress Control Number: 2022943442

To the Fathers and Brothers
of the Birmingham Oratory
and the Oxford Oratory

ACKNOWLEDGMENTS

In 2021 when I completed my book *Tolkien's Modern Reading*, I was wondering what I should write about next. It was then that my friend and colleague Michael Ward suggested that I consider writing a biography centered on Tolkien's faith and that I time it to coincide with the fiftieth anniversary of his death in 2023. Because I was already deeply interested in Tolkien's spirituality, the idea of writing such a book needed no urging. However, since the project required a huge amount of work in relatively little time, it did need encouraging, and without Michael's continual encouragement I would certainly not have completed it. I am grateful for that, for his feedback on drafts of the book, and lastly—and most notably—for his pointing out the hidden initial in Tolkien's monogram.

Many others have also helped me in the process of preparing *Tolkien's Faith* for publication. I wish to thank my colleagues at Word on Fire, particularly Brandon Vogt, Senior Publishing Director, who believed in the project from the beginning; Jason Paone, Editor of Word on Fire Academic; Rozann Lee and Cassie Bielak for the beautiful interior design and cover; Edyta McNichol for assisting in the compilation of the Photo Gallery; and the entire editorial team, including David Augustine, Daniel Seseske, Carolyn Paluch, and Madeleine Cook.

I should like to thank Bradley Birzer and the anonymous peer reviewers for their helpful comments; Peggy Haslar, Megan Prahl, and Miriam Rutegård for providing feedback on some early draft chapters; and Colton Duncan and Michael Hoggatt for their valuable work as research assistants on the Glossary.

I warmly thank the Tolkien Estate for permission to reproduce Tolkien's painting *The Hill: Hobbiton-across-the Water*, as well as the spine of *The Lord of the Rings* and the last photograph taken of him, in the Botanic Gardens, Oxford. I am grateful to Catherine McIlwaine, Tolkien Archivist at the Bodleian Library, for assisting with these images. I also extend my thanks to the Tolkien Society, ArenaPAL, and the estate of Pamela Chandler for permission to use the photograph of Tolkien reproduced on the front cover.

My research has benefited hugely from the assistance of archivists and librarians both in Britain and America. I thank first those in the United Kingdom. At the Birmingham Oratory, I received invaluable assistance from Daniel Joyce, Br. Zachariah Heritage, and Br. Edmund Mirassou; and at the Oxford Oratory, from Fr. Dominic Jacob. Elsewhere in Oxford, I have been greatly helped by Robin Darwall-Smith (University College and Jesus College); Amy Ebrey (The Queen's College); Emily Jennings (Magdalen College); Victoria Northridge (Exeter College); Julian Reid and Julia Walworth (Merton College); the staff of the Weston Library Special Collections; the Bodleian Library Scan and Deliver team; Jessica Woodward (Pusey House); Helen Drury and the staff of the Oxfordshire History Centre; and the Sisters of the Work at Newman's College, Littlemore. Beyond Oxford, I received help from Adam C. Green at Trinity College, Cambridge; Jan Smith and James Costin at the University of Aberdeen; and Caroline Lezny at the University of Notre Dame London Global Gateway. In the United States, I have gratefully received assistance from Laura Schmidt of the Marion E. Wade Center at Wheaton College, Illinois; William Fliss of Marquette University Archives and Special Collections; and Melanie Zebrowski at the University of Dayton.

Numerous other people assisted in various ways, and so I extend my thanks to David Bates, Marie Bates, Steven Beebe, Stephen Bullivant, Joel Clarkson, Joshua Copeland, Austin Freeman, Joe Grabowski, Susan Griffith, Don King, Jennifer Kulzer, Jason Lepojärvi, Alexandra Lloyd, John Martin, Marjorie Mead, Robert Mixa, Giuseppe Pezzini, Hal Poe, Giuseppe Scattolini, Zak Schmoll, Haley Stewart, Olga Watkin, and Luke Webster.

The process of writing *Tolkien's Faith* was enhanced by opportunities to give lectures from the work-in-progress, including at the exhibition *J.R.R. Tolkien: The Art of the Manuscript* at Marquette University; the Catholic University of America; Houston Christian University; the University of Tennessee at Chattanooga; Grandpont House, Oxford; and the Oxford University C.S. Lewis Society.

I wish to recognize the kindness and generosity of my scholarly colleagues. I particularly thank John Garth, who permitted me to make use of his unpublished research on the chaplains of the Great War. Peter Gilliver shared material from his archival newspaper research; Michaël Devaux provided extracts of his scholarship that were unpublished in English; Ryszard Derdziński assisted me in tracking down Polish resources; and Sebastiano Tassarini aided with Italian materials.

A biographer's research necessarily touches upon a wide range of topics. I am grateful for specialist advice from Fr. James Bradley on pre-1917 canon law; Fr. Daniel Sedlacek on the preconciliar liturgy of the Mass; Paul Shrimpton on John Henry Newman; and Fr. Hugh Somerville Knapman on the postconciliar development of the liturgy of the Mass in England. Fr. John Saward, pastor of St. Gregory and St. Augustine, Oxford, kindly shared his knowledge about St. Gregory's during Tolkien's time as a parishioner.

The late Priscilla Tolkien was also a member of St. Greg's, where I had the pleasure of meeting her at Mass on various occasions. I am grateful for her willingness to confirm that her father had indeed taken the name 'Philip' after St. Philip Neri, founder of the Congregation of the Oratory.

As I recount in the pages that follow, it was a priest of the Birmingham Oratory, Fr. Francis Morgan, who became Tolkien's guardian and beloved "second father," supporting him in his vocation as a scholar at Oxford. Furthermore, the spirituality of St. Philip Neri was deeply formative for Tolkien, fostering a sense of beauty, giving him scope to develop his intellect, and providing a framework for a spiritual and literary life that encompassed both joy and sorrow. Tolkien owed much to the Oratorians, and, as a result, all those who delight in Tolkien's imaginative creations owe something to them too, indirectly. In partial honor of my own share in that debt, I dedicate *Tolkien's Faith: A Spiritual Biography* to the Fathers and Brothers of the Birmingham Oratory and the Oxford Oratory.

Holly Ordway
La Crosse, Wisconsin
Feast Day of St. John Henry Newman

CONTENTS

Beginning: 1892–1916

Middle: 1916–1952

End: 1952–1973

A Photo Gallery appears after page 228

BEGINNING: 1892–1916

1

"I am in any case myself a Christian"

In 1953, while *The Lord of the Rings* was being prepared for publication, Tolkien wrote:

> *The Lord of the Rings* is of course a fundamentally religious and Catholic work; unconsciously so at first, but consciously in the revision. That is why I have not put in, or have cut out, practically all references to anything like 'religion,' to cults or practices, in the imaginary world. For the religious element is absorbed into the story and the symbolism. However that is very clumsily put, and sounds more self-important than I feel. For as a matter of fact, I have consciously planned very little; and should chiefly be grateful for having been brought up (since I was eight) in a Faith that has nourished me and taught me all the little that I know.[1]

The "of course" is very interesting: *of course* his epic work is religious and Catholic. It seems natural and obvious to Tolkien that it should be so. *The Lord of the Rings*, he says, is not superficially religious and Catholic but *fundamentally* so—at its roots, in its essence. This religious and Catholic element, however, "is absorbed into the story and symbolism," woven into the warp and woof of the text, implicit, indirect. It was not "consciously planned"; that is to say, *The Lord of the Rings* is not an allegory of the Gospels or a tale didactically expressing Christianity. Rather, the whole world of Middle-earth and everything in it is infused with, rooted in, its author's Christian vision of reality. And he says that this rootedness, this unplanned but essential quality to his work, comes about because he has been raised and nourished in the Catholic faith.

Commenting elsewhere on the inspirations for *The Lord of the Rings*, Tolkien noted that "On a lower plane: my linguistic interest is the most powerful force."

What, then, was on a higher plane? He explains, "if I may say so, with humility, the Christian religion (which I profess) is far the most powerful ultimate source."[2]

Tolkien's faith was lifelong and deep. He was a committed Christian. To put a complex thing very simply, his faith was in Jesus Christ.* He was not shy about this, frankly declaring his religious identity in various letters and interviews: "I am a Christian, and indeed a Roman Catholic"; "I am in any case myself a Christian"; "I am a Christian (which can be deduced from my stories)."[3]

Which can be deduced from my stories. This statement is highly intriguing. Tolkien was always emphatic that his writings could not be read as simple allegories. As he remarked rather tartly, *The Lord of the Rings* "is not 'about' anything but itself. Certainly it has *no* allegorical intentions, general, particular, or topical, moral, religious, or political." In this story, he said, "I neither preach nor teach."[4] Furthermore, his tales of Middle-earth are loved by millions of readers who are not Christian and may have little or no awareness of Tolkien's own religious identity. If his faith can be "deduced" from his stories, the deduction is evidently not one that is easily arrived at.

What are we to make of this? How are we to understand the relationship between his faith and his fiction? This book attempts to address that question biographically. In other words, this book focuses on Tolkien's life—his life of faith—in order to provide context for his works. Once we have a secure grasp of his spiritual identity, we will be able to gain a richer, deeper, more comprehensive and nuanced understanding of his writings—and their fundamental but implicit religious dimension.

A life of faith

There has been, to date, no full biographical treatment that presents Tolkien's faith in detail.[5] As a result, it has been all too easy simply to overlook the significance of

---

* The Christian religion considered in its total breadth and depth—historically, scripturally, doctrinally, philosophically, liturgically, etc.—is at least as complex as mathematics (a child can learn basic addition, but Fermat's Last Theorem took 358 years to solve!). To try to summarize it in a single sentence is extremely difficult. However, focusing on Jesus Christ directs attention to its personal and historical character and, by implication, introduces the all-important fact of God's Trinitarian nature, for *Christ* means 'anointed one' (*Messiah* in Hebrew), and Jesus can only be anointed if there is someone to do the anointing (namely, God the Father) and 'ointment' with which to be anointed (namely, God the Holy Spirit). For more on this, see the accounts of Jesus's baptism in the New Testament (e.g., Matthew 3:13–17).

his religious life, to allow unexamined historical or cultural assumptions to color our view of it, or to view it as a purely private expression of his personality.

Without even realizing it, we can end up taking Tolkien as a sort of cardboard Catholic, viewing his faith as a generic, static background to the supposedly more interesting and dynamic aspects of his life. Alternatively, we can regard him as a plaster saint to be put on a pedestal, someone whose religious life was ideal and equable. But his faith was not made of cardboard or plaster; it was neither boring nor easy.

As we look back on his completed life, it may seem inevitable or obvious that he could declare to an interviewer, "I'm a Roman Catholic. Devout Roman Catholic,"[6] but in fact Tolkien's faith was hard-won. His spiritual biography was one of drama and difficulty. In what follows, we will see that, although Tolkien was introduced to the Catholic faith by his beloved mother, Mabel, he also had many reasons to relinquish it and return to the Anglican church in which he had been baptized. As a young man, his experience of thwarted love could have embittered him against the Catholic priest who was his guardian. He fought on the front lines of the Great War, a conflagration in which most of his close friends were killed, and which caused some of the finest writers of his generation to abandon their Christian faith entirely. In a time when the Church of England's status as the Establishment religion meant a great deal and Catholics were a socially disadvantaged minority, it would have made his career, his social life, and even his marriage smoother if he had muted his Catholicism or exchanged it for something more conventional. The experience of a *second* World War, this time with his own sons serving in the armed forces, could have caused him finally to abandon his faith altogether. The turmoil caused by Vatican II, and the loss of the Latin liturgy of the Mass that he loved so much, could have caused him to reject the authority of the Church or withdraw from engagement in Catholic life.

But he did none of these things: his convictions grew stronger and deeper even as he lived through fresh opportunities to set them aside. And, as we will see, this process of spiritual growth wasn't easy. He went through a barren patch as an undergraduate and later a years-long stretch when, by his own account, he "almost ceased to practise" his religion. A full treatment of his faith uncovers a life marked by determination and decision.

This full treatment is important because Tolkien's spirituality was central to his identity, as his family and friends constantly attest. His daughter, Priscilla, remembers him as "a devout Christian" with "a strong religious faith"; "he cared deeply about his religious faith."[7] His son John says that his faith "pervaded all his thinking and beliefs and everything else. . . . he was very much, always a Christian."[8] His nephew Julian recalls his uncle's "strong faith" and "strong Christian principles."[9] His grandchildren concur: Simon describes him as "a devout Roman Catholic"; Joanna refers to "his profound belief in God"; Michael George notes that "my grandfather had a deep and nourishing faith."[10]

His friend Robert Havard described "the depth of feeling behind his Roman Catholic religious convictions."[11] The chaplain who attended Tolkien during a hospital stay late in his life stated that "he was a committed Christian and a committed Catholic, and his faith meant everything to him. His faith came from the core of his being."[12] Fr. Martin D'Arcy, one of the most notable English Jesuits of the twentieth century and an Oxford colleague, called Tolkien "a very good Catholic."[13]

Clearly, then, Tolkien's faith was an essential part of his life and how he viewed the world: it shaped what he valued, the choices he made, and how he related with other people. Even if it were for that reason alone, an account of his religious commitments and practices is of interest to readers of his stories, or at least to those readers who want to gain a fuller picture of the man who could create such powerful and memorable works. It mattered to him, and that is a good reason for it to matter to us.

"Impossible to disentangle"

But it also matters if we wish to have a deeper understanding of Tolkien's creative output. Tolkien explained that there is "a scale of significance" in the types of facts that are relevant to understanding a writer's work. In his own case, these facts include—at the bottom of the scale—his preference for certain languages over others. Other facts, he says, "however drily expressed, are really significant," such as his rural childhood before the age of the machine. But then he goes on to say, "more important, I am a Christian."[14] We know that his linguistic interests and his early life in a Worcestershire village were indeed imaginatively formative: to note one influence is not to deny another. But by Tolkien's own reckoning, his faith was *more important* for understanding his writings than either of these.

The world of Middle-earth is not a religious allegory. But that is not to say it is unconnected to the Christian religion that Tolkien actually believed in. In fact, he could get a bit testy when interviewers missed this point. "Of course God is in *The Lord of the Rings*. The period was pre-Christian, but it was a monotheistic world." The interviewer asked, "Monotheistic? Then who was the One God of Middle-earth?" Tolkien, taken aback, replied: "*The* one, of course! The book is about the world that God created—the actual world of this planet."[15]

Tolkien once described *The Lord of the Rings* as "an exemplary legend. But this sounds dreadfully priggish when said."[16] The reason that he feared it sounded priggish (overly moralistic) was that "exemplary" literally means setting a good example for others to follow. He elaborates on this point elsewhere, saying that one of his aims in writing *The Lord of the Rings* was "the elucidation of truth, and the encouragement of good morals in this real world, by the ancient device of exemplifying them in unfamiliar embodiments, that may tend to 'bring them home.'"[17] It is important to do so because unless one's understanding of "truth" and "morals" is integrated into day-to-day life, it remains abstract and irrelevant. This is a point that Tolkien's friend C.S. Lewis brought out in his book *Letters to Malcolm: Chiefly on Prayer*,* where he writes that "there is danger in the very concept of religion":

> It carries the suggestion that [religion] is one more department of life, an extra department added to the economic, the social, the intellectual, the recreational, and all the rest. But that whose claims are infinite can have no standing as a department. Either it is an illusion or else our whole life falls under it. We have no non-religious activities; only religious and irreligious.[18]

Tolkien did not compartmentalize his faith. A repeated theme in the recollections of those who knew him is how integral his faith was with his whole person; it manifested itself in a natural manner and was not put forward awkwardly or ostentatiously. His friend Havard noted that his convictions were "apparent . . . but never paraded."[19]

* Tolkien had strong objections to parts of *Letters to Malcolm* (see chapter 34), but undoubtedly he would have endorsed what Lewis says here about the all-encompassing nature of religion.

The hospital chaplain remarked, "he didn't lay it on the counter for you and say, 'that's it, boys.' But you knew that all the glory that he had meant nothing except his faith."[20] Clyde Kilby, who assisted him with his work on the *Silmarillion*, could recall "not a single visit I made to Tolkien's home in which the conversation did not at some point fall easily into a discussion of religion, or rather Christianity. He told me that he had many times been given a story as an answer to prayer." Kilby added that he had been struck by the naturalness of Tolkien's faith: "he would just fling out these things: talking on the phone with a priest friend, I heard him say at the end of a conversation, 'Well, may the Lord bless you' in the most sincere feeling tone."[21]

Tolkien admitted (as we will see) that at times he did not live his faith as he felt he ought to, but it was never just one activity out of many in his very busy life. To understand this is to grasp a key insight into Tolkien's personality and his creative process.

He once remarked that he found it "impossible to disentangle" faith and art.[22] In his important essay "On Fairy-stories," he declared that the writing of fantasy (and by extension, all literary creation) is "a natural human activity . . . a human right." This conviction was based on his belief that human beings have been made in the image and likeness of God, and since God is creative, we would be less than human if we were not to express that side of our nature: as Tolkien put it, "we make in our measure and in our derivative mode, because we are made: and not only made, but made in the image and likeness of a Maker."[23] As Clyde Kilby recalled, "He believed that creativity itself is a gift of God."[24]

Art will necessarily reflect something of the artist's most deeply held beliefs, whatever they may be, at least at some level, however subtle or implicit. For Tolkien, faith was not merely a set of superficial opinions but something integral to his real character—and to his own self-understanding as an author.

So, it follows that if we are to understand and appreciate Tolkien's writings to the fullest degree, we need to come to an understanding of what he himself identified as central to his identity: his faith, which could not be disentangled from his art.

As we do this, we should keep in mind that the word 'faith' can be understood in several ways, all of which are relevant to our project. As '*the* faith' it can refer to the doctrines and teachings handed down by the Apostles to the present day, which Catholics believe to be comprehensively conveyed and authoritatively interpreted by the Church that Jesus established. In order to understand Tolkien's spirituality, we need to know what the content of that faith was, especially in areas that were important to him as an individual or distinct from the wider cultural and religious context in which he lived. 'Faith' can also refer to personal trust in Jesus Christ and to the action of the will in assenting to, and attempting to follow, the teachings of Christ and his Church; in this sense, we can speak of 'Tolkien's faith' as his personal engagement with 'the faith' as he understood it. And as a Christian, Tolkien would also have considered 'faith' to be a gift from God, part of the "immeasurable riches of his grace in kindness toward us in Christ Jesus. For by grace you have been saved through faith; and this is not your own doing, it is the gift of God" (Ephesians 2:7–8). Being aware of the multilayered texture of 'faith' will help us appreciate the nuances of Tolkien's Christianity.

A twentieth-century English Catholic

How, then, are we to go about understanding his faith in all its complexities?

First, we must do so by making full use of chronology.* Tolkien's religious life was not static; he would himself have seen it as a constant process of growth and maturation, developing from infancy "to mature manhood, to the measure of the stature of the fulness of Christ; so that we may no longer be children," in the words of the Apostle Paul (Ephesians 4:13–14). The faith that he expressed as a mature man had its beginnings in his childhood, but was challenged, formed, and deepened throughout his life—which is why a narrative treatment is appropriate.

Second, we must pay close attention to his personal context. He was a Christian in an increasingly secular world. More specifically, he was a Catholic in a society that was still, at least residually, Anglican. He lived in a period when significant changes occurred in the way the Catholic Church understood and expressed itself; most of his life came before the Second Vatican Council, but he saw the conciliar years and had views on the changes that the council brought about. Furthermore,

* Although I will be recounting Tolkien's life of faith chronologically, I have felt free to refer ahead, as appropriate, to relevant parts of his literary output as a way of showing the relevance of his faith to his fiction. Furthermore, some chapters are thematically focused, to enable a fuller understanding of particular aspects of his spirituality, and these often cover a wider range of his life before shifting back into a chronological sequence. The Timeline of Tolkien's Life in Appendix A provides a strictly sequential outline for reference.

he was a Catholic Englishman and therefore part of a faith community that had undergone persecution, marginalization, and restrictions on civil rights, some of which lasted into Tolkien's adulthood. Lastly, his perspective was greatly shaped by the close connection he had throughout his life to the Congregation of the Oratory of St. Philip Neri.

By examining Tolkien's experience of his faith in the time and place and circumstances in which he found himself, we will come to a better understanding of him as a man—and therefore to a deeper appreciation of his writings.

Here I will put my cards on the table. I am, myself, a Christian and a Catholic; I believe the same things that Tolkien believed, albeit from the vantage point of a twenty-first-century American woman. I have been thinking seriously and writing about Tolkien for thirty-odd years: he was of interest to me as an agnostic undergraduate; his work provided the focus of my dissertation as an atheist graduate student; and, later, as a Protestant Christian working at a secular college, I taught his writings for the better part of a decade. In those years, I knew the bare fact that he was a Christian but nothing of the depth and texture of his spirituality, what his faith meant to him, or how it influenced his life and shaped his writings. This book is one I would have found useful at that time.

I have had the tremendous privilege of spending a great deal of time in England over the last fifteen years and, as a Catholic, regularly worshiping in many of the same places that Tolkien did. At the church of St. Gregory and St. Augustine, Oxford, I have frequently sat in the pew that he usually occupied and have had the privilege of speaking there with his daughter, Priscilla, who attended that church herself until her death in 2022. My own faith has been significantly shaped by English Catholicism and indeed by Oratorian spirituality, which has allowed me to gain insights into Tolkien's experiences that would otherwise have been elusive.

But this book is not an attempt to express my own particular perspective. A degree of subjectivity is inescapable, of course, but I will attempt to portray Tolkien's faith with its own colors, contours, and emphases as accurately and objectively as I can. I endeavor to serve as a guide, to help the reader see into Tolkien's experiences as an English Catholic Christian of the twentieth century, grounded in two important locations, Birmingham and Oxford.

Here I wish also to note my choice of subtitle: *A Spiritual Biography.*

This book is a *spiritual* biography; it focuses, necessarily, on his faith. Other events come into my account only insofar as they are relevant to the consideration of his religious life. The relative lack of detail given to matters such as his teaching, his scholarship, and his linguistic work is not a reflection of their importance but simply a necessary feature of this study's parameters. A concise timeline of his life is included to help readers keep the general contours of his life and work in view (see Appendix A).

It is also a spiritual *biography*: it does not include an extended treatment or analysis of his writings, not even from a spiritual point of view. As interesting and valuable as that would be, it is beyond the purview of this book. I have tried to tie my (relatively brief) discussion of the religious aspects of his writings to the developing story of his life, not to make literary-critical comments an end in themselves. There are already many other studies available in that area.[25]

It is also, specifically, a spiritual biography of *Tolkien*. I mention his wife and children where it is necessary for an understanding of Tolkien's life of faith, but this book does not consider their own faith commitments or indeed their lives apart from their intersection with the subject of our study.

I have drawn on a wide variety of sources in my research (which interested readers can trace in the endnotes and bibliography), aiming to get as close to Tolkien as possible. The most important sources are of course his own words in his published works, private correspondence, interviews, and in the recollections of those who knew him best.* I have given particular attention to what he says in his letters, which are a rich source of information about, and insight into, his spiritual life. In considering his personal correspondence, I have endeavored always to keep in mind chronology and context: when he was writing, to whom, and for what purpose.

His daughter, Priscilla, was of the opinion that Tolkien's letters are of great interest because they offer "an authentic means of understanding" an author; indeed, "his letters are his authentic, conscious voice." Here, we are presented with both an opportunity and a challenge as readers seeking to understand the man and his faith. As Priscilla puts it, "I wonder if fiction is more generally appreciated because it can become so easily susceptible to the reader's own projections, fantasies and

* Tolkien's willingness to speak of his faith in public interviews and in letters to a variety of correspondents shows his own understanding of the Catholic faith as a commitment that is personal but not private, individual yet necessarily involving a responsibility to the wider community.

preoccupations, whereas when the writer speaks to you directly in his own voice, it is harder to ignore what he is actually saying, and this you may not like."[26] If we are to gain a fuller picture of Tolkien's life, his personality, and ultimately his creative art, we must attend to what his faith meant *to him*: not what it means to us (whether negatively or positively), or what we wish or assume it meant to him.

In studying a figure this well-known and well-loved, we can easily be tripped up by assumptions or misunderstandings that we do not even realize we have, and for that reason, I have tried to explain anything that might not be clear. I beg the patience of those who find that I occasionally explain what seems self-evident. For those who, on the other hand, find that I use too many unfamiliar terms, I have provided a glossary at the end, which I hope will be of assistance. Additionally, in Appendix B, the interested reader will find a number of prayers and liturgical excerpts that we know to have been part of Tolkien's devotional life, to give a full flavor of the kind of spiritual exercises that he engaged in.

As we explore his spiritual life, we must be careful to attend to his experiences in their chronological, cultural, social, and ecclesiological context as much as possible, not abstracting them out and creating an ahistorical or static account. It is easy to picture Tolkien dressed in tweed and smoking a pipe, bent over a medieval manuscript, enjoying a pint of beer at The Eagle & Child with C.S. Lewis, or even in his army uniform in the trenches of the Somme. Our mental image gallery, to be more complete, must include tableaux such as Tolkien receiving Communion, reading the Bible, kneeling in his pew at Mass, praying with rosary beads in hand while on air-raid duty, or standing in line for the confessional. (The Photo Gallery may assist in this endeavor.) That these images may be less familiar to us does not mean they were less important for him: and so, this book is an attempt to treat Tolkien's faith on its own terms, neither critiquing it nor recommending it.

He was not a saint, if by that we mean an idealized figure who led a supposedly perfect life. As Priscilla remarked, "I don't think you get that picture of my father even from the published letters. You certainly don't if you read a great many of the letters!"[27] A plaster saint? No. A cardboard Christian? No. A complex, fascinating, flawed, devout, funny, and brilliant man—yes, I think so. Read on and decide for yourself what to make of his life and work when they are seen within the all-encompassing context of his faith.

2

Two Worlds

When Tolkien was born in 1892, Queen Victoria was on the throne and Britannia ruled the waves with the world's mightiest naval and merchant fleet. The British dominated territories covering a quarter of the globe, so it was possible quite literally to say that this was an empire upon which the sun never set.

The Church of England, too, had an international reach. Wherever Englishmen went in the Empire, they could be sure to find an Anglican church in which to worship, with the same Book of Common Prayer—albeit not necessarily with the same understanding of the faith they were practicing. Within Anglicanism, many clergy taught a 'low-church' Evangelical faith and considered themselves as firmly Protestant; others viewed themselves as 'Catholic but reformed,' that is, part of the universal 'catholic' body of believers, of which 'Roman' Catholics were another part, in need of reform; and still others, the 'high-church' party, called themselves 'Anglo-Catholics' and considered themselves a branch of the Catholic Church, equal to the Roman and Eastern Orthodox branches. But whatever the disagreements about the propriety of candles on the altar, whether one ought to go to confession, or how to interpret the Bible, Anglicans had one thing in common: their church was established by law as the official state church, of which the monarch was the Supreme Governor, and it was the socially recognized and culturally endorsed religion of the nation and the Empire.

Its reach extended even to South Africa, where the protagonist of our story first drew breath. In the hot summer month of January 1892, a new-born infant, little John Ronald Reuel, the first child of Arthur and Mabel Tolkien, was baptized at the Anglican Cathedral of St. Andrew and St. Michael in Bloemfontein.[1] (See figures 1–4.) Built only twenty-six years earlier, the impressive edifice was a visible sign of Britain's imperial sway and of Anglican self-confidence.

His father, Arthur, was a branch manager for the Bank of South Africa. As was not uncommon in those days, Arthur had elected to work abroad so as to have better prospects for advancement and financial security than were available at home in England. Mabel Suffield, his fiancée from Birmingham in the English Midlands, had joined him in 1891; they were married at the Anglican Cathedral of St. George in Cape Town and took up residence in Bloemfontein, the capital of the Orange Free State.[2]

Both Arthur and Mabel came from Nonconformist backgrounds, meaning that the Tolkien and Suffield families held a strongly Protestant understanding of Christianity that dissented from doctrines about ordained clergy, episcopal authority, and other features of the Anglican establishment. Most of the Tolkiens were Baptists—that is to say, they rejected the practice of infant baptism, holding instead to adult baptism as the symbolic affirmation of a Christian faith already adopted consciously and individually. Mabel's family, the Suffields, were Methodists, but her father, John, had embraced Unitarianism,[3] which affirmed the existence of one God but denied the Trinity of divine Persons (Father, Son, and Holy Spirit).

Being part of the Anglican Church certainly made professional advancement and social interactions easier for Arthur and Mabel in the small English expatriate society of South Africa, but it evidently also had a grounding in the genuine religious convictions of the young couple. Arthur Tolkien served as treasurer for the Diocese of Bloemfontein, and the bishop intended for him to become a member of the Society for the Propagation of the Gospel,[4] an Anglican missionary society. And soon after their marriage, Mabel gave an indication of the strength of her own Christian faith, getting baptized as an Anglican at the cathedral in Bloemfontein, with Arthur as one of the witnesses.[5] Presumably, her father's Unitarianism meant that she had never received baptism in the Triune Name.*

We can get a sense of Arthur and Mabel's spirituality in the choice of G. Edward Jelf as godfather to their new baby. Jelf taught at St. Andrew's College, a diocesan boys' school in Bloemfontein. He provided a solid connection to the Church of England and to one particular strand within it.[6] Jelf's own father was Canon G.E.

---

* Mabel's decision to be baptized as an adult indicates a conscious rejection of Unitarianism and affirmation of Trinitarian theology, as expressed in Christ's command to his disciples, "Go therefore and make disciples of all nations, baptizing them in the name of the Father and of the Son and of the Holy Spirit" (Matthew 28:19).

Jelf, a well-known author of sermons and devotional works and a friend of the great Edward Bouverie Pusey, one of the key members of 'the Oxford Movement,'[7] a Catholicizing movement within Anglicanism that featured among its other leading lights John Keble and John Henry Newman. (Newman's mighty name will meet us many times in the story that is to follow.) By selecting the younger Jelf as godfather to their firstborn child, Arthur and Mabel were providing John Ronald with a spiritual pedigree in the Church of England that had a very definite stripe. In addition to Jelf, the baby received a second godfather in the form of his uncle Tom Hadley, Arthur's brother-in-law, and a godmother in the shape of Edith Mary ('May') Incledon, Mabel's sister.*

A brother, Hilary, was born two years after John Ronald,† in 1894. The Tolkiens' marriage was a happy one, and their life was comfortable. Arthur built a verandah onto the house and planted fruit trees in the garden; Mabel hosted frequent dinners and parties, with the assistance of a staff that included a cook, nursemaid, and house-boy.‡

From Bloemfontein to Birmingham

However, the intensely hot, dry summers were a strain on the health of three-year-old John Ronald, and in 1895 Mabel took the two boys on a visit home to England. It was intended to be only temporary, but, as it turned out, the boys never saw South Africa, or their father, again.

In February 1896, Mabel began preparations for their return to Bloemfontein; John Ronald, now four years old, dictated a letter to his father: "My Dear Daddy, I am so glad I am coming back to see you . . . Mamie says you will not know Baby or me we have got such big men . . . lots of love and kisses . . . your loving Ronald."[8]

---

* She had the same Christian names, as it happens, as Tolkien's future wife, Edith Mary Bratt.

† Tolkien used various versions of his name with different people. He was 'Ronald' to family and close friends; some friends and classmates called him 'John' or sometimes 'John Ronald'; to his adult friends and colleagues he was 'Tolkien' or 'Tollers.' Since the closest friends of his boyhood called him 'John Ronald,' I have chosen to use that name when referring to Tolkien up to the point of his young adulthood.

‡ Unusually for that time, the household servants were included in a family photograph that became the Tolkiens' Christmas card for 1892. Mabel disapproved of the prejudicial Boer attitudes she observed (*TFA*, 16–17).

But the letter remained unsent. The same day it was written, a telegram arrived: Arthur was seriously ill with a relapse of fever—probably typhoid—and died the following day, February 15, 1896.

A newspaper report of Arthur's death recounted that he was attended by the Dean of the Cathedral and had "received the sacrament" (i.e., the Eucharist) shortly before his death, suggesting an inclination toward a high-church position, since bringing the sacrament to the sick was not a practice that a more Evangelical-minded Anglican would have favored. Arthur was accorded the dignity of a funeral in the cathedral consisting of a "full choral service."[9]

Mabel Tolkien was now, at age twenty-six, a widow. She set out, with the help of her family, to make a home for her two fatherless boys in the rural community of Sarehole on the outskirts of Birmingham, a burgeoning industrial city in the English county of Warwickshire.

Here, Mabel kept up the practice of her Christian faith, taking her sons to church each Sunday. She found it worthwhile to take "a long walk" in order to get to a 'high' Anglican church[10]—that is, one that in its doctrinal commitments and liturgical style reflected the beliefs of the Oxford Movement. At some point in the next four years, she began to investigate the Catholic Church, into which she would be received in 1900. We will return to this pivotal point in Mabel's (and therefore in Tolkien's) life later in our story. First, we should consider what an interest in Catholicism would have represented to her at that time.

A minority faith

The English Catholic world stood in sharp contrast with the Anglican world that Mabel had been part of, and in which—all things being equal—she would have been expected to continue. Catholics in England were part of a minority faith and still suffered under legal restrictions in certain respects. It will be worth quickly sketching some of the history looming over Mabel and her sons as they settled into their Warwickshire home.

The Reformation that began in 1517 had lasting effects worldwide, but not in the same way everywhere.* For instance, in countries such as Italy and Spain,

* In 1517, an Augustinian friar called Martin Luther published in Wittenberg, Germany, a list of "Ninety-five Theses" disputing points of Church teaching. His willingness to object publicly

Catholicism remained the majority religion and the culture was relatively unchanged. But the repercussions for English Catholics were considerable, to say the least.

In England, King Henry VIII had previously been such a staunch Catholic that the pope had given him the title 'Defender of the Faith.'* However, when it transpired that his wife Catherine of Aragon could not bear him a son, Henry sought to have the marriage annulled. The pope refused Henry's request to declare the marriage with Catherine null, and he declined to recognize the legitimacy of the king's new liaison with Anne Boleyn. In response, Henry overthrew papal authority and declared himself head of the Church in England. This was a shocking move for a layman and one that rendered the Catholic Church in England subservient to the political requirements of the monarch. Henry's Lord Chancellor, Sir Thomas More, refused to endorse this sudden change and was executed by beheading. (More is another figure who will appear again in the story of Tolkien's faith. See figure 48.) Royal supremacy—as opposed to papal supremacy—became the law of the land; Catholic monasteries were abolished, with their wealth and property confiscated by Henry and distributed to his followers.†

After a brief return to the 'old religion' under Queen Mary, whose reign lasted just five years (1553–58), Henry's daughter Elizabeth I came to the throne. Her reign was long and stormy, and after the pope in 1570 declared her to be a heretic, thereby releasing all Catholic subjects from allegiance to her, it was an easy—and

---

to Catholic doctrine, and implicitly therefore to Catholic authority, led to a widespread protest movement (hence 'Protestant') across Europe that included such figures as John Calvin in France and Ulrich Zwingli in Switzerland, and which, in England, gave political cover to King Henry VIII in his long-running battle with the pope about his marital status.

* The monarch bears the title to this day. Every single coin minted in the United Kingdom during the reign of King Charles III will bear both an image of the sovereign's head and the Latin abbreviation 'Dei Gra Reg Fid Def' (*Dei Gratia Rex Fidei Defensor*), which means 'By the grace of God, King, Defender of the Faith.'

† This tumultuous period in English history may have contributed to Tolkien's later story of Númenor. John Garth observes that "There are striking parallels between Henry VIII and Númenor's king, Tar-Calion (better known to Tolkien fans under a name coined later, Ar-Pharazôn). In Tolkien's story 'The Lost Road,' Tar-Calion decrees himself 'Lord of the West.' But only the chief of the Valar—God's archangelic representative in the mortal world—is supposed to bear that title. It is the Middle-earth equivalent of Henry claiming to be head of the church in place of the pope" ("How J.R.R. Tolkien Came to Write the Stories of 'The Rings of Power'").

indeed politically understandable—move for Elizabeth to paint all Catholics as traitors and enemies of the state.*

In just three short decades, the situation had been completely reversed. In 1521, the pope had proclaimed Henry 'defender of the faith'; in 1558, Parliament declared that Henry's daughter Elizabeth, and not the pope, was the head of the Church in England.

It is hard to overstate the devastating—and long-lasting—effects upon Catholics of what occurred in England during the sixteenth century. The Penal Laws instituted by Elizabeth became more detailed and restrictive. It was illegal for priests to celebrate Mass or for anyone to attend it. Weekly attendance at an Anglican service was required, with steep fines for truancy. It was high treason for an Englishman to become a priest and return to England (the only places for seminary training were now overseas) and a felony for anyone to shelter them. It was illegal to be reconciled to the Catholic Church or to assist anyone in becoming a convert. Parents were prohibited from teaching 'the old religion' to their children. Catholics could not move more than five miles without permission and were restricted in their employment. Various acts of Parliament excluded Catholics from practicing as doctors or lawyers, from holding any public office, and from having a commission in the army or navy.[11]

Nor were the penalties mild for breaking these laws. The usual punishment in those days for publicly and persistently advocating 'heresy' was death, something that was culturally accepted in those days (and some Protestants suffered it under Queen Mary), but the Penal Laws went much further and targeted the very practice of the faith—even in secrecy by ordinary people. Raids on private homes were carried out in the hopes of arresting Catholics caught in the act of attending Mass. Imprisonment, crippling fines, and the confiscation of property were commonplace. Priests, if found, were tortured and executed; so too, on occasion, were lay people. Tolkien would have known of the fate meted out to Humphrey Pritchard, one of the martyrs of Elizabethan times. The bartender at The Catherine Wheel Inn, an Oxford pub, Pritchard was captured and executed for sheltering priests. Today, a small plaque on the corner of Holywell Street commemorates his name.

---

* This papal bull, *Regnans in Excelsis*, applied only to Elizabeth; Catholics were allowed to be loyal to subsequent monarchs.

All parish churches were reconfigured to conform to the new beliefs and priorities; sacred architecture, statuary, and artworks were destroyed on a massive scale. New articles of faith were drawn up for Anglican clergy to swear to; many of these articles were expressly worded to exclude 'Romish' beliefs.* Laws ecclesiastical and civic, and the wholesale changes in national religious culture, were, in short, designed to eradicate the practice of the Catholic faith and to make the very word 'Catholic' synonymous with *traitor* and *idolater*.

Penal Laws and civic disabilities lasted for a long time and were only gradually lifted. In 1778, the first Relief Act removed some of the restrictions but also provoked the anti-Catholic Gordon Riots (a week of public violence led by Lord George Gordon, head of the Protestant Association), an indication that England was still something of a tinderbox when it came to this issue.[12] The Catholic Emancipation Act of 1829 allowed Catholics to be members of Parliament, to work as civil servants, and to vote.†

As late as 1901, when John Ronald was nine years old, the sovereign's coronation oath required the new monarch (King Edward VII) to declare that "in the Sacrament of the Lord's Supper there is not any Transubstantiation of the elements of bread and wine into the Body and Blood of Christ . . . and that the invocation or adoration of the Virgin Mary or any other Saint, and the Sacrifice of the Mass, as they are now used in the Church of Rome, are superstitious and idolatrous."[13] At King George V's coronation in 1910, the requirement was dropped, but to this day, a declaration of Protestant faith is included in the Coronation Oath, and the monarch is still not allowed to be a Catholic, although as a result of an Act of Parliament in 2013, he or she is now permitted to marry one.[14] British monarchs of the twenty-first century, like Henry VIII five centuries earlier, remain (at least in theory) supreme not only over the state but over the church too.

* For instance, Article XXII declares that the "Romish Doctrine" of purgatory, pardons, and the invocation of saints in prayer "is a fond thing vainly invented"; XXV denies that Confirmation, Confession, priestly Ordination, Marriage, and Extreme Unction (last rites) are sacraments; and XXVIII rejects the Catholic doctrine of transubstantiation and prohibits the practice of Adoration of the Blessed Sacrament or processions carrying the sacrament. The Articles of Religion are included in the Book of Common Prayer, the Anglican guide to worship.

† Edward Norman observes, "The shadow of the penal laws lay still across English Catholic life long after they had been abolished"; for instance, until the Roman Catholic Relief Act of 1926, "Property bequeathed for what the law continued to regard as 'superstitious uses'—which might mean anything from the endowment of masses to the building of conventual establishments—was liable to confiscation" (*The English Catholic Church in the Nineteenth Century*, 15–16).

Today, in the twenty-first century, the British sovereign's requirement to affirm Protestantism as the state religion is only a historical curiosity, not an indication of national attitudes. But Tolkien was, of course, born at the end of the nineteenth century, a period in which, as historian Edward Norman puts it, "Ignorance of Catholic doctrines, a sensationalized popular literature about Catholic practices, a political tradition of civil liberty which associated Catholicism with autocracy, treason, and intellectual enslavement: all tended to foster a widespread dislike—some would even express it as loathing—of the Roman Church."[15]

Those who joined the Catholic Church were often viewed by their former coreligionists with suspicion or hostility. When Lord Ripon, a former cabinet minister and a friend of the prime minister, William Gladstone, became a Catholic, a leading article in *The Times* declared that he had lost the confidence of the English people, "for to become a Roman Catholic and remain a thorough Englishman are—it cannot be disguised—almost incompatible conditions.'"[16] Historian Pauline Adams observes that converts had to "take seriously" the "possibility of permanent alienation from their family." [17] Indeed, John Henry Newman's sister Harriet never spoke to him again after he became a Catholic. It was not uncommon for converts to be referred to as 'apostates' or 'perverts.' Wilfred Childe, who would become Tolkien's friend and colleague at Leeds, was called both of these by his father.[18] In 1917, when the celebrated Oxford figure Ronald Knox became a Catholic (Tolkien came to know Knox well), he was cut out of his father's will.[19]

Tolkien later recalled that in his childhood, Mary, the mother of Jesus, "was never mentioned except as an object of wicked worship by the Romanists."[20] This passing remark is notable in how matter-of-factly it sums up the sorts of comments that were routinely made about Catholics. 'Bloody Mary' was the tag given by Protestants to Queen Mary, whose brief reign—as we saw above—marked a temporary return to Catholicism as the national religion. Catholics were considered idolaters, worshiping the Virgin instead of God. The very term 'Romanists' is a slur, implying loyalty to Rome, a foreign city with its alien papal overlord, as opposed to honest Anglican patriots. John Ronald might have observed a common practice of Protestant schoolboys "to stick pins through the eyes of Queen Mary in the illustrations of history books."[21]

There were a few high-born families—such as the Howards, the Throckmortons, and the Vavasours—who had somehow managed to maintain both a tradition of Catholic faith and their social status. As a general rule, however, to be a Catholic in England at the end of the nineteenth century was to be poorer than your Anglican counterpart (wherever you found yourself on the social scale) and to have fewer connections and inferior prospects. You would tend to congregate in the shabbier corners of your town or city and might well count yourself lucky that you had the freedom to be a Catholic at all.

For Mabel Tolkien, newly returned home from South Africa and beginning to consider whether she should remain a member of the Church of England, the surrounding Catholic culture, such as it was, would have had little outwardly to attract her. Even the architecture and art would have been sub-par compared to what she was used to—especially coming from a relatively 'high' expression of Anglicanism as she did, for high churchmanship usually went hand-in-hand with an emphasis on beauty in buildings and liturgy and on excellence in music. Catholic places of worship, by contrast, were newer and were often ugly or plain, made of corrugated iron and cheap brick, or repurposed from other uses.* The first building used for worship by Newman's Oratorians in Birmingham was an old gin distillery.†[22]

Nevertheless, in 1900, Mabel began to receive instruction in the Catholic faith, the necessary step before being officially received into the Church. John Ronald was then eight years old—mature enough to know that something important was happening, even if he did not yet have any idea how much his world was about to change.

* At the Reformation nearly all of the historic buildings (parish churches, abbeys, minsters, cathedrals, etc.) that had once been home to the 'old religion' (i.e., the Catholic Church *in* England) were made to serve the new Church *of* England; until 1791, Catholics were barred from erecting new buildings, and for a time thereafter were prohibited from including bells or steeples in any churches that they did construct (Historic England, "19th- and 20th-Century Roman Catholic Churches," 3).

† We will have more to say about the Oratorians in the chapters ahead.

3

Mabel's Choice

In Victorian England, becoming a Catholic was not merely a private change in religious opinion or practice. It was of necessity a public act. Attendance at worship in the Church of England was part of middle-class social and cultural expectations (quite aside from an individual's personal beliefs). Once a person was received into full communion with the Catholic Church, he or she could no longer attend Anglican services—nor, with the Sunday obligation to hear Mass, was it possible merely to stay home and read spiritual literature. For a family member to 'cross the Tiber,' as the saying goes, was literally as well as spiritually a parting of ways. As historian Pauline Adams points out, "Many views were current at this period as to the wisdom and morality of becoming a Roman Catholic, but few people would have doubted that it was a serious act which was likely to have serious consequences."[1]

For Mabel Tolkien, the consequences were more serious than for most people. As a widow with limited resources and two young children, she would be hit hard when her disapproving family cut off their financial support. Mabel's conversion also had an immediate impact on her two sons, eight-year-old John Ronald and six-year-old Hilary.

It is often assumed that Tolkien was a lifelong Catholic. He wasn't. He was an Anglican for his first eight years, more than enough time to remember what it was like to belong to the Established Church. Tolkien had an exceptional memory, especially with regard to visual impressions; he even retained vivid recollections of the voyage from South Africa to England when he was only three years old. During the first eight years of his life, he had become accustomed to the familiar, English-language liturgy of the Anglican church, celebrated by a (usually) married clergyman in a beautiful, ancient parish church. Once his mother became a Catholic, all that changed. Now he had to get used to attending a crowded, newly built church, surrounded by people lighting candles and handling beads, listening to a celibate priest celebrate an unfamiliar liturgy in Latin, which he didn't (then) understand.

His mother's conversion also presented him with a choice, though he might not have been immediately aware of it. At eight years old, he was above the 'age of reason,' the age when a child knows the difference between right and wrong (usually calculated at seven years old). Therefore, he was *not* automatically received into the Church when his mother became a Catholic, as a younger child would have been. Rather, he would have to be formally received as an 'adult' at the time of his First Holy Communion, which at that time was around the age of twelve.[2] (We will return to this point in chapter 4.)

That John Ronald would follow his mother into the Church was not a foregone conclusion. As Adams explains, "it was by no means invariable—at least in the middle and upper classes—for a family to be received into the Church *en masse*. Conversion divided husbands from wives as surely as parents from children and siblings from one another."[3] In fact, as we will find, Protestant families often exerted moral pressure, or even initiated legal proceedings, to draw the children of converts away from the Catholic Church.

Mabel's conversion, then, changed Tolkien's life but did not set it on an irreversible course toward Catholicism. Indeed, we can readily imagine a counterfactual situation in which the orphaned boy became resentful of his mother's foolhardy choice that had landed the family in poverty and disgrace, such that he rejected the Church (and perhaps Christianity altogether) when he reached young manhood. If he had done so, he would have been in company with other significant figures of his generation, such as the poet Robert Graves, whose bitter memoir *Goodbye to All That* recounts how his childhood Anglican faith was part of "all that" he took his leave from as he grew up.

Tolkien, of course, did not go down that road, but recognizing that he might have done so will help us be more attentive to the formative influences on his spiritual life as a child. His faith was not a *fait accompli*. And it is for this reason that it is worthwhile to explore, as best we are able given the limits of our information, the circumstances of his mother's conversion.

St. Anne's

Mabel Tolkien received her instruction in the Catholic faith at St. Anne's Church on Alcester Street in Birmingham from a septuagenarian Irish priest, Fr. John Dowling.[4] Why St. Anne's, which was inconveniently far from their house in Sarehole?

St. Anne's was established by the great Oxford figure John Henry Newman, who had rocked the Victorian world when he entered into full communion with the Catholic Church in 1845. After his priestly ordination in Rome, Newman and his newly formed group of Oratorians settled in Birmingham and founded St. Anne's as a 'mission church.' The disused gin distillery that provided their first place of worship was repurposed once again as the parish school building when, in 1859, a new red-brick church was built in the English Gothic style.[5]

Though the church was architecturally pleasing, its location was not. St. Anne's was located in the sort of place Mabel's family would certainly have preferred her to avoid: Digbeth, one of the poorest districts of Birmingham. A reporter for the *Birmingham Gazette* described it in 1901 as a "slum-land" with "poor housing . . . intermixed with industry and suffering some of the worst social conditions in Birmingham."[6]

Poor Irish immigrants formed the larger part of the congregation, but the parish retained a distinctive character from its founding by Newman. It was here that Newman, nationally famous (or infamous) as a convert from the Established Church, had first preached as a Catholic priest, and it was while he was the rector at St. Anne's that he traveled to London to give the lecture series that was soon afterward published as *Certain Difficulties Felt by Anglicans in Catholic Teaching* (1850).[7]

St. Anne's retained an element of this intellectual focus and outreach to Anglicans in the work of Canon Arthur Villiers, who served first as a curate to Fr. Dowling and later returned as rector. Villiers was remembered at the parish as one who "had been our great protagonist in the Press, and won the admiration of many by his brief, lucid and logical exposition of the Catholic Cause, whether in defence of Catholic schools or Catholic doctrine itself."[8] Villiers' newspaper writings might well have caught Mabel's attention and suggested that St. Anne's was a place where her inquiry into the faith would be taken seriously.

Mabel's instruction would have taken the form of regular meetings with Fr. Dowling, who would have explained the basic teachings of the Church, almost certainly going through a 'penny catechism,' one of the booklets of instruction known for their sales price of only a penny.[9] She did not go through this process alone; her sister May Incledon, Tolkien's godmother, was also receiving instruction. The two daughters of the Unitarian John Suffield were received into the Catholic Church in June 1900.[10]

Mabel was recorded in the parish baptismal register as *conversa ab hæresi*—literally, as "a convert from heresy." (See figure 5.) This was not an insult but rather a technical description of how the Catholic Church viewed Anglicanism (and, conversely, how the Church of England viewed Catholicism).[11] The word 'heresy' derives from the Greek word for 'choosing'; it denotes private judgment, personal choice about what to believe, as opposed to accepting the Apostles' teaching as handed down authoritatively by the Church. To our modern ears, it sounds unambiguously positive to embrace personal choice about one's creed and intolerant to make distinctions about right or wrong beliefs. But as the Anglican theologian Ben Quash explains, this concern with orthodoxy (right belief) is crucial to Christian identity: "From its very beginnings, Christianity said that neither your race, nor your sex, nor your social class, nor your age could ever be a bar to full membership of Christ's body, the Church. Anyone could be a Christian. . . . What, though, was left to mark a Christian out . . . ? The answer was: your faith—what you believed in, as embodied in your practices and confessed with your lips. . . . Christianity was open to everyone, but it had definite convictions."[12] The delicate question of the Catholic Church's attitude to those who don't subscribe to its teachings is a subject we will discuss fully in chapter 30. Difference about what constitutes orthodox belief is an indication that the question is taken seriously: it matters what people believe.

A rift

Mabel and May would have expected their decision to cause displeasure in the family. Most converts faced an initial response of anger: in the previous chapter, we noted the difficulties experienced by, among others, Newman when he 'poped' and one of his sisters never spoke to him again. Another striking example was Thomas

Arnold (brother of the poet Matthew Arnold): when he became a Catholic, his wife, Julia, expressed her views by throwing a brick through the cathedral window.[13] But the Suffield sisters undoubtedly also hoped that if the first harsh reaction could be weathered, time would bring greater acceptance.[14]

However, as it happened, May's husband, Walter Incledon, a committed Anglican, objected so strongly to his wife's conversion that he "forbade her to enter a Catholic church again."[15] Suddenly, Mabel found herself alone.* And not only alone but poor, because the financial help she had been receiving from her brother-in-law was cut off.[16] In addition, she found herself increasingly frail as the diabetes that would eventually kill her began to disclose itself.

Conversion indeed had serious consequences, and these were distressingly unpredictable. But despite familial disapproval, despite an element of loneliness and a degree of poverty, and despite growing ill health, Mabel persisted in her newly adopted faith and began to provide religious instruction to her sons.

---

* At this point it is interesting to engage in another counterfactual experiment and conjecture what might have happened if Mabel's husband, Arthur, were still alive and, like Walter Incledon, opposed his wife's becoming a Catholic. Would Mabel's story have ended up like May's? And if so, how would that have affected Tolkien and his creativity? Would he have written *The Lord of the Rings* and, if he had, how would it have been different from the "fundamentally religious and Catholic work" that he actually wrote? Of course, there is no way of knowing the answers to these questions, but it is perhaps worth considering Arthur's death in light of some searching words Tolkien wrote about mortality, or at least mortality from the Elven point of view: "A divine 'punishment' is also a divine 'gift,' if accepted, since its object is ultimate blessing, and the supreme inventiveness of the Creator will make 'punishments' . . . produce a good not otherwise to be attained" (*Letters*, 286). Was Arthur's death, such a punishment from one point of view, also a 'gift' to Mabel, and therefore to Tolkien? They would rather it had not happened, but they accepted it and the freedom it provided. These thoughts about the mysterious workings of providence have profoundly affected the American comedian Stephen Colbert, who also lost his father (and two brothers) in childhood. Indeed, Colbert has referred to these words of Tolkien's (about punishments being also gifts) in describing how he came to terms with his own loss: "It's that I love the thing I most wish had not happened" (Lovell, "The Late, Great Stephen Colbert.")

4

J.R.P.R.T.

Eight-year-old John Ronald was now part of a Catholic family, but the transition was far from easy. Mabel and her sons had moved from highly respectable Anglicanism to hardly tolerable Catholicism—and that was just the social side of the equation. The more purely religious side also had its difficulties. As an article in a 1924 Catholic magazine remarked, "Everyone is well aware how utterly lost the average convert is on reception into the Church."[1]

Cradle Catholics—those who have been raised from birth in the Church—take in with their mother's milk any amount of religious information and learn any number of religious codes of conduct, which are accepted so naturally and organically that they can hardly conceive of life as being lived in any other way. As a new adult Catholic, Mabel enjoyed no such process of gradual osmosis. She was learning unfamiliar prayers, getting used to a bewildering variety of devotional practices, and learning to navigate the difference between required observances (such as holy days of obligation) and those which were optional. After he crossed the Tiber, John Henry Newman wrote to a fellow convert friend who evidently disliked praying the Rosary (a characteristic Catholic devotion), "I would not burden myself, if I were you, with what is unpleasant to you." He added, "I certainly think you *should* get into the Catholic ways of devotion by degrees," but he recognized that this would not come instantly or automatically. A great and gradual adjustment had to take place.[2]

A priority for Mabel would have been to become a regular member of a parish church, where she and the boys could settle into their religious and social lives, but her options were limited. In 1900, there were a dozen Catholic churches within the city of Birmingham itself but very few in the rural communities south of the city.[3]

At first, they kept attending St. Anne's, but the two-mile walk from Sarehole was now more of an obstacle than it had been. At that time, a Catholic intending to receive Holy Communion at Mass—as Mabel now could—was required to abstain from both food and water from midnight. The boys, who were not yet communicants, could have their breakfast as usual, but for Mabel, a lengthy walk on an empty stomach (while supervising two energetic young sons) would have been a somewhat daunting prospect. Fasting was of course not necessary if Mabel did not receive communion—and it was by no means the norm at that time to receive every Sunday—but as someone who had made a great personal sacrifice to become a Catholic in the first place, she presumably made an effort to receive communion frequently. We will see that, as an adult, Tolkien placed a very high value on receiving communion; perhaps he had his first impressions of the positive value of this practice from seeing his mother do so often and at some personal cost.

There were other factors that made a change of address desirable. Until this point, Mabel had been teaching both Ronald and Hilary at home. However, in the autumn of 1900, Tolkien began attending King Edward's School. If the family were to go on living in Sarehole, it would mean a journey each day to school that was "too long for a little boy on his own."[4] Accordingly, Mabel moved the family to 214 Alcester Road, Moseley, which was on the tram route.

Now they could also take the tram to St. Anne's, though this was an extra expense. The church's location in a slum neighborhood may also have begun to weigh on Mabel now that she was counting on St. Anne's for the boys' sacramental preparation. Whatever the precise balance of considerations in her mind, a few months later, Mabel moved the family once again, to 86 Westfield Road in King's Heath. Her choice was motivated by its proximity to St. Dunstan's Church, which was the only other parish within ten miles of St. Anne's on the south side of Birmingham.[5]

St. Dunstan's

The scarcity of Catholic churches in the rural areas south of Birmingham was the reason St. Dunstan's had been built just four years earlier in 1896.[6] Referred to at the time as an "iron church," it had an exterior of corrugated iron and a pine-wood interior, very different from and less attractive than traditional brick or stone.[7] The location was ideal, only a half mile from their new lodgings, but Mabel soon began looking once again for a new home parish.[8] We do not know exactly why Mabel found St. Dunstan's unsuitable, but we can reasonably assess some contributing factors. Mabel may have shared with fellow converts from high-church backgrounds a sense of "a cultural shock" at "the dryness of English Catholic liturgy" in general.[9] She would have felt the loss of beauty all the more keenly in an unprepossessing, cheaply built church like St. Dunstan's.

Furthermore, as a new Catholic now attempting to teach the faith to her sons, Mabel needed a knowledgeable parish priest to help her navigate the strange new world of Catholic devotion and practice. Fr. Michael Dolan probably did not fit the bill. He had been brought out of retirement to serve as St. Dunstan's first pastor; he would have had a great deal to do in a parish with a large population of the rural poor and no curate to assist him.[10] Fr. Dowling of St. Anne's had also been elderly and close to retirement. Mabel might well have hoped both for someone who could better understand her needs as a convert and who was young and active enough to be a male role model for her sons.

The Oratory

Mabel therefore began to search for a new parish. By venturing further into the city, she had more choices, including St. Chad's Cathedral; designed by Pugin and completed in 1841, it was notable as the first new Catholic cathedral built in England since the Reformation.[11]

The place she settled on was the parish church of the Immaculate Conception—better known as the Birmingham Oratory—on Hagley Road. At the time Mabel knew it, it was very different from the impressive building that stands there today. Built in 1852, when the Oratorians' funds were severely limited, it "had no pretensions of any sort to architectural beauty; in fact, it simply consisted of four plain brick walls and a roof; and the roof itself was bought, ready-made and second-hand, from a disused factory."[12] It was, according to the Oratory's own historian, "dingy, shabby and dowdy, although quaint and attractive in many ways, and entirely devotional."[13]

But for Mabel, one of the significant features of this parish, over against any other in Birmingham, was that the Oratorians were particularly supportive of convert women.

Both her in-laws and her own family were exerting pressure on her to reject her newly adopted faith. Her sister May had already given in to her husband's demand that she cease practicing as a Catholic.[14] May's agreement with or capitulation to her husband (depending on how one views it) was no doubt influenced by the fact that she had two young daughters; if her husband had chosen to separate from her, he could have taken custody of their children, denying her access to them, with confidence that this would be upheld by the courts.

Despite being a widow, Mabel was not immune from family interference with her sons. At that time, convert mothers were not infrequently taken to court by their non-Catholic relatives, who wanted to get custody of the children. In fact, after Mabel's death, there was talk amongst the Tolkien and Suffield relatives "of contesting Mabel's will and of sending the boys to a Protestant boarding-school."[15] Several famous cases of the 1850s had revealed the Protestant bias of the courts: the presumed wishes of a deceased father or of the extended family would often overrule the known wishes of even a living mother. In one dramatic case, a husband who was receiving instruction to be received into the Church alongside his wife died in an accident. When his widow became a Catholic, her mother-in-law and sister-in-law sued to prevent her offspring from being raised Catholic and were awarded custody of the four children. In another case, in 1851, the widowed sister of the headmaster of Harrow "fled to the continent with her children, under Oratorian escort, to prevent their being made wards of Chancery by their uncles."[16]

Convert women who had to support themselves, as Mabel did, were particularly vulnerable, "both to the effects of anti-Catholic prejudice and to the difficulties of obtaining employment as Catholics." In fact, it was to help this population that, shortly after their arrival in Birmingham, the Oratorians bought a house in Warwick Street to provide "a base for the floating population of pious ladies, mostly converts" who were inspired by Newman and wished to be useful in the Church.[17]

We can see, then, the importance of Mabel's eventual selection of Fr. Francis Morgan as the executor of her will and the guardian of her sons. Not only was he a Catholic priest, but as a member of the Birmingham Oratory, he was part of a community that had practical experience in dealing with convert families who were threatened by lawsuits or family pressure to give up custody of their children. It was a prudent choice.

Since the Oratorian Fathers themselves were mostly converts from Anglicanism, Mabel could be assured of respect and understanding and might legitimately hope for some measure of practical support. The Fathers even had a school—two of them, in fact: the Oratory School, a moderately expensive boarding school, and St. Philip's Grammar School, a more modest establishment. Here was a religious community that valued education as well as religious formation.

So it was that in early 1902, Mabel chose to move with her two boys to 26 Oliver Road, Edgbaston, in the district of Ladywood, a short walk from the Oratory. The house itself seems to have been in disrepair,[18] but the neighborhood overall was different from the slum streets near St. Anne's. Ladywood was primarily a working-class district, and though parts of it would later decay, in 1902 it was a pleasant neighborhood. Extant photographs of the area near the Oratory show wide streets and substantial houses with gardens, one of which was the home for many years of the famous Birmingham businessman and author J.H. Shorthouse, whose best-selling novel *John Inglesant* Tolkien would eventually come to read with some interest and admiration.

At the Birmingham Oratory, the community of Fathers took it in turn to serve as the parish priest, and it was in this way that Mabel, John Ronald, and Hilary Tolkien met Fr. Francis Xavier Morgan,[19] a good-natured, intellectually cultivated man, half Spanish and half Welsh. (See figure 8.) It was Mabel's good fortune (and the boys') that they got on so well with this cheerful, middle-aged priest who came to see how they were doing.

The Oratorians

The Oratorians would end up having a substantial and lasting effect on Tolkien's life and his spirituality, which we will explore in detail in later chapters. But we should start with the simple question "Who are the Oratorians?"

The Congregation of the Oratory was founded by St. Philip Neri, who, despite little name recognition in the wider world, is a major figure in Church history—he is known as the 'third apostle of Rome,' coming in only after St. Peter and St. Paul.* Born in 1515 in Florence, Italy, Philip came to Rome as a young man,

* The book of Acts tells of how the Gospel was taken from Jerusalem to Rome, the center of the Mediterranean world and an apt symbol for how divine revelation had spread from its Judaic

where he was ordained a priest and gathered around himself a company of men, all seeking holiness of life during a period of decadence and moral corruption. By his remarkable character and personal example, Philip effected a considerable and long-lasting renewal of the spiritual life of 'the eternal city'; he was declared a saint only a few years after his death in 1595.[20]

A community formed from the young men who were drawn by Philip's approach to prayer and the Christian life, and eventually it was formally recognized as the Congregation of the Oratory. The name 'oratory' comes from the Latin *orare*—'to pray.' As time went on, new Oratories were founded in Italy and beyond.

Each Oratory is independent of all the others. They do have certain characteristics in common, however, based on the Oratorian Rule and on the example of their spiritual father, St. Philip. Oratories are always established in cities; their mission is to the more highly educated in the community; and they emphasize outreach and evangelization through the beauty of liturgy and music and through the sacrament of Reconciliation ('confession').

The men who join a particular Oratory live in community under the Oratorian Rule and with an elected Provost, but they do not take vows, they retain their own personal property, and are free to leave at any time, though the Fathers normally live out their lives in the particular Oratory they have joined. An Oratory is conceived of as a family, bound by ties of affection, so the building up of fellowship in community is a major value. Therefore, they are not actually a religious order but rather a *congregation*. Just as the Dominicans add to their names the initials OP (for Order of Preachers) and Benedictines OSB (for Order of St. Benedict), the Oratorians use, variously, Congregation of the Oratory, CO, or Cong. Orat. This last abbreviation gives rise to the in-house Oratorian joke—at least among the Oxonian Oratorians—of calling themselves 'Congo Rats.' As we will see in chapter 9, humor and playfulness are part of the heritage of Philip Neri, who is known not only as 'the third apostle of Rome' but also as 'the apostle of joy.'

The Oratory in Birmingham was the first to be established in England, founded by John Henry Newman. Newman served as the superior of the Birmingham

---

roots to become a worldwide message for Jews and Gentiles alike. Rome thus became the spiritual headquarters of Christianity, so to speak, something intensified by the martyrdoms there of Peter and Paul. It is for these reasons, among others, that Tolkien, on his visit to Italy in 1955, recorded in his journal his sense "of having come to the heart of Christendom, an exile from the borders and far provinces returning home, or at least to the home of his fathers" (*TCG:C*, 489).

Oratory from its establishment in 1852 until his death in 1890. (See figure 9.) He was made a cardinal in 1879, and thereafter the Oratorians affectionately came to refer to him as "our Cardinal."

It was a remarkable place for any young man to grow up—especially for one as sensitive and brilliant as the young John Ronald. The Fathers of the Oratory were not distant and forbidding ecclesiastical figures; nor were they all elderly, in contrast to the only other Catholic pastors that he had known up to that point. A remark in one of Mabel's letters gives a vivid picture of Tolkien being drawn into the life of the community: in 1903, she commented that "One of the clergy, a young, merry one, is teaching Ronald to play chess—he says he has read *too* much, everything fit for a boy under fifteen, and he doesn't know any single classical thing to recommend him."[21] They had been at the Oratory parish for slightly less than two years, and the priests there—not just Fr. Francis—were investing time and energy into befriending, mentoring, and encouraging John Ronald.

Tolkien the convert

Tolkien was received into the Church in his own right at Christmas, 1903. At this time, he was only nine days from his twelfth birthday,* and hence could well remember his pre-Catholic life and the point at which he crossed the Tiber.

That he did remember this transition and found it deeply significant is shown in later references to the event. In one letter reflecting on his faith, he remarks, "I am one who came up out of Egypt, and pray God none of my seed shall return thither."[22] In another, he says that his experience of the Church is unlike that of cradle Catholics: "Canaan seems different to those who have come into it out of the desert."[23] Both are allusions to the Exodus, in which Moses led the Israelites out of slavery in Egypt and, after forty years wandering in the wilderness, guided them to the Promised Land of Canaan. Framing his experience in these scriptural terms suggests that Tolkien came to regard his conversion as a movement from Erastianism (a situation in which the state constitutionally controls the church)

* At that time, a young person's First Holy Communion was typically not until age twelve, or even a little later. It would not be lowered to the current age of around seven years old until 1910, with Pope Pius X's decree *Quam Singulari* (John McNicholas, "Quam singulari").

into religious freedom (where the pope and the magisterium are not constrained by secular authority), a testing journey but worth it.

The sacrament of Confirmation was also conferred at the same time, and Tolkien took an additional name: Philip. This is worth pausing to explain in some detail.

When people are confirmed in the Catholic Church, they usually take a 'confirmation name,' the name of a saint to whom they feel some special connection.* The name is not just an indication of admiration for a holy figure from the past. It goes with a belief in 'the communion of saints'—a bit like the ethos or spirit of a family, where brothers, sisters, uncles, aunts, and cousins all have something in common. What Catholics have in common is that they all worship God their Father and Christ their Brother, and they honor or venerate Mary as their mother, for Catholics understand Jesus's words to the Apostle John ("Behold your mother," John 19:27) as applying to them too by a kind of spiritual inheritance. (We will return to the Catholic understanding of saints in chapter 22.) Just as individual people have particular friendships on earth, so too Catholics typically have certain spiritual friends: saints to whom they feel a particular affinity.

When Tolkien received the sacrament of Confirmation, he took the name of *Philip*. There are various holy Philips in the history of Christianity, most famously St. Philip the Apostle, one of the Twelve, and St. Philip the Deacon, one of the original seven deacons mentioned in the Acts of the Apostles (Acts 6:5). But the Philip whom Tolkien chose as his confirmation saint was in fact Philip Neri, the founder of the Oratorians. I have checked this with Tolkien's daughter, Priscilla, who confirmed that this is the case.[24]

Taking the name 'Philip' was more than just a pious convention; it was important to Tolkien and became part of what he considered to be his set of Christian names. We get a glimpse of this in some notes he made in Elvish script in the 1930s, listing the names of each member of his family and giving his own name as "John Ronald Philip Reuel Tolkien."[25] He places the name that he had taken at confirmation alongside the names he was given at baptism.

This helps explain an otherwise puzzling remark in his academic lecture "English and Welsh," which he delivered in Oxford the day after the publication of *The*

* Thus, for example, the fantasy writer George R.R. Martin, who was raised Catholic, was born George Raymond Martin, adding the name 'Richard' when he was confirmed at age thirteen (George R.R. Martin, NPR interview, April 28, 2011).

Return of the King in 1955. "My surname is German," Tolkien announced, "my other names are Hebrew, Norse, Greek, and French."[26] Why does he refer to four languages when he had three Christian names—as represented by his initials, J.R.R.? It is because he is including Philip among his "other names." His Hebrew name was Reuel, his Norse name was Ronald, his Greek name was Philip, and his French name was John (John has a Hebrew origin in Johanan, but Tolkien is presumably referring to the influence of the French version, Jean).

Tolkien's assimilation of the name 'Philip' may also explain an odd detail in the famous monogram of his initials. (See figure 56.) Looking carefully at this monogram, with its partially superimposed letters, the T for Tolkien and the J for John are readily recognizable, with the mirror-image Rs (Ronald Reuel) on either side; but one can trace the P as well, almost hidden. It shares the loop of the right-hand R and the vertical line of the T, but is made visible by the otherwise irrelevant spur on the side of the T upright, which marks the foot of the P. Because the little spur appears on only one side, it is not part of the mirrored Rs and would be awkward as only half the base of the T. Nor does it seem that Tolkien would put in an extraneous element in an otherwise highly balanced and carefully composed design. But once we are aware that Tolkien had the name 'Philip,' every detail can be accounted for.*[27] If this reading of his monogram is correct, it could even be considered a sort of visual pun or homage to St. Philip, who placed a great emphasis on humility and hiddenness and humor.

"A very great feast indeed"

Tolkien's First Holy Communion and Confirmation took place at Christmas 1903 in the Birmingham Oratory, where he also made his first confession. It was an important enough day that Mabel even shared the news with her mother-in-law, writing that "Ronald is making his First Communion this Christmas—so it is a

* Tolkien used various versions of this monogram throughout his life as an artistic signature; the earliest versions (ca. 1906) do not contain the P-spur, but the fully developed version appears in *The Book of Ishness*, a book of drawings from around 1913–15. In later years, the monogram (with the P-spur) would appear in simpler forms as an artistic signature, as in his illustration of Hobbiton for *The Hobbit* (see figure 42, lower right-hand corner). This gradual appearance of the 'P' in his monogram is consistent with a natural growth in his understanding of what St. Philip Neri meant to him (Tolkien, *J.R.R. Tolkien: Artist and Illustrator*, 43; Tolkien, *The Art of "The Hobbit,"* 138, 104).

very great feast indeed to us this year." Mabel was aware that this would emphasize her son's Catholic identity to his Protestant grandmother, but she closes her letter with these words: "I don't say this to vex you—only you say you like to know everything about them."[28]

And so, shortly before his twelfth birthday, Tolkien was confirmed. From then on, he would carry in his very name a recognition of his strong link to the Congregation of the Oratory of St. Philip Neri, which would become his second home and spiritual family: he was John Ronald *Philip* Reuel Tolkien, a Christian in full communion with the Catholic Church.

5

Learning to Pray

January 3, 1904 was John Ronald's twelfth birthday and his first as a fully-fledged member of the Catholic Church. Naturally, he had received catechetical teaching from a priest in the run-up to his first Holy Communion and Confirmation, a great milestone in his religious life, but much of his spiritual education would have happened at home.* The Catholic Church strongly emphasizes the family as the 'domestic church' where children receive their first instruction and where the whole family joins together in regular prayer and worship. Mabel took this responsibility seriously. All the way to the end of his life, Tolkien recalled the great "effort" that his mother made "to hand on to us small boys the Faith,"[1] despite the burdens of poverty, illness, and familial opposition.

His choice of words is significant: it wasn't just that Mabel persisted in her own Catholic faith—and was therefore a good role model—but that she *handed it on* to her sons. 'Tradition' is a key concept for Catholics and literally means 'handing on': it has a biblical foundation in the example of St. Paul, who twice tells the Christians at Corinth that what he received from the Lord he is now passing on to them (1 Corinthians 11:23; 15:3). Tolkien recalled that his mother "brought me into the Church,"[2] by which he meant that she gave him the formation that equipped him, as we have seen, to enter into full communion himself.

His mother would have taught him the basic tenets of the faith from a catechism, probably the same penny catechism that she had used before entering the Church. But in addition to teaching him *about* the faith, she would also have taught him how to *practice* his faith by instructing him in Catholic prayers, just

* 'Catechesis' essentially means 'teaching,' but literally it means 'down-echo,' reflecting the way that, in days before mass literacy when instruction was carried out by word of mouth, the teacher would say something and it would be repeated back by the student. With the advent of mass literacy and the printing press, guidebooks to the content of the faith became increasingly common, so that 'catechumens' (students of the faith) could 'catechize' (teach) themselves simply by reading 'catechisms' (manuals of the faith).

as she had undoubtedly taught him the basics of prayer in his earliest years. Here, she established a basic pattern that would influence his entire life.

The basic underlying premise of Tolkien's prayer life was one common to all Christians—the importance of "raising up one's mind and heart to God," as the English Catholic Catechism of 1900 put it.[3] To consider Tolkien's prayer, then, is to gain a better sense of his spiritual personality, as it were, and his understanding of what it meant to live a life of faith.

The actual practice of prayer has extraordinary variety: it includes such things as a child's simple bedtime prayer; giving thanks before meals; extemporaneous prayer; prayer using memorized texts; liturgical prayer; adoration; *lectio divina* (that is, prayer while reading the Scriptures); and so on. The Christian tradition puts no limit on the number of possible approaches, encouraging prayer to be undertaken at all stages of life, by people of every kind of temperament, and covering every conceivable situation. Even the handful of prayers that we will discuss in this chapter can be, and are, used in a variety of different contexts.

Mabel's 'prayer book'

The one surviving document providing insight into what Mabel taught Tolkien is a booklet held in the archives of the Birmingham Oratory, among a few other possessions from Tolkien's childhood. It is usually referred to as 'Mabel's prayer book,' but in fact it is not a book of prayers, but rather a book *about* prayer, and an unusual one.*

The book is *The Lord's Prayer and the Angelical Salutation*, by Fr. Jerome Savonarola, OP, published in 1899 by the Catholic Truth Society.† The book examines first the Our Father (the Lord's Prayer) and then the Hail Mary (the Angelic

---

* Mabel almost certainly gave the book to Tolkien. As we will see in chapter 10, the boys' Aunt Beatrice burned Mabel's letters and papers without consulting her sons. The survival of this book suggests that it was already in John Ronald's possession.

† An Italian Dominican friar, Savonarola (1452–98) became famous for his fiery calls to repentance and his sermons against the immorality of the clergy. After getting involved in the tumultuous politics of Florence and disobeying the pope's commands to stop preaching, Savonarola was eventually executed as a heretic. This explains the book's prefatory note: "Most people know Savonarola only as a demagogue, a reformer, a leader of the people. These two little treatises give us some insight into the other side of his character as a man of study, prayer, and contemplation" (Robinson, *In No Strange Land*, 92–97; Prefatory note, Savonarola, *The Lord's Prayer and the Angelical Salutation*, 3).

Salutation) in detail, phrase by phrase. Savonarola explains that this in-depth study has a larger purpose:

> If a man desires to have a true understanding of God's Holy Scriptures, he must read them again and again, and make himself familiar with them. When he has mastered the first or literal meaning, he must meditate upon the words, so as to discover their more hidden sense, and this he will be able to do with the aid of other and less obscure passages. Knowledge is worthless without action; so when a man has understood the spiritual meaning of the words of Holy Scripture, he must ask of God grace to lead him on to love and good works. If he act thus day by day, he will make such progress as to proceed readily to contemplation.[4]

By leading the reader through all four stages of this process with the familiar texts of these prayers and showing how they are rooted in Scripture, Savonarola proposes to teach a model for reading the Bible in general. Tolkien thus not only gained a fuller understanding of these Catholic prayers but also learned the importance of a thorough knowledge and understanding of Scripture, something that he pursued throughout his life (as we will explore further in later chapters).

The Our Father and the Hail Mary prayers were simple enough that young John Ronald would have committed them to memory with ease, yet they provided him with abundant material for meditation throughout his life. Here, it is a suitable moment to consider what place they had in his spirituality.

Our Father

The Our Father, *Pater Noster* in Latin, is named from its opening words; it is also called the Lord's Prayer since it was given to the disciples by Jesus (Matthew 6:9; Luke 11:2). It is prayed at every Mass and is included in many common devotions, such as the Rosary and the Stations of the Cross, as well as being frequently used in personal prayer. Tolkien would have learned this prayer as a young boy, even before Mabel became a Catholic, and it was an important part of his devotional life as an adult.* (See Appendix B.)

It also formed material for reflection on the theological underpinnings of Middle-earth. In the 1950s, he worked extensively on translating the Our Father into his Elvish languages (for instance, making six different versions in Quenya), and his linguistic efforts show that he was ruminating seriously on the prayer in theological terms. Tolkien was not simply making a translation into already-developed languages but rather contributing to the development of his invented languages through the process of translation. When he tested out different ways to express, for instance, 'heaven' in Quenya, he was ensuring that the language he was creating for his Elves was theologically coherent and correct.[5]†

His theological meditations found their way into *The Lord of the Rings*. Tolkien explained that the scene on Mount Doom in which Frodo refuses at the last to give up the Ring had a significance beyond that of the story and characters: he says that "within the mode of the story the 'catastrophe' *exemplifies* (an aspect of)" the words of the Our Father: "Forgive us our trespasses as we forgive them that trespass against us." Frodo's failure is redeemed precisely because of his earlier pity and mercy toward Gollum: "By a situation created by his 'forgiveness,' he was saved himself, and relieved of his burden."[6]

Tolkien considered that the final phrase of the Our Father ("Lead us not into temptation, but deliver us from evil")‡ is in fact "the harder and the less often considered petition." Elsewhere, he observed that the "mysterious last petitions" of this prayer indicate the potential to be tested beyond the limits of endurance as Frodo

* An early memory Tolkien had was of his grandfather John Suffield taking a sheet of paper and selecting a pen with an extra fine nib. "Then he would draw a circle around a sixpence, and in this little space would write in fine copperplate the words of the entire Lord's Prayer" (*Biography*, 26).

† For instance, in the opening line, "Our Father, who art in heaven," Tolkien initially used forms of the Quenya word *menel*, meaning 'firmament, high heaven, the region of the stars.' However, he evidently realized that "the idea of God dwelling in 'the region of the stars' or 'the firmament' was an inaccurate representation of the Elvish conception of Eru [God], as well as of present-day theological concepts of Heaven" and made an emendation, adding "an alternative phrase above *meneldëa* in line 1: *i ëa pell' Ëa*, which must mean 'who is beyond Ëa (the World that Is)'" (Wynne, Smith, and Hostetter, Notes to Tolkien, "'Words of Joy,'" part 1, 13).

‡ This is the ending of the Catholic version of the prayer; the doxology "For thine is the kingdom, and the power, and the glory, for ever and ever" is part of the liturgical response to the prayer in the context of the Mass, but, unlike in Protestant usage, is not treated as part of the prayer itself.

was. Frodo, he said, was honored not because he was able to complete the Quest by his own power but because he had "spent himself completely (as an instrument of Providence)." Here we can see Tolkien's balance of realism and compassion, his recognition of human weakness, and his emphasis on the need for divine grace. In a 1963 letter, he explained that we must hold ourselves to an ideal for the moral life but that any judgment of others must be "tempered by 'mercy'" and that this "double scale"—rigor for oneself, mercy for others—is often used "by the saints."[7] He might have had in mind, for instance, St. Paul's description of himself as the foremost or chief of sinners (1 Timothy 1:15). We should pray "lead us not into temptation, but deliver us from evil" precisely because none of us can be sure that we will successfully resist a time of trial.

Tolkien viewed the Our Father as the gold standard of prayer—and for good reason, given that it is the prayer that Jesus taught his disciples. It is perhaps for this reason that Tolkien recited the *Pater Noster* when venturing into new territory, such as the initial mechanical recording of his own voice. When his friend George Sayer invited him to test out an early tape recorder—a rather daunting-looking "large black box"—Tolkien startled him by doing a sort of 'exorcism' of it: "First he recorded the Lord's Prayer in Gothic to cast out the devil that was sure to be in it since it was a machine." Then, "surprised and very pleased" by the results, he went on to record several poems from *The Lord of the Rings*.[8] There was doubtless a touch of playfulness in Tolkien's actions, but even Sayer remarked that it was "not just whimsey." Though he was no Luddite, Tolkien had profound concerns about the way that machines were so readily abused for purposes of coercion and dehumanization.* He also had a deep sense of personal humility regarding his work. If this machine were to be useful, better that it should first hear him reciting the Lord's Prayer than any of his own words.

His attitude toward this prayer even included an element of literary-critical pedantry. Clyde Kilby recalled that Tolkien "had a little objection" to the "hallowed be thy name" clause; he said that Tolkien claimed it "was unnecessary, since you've already hallowed the name when you say 'Our Father.'"[9] In other words, he thought

* His son John recalled that Tolkien was skeptical about so-called labor-saving machinery: "He used to say, you only move the slavery out of sight, so it's much more effective, because nobody knows what's going on" (*J.R.R.T.: A Film Portrait*). For more on Tolkien's surprisingly nuanced views on technology, see my *Tolkien's Modern Reading*, chapter 9.

the phrase was redundant. That Tolkien should exercise his linguistic precision on critiquing the wording of the prayer Jesus taught his disciples might seem irreverent—and indeed it is entirely possible that he was expressing a bit of deadpan English humor. But it speaks to the familial confidence that characterized his life of faith: God is not kowtowed to as a distant aristocratic dignitary but loved and known—and hallowed—as Our *Father*.

Hail Mary

The Hail Mary is the second prayer discussed in Mabel's book about prayer, and—unlike the Our Father—would have been new to John Ronald in his experience of Catholic spiritual life.

The Hail Mary (*Ave Maria* in Latin) is a short prayer that comes mainly from two scriptural passages. "Hail, Mary, full of grace, the Lord is with thee" comes from the Archangel Gabriel's salutation to Mary at the Annunciation (Luke 1:28). "Blessed art thou among women, and blessed is the fruit of thy womb, Jesus," comes from Elizabeth's greeting to the pregnant Mary at the Visitation (Luke 1:42). This is followed by a petition for Mary's intercession: "Pray for us sinners now and at the hour of our death. Amen."*

In later years, Tolkien wrote out this prayer in both English and Latin, using Elvish script, and made four different translations of it into Quenya.[10] His translation of the opening words reflects the Catholic understanding of the Scripture it references, Luke 1:28, in which the angel Gabriel addresses Mary as "full of grace," a salutation indicating that the Virgin is as full of God's grace as it is possible for a human to be, which in turn lends support to the dogma of the Immaculate Conception (a teaching that was important to Tolkien and which we will return to later). Hence, Tolkien's rendering of the words "full of grace" is "*quanta Eruanno*." "Eruanno" is literally "of the gift of Eru," and "quanta" means "full," with associations of "full to the brim."[11]

* That is, asking Mary to pray to God on behalf of the person praying. Catholics believe that, in addition to directly addressing God, believers can and should ask others to pray on their behalf—both friends who are alive on earth and the saints who are in heaven. The intercession of the saints depends upon and is enabled by the unique and foundational intercession between God and man achieved by Christ and does not detract from it, but rather displays an aspect of its meaning.

The Rosary

The third prayer that Tolkien would have learned at his mother's knee was the Glory Be (*Gloria Patri* in Latin), offering praise to God the Holy Trinity: "Glory be to the Father, and to the Son, and to the Holy Ghost,* as it was in the beginning, is now, and ever shall be, world without end. Amen." In later life, Tolkien counted it among the "praises," which he used often (and to which we will return in chapter 27) and made a partial translation of it into Quenya.[12]

The Glory Be, the Our Father, and the Hail Mary form the basic elements of the Rosary, a characteristic Catholic devotion that Tolkien would have learned early on. The Rosary is a way of meditating prayerfully on a specific 'mystery' from the life of Christ. In Tolkien's day, there were three sets of mysteries: the Joyful (the conception, birth, and childhood of Jesus), the Sorrowful (his suffering and death on the Cross), and the Glorious (his Resurrection and events following it).†

The word 'rosary' comes from the Latin word *rosarium* (a garland of roses) and refers both to the devotion itself and to the string of beads used to keep track of the prayers said. (See figure 41.) Since the Virgin Mary is often associated with the rose (one of her titles in the Litany of Loreto, for instance, is the Mystical Rose), this devotion came to be envisioned as a spiritual gathering of roses to offer to the Blessed Virgin, which she in turn would bestow on her Son. It was not uncommon in Tolkien's day to refer to praying the Rosary as 'saying one's beads,' and Tolkien would have been well aware that the word 'bead' comes from the Old English word for 'prayer.' The repetition of familiar prayers while using the string of beads to keep one's place in the series is intended to occupy the surface level of one's attention, reducing distractions as one meditates on each mystery in the story of salvation.

Tolkien's translations meant that he eventually created almost a complete set of Rosary prayers in Elvish. The point is not that he ever prayed the Rosary in Elvish (there is no indication that he did so, and the texts are clearly experiments in translation). Rather, his work with Elvish reveals that these prayers were meaningful

* In Tolkien's time the English usage was more commonly 'Holy Ghost' rather than the modern-day 'Holy Spirit.' The meaning is the same.

† In 2002, Pope John Paul II added a fourth set of mysteries, the Luminous, related to the ministry of Jesus. They are the baptism in the River Jordan, the wedding at Cana, the proclamation of the Kingdom, the Transfiguration, and the institution of the Eucharist.

and deeply familiar, and so he turned readily to them as material for linguistic exploration and for practice of his Elvish scripts.*

We can get a sense of Tolkien's approach to praying the Rosary in some comments he made in his diary of a 1955 trip to Italy that he took with his daughter, Priscilla. Remarking on the public recitation of the Rosary, he noted at one point that it was said "badly" and at another that it was "very well said."[13]† What would the difference have been? When the Rosary is recited communally, it is led by one person who says the first part of each prayer with the congregation supplying the second part and following the pace established by the leader. A badly done Rosary is rushed, gabbled, mumbled, or said without attention to the meaning of the words; a Rosary when said well is led audibly and at an appropriate pace, such that the meaning of the prayers is apparent.

In his letters, we get occasional glimpses of how frequently Tolkien prayed the Rosary and how it wasn't just something he did at home. He brought his beads with him when traveling, as we have just seen, and was sure to have them by him when sleeping in a bomb shelter as part of his wartime service as an air-raid warden.[14] One of his illustrations for *The Hobbit* even seems to include a visual nod to the rosary. His painting of Hobbiton depicts a tree on a green hill surrounded by a circle of hedges that looks very much like a string of rosary beads. (See figure 42.) If this is indeed what he intended, it would be exactly the kind of subtle and playful detail that would fit his personality and also a latent testimony to the essential role prayer played in his spiritual life.

---

* He used other texts as material for transcriptions as well, including the "Walrus and the Carpenter" poem from Lewis Carroll's *Alice in Wonderland* and "God Save the King" (Tolkien, "The Qenya Alphabet," 20, 41, 85), but the prayers are the texts that he used and re-used most often.

† In the latter instance, Tolkien added, "and entirely in Latin to my pleasure and surprise"; but it is evident that he thought it well said apart from it being in Latin. He enjoyed praying in Latin, and undoubtedly this contributed to his feeling that the devotions were "homelike and delightfully familiar"; he was probably also pleased because he knew Latin fluently, but he admitted elsewhere that his command of Italian was "embryonic" (*TCG:C*, 493).

6

Formation

Mabel's decision in 1902 to move house where she could be part of the Oratory parish meant that John Ronald's moral and religious education was now taking place in a supportive and stable environment. But the formation of her exceptionally intelligent and creative son included other dimensions—intellectual, social, and aesthetic—that had to be considered as well.

John Ronald had been enrolled since 1900 at King Edward's School, a logical choice since it was academically strong, the alma mater of Mabel's late husband, Arthur, and her brother Roland, and the fees were being paid by a kindly uncle.[1] This exception to her family's withdrawal of financial support might have been related to the fact that King Edward's was a Protestant school, and it might have seemed a means to draw the boys (and perhaps Mabel) back into the Anglican fold. But after two years of becoming more well-grounded in her adopted faith, Mabel realized that King Edward's was no longer self-evidently the best place for John Ronald's education.

Mixed blessings

Mabel had encountered one of the ongoing issues in Catholic life at that time: the question of 'mixed' education. At that time, most Catholic parents were hesitant to send their sons to a Protestant school; and not without reason, because anti-Catholic sentiment was still strong in Church of England schools and in the Anglican establishment more generally. The concern was not merely what was taught in class, but the influence of other students (since as a general rule children want to fit in with their peers) and the fact that at that time, schools usually had communal prayers and chapel attendance, which could easily lead to Catholic students being gradually assimilated into the Protestant faith of their classmates.

The trajectory of Tolkien's life was at this crucial point significantly influenced by the approach that the Oratorian Fathers took toward education. To begin with, the Birmingham Oratorians were particularly committed to education. Their founder, Cardinal Newman—a scholar, writer, and teacher—was himself one of the most powerful intellects of his day. Before his entrance into the Catholic Church, he had been one of the leading lights of Oxford (Fellow of Oriel College, Vicar of the University Church), and, following his conversion, he was also involved with the establishment of the Catholic University in Ireland (now University College Dublin). One of the reasons Newman felt that the Oratorian Rule was a good fit for himself and his fellow well-educated converts was that it "allowed the retention of personal property, such as books, and it encouraged scholarly pursuits among its members."[2] Many of the Oratorian priests in Mabel's day (including Fr. Francis) had known, worked with, and been personally taught by Newman.

Mabel could therefore be confident that her ideals regarding the education of her unusually gifted older child would be taken seriously, as they might not have been in a more ordinary Catholic parish. Undoubtedly, she consulted Fr. Francis and probably others of the Fathers as well to determine what the best step was for the boys' education. The Oratory School would have been ideal, except that it was a boarding school, and its fees far outstripped Mabel's ability to pay. Lacking an endowment, the school's finances were so tight that no scholarships were offered.[3]

Mabel's decision was to enroll John Ronald and Hilary at St. Philip's Grammar School, a day school run by the Oratory Fathers. The fees were somewhat lower than King Edward's, but the key factor was that at St. Philip's he would get a fully Catholic education.[4] However, John Ronald soon outpaced all his classmates at St. Philip's, and it was clear that he needed a more challenging academic environment. But would it be wise to send him back to King Edward's?

Fr. Francis and Fr. Robert Eaton, the headmaster of St. Philip's Grammar School, would have helped Mabel discern that the boys could be academically educated in a non-Catholic setting; the Oratory priests would ensure that they received proper spiritual formation. For instance, Tolkien recalled that he and his brother "were supposed to, and usually did, serve Mass before getting on our bikes to go to school."[5] In November 1902, John Ronald re-took the entrance examination at King Edward's and was awarded a scholarship that covered all his fees,[6] thus ensuring that the financial question was resolved with no question of strings attached from Protestant relatives.

This decision would have been all the easier to make since, as it happened, although King Edward's was officially a Church of England school, it had an ecumenical and indeed inter-religious character that was exceptional for the time. E.W. Badger, an alumnus and later a teacher at King Edward's, wrote in 1908 that "Religious education in the school is entirely unsectarian; Anglican, Nonconformist, Roman Catholic, and Hebrew, all meet for scripture lessons."[7]

The school's irenic religious ethos is probably why Tolkien was allowed to attend classes on the Greek New Testament, taught by the King Edward's headmaster. This permission was even more unusual than his attendance at the school, since it could be argued that the class was a form of Protestant religious education and therefore forbidden for a Catholic. It is highly unlikely that Tolkien would have been granted this permission by anyone other than the Oratorians, who were mostly converts themselves and therefore understood and were not afraid of Protestantism. And as Tolkien later recalled, "I certainly took no 'harm,' and was better equipped ultimately to make my way in a non-Catholic professional society."[8]

Barrovians and Boy Scouts

At King Edward's, Tolkien made friends who would have a lasting impact on his life. One of these was Christopher Wiseman, who was a devout Methodist. Oddly enough, this would have given him something in common with Tolkien. Although Methodists were Protestants, they were 'Nonconformists,' and so Wiseman, like Tolkien, did not enjoy 'Establishment' respectability.

Another two friends were Rob Gilson and Geoffrey Smith, who, along with Tolkien and Wiseman, were the core members of the 'Tea Club, Barrovian Society' or TCBS. (See figure 25.) This informal society took its name from the fact that the boys gathered for tea and snacks in the library of King Edward's School and in the tearoom of the nearby Barrows' department store. As John Garth puts it, the boys' "humour was quickfire and often sophisticated; their interests and talents were many"[9]—ranging from playing rugby to debating (in English and in Latin), writing poetry, and performing plays in Greek verse. The TCBS also had a morally serious side, which would grow stronger as they went up through the ranks of King Edward's and then departed for university. The quartet called themselves the "Immortal Four"; their aim, according to Geoffrey Smith, was to "reestablish sanity, cleanliness, and the love of real and true beauty in everybody's breast." Tolkien declared that their destiny was "to testify for God and Truth."[10]

Tolkien seems to have acquired, at least briefly, the nickname 'Gabriel' among the TCBS: in 1911, Wiseman wrote him a note addressing him as "My dear Gabriel" (signing himself "Beelzebub").[11] Since Gabriel is the name of the archangel who announced to Mary that she would conceive the Christ-child, it might be a teasing reference to Tolkien's Marian devotion, a way that he would have stood out as a Catholic in the group. But despite their ecclesiological differences, the TCBS shared a commitment to living out Christian principles; later, Gilson wrote, "I believe we can never thank God enough for the purity of our school." England was in need of moral reform, and this would be the "great task" of the Immortal Four.[12]

Because King Edward's was a day school, not a boarding school, Tolkien had no interruption in the pattern of his worship as a Catholic, and he also had opportunities for socializing with Catholics of his own age. An important part of Oratory life was The Brothers of the Little Oratory, a group of boys and young men from the local community who gathered with the Fathers for prayer and social activities, and encouraged one another in a life of holiness.* The extant records are too fragmentary to know whether John Ronald was a member of the Little Oratory, but we do know that later, in 1909, he and his brother, Hilary, became leaders of the newly formed Oratorian Boy Scout troop, overseen by Fr. Charles Heurtley.[13] The Oratory was an early adopter of Scouting, which had been launched only the year before by Robert Baden-Powell with his guidebook *Scouting for Boys*. The Boy Scout program, which spread widely across England, was not specifically Catholic, but it had a Christian basis. As Scout leaders, John Ronald and Hilary were in charge of three patrols, a total of about eighteen or twenty boys: a not inconsiderable number, representing a genuine exercise of responsibility on the brothers' part. We can get a sense of how Scouts were integrated into the social and religious life of the Oratory by their activities on Easter Monday of 1909: the Scout patrols "marched smartly

* That the discipline of the Little Oratory was not unrealistically austere can be seen, for instance, in one of the Lenten pledges: to abstain from alcoholic drinks . . . between meals (Birmingham Oratory Archives).

in the wake of the Boys' Brigade," a visiting Catholic group from Coventry; they processed up the Hagley Road "to the strains of a fine Bugle Band," played two football matches, had tea, and returned to the Oratory for Benediction.[14]

"The arts as means to draw people closer to God"

In addition to valuing the intellectual life, the Oratorian Rule, as Newman explained, "sets great store by the arts as means to draw people closer to God, especially music."[15] Newman himself was not only a theologian and preacher; he was also a talented violinist, a writer of hymns, a poet, and a novelist (the author of *Loss and Gain* and the historical tale *Callista*). His positive attitude toward the arts had a shaping effect on the ethos of the Birmingham Oratory. The cultural tone was high, achievements in the arts were prized, and the *Oratory Parish Magazine* of Tolkien's youth was full of poetry and articles about literature and music. At the same time that John Ronald was getting his academic education at King Edward's, he was also being formed aesthetically as well as morally and spiritually at the Oratory.

A 1903 letter from Mabel gives us a glimpse of the way John Ronald's artistic interests were encouraged. She wrote to her mother-in-law—who had been pleased with drawings that the boys had sent her—that John Ronald had done very good work in the past year: "he has just been having quite an exhibition in Father Francis' room."[16] Few things are as encouraging to an artist as having an appreciative audience, and for Fr. Francis to allow a miniature "exhibition" in his own room is an indication of his good-humored support of Tolkien's burgeoning artistic sensibilities.

The Oratorians' special attention to music derives from Philip Neri, who decided that a good way to engage the young men of his day was to provide musical evenings interwoven with Scripture readings, lectures, and discussions. Because of this interest in music, composers began to compose 'oratorios,' pieces written specifically for the Oratory in Rome (though over time they became less obviously related to sacred space and moved into the concert hall). The Birmingham Oratorians continued in this tradition, producing new programs for musical evenings. One such was entitled "The Creator and the Creature." The first part of this oratorio is a musical expression of the creation account in Genesis, followed by the fall and the redemption made possible by the Incarnation.[17] It was first presented sometime before 1902. Might this have contributed something to the inspiration for Tolkien's account, in the *Silmarillion*, of the creation of Middle-earth expressed in musical terms? Perhaps.

Music in worship was taken seriously at the Birmingham Oratory. Newman had a particular interest in encouraging congregational singing and produced a book of hymns to be used both at Mass and at services of Benediction.[18]* Plainchant, often called Gregorian chant, was also used, something which Tolkien had probably not heard as an Anglican. Chant is a mode of singing or intoning a text without accompaniment; on particularly high or solemn liturgical occasions, the Scripture readings are chanted, as well as other parts of the liturgy. It evidently made a great impression on Tolkien; Priscilla later recalled of her father that "The only kind of music I knew him to love dearly was Gregorian Plain Chant."[19]

Here we can trace a direct influence on Middle-earth. Soon after the publication of *The Lord of the Rings*, Tolkien explained that a few of the songs in it were written to specific "tunes." One of these was the "Elvish chant" *Namárië* that Galadriel sings to the Fellowship as they depart from Lothlórien, which, he says, "has in mind the tones used in the *Lamentatio* of Tenebrae."[20] The *Lamentatio* is a chant of the readings from the Old Testament book of Lamentations during the Tenebrae prayer service of Holy Week. Tenebrae (*darkness* in Latin) was visually dramatic, involving the progressive extinguishing of fifteen candles set upon a stand (known as a 'hearse') in the sanctuary so that the service ends in darkness, with the congregation leaving in silence.

Sermon in stone

Another influence on John Ronald, both aesthetic and spiritual, was a 'sermon in stone': the new Birmingham Oratory church.

* At that time, the Oratory was somewhat exceptional in this regard. Unlike today, when a Sunday Mass will typically include one, two, or even three hymns, in Tolkien's youth congregational singing was relatively uncommon. This was due largely to historical influences: as Fr. Guy Nicholls explains, "Music in most English Catholic churches was far from elaborate" because for nearly three hundred years, "Catholics had been obliged either by periods of direct persecution or at least by grave social disadvantages to conduct their worship in a hidden and somewhat hurried manner, generally without singing of any kind" (*Unearthly Beauty*, 188).

During his boyhood, Tolkien witnessed the complete transformation of the building. The 'Old Church' had been erected quickly and cheaply, out of necessity, and as the size of the congregation increased, it became crowded and inadequate. The decision was made to replace it with a new, classical-style basilica as a memorial to Cardinal Newman. The foundation stone was laid on March 25, 1904 (the Solemnity of the Annunciation), in a major ceremony.[21] Since the Oratorians had no other land on which to build, the Memorial Church was constructed around the 'Old Church,' which remained in use for two years before it was finally demolished, having been "gradually pulled down as its successor was built."[22] The first Mass was celebrated in the partially completed new building on October 9, 1906, the anniversary of Newman's Tiber-crossing; it was officially opened on December 8, 1909 (the Solemnity of the Immaculate Conception).[23] It is probable that Tolkien was present on all of these dates, especially since the first and third are also major days in the liturgical calendar.

The new church, nearly 200 feet long, has a tunnel-vaulted ceiling with a row of massive pillars of Italian marble. (See figure 11.) The sanctuary, paneled in onyx and marble, has an ornately decorated tabernacle at the center of the high altar. Soaring above is a dome, covered on the outside with bronze. Inside, to the right of the sanctuary, is the organ gallery; to the left is a Marian shrine featuring a replica of the statue of Notre Dame des Victoires in Paris.* Around the walls run the Stations of the Cross. The side altars are dedicated respectively to the Sacred Heart of Jesus, St. Charles Borromeo, St. Anne (mother of the Virgin Mary), St. Joseph (foster-father of Jesus), St. Patrick (patron saint of Ireland), the English Martyrs, the Holy Souls (the dead in purgatory), and lastly, St. Valentine—though not the one associated with Valentine's Day.[24] A large chapel is dedicated to St. Philip Neri,[25] and the main church also features a Shrine of St. Philip Neri. This includes a painting of the saint (see figure 10), a full-sized wax effigy, and a glass case displaying several relics, including his spectacles-case, brought back by Newman

---

* Our Lady of Victories appears in the Birmingham Oratory because in 1836, Abbé Desgenettes, who had taken over the Church of Notre Dame des Victoires in Paris, dedicated his parish to the Immaculate Heart of Mary, and founded a Confraternity of Prayer. In the days before Newman's conversion, intense prayer was offered for him in this Church by the members of that very same Fraternity. For that reason, Newman stopped off in this church on his way to Rome in 1846 in order to give thanks for his conversion—and later named the Marian shrine at the Oratory with this same designation.

from Rome; these would all have helped the young Tolkien get a sense of Philip as a real person, and one with a tangible connection to the Oratory where he was now spending so much of his time.

The slow-motion transformation of an unprepossessing, utilitarian church into a place of great beauty could not have failed to make an impression on the young John Ronald, who was twelve when the construction began and seventeen when it was completed. Here was an outward and visible indication of the Oratorians' commitment to beauty in the Christian life and a representation in art and architecture of what they believed as Catholics. The structure and the design of the new church underscored the importance of the Eucharist, with the sightlines drawing the eye to the dramatic high altar and tabernacle. It showed the importance of honoring Mary, the Mother of God, with the Lady Altar and various paintings and statues of her. And the communion of saints was brought to mind by the little chapels and side altars whose figures often had dramatic histories, as with St. Patrick and the English Martyrs.

The choice of liturgically significant dates for the key stages in the opening of the church would have been Tolkien's first exposure to the way that layers of meaning can be created and the significance of events heightened by the deliberate intersection of the religious calendar with outward events. Here we may perhaps trace an early influence on his later decision, when writing *The Lord of the Rings*, to arrange the schedule of events in his fictional world so that they corresponded (for those who were observant enough to notice) with key dates in the life of Christ: the Fellowship set out from Rivendell on December 25 (the date of Christ's Nativity), and the Ring is destroyed on March 25 (the date of the Annunciation).*

---

* How intentional were these dates? On the one hand, Tolkien remarked in a 1966 interview that the December 25 date "occurred strictly by accident, and I let it in to show that this was not a Christian myth anyhow" (Resnik, "An Interview with Tolkien," 43). On the other hand, in the *Nomenclature*, a guide for translators that he prepared for his publisher, he wrote that in the world of the story, December 25 "had then no significance" but continued, "Though Dec. 25 (setting out) and March 25 (accomplishment of quest) were intentionally chosen by me" (781). December 25 evidently arose first from the narrative chronology, and the story is "not a Christian myth" because it is set in a pre-Christian world. However, having settled on the date, Tolkien seems to have appreciated its liturgical resonance and deliberately chose March 25th to heighten the effect. In the interview, as he was responding to the question "How do you feel about the idea that people might identify Frodo with Christ?" he probably emphasized the first aspect in order to squash a potential (and erroneous) allegorical reading.

The dismantling and rebuilding of the Oratory Church was, in a sense, an objective correlative to Tolkien's own life at this time. When the foundation stone was laid in the spring of 1904, his mother was still alive and his domestic situation, though circumscribed by a degree of poverty and familial exclusion, was solid and sound. Soon, however, the security of home life would be torn apart by Mabel's death. And then a new stability would emerge, slowly, painfully, in a gradual process of reconstruction.

7

Death in a Cottage

At the start of 1904, when John Ronald celebrated his twelfth birthday, it might have seemed that the tiny family of Mabel and her two sons was at last reasonably secure. They were poor, but at least the older boy had won a scholarship to King Edward's School. Although the extended family still disapproved of Mabel's Catholicism, she had maintained communication with them. John Ronald had made his First Holy Communion, and they enjoyed the friendship and support of Fr. Francis and other Oratorian Fathers. Prospects, though not exactly bright, were brightening.

But 1904 was to be an *annus horribilis* for the Tolkien brothers. As the New Year opened, both John Ronald and Hilary were seriously ill: they went down with measles and whooping cough, and then (for Hilary) pneumonia. These illnesses were highly dangerous in those days before antibiotics, and Mabel exhausted herself in caring for the boys. Her own health deteriorated further, and she was hospitalized in April, when she was diagnosed with diabetes.[1]

At that time, it would have been a terrifying disease—poorly understood, incurable, untreatable. Mabel had what we now call Type 1 diabetes. Though often called 'juvenile diabetes' because it most often appears in childhood, Type 1 can strike suddenly in adulthood. It is an autoimmune disorder in which the body attacks its own pancreatic cells and thus becomes unable to produce insulin at all (as opposed to Type 2 diabetes, in which the supply is insufficient and the body is also unable to respond properly to the insulin it has). The only effective treatment is the injection of insulin—a discovery that was not made until the 1920s. Without insulin, excess sugar builds up in the blood, permanently damaging the heart, kidneys, nerves, and eyes. Furthermore, as the body, unable to access sugars to produce energy, begins to burn fat instead, acids can accumulate rapidly in the bloodstream and trigger a sudden, life-threatening attack of diabetic ketoacidosis. Other effects of the disease include fatigue, stomach pain, confusion, blurred vision, constant thirst, and slower healing of cuts and bruises, which can lead to serious infections.

The cause of Type 1 diabetes is still unknown, but it is worth noting that researchers today recognize potential triggering factors in the environment, such as pollution, poor diet, and stress.[2] Mabel's environment contained all three factors. The urban environment of Birmingham—England's second largest city after the capital—was heavily polluted, and the Clean Air Act of 1956 (brought in after a London smog killed literally thousands of people) was decades away. When, following her conversion, Mabel's family cut off financial support, it was much harder for her to maintain a nutritious, high-protein, vitamin-rich diet. And the emotional support that she had previously enjoyed from her family was also withdrawn, leading to personal turmoil and private distress. In short, Mabel had a lot to deal with and worry about, some of it directly connected to the new form of Christian faith she had recently adopted. It was not unreasonable that Tolkien later concluded that his mother's disease had been "largely consequent" upon the situation that she experienced after becoming a Catholic[3]—a form of suffering that she could have ended at any time by reverting to Anglicanism but chose, instead, to endure.

John Ronald and Hilary were packed off (separately) to relatives while Mabel had a long hospital stay. In June, when she was released, Fr. Francis put into effect a plan to help her convalesce. He arranged that she and the boys would move for a few months to the countryside and stay in a cottage at Rednal, on the southwestern edge of the Birmingham suburbs, part of a property established by John Henry Newman as a retreat center for the Oratorians. Newman himself was buried in the Rednal cemetery alongside other Oratorian fathers, and there was a chapel and wooded grounds that the family would have access to. The move enabled Mabel to get a change of air and to enjoy the company of her boys again in a relatively peaceful place as she sought to regain her health.

It was a delightful summer, with the boys enjoying the freedom of the countryside, playing with Fr. Francis's dog, 'Lord Roberts,' which resided at Rednal, and spending time with Fr. Francis himself on his visits. If an Oratorian priest was in residence at the retreat house, they could attend Mass right there in the chapel; otherwise, the gardener and his wife gave them a lift into the town of Bromsgrove, a fifteen-minute ride away, where they could worship at the church of St. Peter's.[4]

The parish of St. Peter's had a rich recusant history, and the church itself, an attractive Gothic Revival edifice built just forty years earlier, continued to nourish Tolkien's understanding of the aesthetic dimension of the Catholic faith.* It contained a beautiful high altar built by Augustus Pugin (who also designed London's iconic Big Ben tower)[5] and a statue of Our Lady of the Immaculate Conception, underscoring an element of Tolkien's faith that we will return to in chapter 16.[6]

Sadly, this peaceful interlude was all too brief. Rest and a change of scene could mitigate but not arrest the progress of Mabel's diabetes. In the absence of insulin, there was only ever going to be one outcome; it was simply a matter of timing. In early November of 1904, she suffered a sharp decline and slipped into a coma. Six days later, on November 14, she died.

The postman's cottage at Rednal

Mabel's death was a watershed moment in Tolkien's childhood, and indeed in his life. He had now lost both his parents, and he was only twelve years old. Given what we know of his future development and the fact that he retained his faith, we might naively assume that such an outcome was predictable, inevitable. But on that heartbreaking November day as his mother slipped away, there was nothing inevitable about it. It was not an assured fact that he would remain a Christian. The death of a parent always has complex psychological and spiritual effects, and all the more so when the circumstances are as tangled as those that the Tolkien family found itself in. The emotional possibilities for young John Ronald, now an orphan, included rebellion and rejection of the faith that had cost his mother so dearly.

In this light, it is worth pointing out a parallel in the life of Tolkien's future friend C.S. Lewis. Like Tolkien, Lewis had lost his mother at a young age; he was not quite ten years old when his mother, Flora, died at home from cancer. Though Lewis was not entirely rendered an orphan, he soon found that he was effectively losing his father as well as his mother, as Albert Lewis withdrew emotionally and sent the young boy away from home in Ireland to a boarding school in England within a few weeks of Flora's death. Lewis loved his mother and had prayed earnestly for

* The composer Sir Edward Elgar, who in 1900 had set to music Newman's poem *The Dream of Gerontius*, attended Mass at St. Peter's whenever he was in the area to visit his sister, who lived nearby; he even composed a Mass setting for the church ("Bromsgrove—St Peter").

her healing—as we can expect Tolkien did for Mabel. But the two boys took very different trajectories in their response to the Christian faith in which they had been raised. Within a few years of the trauma of his mother's death, Lewis abandoned his faith without regret but rather with a huge sense of relief, and considered himself an atheist for most of the next two decades.

Tolkien did not take that path. *Why* he did not is, of course, an unfathomable question, with many contributing factors, including the mystery of Tolkien's own personality and what he would have called the workings of providence. But given the significance of this death and its impact on his spiritual development, we will certainly benefit from exploring, as best we can, what John Ronald experienced when his mother passed away and what it meant to him.

Mabel "died in the postman's cottage at Rednal,"[7] as Tolkien put it decades later. That he remembers not just the brute fact of her death but also situates it so carefully indicates how deeply the place was imprinted on his memory. Her death did not occur far removed from his experience in an impersonal hospital, but in the temporary home where she and he and his brother were staying. And since John Ronald and Hilary were day boys, not boarders, at King Edward's School, they would presumably have been present during her last days. What were these days like?

Tolkien's biographer Humphrey Carpenter writes that Mabel died "with Father Francis and her sister May Incledon at her bedside in the cottage."[8] Yet Tolkien, late in his life, recalled in some bitterness that his mother died "alone, too ill for viaticum."[9] Both parts of this comment are worth considering.

We should first consider the apparent inconsistency in Tolkien's recollection of Mabel dying alone when, in fact, her sister and Fr. Francis were present. To begin with, there may not even be an inconsistency. With Mabel in a coma, her carers could not know exactly when the end would come, and both of them had to sleep sometime. It is possible that Mabel passed away in the small hours of the morning, when Fr. Francis or May were perhaps even in the room but sleeping and so unable to be with her in her last moments. This is the more likely since Carpenter does not record that John Ronald or Hilary were present at the death, which they perhaps would have been if the adults had been aware that their mother was close to her end. An imaginative boy like John Ronald might have felt that his mother had been abandoned to a lonely death, if he had woken the next morning to the news that she had passed away in the night while everyone else slept.

Another scenario, perhaps more likely, is that Tolkien, reflecting on this childhood trauma, was using slightly hyperbolic language to convey his sense of the abandonment of his mother not by her sister May in particular but by her family in general. There was to be no touching deathbed reconciliation between Mabel and her parents or her in-laws. Though her death was preceded by six days of coma, which gave plenty of time for family to arrive if they had wanted to, her mother and father chose to stay away while their daughter died. So, too, Arthur's parents apparently left their grandchildren to brave their mother's death without family support. May Incledon's presence perhaps only underscored the hard line that the Tolkien and Suffield families were taking. If May knew about Mabel's impending death, the rest of the family must surely have known as well. But only the sister who had (however briefly) shared Mabel's Catholic convictions came to her side.* The Protestant relatives, it seems, stayed away.

This is worth emphasizing not to lay blame on Tolkien's extended family but rather to highlight how remarkable it is that in the not-too-distant future he would develop genuine relationships with his grandparents, uncles, and aunts. John Ronald would have had ample reason to feel resentment and hostility, but somehow this path was avoided. It is not without reason that Tolkien would later say that he learned "forgiveness" from Fr. Francis, a topic which we will explore further in chapter 23.

Last rites

The other grief that Tolkien kept with him throughout life was that Mabel had died "too ill for viaticum."[10] This comment, though brief, is significant enough to merit a full explanation.

Fr. Francis was not just a family friend: he was a priest present at the deathbed of a faithful Catholic who was also one of his parishioners. He was not only

* Though May never did return to the practice of Catholicism after her brief entrance and retreat, it was a generous gesture. And perhaps it did not go unnoticed on the part of her children; her daughter Mary, Tolkien's cousin, would eventually become a Catholic and be the godmother of his first child.

expected but indeed required to help Mabel prepare for her death—something that would have involved several different elements and may well have taken place over several days.

Ideally, an important part of this preparation would have been giving her 'viaticum': that is, the reception of the Blessed Sacrament in preparation for death. The word 'viaticum' comes from the Latin word meaning "provision for a journey" and is viewed spiritually in exactly that sense: the final and most important provision for the last passage that a human being makes. Such importance is placed on it that, even in those days of an extended Eucharistic fast, the person receiving viaticum was not required to have fasted at all.

Sadly, however, Mabel was not able to receive viaticum, which suggests that her collapse was so rapid that she was already in a coma when Fr. Francis arrived at her side. Being unconscious, she was physically incapable of swallowing the consecrated Host and so could not receive it. As we will explore in detail in chapter 13, Tolkien developed a strong personal devotion to the Blessed Sacrament. We do not know how much it struck him at the time, but certainly when he recalled his mother's death, he was grieved to remember that she had been too ill to partake of the Eucharist in her last illness.

Even with Mabel in a coma, however, Fr. Francis would have provided Extreme Unction, prayers, and the 'last blessing.' These could have been done at any time during the final six days of her life and would almost certainly have been done sooner rather than later. We do not know for certain that John Ronald and Hilary were present at these rites, but it is probable they were. The last rites are intended to be done in the presence of family and friends with their active participation through responses and prayers. Furthermore, the rubrics for Extreme Unction include the assistance of at least one server if possible.[11] Since both John Ronald and Hilary regularly served at Mass for Fr. Francis, he would naturally call upon them, if available, to assist him as he fortified their mother with the rites of the Church.

The first of these would have been Extreme Unction. This is a sacrament of healing, both physical and spiritual: 'unction' means 'anointing' and refers to the use of consecrated oil in the rite. It is given to those who are in 'extreme' need: that is, either dying or in danger of death. It has its scriptural basis in James 5:14–15: "Is any among you sick? Let him call for the elders of the church, and let them pray over him, anointing him with oil in the name of the Lord; and the prayer of faith will save the sick man, and the Lord will raise him up; and if he has committed sins, he will be forgiven."

Fr. Francis would have sprinkled Mabel with holy water as a reminder of her baptism and prayed, finishing with the *Confiteor* or confession; since she was unconscious, he would have given her a conditional absolution of her sins.* He would then have anointed her with consecrated oil, making the sign of the cross over her eyes, ears, nose, lips, and hands, as symbolizing the five senses, saying in turn, "Through this holy unction and His own most tender mercy may the Lord pardon thee whatever sins or faults thou hast committed by sight" (and so on). While he did this anointing, the others in the room—including John Ronald if he was present—would have recited the Seven Penitential Psalms and also the Litany of the Saints. At some point as death grew nearer, Fr. Francis would also have given Mabel the "Apostolic blessing for the hour of death."[12]

Witness to the faith

Mabel's death was therefore an occasion of serious religious significance for Tolkien. He later wrote, "I witnessed (half-comprehending) the heroic sufferings and early death in extreme poverty of my mother who brought me into the Church"[13]—only half-understanding because of his youth and the intense emotion and anxiety of the moment, but taking it in. The solemn words and gestures of the last rites would have framed his experience of her death, giving him a structure by means of which he could ponder it as he matured. In 1913, when he was twenty-one, Tolkien wrote, "My own dear mother was a martyr indeed, and it is not to everybody that God grants so easy a way to his great gifts as he did to Hilary and myself, giving us a mother who killed herself with labour and trouble to ensure us keeping the faith."[14]

* Conditional absolution is given on the assumption that the person, if conscious, would have repented of any remaining sins. The inclusion of confession is intended to spiritually cleanse and prepare the Christian before entering into the next life. For a Catholic fallen away from the Church or living an immoral life, the last rites provide an opportunity for repentance and confession (illustrated by the death of the fictional Lord Marchmain in Evelyn Waugh's novel *Brideshead Revisited*), but for practicing Catholics such as Mabel, it was a source of additional spiritual strength at a time of need.

But perhaps of equal importance is that he also saw what it meant to die in the Christian faith. Tolkien had already lost one parent, his father, Arthur, who died in 1896. But at that time, John Ronald was only four, and they had been away from him in England for the better part of a year; his funeral took place without them, and they did not return to South Africa, so Tolkien never even saw his father's grave. For him at least, Arthur's death was an absence rather than a wound. Mabel's death was very different. Although she was too ill to receive *all* the strengthening preparations that the Church had to offer, such as viaticum, Tolkien would have seen that she had not made her passage unsupported or unprepared. The determination of Fr. Francis to do all he could for Mabel, even in the face of her inexorable decline, seems to have impressed Tolkien with a realization that, though death is unavoidable, it is worth resisting and assuaging as much as reasonably possible. As he grew into adulthood, he would come to adopt a view of history as a "long defeat," an inescapable loss ameliorated only by temporary and incomplete victories, a view that perhaps struck its first root at this point.

Mabel's funeral Mass was held at St. Peter's, Bromsgrove, where she was buried in the cemetery in the churchyard. In a remarkable tribute, Fr. Francis gave her a headstone in the identical style to that used for the graves of the Oratorian Fathers—including Newman himself—who are also buried at Rednal. (See figure 7.) In a sense, it was an image of a promise: that the link with the Oratorians which Mabel had formed for herself and for her sons would not be broken by her death but would endure.

8

A Home in the Highest

Mabel Tolkien died on Monday, November 14, 1904, and was buried three days later. Shortly thereafter, the season of Advent began, marking the beginning of a new liturgical year, since in the calendrical cycle of the Church the year begins not on January 1 but on the First Sunday of Advent.

Advent is a penitential period, not as strict as Lent, but one that takes as a theme the Four Last Things: death, judgment, heaven, and hell. The color of the season is a somber purple; no flowers decorate the altar; the *Gloria* is omitted from the Mass.[1] Yet it simultaneously looks forward to the joyful festival of Christmas, the celebration of the Nativity of Christ. The particular quality of the Advent season is hopeful expectation—of the coming of the Redeemer at Christmastide and of his coming again on the last day to judge the living and the dead.

At the Oratory, the Advent hymn "Creator alme siderum"* was sung at Vespers:

> Creator of the starry frame!
> Eternal Light of all who live!
> Jesu, Redeemer of mankind!
> An ear to thy poor suppliants give . . .
>
> Great Judge of all! in that last day,
> When friends shall fail, and foes combine,
> Be present then with us, we pray,
> To guard us with thy arm divine.[2]

It might well have seemed to John Ronald and Hilary that it was a fitting backdrop to their grief. They were now orphans: impoverished and seemingly abandoned by

* It is best known today by the English title "Creator of the stars of night."

their grandparents who had not even bothered to come to their daughter's deathbed. It was a grim situation—but, fittingly for the Advent season, one that had the hidden beginnings of hope and new life. As Tolkien recounted years later, "From [this] plight we were rescued by Fr. Francis Morgan of the Oratory."[3] In her will, Mabel had appointed Fr. Francis to be the guardian of her sons.[4] His guardianship was no mere legal formality on his part, as it might have been. Rather, the priest stepped up with what Tolkien called "astonishing charity"[5] to look after the boys and become their "second father."[6]

Francis Morgan is, therefore, a figure of central importance in our story. But we must remember that the Oratory was a community, a family, with, as Tolkien recalled, "many learned fathers."[7] The Birmingham Oratory was a large and lively Congregation, with fifteen to twenty priests in residence during Tolkien's boyhood. Apart from having an elected superior or provost, there was very little by way of the traditional monastic hierarchy at the Oratory. Each priest had scope for the expression of his own particular personality—and these personalities were highly individual.

Before we discuss Fr. Francis, then, we should meet some of those Fathers who became Tolkien's mentors and in some cases lifelong friends. These included Fr. William Neville, who was John Henry Newman's literary executor; Fr. John Norris, who had also known Newman well and was provost of the Oratory when the Tolkien family arrived at the parish; Fr. Henry Tristram, a specialist in Classics, especially Greek; and Fr. Anthony Pollen, who was a cycling enthusiast and a composer of classical music.[8]* Another important figure was the elderly Fr. Ignatius Ryder, a distinguished theologian and the first provost after Newman; Tolkien later came to possess his Latin dictionary.[9] When Tolkien joined the Oratory Scouts (as we saw in chapter 6), he got to know Fr. Charles Heurtley, who had them in his charge. Fr. Charles was recalled as "a benevolent, happy man" who had a particular gift of preaching at the Sunday children's Mass in a way that young people understood, and under his care, the Scouts became a "flourishing and successful group."[10]

Over the years, Tolkien kept in touch with some of the Oratorian Fathers he had known as a boy and also made new friendships among them. One such was

---

* Fr. Anthony went on to serve as a chaplain in the Royal Navy during the Great War and became the only chaplain to be awarded the Distinguished Service Cross for Gallantry in Action ("F. Anthony Pollen," Birmingham Oratory).

with Fr. Basil Lynch, who was ordained a priest of the Oratory in 1932. Fr. Basil was, in the view of his brother Oratorians, a true son of St. Philip, "a sharp-witted, learned, happy man who loved people" and "believed in not being serious," and he was, like Tolkien, a great reader; his favorite author was Jane Austen.[11] According to Oratory tradition, Tolkien consulted Fr. Basil on "what to do about Aragorn,"* but precisely what this means is a mystery.

Three of the Fathers deserve closer attention, before we turn back to Fr. Francis Morgan.

Fr. Vincent Reade (1874–1958)

Fr. Vincent Reade became a lifelong friend of Tolkien. Known affectionately as "Vink," he was a cultivated man with a degree from Cambridge; he was also a convert, having previously been an Anglican cleric.[12] Fr. Vincent served for many years as the headmaster of St. Philip's Grammar School, where he was remembered for his gentleness and warmth: "He called us all 'Dear Boy,' which made us feel at home and not just one in a crowd."[13] This kindness extended even to looking after boys who were not actually students at St. Philip's, for he was generous with his time and attention to the orphaned Tolkien brothers.

In the summer of 1914, he took John Ronald and Hilary on a walking holiday in Cornwall, with the party staying at the home of Fr. Vincent's mother.[14] They went all the way to the tip of Cornwall, where Fr. Vincent celebrated Mass at the chapel of Our Lady of the Lizard[15]—which certainly is an eye-catching Marian title, though in fact it merely refers to the place, the Lizard Peninsula. It was a tour with plenty of strenuous walking but also time to contemplate the landscape. At the Oratory, Tolkien was encouraged to develop his artistic talents, and on this tour, he exercised his skills, making a number of striking drawings and paintings.[16]

Tolkien recalled that as a young man, he wrote letters "grousing . . . to poor old Fr. Vincent Reade,"[17] who evidently offered a sympathetic ear. A lasting friendship developed, and as a student at Oxford, Tolkien even found room in his busy exam-time schedule to pay a visit to Fr. Vincent's mother, who then lived far out

* Personal communication from Fr. Guy Nicholls, who heard it from the archivist Gerard Tracey, who heard it from Fr. Basil himself. For biographical details, see "Father Basil Lynch," *O.S. Lives*, 107–8.

on the Banbury Road.[18] Fr. Vincent repaid the compliment, visiting the Tolkien family not long before the outbreak of World War II and relating alarming accounts of what he had recently witnessed during his travels in Germany.[19]

Fr. Vincent was described by a fellow Oratorian as "an outstanding man of deep and wide learning, meticulous in his speech and caring nothing for worldly things."[20] His students appreciated his encouraging manner. One recalled, "when I apologetically told him I'd managed only a Second Class Degree, he said, 'Well, I must tell you, I also got a Second—and so did Cardinal Newman.'" Indeed, Newman had barely squeaked through with a lower-second-class result in Classics and had failed altogether in mathematics. Here we may find an early role model for Tolkien's own supportive manner with his students. One of them, Daphne Castell, recalled, "No one could have been kinder, or more genuinely interested in the sometimes dull excursions of youthful delvers into philology. One of my own earlier memories is of failing some minor examination, and being awarded a glass of sherry by him, and the consoling remark, 'But, my dear girl, *everyone* fails that!'"[21]

Fr. Robert Eaton (1866–1942)

Fr. Robert Ormston Eaton was a dynamic figure at the Oratory, well known for his preaching, which attracted large crowds, and for his extensive involvement with the Oratory's choir and music program. He was also headmaster of St. Philip's Grammar School at the time that Tolkien attended for a few months in 1902. John Ronald moved so swiftly to the top of his class that he was sure to have come to the attention of Fr. Robert.

A skilled boxer and cricketer as a young man, Fr. Robert ("Burby" to his students)[22] was also a talented amateur actor, who continued as a priest to coach student actors in Latin plays, a tradition of The Oratory School. John Ronald would thus have had a Catholic mentor to encourage him both in his love of sport (in his case, rugby) and his acting in classical plays, two passions which he developed at King Edward's School.

Fr. Robert was also a prolific writer of spiritual works, including *The Mirror of Justice: Chapters on Our Blessed Lady* (1916) and *The Divine Refreshment: Chapters on the Blessed Sacrament* (1927). Though published in later years, these titles would have reflected Fr. Robert's preaching and general attitude, which Tolkien would have encountered as a boy and which no doubt contributed to his developing spiritual interest in Marian devotion and his love of the Eucharist (to which we will return in later chapters). Fr. Robert writes, "To receive our Lord in Holy Communion is not a mere mechanical exercise of the spiritual life. . . . It is a stupendous communication of our Lord's sweetness and strength to a soul for which He died, and which He would make all his own. It is an outpouring of the choicest graces of the Sacred Heart . . . a bestowal of precisely those graces which every individual soul needs."[23]

Fr. Denis Sheil (1865–1962)

Six feet four inches tall, Fr. Denis Sheil was a remarkable figure of "impressive dignity, gentle manliness and Victorian courtesy," recognizable in the Ladywood neighborhood for his "big black cloak." He had a very long career in the Congregation (seventy-two years), and it was recalled that he "exercised great influence especially about the appearance of the Church building, in which he received much help from Fr. Francis Morgan."[24]*

Fr. Denis also provided a strong link with the Oratory's founder, Cardinal Newman, for he was the last novice received by Newman himself and served as a priest alongside him during his final years. Furthermore, Fr. Denis made such a detailed study of Newman's life and works that, when the Archbishop of Birmingham began the process of introducing the cause of Newman's canonization, he was called as the principal witness. Considering Tolkien's later great interest in the reforms of Pope Pius X, he was undoubtedly interested in the fact that Fr. Denis had, in 1914, been present in the antechamber when the pope died.[25]

It's very likely that Fr. Denis heard Tolkien's confession at least on occasion. He was highly regarded as a confessor: one parishioner recalled him as "the wonderful priest who lived, or so it seemed, inside the confessional box in the shadow of the pulpit. . . . Every evening, immediately after dinner, Fr. Denis would enter his box, and there he stayed until the lights went out."[26] As we will see in chapter 9, in later years, Tolkien put a high value on the sacrament of Confession, and it is not

* In fact, in the summer of 1904, John Ronald had scolded his future guardian for letting Fr. Denis take up so much of his time: "You are too bad not to come [to Rednal] in spite of Fr. Denis" ("Rebus Letter," 1).

unlikely that this positive attitude was shaped in part by his experiences with Fr. Denis, who was known for his "sympathetic and constructive help" and for being "encouraging, telling us 'not to worry.'"[27]

Fr. Francis Morgan (1857–1935)

Now we return to Fr. Francis Morgan. (See figure 8.) When Mabel Tolkien chose him to be the executor of her will and the boys' guardian after her death, he was already a close friend of the family. He gave the boys the gift of time and attention, indulging in boyish pastimes such as flying kites, and they responded with warmth. We can see this in a charming letter that Tolkien wrote in the summer of 1904, addressing him as "My dear wise owl Francis" and closing as "your loving Ronald," and declaring that "We each have found two lovely walks" that they hope to take him on when he visits.[28]

Who was Fr. Francis? To begin with, he was almost exactly the same age that Tolkien's own father would have been; the two men were born only a few weeks apart in 1857, Francis in Spain, Arthur in England. Francis's mother was a Spanish Catholic, and his father was an English Protestant; as an adult, he held dual British-Spanish citizenship. From an early age, Francis was educated in England, including at Newman's Oratory School, known as something of a 'Catholic Eton,'* where he had Newman as a teacher.

He studied for a time in London and France before entering as a novice at the Birmingham Oratory; he was ordained as a priest in 1883. Francis traveled regularly on Oratory business and sent reports to Cardinal Newman—"my dear Father"—while on trips to London, Rome, and Spain.[29] Francis even accompanied Newman on a visit to the Duke of Norfolk as his sacristan and attendant. Since Newman at that time was both elderly and recovering from a bad fall, choosing Francis as his attendant shows how reliable he considered the younger man. Francis

* Eton College is perhaps the best-known school in England. A boys' boarding school founded in 1440, it is famous for its alumni becoming part of the governing elite of England. It has traditionally placed a great emphasis on sport as a means of building character; hence the saying attributed to the Duke of Wellington that "The Battle of Waterloo was won on the playing-fields of Eton." Obviously, a 'Catholic Eton' would not have the same direct route to top positions in politics, law, and business, but it did what it could to equip its students for leading roles in society.

also served as his personal secretary, handling correspondence and financial matters. Over the years, he held numerous pastoral and administrative roles at the Oratory, serving at various times as the pastor of the parish, as treasurer, and as the Father Minister, responsible for overseeing the employees of both the Oratory House and the Oratory School.[30]

His family on the Spanish side, the Osbornes, had an extensive sherry business from which Fr. Francis had some income. He was not himself rich and was pleased to remark that he was glad to have rich friends; in fact, when the new Oratory Church was built, its sanctuary was financed by wealthy relatives of his.[31] But he was moderately well-off, and since Oratorians do not give up their private property upon joining the community, he could (and did) use his private means to support a diverse array of charitable causes; he was remembered at the Oratory "for his many deeds of charity, all done in the most unassuming and secret way."[32] The causes he supported included the Catholic Prisoners' Aid Society, the Birmingham Catholic Cripples' Care Society, and the Little Oratory Cricket Club.[33] And from 1904 onwards, Fr. Francis drew on his own funds to supplement the small income that the Tolkien boys had after their mother's death.

He loved music and had a pleasing singing voice. He was also an avid reader, with his room crammed full of books, including a rotating bookcase in the center. He purchased titles on a wide range of subjects—devotional, apologetics, literary—and his personal library included various volumes in Spanish, which Tolkien later used in an attempt to learn the language by himself. Fr. Francis also made use of his bilingual competence by serving in the Oratory's Spanish-language confessional and occasionally doing a bit of translation work.[34]

That his personal spirituality included a devotion to the Blessed Virgin Mary is indicated by the fact that when he was not celebrating a public Mass at the main altar of the church, he chose to celebrate it at the Lady Altar.

What was he like? He was remembered by the Oratory School boys as being "always ready to cheer everyone with his hearty laugh and witty remarks, or to console them with good advice and words of encouragement."[35] Tolkien once declared that in the course of his life, he had met "hypocritical . . . cynical . . . mean . . . and even (at a guess) immoral priests," yet "for me one Fr Francis outweighs them all, and he was an upper-class Welsh-Spaniard Tory, and seemed to some just a pottering old snob and gossip. He was—and he was *not*."[36]

That Tolkien could admit to Francis having been something of a snob and gossip indicates the clear-eyed view he came to have of his guardian; he was too honest to indulge in hagiography. But the fact that, despite this honesty, he could also maintain the opposite—that Francis was *not* a snob and a gossip, or that he was certainly more than just those things—speaks to Tolkien's grasp of the complexity of human personality and of his love for Fr. Francis, for love "covers a multitude of sins" (1 Peter 4:8). Having learned lessons from Fr. Francis himself about how to forgive sins far worse than snobbery and gossip (as we shall see further in chapter 23), Tolkien knew that these relatively mild vices could and should be overlooked and attention paid instead to the man's many virtues: generosity, goodness, kindness, patience.

Fr. Francis was well educated and cultured,* but he had no particular calling to the scholarly life. That one of his brother priests warmly recalled having "a fellow feeling for him, as he was not academic"[37] indicates the high (perhaps even intimidating) intellectual tone of the Congregation at that time. But he felt no need to compete with the theologians and writers among his brother priests. His service as personal secretary to Newman indicates that he was an intelligent and competent man, and perhaps this early opportunity to serve 'their Cardinal' in a supporting role suggested the path that he would take in his mature years at the Oratory, serving in ways that were more pastoral and practical, making use of emotional intelligence and interpersonal skills as much as intellect.

As guardian, he was an unselfconscious and relaxed man who could genuinely enjoy the company of children and understood what they needed. He took John Ronald and Hilary on holidays every summer to Lyme Regis in Dorset,[38] a seaside town on the south coast of England, notable for its beaches and its fossil-studded cliffs—a good choice for two active yet thoughtful boys.

Tolkien came to consider Fr. Francis his "second father," recalling into his old age "the sudden miraculous experience" of his "love and care and humour" for himself

* For instance, his papers in the Oratory Archives reveal that in 1911 he carried on a detailed three-way correspondence as a sort of pastoral mediator between a non-Catholic, one Mr. Shore, who was concerned about the Catholic Church's position regarding the papacy, and a Catholic theologian or controversialist whose works Shore had read (Birmingham Oratory Archives).

and Hilary.[39] The brothers had suffered the tragic loss of both their parents, a loss that could never be put right, but they were not left alone. Under the particular oversight of Fr. Francis and in the bustling, fatherly-brotherly atmosphere of the Birmingham Oratory, the boys gained a new family: not a replacement for what they had lost but something still good in itself. And although he came under Fr. Francis's guardianship at the lowest point of his life, no bitterness tinges Tolkien's recollection of the place that became his substitute home. In fact, he made a promise that any sons of his would be educated at The Oratory School—the boarding school that he had not attended but whose spiritual, intellectual, and emotional atmosphere he evidently judged to be the closest equivalent that he could offer his own boys.[40*]

Many years later, Tolkien would recall that, growing up at the Oratory, he "had the advantage . . . of a 'good Catholic home'—'in excelsis.'"[41] We should note the exuberant quality of his praise: "in excelsis" means 'in the highest,' and would have been immediately associated in Tolkien's mind with the opening of the Gloria in the liturgy of the Mass: *Gloria in excelsis Deo* (Glory to God in the highest). And so, to speak of the Oratory House as a home "in excelsis" is no small compliment. It was a home elevated by friendship with divine things, a home touched with a heavenly light.

---

* And he kept his promise: John, Michael, and Christopher were all educated at The Oratory School, which had relocated in the 1920s from Birmingham to Caversham, near Reading. At that time, the school was not coeducational, but Priscilla did also receive a private Catholic education at Rye St. Antony School in Headington.

9

Horsemaster

From age twelve until nineteen, when he left for his university studies, Tolkien was, as he put it, "virtually a junior inmate of the Oratory house."[1] The seven years in which he was wholly under the care of the Oratorian Fathers was an intensely formative time.

Tolkien had lost first his father, then his deeply beloved mother. Not many years later, he would go through the horrors of the Great War. These experiences would be more than enough to account for a bleak view of life, and indeed Tolkien had a depressive streak in his character. What is surprising is not that he experienced times of intense melancholy but rather that he also had such a deep-seated streak of joy and fun. His extraordinarily complex intellect was balanced by what he described wryly, in later years, as "a very simple sense of humour (which even my appreciative critics find tiresome)."[2] William Cater recalled his "sudden grin which would charm birds off trees" and that he had "the most humorous eye I've ever seen on mortal man."[3] (See figure 70.) This aspect of Tolkien's personality is reflected in his most famous creation, the Hobbits, a people who are by nature merry and full of laughter, "fond of cheerful jests at all times"; they are "hospitable, and delighted in parties."[4]

But in noting Tolkien's famous remark that "I am in fact a *Hobbit* (in all but size),"[5] we will do well to recall his description of the hobbits as also being "curiously tough." As he puts it in the prologue to *The Lord of the Rings*, "they were, perhaps, so unwearyingly fond of good things not least because they could, when put to it, do without them, and could survive rough handling by grief, foe, or weather in a way that astonished those who did not know them well and looked no further than their bellies and their well-fed faces."[6] *The Hobbit* and *The Lord of the Rings* take the characters, and the reader, through darkness, sorrow, and loss, but the stories are deeply grounded in the simple, joyful life of the hobbits in the Shire—where both books begin and end.

Priscilla Tolkien considered that "Humour is an essential, or the essential, element if this balance [the balance between vision and practicality] is ever to be achieved, and humour is thus seen to be the core of any morality. This awareness is crucial to my father's creation of the hobbits and the world of the Shire."[7] If we are to understand how this could be so—how humor could be at the "core" of Tolkien's moral sense and how, despite the trauma of his early years, joy was so interwoven into his sense of self—then we must consider those formative years at the Oratory of St. Philip Neri, during which the distinctive charism of the Oratorians shaped his spiritual, emotional, and even temperamental development.

The 'spiritual father' of the Oratorians is known as the 'apostle of joy.' As *The School of St. Philip Neri* puts it, Philip "would always have us cheerful, for he says that melancholy is prejudicial to spirituality." A key characteristic of Oratorian spirituality is therefore a certain levity, with a serious purpose. As Philip taught, the first remedy against melancholy was "to have a good conscience, wherefore the Saint prescribed the powerful means of a general confession." Hence his maxim that "they should maintain cheerfulness and preserve themselves from sin."[8]

Reconciliation

One important element of Oratorian spirituality is, therefore, its emphasis on the sacrament of Reconciliation. John Ronald had made his first confession in preparation for his First Holy Communion and confirmation, as we discussed in chapter 4. The Oratorian Fathers would have been sure to explain clearly what this sacrament entails, as, being mostly converts themselves, they were aware that it was not practiced in the Church of England in the same way as in the Catholic Church. For Anglicans, the approach to confession was 'all may; some should; none must,' and there was a wide range of views among clergymen as to whether auricular confession (that is, a confession heard by a priest from a penitent speaking aloud) was allowable or an unacceptable Romish practice.

In contrast, the Catholic rule can be summed up as 'all should, all must': every Catholic above the age of reason must make their confession at least once a year, preferably more often. In Tolkien's day, when people did not necessarily receive Holy Communion each time that they attended Mass, it was the usual practice to make one's confession if one intended to receive at the Sunday Mass.

The scriptural basis for confession rests on two main pillars. First, the idea that honesty among believers is a good thing in general, including honesty about one's sins; hence, the Epistle of St. James recommends, "Confess your sins to one another, and pray for one another, that you may be healed" (James 5:16). And second, the idea that Christ, through his Apostles, will forgive sins if they are confessed honestly and sincerely: "If you forgive the sins of any, they are forgiven; if you retain the sins of any, they are retained" (John 20:23).

Preparing for confession meant that John Ronald would make an 'examination of conscience.' Many devotional guides were available to help the penitent be honest and thorough, not skipping things or making excuses, and, conversely, to avoid scrupulosity—that is, being overly self-critical and trying to confess things that were not actually sins at all. (For instance, missing Sunday Mass is not a sin if one needs to stay home to take care of someone who is ill.) The priest acts *in persona Christi*: that is, 'in the person of Christ.' After hearing the confession and perceiving that the person is genuinely contrite, he gives the person a penance (usually some prayers to say) and absolves him of his sins in the name of the Father, the Son, and the Holy Spirit. The priest does not himself forgive sins but rather channels to the penitent God's forgiveness, which he is authorized to communicate. The priest may also provide some spiritual counsel after hearing the confession and ask the penitent to pray for him as a fellow sinner.

The Oratorian approach to confession is not punitive or shaming but rather places the act in the context of love, healing, and spiritual growth. Here, Tolkien would have learned that confession is more than a 'hoop-jumping' act of obedience to the requirements of the Church, a conventional behavior before receiving communion, or a psychological maneuver to assuage guilty feelings. Rather, it is an act of re-conciliation (literally, a calling together, with a shared etymological root in 'council,' an assembly with a shared purpose), for it is only by receiving God's forgiveness that there can be any true peace in a congregation or a family or indeed internally within an individual. With reference to the making of a 'good confession,' Tolkien later observed that "gaiety proceeding from a 'lightness of heart' may be and often is a result of the fitting reception of a sacrament by one of the faithful, and that quite independently of other pains, or cares."[9]

His appreciation for the re-integrating effect of confession can be seen, many years later, in the gratitude he expressed for the advice of his friend and doctor, Robert 'Humphrey' Havard: "I've been in a very bad state. Humphrey came here and told me that I must go to confession and that he would come early on Sunday morning to take me to confession and communion. That's the sort of doctor to have."[10]

Regular confession became an important part of Tolkien's spiritual life. As a mature man, he said that "he always liked to go to confession before receiving communion," even inquiring if he would be able to go to confession while visiting friends over a Sunday.[11] The routine of confessing one's sins on a regular basis means, of course, that the same ones tend to turn up repeatedly, but this, in the Catholic understanding of it, is simply an indication of the way God's grace most usually works slowly and organically, not all in a flash. As Tolkien remarked, repentance "works spirally and not in a closed circle."[12]

Prancing ponies

The approach of the Oratorians, in nurturing spiritual health through fostering cheerfulness even (or especially) in difficult times, would certainly have been of assistance in helping the orphaned John Ronald to ease back into enjoyment of life. He could indulge in boyish pranks—as when he tampered with the corkscrew-like contraption that carried trays of food from the basement kitchen up for the priests to collect in the refectory above. On at least one occasion, he mischievously placed the Oratory's cat in the serving drum and sent it up, where a hungry priest found, not his tea and toast, but a fretful feline.[13]

There is a subtle nod to the playfulness of St. Philip in his unfinished story *The Notion Club Papers*, in which the characters are members of a very Inklings-like group and indeed share certain traits of Tolkien and his friends. One of the cast is Philip Frankley, the "Lover of Horses and Horseplay!"[14] The name Philip (as Christopher Tolkien reminds us in the notes) comes from the Greek *phil-ippos* and means 'horse-loving.' This is the sort of etymological joke that is characteristic of

Tolkien—and tellingly he refers to Philip not just as an equine aficionado but also as a lover of *horseplay*: rough-and-tumble, boisterous play.

Tolkien exhibited a readiness to be silly throughout his life. Hugh Brogan recalled an episode from his childhood when Tolkien came to visit the family and showed off his 'party trick': he "went up to the first-floor landing and fell all the way down quite spectacularly—about a dozen steps, I guess—arms and legs splaying about in all directions, and an immense clatter. We were literally breathtaken."[15] On another occasion, Tolkien dressed as a bear for a children's Christmas party, held at the University Catholic Chaplaincy, and walked home late at night still in full costume.[16] George Sayer recalled a visit when he found the elderly Tolkien playing trains with one of his great-grandchildren: "I'm Thomas the Tank Engine. Puff. Puff. Puff"—and immediately "conscripted" Sayer into the game as a train signal.[17]

Some of the stories of Tolkien's adult sense of humor can strike the reader as rather undignified, even embarrassing. At a literary society meeting in 1938, he exhibited from his pocket a curious green object, claiming "stoutly and with apparent sincerity that it was the shoe of a Leprechaun."[18] According to his biographer Humphrey Carpenter, he once dressed up "as an Anglo-Saxon warrior complete with axe" and chased "his astonished neighbor down the road."[19] As an elderly man, on one occasion he disconcerted a shopkeeper by paying with a handful of coins that included his false teeth; presumably he had sneezed or coughed, and on finding his dentures having come loose and fallen into his hand, he jokingly offered the whole lot.[20]

Surely, we might think, a professor at Oxford, and later the author of the worldwide best-seller *The Lord of the Rings*, ought to live up to his status as a figure of high academic repute and a literary lion? Not according to the teachings of St. Philip, who considered spiritual pride to be a serious danger and humility the best remedy. Philip remarked, "Charity and cheerfulness, or charity and humility, should be our motto." He also said, "Let us pray God, if He gives us any virtue or any gift, to keep it hidden even from ourselves, that we may preserve our humility, and not take occasion of pride because of it."[21]

Philip was himself an exceptionally gifted and holy man, widely considered a saint in his own lifetime. However, he deliberately sought to undercut this image of sanctity—the *image* of it, not the reality of his devotion to God, his mentoring of the young Oratorians, or his care for the poor of Rome, all of which he pursued unabated. For instance, Philip once showed up at an important social event with half his beard shaved off. He knew he'd only been invited to the party so that his wealthy host could show off his piety by having the holiest man in Rome in attendance: to undercut those pretenses, he deliberately made himself look like a fool. Philip took the spiritual life seriously but never took himself too seriously.

This emphasis on humility in John Ronald's teen years seems to have helped check any tendency for the devout young man becoming a prig or a pious show-off, as we can see in the recollections of Colin Brookes-Smith, a friend of the family who spent time with John Ronald and Hilary at their aunt Jane Neave's farm. He remarked that Tolkien had a "robust attitude to religious matters. He took them seriously, but there was always an element of humour in it which he could not resist." One particular incident stood out in Brookes-Smith's memory. He, John Ronald, and Hilary had been given a shared bedroom.

> Either in a sense of bravado or perhaps the need for a display of religiosity in the presence of the two Roman Catholics I knelt down by my bedside ostensibly to say or pretend to say my prayers. At which point, Ronald threw a boot at my head with a roar of laughter. This, needless to say, cured me for ever of ostentatious religious practices and fitted well with my agnosticism.[22]

The point here is not that Tolkien disapproved of his friend saying unaccustomed prayers but rather that he could tell it was pretense, and therefore ought to be squelched. False piety was not the sort of thing a son of St. Philip would put up with.

The Philippine teaching on humility that Tolkien absorbed as a young man did not preclude achievement or even pride in achievement—rather, it sought to keep the right perspective. Philip warns against pursuing achievements for the sake of worldly praise. However, he was also aware of a kind of scrupulosity that could arise, and "did not wish to keep us back from doing good, that we may avoid vain-glory";[23] therefore, Philip explained that "it does not take away our merit" in the spiritual life if we enjoy praise and acclaim for our work as long as it wasn't deliberately sought after for its own sake.[24] If we have done good work, then we are to accept whatever praise or acclaim comes from it, but not dwell upon it or treat it as important—or to start considering ourselves as important.

Looking much further ahead in Tolkien's life, this early formation in humor and humility would stand him in good stead. When *The Hobbit* and *The Lord of the Rings* brought him fame, fan mail poured in, often of the most adulatory kind. Tolkien, however, was from the start alert to the spiritual dangers this presented. His correspondence shows a keen awareness of the danger of uncritically accepting lavish praise from admirers—what he calls "incense," as in the incense offered before idols.

Writing to Christopher in 1944, he shared a fan letter he had received from an American boy who declared that he had read *The Hobbit* no fewer than eleven times. Tolkien's comment is telling. Though he admitted that the "smell of incense" was pleasing, letters like these, he said, "make me rather sad. What thousands of grains of good human corn must fall on barren stony ground, if such a very small drop of water should be so intoxicating! But I suppose one should be grateful for the grace and fortune that have allowed me to provide even the drop."[25]

In 1958, after a celebratory dinner thrown in his honor in Holland, he wrote to his publisher to give a report of it, now that he has "had time to simmer down a bit, and recover some sense of proportion. The incense was thick and very heady; and the kindness overwhelming."[26]

And in the last year of his life, he commented, "Being a cult figure in one's own lifetime I am afraid is not at all pleasant. However I do not find that it tends to puff one up; in my case at any rate it makes me feel extremely small and inadequate. But even the nose of a very modest idol . . . cannot remain entirely untickled by the sweet smell of incense!"[27]

He could laugh both at excessive veneration and at his own readiness to enjoy it. But insofar as he managed to stay down to earth, it surely had much to do with his early rootedness in the humor and humility of St. Philip Neri.

10

Love's Labors

The Birmingham Oratory became a home for young John Ronald in the emotional, social, and spiritual sense, but he still needed a roof over his head, meals, and someone to look after him and his brother.

This presented Fr. Francis with a practical problem. There were no accommodations suitable for them at the Oratory House. For a month or so after their mother's death, John Ronald and Hilary stayed with a Tolkien uncle in the Birmingham suburb of Kings Norton.[1] Almost five miles from the Oratory, it was acceptable as a temporary measure but not at all suitable for their access to Catholic worship; it was also too far away for Fr. Francis to keep a close eye on their well-being. In January 1905, he found an adequate, if not ideal, solution: they would stay with their Aunt Beatrice Suffield in Edgbaston, conveniently near the Oratory, so that each morning the brothers could start the day by assisting at Mass with Fr. Francis before heading off to school at King Edward's. Aunt Beatrice did not have any particular religious faith, which meant that although the boys would not have active support for their Christian faith at home, they also would not face resistance to growing up as Catholics.

Recently widowed, childless, and not well-off, Beatrice might have seemed like someone who would respond warmly to having her nephews under her care. Unfortunately, that was not the case. She provided their meals and a place for them to stay but nothing by way of substitute motherly love. Indeed, early on, she dealt John Ronald a serious emotional blow. Walking by chance into the kitchen, he discovered that she had burned Mabel's personal papers without consulting him or his brother and, apparently, without even realizing that they might wish to keep them.[2] It was an extraordinarily insensitive thing to do.

Nevertheless, it was not until the summer of 1907 that Fr. Francis learned that the boys were unhappy there. Perhaps they were exhibiting the curious reticence that children often have about unhappiness; perhaps they simply accepted the situation; and perhaps they were, at some level, anxious about the alternatives. If they didn't live at Aunt Beatrice's, would they be sent away from the Oratory?

John Ronald would have been uncomfortably aware that just down the street from where they had lived on Oliver Road was St. Philip Neri's Orphanage for Boys. Established in 1861 by the Oratorians, it was run by Mr. and Mrs. Rawlins, whom Fr. Francis knew, and was supervised by another Oratorian priest, Fr. Edmund Hodgson.[3] Fr. Edmund had visited the boys at one point during their summer in Rednal, which seems not to have gone over well. John Ronald sent Fr. Francis a note containing a sarcastic limerick, adding, "This is to pay you out for not coming, and sending Father Edmund instead."[4]

If he had fears about Fr. Francis committing him and Hilary to the orphanage, he underestimated his guardian. It took several months, but in early 1908, Fr. Francis found new lodgings for them at 37 Duchess Road, within sight of the Oratory church.* It was the home of Mr. and Mrs. Faulkner, who were active members of the parish; some of the Oratorian Fathers attended musical soirées in their home.[5] And it was this house that Tolkien described many years later as having been "of supreme importance" to his life.[6] Here it was that he met the young woman who would eventually become his wife and the mother of his four children, his Lúthien: Edith Mary Bratt.

Edith

She was a fellow lodger with Mrs. Faulkner and, like Tolkien, an orphan.† (See figure 13.) Beautiful, musical, high-spirited, and intelligent, she was kind to both brothers, particularly winning their favor by conspiring with the maid to smuggle them extra

* The Oratory archivist noted that Beatrice Suffield "was not too well off financially and so the four pounds and sixteen shillings which Father Francis paid over every month must have been very useful (indeed, he continued to pay varying amounts to her even after the boys had moved on)." Here is a notable instance of Francis generously putting his money to good effect: paying Mrs. Suffield more than was strictly necessary in order to tide her over (until, presumably, she found other lodgers), thereby ensuring she suffered no loss even as his prime purpose was to help his two wards (Tracey, "Tolkien and the Oratory").

† Her mother, Frances Bratt, died when Edith was fourteen. Her father, Alfred Warrilow, who was not married to her mother and was not named on her birth certificate, had died in 1891 when she was only a toddler. She never knew him. It was only after her marriage to Tolkien that Edith revealed she was "illegitimate," and he encouraged her not to let it trouble her as it didn't

food. Teenaged boys are notoriously always hungry, but it was also undoubtedly more fun to receive food in a basket sent up to their window by a pretty girl than simply to ask their landlady for extra helpings. This playful attention gave John Ronald an excuse to interact with Edith. Though he went to an all-boys school, Tolkien had the benefit of some practice talking to girls, since by this time he spent many of his holidays with the Incledon family, sharing in family games and even in the hobby of inventing languages with his cousins Marjorie and Mary.

In any case, sixteen-year-old John Ronald and nineteen-year-old Edith soon became good friends, and over the next year or so, their friendship developed into love. In his old age, Tolkien would recall that they had "rescued one another" from "the dreadful sufferings of our childhoods."[7] They had suffered much; they would go on to suffer much; but they would do so together.

In the meantime, their romance blossomed in mischievous visits to Birmingham tea shops (throwing sugar lumps onto the hats of passersby) and in late-night conversations, with John Ronald leaning out of his window to whisper to Edith in her room below.[8] But they kept it quiet and in fact tried to keep it secret. One day they arranged for a surreptitious bicycle outing, each giving separate (untrue) destinations but meeting up for a walk in the hills and tea in Rednal, then arriving separately back at Duchess Road.[9]

When Fr. Francis caught wind of it, he was troubled. To be sure, the relationship was an innocent one, with no more than kisses exchanged.* But what would have disturbed him was that Tolkien had lied about this outing: not a hasty lie on the spur of the moment, stemming from embarrassment about revealing his feelings for a girl, but a deliberate deception. He would have considered—and Tolkien would have had to concede—that this was a sin against the Eighth Commandment,

---

matter to him. He wrote to her: "I think I love you even more tenderly because of all that, my wife, but we must as far as possible forget it and entrust it to God" (*Biography*, 86).

* This was in line with the Christian faith that John Ronald and Edith shared, as well as the cultural and social expectations of the time; indeed, one of the ideals of Tolkien and his friends in the TCBS was of moral purity, in emulation of the Pre-Raphaelite Brotherhood. The fact that in a later letter Tolkien refers to Edith as his 'lover' may be confusing to modern readers, but what he meant by it was, as the *Oxford English Dictionary* explains, "A person who is in love with, or who is enamoured of, another person" (*OED*, lover, n., 3a), which was a typical use in his day. Only in the second half of the twentieth century did the usual usage of the word shift to have a sexual meaning. As the *Oxford English Dictionary* dryly notes, "There is considerable semantic overlap between the subsenses at sense 3, esp. as a result of historical changes in the nature of love and courtship."

"Thou shalt not bear false witness against thy neighbor," which, the Catechism said, "forbids all false testimony, rash judgment, and lies."[10] Fr. Francis was responsible for the moral as well as the practical well-being of his ward, so this was a cause for concern. What had begun as youthful poor judgment might take root as a habit of dishonesty.

And so Fr. Francis made it clear that their relationship must end, at least for the time being. To ensure that this happened, he arranged for John Ronald and Hilary to move to different lodgings a few streets away. He had not at that point forbidden the young couple to see each other, so Tolkien was not technically disobeying him in meeting up with Edith to spend the afternoon together and exchange birthday presents (their January birthdays were about a fortnight apart). It was at this time that Edith explained that she had decided to move to Cheltenham to stay with family friends. He wrote "Thank God" in his diary, recognizing that this was for the best.[11]

But the fact that John Ronald had again concealed their meeting caused his guardian fresh heartburn. This time he forbade Tolkien to see Edith at all, except to say goodbye when she left for Cheltenham; he also forbade him to write to her.

Tolkien made an effort to obey, not with entire success at first. He wrote in his diary on February 16, 1910: "Last night prayed would see E. by accident. Prayer answered . . . Told her I could not write . . . Happier but so much long to see her . . . Cannot think of anything else." A few days later he chanced to see her again and "could not resist" going over to speak with her: "This cheered me up for a while. Prayed and thought hard." Two days on and he bumped into her once more, "coming from the Cathedral to pray for me." These meetings were not planned, but when Fr. Francis learned of them, he laid down the law even more firmly, writing a stern note to Tolkien describing his behavior as "evil and foolish"[12]—possibly an overreaction, but one that he felt consistent with his responsibility for the young man's moral and practical well-being. His final ruling was that there was to be no contact of any kind between them for three years, by which time Tolkien would be twenty-one years old and no longer his ward.

Here the story takes an unexpected turn for most modern readers. Tolkien obeyed—not without pain, but, in the end, with complete fidelity. And, as we will see in chapter 14, his relationship with his guardian, though it was understandably strained, was not broken, and his relationship with Edith survived. It was, in some ways, the first serious test of Tolkien's ability to keep faith with other people. His romantic love for his girlfriend and his filial love for his guardian were pulling him in different ways. How could he continue to love them both?

A moral crisis

When Fr. Francis forbade him to see Edith, Tolkien wrote in his diary, "I owe all to Fr. F and so must obey."[13] What did he mean by *must*?

John Ronald and Edith were intelligent, resourceful, and perfectly willing to work around 'the system' if they felt it right to do so. (Later, when Tolkien was serving on the front lines in the Great War and was forbidden to reveal his location, they devised a code of pinholes in the letters so that Edith could work out where he was.[14]) Tolkien recalled, "I had to choose between disobeying and grieving (or deceiving) a guardian who had been a father to me, more than most real fathers, but without any obligation, and 'dropping' the love-affair until I was 21."[15] He had a choice and knew that he did. He could have found a way to circumvent the strictures, but he realized he "must obey": the *must* was a moral imperative coming from his own conscience, not imposed upon him from without.

In later years, when Tolkien recounted this episode, he admitted how "extremely hard, painful and bitter" the separation was, especially at the beginning,[16] but he showed no resentment toward his guardian. As he summed up the situation to his son Michael:

> Your mother was older than I, and not a Catholic. Altogether unfortunate, as viewed by a guardian. And it was in a sense very unfortunate; and in a way very bad for me. These things are absorbing and nervously exhausting. I was a clever boy in the throes of work for (a very necessary) Oxford scholarship. The combined tensions nearly produced a bad breakdown.[17]

In other words, he came to see that Fr. Francis's objections were not without reason, and we can get a sense of what those reasons were.

Edith had made "no vow"[18] to Tolkien (so he later explained to his son Michael), and she was thus free to marry someone else during their separation if she chose to. But what vow might Tolkien have made to her? This would have been a potential cause of concern to Fr. Francis. English law at that time held that if a man promised to marry a woman but broke off their engagement, she could sue him for 'breach of promise.' We should remember that Fr. Francis knew very little about Edith except that she was an orphan. Was she the sort of woman who, desirous of social and financial security, would pressure a younger man into marriage or seek financial damages for a broken engagement? He would have been protective of Tolkien in this regard, and eager to separate the two before the young suitor had irrevocably committed himself.

Another concern was that Tolkien's romance would distract him and destroy his chances of getting a place at Oxford—for which he needed to win that "very necessary" scholarship.[19] Fr. Francis's resources were not limitless, and what was sufficient to support a teenage boy was not going to cover a married man with children. And of course, he was responsible for Hilary too.

Fr. Francis would also, quite reasonably, have wondered whether the romance was not just a passing fancy; if it were a genuine love, it would survive a three-year separation. Tolkien eventually came to the same view, acknowledging that although the separation was difficult, "I don't think anything else would have justified marriage on the basis of a boy's affair; and probably nothing else would have hardened the will enough to give such an affair (however genuine a case of true love) permanence."[20]

And she was not a Catholic: if they were serious about marriage, this matter had to be worked out, as we will discuss further in chapter 14. Fr. Francis may well have considered that if the young couple were not ready to face this issue, then they were not ready for a relationship. Tolkien's silence would have been troubling in itself. Did he not understand the seriousness of marriage? Fr. Francis was more than a legal guardian; he had been entrusted by Mabel with the spiritual care of her sons.

It is easy to see this cautious priest as an interfering figure, squashing young love and exercising oppressive management over Tolkien's life. But that's not how Tolkien himself saw him. The "all" that he owed to his guardian was far more than a financial debt. Fr. Francis was his substitute father, and a generous, loving, caring one. He owed obedience to Fr. Francis, not out of fear, but out of love and respect.

Perhaps he had in mind St. Paul's advice: "Children, obey your parents in the Lord, for this is right. 'Honor your father and mother' (this is the first commandment with a promise) 'that it may be well with you and that you may live long on the earth'" (Ephesians 6:1–3). Here, Tolkien was obeying the spirit, and not just the letter, of St. Paul's admonition, for if Fr. Francis was unrelated by blood, still he was his spiritual father and had lived out the exhortation that Paul gives in the next verse: "Fathers, do not provoke your children to anger, but bring them up in the discipline and instruction of the Lord" (Ephesians 6:4).

"A three years' fast"

Tolkien accepted his guardian's ruling, painful though it was. When he reached his twenty-first birthday and obtained his legal adulthood, he would be free of his bond, but until then, he was not to see Edith nor write to her.[21] His situation was akin to that of Longaville in Shakespeare's play *Love's Labour's Lost* after he agrees to forgo female company for a set period: "I am resolved: 'tis but a three years' fast."

Once the two young people were separated and no more deceptions were being practiced, Fr. Francis gave the now eighteen-year-old Tolkien permission to write a long letter to his sweetheart. The date on which he chose to write to her is significant: March 26, 1910, which was Holy Saturday, the day before Easter Sunday.[22]

The week before Easter is called Holy Week, culminating in the Triduum, the three-day period beginning on Thursday and concluding with Easter Sunday. Thursday is known as Maundy Thursday: 'Maundy' from the Latin *mandatum*, meaning "command," from Jesus's words at the Last Supper, "A new commandment I give to you, that you love one another; even as I have loved you, that you also love one another" (John 13:34). Friday is known as Good Friday because it commemorates the goodness of Christ's sacrificial love, poured out for the world in his Crucifixion and death. Holy Saturday marks the silence of the tomb and Christ's descent to the dead.

Holy Week is a time of great solemnity at every Catholic Church in every part of the world. Churches run by Oratorian priests tend to have especially rigorous observances and solemn liturgies, as that is part of the charism of the Congregation established by St. Philip Neri. The Birmingham Oratory's marking of Holy

Week would have been a time of rich immersion in the liturgical expression of the Passion and Death of the Lord in preparation for the highest of high days in the ecclesiastical calendar, Easter Day, celebrating Christ's Resurrection. Tolkien would almost certainly have made his confession sometime during Holy Week in order to be prepared to receive communion at Easter.

At that time, before the reform of the Holy Week schedule in the 1950s, the most important Mass of the Church year, the Easter Vigil, was celebrated on the morning of Holy Saturday. Easter Sunday had its own High Mass the following day.

Anthony Kenny's description of his experience of the Easter Vigil at a Catholic seminary gives us a picture of what that Saturday morning would have been like for Tolkien, participating in the elaborate liturgies at the Oratory:

> We rose early in the morning to bless the new fire, to sing a dozen 'prophecies' from the Old Testament, and to bless the paschal candle with the triumphant chant '*Exultet*.' . . . At the *Gloria in Excelsis* of the Holy Saturday Mass, the bells, which had been silent for the last three days, were all rung out, large bells in the tower and tiny bells in the hands of the altar boys; the organ sounded for the first time since the beginning of Lent; and the black and purple vestments gave place to white and gold.[23]

The day on which Tolkien wrote to Edith was therefore rich with spiritual significance. Their relationship was on hold, but it was not over. Admittedly, the wait would feel like an eternity to a young man, but after all, the season of Lent provided a training in deferred gratification, with its emphasis on abstinence and self-control. Tolkien had just completed the most penitential time of the entire Catholic year, having been immersed in a forty-day period of prayer, fasting, and almsgiving. He had recently gone through the self-examination necessary for confession.

Accompanying his long letter, Tolkien sent Edith two devotional booklets: *The Stations of the Cross* and *The Seven Words of the Cross*.[24] Given that this is the last time he would write to her for three years, these hardly seem romantic choices, so it is worth considering more closely what these booklets are and what they reveal about Tolkien's spiritual life.

The Stations of the Cross is readily identifiable as to its content. Its title refers to a devotional practice, most common during the Fridays of Lent, in which participants meditate on fourteen 'stations' or stages of Jesus's Passion and death. Every Catholic church has a series of plaques on the walls with images of the stations so that one can pray this devotion by physically moving from one place to another around the church. (See figure 66.) Booklets such as this one, with meditations and prayers for each station, were used for private devotion at home.

What Tolkien sent Edith was almost certainly Newman's *Stations of the Cross* (1908),* an inexpensive edition that was readily available; he probably bought it at the Oratory. It is a short, accessible introduction to the devotion, and he may well have felt that Edith, not yet a Catholic, would be more receptive to material written by Newman, the former Anglican. In addition to the Stations, the booklet contains other prayers, including the "Prayer for the Light of Truth," entirely suitable for both of them as they discerned how to proceed in their relationship: "O my God, I confess that Thou canst enlighten my darkness. . . . I hereby promise that by Thy grace which I am asking, I will embrace whatever I at length feel certain is the truth, if ever I come to be certain"; it closes with a petition to be guarded "against all self-deceit."[25]

The second booklet, *The Seven Words of the Cross*, is an example of the Catholic devotional tradition of meditations on the seven last 'words' (utterances) of Christ as he hung on the cross as recorded in the Gospel accounts of the Crucifixion.† It was almost certainly comprised of reflections taken from sermons by an Oratory Father during a Lenten series, a frequent practice at that time.[26] These booklets

* Newman lists the fourteen stations as follows: Jesus is condemned to death; Jesus receives his Cross; Jesus falls for the first time beneath the Cross; Jesus meets his Mother; Simon of Cyrene helps Jesus to carry the Cross; Jesus and Veronica; Jesus falls a second time; Jesus comforts the Women of Jerusalem; again, a third time, Jesus falls; Jesus is stripped, and drenched with gall; Jesus is nailed to the Cross; Jesus dies upon the Cross; Jesus is taken from the Cross, and laid in Mary's Bosom; Jesus is laid in the Tomb.

† These are (as ordered in Fr. Ignatius Ryder's sermon): 1) "Father, forgive them, for they know not what they do"; 2) "Amen, I say to thee, this day shalt thou be with Me in Paradise"; 3) "When therefore Jesus had seen His mother and the disciple whom He loved, standing, He saith to His mother: 'Woman, behold thy son.' Then he saith to His disciple: 'Son, behold thy mother'"; 4) "And about the ninth hour, Jesus cried out with a loud voice ELOI, ELOI, lamma sabacthani, which is interpreted, My God, My God, why hast Thou forsaken Me?"; 5) "I thirst"; 6) "It is finished"; and 7) "Father, into Thy hands I commend My Spirit" (*Sermons and Notes of Sermons*).

were typically ephemeral productions and seldom survive, but it seems probable that this particular one was derived from sermons by Fr. Ignatius Ryder.[27]

We might ask why Tolkien would send specifically *Lenten* booklets to Edith at the beginning of *Easter*. One possibility, considering that he wrote with Fr. Francis's permission, is that Tolkien had had a discussion with his guardian about his future. If he was determined to remain loyal to Edith during their three-year separation, the topics covered by the *Stations* and the *Seven Words* would be valuable in helping her understand more fully what Tolkien believed about the value of patience and endurance. He was facing up to suffering, not as something to be avoided or dismissed, but as a real part of his life—of *their* life, in this period of enforced absence from each other—and something with genuine spiritual merit. The message of the booklets was, consciously or unconsciously, that the two of them had a Lenten time ahead of them.

The *Stations* and the *Seven Words* offer meditations of special relevance in times of distress. For example, the fourth 'word' offers the comfort of knowing that, as Jesus cried out "My God, My God, why hast Thou forsaken Me?" he sympathizes with every aspect of human suffering. Likewise, the closing word—"Father, into Thy hands I commend My Spirit"—is a meditation about trusting in God that applies both to facing death and to facing any great loss or difficulty.

Fr. Ignatius's sermon closes with the affirmation that Christ's death on the Cross is followed three days later by the Resurrection and with a prayer asking the Lord that, "as Thou comest to Thy kingdom, remember us, and lift us up with Thee, to a new and better life."[28] Tolkien and Edith were facing three long years apart. What realistic chance was there for them of a new and better life on the other side?

11

Towery City

Tolkien sat for his first scholarship examination for Oxford in December 1909—and he "muffed" it.[1] The emotional strain of first falling in love with Edith and then painfully parting from her distracted him, and he failed the exam. Still, in later years, he wryly noted that his failure was in large part "due simply to not working . . . not because I was in love, but because I was studying something else: Gothic and what not."[2] Throughout his life, he tended to procrastinate by working hard at something totally unrelated to what he was meant to be doing. His ability to focus was extraordinary—but he was exceptionally capable of focusing on distractions.

A year later, he tried again for a scholarship and this time was successful: he won an Open Classical Exhibition for Exeter College worth £60. With his intellect and a whole year to prepare, he ought to have won a more substantial award, but it was just enough, when combined with a scholarship for King Edward's School alumni and Fr. Francis's ongoing financial support, to get him started.

And so, he was heading to Oxford, the city of dreaming spires, the place that Victorian poet Gerard Manley Hopkins* had immortalized as

> Towery city and branchy between towers;
> Cuckoo-echoing, bell-swarmèd, lark charmèd, rook racked, river-rounded . . .

It seems obvious, inevitable even, that Tolkien would study at the University of Oxford—but it would not have been obvious at the time. Even the fact that he, a Catholic, *could* go was a relatively recent development. Here we should take a

* Hopkins (1844–99), like Tolkien, had begun life as an Anglican and studied Classics at Oxford, graduating with First Class Honours. In 1866, he was received into the Catholic Church by Newman in Birmingham. Having become a Jesuit priest, Hopkins returned to Oxford in the late 1870s, serving briefly as curate at the church of St. Aloysius and helping found the Newman Society. Tolkien knew Hopkins's poetry and took an interest in his published correspondence.

brief historical excursus, as it will help us better understand Tolkien's experience at Oxford. (See figure 15.)

Until 1854, Oxford University required all matriculating students to assent to the Thirty-Nine Articles, a specifically Anglican declaration of faith that excluded both Catholics and Nonconformists. It was only in 1871, by act of parliament, that all barriers were finally removed to Catholics earning university degrees or holding university positions.[3] The Catholic hierarchy responded cautiously. From 1871 to 1895, Catholic students wishing to study at Oxford had to receive special permission from their bishop to do so. The prohibition was imposed because the university was officially and culturally Protestant—chapel attendance was expected—and, furthermore, because the intellectual environment of the university showed a strong tendency toward theological modernism, treating the Christian religion as chiefly a cultural and social phenomenon rather than in terms of divinely revealed truth. Given that Catholics were a tiny minority in this environment, the ecclesiastical hierarchy believed that Catholic students would be at serious risk of losing their faith. In 1895—just sixteen years before Tolkien's matriculation at Oxford—this restriction was lifted, with the concurrent establishment of a chaplaincy within the university to support the faith of Catholic students.

A habit of exclusion does not cease overnight, even once the legal barriers are removed. Restrictions may have been lifted at Oxford, but a kind of religion-based apartheid still obtained in education for younger children, either *de jure* or *de facto*; this was all the more true of the rich and well-connected educational echelons where future Oxford students were typically incubated. Oxford was still largely fed by the great (and exclusive) public schools*—Eton, Winchester, Westminster, Harrow, to name but four—which were all bastions of the Establishment religion. A handful of Catholic schools had acquired wealth and reputation, the most notable being Ampleforth, Downside, and Stonyhurst, but Catholics had been marginalized in British society for so long that there was no automatic assumption, as there was among Anglican families, that their brightest sons should go up to Oxford.†

---

* An English 'public school' is what Americans would call a 'private school.'

† If a university *were* being considered, Oxford was the most Catholic-friendly choice. Oxford was associated with the Catholic-supported Royalist side in the Civil War, had given rise to the Tractarian Movement, and was the *alma mater* of England's most famous Catholic convert, John Henry Cardinal Newman, whereas Cambridge had been the breeding-ground of the English Reformers, meeting in The White Horse Tavern, and was linked to the dissenter-friendly

Fortunately for Tolkien, the Birmingham Oratorians were somewhat atypical in that they were strongly in favor of university education in general and of allowing Catholics to go to Oxford in particular. Newman himself was a thoroughly Oxford man, and many of the Fathers whom Tolkien knew personally were converts who had been educated at Oxford or Cambridge. Even so, Fr. Francis might have insisted that Tolkien attend University College Dublin, a Jesuit-run institution that had just been formed out of the collapse of the Catholic University of Ireland. However, he would have been well aware that Dublin was academically inferior to Oxford and that Tolkien's intellectual potential could only be fulfilled if he went to one of the great universities. And since his resources didn't extend to paying for the entirety of Tolkien's university education, he was understandably anxious for Tolkien to win a scholarship—and alarmed when his ward failed on the first try.

New (and old) territory

Tolkien began his time at Oxford in 1911 and left four years later with a First Class Honours degree in English Language and Literature,[4] a brilliant achievement. In hindsight, it seems natural that he should have thrived there. But in fact, Oxford was new and challenging territory for him as a Catholic, and it is worth sketching the scene in some detail.

The structure of Oxford University is difficult for most outsiders to understand. The University describes itself as "a kind of federal system," and the federal system of government in the United States of America may provide a helpful analogy. An Oxford college is analogous to an American State: self-governing, financially independent, responsible for admitting students, supplying housing, and providing teaching. Analogous to the federal government is the central University authority,

---

Roundheads during the Civil War. (Such historical associations linger.) The more recently founded Durham University and Kings College London were solidly Anglican, and University College London was associated with secularists. That being said, Oxford, for all its relative openness to Catholics, was still very much an Anglican university. It is worth noting that in 1843, as a deliberate response to the Catholicizing effects of the Tractarians, more Protestant-minded Anglicans had erected the Martyrs' Memorial, a stone spire at the intersection of St. Giles', Magdalen, and Beaumont Streets, to perpetuate the memory of the Protestant martyrs Thomas Cranmer, Nicholas Ridley, and Hugh Latimer, who died, as the inscription on the memorial reads, "bearing witness to the sacred truths which they had affirmed and maintained against the errors of the Church of Rome."

which coordinates admissions, establishes requirements for degrees, and sets and marks examinations.[5]*

When Tolkien arrived at Oxford as a nineteen-year-old student, he would have found that the university landscape was surprisingly varied. Some of the colleges date from Oxford's medieval founding, such as Exeter College (1314), which is where he enrolled as an undergraduate, and (the now inaptly named) New College (1379); these were originally Catholic but were taken over by the Church of England at the Reformation. Other colleges are of later foundation and thus part of the Anglican establishment from the beginning, such as Pembroke College (1624), where Tolkien would have his first professorial chair, and St. Hilda's (1893), where he did some of his first teaching.

Some are richly endowed; others are relatively poor. (Pembroke is known for belonging to the latter category and is sometimes therefore nicknamed Pem-*broke* College.) Although today Oxford has a reputation across the board for academic excellence, in the nineteenth century the academic quality of the colleges was varied: some were noted for their rigor and excellence, such as Trinity and Balliol, while others were places where the sons of wealthy families could make social connections and scrape by with the lowest degree, sometimes referred to as 'a gentleman's Third.'

Each college has its own buildings, typically including lecture rooms, a dining hall, and student lodgings arranged around a quadrangle of lawn. It is from the college that students receive most of their instruction. A student's main instructor is called a 'tutor' (what Americans would call a 'professor'). Normally, a student meets weekly with the tutor, who assigns readings and an essay to write before their next session. Students are said to be 'reading for' a particular degree, which indicates the importance of first-hand immersion in the relevant texts, both primary and secondary. They may also attend lectures, which are organized at the university

---

* In addition to the colleges, there are 'Private Halls' which, after 1918, could become 'Permanent Private Halls'; these are the functional equivalent of Oxford colleges, except that they are much less wealthy than the colleges and have different internal constitutions. There were twenty-one colleges and three private halls (not yet permanent) in Tolkien's day. It is worth specifying the existence of these PPHs, as they enabled Catholic religious orders to regain a foothold in Oxford after their expulsion following the English Reformation. For example, Blackfriars, the Dominican house of study, was founded in 1221 and then abolished by Henry VIII in 1538; the Priory was re-founded in 1921 after an absence from Oxford of nearly four hundred years. Its studium (seminary) in Oxford was established in 1929, and it became a PPH in 1994. It was at Blackfriars that Tolkien gave a public reading of *Smith of Wootton Major* in 1966.

level and are entirely optional. These lectures could be given by any members of the faculty but are especially the responsibility of those who hold specific (i.e., named) professorial chairs. These academics, and these only, have the title 'professor'; all other faculty hold various titles depending on their particular post ('lecturer,' 'reader,' etc.) and are generically called 'dons.'

Although students are given grades for individual essays by their tutors, these grades have no bearing on their eventual degree, which is determined by a grueling multiday exam at the conclusion of their period of study. This exam will determine whether they pass and earn their degree at all and, if so, at what level of honor. As a result, there is considerable freedom for undergraduates as to how they do their work—or whether they do it at all.

Catholics at Oxford

When Tolkien started in Oxford, there were approximately 3,000 undergraduates,[6] the overwhelming majority of whom were men. At that point, women could study at a handful of women-only colleges, but they were not awarded degrees until the 1920s.*

Catholics were a small minority—small enough that *The Tablet* ran a report each year listing the incoming 'freshers' and their respective colleges. In 1911, Tolkien was one of thirty-seven new Catholic students, comprising a mere four percent of the 911 freshmen. *The Tablet* was delighted at this "record number," noting that there was now a total of one hundred Catholic students studying for degrees at that time.[7]

* Lady Margaret Hall (founded 1878), Somerville (1879), St. Hugh's (1886), and St. Hilda's (1896) were the women's colleges when Tolkien was an undergraduate. Oxford did not become coeducational, in the sense of (some) colleges admitting both men and women, until 1974, but during Tolkien's lifetime opportunities for women steadily increased, a development he supported. His daughter, Priscilla, attended Lady Margaret Hall and emphasized her father's "complete belief in higher education for girls; never at any time in my early life or since did I feel that any difference was made between me and my brothers, so far as our educational needs and opportunities were concerned." She recalled that he was pleased at her choice of LMH, "the one he knew best" of the women's halls, and that he enjoyed "many years of friendship" with Dorothy Everett, one of its Fellows. He also "spoke with appreciation of his visits to the High Table in the days when Miss Grier was Principal." Lynda Grier, a pioneering figure in women's higher education, headed LMH from 1921–45 (Priscilla Tolkien, "Memories of J.R.R. Tolkien," 12).

Not every college had the same proportion of Catholic students, and some had no Catholic freshmen at all. Exeter College had a history of being Catholic-friendly; in previous decades, its Fellows had included supporters of the Oxford Movement, leading John Henry Newman to remark (while still an Anglican), "At Exeter, right opinions are strong."[8] At the time of Tolkien's matriculation, Exeter stood out as the college that had "of recent years been more frequented by Catholic students than any other college."[9]

Tolkien soon became friends with fellow Catholics Anthony Shakespeare and B.J. Tolhurst; they were a year ahead of him and took him "under their wings" when he first arrived.[10] But he also immediately immersed himself in the vibrant culture of Exeter College, joining (and helping to form) various societies, going to concerts, and, of course, also attending tutorials and lectures. He was at his most extroverted in his first year: a report in the King Edward's School *Chronicle* remarked humorously that "Tolkien, if we are to be guided by the countless notices on his mantelpiece, has joined all the Exeter Societies which are in existence."[11] In some ways a shy personality, Tolkien also had a highly companionable side. Having been raised such that he was comfortable socializing outside the Catholic community, he immediately made friends with those who shared his interests whether they happened to be Catholics or not, an approach that he would continue his entire life.

When it came to practicing his faith, he was severely limited in his options compared with his non-Catholic friends. Anglicans at Exeter had a beautiful college chapel to worship in, rebuilt as recently as 1859 in a French Gothic style that was much indebted to the (Catholic!) church of Sainte-Chappelle in Paris. In the wider university, Anglicans had their pick of numerous fine old places of worship, chief among them St. Mary's on the High Street with its soaring spire, which had been the titular 'university church' since the thirteenth century, and Christ Church Cathedral, part of a college founded by Cardinal Wolsey in 1525 with monies derived from suppressed priories. Tolkien and his co-religionists had to make do—at least as far as official university provision was concerned—with a rather cramped attic space that served the Catholic Chaplaincy. (See figure 18.)

However, there was also a much more handsome place of worship available to him in the form of the parish church of St. Aloysius (see figure 19), and this he attended from time to time while a student. Tucked inconspicuously back from the Woodstock Road, St. Aloysius's was run by the Jesuits and had the distinction of being a place where Newman had preached (in 1880) and where Hopkins had served as a curate.*

St. Aloysius's Church was relatively new, having been built in 1875. Although it has an unassuming brick facade, the interior of the church would have been a visual delight to Tolkien, who loved intricate designs in the style of William Morris's Arts and Crafts Movement. Indeed, he might well have noticed that the enamel, copper, and silver altar of the Lady Chapel was designed by Morris & Company. A double rank of statues of saints and angels curves above and to either side of the main altar; Tolkien would have observed among them his patron, St. John the Evangelist, and the Archangel Gabriel, after whom he had been nicknamed by the TCBS. In later years, Tolkien would regularly attend Mass at St. Aloysius's, but as a student, the Catholic Chaplaincy was—or at any rate, was supposed to be—his center of gravity.

A difficult start

Tolkien arrived at an in-between time for Catholic students. For fifteen years, they had been looked after by the very first chaplain, Monsignor Charles Kennard, who paid many of the chaplaincy's expenses out of his own pocket. Kennard had been admired and loved, but for the ten years after his retirement, "the chaplaincy was to wander under various masters with a flock which was sometimes very small."[12] Without his private chapel to use, even the physical location of the chaplaincy was in flux. When Tolkien matriculated, the chaplaincy rented from Pembroke College a building on the street called St. Aldate's, setting up a chapel on the top floor. Then, from 1913–15, they used "a temporary 'iron chapel'" at 7 St. Cross Road, which saw double duty for Mass and for lectures.[13] It was only after Tolkien's time as an undergraduate that the chaplaincy managed to purchase a building opposite the gardens of Christ Church and establish a permanent home in what is known as 'The Old Palace,' as it had been the palace, or residence, of the first bishop of Oxford.[14]

* Today, it is also the Oxford Oratory, but this was not the case during Tolkien's lifetime. Although Newman had made several attempts to establish an Oratory in Oxford, it did not happen until 1990.

Catholic students at Oxford were required to attend weekly lectures, called 'conferences,' in order to educate and strengthen them in their faith. These were usually given by the chaplain himself, but in the Trinity Term* of Tolkien's first year, these were handled by two guest speakers, the Jesuit priests Fr. Alban Goodier and Fr. Joseph Rickaby.[15]

It was an indication of the unsettled state of the chaplaincy. The chaplain when Tolkien arrived at Oxford was Fr. Algernon Lang. A former Anglican who had been ordained as a Catholic priest only two years earlier, Lang had little experience to draw upon for the pastoral side of his role.[16] Some of the students found him "invariably kind and accessible and hospitable," but unfortunately, he was also "eccentric and tactless," and by the spring of 1913, the chaplaincy's board concluded that "he does not exercise the influence on the undergraduates or occupy the position in the University that could be wished: but it would be a great exaggeration to say that he had brought his office into disrepute or that men were giving up the practice of their religion on account of his fault or inefficiency."[17] This, in its understated English style, was quite a strong critique, and the Board decided that June to remove him from his post.[18]

Lang's replacement did not arrive until the beginning of 1914, leaving the chaplaincy leaderless and the Sunday conferences "in abeyance" for the entire Michaelmas Term of 1913.[19]

As a result, during the first year and a half of Tolkien's time at Oxford, there was first an ineffective chaplain and then none at all; there were different speakers for the conferences and then no conferences whatsoever for a term. Even the place of worship was unsettled. And we should consider that the board would not have needed specifically to exonerate Lang as a cause of students "giving up the practice of their religion" if such a concern had not arisen.

During this time, Tolkien was getting accustomed to a new environment with considerably more freedom than he had previously enjoyed—and struggling with the emotional and spiritual challenge of obeying Fr. Francis's strictures on not

* Trinity Term is the third of three eight-week terms that make up the academic year at Oxford. The first, called Michaelmas Term, stretches from October to December and is named after the Feast of St. Michael and All Angels on September 29; the second, called Hilary Term, runs from January to March and is named for the Feast of St. Hilary on January 13; and the third, from April to June, is called Trinity because it usually coincides with Trinity Sunday, the first Sunday after the Feast of Pentecost.

communicating with Edith, when he could have disobeyed secretly. The lack of a chaplain in whom he could put his confidence, and the unstable environment for Catholic students, were both perhaps contributing factors to what Tolkien would later call his "slackness" during this time.

A misspent youth?

Writing to his son Michael many years later, Tolkien recalled that "I fell back into folly and slackness and misspent a good deal of my first year at College."[20] What precisely did he mean by that? At the time, he kept a diary of his failings, but John Garth points out that "it seems unlikely to contain anything shocking: as Priscilla Tolkien has cautioned, he was 'intensely scrupulous' in religion and prone to self-recrimination over the slightest lapse."[21]

But some faults in Tolkien's first year at Oxford seem fairly clear and objective. He was sufficiently lackadaisical about his studies that in his second term, the subrector of Exeter College noted that he was "v[ery] lazy" and warned him that he might lose his scholarship.[22] And on occasion, he was not just indolent but, as John Garth puts it, "reckless" in "pursuit of anarchic fun." In his role as Secretary of the Stapeldon Society, the closest thing Exeter had to a student union, Tolkien minuted a meeting of December 1913 in which "large quantities of contraband [i.e., "spiritous liquors"] were freely circulated throughout proceedings imparting a fervour and a liveliness to them never, we believe, before approached."[23] (See figure 17.) He also joined in with student pranks, as when he and a friend "'captured' a bus and drove it up to Cornmarket making various unearthly noises followed by a mad crowd of mingled varsity and 'townese.'"[24] He even had a run-in with the police: on May 11, 1913, he was briefly arrested and then released for his involvement in another town-and-gown imbroglio.*

He also had a tendency toward overspending, not from any particular extravagance, but from all the incidentals that added up. His 'battels,' or college bills, show plenty of regular food, from crumpets to sardines, to supplement meals "in hall," as well as orders for "cider, claret cup (similar to Pimm's) or mulled claret;

* Tolkien seemed to be more amused than dismayed by his youthful riotous behavior. "Telling the story to his family many years later, Tolkien recalled hearing one policeman say, 'Let's take this little one,' before officers grabbed him from behind" (*TEC*, 23).

and for cigarettes and tobacco."[25] He played rugby and tennis, and the club he started, the "Apolausticks," was devoted to "self-indulgence"; they enjoyed excellent meals, including, on one memorable occasion, a nine-course dinner at the elegant Randolph Hotel.[26]* Like other students at the time, he bought furnishings and prints for his rooms.[27] He even managed to run up a substantial fine for overdue books at the Oxford Union Library.[28] The result was that his expenses consistently exceeded his scholarship money, and Fr. Francis had to pay the difference.[29]†

Overspending is a typical failing for students, but Tolkien, aware of how much he owed to Fr. Francis (and that his guardian still had his brother, Hilary, to look after), might well have felt that he had been ungrateful as well as a poor steward of resources.

Another fault, of which he was keenly conscious, was his failure to attend Mass regularly,[30] which would have had a dampening effect on his spiritual life as a whole. He made a regretful note in his diary that his activities in his first terms at Oxford had included "practically none or very little practice of religion."[31] There is even the hint of a crisis of faith during that first year: in November 1914, Tolkien's Methodist friend from King Edward's School, Christopher Wiseman, wrote, "I was at one time afraid that Oxford had killed your religion."[32]

Skipping Mass was not merely a question of failing to live up to his own standards but of disobedience to the Church. All Catholics are required to attend Sunday Mass if it is possible for them to do so. It is important to note 'if it is possible.' In later years, Tolkien might have been troubled by scruples about missing Mass when he or Edith was feeling unwell, but this would not, in fact, have been a sin. What would be a sin—more serious or less so depending on how premeditated it was—was deliberately choosing not to attend Sunday Mass when it was otherwise possible to do so. Disobedience could also come more subtly in allowing himself to stay up late on Saturday night, aware that it would probably result in oversleeping the next day.

* The name "Apolaustick" is, as John Garth explains, "a spoonerism for *apostolic*, and there were usually a dozen members. Rather than referring to the biblical Apostles, it was probably a send-up of the famous Cambridge Apostles, an undergraduate club that, at one time or another, counted Alfred Tennyson, Bertrand Russell and Ludwig Wittgenstein as members" (*TEC*, 13).

† In fact, he continued to carry over a balance owed from term to term, which he didn't settle until after he had taken his final exams (*TEC*, 38–39, 46).

For Tolkien, the 'Sunday obligation' would have been one of the first things that marked him out from most of his companions at Exeter College and even from the devout Anglicans among his friends, since the Church of England places no such obligation for attendance on its members. At that time, the 'anticipated' Mass of the evening before, and Masses later in the day, were not yet a practice: it was morning or nothing. Tolkien struggled with this mightily as a sociable extrovert and a night owl in general. And it was not only a matter of obedience. As we will see in chapter 13, Tolkien had from early on a strong devotion to the Eucharist; he would have felt it a real deprivation to miss the opportunity to receive communion and the graces flowing from it—and all the more so if it was his own fault from laziness or self-indulgence.

Love's labor's lost . . . and won

At Oxford, Tolkien kept his word to Fr. Francis. For a whole year and half, he neither saw Edith nor wrote to her. But he had not forgotten her.

As midnight struck on Thursday, January 2, 1913, and the clock began to mark the start of Friday the third, Tolkien reached his twenty-first birthday and was released from his promise to his guardian. Immediately, he wrote to Edith, telling her that he still loved her. More than that, he declared his intentions for marriage: "How long will it be before we can be joined together before God and the world?"[33]

He posted his letter and waited for Edith's reply—the first communication of any kind that he would have had from her in three years. When she wrote back, her news was stunning. She was engaged to be married to another man, the brother of one of her school friends. His name was George Field.[34]

Once the shock had passed, Tolkien assessed the situation. Edith's letter still gave him some slight grounds for hope. As she explained, she had not imagined that Tolkien would still care for her, and George was a kindly man whom she felt that she could love as a husband. If Edith wanted to have a family, she could not leave the question of a marriage partner undecided for long.* Tolkien would naturally

* Whatever Tolkien might have felt about this as a twenty-one-year-old discovering a rival, in later years he better understood Edith's perspective. He advised his son Michael that it is wrong to ask a woman to wait too long for marriage, because the years of her youth are "precious and necessary to a would-be mother." Especially in the days before the invention of antibiotics, the later a woman left the start of her childbearing, the more dangerous it was to her health (*Letters*, 50).

have had to give up all idea of gaining Edith's hand if she and George were already married. As it was, they were only engaged; there was still a chance.

Undaunted, Tolkien wrote back, and they agreed to meet. He took the train from Oxford to Cheltenham, and Edith met him at the station; they walked out into the countryside until they came to where the railway crossed over a stream and sat beneath the viaduct to talk. It was an appropriately liminal place—under a bridge, a brook flowing in front of their feet—since whatever would come of their conversation, it would mark a change in both their lives.

That day, Tolkien convinced Edith to break off her engagement to George Field; he then proposed marriage to her, and she accepted.[35] It was quite a turn-around, to put it mildly. They decided to defer public announcement of their betrothal; it would probably have caused more wondering commentary than either of them was prepared to deal with, especially since, with Tolkien still a student, their wedding would be at some indefinite point in the future.

There was one exception: when he got back to Oxford, Tolkien wrote straightaway to Fr. Francis, letting him know that he and Edith had reunited and intended to marry. Tolkien had been nervous about his now-former guardian's reaction, but Fr. Francis reassured him with a calm reply.[36] Though he was not enthusiastic about this abrupt and rather dramatically romantic leap into matrimonial commitment, he accepted it and gave his blessing.[37] Tolkien could easily have kept the news concealed from Fr. Francis, but he felt it was his duty to tell him, his "second father." And it was surely relieving to both of them, at some level, that the secret was out. Their paternal-filial relationship had inevitably been tested and strained over the previous three years and would take some time to recover fully, but it was still intact. Tolkien had not lost a (substitute) father and he had gained a (future) wife.

12

A Second Wind

January 1913. Tolkien had come of age and had not only reconnected with Edith after three years' separation but had become (at least privately) engaged to marry her. He still had his Oxford degree to finish, and an uncertain future ahead of him, but one important thing had changed. When he had begun his studies, Edith's remembered love was something to live up to; he had even kept a diary of his own faults, with her in mind as a reason to improve himself.[1] Now she was not just an ideal but a reality: a woman to whom he was morally and spiritually accountable. And although Edith had, of necessity, little to do with his student life on a day-to-day basis, she had a profound impact on the second half of his time at Oxford.

Tolkien recalled that, when he had first fallen in love with Edith, their relationship became for him "the source of effort"—not, admittedly, in his studies for his upcoming Oxford scholarship examination but in the more public arena of the King Edward's rugby team: although he admitted that he wasn't physically brave, he went from being "a despised rabbit on a house second-team to school colours."[2] Edith's affirmation of love for him, and their decision to marry, seems to have provided a similar impetus in his spiritual life at this time. Whatever the cause, 1913 brought a renewed commitment to a serious and intentional practice of his faith.

Tolkien's period of slackness in his religious observance had, as we saw, worried his TCBS friend Christopher Wiseman. But by 1914, Wiseman no longer had fears for his faith. In a letter, he had challenged Tolkien in some way; we do not know what he said, but Tolkien evidently had replied rather hotly on the subject and his very heatedness relieved Wiseman, who commented that "no man can be angry, used in the noblest sense, unless he has an honest and *living* conviction on the subject of the Divinity of Our Lord."[3] Tolkien, responding promptly and agreeably to this letter, declared that "religion is the moving force and at the same time the foundation of both of us."[4]

One of the immediate fruits of his new resolve was better attendance at Mass. We catch a glimpse of this just a few weeks after he reconnects with Edith; on February 1, 1913, he sent her a postcard mentioning, "Went to H. Comm. [Holy Communion] this morning & am going again tomorrow."[5] His inclusion of Mass-going in the limited space available on a postcard suggests that this was important to him: given his self-admittedly slack habits hitherto, he was turning over a new leaf. Furthermore, February 1 was a Saturday, so there was no obligation to attend. He might have gone simply in order to get back into the habit of daily or near-daily Mass attendance, but since in this instance it was the first Saturday of the month, it's possible that he was participating in 'First Saturday' devotions to the Virgin Mary, then a relatively new addition to Catholic devotional practices.

Most importantly, Tolkien specified that he went to Holy Communion—that is, he received the Eucharist. That meant he had gone to confession not too long before, had kept the Eucharistic fast, and intended to repeat it the next day as well; and considering that the fast required abstention from all food and drink from midnight, this would likely have impinged upon his habits of late-night socializing. In short, it indicates a turn toward an increasingly serious practice of his faith.

The commitment held strong. A year and a half later, writing in November 1914 after an evening of officer-training maneuvers on Port Meadow, Tolkien told Edith that although he was "rather tired" the next morning, which was a Sunday, nevertheless "I got up at 7.40 and just reached Church in time, and went to Communion."[6] Once again, he emphasized not just that he met his Sunday obligation to hear Mass but that he received the sacrament.

A "work-diary" that he began in January 1913 also gives insight into his reinvigorated spirituality. Part of its purpose was to serve as an "account book" of time spent at his studies, with the promised reward from Edith of "kisses earned for hours worked"[7]—an indication that he was resolved to be more diligent in his studies henceforth. The cross-markings indicate that, as a general rule, Tolkien seems to have worked fewer hours on Sundays and holy days than on ordinary days, which is in accordance with Catholic teaching that these should be days of rest insofar as it is possible.

But in fact, this was only one aspect of the diary. It also contained "notes (in red ink) of the performance of religious duties and saints' days,"[8] which provide an insight into his personal spirituality. For instance, he labeled the Octave of Corpus Christi as well as the Feast of Pentecost and Trinity Sunday. He also wrote "Sacred Heart" in red ink at the top of the page for June, showing his awareness of the fact that, in Catholic tradition, the month of June is devoted to the Sacred Heart of Jesus. There is also a Eucharistic association: the Feast of the Sacred Heart, celebrated on the Friday after Corpus Christi, was added to the universal calendar of the Church by Pope Pius IX in 1856, who declared it as a day of reparation for sins against the Eucharist, such as irreverence, sacrilege, and indifference—especially by Catholics.

There are other insights we can gain from this work-diary. Its heading is "JRRT and EMB [Edith Mary Bratt] in account together, AMDG."[9] AMDG stands for *ad majorem Dei gloriam*, Latin for 'to the greater glory of God,' which is a fitting motto for the start of this book. Here we can identify an influence from Jesuit spirituality. AMDG is the particular motto of the Jesuits, the Society of Jesus, founded in the sixteenth century by the Spaniard Ignatius of Loyola, a former soldier turned priest. St. Ignatius wrote a set of spiritual exercises that are still used today by the Jesuits and also by lay people; these take an imaginative approach to spiritual reflection, such as picturing oneself in a scene from the Bible and thinking about the sounds and smells and all the other sensory impressions that would have accompanied first-hand experience of it. The Jesuits had a strong presence at Oxford, running Pope's Hall (now Campion Hall) and the parish of St. Aloysius. Tolkien presumably had at least some interactions with Fr. Frederick O'Hare, SJ, who served as rector of St. Aloysius from 1908–21.[10] Another influence might well have come from the two Jesuit priests who, as we observed in chapter 11, gave the conferences for the chaplaincy in Trinity Term 1912, no doubt presenting something of the Jesuit approach to the spiritual life.

One final interesting point about the work-diary appears on the Pentecost–Corpus Christi page. In the upper left corner is written "*Per Umbras Et Imagines*,"[11] meaning 'through shadows and images.' This distinctive phrasing is an allusion to John Henry Newman's epitaph, '*Ex umbris et imaginibus in veritatem*' ('from shadows and images into truth'). Tolkien, having grown up in Newman's Oratory, would not only have been familiar with this famous phrase but would even have seen it engraved on a marble memorial tablet on the wall of its cloister.[12] (See figure 12.) These words may give some indication of how Tolkien viewed (or hoped to be able to view) his spiritual life at that time: moving through the shadows and images of his teenage years into the solid reality of adult faith.

Maturing with Maturin

Tolkien's reinvigorated efforts to practice his faith also now found more resources in Oxford to support his spiritual life. At the start of 1914, Fr. Basil Maturin was appointed as the new university chaplain. An Irishman, he had done extensive mission work as an Anglican cleric before crossing the Tiber and being ordained a Catholic priest in 1897.

Fr. Maturin, in contrast to his lackluster predecessor, was known as "a kindly but exacting spiritual guide," one who was deeply convinced of the Catholic faith but nevertheless "refused to stoop to low or mean attacks upon his former [Anglican] co-religionists."[13] The author of books such as *The Laws of the Spiritual Life* and *Self-Knowledge and Self-Discipline*, he began his tenure at Oxford with a set of lectures on "conflict and victory in the Christian life,"[14] a topic that would have especially resonated with the young men under his care when, a few months later, the war began. He also had a slight link with the Birmingham Oratory, having once given a talk there on "Charity, the Condition of Spiritual Knowledge" as part of an oratorio series.[15]

Tolkien would have found several things in common with his new chaplain. Fr. Maturin was an avid reader, known to "come down to breakfast full of the most intense sympathy with the hero or heroine of the novel of the hour." He was also very fond of ghost stories and even invented some of his own, which he told to his friends,[16] and at this time, Tolkien was intrigued by ghosts, proposing to the Apolausticks the motion "That a belief in ghosts is essential to the welfare of a people" and, later, to the Stapeldon Society, "This house believes in ghosts."[17] On a more serious level, Fr. Maturin had spent six months in South Africa, writing home "vivid and minute accounts" of his visit.[18] Tolkien, who retained a lifelong interest in the land of his birth, might well have appreciated hearing the sociable Fr. Maturin recount his experiences. And lastly, they shared something of the same temperament: like Tolkien, Maturin was often "light-hearted" but had "incidental fits of depression that had haunted him all his life."[19]

Unfortunately, the influence of this literary-minded priest was brief: after just a year of service, Fr. Maturin went on a lecture tour in America to raise funds for the chaplaincy. In May 1915, he returned on the passenger ship *Lusitania*, which was torpedoed by a German submarine. He was one of over a thousand people who died in the tragedy. It was reported that he "gave absolution to the passengers at the end and helped to save an abandoned child."[20] Tolkien probably attended Fr. Maturin's Requiem Mass at St. Aloysius's, which was held on May 21, 1915, shortly before he sat for his final exams.*

There were so few Catholics at Oxford during Tolkien's undergraduate years that one figure would have stood out: F.F. Urquhart, the dean of Balliol and the first Catholic to be a Fellow at Oxford since the Reformation, who was for many years the most visible and high-profile Catholic at the university.[21] Tolkien later knew Urquhart as a fellow Oxford don,[22] and in the small world of Oxonian Catholicism, he very probably got to know him as a student.

Francis Fortescue Urquhart, known as 'Sligger' Urquhart, was a rare figure of the period: an Oxford-educated layman who was involved in efforts to instruct Catholics in their faith at a time when this type of work was more usually left to priests. He contributed more than a dozen articles to the massive *Catholic Encyclopedia*.[23] Most of his energy, however, went into getting to know each successive generation of students. His obituary in *The Guardian* described him as "one of the best-loved and most widely known of Oxford dons . . . a man of deep religious faith and a man of friendships. . . . The foundation of his life was a broad-based Catholicism, having no tincture of intolerance or of propaganda."[24] A Balliol student recalled that he "combined relaxation with authority—authority flowing not from discipline but from his personality and the standards of behaviour which he exemplified."[25] Urquhart would have been an encouraging example to Tolkien. A Catholic scholar at Oxford, well regarded both professionally and personally, held in high esteem

* There would be no new chaplain until 1919, with the arrival of Monsignor Arthur Barnes. Tolkien hardly had any opportunity to know Barnes, as he retired in 1926, the year after Tolkien's return to Oxford to take up his professorial chair at Pembroke. Tolkien would, however, come to know well Barnes's successor, Ronald Knox.

by Christians and non-Christians alike, and a layman to boot, he embodied what Tolkien hoped one day to be.

In certain areas, Tolkien's time at Oxford had taken him from uncertainty to greater clarity about his future. He had entered the college dreaming of a future with Edith; now he was engaged to marry her. When he arrived at Exeter, he was studying Classics, but he showed such talent in philology that, contrary to the usual practices, he was allowed to switch to English and retain his scholarship. Tolkien already had in mind a career in academia; now it was becoming clear that the particular direction of his work would run along linguistic lines. What he did not expect and could not have anticipated was that these unfolding plans would be profoundly shaped by the catastrophe of the Great War. But we must not run ahead of our story.

13

"The one great thing to love on earth"

Thus far in our story, we have seen Tolkien's love for his mother, Mabel; his love for his "second father," Fr. Francis; and his love for Edith. In chapters to come, we will see more fully his love for his friends, already evident in his relations with the TCBS. But none of these loves took the highest place. Writing to his son Michael in 1941, he declared, "Out of the darkness of my life, so much frustrated, I put before you the one great thing to love on earth: the Blessed Sacrament." In another letter, Tolkien recalled that he "fell in love with the Blessed Sacrament from the beginning—and by the mercy of God never have fallen out again."[1]

These are significant words: the Blessed Sacrament is "the one great thing to love on earth," and Tolkien fell in love with it "from the beginning." The ordering of priorities in his spiritual life could hardly be clearer. It behooves us, then, to examine carefully what Tolkien believed the Blessed Sacrament to be and how he demonstrated his love for it.*

Tolkien's belief was specifically Catholic, which may seem obvious, but it needs to be clarified, as other Christian bodies also have rites and doctrines pertaining to the words and actions of Jesus at the Last Supper. Celebrating the Passover meal with his disciples, "he took bread, and when he had given thanks he broke it and gave it to them, saying, 'This is my body which is given for you. Do this in remembrance of me.' And likewise the cup after supper, saying, 'This cup which is poured out for you is the new covenant in my blood'" (Luke 22:19–20). Christians

* Strictly speaking, 'the Blessed Sacrament' means both the Body and the Blood, but in practice it tends usually to refer to the Body, because it is the Body that the faithful always receive at Communion and that is put before them at services of Adoration and Benediction. According to the *Catechism* (§1390): "Since Christ is sacramentally present under each of the species, communion under the species of bread alone makes it possible to receive all the fruit of Eucharistic grace. . . . But 'the sign of communion is more complete when given under both kinds, since in that form the sign of the Eucharistic meal appears more clearly.'"

are largely in agreement that this is a command for all believers but differ over what it means to fulfill the command: Is it a purely symbolic act, only a memorial of the Last Supper, or is it in some way a sacramental act, involving divine grace that comes through or is present in the bread and wine? And if it is sacramental, is the efficacy of the sacrament subjective (based on an individual's spiritual state at the moment of reception) or objective?

Tolkien's view, as a Catholic, was that in the Eucharistic sacrifice*—celebrated by a validly ordained Catholic priest in the direct line of succession from the Apostles—the elements of bread and wine brought to the altar become, through the power of the Holy Spirit at the priest's prayer of consecration, the Body and Blood of Christ. Not in a metaphorical or symbolic way, and not dependent on the belief of those receiving it, but rather that the consecrated elements are mysteriously changed into the Body, Blood, Soul, and Divinity of Christ. The Blessed Sacrament is therefore essentially not a 'what' or an 'it' but a 'who,' a person: the Lord Jesus Christ himself—God the Son, the second person of the Holy Trinity.

This doctrine is generally called the 'Real Presence' of Christ in the Eucharist and is explained by the philosophical concept of 'transubstantiation.' As declared at the Council of Trent, the Church holds that "Because Christ our Redeemer said that it was truly his body that he was offering under the species of bread . . . by the consecration of the bread and wine there takes place a change of the whole substance of the bread into the substance of the body of Christ our Lord and of the whole substance of the wine into the substance of his blood. This change the holy Catholic Church has fittingly and properly called transubstantiation."[2] The word 'substance' is used in a philosophical sense, referring to the essence or identity of something, in contradistinction to its 'accidents,' or superficial outward characteristics. In this way, the consecrated host has become in its substance (its real identity) the Body of Christ, while its accidents—its shape and size, its wheaten texture and flavor—remain the same.

* 'Eucharist' comes from the Greek word for 'thanksgiving' (*eucharistia*), and its use in this sense derives from the account of Jesus at the Last Supper: "He took bread, and when he had given thanks he broke it and gave it to them" (Luke 22:19). By extension, the thanksgiving refers also to what the faithful offer to God in response to Christ's original giving of thanks. The term 'Eucharist' can be applied both to the liturgical service of Mass as a whole and specifically to the consecrated elements.

To natural human senses, no change has come about, but to the eye of faith, the most important change imaginable has occurred. This may fairly put us in mind of an aspect of the Eucharistic significance of the *lembas* bread in *The Lord of the Rings*; Tolkien explains that although this elven "waybread" has exceptional properties when consumed, "No analysis in any laboratory would discover chemical properties of *lembas* that made it superior to other cakes of wheat-meal."[3]

The doctrine of the Real Presence is based on Scripture, most notably the 'Bread of Life' discourse in the Gospel of John, chapter 6, and it is this passage that Tolkien emphasizes when explaining his Eucharistic beliefs. In this long discourse, Jesus tells the gathered crowds, "I am the bread of life." When the crowd murmurs in protest, he reiterates, "I am the living bread which came down from heaven; if any one eats of this bread, he will live for ever; and the bread which I shall give for the life of the world is my flesh." When the Jews protest further, "How can this man give us his flesh to eat?" Jesus says even more firmly: "Truly, truly, I say to you, unless you eat the flesh of the Son of man and drink his blood, you have no life in you; he who eats my flesh and drinks my blood has eternal life, and I will raise him up at the last day. For my flesh is food indeed, and my blood is drink indeed." This so scandalized his hearers that "many of his disciples drew back and no longer went about with him. Jesus said to the twelve, 'Will you also go away?' Simon Peter answered him, 'Lord, to whom shall we go? You have the words of eternal life.'"[4]

Tolkien considered "the promulgation of the Blessed Sacrament" in John 6 to be a critically decisive issue: "We must therefore either believe in Him and in what he said and take the consequences; or reject him and take the consequences." To "deny the Blessed Sacrament," Tolkien wrote, is "to call Our Lord a fraud." But to accept the Blessed Sacrament necessarily entails giving it "the prime place" and according it the "most honour."[5]

We can begin to see, then, why Tolkien considered reception of the Eucharist to be a truly vital part of his spiritual life: it was the reception of Christ himself, sacramentally, into the temple of his body, and conversely, of renewing his membership in Christ's Body, which is the Church.

Tolkien's own respectful attitude toward the sacrament could be seen, for instance, in his granddaughter Joanna's recollection that "he always raised his hat when he passed a church."[6] This was not a generic gesture of respect for churches, but something he would do at a Catholic church because he knew that the sacrament was reserved in the tabernacle inside. It was the same gesture that he might make when acknowledging the presence of a friend on the other side of the road. Most Catholics would make the sign of the cross, but Tolkien appears to have considered that a bit religiose, unnecessarily pious. The Sacred Host was the sacramental continuation of the Incarnation of Jesus Christ in space and time, the presence of a real person, a genuine friend. Crossing oneself, hatless, inside a church would be right and proper, but if one was outside and wearing a hat, why not raise it? The habit speaks to the relaxed and affectionate love for Jesus Christ that he had, which was entirely compatible with the deepest reverence. As a linguist, he would have appreciated the capacity for a single sign to serve multiple purposes, and as a son of St. Philip Neri, he would have enjoyed its playfulness.

The breaking of the bread

Tolkien believed that the frequent reception of the sacrament was of the highest importance for the spiritual life, explaining to his son Michael that "Seven times a week is more nourishing than seven times at intervals."[7] He wasn't just recommending daily Mass attendance—which was not uncommon among devout Catholics at the time—but the reception of the sacrament every time he went to Mass, which was much less common.*

Catholics are obligated to attend Sunday Mass each week if it is possible to do so but are only required to receive the sacrament once a year, during the Easter season. In fact, during Tolkien's lifetime, it was fairly typical for even devout Catholics to receive communion only once a month or a few times per year, partly because of the strictness of the Eucharistic fast at the time. Even on Sundays, many churches offered a 'Mass with communion' first thing in the morning and then a late-morning Mass at which there was a sermon and usually music but without the distribution of communion.

* In modern Catholic practice, it is typical for everyone (or nearly everyone) who attends Mass also to receive Communion, but this was not the norm in Tolkien's day. It was common to refer to 'hearing Mass,' implying that attendance did not necessarily include receiving Communion.

The practice of frequent or even daily communion was brought about, in the worldwide Catholic Church, by the reforms of Pope Pius X (see figure 58), which Tolkien felt were extremely significant. Writing in 1963, he declared that Pius X had established "the greatest reform of our time," one that he felt was sorely needed: "I wonder what state the Church would now be but for it."[8] This is strong praise, so it is incumbent upon us, as we investigate Tolkien's faith, to look carefully at what he felt was so important about these changes.

The reforms unfolded over several years, beginning in 1905 when the pope approved the decree "*Sacra Tridentina*: On Frequent and Daily Reception of Holy Communion" and began to encourage the practice of daily communion. At that point, frequent communion was controversial due to differences of view as to how much preparation was necessary to be worthy to receive the sacrament. With his decree, the pope pushed back against the idea that people had to reach some level of spiritual perfection before they could approach God in the Eucharist. Being 'worthy' does not mean being perfected in sanctity, but rather indicates that one has put oneself through a basic examination of conscience and preparation of heart so as not to receive carelessly or unworthily, something St. Paul warns against in his First Letter to the Corinthian church (1 Corinthians 11:23–29).* The pope's aim was to encourage Catholics to receive communion daily and thus "to derive from this most health-giving Sacrament its more abundant fruits."[9]

Tolkien declared that frequent communion is the "only cure" for weak or "sagging faith"—that is, one does not need *already* to have strong faith before receiving communion. Furthermore, he emphasizes that although the Blessed Sacrament is always "perfect and complete and inviolate" in itself, it "does not operate completely and once for all in any of us. Like the act of Faith it must be continuous and grow by exercise."[10] Here he follows Pius X, who in his decree declared that it is right for a person regularly to seek the remedy of "this most healing sacrament," not out of mere custom or routine, but for the purpose of "seeking this divine remedy for

* In his 1910 decree *Quam Singulari*, Pius X also established the standard for First Holy Communion at the age when "the child knows the difference between the Eucharistic Bread and ordinary, material bread, and can therefore approach the altar with proper devotion," adding that "A full and perfect knowledge of Christian doctrine is not necessary either for First Confession or for First Communion. Afterwards, however, the child will be obliged to learn gradually the entire Catechism according to his ability."

his weaknesses and defects." Furthermore, the pope says that daily reception will aid people to "gradually emancipate themselves" from sin and the desire to sin.[11]

Tolkien's advice to Michael also contains the rather counterintuitive suggestion to strengthen his faith by going to a Mass celebrated by "a snuffling or gabbling priest"—that is, one who mumbles the liturgy or rushes through it in a mechanical manner—or by "a proud and vulgar friar." This, he says, "will be just the same (or better than that) as a mass said beautifully by a visibly holy man."[12] Why would Tolkien, with his great devotion to the Eucharist, consider that a slipshod liturgy could be "the same" or "better" than a beautiful and devoutly celebrated one? It is precisely his Eucharistic spirituality that undergirds his thinking.* Here Tolkien is emphasizing his belief that the Real Presence of Christ in the Eucharist is brought about *ex opere operato* ("by the work worked"), meaning that sacramental grace comes from the validity of the rite and of the priest's ordination; it does not depend on the aesthetically pleasing nature of the liturgy or on the personal holiness of the priest who has consecrated it. Tolkien had by this stage in his life of faith learned to relax into the sheer objectivity of the Blessed Sacrament, undeflected by exterior irritations or distractions—or at least he felt there was spiritual value in making the attempt.

To be sure, he certainly did appreciate the Mass being celebrated with beauty and reverence. For instance, on his visit to Italy in 1955, he was delighted by the fact that at the High Mass, there were "silver trumpets at the elevation!"[13] and deprecated the fact that the celebrant could not sing. The 'elevation' refers to that moment in the Mass when the priest raises up the Host so that it is visible to the entire congregation; he then does the same with the chalice. A bell is usually rung at this moment; silver trumpets are exceptional. But on that same Italian trip, he noted in his diary, "the chapels of the Blessed Sacrament (often commonplace or tawdry in their gear)" nonetheless emitted "a curious glow of dormant life and Charity."[14] Just as St. Paul described Christians as possessing "treasure in earthen vessels, to show that the transcendent power belongs to God and not to us" (2

---

* Tolkien suggests this as an "exercise"—a way of performing an 'act of faith'—and not as a regular practice, though he observes that it is "alas! only too easy to find opportunity for" (*Letters*, 339). In chapter 31 we will return to this exercise to see how Tolkien presents it as an opportunity also to grow in charity.

Corinthians 4:7), so churches and chapels, however unappealing in design or furnishings, contained incalculable riches.

Exposition, Adoration, Benediction

Although Tolkien's emphasis was, as we have seen, on the importance of receiving communion at Mass, this was not the only way that the Blessed Sacrament was present in his life of faith. The doctrine of the Real Presence of Christ in the sacrament also gave rise to the devotional practices of Exposition, Adoration, and Benediction.

In the basic practice of Adoration, the sacrament is 'Exposed'—that is, brought out of the tabernacle and displayed publicly on the altar. It is placed inside a 'monstrance,' a metal stand (usually ornately decorated) in the shape of a cross or sunburst, with the Host visible behind a glass circle at the center. (See figure 28.) Many Catholic churches have times for Adoration every week, and during Holy Week, it is customary to hold such a service on Maundy Thursday, that being the day commemorating Christ's institution of the Eucharist at the Last Supper. At these times, people come to pray individually in the presence of the sacrament, whether for a few minutes or for an hour or more.

Adoration most often takes place as part of the devotion called Benediction, which Tolkien participated in regularly throughout his life, and not just when at home in England. While on holiday in Italy with Priscilla, he made a point of going to Benediction in Assisi.[15] In this service, the Blessed Sacrament is Exposed with lit candles placed around it, it is censed (that is, wafted with incense burning inside a thurible), and hymns are sung.[16] The name 'Benediction' comes from the central action of the service, when the priest takes up the monstrance, turns to the congregation, and makes the sign of the cross with it as a blessing (a 'benediction'). At the conclusion of the service, as the sacrament is put back into the tabernacle, other hymns and Psalms are sung, such as the *Te Deum* and the Psalm *Laudate Dominum*.[17] These were important prayers for Tolkien, and we will return to them in chapter 27.

One variation of Adoration is the *Quarant'ore*, or Forty Hours Devotion, which we know that Tolkien participated in. It consists of approximately forty hours of

Exposition of the Blessed Sacrament for prayer and adoration—corresponding to the forty hours that Jesus's body lay in the tomb—in a single church or sometimes in a sequence of churches. It began in Italy in the sixteenth century and was encouraged by the Oratory of St. Philip Neri. By means of the Oratorians, it made its way to England in the nineteenth century, although it was held by only a tiny fraction of English Catholic churches in Tolkien's day. In 1944, Tolkien recalled "spending half an hour . . . before the Blessed Sacrament when the Quarant' Ore was being held."[18] It was the occasion for his experiencing something akin to a mystical vision of divine love, as we will explore further in chapter 22.

But even on ordinary occasions, when there was no 'sensible consolation,'* Tolkien believed that the Blessed Sacrament communicated God's love to him. As he declares to his son Michael:

> There you will find romance, glory, honour, fidelity, and the true way of all your loves upon earth, and more than that: Death: by the divine paradox, that which ends life, and demands the surrender of all, and yet by the taste (or foretaste) of which alone can what you seek in your earthly relationships (love, faithfulness, joy) be maintained, or take on that complexion of reality, of eternal endurance, which every man's heart desires.[19]

Waybread

With all this in mind, we can return to Tolkien's connection between the *lembas* of *The Lord of the Rings* and the Blessed Sacrament.

Tolkien stated that he was a Christian, "which can be deduced from my stories," and though he added that his specifically Catholic identity "perhaps cannot be deduced," he offered several instances in which attentive readers had in fact done so. One of these was related to the significance of the *lembas*. He noted that a reader saw in the *lembas* something equivalent to "viaticum" and in the reference

* 'Sensible consolation' is a term in Catholic spirituality derived from *The Dark Night of the Soul* by the Spanish mystic St. John of the Cross (1542–91). Sometimes a Christian *feels* comforted by God's presence while at prayer; sometimes nothing is felt; sometimes what is felt seems more like desolation than consolation. The heart of Christian devotion is a matter of faith, not of a particular quality of emotion (Hebrews 11:1).

to "its feeding the *will* . . . and being more potent when fasting, a derivation from the Eucharist." It is an example, he explains, of how "far greater things may colour the mind in dealing with the lesser things of a fairy-story."[20]

His use of 'waybread' as a synonym for the Elvish *lembas* is a signpost toward its spiritual meaning since it is a word that he has, in effect, invented for this very use.

Before Tolkien's writing of *The Lord of the Rings*, 'waybread' had only one meaning: it was the medieval common name for plantain, a wide-leaved plant growing beside the 'way' (i.e., the road). The suffix '-bread' had nothing to do with food but rather comes from the Old English word for 'broad' (referring to the leaves).[21] Tolkien's repurposing of 'waybread' to mean 'food for a journey' converts it into an English equivalent of the Latin *viaticum*, which comes from *via* ('way') and, as the *Oxford English Dictionary* notes, means literally 'provision for a journey.' As we saw in chapter 7 in the discussion of the last rites given to Tolkien's mother, *viaticum* is what the sacrament is called when it is given to a dying person as preparation for the final journey.

Tolkien recognizes that the story-function of *lembas* is to make it plausible that the characters can go on such long journeys with so little provision of food. But that aspect, he says, is "relatively unimportant." Its real significance, he explains, appears in the "Mount Doom" chapter, in which we learn that Frodo and Sam "would long ago have lain down to die" without this waybread, which "fed the will" and "gave strength to endure . . . beyond the measure of mortal kind." This, he says, points to the fact that the *lembas* "has a much larger significance, of what one might hesitatingly call a 'religious' kind."[22] The *lembas* bread is not an allegory of the Blessed Sacrament but rather an image or 'type' of it, such that it has, to use Tolkien's preferred word, "applicability" to the primary world.

It is fitting that in the *Oxford English Dictionary* the word 'waybread' is now defined as more than just 'plantain'; there is an additional entry, illustrated by quotations from Tolkien's writings and corresponding exactly to the dual usage of the word in *The Lord of the Rings*. On the non-religious level, as the *Oxford English Dictionary* notes, 'waybread' means "(after J. R. R. Tolkien's use): a kind of sustaining food made for eating before or during a long journey, typically in the form of flat bread or wafers"; on the religious level, it is "The Eucharist. Cf. *viaticum*," with the first illustrative quotation from the letter we have quoted above. Three more examples follow, from 1993, 1998, and 2003, in which 'waybread' is used as a synonym for the Blessed Sacrament; these citations make no reference to *The Lord of the Rings*, though all are undoubtedly indebted to it.[23]

This is remarkable and something that Tolkien the philologist—who once worked for the *Oxford English Dictionary*—would surely have been delighted by had he lived to see it. 'Waybread,' his invented word in the fictional realm of Middle-earth, has made its way out into the primary world, there bestowing a new name upon "the one great thing to love on earth."

14

"With this ring I thee wed"

The start of 1913 marked the renewal of Tolkien's relationship with Edith. The years of separation were past, they were both now of age, and they had proved the strength of their attachment. All was not smooth sailing, however. Tolkien had no prospects of financial security in the foreseeable future, and it might be years before they could marry. But the most important issue was that he was a Catholic, she was an Anglican, and Tolkien did not want them to have a 'mixed marriage.'

Today, in a different cultural context, it may seem difficult to understand why this mattered: after all, they were both Christians. Was that not enough? Here it is worth attending to the Catholic Church's view on religiously mixed marriages at that time—that is, before the first Code of Canon Law came into effect in 1917—as it provides essential context to understand more fully why it was so important to Tolkien that Edith should become a Catholic before they married.

To be sure, mixed marriages were possible if the proper dispensation had been granted; however, the Church strongly discouraged Catholics from marrying Protestants. The reason for this was not that the marriage would be invalid—a dispensation would avoid that—but because the hierarchy considered such marriages would pose a risk to the faith of the Catholic spouse and also to the proper upbringing of the children of that marriage, a point to which we will return shortly. In Tolkien's day, anti-Catholic attitudes were far more common than they are now and could lead to considerable tensions, to say the least, in the wider family and even within a marriage.* Therefore, the Church placed an obstacle in the way of Catholics who wished to marry non-Catholic Christians by officially declaring that the 'mixed communion' was an impediment to marriage that could only be removed

* Another key point was (and is) that for a Catholic, a validly contracted marriage—one entered into freely and with full understanding and agreement to its conditions—is permanent; it cannot be ended by divorce. The spouses might need to separate, but they would remain married.

by a dispensation, which at first had to come from the pope. Tolkien would have been well aware of this, not least because his own erstwhile guardian, Fr. Francis, was the fruit of just such a marriage between a Spanish Catholic mother and an English Protestant father, who received their dispensation from the pope in 1849.[1]

The year after Fr. Francis's parents married, the situation had changed somewhat. In 1850, the hierarchy was restored to England: 'Mary's Dowry'* had bishops again. As a result, the pope's authority to provide dispensation for a mixed marriage was now delegated to the local bishop. If Tolkien had wished to petition for a dispensation to marry Edith, he would have made the request to the archbishop of Birmingham—a much less formidable procedure than sending a petition all the way to Rome.

The bishop would have then looked into the case. The first step was that he "should endeavour to procure the conversion of the non-Catholic; and if this cannot be had, he should exhort the Catholic to desist from the marriage." If these efforts had been made and proved unavailing, the bishop had authority to "grant a matrimonial dispensation."[2]

The dispensation itself would have contained a threefold requirement: the Catholic spouse was to have complete freedom to practice his or her faith; the Catholic "must promise to do all that is possible to procure the conversion of the non-Catholic"; and all the children were to be brought up Catholic.[3]† This last requirement was by far the most pressing (and divisive) question in the England of Tolkien's time. The compromise approach taken by some Anglicans was that daughters would be brought up in their mother's religion, and sons in their father's religion—but although this tactic was adopted by some Catholics as a way of keeping the peace, it was not in line with the Church's official position.‡

---

* Since the medieval period, England has been known as 'Mary's Dowry' on account of the special devotion of English Catholics to the Blessed Virgin. A late fourteenth-century altarpiece depicts King Richard II kneeling and offering to Mary an orb on which a miniature map of England is depicted; the inscription reads, "This is thy dowry, O Holy Virgin." The Wilton Diptych (ca. 1395, now in the National Gallery) depicts a similar scene.

† This remains true in current Catholic canon law, which states that the Catholic party in a mixed marriage "is to make a sincere promise to do all in his or her power so that all offspring are baptized and brought up in the Catholic Church" (Canon 1125, 1° of the 1983 Code of Canon Law).

‡ It was also not conducive to family harmony. For example, in Newman's day, Tom Arnold, whom we met in chapter 3, attempted to keep the peace in this manner when he became a

On the face of it, the requirements presented no problem for Tolkien. Edith had a generally positive attitude about Catholics, and her former guardian was a Catholic;[4] it is reasonable to assume that even if she had remained an Anglican, she would have agreed that their children be raised Catholic. They would not have been able to have a Nuptial Mass or receive the 'nuptial blessing,' which was only given to marriages in which both parties were Catholic, but their union would have been recognized as a fully valid marriage in the eyes of the Church.[5]

In short, as a devout Catholic, Tolkien could have married Edith even if she had remained an Anglican. It would not even have been particularly unusual for the time, given the minority status of English Catholics in a Protestant culture. Furthermore, at the Oratory, he could easily have found out how to go about such a marriage from Fr. Denis Sheil, who had a deep knowledge of canon law and liturgy, "which he willingly and untiringly placed at the disposal of those who requested his help."[6]

Why, then, was Tolkien so desirous of Edith becoming a Catholic before their marriage?

One reason has to do with their future children and what would happen to them if Tolkien died young. With the shadow of the Great War over their final preparations for marriage, the idea of a widowed Edith being left with small children would have figured as a real concern. If he died, or if they both died, would his extended family support the Catholic education of great-grandchildren, nieces, and nephews, or take the 'mixed' status of the family as a rationale for bringing up the children as Protestants? Tolkien was surely aware that when he and his brother were newly orphaned, the family wished them to be raised as Protestants, in defiance of their mother's wishes. If he and Edith left an orphan daughter, would their Protestant family press their claim on the grounds that the child's mother had been an Anglican? We do not know that this issue was a consideration for Tolkien, only that, given the trauma of his childhood, it would not have been unreasonable for him to be sensitive on this topic.

The really pressing issue was surely Tolkien's faith. His desire for her to become a Catholic was not so much preemptively to guard against unfortunate future possibilities; it was because he wanted her to join him in the Church in which

Catholic, with his daughters raised Anglican and his sons raised Catholic. It did not assuage his wife's anti-Catholic attitude or benefit his relationship with his children.

he believed. He wanted their marriage to receive the fullest blessing possible: the complete approval of the Church and its celebration in the context of a Mass.

An excess of zeal?

As it happens, Edith was content to become a Catholic, and indeed she believed that her family had historically been Catholic.[7] But, not surprisingly, her preference was to wait until closer to their marriage. For one thing, she expected that her Uncle Jessop would react badly, and in this she was correct; in the event, he demanded that she leave his house, so she had to find new lodgings.[8] Becoming a Catholic would also mean breaking off her life as an Anglican in Cheltenham, where she had a meaningful role as a musician in her parish church. For instance, as late as April 1913, after she and Tolkien had reconnected, she gave piano performances for several events in her parish, including the annual parish tea, which had two hundred guests; the newspaper account highlighted "a pianoforte solo by Miss Bratt."[9] She knew that, on announcing her intention to swim the Tiber, she would lose friends and social connections, and all while she would be on her own, without the compensation—yet—of a husband. Tolkien had plenty to occupy him as a student in Oxford; she did not.

Tolkien's understandable enthusiasm for his fiancée to share his Catholic faith meant that he was impatient with any delays, and, as John and Priscilla Tolkien recalled later on, "persuaded" her to begin her instruction right away with Fr. William Murphy, the pastor of St. Mary Immaculate, Warwick.[10]

Tolkien later came to consider that her instruction by Fr. Murphy had been inadequate.[11] He would have remembered that his mother had received catechesis in a similarly lonely (in fact, even lonelier) position, but perhaps didn't fully appreciate that Mabel had sought out first St. Anne's and then the Birmingham Oratory partly in order to connect with priests who knew the particular difficulties faced by Anglicans entering the Church. Fr. Murphy, it seems, was not so used to dealing with converts.

Tolkien also might not have fully grasped that Edith's day-to-day experience as a catechumen was not as aesthetically pleasing as his own had been. Tolkien had grown up in an atmosphere of beauty and reverence in worship at the Oratory.

When she lived in Cheltenham, Edith could worship at the historic Anglican parish church of St. Mary's, dating from the eighth century; it featured a superb rose window, was musically inspiring, and, of course, Edith knew the people there very well.[12] In contrast, the relative newness and plainness of the Catholic church of St. Mary Immaculate, Warwick, on top of its strangeness, made it somewhat "sordid," as Tolkien admitted.[13] (See figure 21.)

Though we have only a few snippets to indicate what Tolkien and Edith discussed before her entrance into full communion with the Catholic Church, we can get a sense of his earnestness in exhorting her to do so. Tolkien wrote to her, "I do so dearly believe that no half-heartedness and no worldly fear must turn us aside from following the light unflinchingly."[14] This image of "following the light" is almost certainly an allusion to a hymn that Edith, as a church organist, would have known well: "Lead, Kindly Light," written by John Henry Newman during his Anglican days, and widely popular in the Church of England.[15] Its opening verse runs as follows:

> Lead, Kindly Light, amidst th'encircling gloom,
> Lead Thou me on!
> The night is dark, and I am far from home,
> Lead Thou me on!
> Keep Thou my feet; I do not ask to see
> The distant scene; one step enough for me.

The fact that Newman had taken the same step that Edith was contemplating would have made the hymn particularly resonant for her situation.

Tolkien had himself dealt with the temptation to "half-heartedness," and his return to regular attendance at Mass meant that he was now in a position to understand more fully the value of the Church's sacramental life. He longed for his beloved Edith to share completely in that life.

But he seems to have been a bit tactless in conveying this, describing the Church of England, on one occasion, as "a pathetic and shadowy medley of half-remembered traditions and mutilated beliefs."[16] No doubt he would have defended his remark by pointing to the fact that within the Church of England some clergymen thought auricular confession necessary while others declared it a popish abomination; some believed baptism to be a sacrament while others thought it a mere symbol; some called the Eucharist 'the Blessed Sacrament' while others considered it more like an *aide memoire*. And alongside such latitude over sacraments, there had been heresy trials in the Church of England over much more minor matters, such as the type of vestments that the priest wore or the number of candles on the altar. You could be Anglo-Catholic, High Church, Broad Church, Low Church: "medley" was not an entirely inapposite word.* Nevertheless, his denunciation in such hyperbolic terms of the tradition in which Edith had grown up and enjoyed Christian fellowship was insensitive and certainly not something that would have been modeled by the Oratory Fathers or the Oxford chaplain, Fr. Basil Maturin.

In later years, the mature Tolkien took a very different approach with his non-Catholic friends, building from shared beliefs when possible and making an effort to restrain his tendency toward hyperbolic rhetoric. It seems likely that this moderation was learned in part from the experience of over-eagerly sharing his faith during his courtship.

Still, his zeal was already achieving something that gave him great joy. In June 1913, during the Oxford Long Vacation, he and Edith attended Benediction in Warwick. From this shared experience, "we came away serenely happy," Tolkien wrote, "for this was the first time that we had ever been able to go calmly side by side to church."[17] The two of them had probably gone to Mass together in Warwick on numerous occasions, but Benediction was something special. It is a distinctively Catholic service,† but it can be participated in by Catholics and non-Catholics on an equal footing. Since it did not include the distribution of Holy Communion, there was no reminder that Edith was not yet a Catholic, and the service would have been more comprehensible to her as it was mostly in English (unlike the Mass) and included hymns, some of which she probably knew from Church of England use. And from Tolkien's perspective, going calmly side by side to Benediction with

---

* Tolkien's Oxford college, Exeter, was located opposite Jesus College on Turl Street, which linked Broad Street to the High Street. A very Oxonian joke was to ask why the Church of England was like Turl Street. Answer: "Because it goes from High to Broad, passing Jesus on the way."

† Benediction does sometimes occur in the Church of England, despite one of the Thirty-Nine Articles (the twenty-fifth) appearing to outlaw it: "The Sacraments were not ordained of Christ to be gazed upon, or to be carried about."

Edith would have been a foretaste of the unity they would eventually enjoy at the Eucharistic table of the Lord, the heart of his faith.

Magna Dei Gloria (Warwick)

They did not have long to wait. Tolkien had the joy of being present when Edith was received into full communion with the Catholic Church by Fr. Murphy in the church of St. Mary Immaculate, Warwick, on Thursday, January 8, 1914; she and Tolkien were formally betrothed by the same priest on the same occasion.* Around this time, Tolkien wrote a poem called "Magna Dei Gloria (Warwick)" and dedicated it to Edith.[18] "Magna Dei Gloria" means 'to the great glory of God.' It signifies something of the spiritual elation with which Tolkien viewed her entry into the Church and their now much smoother path to marriage.

During the next eighteen months of their engagement, Tolkien finished his studies at Oxford; he then "bolted" into the army in the summer of 1915, as soon as he had his degree under his belt. Early in 1916, they set their wedding date for March 22 of that year. Ironically, the choice of date meant that even though Edith was now a Catholic, they still could not receive the nuptial blessing at their wedding. March 22 fell that year during Lent, the penitential season of abstinence preparatory to the festivities of Eastertide. Marriages could be conducted during Lent, but in a somber and curtailed mode; hence, not with a Nuptial Mass or blessing.[19]

The reason for such an infelicitous date was probably the Great War, which was disarranging everyone's lives. Now that Tolkien had finished his degree and completed his officer's training, he knew that he would soon be sent to active duty on the front. That year, Easter was almost as late as it can be, falling on April 23.

* They chose January 8 because it was the first anniversary of their reunion (*Biography*, 76), and there may be further significance to the date. Given that Edith's reception took place at the church of St. Mary Immaculate, it is likely that Tolkien pondered both the date of the Feast of the Immaculate Conception, which had occurred exactly one month earlier on December 8, and the fact that the Feast of Mary's nativity is always marked on September 8, nine months later. Since January 8 marked the rebirth of Tolkien and Edith's relationship, what date would have marked its "re-conception"? Answer: April 8, nine months prior. It is striking that the climax of *The Lord of the Rings*, when Frodo and Sam are praised on the Field of Cormallen, the scene that Tolkien described as "the peak" of the story's music, should be dated to April 8. That date marks no regular feast day of any importance in the church calendar, but it acquires significance in light of the timing of Edith's reception. (I am grateful to Michael Ward for bringing this to my attention.)

Setting a date after Easter, though it would allow them to have a full Nuptial Mass, would be risky: Tolkien might have been posted to the front lines in France by then. Once they realized that they wanted to marry before Tolkien went off to war, they had relatively little time to work with, since the banns had to be announced on the three successive Sundays before whichever date they chose. As it was, the March date allowed Tolkien to combine, in one leave from his officer training, his degree ceremony at Oxford, their wedding, and the honeymoon.[20]

His relationship with Fr. Francis was still in a slightly strained condition (a point that we will return to in chapter 23), and so he delayed disclosing the wedding date until two weeks before the event. But when he did break the news, Fr. Francis not only wished them "every blessing and happiness" but also suggested that he personally officiate and that the ceremony take place at the Birmingham Oratory.[21] Although it was at that point too late to change their plans, his warm response must have gone a long way toward reassuring Tolkien that his father figure harbored no lingering disapproval.

Silver and gold

So, on Wednesday, March 22, 1916, Tolkien and Edith were quietly married by Fr. Murphy after the morning Mass at St. Mary Immaculate, and the "sordid" building must have suddenly seemed a little brighter.[22] The ceremony was a simple one. After the couple exchanged their vows, the priest made the sign of the cross over their joined hands, declaring them to be joined in matrimony. Then followed an action so richly symbolic that it is worth quoting in full from the rubric:

> The husband puts the ring, a piece of gold and a piece of silver [generally gold and silver coins] on the plate held by the server. The priest blesses the ring . . . and sprinkles it with holy water in cross form. The husband takes the gold, silver and ring, and says (in short phrases after the priest) *With this ring I thee wed*, etc. As he says *This gold and silver I thee give*, he hands the pieces to the woman, who puts them away or hands them to someone to hold for her. Then the husband puts the ring on the woman's left hand. He puts it first on the thumb, saying *In the name of the Father*, takes it

> off and puts it on the forefinger, saying *and of the Son*, takes it off again and puts it on the third finger, saying *and of the Holy Ghost*, on the fourth (*Amen*), and leaves it there.[23]

The giving and receiving of a ring in this way expressed how their marriage was a gift from God.* Tolkien had a very high view of the meaningful quality of ritual and ceremony. Many years later, in 1968, he told an interviewer that spoken words are "only one form of language" and that actions are "sometimes much more expressive" than words.†

The expressiveness of giving not just a ring but also gold and silver coins as a symbol of his commitment to love and care for Edith is worth remarking on. It is interesting to observe how often the most beautiful things in Middle-earth are both gold *and* silver.‡ The most notable of these are the Two Trees of Valinor, which appear in *The Book of Lost Tales*, composed soon after Tolkien and Edith's marriage: many details of the Trees changed in later versions, but from the beginning, one tree pours forth "pale gold effulgence" while the other sheds "light like liquid silver."[24] The light from the Trees would, in the later development of Tolkien's mythology, be captured in the Silmarils, the holy jewels that give their name to the *Silmarillion* and form an integral part of the story of Beren and Lúthien.

The newlyweds took a week's honeymoon in Clevedon, Somerset,[25]§ and then settled in lodgings near Tolkien's training camp in Great Haywood. There, on April 30 (the first Sunday after Easter), they finally received a nuptial blessing from the

---

* Although it was typical at that time for only the wife to wear a ring, and the ceremony included only the bestowal of her ring, Tolkien in fact also wore a wedding ring.

† He adds, "To light a candle becomes a beautiful thing, to light a candle and then go away and leave it as a model of your aspiration" (Lee, "Tolkien in Oxford," 149).

‡ For instance, Galadriel's hair is golden but shot through with silver; the fallen statue of the king at the Cross-roads in Ithilien bears a living "coronal of silver and gold"; and when Frodo and Sam are honored at the Field of Cormallen, "the clear voice of the minstrel rose like silver and gold." Michael Ward writes, "In this connection we should note that Cormallen's circle of laburnums is located in *Ithilien*, a Sindarin name which means 'Land of the Moon.' The Field therefore provides yet another pairing of gold and silver, of Solar and Lunar significance. Read in religious terms, this pairing connotes the importance Tolkien attached not only to Christ ('the light of the world,' John 8:12) but also to his mother, for the Blessed Virgin is often represented iconographically in Christian art by means of the Moon, which derives all its light from the Sun (see Revelation 12:1)" ("Peak Middle-earth," 68n62).

§ During their stay, they visited Cheddar Caves, which, as Tolkien later revealed, provided the inspiration for the glittering caverns of Helm's Deep in *The Lord of the Rings* (*Letters*, 407).

local priest, Fr. Augustin Emery,[26] to make up for the fact that they had not been able to have a proper Nuptial Mass. (See figure 23.) The inclusion of this blessing in a regular Sunday Mass created a certain amount of confusion in the parish. Priscilla recalled that "my mother would describe with great amusement how the local people thought that this meant that they were a couple who had been living in sin and now the priest was making an honest woman of her!"[27]

At age twenty-four, Tolkien was now a married man: he would continue in that role for the next fifty-five years till Edith's death in 1971. They would raise four children and endure two world wars, experiencing more than an average share of ill health between them and shouldering many years of financial strain before his writings gained them a measure of wealth.

But the present moment meant yet another enforced separation.

On Friday, June 2, 1916, at their lodgings in Great Haywood, Tolkien received notice that he was being sent to join the British Expeditionary Force in France—on the Western Front. He was granted 48 hours of leave before he had to report to Folkestone, on the southeast coast, where he would then cross the English Channel and enter the front line. He and Edith chose not to spend those last precious hours in their ordinary lodgings; rather, the next day, they traveled together to Birmingham and spent the night at The Plough and Harrow, a pleasant and comfortable hotel conveniently located across the street from the Oratory. Tolkien thus had a chance to make his confession, attend Sunday Mass, receive Holy Communion, and say goodbye to Fr. Francis.

In the afternoon of Sunday, June 4, Tolkien boarded his train to Folkestone. Years later, he recalled the moment: "Parting from my wife then—we were only just married—it was like a death."[28]

MIDDLE: 1916–1952

15

Into Battle

We now need to retrace our steps to January 1914, when Tolkien and Edith were formally engaged. At that juncture, they had no idea that just eight months later, England would be at war with Germany. The British Empire declared war on August 4 and, to begin with, the national mood was exuberant, even enthusiastic. The response to Lord Kitchener's recruiting slogan "Your Country needs YOU" was overwhelming. The initial call, in September 1914, was for a total of 100,000 men. By the end of the month, 750,000 had enlisted. War spirit was high, and people sincerely believed 'it would all be over by Christmas.'

Christmas 1914 came and went, and it began to be apparent that this war would not be brief. Nevertheless, 125,000 men continued to enlist each month until June 1915, when the flow of volunteers finally began to slacken. Still, public opinion in England remained so strongly in favor of volunteering that young women began a campaign of giving a white feather—a symbol of cowardice—to any man of military-service age observed in public not wearing a uniform. This campaign did not spur sufficient numbers of men to sign up. Eventually, to maintain the supply of recruits, conscription was put into effect in 1916.[1]

Tolkien later recalled that "In those days chaps joined up, or were scorned publicly. It was a nasty cleft to be in, especially for a young man with too much imagination and little physical courage." In the fall of 1914, he joined the Officers Training Corps at Oxford. In this way, he could finish his studies while training for the army and go into active service straight after his Finals. He gritted his teeth, withstood the reproaches and abuse that came his way, and stayed at Oxford until he earned his degree—and then "Bolted into the army: July 1915."[2]

Patriots or traitors?

In November 1914, Tolkien declared to his friend Christopher Wiseman that "The duty of patriotism and a fierce belief in nationalism are to me of vital importance"—though he tempered this statement by adding, "I am not of course a militarist."[3]

"The duty of patriotism" was a point of view that many Catholics were eager to express at that time. Their Protestant neighbors often considered them likely to be unpatriotic, even traitorous, because their allegiance to Rome's pope was supposedly higher than their allegiance to England's king.* † The declaration of war against Germany and Austria-Hungary appeared to put British Catholics in something of a dilemma. As James Hagerty notes, these nations had "large Catholic populations [who were] united with British Catholics in acknowledging the religious supremacy of the Pope." But as it happened, the Catholic response in Britain was firmly patriotic: "Whilst deploring war and its dreadful effects, Catholic bishops were unequivocal in their support of the government. At their behest, congregations prayed for peace but only for one that followed victory over a tyrannical and warlike nation that had transgressed Christian principles and violated the integrity of both Catholic Belgium and France."[4]

In joining the army as the other young men of his time did, Tolkien was doing his part to show that 'papists,' too, could be patriotic Englishmen, and in his case, it was perhaps felt to be all the more necessary because of the German origin of his surname.‡ One of the early effects of the war was a rise in anti-German sentiment. The Rector of Exeter College had a "distaste" for Germans and retailed (unconfirmed) stories of Belgians being buried alive by German forces. German Rhodes Scholars at Oxford had their funds withdrawn.[5] For those like Tolkien, with

* William Manchester observes that "It was probably impossible to deepen the contempt of Irish Catholics for the British, but Kitchener had a try at it, issuing orders that under no circumstances would Catholics be permitted to fight under their own officers" (*The Last Lion*, 1:665).

† As a Navy chaplain, Fr. Anthony Pollen of the Birmingham Oratory used Philippine humor to tackle these difficulties. When he reported to the captain of his ship the *Warspite*, "the Captain said, 'I hope we shall get on, but I think it fair to tell you that I don't like Catholics.' To which F. Anthony replied, 'I am sure, Sir, that we shall get on, as, to be candid, I detest Protestants.' They did become friends and played golf together during the short intervals at Scapa when they could get ashore" ("F. Anthony Pollen," Birmingham Oratory).

‡ 'Tolkien' is an Anglicized version of the German *tollkühn*, meaning 'foolhardy' (*Letters*, 218). Tolkien's German ancestors on his father's side had been in England for several hundred years—not that this would have appeased anti-German sentiment.

foreign-sounding names, things could be problematic.* As a result, he would have felt all the more keenly the social pressure upon him to show loyalty to his country, for there were two strikes against him: Roman *and* 'German'! That he insisted on completing his degree before bolting into the army speaks to his strength of purpose as a scholar and his ability to chart a course he believed to be right, even if it was unpopular.

The horrors of war

After nearly a year in camps in England, where he trained as a signals officer, Tolkien was sent to France in June 1916. (See figure 27.)

There he encountered a horror previously unimaginable: the first fully mechanized war. Guns and shells had seen use in previous conflicts but to a limited extent alongside cavalry charges; now machine guns, tanks, and poison gas could cut down soldiers *en masse*. Trench warfare was a horrific stalemate, with men slaughtered in attempts to gain just a few yards of territory.

The death toll was staggering. 880,000 British soldiers died in the conflict: six percent of the adult male population. (By comparison, slightly over 100,000 US soldiers died.)[6] Two million were wounded. Death could come during an assault on German lines, from ordinary shelling and sniping, from accidental 'friendly fire,' or as a consequence of disease contracted in the waterlogged, rat-infested trenches. Away from the front, German U-boats circled in Atlantic waters, torpedoing not just warships but also passenger ships such as the *Lusitania*, a tragedy in which—as we noted in an earlier chapter—Tolkien's Oxford chaplain Fr. Maturin lost his life.

And death struck closer still. The TCBS—that band of brothers from King Edward's School with their earnest moral vision for changing the world through the arts—was cut in two. While Tolkien and Wiseman survived, Gilson and Smith did not. Rob Gilson died leading his men into action on July 1, 1916, the first

* The poet Robert Graves was at one point suspected by fellow officers of being a German spy on account of his family name actually being 'von Graves.' The future poet laureate John Betjeman's family changed the spelling of their name from 'Betjemann' to make themselves seem less German. Even the royal family felt it was necessary to change their name from Saxe-Coburg-Gotha to the reassuringly English 'Windsor,' prompting the celebrated remark of the Kaiser that he looked forward to seeing a performance of Shakespeare's *The Merry Wives of Saxe-Coburg-Gotha*.

day of the Battle of the Somme, when nearly 20,000 men were killed and almost twice as many injured. Geoffrey Smith died in December of that year, succumbing to injuries caused by shell fire.[7]

The men of Exeter College were likewise mown down like grass beneath the sickle. The cohort who matriculated with Tolkien in 1911 was more severely hit than any other class year: 59 served and more than a third were killed.*

"By 1918," as Tolkien wrote years later, "all but one of my close friends were dead."[8]

Spiritual life in the trenches

It is sometimes said that 'There are no atheists in foxholes,' but this is untrue. Robert Graves, in his memoir *Goodbye to All That*, wrote that "Hardly one soldier in a hundred was inspired by religious feeling of even the crudest kind. It would have been difficult to remain religious in the trenches even if one survived the irreligion of the training battalion at home." He recalled a sergeant, who complained of the "damn nonsense" of newspaper stories about wayside crucifixes not being damaged by fire, using one such shrine for target practice and "humorously" (as Graves viewed it) substituting for "concentrate, fire!" the words "consecrate, fire!"[9] Likewise, the young atheist C.S. Lewis, remarking on his service in the trenches, admitted to being frightened all the time, "But I never sank so low as to pray."[10]

Whom would one be praying to? Could God be real when both sides of the conflict claimed divine sanction for their actions? And if God did exist, why did he allow such pointless slaughter as occurred at Passchendaele, that "senseless campaign," as Prime Minister Lloyd George later described it?[11] How could a good God allow *any* of this suffering to fall upon young men in the prime of life?

Quite aside from these theological questions, there were practical moral questions thrown up by the war. The soldiers' environment, with its stresses and deprivations, provided many reasons and opportunities for ethical disintegration, from blasphemy and despair to drunkenness and the visiting of brothels while off duty. It is no surprise that religious leaders were concerned about the effect of the war on the spiritual health of their flock. Immediately after the Armistice, both the Church of

* In total, 143 Exeter College members (students and faculty) were killed, out of 771 who served. Three of Tolkien's fellow Apolaustick members were among the fallen (*TEC*, 50).

England and the Catholic Church in England set out to do comprehensive surveys and interviews with chaplains and combatants. The resulting reports were published in 1919.* These contemporary assessments give us a vivid picture of spiritual life during the war, as well as how its effects were judged in Tolkien's own day.

For Catholic soldiers like Tolkien, their entire structure of religious habits was thrown into disarray. The hierarchy of English bishops did what it could to ensure provision of the sacraments under these difficult circumstances. Many priests went to the front lines to serve as chaplains (including two Oratorians whom Tolkien would have known†) and did so in a proportionately high number considering the minority status of Catholics in England: "over 800 priests, approximately 10% of Catholic clerical manpower in the British Isles, had served in the military by the time of the Armistice."[12] Even that was insufficient to meet the needs of the soldiers on the front lines, at home bases, and in hospitals, and the men and their families complained about the lack of spiritual support.[13]

Chaplains heard confessions and indeed put in a lot of effort to encourage the men to go to confession; they could also give the men a general absolution if there was danger of death and no time for the chaplain to hear individual confessions; in these instances, the chaplain would exhort the men to make an act of contrition—recognizing their sins and being sorry for them—before absolving them as a group. (See figure 24.) One chaplain recalled that "The majority, unless strongly urged, don't come *often* to confession, the real reason being shyness, shame, ignorance, forgetfulness of method of going, fear of reproof, and long absence, but they were eager for Absolution all the same, for almost every man would come to Holy Communion after a General Absolution."[14] The hierarchy also dispensed soldiers from the requirement to fast before receiving communion so that they could receive the sacrament whenever it became possible for them to do so.[15]

Scheduling was a problem. The nature of warfare meant that men might be relocated at a moment's notice, and in the routine of the army, "almost anything

* The Anglican report was entitled *The Army and Religion: An Enquiry and Its Bearing upon the Religious Life of the Nation*; the Catholic report, edited by Charles Plater, was entitled *Catholic Soldiers: By Sixty Chaplains and Many Others*.

† Fr. Charles Heurtley and Fr. Stanislas du Moulin-Browne, whose health was severely damaged from being gassed during his war service. My thanks to Br. Zachariah Heritage of the Oratory for this information.

was allowed to take precedence over religion," with routine troop movements often scheduled for Sundays.[16]

The chaplains would often bring the sacrament directly to the men, even those on duty in the trenches.[17] They celebrated Mass as and when they could—which was seldom under ideal circumstances. Only rarely did they have the opportunity to use a parish church behind the lines in France, as in August 1916 when Tolkien attended a Sunday Mass at a church in Bertrancourt.[18] Most of the time, arrangements were makeshift. On one occasion, Tolkien attended a Mass that was celebrated "in front of a portable altar in a field,"[19] and chaplains recalled saying Mass in places such as "old barns and stables, and in deep dug-outs." One chaplain remembered that "on the morning that we were going into battle I got a fair number for Mass, which I said on a plough drawn up against a haystack." Another recalled that on the Marne, "I went about with the Blessed Sacrament, hunting for the men who had been a long time without facilities. I got them in groups of four or five under the trees—my hat on the ground was my altar." He added wryly, "The Germans did not leave us undisturbed."[20]

Tolkien made a consistent effort to have recourse to the sacraments during his time on the front lines, as we can see from a diary that he kept at this time. A number of days are marked with a 'cross potent' (a cross with equal-length arms barred at the end), which probably indicates that he went to confession; the following day is nearly always marked with an asterisk, evidently signifying that he received Holy Communion. On one instance, September 10, Tolkien wrote "mass" instead of marking an asterisk, suggesting that he had the rare opportunity to attend a proper celebration of Mass in a chapel where he was billeted. The dates he marked with asterisks included seven Sundays, several weekdays, and two holy days: the Assumption of the Blessed Virgin Mary on August 15 and All Souls' Day on November 2.[21] The picture that this concise diary gives us is that Tolkien made an effort to avail himself of the sacraments of confession and Holy Communion on a regular basis, including on days of personal importance, such as the day before he went to the trenches.

His military assignment, the Lancashire Fusiliers, also had an effect on his spiritual life. Tolkien had intended to join the 19th Battalion, where his friend Geoffrey Smith was posted, but in the end, he was assigned to the 11th.[22] Although men could be assigned to any battalion, the largest proportion of the soldiers would be drawn from a particular region—in this case, Lancashire. A fortuitous consequence of his placement was that Tolkien found himself in one of the most solidly Catholic battalions in England. Lancashire had a deep Catholic history. During the penal times, it had retained the largest recusant population of any English county, and it was said that in the nineteenth century, "Lancashire was the backbone of Catholicity in England."[23] A chaplain later recalled that, during the Great War, he "was struck by the really high standard of morality, especially among the men from Lancashire."[24] As it happened, the Anglican 'padre' assigned to their battalion was "averse to Roman Catholics,"[25] but the tension this would have created for Tolkien as an officer would have been mitigated by the fact that he was not isolated as a Catholic.

The 11th Lancs also had fairly regular access to a chaplain, though probably shared with other battalions as circumstances required.[26] The senior chaplain was Fr. Henry Gill, a Jesuit priest, who declared that his "chief care . . . must be to see that his men have received absolution and Holy Communion before going into the trenches."[27] Another who served the Lancashire Fusiliers was Fr. Donal O'Sullivan, who was killed by a shell on July 5, 1916, the first Catholic chaplain to die on the Somme.[28] Their presence made a difference. As Plater noted in his assessment of the survey of chaplains, "Where Catholics are few and scattered they are apt to be less keen on the practice of their religion, partly, no doubt, because they cannot be looked after so well by the chaplain (if they have one) and partly because they lack the backing of public opinion."[29] But in contrast, as one of the chaplains observed, "in a unit with a good religious spirit, generally infused by officers or N.C.O.s [Non-Commissioned Officers], the proportion [of men receiving the sacraments regularly] will be between 90 per cent and 100 per cent."[30]

Cigarettes and sacraments

The fact that Tolkien ended up in a particularly Catholic battalion undoubtedly contributed to the resilience of his faith during the war. But it is also worth noting that his experience was not especially remarkable in that regard. Contemporary reports by chaplains of both the Anglican and Catholic communions indicate that a higher proportion of Catholics than Anglicans came through the Great War with their faith intact. Here it is worth considering the results of the two surveys mentioned above, by the English Catholics and the Church of England, regarding the immediate effects of the war.

The Church of England report is bleak. "Two complaints recur in the evidence: (1) the absence of serious thought about religion; (2) the ignorance of the facts and truths of Christianity."[31] On the positive side of the balance sheet, the chaplains observed that the men showed a "wealth of unselfishness and heroism" despite "the poverty of their religious ideas," but in summing up, they concluded that "The evidence shows how poorly equipped the men were spiritually and intellectually for the crisis" and that "The faith of the future will be that which deals most adequately with the problem of evil."[32]

The view of the Catholic chaplains, when asked to assess the spiritual condition of their men, was in contrast cautiously positive. One observed that in his experience, Catholic soldiers "are not puzzled as non-Catholics are by God's allowing war. They understand it is a consequence of sin—of free-will badly used. I have met no man whose faith suffered: many who for the first time appreciate the faith." The men varied in the practice of their faith; as one chaplain remarked, "the *habitually neglectful* Catholic in peace time did not improve at the front," and another remarked on the "ignorance" of many men, who "had the haziest notions about the Mass, about the essence of sin, of how to make a confession, and so on."[33] But as a rule, where the Catholic chaplains noted weakness, it tended to be not in core beliefs or basic knowledge of the faith but rather in religious practice, which was more easily remedied.

Most notably, the Catholic chaplains encountered fewer difficulties with regard to the problem of evil, which their Church of England colleagues had identified as a crucial issue for the men. As one chaplain explained, "The Catholic Church has so consistently preached the value of 'cross bearing' that . . . pain, and sickness do not lead to blasphemy and unbelief in the case of even ignorant Catholics." Another noted, "I have not found any cases of Catholic men whose faith has suffered through the discussions on 'God's power and the war,' 'the problem of pain,' etc., which used often to take place amongst their companions in their presence."[34] This is not to say that Catholics were untroubled by the horrors of the war—far from it. A representative example was Fr. Peal, on the Western Front, who "was feeling the intense strain brought on by the frequency and proximity of death. . . . 'My God,' he wrote, 'how long, how long? Until men turn to God in sackcloth and ashes, this cruel butchery will go on.'"[35] But the slaughter and miseries of the front could be placed in a theological and devotional framework that enabled the average Catholic to make some rudimentary sense of it in a way not as readily accessible to their fellow soldiers in the Anglican communion.

This difference in the handling of suffering and evil in preaching and religious formation goes some way to account for why the war had a different effect on the spirituality of the average Anglican and the average Catholic. To complete the picture, there are three other important factors worth noting.

One is demographics. The Church of England was the established religion of England and Wales* and, by default, soldiers were listed as 'CofE' if they had expressed no other preference; many undoubtedly accepted this label despite being agnostics or even atheists. Anglican soldiers who were personally devout might well find themselves isolated among their own supposed co-religionists. In contrast, for soldiers to identify themselves as Catholic—part of a socially marginalized minority faith—was an active assertion, not a default social position. It is not surprising, then, that contemporary observers found that "the majority of Catholic soldiers at least knew the fundamentals of their faith."[36]

Another factor was the place of the chaplains in the military establishment. As Hagerty explains, the Anglican 'padre' was expected to "conduct religious services as by law established and, according to military requirements, instil morality, support military discipline, and loudly and frequently espouse the noble cause for which the nation was fighting."[37] This utilitarian approach to religion sometimes backfired as the war dragged on and the men witnessed the contrast between patriotic propaganda and the apparently senseless slaughter on the front lines. One Catholic chaplain found that "It was fatal to start out with the evident purpose of raising the morale of the men, for they were very quick to perceive any attempt at unwarranted optimism."[38] In contrast to Establishment padres, Catholic chaplains were able largely to sidestep this official morale-raising role and focus on providing

* The island of Ireland was still united at this point, but the Anglican Church in Ireland had been disestablished since 1871. In Scotland, the established church was Presbyterian, not Anglican. The Anglican Church in Wales was disestablished in 1920.

the sacraments, which did not go unnoticed by Anglican soldiers. Robert Graves, despite his loss of faith, remarked on how Catholic chaplains "definitely enjoyed to be wherever fighting was, so that they could give extreme unction to the dying,"[39] though the jaundice in his choice of the word "enjoyed" represents no unmixed admiration for their devotion to duty.

Lastly, the Church of England was, as we have already remarked, extremely diverse in terms of theology and religious practice. Offering to hear a man's confession might well be received as a comfort by one man, if he was High Church, and as a blasphemous insult by another, if he was not. Of necessity, then, the Anglican padres had to take a 'lowest common denominator' approach, which had its drawbacks. The Anglican soldier Guy Chapman complained that CofE chaplains "had nothing to offer but the consolation the next man could give you, and a less fortifying one. The Church of Rome sent a man into action mentally and spiritually cleansed. The Church of England could only offer you a cigarette."[40] Evelyn Waugh writes that when one high-church Anglican applied to be a chaplain during the war, he "was refused on the grounds, it was said, that in his interview with the Chaplain-General he was asked what he would do for a dying man, and answered, 'Hear his confession and give him absolution.' The correct answer was: 'Give him a cigarette and take any last message he may have for his family.'"[41] These repeated references to cigarettes reflect the very different attitude to smoking in this period and also serve as a nod to the most famous Anglican chaplain of the Great War, George Studdert Kennedy, nicknamed 'Woodbine Willie' because he was constantly giving out Woodbines. Anglican chaplains, not least Studdert Kennedy himself, served the men under their care with faithfulness, compassion, and even heroism,[42] but the constraints under which they served made their work more difficult.

For all these reasons, then, Tolkien would have encountered more spiritual support during his wartime experiences than we might have expected, helping him to stay committed to his faith.

Trench fever

What took Tolkien out of the front lines, at the end of October 1916, was not a machine-gun bullet or an exploding shell, but another new, and insidious, feature of the Great War. He came down with trench fever, a bacterial disease spread by the lice that were endemic to the trenches. He was admitted to a French hospital and then shipped back to England to recover. By December, somewhat improved but still too ill to serve, he was given leave until mid-January, which he spent with Edith in Great Haywood. It was during this stretch of time that he began to write the first prose tale of the legendarium, *The Fall of Gondolin*,[43] which includes passages of mechanized warfare vividly evocative of what he had seen firsthand. During the next two years, he spent much time in hospitals; he was regularly examined by the Army's Medical Board, and on each occasion was classified as disabled and assigned to light duty at home. A major relapse in the summer of 1918 resulted in his weight dropping by nearly thirty pounds—a drastic decline for a man with a spare, wiry frame—and he was finally declared one-hundred percent disabled and instructed to seek sedentary employment through the Ministry of Labour.[44]

With the war's catastrophic death toll, the army needed soldiers to return to service as soon as they were physically able to do so, and Tolkien's skills as a signals officer would have made him all the more valuable; the fact that he was never sent back to active duty indicates how severely ill he had been.

For Tolkien, trench fever meant suffering from a new, strange, and frightening illness. It produced recurring fever, headache, dizziness, joint and muscle pain, severe discomfort in the shins, and general weakness. The first case was identified in mid-1915 by a doctor on the Western Front, but it was only recognized as a specific disease in the summer of 1916. When Tolkien contracted it in late 1916, not only was there no cure, but none of the treatments had any effect. Most sufferers recover in a couple of months, but if it persists beyond that time, it can become chronic, with lifelong bouts of recurring symptoms. Indeed, the disease could become "debilitating": "In 1920, 6,000 men in Britain still attributed their war disability to trench fever."[45] It is not unlikely that Tolkien's recurring health problems throughout his life were due in part to his particularly serious case of this disease.[46]

Tolkien experienced suffering, sickness, and loss during the Great War, but he did not—as did many others—have a crisis of faith, let alone lose his faith. (A different kind of spiritual crisis would come later, as we shall see.) As one of the Catholic chaplains observed, the men who "came to the war with a good working religion, with faith and instruction and a clear and definite rule of Christian life" were those who "stood the test, the supreme test of war and the awful temptations of a soldier's life in foreign towns."[47]

Part of Tolkien's spiritual resilience was due, no doubt, to having come through early experiences of bereavement with his faith intact. Having lost both his parents by the time he was twelve, he was no stranger to sorrow and death: he was not surprised that life could be short and end cruelly, or that blessings could be portioned out with little apparent reason to some yet not to others. His faith rested on a crucified Savior who suffered for him, alongside him, and alongside all mankind, and who rose again from the dead, a risen life that he could mystically partake of in the Eucharist. Tolkien had developed real spiritual muscle even before 1914 and, though the war undoubtedly deepened his depressive tendencies and confronted him with a depth of darkness that he could never forget, it did not provoke a wholesale shaking of his foundations.

16

Stella Vespertina

Tolkien's practice of the faith under wartime conditions was in large part dependent on factors out of his control, such as assigned duties, troop movements, access to chaplains, and the attitudes of his fellow officers—not to mention the attentions of the enemy. But he also made a deliberate personal effort to maintain his religious commitment during this extraordinarily testing time. Having seen his efforts to participate frequently in the sacraments, we now turn to consider his devotional habits during his wartime service and what we know of his own particular habits and observances as a Christian. They will give us an insight into how his faith sustained him during the war and was in turn shaped by the war.

The Canon of the Mass

Tolkien's diary reveals that he regarded Mass attendance as worth recording, and his complaint about a whole "sunny Sabbath"[1] being given over to a military parade indicates that he thought there could have been better uses made of it—which presumably would have included Holy Mass. What did he do when he couldn't get to Mass? A common practice for Catholics is to make what is called 'a spiritual communion,' raising one's heart and mind to the Eucharistic mystery of the altar and saying a prayer to that effect.* An important part of this spiritual communion for Tolkien included recollecting the words of the liturgy. During the Second World War, when his son Christopher was serving in the Royal Air Force, Tolkien wrote

* A typical prayer for spiritual communion of the time was: "O my most loving Saviour, since I cannot have the happiness of receiving thee this day, suffer me to gather up the precious crumbs that fall from thy table, and to unite myself to thy divine heart by faith, hope, and charity. I confess I do not deserve the children's bread; but I venture humbly to declare that, away from thee, my soul is dried up with thirst, and my heart cast down with faintness. Come, then, into me, O my divine Jesus! come into my mind, to illuminate it with thy light; come into my heart, to enkindle in it the fire of thy love, and to unite it so intimately with thy own, that it may be no more I that live, but thou that livest in me, and reignest in me for ever" (*The Catholic's Vade Mecum*, 89).

to say that it is "a good and admirable thing to know by heart the Canon of the Mass, for you can say this in your heart if ever hard circumstance keeps you from hearing Mass."[2] He certainly knew firsthand the "hard circumstance" that was all too common for soldiers in wartime, and it seems nearly certain that his recommendation is drawn from his own practice during the Great War.

Having prayers committed to memory is an ordinary Catholic practice; having the Canon of the Mass memorized is decidedly *not* typical. Hence it behooves us to consider what, precisely, Tolkien was recommending.

The 'Canon' of the Mass is the name for the section of the liturgy between the *Sanctus* and the *Pater Noster* or, in English, between the acclamation that begins "Holy, holy, holy, Lord God of hosts" and the Lord's Prayer. The Canon is fixed and unchanging, whereas other parts of the Mass vary, depending on the season and day. By mentally praying through the Canon (in Latin, of course), Tolkien would be able to participate spiritually in the celebration of the Mass when he was prevented from attending in person; it is testimony to the seriousness of his Eucharistic devotion. Tolkien's recommendation of the *whole* Canon also indicates the strength of his memory. To be sure, he would already have been familiar with it from the innumerable times when he served as an altar boy at the Oratory, but it still represents a substantial amount of material to be able to recall at will. (See Appendix B.) Since he recommends this entire section, and not just a few more easily memorized prayers within it, we need to consider its contents in some detail.[3]

The Canon begins with intercessory prayers for the Church, asking God to "keep her in peace under thy protection, to bring her to unity, and guide her throughout the world," and for the people who are themselves present at Mass and their friends and family, "for the redemption of their souls; for their hope of safety and salvation"—all of which would seem particularly relevant in wartime. Next are prayers "in communion with" Mary the Mother of God, the Apostles, and other saints, asking God, for the sake of their "good deeds and prayers," to "grant that in all things we may be guarded by the help of thy protection. Through the same Christ our Lord."

The Eucharistic prayer comes next. In this extended prayer, the priest consecrates the bread and wine of the offering. The bread is consecrated with the words "*Hoc est enim corpus meum*" ("This is my Body"), words which for Tolkien were a sacred re-expression by the priest of the very words of Jesus himself at the Last Supper and the means by which his sacramental presence was brought about or 'confected,' to use the technical liturgical term. Next come prayers for the dead (again, all too relevant on the front line) "who are gone hence before us with the sign of faith, and sleep the sleep of peace. To these, O Lord, and to all that rest in Christ, we pray thee grant a place of refreshment, light and peace. Through the same Christ our Lord. Amen."

The last part of the Canon is a prayer entrusting those at Mass to God's mercy and asking that they be brought into fellowship with the Apostles and martyrs, "not weighing our merits but pardoning our offenses." It concludes with a Trinitarian prayer that all this be done "Through Christ our Lord. By whom, O Lord, thou ever dost create, hallow, quicken, bless and bestow upon us all these good things. Through him, and with him, and in him, is unto thee, God the Father almighty, in the unity of the Holy Ghost, all honour and glory. For ever and ever. Amen."

The Canon, the heart of the Mass, offered Tolkien the opportunity to meditate on the Body and Blood of Christ—a meditation perhaps heightened now that he no longer could count on receiving Holy Communion whenever he wished to. It was undoubtedly sustaining to him in wartime to remember the words of consecration and reflect on "the mystery of faith" that is communicated to believers by Christ's death on the Cross and Resurrection from the grave.

Marian devotion

As we noted above, the Canon of the Mass includes prayers in communion with Mary the Mother of God. The Blessed Virgin Mary holds a special place in the life of all Catholics, though the personal relationship of individual believers with Mary shows considerable variation, from simple acceptance of her importance without having any particular Marian devotion, to Ronald Knox's habit of including a reference to her, however oblique, in every sermon he preached.

By Tolkien's own account, Mary had an important role in his spiritual life. He once told George Sayer, "I attribute whatever there is of beauty and goodness in my work to the influence of the Holy Mother of God."[4] He reiterated the point in a letter explaining that it was upon "Our Lady" that "all my own small perception of beauty both in majesty and simplicity is founded."[5] Clyde Kilby recalled that Tolkien had "a special reverence for the Virgin Mary."[6] As the mother of Christ, who is God the Son, Mary can properly be said to be the mother of God, but she is also considered by Catholics to be the 'mother of the Church' and thus the spiritual mother of every Christian. This understanding of Mary is based on the biblical account of Jesus's words from the cross to his mother and John, the beloved disciple: "He said to his mother, 'Woman, behold, your son!' Then he said to the disciple, 'Behold, your mother!' And from that hour the disciple took her to his own home" (John 19:26–27). Disciples of Jesus likewise take Mary—spiritually speaking—into their home, into their lives, to learn from her about her divine Son. For Mary is also the perfect disciple, always focused on leading others to Jesus, as in the wedding at Cana, when she calls her son's attention to the lack of wine and tells the servants, "Do whatever he tells you" (John 2:5).

Tolkien's earliest years, as an Anglican, would not have included devotion to Mary as a regular part of his prayer life. Most Anglicans, as well as Nonconformists like Tolkien's grandparents on both sides, viewed devotion to Mary as an idolatrous practice and an indication that the Roman Church was corrupt. With the rise of the Oxford Movement and the example of pastors such as John Henry Newman while he was still in the Church of England, more Anglicans came to admire or even cautiously venerate Mary ('veneration' being a key term and importantly distinct from 'worship,' which Catholics reserve for God alone).* Nonetheless, Marian prayers and devotions would have been (as they still are now) alien to the experience of the average member of a Church of England parish. However, once his mother, Mabel, had crossed the Tiber, he would immediately have begun to absorb the Catholic view of Mary.

The difficulties that attended Mabel's life of faith may even have helped Tolkien sympathize with those experienced, at a supremely higher level, by Mary herself. He was alive to the practical problems that Mary faced as the appointed mother of the Savior. Clyde Kilby recalled that "one of his observations was that she must have jealously guarded her pregnancy since, had it been discovered, Mary would either have been stoned as an adulteress or, if she had tried to explain, stoned for

* In Catholic terminology, *latria* is the Latin word for the form of adoration or worship that may properly be given to God alone. The saints may receive only respect or veneration (*dulia*), and the Blessed Virgin Mary, as the archetypal disciple, may receive special veneration (*hyperdulia*).

blasphemy." Tolkien, he said, was also deeply moved by the degradation involved in God's becoming one of us, by "the birth of Christ in a stable with its filth and manure," which he saw as "a symbol of the real nature of holy things in a fallen world."[7]

Mary also had to witness her own Son's suffering, an example of faithful endurance that Tolkien evidently found especially moving and helpful in his own life of faith. We know this from the gift he made to his son Michael of a book entitled *The Same Scourge* by John Goldthorpe, a novel of historical fiction depicting the events surrounding the Crucifixion. (See figure 44.) Michael noted that his father had made "particular reference to the passages on pages 308 and 353."[8] In the first of these, the centurion at the foot of the cross (whom tradition names Longinus) recalls that Mary "had the most wonderful face I have ever seen. Her voice was the most wonderful I have ever heard. She looked at her son on the cross as though she saw something hidden from the rest of us." In the second passage, Longinus again recalls Mary being present at the foot of the cross: "The mother and the son seemed to be talking together, without words."[9] Mary is a character who appears throughout *The Same Scourge*, not just at the Crucifixion; Tolkien's singling out of these two passages for special attention suggests that he had a particular feeling for the suffering experienced by the Blessed Virgin when she saw her son crucified.

We have seen Tolkien's deep roots in the Birmingham Oratory, but that church is not just 'the Oratory': it is the parish Church of the Immaculate Conception—a title of significance. Tolkien later noted that he had "a special devotion"[10] to the feast of the Immaculate Conception. This feast is celebrated every year on December 8 and would have been kept with particular solemnity at the Birmingham Oratory as its patronal festival; it was also the date that the completed 'new church' was opened in 1909,[11] a celebration at which the young Tolkien was almost certainly present.

The 'Immaculate Conception' had been formally defined and declared as a dogma (a requirement for Catholics to accept as part of the Christian faith) in 1854. This dogma (often confused with the Virginal Conception of Jesus) states that Mary "in the first instance of her conception, by a singular privilege and grace granted by God, in view of the merits of Jesus Christ, the Saviour of the human race, was preserved exempt from all stain of original sin."[12] Thus preserved from the effects of original sin, Mary was able to carry God the Son in her womb and provide her own flesh to form his body. She became a human version of the Old

Testament ark of the covenant, in which had been placed the manna from heaven (Hebrews 9:4).

Tolkien believed that Mary was, as he put it, "the only *unfallen* person," by which he means, of course, the only unfallen person other than Christ himself. When St. Paul declares that "all have sinned and fall short of the glory of God" (Romans 3:23), he assumes the same two exceptions, for just as Christ is the 'second Adam,' so Mary is the new Eve, the woman who reverses Eve's disobedience. Tolkien noted that Mary lived after the fall, not in the innocence of the Garden of Eden. But "her destiny (in which she had cooperated) was far higher than that of any 'Man' would have been, had the Fall not occurred."[13] Mary "cooperated" with her destiny by saying 'Yes' to her vocation as the mother of God the Son. As a result, she brought the Savior into the world, and—as Pope Pius IX defined it—it was "in view of" the Savior's merits that she had been conceived without sin.*

The Immaculate Conception is linked to another Marian dogma, that of the Assumption. There is sometimes confusion between this and Christ's Ascension: the latter marks the end of his post-Resurrection ministry, in which after giving final instructions to his disciples, he "was taken up into heaven, and sat down at the right hand of God" (Mark 16:19; see also Acts 1:6–11; Luke 24:50–51). The dogma of Mary's Assumption states that when her earthly life was ended, she was taken up to heaven in both body and soul.† As Tolkien explained, since she had been the special vessel of God Incarnate, it was "unthinkable" that her body "should have been disintegrated, or 'corrupted,' nor could it surely be long separated from Him after the Ascension." This does not put her on an equal footing with her Son. Tolkien clarified that Mary's Assumption was different from her Son's Ascension

* The logic of the Immaculate Conception can only be understood if one steps out of a linear understanding of time in which the chain of causation only works in a forward direction. God, *foreseeing* the graces that his Son would procure for the world, by a unique, *anticipatory* act, bestows those graces on Mary from the first moment of her conception so that, whereas all other believers would be *delivered* from sin, she would be *preserved* from sin. As a result, her salvation by grace would be an even more wonderful testimony to God's generosity than that of other Christians. In other words, Mary's Immaculate Conception is the archetypal example of 'prevenient grace,' divine action that precedes human response (see, e.g., 1 Corinthians 12:3).

† It is important to note that 'up' is not to be taken literally. Catholics do not believe that Mary and Jesus, with their human bodies, are somehow physically 'up there' (as if they were orbiting in outer space). Rather, they have been, as it were, transposed into what we might call a different dimension, a higher order of being. Her Assumption is not unprecedented: the Bible records that the Old Testament figures of Enoch and Elijah were assumed, or 'translated,' into heaven (Genesis 5:24; 2 Kings 2:11).

in the same way that Lazarus being raised from the dead by Jesus (John 11) was distinct from Jesus's Resurrection:[14] that is, Mary did none of this by her own power but—like Lazarus—was the recipient of divine action.

Having described some of the beliefs Tolkien held about Mary, we can now consider how she came to be important to his devotional life under the extraordinary strains of wartime conditions. He had no saccharine or sentimental fondness for the Blessed Virgin Mary, but a devotion tested and proved in the fires of war.

Consoler and Evening Star

While he was on the front lines, Tolkien wrote a poem in honor of Mary, which begins with the line "O Lady Mother enthroned amid the stars." He gave the poem two different titles, "Consolatrix Afflictorum" and "Stella Vespertina."[15] Each of these titles provides a valuable indication of the place of Mary in Tolkien's spirituality.

Both titles are connected to a prayer called the Litany of Loreto,* which we know Tolkien found deeply meaningful, as he recommended it to Christopher as one of the prayers to learn by heart.[16] (See Appendix B.) He would later translate a portion of it into his Elvish language of Quenya.[17]

A litany is a series of invocations followed by a response, the response in this case being *ora pro nobis*, "pray for us." In the Litany of Loreto, Mary is addressed under various titles. Many highlight some aspect of her role in salvation history and the life of the Church, such as "Mother of God," "Cause of Our Joy," "Queen of Apostles." Others present her in symbolic terms, such as "Mirror of Justice," "Seat of Wisdom," and "Mystical Rose."

One of these titles is *Consolatrix Afflictorum*, meaning "Comforter of the Afflicted," and it is this that Tolkien chose as the first of the titles for his 1916 poem.

Given the circumstances, it is not surprising that he chose to reflect on Mary as *Consolatrix Afflictorum*. In the Bible, Mary is shown "standing by the cross of Jesus" (John 19:25) in fulfillment of what had been told to her when Jesus was still an infant: "a sword will pierce through your own soul also" (Luke 2:35). Given the communion of saints as "a cloud of witnesses" (Hebrews 12:1), Christians believe that Mary, from her heavenly vantage point, can console people on earth because

* A prayer officially approved by Pope Sixtus V in 1587, it takes its name from its first use at the Shrine of Our Lady of Loreto in Italy.

of her own experience of seeing her only son betrayed, tortured, and crucified. Tolkien would have meditated on the sorrows of Mary while praying the Stations of the Cross during Lent; these Stations include Jesus meeting his mother while carrying the cross to Golgotha, and the taking down of his body from the cross, an image which is frequently depicted in art and known as 'the Pietá.' (See figure 66.) With the slaughter of so many men—often barely more than boys—on the Western Front, the image of the sorrowful Mary cradling the dead body of her son in her arms would have taken on even more resonance: here is a spiritual mother who can offer comfort, having gone through such horrors herself.

Tolkien's second title for his 1916 poem, "Stella Vespertina," is connected to the Litany of Loreto at one remove. It is Tolkien's own invention and is an intriguing variant of one of the Litany's titles for Mary, namely *Stella Matutina*. Whereas "Stella Matutina" means "Morning Star," Tolkien's variant means "Evening Star."*

The 'morning star' is, astronomically speaking, the planet Venus; visible just before sunrise, it heralds the rising Sun. Its Christian symbolism is rich and complex; in the Litany of Loreto, Mary is the Morning Star because Christ is traditionally symbolized by the Sun. Therefore, his mother, Mary, who brought him into the world at the Nativity, is associated with the Morning Star: a lesser light that indicates the imminent arrival of the greater light.†

Tolkien was interested in and knowledgeable about astronomy and would have known that Venus is also called the evening star since it becomes visible in the western sky after sunset as well as in the eastern sky before sunrise. And these celestial appearances would have become weighted with deep emotional and spiritual significance once he began to serve on the front lines of the Great War. Soldiers were required to 'stand-to' at dawn and dusk each day. As historian Paul Fussell

---

* 'Vespertina' comes from the Greek word for 'west,' that part of the sky where the sun sinks at evening. Hence another name for the planet Venus is Hesperus, and 'Vespers' is the name given to the evening office of prayer.

† Christ is himself sometimes symbolized by the morning star (e.g., Revelation 2:28). It was in connection with this image that the Old English poet Cynewulf wrote, in his poem *Crist*, "*Eala earendel, engla beorhtast, ofer middangeard monnum sended*," which Tolkien later translated as "Here Eärendel, brightest of angels, sent from God to men." When Tolkien encountered the poem in 1914, he took Earendel as a reference to the morning star, though at first he thought it represented John the Baptist (also a herald of Christ). As Tolkien put it, from Cynewulf's words "ultimately sprang the whole of my mythology" (*Biography*, 72; Kilby, *Tolkien and the Silmarillion*, 57; see also Hostetter, "Over Middle-earth Sent Unto Men: On the Philological Origins of Tolkien's Eärendel Myth").

explains, "Stand-to was a solemn moment. Twice a day everyone stared silently across the wasteland at the enemy's hiding places and considered how to act if a field-gray line suddenly appeared and grew larger and larger through the mist and the half-light." The military routines of 'standing to arms' in combat readiness at daybreak and nightfall were, as Fussell notes, "the occasions when the sky especially offered itself for observation and interpretation"; they were also "moments of heightened ritual anxiety," all the more cruelly wrenching in contrast with the prevailing literary conceit of dawn and dusk as images of peace and tranquility.[18]

Tolkien's adaptation of the Litany to address Mary as "Stella Vespertina," as opposed to "Stella Matutina," is thus both astronomically and theologically apt—all the more so when we consider his other title, "Consolatrix Afflictorum." The image of Mary as the *Evening* Star invites us to consider how she is visible when the Sun—her son—has disappeared beyond the horizon. Christ may have died, but his mother is still present, consoling those who, like her, mourn his loss. In the nightmarish situation of the trenches, with the problem of evil and suffering all too present, this is a powerful image of faith as experienced, or at least as hoped for, in darkness.

Years later, Tolkien gave his character Arwen in *The Lord of the Rings* the name 'Undomiel,' meaning 'Evening Star.' In calling her the Evening Star, he was giving her a title that had Marian associations for him, and specifically, ones that were rooted in his Great War experiences. The significance of this title is underscored by the fact that it is twice contrasted with the beauty of full daylight, as signified by Galadriel. Gimli the dwarf prefers Galadriel's beauty and challenges Éomer to agree with him, but when Éomer puts Arwen first, Gimli concedes: "You have chosen the Evening; but my love is given to the Morning. And my heart forebodes that soon it will pass away for ever."[19] Likewise Frodo, after seeing Arwen, the "Evenstar of her people," declares, "Now not day only shall be beloved, but night too shall be beautiful and blessed."[20]

Evidently, this finding of beauty in the night was of tremendous importance for Tolkien; it allowed him to explore in *The Lord of the Rings* images and tales of great darkness, such as the passage through the Dead Marshes and Sam's despair when he believes Frodo to be dead, without losing hold on hope. In his 1916 poem, Tolkien described Mary as "enthroned amid the stars,"[21] another indication that he sees her as a figure present in the darkness of night, not just in the brightness of day.* We can perhaps see the influence of this celestial image of Mary in the scene where Sam and Frodo, having escaped from the orcs, begin their seemingly hopeless trek into Mordor. Sam looks up and sees a single star shining through the "cloud-wrack" above the mountains:

> The beauty of it smote his heart, as he looked up out of the forsaken land, and hope returned to him. For like a shaft, clear and cold, the thought pierced him that in the end the Shadow was only a small and passing thing: there was light and high beauty for ever beyond its reach.[22]

---

* He is glancing here at Revelation 11:19–12:1, where the Ark of the Covenant is revealed in heaven and, not coincidentally, a great woman appears wearing "a crown of twelve stars" upon her head.

17

Demobilization

The Great War finally staggered to its end. Hostilities ceased at the eleventh hour on the eleventh day of the eleventh month, November 1918.

But for the soldiers who had fought and suffered, and who bore wounds and disabilities both visible and invisible, the war did not end quite so neatly. They came back, changed, to an England that had little understanding of what they had gone through.

One of the strangest things about the Great War was the paradox of proximity. The front lines in France were only seventy miles from England, so near that the guns could be heard in Sussex and Kent; the postal service operated smoothly with letters and parcels promptly delivered to and from the trenches—the London newspapers arrived only a day late—and soldiers on leave could hop on board a Channel boat just as in peacetime: one officer "breakfasted in the trenches and dined in his club in London."[1] Yet those seventy miles represented a tremendous gulf between the horrors and privations of the war as experienced by the soldiers and by the uncomprehending civilians back home. One soldier, visiting the battlefields years later, remarked, "What is most disquieting on such a visit is to realize how little space . . . separated the line, the soldier's troglodyte world, the world which might have been another planet, from home, from England, from sanity."[2]

Martin Gilbert, who was Tolkien's colleague at Merton in the 1960s, said that Tolkien was "reticent, yet when he did open up, full of terrible tales. . . . [He] remembered, as vividly as if it were yesterday, the constant danger of German artillery shells, ranging throughout the area, falling with their screech and roar, and clouds of earth and mud, and the fearful cries of men who had been hit." Gilbert recalled that "There was never any boasting. The war's scars were too many, its reality too grim, to lead to self-glorification, or even to embellishment."[3] John and Priscilla remembered that their father "would occasionally talk of being at the Front: of the horrors of the first German gas attack, of the utter exhaustion and ominous quiet after a bombardment, of the whining screams of the shells, and the endless marching, always on foot, through a devastated landscape, sometimes carrying the men's equipment as well as his own to encourage them to keep going."[4]

Tolkien can rightly be placed, as Tom Shippey suggests, in the company of the "traumatized authors";[5] for him as for so many of his compatriots, the war had lingering effects—physical, emotional, spiritual. The trench fever that he contracted in 1916 may well have saved him from death at the front, which was the fate of so many of his friends and classmates, but it also probably damaged his health permanently. And although he did not suffer what was then called 'shell shock'—now considered a form of post-traumatic stress disorder—he felt the effects of the war at a profound level. After the Second World War, he wrote, "One has indeed personally to come under the shadow of war to feel fully its oppression. . . . it seems now often forgotten that to be caught by youth in 1914 was no less hideous an experience than to be involved in 1939 and the following years."[6]

The immediate aftermath of the war would have been, in some ways, as difficult to endure as the war itself. The day-to-day grind of survival in the trenches had come to an end, but from 1918 through the early years of the 1920s, Tolkien, like so many veterans, was still just getting by, and processing (partly at a subconscious level) what he had been through at the front. This process took decades and would ultimately be aided by the writing of *The Lord of the Rings*. In 1944, on a visit to Birmingham, Tolkien was distressed by the memories of his dead friends from King Edward's School, whose "ghosts" seemed to meet him as he walked.[7] Until then, he had been stuck with a bad case of writer's block as he composed *The Lord of the Rings*, but this disturbing experience back in Birmingham provided a sort of "artistic catharsis";[8] a few weeks later, he wrote the "Dead Marshes" scene and was able to carry on with the tale. Perhaps part of the release was that he had found a way to distinguish the noble honoring of sacrifice from a morbid fascination with death and decay. Frodo and Sam must follow Gollum across a place of horrors, but they must not look at the tricksy lights.

He had much to grieve over. The TCBS had developed a profound vision for their future endeavors, but their fellowship had been shattered. Robert Gilson and Geoffrey Smith were both dead, killed at the Somme in 1916.[9] Earlier that year, before he set out on a nighttime raid across no-man's-land, Smith had written what he thought might be his last letter to Tolkien:

> Death can make us loathsome and helpless as individuals, but it cannot put an end to the immortal four! . . . Yes, publish! You I am sure are chosen, like Saul among the Children of Israel. . . . May God bless you, my dear John Ronald, and may you say the things I have tried to say long after I am not there to say them, if such be my lot.[10]

Tolkien had survived and had a promising future ahead of him with his wife and growing family. But the past could not easily be left behind. Most of his friends had died. Why had he lived? Had he indeed been preserved for some great task, a pioneering destiny, like Saul, the first of Israel's kings (1 Samuel 9–11)? Would he be able to live up to the charge placed upon him by Smith?

In 1948, in a long and thoughtful letter to C.S. Lewis, Tolkien drew Lewis's attention to an observation made by Gerard Manley Hopkins about the nature of literary fame. Tolkien was clearly interested in Hopkins's perception that an author's hopes can be "frustrated" in this world, his work entirely neglected or even destroyed.[11] He paraphrased to Lewis the following passage from Hopkins's letter:

> The only just judge, the only just literary critic, is Christ, who prizes, is proud of, and admires, more than any man, more than the receiver himself can, the gifts of his own making. And the only real good which fame and another's praise does is to convey to us . . . some token of the judgment which a perfectly just, heedful, and wise mind, namely Christ's, passes upon our doings.[12]

In reflecting on Hopkins's words, Tolkien gave as an example the protagonist of his own story "Leaf by Niggle": Niggle is a painter who has been laboring for years over a picture of a tree, and having spent his whole life and all his creative energies upon it, the picture is in the end burnt up and forgotten. Likewise, any number of 'pictures' had been burnt up by war; death had silenced many stories that would otherwise have been told—by his TCBS friends Smith and Gilson and by countless others. Only the critic who knows the whole, who has a divine perspective, can securely judge the worth of these tales, the stories left untold, the potential cut off before its flowering. Tolkien's meditation on this idea helps explain why he felt that "it is the untold stories that are most moving."[13] His dead comrades had many stories that would never be told, but Christ knows what they are.

In *The Lord of the Rings*, Frodo—who has not yet experienced any suffering—declares that Gollum deserves death for his crimes. Gandalf replies: "Many that live deserve death. And some die who deserve life. Can you give it to them? Then do not be too eager to deal out death in judgement. For even the very wise cannot see all ends."[14]

In the Great War, Tolkien came face to face with violent death: men cut down by machine guns as they went 'over the top'; the horrors of poison gas; corpses littering the bomb-cratered no-man's-land. But it did not make him callous or indifferent. Rather, it roused in him a profound respect for the mystery of life—and of death. We do not know what the story might have been of *anyone* killed in the war, including enemy combatants, and therefore we should not be too ready to sit in judgment. Hence his anguished lament, in 1945, that anyone should "gloat" over the destruction of Germany or the floods of refugees, and that he sees "no bowels of mercy or compassion" in this dark time.[15]

His unusual phrasing comes from the words of Scripture in the Douay translation he knew so well, as in Psalm 25:6: "Remember, O Lord, thy bowels of compassion: and thy mercies that are from the beginning of the world," and the exhortation of St. Paul to the Colossians: "Put ye on therefore, as the elect of God, holy and beloved, the bowels of mercy, benignity, humility, modesty, patience" (Colossians 3:12). "Bowels" can be rendered as "the heart," as the seat of the emotions and center of the self; but more than that, it means the seat of "the tender and sympathetic emotions," specifically "pity and compassion."[16] And Tolkien would have well known that 'pity,' meaning sympathetic concern for someone who is suffering, has deep roots in Old English, in which it meant, even more fundamentally, "a *disposition* to mercy or compassion."[17]

For Tolkien, mercy and pity are not merely superficial qualities but should be part of one's inmost being, a belief that forms a core theme in *The Lord of the Rings*. When Frodo exclaims about Gollum, "What a pity that Bilbo did not stab that vile creature, when he had a chance!" Gandalf turns this thoughtless use of 'pity'—meaning simply 'too bad'—into a profound reminder of the workings of providence: "It was Pity that stayed his hand. Pity, and Mercy: not to strike without need. . . . Be sure that he took so little hurt from the evil, and escaped in the end, because he began his ownership of the Ring so. With Pity."[18]

The war and its aftermath had lingering effects on Tolkien—on his health; on his tendency toward depression; on his lifelong emphasis on gentleness, pity, mercy, and peace, over against 'Power' and 'the Machine'; and on his attitude toward his creative work in light of mortality. But it would take time for the traumatic experiences of the war to be assimilated and fully integrated into his life, his spirituality, and his literary art. In 1918, this process had only begun. He was one of thousands of newly demobilized soldiers in England, picking up the threads of his life that had been so cruelly interrupted and moving slowly forward into an uncertain future.

18

"I almost ceased to practise my religion"

After the tragedies of his childhood and the grimness of the Great War, Tolkien would have hoped that with marriage and a young family, and a developing career as an academic, he could settle into a life of peace and security.

In January 1919, after he was demobilized, he took up a post as an assistant lexicographer for the *Oxford English Dictionary*, where he worked on entries for a number of words beginning with the letter W, such as 'walrus' and 'waistcoat.' He also began to do some teaching for Oxford University,* but being a tutor rather than a Fellow, he didn't have a set of rooms of his own at any of the colleges, so he taught from home. He was favored by the women's halls such as St. Hilda's and St. Hugh's, in part because, with Edith present in the house, they could send women students to his home without a chaperone.†

Meanwhile, he sought a full-time post at a university, and in October 1920, the same month that his second son, Michael, was born, Tolkien accepted a teaching position at the University of Leeds in the north of England, taking up the Readership in English Language.

---

* He was a 'tutor,' which at Oxford means an instructor in a subject who teaches students either in one-on-one sessions or in small group seminars. He was not yet a 'Fellow,' which denotes a faculty member holding a Fellowship at one of the colleges, as he would later at Pembroke (1925–45) and then Merton (1945–59). The term 'professor' is reserved for a faculty member who holds a named professorial chair.

† The rationale for the chaperones in the first place can be gauged from experiences of women students in the years shortly after the policy was discontinued. Mary Midgley, in her memoir *The Owl of Minerva*, mentions matter-of-factly a number of incidents during her Oxford student days, in 1937–42, of what would be today described as sexual harassment or assault by male dons. But Tolkien's popularity with the women's colleges—which continued through his career—stemmed mostly (and more lastingly) from the respect and fair treatment he gave his female students. In contrast, recollections from St. Hugh's in the 1920s, for instance, include many references to dons who "disliked women" and even one who "commonly made the women sit at the back of the hall where, he hoped, he could not see them" (*St. Hugh's: One Hundred Years of Women's Education in Oxford*, ed. Penny Griffin, 95). See also Rateliff, "The Missing Women."

He had also applied for a newly created professorial Chair at the University of Cape Town, South Africa, and in 1921 he was actually offered the position. However, he declined it because Edith and baby Michael were not yet well enough to face the rigors of international travel.[1] After the separations from Edith and John during the war and with the knowledge that his own father had died while away from his wife and sons, it is understandable that Tolkien chose to stay in England, but it is still a sacrifice worth noting. Tolkien might well have liked to move to the land of his birth.

The Leeds position, though only a Readership and not a Professorship, was a valuable step up from college-less tutoring in Oxford. In order to avoid a disruptive move with a newborn baby, Edith and the children stayed in Oxford for the autumn term while Tolkien commuted, spending the week in Leeds, the weekend at Oxford. Only in January 1921 did the family move north to Leeds: first as tenants of Cardinal Newman's great-niece, as we will discuss in the next chapter.

There was much to appreciate about life at Leeds. Edith was happy in the social circle of faculty wives there, and in 1924, the year of Christopher's birth, the Tolkiens also bought their first house, at 2 Darnley Road in West Park, with open fields nearby so that the family could get out for walks.[2] Professionally, he was well regarded by his colleagues. He had an important role in building up the Language program at Leeds, and in 1924 he was made Professor of English Language, a chair created specifically for him. And he was expressing his literary creativity in published poetry as well as in the gradual and still private development of his Middle-earth legendarium.

But it was not uniformly sunny. With a growing family came growing expenses; it was at this point that Tolkien began the tedious, poorly paid, but reliable job of marking exams over the holidays for extra money.[3] Leeds was an industrial city, with horrific air pollution,[4] and Tolkien sometimes doubted whether he had done right in turning down the job offer from South Africa: "I have often wondered since if that was not our chance that came then, and we had not the courage to seize it."[5]

Little biographical material is available for this part of his life,[6] but it seems to have been a difficult time in his marriage as well. Certainly, he and Edith had to learn how to have a settled life together; their first four years of marriage had been one long medley of separations and moves, both during and immediately after the war. They also experienced conflict over his practice of the faith. Family Mass attendance seems to have become a particular point of tension; according to Carpenter, Edith had developed conflicting feelings about having become a Catholic and "by the time the family returned to Oxford in 1925 she was showing resentment of Ronald taking the children to church."* It may be to this painful time that Tolkien alludes after Edith's death, writing to Christopher of "the lapses and darknesses which at times marred our lives."[7]

Tolkien was also a war veteran, adjusting to life as a civilian. As we saw in chapter 15, he made a diligent effort to practice his faith even in the trenches. But he often had to rely on personal prayer instead of Mass attendance, and access to the sacrament of Confession was limited: his habits were thrown into confusion. Understandably, the Catholic hierarchy had given soldiers an official dispensation from the Eucharistic fast and the Sunday obligation, but these necessary short-term relaxations of discipline might have unintended long-term effects.

"Wickedness and sloth"

One of the chaplains surveyed after the war made a prescient comment about the impact of these disruptions on the habits of faithful Catholics: soldiers "have not been able to practise their religious duties regularly, and have in consequence come to regard the obligation as less binding: and there is a great danger that they will retain the same tendency at home."[8] Indeed, this is precisely what appears to have been the case with Tolkien. Years later, writing to his son Michael, he admitted that for some years he had "almost ceased to practise my religion—especially at Leeds, and at 22 Northmoor Road."† It is a striking statement and worth our careful attention. We should begin by considering it in the context of his self-examination:

* *Biography*, 159–60. After one particularly strong disagreement in 1940, however, "there was a true reconciliation between her and Ronald, in which she explained her feelings and even declared that she wished to resume the practice of her religion," though her attendance at church remained irregular (*Biography*, 160).

† Tolkien began his teaching at Leeds University in the autumn of 1920. 22 Northmoor Road was the first house that the family owned after their return to Oxford; they lived there from 1926–30. These locations signify a range of nearly ten years.

> I fell in love with the Blessed Sacrament from the beginning—and by the mercy of God never have fallen out again: but alas! I indeed did not live up to it. . . . Out of wickedness and sloth I almost ceased to practise my religion—especially at Leeds, and at 22 Northmoor Road. Not for me the Hound of Heaven, but the never-ceasing silent appeal of Tabernacle, and the sense of starving hunger.[9]

The qualification of "almost" and the precision with which he establishes the time period suggest that he was not simply being hyperbolically self-critical about his spiritual life in general.

Exactly what Tolkien meant when he confessed that he "almost ceased to practise" his religion, we do not know. It may point to irregular Mass attendance or ceasing to go regularly to confession (which, ironically, might well have exacerbated his tendency toward scrupulosity, since regular confession would help him distinguish genuine faults from undue self-recrimination).* It might indicate the loss of a regular habit of personal prayer. Among colleagues who were mostly non-Catholics, he might have fallen out of the observance of abstaining from meat on Fridays.†

He does, however, provide key insights into his spiritual state at that time. Tolkien said that his near failure to observe his religion came from "wickedness and sloth." Though he often used 'sloth' to mean simply 'idleness or laziness,' here he seems to be using it in its specifically religious sense, as a spiritual affliction. He

* Even in the context of a spiritual tradition that emphasizes the value of confession, Catholic teaching does not require confession before each and every time that one receives Communion (especially after Pius X's encouragement of daily Communion, which as we saw in chapter 13, Tolkien approved of). Tolkien, however, seems to have been particularly committed to making his confession before Communion, a level of rigor that seems at times to have had a deleterious effect on his spiritual life. Carpenter says that Tolkien "set himself a rigorous code of behaviour, especially in the matter of making his confession before receiving communion, and when (as often happened) he could not bring himself to go to confession he would deny himself communion"; thus he sometimes refrained from receiving the Sacrament when there was probably no need for him to do so. This unnecessarily deprived him of the graces of the Sacrament and contributed to what Carpenter calls a "state of spiritual depression" (*Biography*, 133).

† This practice is not just a dietary custom but a spiritual discipline meant to turn one's mind and heart to Christ's sacrifice on the cross on Good Friday, and in Tolkien's day it was an obligation for adult Catholics, as now in England and Wales. (In 1985, the Catholic Church in England and Wales allowed Catholics to choose their own penance for Fridays; in 2011, the bishops reinstated the specific penance of abstaining from meat, recognizing that the traditional shared penance was an act of common witness.)

had already recognized his susceptibility to this sin, admitting in a 1913 letter to Edith, "I am so dreadfully tempted to sloth."[10]

Sloth (or *acedia* to use the Latin term) is considered a 'deadly' or 'capital' sin: that is, one that gives rise to other sins.* But it is not simple laziness. St. Thomas Aquinas describes sloth as "an oppressive sorrow, which, to wit, so weighs upon man's mind, that he wants to do nothing."[11]† Sloth is a sin insofar as it leads to a neglect of one's spiritual duties. A devotional book of Tolkien's day gives, as an aid to examination of one's conscience, various questions to determine whether one has been guilty of sloth: "Have you neglected your spiritual duties? or discharged them with tepidity or indolence? Have you studied too much your own ease, leading an unmortified and unchristian life?"[12] The 1912 *Catholic Encyclopedia* relates the sin of sloth to a lack of love: by failing to make the effort to cultivate his relationship with God in prayer, a Christian "violates, therefore, expressly the first and the greatest of the commandments: 'Thou shalt love the Lord thy God with thy whole heart, and with thy whole soul, and with thy whole mind, and with thy whole strength' (Mark 12:30)."[13] Tolkien's regret in this context that he "did not live up to" his love for God in the Blessed Sacrament would therefore seem to be almost a textbook example of sloth.

"Starving hunger"

He goes on to explain that, during this time, "Not for me the Hound of Heaven, but the never-ceasing silent appeal of Tabernacle, and the sense of starving hunger"[14]—a remark that merits a great deal of unpacking.

"The Hound of Heaven" is a reference to the poem of that name by the Catholic poet Francis Thompson, whom Tolkien considered "among the very greatest of all poets."[15] It recounts the story of a soul who is resisting God, while God is imagined as a hound pursuing the speaker wherever he may go. The opening lines are the most famous:

* The other six deadly sins are pride, lust, gluttony, avarice, anger, and envy.

† Tolkien would have been familiar with St. Thomas's analysis of *acedia*, as in the 1920s he purchased a complete set of the *Summa Theologica*, in Latin (Cilli, *Tolkien's Library*, 300).

I fled Him, down the nights and down the days;
  I fled Him, down the arches of the years;
I fled Him, down the labyrinthine ways
  Of my own mind; and in the mist of tears
I hid from Him, and under running laughter.
  Up vistaed hopes I sped;
  And shot, precipitated,
Adown Titanic glooms of chasmèd fears,
From those strong Feet that followed, followed after.

Thompson's poem sums up a certain type of struggle with the faith: the experience of suffering loss, failure, and bitterness trying to find satisfaction anywhere other than in God.

Tolkien, however, defines his spiritual struggle by contrast with this poem: "*Not* for me the Hound of Heaven." He did not feel that God was chasing after him, or that he was actively trying to flee from God, but that God was waiting patiently, issuing a "never-ceasing silent appeal" from the tabernacle.

A tabernacle is the box, usually metal and ornately decorated, in which the Blessed Sacrament is reserved in a Catholic church. With his profound devotion to the Eucharistic presence of Christ, Tolkien felt that the tabernacle was making a "silent appeal" to him, reminding him that his "starving hunger" could only be assuaged by the Bread of Life. His spiritual state was not one of dramatic flight from a pursuing heavenly hound but one of desperate need for sacramental nourishment.

It seems probable that Tolkien went through a time in which he seldom received communion. Whether this was because he did not attend Mass, had neglected the practice of going to confession, had not been sufficiently diligent to keep the Eucharistic fast, or simply did not feel spiritually prepared to receive, we do not know.* But whatever the reason, during this time he felt an intense hunger for God in the Blessed Sacrament, the "daily bread" that Christians pray for in the words of the Lord's Prayer.

* To the extent that he did practice his faith in Leeds, Tolkien probably attended St. Anne's Cathedral, since it was there that his son Christopher was baptized in 1924 (Buck, "An Inspired Alias?," 197). This centrally located church was relatively new, built in 1904 in the Arts and Crafts Gothic style (Little, *Catholic Churches Since 1623*, 167).

For Tolkien, one result of these seemingly fallow years of "starving hunger" in his spiritual life seems to have been greater insight into the role of the will in the life of faith. As he explained to Christopher in 1944, "If you cannot achieve inward peace, and it is given to few to do so (least of all to me) in tribulation, do not forget that the aspiration for it is not a vanity, but a concrete act."[16] To make an effort toward that kind of peace is not mere emotion or sentiment but a movement of the will, which in Catholic devotional practice is called an 'act of hope' or an 'act of faith.' A typical expression of this is given in a prayer manual of the time:

> O my God, relying on thy gracious promises, I hope, by the merits of Jesus Christ, for the pardon of my sins, grace to serve thee faithfully in this life by doing the good works which thou hast commanded, and eternal happiness in the world to come, through Jesus Christ our Lord.[17]

In his brief comment on an aspiration being a concrete act, Tolkien is giving voice to an important aspect of his faith, learned, it seems, through hard experience: to pay little attention to sensible consolation and focus on deliberate action. Feelings may come and go, but one can determine to attend confession and receive Holy Communion even in an arid state. In such periods, faith is more a matter of obedience than emotion.

And around 1930, by Tolkien's reckoning, he began once more to fully practice his faith. As with the onset of this time of spiritual dryness, we do not know exactly what brought about its end. Christopher's birth in 1924 had already been, for Tolkien, a "gift" during this difficult time, so the arrival of Priscilla in 1929 may have been a factor as well; the joy of a long-hoped-for daughter might have helped to shift Tolkien out of his spiritual rut.

In any case, Tolkien himself might not have been able to explain the reason behind this new season in his spiritual life. He would have considered any growth in faith to be entirely dependent on God's grace, though not without the freely chosen participation of the person in question. As Paul writes in his Epistle to the Philippians, "with fear and trembling work out your salvation. For it is God who worketh in you, both to will and to accomplish, according to his good will." The Christian works out his salvation, but it is "God who worketh in you."[18] There is no reason why the two workings cannot coincide, for "thou hast wrought for us all our works" (Isaiah 26:12). This mysterious cooperation of divine and human action is something Tolkien meditated upon: "As souls with free-will we are, as it were, so placed as to face (or to be able to face) God. But God is (so to speak) also behind us, supporting, nourishing us."[19]

19

The Domestic Church

War had disrupted Tolkien's life, and the first years after demobilization were unsettled as well, with his career as an academic still taking shape. During his time at Leeds and his early years back at Oxford, he felt his spiritual life to be at a low ebb. But even during that difficult stretch, he and Edith had begun new friendships that would be important and fruitful in the years to come. And they had been fruitful themselves, welcoming four children into the world: John, born in 1917; Michael, 1920; Christopher, 1924; and Priscilla, 1929.

From his children's earliest days, Tolkien showed himself to be very much a family man, telling bedtime stories to the children and delighting in spending time with each of them.* Simonne d'Ardenne, who lived with the Tolkiens for a time in the 1930s and became an "unofficial aunt," recalled that Tolkien, despite his busy schedule, "always found time to rush home and kiss his younger children goodnight."[1]† He delighted in them; he had the rare ability "of combining fatherhood with friendship," as Michael recalled. But, of course, it was not always smooth sailing. Michael also admitted that "he was not a super-human father, and often found his children insufferably irritating, self-opinionated, foolish and even on occasions totally incomprehensible."[2]

For Tolkien, as a Christian, fatherhood had a significant spiritual dimension. His children were immortal souls in his care, not just 'his,' but God's, entrusted to

---

* He often included the children's toys in these stories. For instance, Tom Bombadil, who first appeared in poetry before making his way into *The Lord of the Rings*, was inspired in part by a Dutch doll the children had, and *Roverandom* was written to console Michael for the loss of a toy dog at the beach during a family holiday. At least some parts of *The Hobbit* were either told or read to the children (and in an early draft, Bilbo the hobbit is named 'Bingo' after Priscilla's stuffed bear), but the compositional history of that book is highly complex and there is no scholarly consensus as to its earliest origins.

† When he did so, he probably also blessed them with the sign of the cross on their forehead (a common Catholic family blessing), since this was his practice in later years; his granddaughter Joanna recalled that on her visits, "Grandfather always crossed my forehead before I went to bed" ("Joanna Tolkien speaks," 34).

him for his care, as he would have read in St. Paul's Epistle to the Ephesians (3:15). His responsibility was not just to feed them and shelter them physically, but to provide teaching and spiritual formation in what the Church calls the 'domestic church.' The *Catechism of Christian Doctrine* (1900) put it plainly: "The duty of parents towards their children is to provide for them, to instruct and correct them, and to give them a good Catholic education."[3]

Tolkien evidently felt the weight of this responsibility, for in later years, he regretted that he had not done more. Writing in 1963 to his now adult son Michael about the children's religious formation, he lamented, "I brought you all up ill and talked to you too little. . . . I failed as a father." He prays "unceasingly" that Christ the Healer "shall heal my defects, and that none of you shall ever cease to cry *Benedictus qui venit in nomine Domini*."[4] This Latin phrase means "Blessed is he who comes in the name of the Lord" and refers to Christ himself: it is the acclamation as king, recorded in all four Gospels, that Jesus receives from the crowd on entering Jerusalem before his Crucifixion,* and also appears in the liturgy of every Mass.

Priscilla confirms her father's reticence about direct instruction in religious matters: "Though I am profoundly aware of my father's piety and faith, I do not remember him ever intent on speaking of dogma or doctrines in intellectual or abstract terms." She goes on to draw the conclusion that "I do not think it was ever in his heart to write or speak of religion didactically: his mode was to express religious themes and moral questions through the medium of story-telling." He did encourage their reading on religious topics, as with his gift to Priscilla of *The Pageant of the Popes* (1943), a history of the papacy, and his published correspondence shows his readiness to discuss theology with his children once they were grown up, but when they were younger, he seems to have been less inclined to address such topics directly.[5]

Priscilla described her father as "a shy man, to whom intimacy did not come easily."[6] As dearly as he loved his children and as much as he enjoyed spending time with them, and they with him, he may have found it difficult to speak to them directly about the faith that meant everything to him. How does one communicate 'everything'? He seems to have had a similar difficulty with Edith; Carpenter says that Tolkien found it difficult to discuss the faith with her "in a rational manner. . . . he presented only his emotional attachment to religion, of which she had little

* See Matthew 21:9, Mark 11:9, Luke 19:38, John 12:13.

understanding."[7] To write his thoughts in letters sent to his adult children was no doubt easier for him than to speak to them one on one while they were all living under the same roof. And so it seems probable that Tolkien did not *speak* very much about his faith to his children as they were growing up. Whether or not he could have done better in this regard is impossible to adjudicate, but what is significant for our purposes is that it shows how keenly he felt the importance of the family as a place of spiritual formation.

Even if he provided relatively little direct instruction of his children on religious topics, he took up his role as the head of his 'domestic church' in other ways. For one thing, as Priscilla's comment shows, his "piety and faith" were evident to his children, so he was leading by example, more telling than any amount of verbal exhortation. References in his letters show that he prayed for them regularly, and the very names that he chose for the children spoke to the centrality of his faith. All four children, the daughter as well as the sons, received the Old Testament name 'Reuel,' a point we shall return to later in our story. Their other names were also either biblical or came from saints in the later history of the Church. It was evidently essential for Tolkien (and Edith) that their children should have not just 'forenames' in front of their surname, but *Christian* names, names publicly announced at their baptisms (that sacramental initiation into the life of the Church), which would link them to characters from Scripture and Tradition.*

Mention of baptism brings us to one of the most important ways that Tolkien built up the domestic church: by ensuring that all of his children had baptismal sponsors (that is, godmothers and godfathers) who were serious about the faith.

In the Catholic rite of baptism, the godparent has "a general duty of looking after the child's spiritual welfare."[8] Being asked to be a godfather or a godmother represents a judgment by the child's parents that the person concerned has a certain degree of spiritual maturity, and that the parents want the relationship to be a lasting one. Godparents are, in a very real sense, considered to be members of the extended family.

---

* This appears to have been a deliberate strategy, especially when we consider the two names that did not get handed on. None of their sons received the name 'Ronald' and their daughter did not receive the name 'Edith': these are names that do not appear in the Bible and were not saints at the time. 'Edith' is now notable for St. Edith Stein, the Jewish convert to Catholicism who took the name Teresa Benedicta of the Cross and was murdered at Auschwitz in 1942. She was canonized in 1998.

Canon law requires at least one godparent for each child, though two are preferred (a godmother and a godfather). A godparent can serve as a sponsor to more than one child in a family, and older children can serve as godparents for their younger siblings if the family so chooses. Tolkien and Edith arranged to have a godfather and a godmother for all of their four children, and different ones for each. This gives us some sense of what this spiritual relationship meant to them. For Tolkien and Edith, who as orphans and converts could not lean on an extended network of biological family for spiritual help, establishing such links with fellow Catholics would have been an important contribution to their growing family's faith tradition. It is no surprise, then, to learn that the godparents whom Tolkien and Edith selected for their children became in many cases lifelong friends of the family. We can gain insights into Tolkien's faith by examining the names he gave his children and by surveying the four men and four women selected as baptismal sponsors.

John

Their first child, John Francis Reuel, was born in November 1917, a year into Tolkien's convalescence from trench fever. 'John' was traditionally handed down in the Tolkien family as the name of the eldest son but is also the name of St. John the Evangelist, the author of the fourth Gospel, to whom Tolkien had a special devotion. (See figure 46.) 'Francis' was in honor of Fr. Francis Morgan, who also baptized him, and refers to St. Francis Xavier, the great Jesuit missionary for whom Fr. Francis himself was named.[9]

The choice of John's godparents shows the young couple's wish to strengthen ties with their biological family as much as they could. His godfather was Tolkien's brother, Hilary,[10] who was at that time also in the army.* Hilary was an obvious choice given the good relations between the brothers, which would endure all their lives; the Tolkien family would regularly receive visits from Uncle Hilary

* Hilary served in the Royal Warwickshire Regiment as a bugler and stretcher bearer. He was wounded several times and awarded the British War Medal and Victory Medal (The National Archives of the UK; Kew, Surrey, England; War Office and Air Ministry: Service Medal and Award Rolls, First World War. WO329; Ref: 743).

and, in due course, visit him and his own growing family at his farm in Evesham, Worcestershire.

John's godmother was Tolkien's cousin Mary Incledon.[11] Mary was the daughter of Tolkien's Aunt May, Mabel Tolkien's sister. As recounted in chapter 3, May had become a Catholic the week before Mabel did but then, under pressure from her husband, left the Church. Tolkien's cousin Mary had therefore not been raised a Catholic—indeed, quite the reverse, as her father, Walter Incledon, remained staunchly opposed. Despite this, after Mabel's death, good relations were restored with the Incledon family, and Tolkien and his brother had spent many of their school holidays with them. We do not know exactly when Mary became a Catholic, but it must have been prior to 1917, since godparents of Catholic children are required to be in full communion with the Church.[12] The Tolkiens' decision to invite her to be their first child's godmother would have been an affirmation of her own new religious identity.* Sadly, she died of cancer in 1940, aged only forty-five. In her will, she "left a large number of shares in her father's business to the Catholic Archbishop of Liverpool, to help in the building of a new cathedral. Her father, still anti-Catholic, bought back the shares at great expense."[13]

Michael

Their second child, Michael Hilary Reuel, was born in 1920, as Tolkien was beginning his academic career at the University of Leeds. 'Michael' is the name of the warrior archangel who casts down Satan in the Apocalypse, the final book of the Bible (Revelation 12:7). 'Hilary' was in honor of Tolkien's brother, and it is also the

* His cousin's example provides a possible answer to the counterfactual question asked in chapter 3 about what might have happened to Tolkien had his father lived and opposed Mabel's conversion. In that eventuality, his own path to Catholic faith might not have been prevented, but rather achieved by other means. C.S. Lewis remarked in this connection: "Parents are not Providence. . . . Perhaps prayers as a secret indulgence which Father disapproves may have a charm they lacked in houses where they were commanded" (*CLII*, 507). Likewise, in Tolkien's understanding of providence, apparent evils (like the breaking of the Fellowship in *The Lord of the Rings*) can turn out to have beneficial effects; contrariwise, moral heroes can frustrate the good they are trying to bring about (like Sam's protectiveness of Frodo forestalling Gollum's possible moment of penitence). In light of these complexities, Tolkien tended to resist absolutist judgment about individual persons or acts. It is not that he had no convictions about the intrinsic evil of certain actions, but that he declined to draw final conclusions about the implied destiny of the actors involved: "Judge not, that you be not judged" (Matthew 7:1).

name of a prominent saint from the fourth century: St. Hilary of Poitiers (315–67), a Doctor of the Church.

Michael's godparents represent friendships formed in wartime. His godfather was Fr. Augustin Emery, the pastor of St. John the Baptist Church in Great Haywood who had blessed the young couple's marriage in 1915. Priscilla recalls that it was her mother who initially "made friends with" Fr. Augustin and that he "was to remain a friend of my parents for the rest of his life"; he was known in the family as "Uncle Gus." This friendship evidently meant a lot to them, and especially to Edith, a new convert in a new place. Priscilla says, "I remember my mother, who was at that time a pianist of professional standard, telling me of the comfort and pleasure she had during this time from making music with Fr. Emery, who played the violin."[14] Years later, in 1931, the Tolkien family would take a holiday in Milford-on-Sea, where Fr. Augustin then lived.[15]

Michael's godmother, Sister Mary Michael, represents an unexpected friendship that came about during the war.[16] In the summer of 1917, during one of the relapses of his trench fever, Tolkien spent several months convalescing in the Brooklands Military Hospital in Hull, East Yorkshire. Mary Michael was one of the Sisters from the nearby convent of the Congregation of the Sisters of Mercy who took on the ministry of visiting the patients in the Brooklands hospital, which would have been very much appreciated by the Catholic soldiers, since chaplains were in short supply on the Home Front.[17]* Though the Sisters could not provide the sacraments as a chaplain could, they did provide spiritual care simply by the friendly visits that relieved the tedium of the men's days and also by praying with them, giving counsel, and supporting them in their faith. For soldiers grieving the loss of friends and comrades and dealing with their own injuries and trauma, such consolation would have been a lifeline.

As Tolkien later recalled, Sister Mary Michael "befriended me in hospital as a lonely soldier in 1917" and became "a very dear old friend."[18] The fifty-one-year-old nun—remembered by one of her students as "only short, but very formidable"[19]—would have provided a positive maternal presence in the life of the twenty-five-year-old Tolkien, something that had been lacking since the death

* Dedicated to Mary under the title of Our Lady of Mercy, the sisters' work focused on caring for the sick and vulnerable, educating the poor, and founding hospitals and orphanages (Austin, "Sisters of Mercy").

of Mabel. In 1945, Tolkien returned something of the kindness he had received from her by visiting her at the convent's retirement home in Whitby. A few years later, he arranged for her to be sent flowers in honor of her Diamond Jubilee as a nun; he affectionately remarked that "the old darling . . . would be much mystified how I had arranged it" and adds that the card should read "Mother Mary Michael with love from Ronald Tolkien."[20] Their friendship would continue until her death, aged eighty-five, in 1951.

Christopher

Christopher John Reuel, Tolkien's third son, was born in 1924 and baptized at St. Anne's Cathedral, Leeds.[21] 'Christopher' was in honor of Tolkien's TCBS friend Christopher Wiseman and is also the name of St. Christopher, the 'Christ-bearer.' 'John,' repeated here, underscores Tolkien's devotion to the fourth Evangelist.

Christopher had as his godmother Eleanor Mozley, the landlady of 5 Holly Bank, where the Tolkiens lived in the spring of 1921 on their first arrival in Leeds.[22] A landlady seems an unlikely choice for a godmother, but as it happens, here we find a fascinating link. The forty-nine-year-old 'Miss Mozley' was none other than the great-niece of John Henry Newman; her grandmother was Jemima Newman—John Henry's sister. Almost certainly Tolkien had been put in touch with her through the Birmingham Oratory, probably by Fr. Francis Morgan, who, having known Cardinal Newman personally, was no doubt aware that his great-niece had become a Catholic and was living in the city where Tolkien had just taken a job.

Eleanor Mozley was baptized in the Church of England, and at age eighteen, she was living at home with her parents, two brothers, one sister, and three servants: the very picture of an upper-middle-class Anglican family. A decade later, the 1901 census gives a complete change of scene: she was now a trained staff nurse living in lodgings with a large group of student nurses; she later enrolled as a midwife, a field she worked in for years.[23] By 1921, when the Tolkiens met her, she was sufficiently well-off to have a home of her own in addition to being a landlady.[24] Then in 1930, at age fifty-eight, she married a widower twenty years her senior, by name Timothy Louis Eugene Spilmont, a wholesale merchant from France who had become a naturalized Englishman before the Great War. Their wedding at St. Anne's Cathedral made the news: as the *Leeds Mercury* reported, the couple "received special greetings from the Pope"[25] on account of her family connection to Cardinal Newman. Eleanor died in 1964 at the age of ninety-one.

The Tolkiens stayed at 5 Holly Bank for only a few months in 1921 before moving to lodgings closer to the university,[26] but they got to know Eleanor Mozley well during that time and kept up the friendship, such that they felt able to ask her to be Christopher's godmother three years later. Their shared experiences as converts and the link with Newman made her an obvious choice to become part of their extended family in this way.

Christopher's godfather was Wilfred Childe (1890–1952), one of Tolkien's new colleagues in the English faculty at Leeds and also a poet. He had been co-editor of *Oxford Poetry* alongside Aldous Huxley and Dorothy L. Sayers and was part of the literary circle established by the poet Edith Sitwell and her brothers, a group that included Siegfried Sassoon and other notable modern writers.[27] Tolkien later showed him *The Hobbit* in manuscript, and Childe liked it; Tolkien suggested that his publishers ask him to help publicize the book when it was released.[28] Childe, like Tolkien, was a Catholic convert, having been received into the Church in 1914 and taking 'Mary' as his confirmation name.[29] Catholics often choose a patron saint who is their same sex, but this is by no means the general rule (as we saw with Tolkien's friend Sister Mary Michael). Childe's choice of 'Mary' signals a Marian devotion, which would have been a connecting point between the two men, as would his poem "Hoc Est Corpus Meum" ('This is my Body') in honor of the Blessed Sacrament.

Priscilla

Priscilla Mary Reuel was born in 1929 in Oxford, their fourth child and only daughter. 'Priscilla' is the name of one of the helpers of Paul the Apostle in his missionary journeys and is mentioned twice in the New Testament (Acts 18:26, Romans 16:3–4). 'Mary,' in addition to being her mother Edith's second name, is of course the name of the Blessed Virgin. Tolkien remarked on how happy and proud he was to have a daughter at last, and Edith, who had been hoping for a daughter when Christopher was born, was delighted finally to have a girl in the family.[30]

Priscilla's godfather was Francis de Zulueta, a significant figure in the Oxford Catholic scene.[31] (See figure 36.) The son of a Spanish diplomat, de Zulueta, a naturalized British citizen, served as an officer in the Worcestershire Regiment during the Great War. A 'cradle Catholic,' he was a nephew of Fr. Denis Sheil of the Birmingham Oratory and had attended The Oratory School.[32] In 1919, he was elected as the Regius Professor of Civil Law at All Souls, Oxford: the first Catholic to hold this chair since the Reformation. De Zulueta helped to draw Tolkien into the Catholic life of Oxford—for instance, inviting him in 1930 to a dinner given at All Souls for the Archbishop of Birmingham, with Sligger Urquhart among the guests as well.[33]

Priscilla's godmother was Helen Buckhurst, a Catholic convert who had been a student of Tolkien's; he supervised her thesis, "The Historical Grammar of Old Icelandic." She was a Fellow and tutor in English at St. Hugh's College and went on to teach at a Catholic girls' school in Hertfordshire; she evidently stayed in touch with her goddaughter, for instance giving Priscilla a copy of Lord David Cecil's *The English Poets* as a birthday present in 1947.[34] We know little else about Buckhurst, except that she became a family friend; Tolkien sent her a copy of *The Hobbit* when it was published and later had Allen & Unwin send her *The Lord of the Rings* as each volume came out.[35]

Formation and festivals

As well as giving the children biblical and saints' names and devout godparents, Tolkien ensured that they were taught in an environment that was supportive of their faith, sending each of them to Catholic schools—the boys to The Oratory School, Priscilla to Rye St. Antony.

We can also trace some ways that he found to embody or enact their faith at home. One of these is the long-running series of illustrated letters that he wrote for his children, beginning in 1920, when John was three years old, and continuing until 1943, when Priscilla was fourteen.* Each year at Christmastime, Tolkien

* His delight in Christmas continued when he became a grandfather. Joanna Tolkien recalled that in the late 1950s and early 1960s, "I stayed with my grandparents at Sandfield Road, and this included spending several Christmases there, which were fond memories which I'll always cherish. I remember in particular the delight he took in decorating the tree, the crib and the house, and his insistence on my helping him, and our going together to midnight mass" ("Joanna

would pen a letter purporting to be from Father Christmas, who lives at the North Pole alongside a growing cast of remarkable characters, including the North Polar Bear, an elf called Ilbereth, and a horde of antagonistic goblins. The letters were a pure delight to the children: "Sometimes the envelopes, dusted with snow and bearing Polar postage stamps, were found in the house on the morning after his visit; sometimes the postman brought them; and the letters that the children wrote themselves vanished from the fireplace when no one was about."[36] As time went on, they provided a subtle way for Tolkien to ensure that the gift-giving, "Father Christmas" aspect of the holiday did not conflict with the celebration of the Nativity of Christ but rather was made harmonious with it. Many aspects of real-world Christianity are woven into the Father Christmas Letters: there are references to the Church calendar, including mentions of St. Nicholas, St. Stephen, and All Saints.[37] Tolkien gives Father Christmas the same birthday as Jesus, December 25, conveniently enabling him to fit this folkloric figure into the Nativity season without disrupting its religious meaning, and his name is even given at times as "Fr. Christmas," as if he were a priest.*

Another instance of the way he approached forming the children in the practice of their faith has to do with his perspective on the traditional annual celebration of 'Bonfire Night.' It commemorates the attempt made on November 5, 1605, by Guy Fawkes and other political agitators to assassinate Queen Elizabeth I's successor, King James. Fawkes and his co-conspirators were discovered, tortured, and executed, and by Act of Parliament, November 5 was declared a national day of thanksgiving, a status it retained until 1859. Because Fawkes and his crew were all Catholics, 'Bonfire Night' became a cultural expression of approved anti-Catholic sentiment.†

It's no surprise, then, that Tolkien was less than enthusiastic about his children participating in what he declared was "one of the wickedest, cleverest, and most successful pieces of Government propaganda in history!"—a statutory seizing

Tolkien speaks," 34). A 'crib' is a Nativity scene; this small-scale replica of the Holy Family at Bethlehem is commonly used as a devotional focus for family prayers and a way for even young children to reflect on the birth of Christ.

* This detail is obscured in published editions of *Letters from Father Christmas*, where 'Fr. Christmas' is almost always expanded into 'Father Christmas' in the transcriptions of the handwritten letters. There are numerous editions of *Letters from Father Christmas*; the 2019 deluxe edition (London: HarperCollins, 2019) is the only one to include images of every letter and envelope.

† On Bonfire Night to this day, the pope is burnt in effigy every year in the town of Lewes, East Sussex.

upon the hot-headed actions of a few papists as an excuse to perpetuate suspicions that all Catholics are inherently traitorous. To avoid giving parental approval to this negative aspect of Bonfire Night while not depriving the children of the fun of bonfires, he came up with the idea of making it a "great Festival" for the boys' birthdays, which fell on October 22, November 16, and November 21. They had "a 'continuous birthday' jamboree" which doubled as "a carrying on of the ancient Incoming of Winter Festival, so that no shadow of that abominable business of 1605 was allowed to fall on it."[38]

Here, we find a good example of Tolkien teaching his children to resist the encroachment of the prevailing Protestant culture in a playful manner that St. Philip Neri would have endorsed, not retreating into a recusant or persecuted mentality but turning a serious religious matter into a long-running "jamboree."*

And if Tolkien formed his children, his children formed him too, teaching him much about love and about hope, indeed, the hope of everlasting life. We can see this especially in letters he sent to Christopher and Michael after they were grown men. To Christopher, he recalled the profound "gift" that his son's love was to him, providing the deep consolation that "there is no end to this. . . . we have some special bond to last beyond this life." And to Michael, he wrote, "The link between father and son is not only of the perishable flesh: it must have something of *aeternitas* about it. There is a place called 'heaven' where the good here unfinished is completed; and where the stories unwritten, and the hopes unfulfilled, are continued."[39]

Tolkien had seen his children come into the world: he had seen too that they brought with them something that reached beyond the walls of the world.

---

* Tolkien's desire to connect faith with fun is seen also in his involvement with the Sacred Heart Convent at 11 Norham Gardens, Oxford, where his children went to summer and Christmas parties; Priscilla recalled that Tolkien was "a famous entertainer" at these gatherings. He also published the poem "Firiel," an early version of "The Last Ship," in the 1934 *Chronicle of the Convents of the Sacred Heart* (*TCG:RG*, 1071).

20

Fellow Pilgrim

In 1925, Tolkien applied for and was elected to the Rawlinson and Bosworth Chair of Anglo-Saxon at Oxford.* Thus far in our story, we have met three of the four people who were the most formative in his life: Mabel Tolkien, Fr. Francis Morgan, and Edith Bratt. When he returned to Oxford after his stint at Leeds in order to take up his new chair, Tolkien encountered the fourth of these formative figures, though the person in question seemed an unlikely candidate for such a role.

His new acquaintance was a Northern Irishman of Protestant family who had been raised to distrust 'papists.' What was more, he was an atheist, having abandoned his childhood Christianity around the same age that Tolkien had fully embraced his own faith. After beginning his academic career in philosophy, he had secured a Fellowship in English at Magdalen College, Oxford, and so it was that his first encounter with Tolkien occurred—in May 1926—at a meeting of the English Faculty. This anti-papistical atheist recorded the event in his diary, saying of Tolkien, "He is a smooth, pale, fluent little chap. . . . No harm in him: only needs a smack or so."[1]

The man in question was, of course, C.S. Lewis (see figure 30), known to his friends as Jack.† If this thumbnail portrait of him seems unexpected, it is because

* The chair came with a Fellowship at Pembroke College, founded in 1624. One of the college's most famous alumni was Dr. Samuel Johnson, the eighteenth-century essayist, lexicographer, and Anglican moralist. Although he left Oxford before taking his degree (owing to lack of funds), Johnson remembered Pembroke fondly. Tolkien remained at Pembroke for two decades, 1925–45, and shared not only his lexicographical interests with 'Dictionary' Johnson: he also "had a Johnsonian horror of going to bed" (Obituary, 15).

† Lewis disliked his given names (Clive Staples) and was known as Jack from boyhood; Tolkien soon came to use the nickname. Lewis usually referred to Tolkien as 'Tollers,' on the same principle whereby Addison's Walk became 'Adder's,' the Radcliffe Camera (part of the Bodleian Library) became 'the Radder,' and the wastepaper basket 'the Wagger Pagger Bagger.' Tolkien is on record calling the Martyrs' Memorial in Magdalen Street, Oxford, "the maggers' memugger" (*Biography*, 62). This habit was not peculiar to Lewis and Tolkien but was a standard piece of

we are accustomed to viewing Lewis in light of his later achievements: as a popular theologian rather than a philosopher, as the author of *Mere Christianity* rather than as a strident unbeliever, and as a firm friend of Tolkien rather than as someone who wanted to give him a smack.

Their friendship was transformative for both men; indeed, if they had never met, it is entirely possible that we would know nothing of either of them today.

If Tolkien had not become friends with Lewis, then *The Lord of the Rings* would never have been finished, let alone published. As Tolkien put it years later, "But for his interest and unceasing eagerness for more I should never have brought *The L. of the R.* to a conclusion."[2] Given how much of Tolkien's output remained unfinished or unpublished in his lifetime, this is an entirely plausible scenario. Conversely, without Tolkien, Lewis quite possibly would not have become a Christian, or at least not during this pivotal stage, with his literary career ahead of him—and thus we would not have had *Mere Christianity*, *The Screwtape Letters*, and the *Chronicles of Narnia*. As Lewis recalled years later, Tolkien gave him "much help in getting over the last stile" of his conversion.[3]

Reflecting on their friendship after Lewis's death in 1963, Tolkien acknowledged their crucial mutual influence: "we owed each a great debt to the other, and that tie with the deep affection that it begot, remains."[4] With the many differences between them when they first met, their friendship was, on the face of it, unlikely. But friends they did become, through a shared interest in Norse sagas. Tolkien had started a little club to foster knowledge of Old Icelandic; it was called the 'Kólbitar,' which means literally 'coal-biters,' an Icelandic word for old cronies who sit so closely around the fire that they look as if they were biting the coals.[5] Lewis joined the Kólbitar and thus one of the great literary friendships of the twentieth century was put in train.

A friendship that began in a shared enthusiasm for Old Icelandic tales extended, a few years later, to include their own creative endeavors. In 1929, Tolkien cautiously showed Lewis the draft of "The Lay of Leithian," a long narrative poem about the love of Beren, a human man, and Lúthien, an Elvish princess. It was a significant gesture of trust. This was no ordinary poem; it was one of the 'Great Tales' from the heart of Tolkien's legendarium, and the character of Lúthien was inspired by

linguistic play among men of their generation. Hence Rugby Football was known as 'rugger,' whereas Association Football, shortened to *Assoc* Football, became 'soccer.'

Edith. Lewis's response was warm: "I can quite honestly say that it is ages since I have had an evening of such delight: and the personal interest of reading a friend's work had very little to do with it. I should have enjoyed it just as well as if I'd picked it up in a bookshop, by an unknown author. The two things that come out clearly are the sense of reality in the background and the mythical value: the essence of a myth being that it should have no taint of allegory to the maker and yet should suggest incipient allegories to the reader."[6]

Lewis went through the draft of the poem and wrote a detailed commentary, in many cases being so bold as to suggest not only the rephrasing of certain lines, but even providing entire rewritten passages. It could easily have come across as overbearing, but Lewis adopted the conceit that the poem was an ancient text being critiqued by four different scholars (Peabody, Pumpernickel, Schuffer, and Schick) arguing over the authentic reading of the manuscript. In this way, he could take the sting out of remarks that are otherwise strongly critical, as when he commented, "Many scholars have rejected lines 1–8 altogether as unworthy of the poet."[7] Tolkien accepted much of the feedback, making many changes to the text in light of Lewis's remarks. As it happens, he never finished "The Lay of Leithian," but the exchange had an immediate positive result: it greatly strengthened their friendship.[8]

From friend to fellow Christian

Lewis was at this time gradually moving toward belief in God, partly through his philosophical engagement with the idea of objective value[9] and partly through his steadily advancing intimacy with Tolkien. Lewis recorded that on one occasion they "sat discoursing of the gods & giants & Asgard for three hours. . . . the fire was bright and the talk good";[10] it went on till 2:30 in the morning.

The most significant of these nighttime conversations occurred in September 1931. Tolkien joined Lewis and his visiting friend Hugo Dyson for an evening at Magdalen College.* Dyson was an Anglican. Tolkien, the Catholic, had

* Henry Victor Dyson Dyson (1896–1975) signed his academic work as 'H.V.D. Dyson' but was known to his friends as Hugo. (See figure 31.) A Shakespearean scholar, Dyson was teaching at the University of Reading in 1931. He would later become a fellow at Merton College, Oxford, and a member of the Inklings. We will meet him again in chapter 26.

recently emerged from a relatively barren stretch in his spiritual life. Lewis was a newly-minted Theist—a believer in God—but not yet a Christian.

After dinner, the three men took a stroll around Addison's Walk, the beautiful tree-lined path circling parkland where the college's fallow deer roam (see figure 32). They began with discussions of myth and metaphor, then turning to the topic of Christianity. Lewis recalled that their talk was "interrupted by a rush of wind which came so suddenly on the still, warm evening and sent so many leaves pattering down that we thought it was raining. We all held our breath . . . appreciating the ecstasy of such a thing." A week after this conversation, Lewis "passed on from believing in God to definitely believing in Christ—in Christianity. . . . My long night talk with Dyson and Tolkien had a good deal to do with it."[11] Obviously, we do not have a verbatim account of what they said, but we can piece much of it together from Lewis's letters and from a poem that Tolkien wrote that was directly inspired by the occasion.

Lewis's problem with Christianity at this point, so he explained, had to do with his inability to grasp the *meaning* of certain Christian doctrines, "in what sense the life and death of Christ 'saved' or 'opened salvation to' the world." The theological expressions of this mystery (such as "sacrifice" or "the blood of the Lamb") seemed to him "either silly or shocking." He was focusing intellectually upon "doctrines" and finding that they left him cold.

> Now what Dyson and Tolkien showed me was this: that if I met the idea of sacrifice in a Pagan story I didn't mind it at all: again, that if I met the idea of a god sacrificing himself to himself . . . I liked it very much and was mysteriously moved by it: again, that the idea of the dying and reviving god (Balder, Adonis, Bacchus) similarly moved me provided I met it anywhere *except* in the Gospels. The reason was that in Pagan stories I was prepared to feel the myth as profound and suggestive of meanings beyond my grasp even tho' I could not say in cold prose 'what it meant.'[12]

The irony was that Lewis already knew very well that myths could not be adequately rendered "in cold prose." Myths were different from allegories (as shown in his response to "The Lay of Leithian"), yet his approach to Christianity was essentially allegorical, not mythical: Lewis had been trying to understand the faith by translating it into another set of terms, a doctrinal, intellectual, systematic language. But as his talk with Tolkien and Dyson progressed, he began to see that Christianity was primarily a story, not a system of thought, and that it had to be approached with the same imaginative embrace that enabled him to enjoy myths in general. The "tremendous difference," Lewis realized, was that the Christian story was historical; it was a *true* myth—indeed it was *the* true myth. It "*really happened*."[13] Or as Tolkien put it: in the Gospels, "Art has been verified. . . . Legend and History have met and fused."[14]

As Lewis acknowledged within days of this life-changing conversation: "The 'doctrines' we get *out* of the true myth are of course *less* true: they are translations into our *concepts* and *ideas* of that wh. God has already expressed in a language more adequate, namely the actual incarnation, crucifixion, and resurrection." Tolkien and Dyson had helped him see that Christianity was a series of events that shone by its own light; doctrinal expressions had their use, but they were secondary and derivative. The thing that had to be believed was not contrary to reason but was opaque to reason in the sense that it couldn't be explained better in any other terms; one couldn't see through the story to some more fundamental explanatory framework.

The specifics that Dyson contributed to the conversation are lost to history, but the way that Tolkien helped to shape Lewis's new perspective comes across in "Mythopoeia," the poem he wrote soon after their Addison's Walk discussion.

"Mythopoeia" opens by describing a way of looking at the world merely as an "endless multitude of forms," an aggregate of objects to be named and categorized but without real intrinsic value. A star is just "some matter in a ball / compelled to courses mathematical." But this, Tolkien says, is "cold" and "regimented," an inadequate understanding of the world. One cannot be said to really see the stars without seeing them as "living silver"; outer space is "only a void" unless and until it is perceived as a "jewelled tent / myth-woven." To be "myth-woven" means that the universe carries its meaning with it. The cosmos does not find a richer meaning by being put in other terms, for that would be to tread a "dusty path and flat, / denoting this and that by this and that." It would be to "ceaselessly revolve the same / unfruitful course with changing of a name."[15]

As well as defending a mythic reading of reality, "Mythopoeia" celebrates human creativity in light of such a reading. Although human beings have become "estranged" from God, they can still show forth his wisdom and truth in their own literary sub-creations. And so Tolkien pronounces a blessing on the "legend-makers," whose stories help to pull people away from the flatness of materialism. In the final lines of the poem, he affirms that poets, and by extension storytellers and artists of all kinds, will still create art in heaven: "Be sure they still will make, not being dead, / And poets shall have flames upon their head"—a bold image, for here he uses the imagery of Pentecost, in which the Holy Spirit appeared as tongues of fire on the heads of the Apostles (Acts 2:2–4).[16]

"Mythopoeia" is a passionate poetic testament to Tolkien's belief in the meaningfulness of both God's creation and of artistic "sub-creation." This insight into the meaningful quality of stories, both divine and human, helped erode Lewis's tendency to overvalue abstraction and after-the-fact conceptualizing, enabling him to arrive at belief in Christ and Christianity.[17] A decade later he hadn't forgotten his debt to them, remarking in a 1941 letter, "Dyson and Tolkien were the immediate human causes of my own conversion."[18]

Tolkien influenced not just Lewis's faith but also his literary imagination. His manifesto of belief, "Mythopoeia," inspired Lewis to pen a poetic reflection of his own, drawing upon their momentous conversation. Tolkien's poem had cleverly drawn upon the circularity of Addison's Walk in order to symbolize Lewis's pre-Christian and un-mythic tendency to "ceaselessly revolve the same / unfruitful course." Now Lewis, in his own poem, declares that the summer will not lead him "round and back / To autumn, one year older, by the well-worn track." Rather, "as all these flowers foretell, / We shall escape the circle and undo the spell."* A new life in a larger, freer world will be entered upon as the imprisoning gates of doubt are drawn apart.

---

* Lewis's poem, entitled "Chanson D'Aventure" (Song of Adventure), was first published in 1938 in *The Oxford Magazine*. He made several revisions, and the final version, with the title "What the Bird Said Early in the Year," is now inscribed on a circular stone plaque on a wall within Addison's Walk at Magdalen College. It was unveiled in 1998 to mark the centenary of Lewis's birth.

The Christian apologist

Tolkien's line of argument about Christianity as a true myth resembles, and was probably influenced by, G.K. Chesterton's 1925 book *The Everlasting Man*.* There, Chesterton contends that Christianity "met the mythological search for romance by being a story and the philosophical search for truth by being a true story."[19] Lewis had also read *The Everlasting Man*, and it did a great deal to shift his views toward his acceptance of theism, but it was Tolkien (with help from Dyson) who finally persuaded him to go all the way and embrace Christianity. In taking the baton from Chesterton, as it were, Tolkien was making good on some famous words of John Henry Newman: "I am a link in a chain, a bond of connection between persons."

Newman and Chesterton are both known as defenders of the faith, and Lewis too, in due course, became a great Christian apologist. Because Tolkien never did public speaking or writing about Christianity, it's easy to assume that he wasn't interested in apologetics or evangelism. However, he was indeed willing to make a defense of the faith in personal interactions—as in the Addison's Walk conversation and in other instances which we will discuss in chapter 31—if he could do so in a way that fit his preference for a mythic approach.

For now, though, let us briefly look again at "Mythopoeia" to see how Tolkien presents the faith in persuasive fashion. He makes three significant points to address the objection that Christianity is nothing more than a wish-fulfillment story. First, he observes that although humans are "estranged" from God, human nature still "recalls" its Maker and "draws some wisdom" from him. This is the concept of natural theology (as summed up in Romans 1:19–20). Second, he asks, if we entertain "wish-fulfillment dreams," where did we get the power to wish or dream in the first place? The answer: because we are created (Genesis 1–3). The power is a pointer to the fact that human beings have a Creator who is personal and creative: "We make still by the law in which we're made." Third, Tolkien notes that wish-fulfillment dreams require us to distinguish between the "fair" and the "ugly."[20] The ability to judge some things as good, true, or beautiful and others as evil, false, or ugly depends on the existence of objective value, a reality that individual

---

* George Sayer recalled that Tolkien had "a great liking and appreciation for *The Everlasting Man*" and felt its arguments to be "absolutely valid" (Carpenter et al., "A Dialogue," 21).

people can access that is independent of themselves. In short, we are created with a conscience (Romans 2:14–15).

These theological concepts that Tolkien shared with Lewis in 1931 were rendered in poetic form. What he said in actual dialogue we do not know, but presumably things very similar. That he felt comfortable transposing his thoughts into a poem (and publishing it) but not into a prose apologia tells us a lot about where he thought his own strengths lay.

A rising tide

When Lewis and Tolkien first met in 1926, Tolkien was still at a low point in his religious life. It is not unlikely that the discussions and inevitable lively disagreements with his non-Christian friend over the next few years contributed to the gradual revitalization of Tolkien's own spiritual health. In explaining Christianity to an intelligent, thoughtful friend and colleague, who would have actively challenged him, Tolkien would have found himself compelled to think more deeply about his own beliefs: what he held to be true and why. Iron sharpens iron (Proverbs 27:17): in helping Lewis toward Christian conversion, Tolkien was helping his own faith too.

Tolkien undoubtedly hoped that Lewis would become a Catholic and was presumably disappointed that Lewis chose to reaffiliate himself with the Anglican tradition in which he had been raised. Nevertheless, he was perfectly clear that Lewis was a Christian, even if not fully in the 'one fold' of the Catholic Church (we will have more to say about Tolkien's ecumenical views in chapter 30). In the same letter in which Tolkien affirms his own fidelity to the Catholic Church, he adds, "God cannot be limited . . . and may use any channel for His grace. Even to love Our Lord, and certainly to call him Lord, and God, is a grace, and may bring more grace."[21]

As late as 1931, Lewis was still describing Tolkien as "one of my friends of the 2nd class."[22] But this was to change as Lewis underwent the central transformation of his life, becoming an adult Christian at Tolkien's encouragement, and not just any old Christian but one of the most influential apologists of the twentieth century. The newfound unity on spiritual matters that the two men enjoyed allowed their friendship to deepen and flourish, and as the 1930s unfolded, they grew closer and closer, sparking ideas off each other "like two young bear cubs sometimes, just happily quipping with one another."[23] Tolkien wrote in his diary that not only did he enjoy Lewis's friendship, but it "has done me much good from the contact with a man at once honest, brave, intellectual . . . and a lover, at least after a long pilgrimage, of Our Lord."[24]

It was out of their friendship that one of the great literary circles of all time developed, a group that in its global influence would rival and perhaps surpass that of the Bloomsbury set and possibly even that of the Lake Poets: namely, the Inklings, whom we will discuss later in this story. Whatever ranking we give to that circle, it is hard to imagine how any such group could or would have developed if it hadn't been for that crucial nighttime conversation in Addison's Walk, when Tolkien, with Dyson's help, convinced Lewis that the story of Christ was the fulfilment of paganism, the culmination of philosophical search and imaginative desire—in short, "the true myth."

21

An Academic Vocation

Tolkien was unlike Lewis in that he never became a public apologist for the Christian faith. However, just like Lewis, Tolkien had a calling to the academic life. After returning from Leeds in 1925,[1] he would spend the remainder of his academic career and most of the rest of his life in Oxford. Here, he would become a world-class expert on Old English and Middle English language and literature, his days full of writing, lecturing, supervising—in short, living out his Christian vocation as a scholar, one of only four Catholic Professors in the entire University of Oxford at that time, the others being Francis de Zulueta, Cesare Foligno, and John Fraser.* (See figure 36.) He was thirty-three years old and was becoming a public intellectual with an increasingly high profile.

As the Rawlinson and Bosworth Professor of Anglo-Saxon and Fellow of Pembroke College, Tolkien had attained a higher rank in the academic world than he had enjoyed at Leeds and certainly higher than his previous work at Oxford as a tutor without a Fellowship.† But he really only made his name in 1936 when he gave the prestigious Gollancz Memorial Lecture to the British Academy, speaking

* Francis de Zulueta, Regius Professor of Civil Law (appointed in 1919); Cesare Foligno, Serena Professor of Italian (also appointed in 1919); and John Fraser, Jesus Professor of Celtic (appointed 1921).

† The history of his own professorial chair offered a reminder of how new the Catholic foothold in Oxford was. We briefly met Tom Arnold in chapter 3: brother of the poet Matthew Arnold, he scandalized the family by becoming a Catholic. After a stretch of penurious years, he reverted to Anglicanism and returned to a successful career at Oxford. In 1876, he was in line to be elected as the Rawlinson Chair of Anglo-Saxon, as it was called then. However, he had been struggling with his conscience and publicly announced that he intended "to join, or rather to return to, the communion of the Catholic and Roman Church." He was not elected, and as his daughter's biographer put it, this action was "destructive" of his career (Sutherland, *Mrs Humphry Ward*, 67–68). In 1925, when Tolkien was elected, it was a scant fifty years from the time when declaring one's intention to become a Catholic could be perceived as a total disqualification for the post.

on "Beowulf: The Monsters and the Critics." *Beowulf* is an epic poem of about three thousand lines, written sometime between the eighth and eleventh century, and one of the most important pieces of literature in Old English to have survived from the period. (See figures 33 and 35.) The poem is in the tradition of Germanic heroic legend and recounts how the warrior Beowulf slays two monsters and is then at last mortally wounded in a fight with a dragon. By subtitling his lecture "the monsters and the critics," Tolkien, with characteristic wit, was putting them on a level and, by implication, suggesting that it might not be easy to tell which was which. Were the critics of this celebrated poem insightful scholars or dangerous beasts? His lecture permanently transformed *Beowulf* scholarship and, it may be fairly said, transformed his own academic reputation too, from that of a standard Oxford professor—worthy but unexceptional—to that of a truly innovative thinker who made a deep and lasting impact on the field.

Of course, the field in question—Old English language and literature—was a relatively small patch of turf, and few people working outside that field would ever have come to know Tolkien's name if he hadn't also written *The Hobbit* and *The Lord of the Rings*. Still, it is a major scholarly achievement to change the landscape of one's chosen specialty, and with his *Beowulf* lecture, Tolkien certainly did that.

But what does it have to do with his faith? Two answers suggest themselves, one particularly related to arguments of the lecture and the other more generally related to the fact that it was he who was delivering it.

Tolkien's basic contention was that *Beowulf* scholarship had overlooked the sheer literary value of the poem and had merely quarried it for its historical content. Indeed, he begins his critique with an allegory of the poem as a tower built from a more ancient ruin. People come and push the tower over so they can study the stones. "They all said: 'This tower is most interesting.' But they also said (after pushing it over): 'What a muddle it is in!'"[2] It is as if Tolkien is telling his fellow experts: 'You're too serious. Forget your geological and architectural assessment of the stones out of which this poem is made! Run up the stairs of the tower and look out from the top—you'll catch a glimpse of the sea!' By focusing on the adventure of *Beowulf*—a man slaying monsters—Tolkien showed that, even with all his great learning, he was not afraid to adopt a simple and humble immersion in an exciting story. In this respect, we may see yet again the influence of St. Philip Neri, and behind him, of course, the influence of Christ's own teaching: "Unless you turn and become like children, you will never enter the kingdom of heaven" (Matthew 18:3). This is not to imply that only Christians can be humble, but it is to help account for the roots of Tolkien's own humility.

Tolkien's approach to Christianity as "the true myth" is also relevant when we try to assess his scholarly engagement with *Beowulf*, for he took it in mythic terms too:

> The significance of a myth is not easily to be pinned on paper by analytical reasoning. It is at its best when it is presented by a poet who feels rather than makes explicit what his theme portends; who presents it incarnate in the world of history and geography, as our poet has done. Its defender is thus at a disadvantage: unless he is careful, and speaks in parables, he will kill what he is studying by vivisection, and he will be left with a formal or mechanical allegory, and, what is more, probably with one that will not work. For myth is alive at once and in all its parts, and dies before it can be dissected.[3]

The use of the theological word "incarnate" in this passage is telling. To be sure, a non-Christian scholar might equally have contended that *Beowulf* could be over-analyzed. But Tolkien's Christian appreciation of reality itself as mythic, something that the Creator has honored by incarnating himself alongside his creatures—and which needs no allegorical explanation, no analytical set of terms in order to become meaningful—helped him become alive to this aspect of the poem.

But most people are never going to read either *Beowulf* or Tolkien's lecture, so the question is worth asking: What does such a specialist line of scholarship have to do with his faith? Here we turn to the more general point that the academic life is a calling that a Christian can enter as a way of glorifying God and serving his neighbor. As we saw in an earlier chapter, religion properly understood is not a mere compartment of life but saturates every part of it, including the life of the mind, however obscure its activities. Tolkien undertook his scholarly career in the spirit of St. Paul's injunction: "Whatever you do, do all to the glory of God" (1 Corinthians 10:31).

A vocation

A 'vocation' means a calling to a particular mode of life. For Catholics of Tolkien's day in particular, the word 'vocation' would have been primarily associated with the priesthood or the religious life, or the idea of a calling to marriage rather than the single life. But the idea of 'vocation' is much broader.

In 1949, the historian Outram Evennett (Fellow of Trinity College, Cambridge, best known for his book *The Spirit of the Counter-Reformation*) described what he called the 'vocation' of Catholic faculty members at Oxford and Cambridge, in terms that are significant for the light they shed on Tolkien's approach to his role. Writing in the *Catholic Herald*, Evennett suggests that the work of a 'don' (a faculty member) is "partly 'contemplative,' partly 'active,' in nature." It comprises intellectual work, research, "concentrated thought on one subject," and teaching; and it also allows for the possibility of "a more self-conscious Apostolate." He argues that, while avoiding polemics and aggressive argument, "the Catholic attitude to life or to a given subject" should be expressed at the university in appropriate terms and "by the methods natural to each individual's temperament." Indeed, he says, "It is therefore the duty of Catholics in the universities to display the Faith."[4]

As Tolkien settled into his teaching at Oxford, he found himself in a position to be a witness to other believers. An editorial in the *Catholic Herald* in 1936 welcomed "the protection afforded to Catholics at Oxford and indeed the great chance they now receive there of deepening their Catholic mind." Nevertheless, the writer cautioned that students still faced an environment of "indifference and the self-sufficiency of wholly secular learning" and teachers "who find the Faith both antiquated and unnecessary"; it was vital for students to have the "balancing and steadying effect" of academics who were devout believers.[5] But in order for students to benefit from the mentoring of such figures, they had to know who they were. It seems to be with this in mind that the *Catholic Herald* began regularly to publish lists of each term's Catholic lecturers at Oxford, a practice that continued for about a decade.

The extant lecture lists cover the period from Trinity Term 1938 through Hilary Term 1942, with one final list published for Hilary 1949. The numbers are low: around four or five names listed per term in the earlier lists to a high of thirteen for one term (Michaelmas 1939), and mostly around eight or ten. Notably, while some lecturers appear regularly, there is only one name that occurs in every lecture list: that of J.R.R. Tolkien.

He was hardly the world's greatest lecturer (he spoke too fast and too indistinctly), but he was exceptionally diligent, not only providing lectures more often and more regularly than was the norm for a professor, but also—as these lists show—providing lectures on a larger number of topics than his colleagues and without the gratification of packed lecture-halls or appreciative audiences.* It highlights the extent to which he worked hard to ensure that students in his field had the opportunity to receive the instruction needed to pass their exams.

It also meant that Tolkien stood out as an example. The best-known Catholics at Oxford were priests, such as Fr. Martin D'Arcy and Fr. Ronald Knox. At this time, the idea of active engagement by the English Catholic laity in the wider professional and cultural world was still relatively new. Tolkien's role as Professor of Anglo-Saxon was sufficiently important that it was considered newsworthy in the Catholic press even as far afield as Australia. (See figure 34.)

Catholics in higher education

Tolkien had experienced Oxford University as an undergraduate—first as one not very diligent about his Christian faith and then with renewed seriousness. Now he was back on familiar territory but approaching it from the other angle: as a faculty member who could support the faith of students like his younger self and knowing, from personal experience, just how much they might need such support. As the dry spell in his faith faded away, he took up the role with an increasing sense of purpose. We might say that at Leeds, he had been an academic who happened to be a Catholic; now he accepted a more visible and active role in which his faith was far more than incidental to his professional identity.

Catholic students were still very much the minority. For instance, the chaplaincy's report for 1936 noted a total of 172 Catholic undergraduates,[6] and coreligionist

* We should not exaggerate his faults as a lecturer, however. Tolkien's colleague at Merton College, Courtney Phillips, who knew him well, noted that "he had a typical audience between 20 and 40 people," adding that an outstanding lecturer might have two hundred students and a very bad lecturer as few as five. "He was in the middle" (di Noia, "Best wishes from Thorin and Company!", 21).

lecturers were rare. As time went on, the topic of university education was increasingly discussed in the Catholic press across the United Kingdom and was seen as a matter of wider cultural and religious significance.

In 1933, at a meeting of the Universities' Catholic Education Board, Fr. Bede Jarrett spoke about the important role of the university chaplains and then "appealed to the audience to interest others in this necessary and vital work. What was needed to-day was leadership, and the natural leaders were those who had been to the University."[7] A number of leading Catholics at Oxford were present, including Fr. Martin D'Arcy, Francis de Zulueta, and Fr. Ronald Knox, and they evidently felt that Tolkien fit the description, for two years later, in 1935, he was appointed as a member of the board.[8]

Tolkien was characteristically self-deprecating about his suitability for the role, remarking that he had found himself "foisted upon the University Education council. . . . Not that I am likely to be of any use. I meet other more able and more apostolic men. But I never can make head or tail of 'public business' even of a minor sort. From a balance-sheet to an encyclical such matters are almost equally dark to me."[9] His use of the word 'apostolic' is interesting and probably carries a double meaning. Since the word 'apostle' means literally 'one who is sent,' Tolkien is saying that other men are, in his view, more suitable to be sent for work on this council than he is; but he is also surely saying that other men are better equipped than he is to carry on the evangelizing mission of Jesus's twelve Apostles—in other words, better Christians.

He might have had doubts about his ability and suitability, but not about the value of the work. As a representative of the Oxford side of the Universities Board, Tolkien was taking the place of the late Fr. Edward Butler, an Irish Benedictine who was a highly regarded historian, preacher, and author, and he was serving alongside some of the best-known names in English Catholic public life—"apostolic men" indeed. And so, we should not make too much of Tolkien's self-professed incapacity, nor indeed of his inability to understand an encyclical! These are precisely the sorts of things that St. Philip Neri would advise him to downplay, lest they make him vain or sanctimonious.

Increasing involvement

Tolkien began his contributions to Catholic university life in the late 1920s and 1930s at the local level. The first indication that we have of Tolkien's professorial involvement in the Catholic life of the University comes in the spring of 1928, when he read a paper at a meeting of the Newman Society. His talk was titled "The Chill Barbarians of the North" and challenged the views of the Catholic journalist, author, and politician Hilaire Belloc. The essay has not survived, though it was considered notable enough to merit a summary in *The Tablet*. Tolkien seems to have been in fine pugnacious form: he "criticized the views associated with Mr. Belloc and maintained that the Northern culture was quite as real as the Latin, and that so far as observation of foreign lands was concerned the Romans were stupid and devoid of imagination."[10]

Later that year, Tolkien participated in another student-oriented activity: the visit to Oxford of the Annual Congress of the Pax Romana organization. Founded in Switzerland in 1921 with papal approval, Pax Romana was first known as "The International Secretariat of the (National) Federations of Catholic Students' Societies"—"an unwieldy but explanatory name,"[11] as *The Tablet* drily reported. Pax Romana's aim was to bring together Catholic students "for a better mutual understanding and friendship."[12] In August 1928, Pax Romana had its Annual Congress in England, with the theme of "the examination, from the triple point of view, historical, philosophical, and ethical, of the causes of the divorce between the spirit of the world to-day and that of Catholicism."[13] The main event took place in Cambridge; about 150 attendees continued on to Oxford, where they were treated to an evening lecture and dinner. We don't know exactly what role Tolkien had, but he did serve as a tour guide and was present at the dinner.[14] In any case, he was involved enough to merit acknowledgment from the organizer of the Oxford leg, Fr. Leslie Walker, SJ, who reported that he was "fortunate to have secured the help of Professors Fraser and Tolkein [sic]."[15]*

By the 1930s, the Catholic student population at Oxford had grown enough under Fr. Ronald Knox's leadership that the chaplaincy was enlarged, with a new

* Walker was a lecturer in Literae Humaniores ('Classics') at Campion Hall.

meeting room for the Newman Society to host its public lectures.[16]* Tolkien was present when, in the Trinity Term of 1931, Hilaire Belloc gave the inaugural talk to an audience of nearly two hundred people.[17] Fr. Martin D'Arcy recollected Tolkien's reaction with amusement:

> In his talk Belloc came out with one [of] his pet themes: that the Anglo-Saxons were utterly unimportant in the history of England. . . . Well, Tolkien disagreed profoundly with Belloc on this question of the Anglo-Saxons. He was sitting just in front of me, and I saw him writhing as Belloc came out with some of his more extreme remarks. So during the interval, I said to him, 'Oh, Tolkien, now you've got your chance! You'd better tackle him.' He looked at me and said, 'Gracious me! Do you think I would tackle Belloc unless I had my whole case very carefully prepared?' He knew that Belloc would always pull some fact out of his sleeve which would disconcert you![18]

D'Arcy called Tolkien's comment a "tremendous tribute" to Belloc, as indeed it probably was. It was also an indication that at age thirty-nine, Tolkien was in better control of his temper than he would prove to be in later years; the elderly Tolkien might well have had a few choice words to say to Belloc on the subject.

Tolkien's participation in the life of Catholics at Oxford often now took the form of simply 'showing up' at relevant events. For instance, in 1931, he attended the opening of Greyfriars, the Oxford friary of the Capuchin Franciscans, now reestablished after having been suppressed at the Reformation; the distinguished guest list included the mayor of Oxford and the vice-chancellor of the university.[19] In 1936, he returned to Greyfriars to mark the 700th anniversary of the death of the founder of the English Province of the Franciscans.[20] That same year, he and Edith attended the opening of Campion Hall, the private hall run by the Jesuits, a splendid occasion where they met and mingled with the expected representatives of the university but also with grandees from broader Catholic society, including the Earl of Oxford and Asquith and the novelist Evelyn Waugh.[21] Tolkien was

---

* The new building also prominently featured the heraldic device of Blessed Thomas More (as he then was: his canonization occurred in 1935), the patron of the chaplaincy and a figure whom Tolkien admired greatly, as we will see in chapter 22.

considered prominent enough, as the Professor of Anglo-Saxon, to be listed by name in the reports of these events in the Catholic press.

At the end of Trinity Term 1939, Tolkien attended the farewell dinner given by the Newman Society to their chaplain: Fr. Ronald Knox was retiring in order to devote himself to producing a new translation of the Bible. It was another major occasion, with over a hundred people present. *The Tablet*'s full-page report highlights Tolkien as one of the attendees, along with the usual suspects from the University and notable figures such as economist Christopher Hollis, biographer Robert Sencourt, and—giving a toast to Knox—again, Evelyn Waugh.[22]

In the 1940s, Tolkien expanded his engagement with Catholic academic life from the local to the national level as he became involved with the Newman Association. Established in 1942, its aims included "fostering Catholicism at the British universities" and "encouraging Catholic graduates to assume positions of responsibility in public life," for both of which Tolkien was a good representative.[23]*

Tolkien began serving as an honorary vice president no later than 1947 (possibly as early as 1942) and served continuously from that point until 1955.[24]† His willingness to put his name on the register as a high-ranking academic was valued by the Newman Association. In 1953–54, the association's report included a section on university professors, noting that "Few things are more encouraging in our university work than the striking increase in rank and quality of the men and women on this 'academic register' [of Catholics with university appointments]; at Oxford alone some forty Catholics hold teachers appointments and of these eight hold full professorships. It is worth mentioning that an increasing number of these dons are associating themselves with the work of the Association."[25]

---

* Despite the similar name, it was a different organization than the Newman Society, with which, as we have seen, Tolkien was also connected. It was a spin-off from the University Catholic Federation of Great Britain.

† During Tolkien's time of involvement with the Association, two events stand out. In 1952, the Association hosted a series of Centenary Lectures on Newman's *The Idea of a University*, later published as a book, with a copy sent to each member. The following year, the Association showed early interest in the cause of canonizing Newman; a letter to members gave details of the first public discussion of the cause and noted that the Archbishop of Birmingham had offered Mass at St. Chad's Cathedral for its success (Palace Green Archives, Newman Association, D1/C/1/2). Newman was eventually canonized in 2019 by Pope Francis.

We don't know how involved Tolkien was at the national level, but he did participate in the Oxford Circle of the Association, featuring, for instance, alongside three other contributors as a panelist in a mid-1950s "Brains Trust" event.[26]

A link in a chain

Another indication of Tolkien's growing confidence as a Catholic with a role to fill and a responsibility to fill it is his involvement with the Catenians, an association of Catholic laymen that focused specifically on businessmen and professionals. In 1943, he became the Oxford Circle's first vice president and later served as president for a year.[27] The Catenians, founded in Manchester, England, in 1908, was an innovative venture for the time. Although there were various social organizations for Catholic working men, and Catholic gentry had their own social circles, there was no equivalent for the middle class; furthermore, priests were excluded from membership in the hope that "freed from clerical supervision and control, Catholic laymen might the better learn how to act independently."[28]

The name 'Catenian' comes from the Latin *catena*, meaning 'chain,' and indicated that the members were linked in support of one another. The emblem of the association, "interlocking but unbroken links with the Cross at the centre," represented "the centrality of Christ, His teachings and His example in the corporate activities of the Association and in their own lives."[29]

Tolkien and the other twenty-five initial members of the Oxford Circle represented a cross-section of professionals: the *Catholic Herald* reported that these included "several University men, a novelist, four civil servants, three medical men and five serving officers in H.M. Forces."[30] The Circle aimed to support Catholic laymen in all aspects of their lives. When he served as president, Tolkien would have officially exhorted new candidates with these words: "in your domestic relationship we look to find you if husband affectionate and trustful, if father regardful of the moral and material well being of our children and dependents, as son dutiful and exemplary, and as friend steadfast and true."[31]

Tolkien wanted the group to avoid becoming exclusive: he was concerned that, meeting as they did in restaurants, "the Catenians is already becoming very expensive for anyone with any limit of good income and many domestic commitments."[32]

In addition to such practical considerations, Tolkien also could relax with fellow members and show his sense of fun: in 1945, he raised a glass to the provincial council "in a most amusing way which included an actual toast in Anglo-Saxon." In 1950, the Brothers of the Oxford Circle officially (if belatedly) congratulated "their former president" on the publication of *The Hobbit*, which must have been a pleasant note of affirmation during a time when he was still struggling to get *The Lord of the Rings* published. Tolkien remained a member of the Catenians until 1956, shortly before his retirement, making for an involvement of more than a decade at a busy time in his life.[33]

Bearing the baldachin

We can perhaps best discern Tolkien's understanding of his role as a Catholic academic in an observation he made near the end of his life. To his son Michael, he remarked about his education under the guardianship of Fr. Francis, "I owe a great deal (and perhaps even the Church a little) to being treated, surprisingly for the time, in a more rational way [that is, being permitted to study in non-Catholic schools]."[34] Tolkien, in typically self-deprecating fashion, has slipped in the most important part in a parenthetical: "*and perhaps even the Church [owes] a little.*" His education and subsequent professional career have benefited himself, and, he suggests, have also benefited the Church. How? By providing a visible role model to students and younger professional men and women who needed an example of how to navigate the academic world as a believer.

That example achieved a notably public and visible expression in June 1934 when, on the Sunday in the Octave of Corpus Christi, the Blessed Sacrament was processed through the streets of Oxford from the Church of St. Aloysius to Blackfriars Priory—the first such procession since the Reformation three centuries earlier. It was an occasion of immense pageantry. Sr. Mary Madeleva, a teacher at St. Mary's College, Notre Dame, Indiana, who was studying in England that year, described the scene:

> The great religious orders of men were there: Benedictines, Franciscans, Dominicans, Servites, Jesuits, Salesians; the religious orders of women:

> Sisters of the Holy Child, Mercy, Nazareth House, Holy Cross; the Oxford undergraduates in academic costume; the Sodalists; the children of the Catholic schools; the bodyguard of the Knights of St. Columba; the four Oxford professors in doctoral robes of crimson and scarlet and black, bearing the baldachin; the great congregation of the faithful. . . . the long procession stopped for Benediction in the fine chapel of Blackfriars. Then the singing progress took its way back to the Church of St. Aloysius where, with a second Benediction, this most significant pilgrimage to honor the Blessed Sacrament ended. Among those officiating were the flower of the priesthood in England today, Fathers Carpenter and D'Arcy, Monsignor Ronald Knox. And who shall forbid the spirit of Newman that paradisal walk in the evening air of his Oxford![35]

Let us return to a central detail: "The four Oxford professors . . . bearing the baldachin." These were the *only* four Catholic professors, none other than de Zulueta, Foligno, Fraser, and—J.R.R. Tolkien.* Each held a pole supporting the baldachin, the square canopy raised over the Blessed Sacrament when it is carried in procession outdoors. (See figure 37.) In what more public way could he declare his faith to students and colleagues than, dressed in academic regalia, to be a guard of honor for Christ himself in the monstrance, borne aloft through the Oxford streets?

* Very unusually, Tolkien held *two* professorial chairs at Oxford: the Anglo-Saxon Chair at Pembroke from 1925–45 and then, from 1945 until his retirement, the Merton Chair in English Language and Literature. Merton is one of the oldest, wealthiest, and most prestigious of the Oxford colleges. Raymond Edwards observes that, upon his election, Tolkien had "reached the highest position open to an English scholar of philology; he was the undisputed head of his profession" (*Tolkien*, 209). He was also the first Catholic to hold this post.

22

Saints and Angels

In later years, when Clyde Kilby spoke to Tolkien of his successful work as a teacher as well as a scholar and writer, "he responded that he had been blessed with a sense of the human."[1]* Though obviously fully capable of operating in the realm of high linguistic abstraction, he never lost touch with the humanity of the students he oversaw and the bearing upon human concerns of the ideas he explored. This was something he knew about himself and regarded as a 'blessing'; it was not just an accidental character trait but a gift, a Godsend.

For him to say he had been *blessed* was not merely a figure of speech, nor was it just a pious thought. Tolkien was a philologist, with an extraordinarily detailed knowledge of etymologies. He would have known that the word 'blessing' derives from Old English and Proto-Germanic sources that could fairly be rendered as 'blooding': to bless something was, originally, to hallow it with the blood of sacrifice on an altar. Later, a blessing meant a hallowing that was brought about by speech rather than bloodshed, from the Latin *benedicere*: 'to speak well of, to praise.' And later still, by association with the unrelated word 'bliss,' a blessing came to mean good fortune and happiness of any kind, whether or not it was effected by words. To be blessed, therefore, in Tolkien's lexicon, if all the shades of meaning were present, was to receive bliss that related to worship and rested on a foundation of sacrifice.

---

* Carpenter reports in his biography that Tolkien's students found him "thoroughly humane, certainly more humane than some of his colleagues, who lecture with a total disregard for their audience. . . . There had been no one before him who brought such humanity, one might say such emotion, to the subject; and it was an approach which influenced many of his most able pupils who themselves became philologists of distinction" (*Biography*, 123, 139). And it was not just his emotional intelligence that was remembered, but also his practical realism. Tolkien helped bring about John Lawlor's first appointment at Oxford; Lawlor recalled, "Meditating on the salary I was very ready to accept, he said pensively that a married man with two young children really needed a thousand pounds. . . . entirely typical coming from a man with a thriving family—and utterly unlike anything that would remotely occur to any others among the dons of that day" (*C.S. Lewis: Memories and Reflections*, 37).

Speaking of bliss, he once wrote these two lines of poetry:

> Christ's mercy, Mary and John: I dare
> Only on these to found my bliss.

Tolkien is here translating words that come from the great Middle English poem *Pearl*, written in the fourteenth century.[2] Although they are a translation, not his original composition, they well represent his own belief that happiness, blessing, bliss must rest fundamentally on Christ's mercy, communicated to humanity through the blood of his cross, and—subsequently, derivatively—on the love and obedience of Mary and John, who beheld his suffering and death (John 19:26) and praised it in their respective ways: Mary in her Magnificat (Luke 1:46–55), and John in his various canonical writings. Mary, the Mother of God, and St. John the Evangelist have a role in the acquisition of "bliss," not because they are themselves divine, but because they help mediate to the rest of mankind the reality and meaning of the one perfect mediation accomplished by Christ.

Tolkien said that these lines from *Pearl* expressed "my vision of a great rood-screen through which one could see the Holy of Holies."[3] This remark takes some unpacking. 'Rood' is another word for the Cross; a 'rood screen' is a screen of wood or stone that divides the nave of a church (where worshipers sit) from the sanctuary (where the priest celebrates the Mass and where the tabernacle is located). The "Holy of Holies" in this context is the sanctuary, containing the tabernacle with the Blessed Sacrament. A rood screen is usually elaborately carved, topped with a crucifix in the middle and with statues of Mary and John standing on either side. Though called a 'screen,' it is not a wall but a series of uprights or pillars connected at the top by a 'rood loft.' As an undergraduate, Tolkien would have seen a simple 'rood beam' (the basic element of a rood screen) in the attic chapel of the university's Catholic chaplaincy: small figures of Christ on the cross, Mary, and John placed on a tie-beam. (See figure 18.)

We should picture Tolkien sitting in church, gazing between the uprights toward the receptacle of the Living Bread in the sanctuary. His vision takes in and passes beyond the dying Christ, the sorrowing Virgin, and the beloved disciple. In other words, the rood screen is a kind of lens that focuses his sight; it is a means "*through which* one could see the Holy of Holies," the tabernacle containing "the one great thing to love on earth." In this chapter, we will consider why Tolkien considered Mary and John—and by extension all the saints—to be an essential part of that lens.

The communion of saints

At every Sunday Mass, Tolkien affirmed, in the words of the Creed, that he believed in "the communion of saints": the active spiritual union of all the faithful, both living and dead. The latter, after going through the cleansing of purgatory as needed, are now enjoying the full presence of God in heaven (Hebrews 12:1, 23). These saints, while they await the general resurrection, in which the heavens and earth will be remade and all the dead will receive new glorified bodies (the resurrected Christ is the 'firstborn' of these: see Colossians 1:18), are fully alive, aware, and actively interceding with God for the needs of people on earth. The saints are the same persons (and personalities) that they were during life, but now, freed from the harmful effects of sin on their desires or judgments, their whole aim is to help others to know and love God. They belong to what is sometimes called 'the Church Triumphant,' that state of the Church in which its members enjoy the beatific vision, the contemplation of God himself in his fullness. They are especially celebrated on All Saints' Day (November 1), one of the major feasts of the Christian calendar. (See figure 19.)

It is therefore a basic part of ordinary Catholic devotion to ask the saints for their intercession—that is, their spiritual assistance and their prayers to God on one's behalf—just as any believer would routinely ask a fellow Christian to pray for them. It is a key way in which the Mystical Body of Christ is held to operate: the saints in heaven praying for those members of Christ's Body who still belong to the 'pilgrim Church on earth' or 'the Church Militant' as it is sometimes called. And just as individual people have particular friendships on earth, so too Catholics typically have certain 'spiritual friends': saints to whom they feel a close connection or affinity.

Tolkien reflected this understanding when he remarked that the Valar, the 'gods' of Middle-earth, are in fact "created spirits—of high angelic order we should say, with their attendant lesser angels." He goes on to explain that the people of Middle-earth may call for help on one of the Valar, such as Elbereth, "as a Catholic might on a Saint, though no doubt knowing in theory as well as he that the power of the Vala was limited and derivative."[4]

Here he makes an important point: a Catholic knows that a saint's power is "limited and derivative." All graces come only from God through Christ, the perfect mediator between God and humankind; but, so Catholics believe, Christ's Body, the Church, is filling the universe (Ephesians 1:23), and thus God, who wishes for his people to participate in his generosity, allows the saints to assist in the sharing of those graces. It is not strictly necessary to invoke the aid of the saints, and the Church does not require individuals to do so in their private devotions, but not to do so would be as weird as speaking only to the father of your family and never to your mother or siblings or uncles or aunts. It is a central point of Catholic belief that all the faithful in the Body of Christ, both living and dead, are part of an objectively real communion and are called, in St. Paul's words, to feel concern for one another (1 Corinthians 12:25), pray for one another (Ephesians 6:18), and "bear one another's burdens, and so fulfil the law of Christ" (Galatians 6:2). In this brief remark about the Valar, we find an echo both of Tolkien's Christocentric theology—that he emphasizes the *derivative* quality of a saint's intercession—and his sense of the reality of the Communion of Saints.

But what does Tolkien mean by "saint"? It has two related meanings. On the one hand, all living Christians are 'saints' (*hagioi* in Greek: see, for example, Acts 26:10; Romans 1:7; 1 Corinthians 1:2). But the word also refers to 'canonized' saints, that is, those people whom the Church has authoritatively recognized as being in heaven, and worthy of public recognition.* Each canonized saint has a feast day, some only observed on a local or national level and some globally. The important point here is that the Church does not make saints; God makes saints. The canonization process is one of recognizing that a particular Christian has attained perfect sanctity with God in heaven, the evidence for this being either the miracles that have occurred as a result of prayers for their intercession or their example of sanctity, as with those who accepted martyrdom rather than deny Christ. The Church continually recognizes new saints, and Tolkien kept abreast of these

* This does not mean they all lived perfect lives; indeed, the Church has canonized people with very disreputable pasts.

canonizations. For instance, he referred in 1963 to Pope Pius X as "St Pius X";[5] Pius, who died in 1914, had been canonized in 1954. (See figure 58.)

There are undoubtedly many saints who were important to Tolkien in one way or another, whether as spiritual intercessors or simply as models of faith.

For instance, he worked for years on various versions of a poem with the working title "The Death of Saint Brendan," published in 1955 as "Imram" (the word for medieval Irish tales of fabulous sea voyages). In the poem, the saint on his deathbed recounts a visit to a mysterious blessed island that seems to lie beyond the edge of the world. It is based on a legendary tale, but St. Brendan himself is a real figure, a fifth-century monk who is known as one of the Twelve Apostles of Ireland. Tolkien ends his poem by relating that

> Saint Brendan had come to his life's end
> under a rainclad sky,
> and journeyed whence no ship returns,
> and his bones in Ireland lie.[6]

There is a resonance between the imagery of this poem about Brendan's death "in green Galway" and the account of Frodo's journey at the end of *The Lord of the Rings* when "on a night of rain" he boards a ship that passes into the West where the "rain-curtain" rolls back revealing "a far green country." This is not to imply in any way that Frodo is a representation of St. Brendan; only to point out how Tolkien's explicit engagement with religious subjects naturally finds an echo in his mythic fiction.

On his visit to Italy in 1955, he was "much moved" by viewing a painting of St. Jerome,[7] the irascible translator of the Vulgate edition of the Bible. (See figure 47.) On that same trip, he showed a keen interest in the two saints of Assisi, Clare and Francis, taking time to see the various churches associated with them.[8] Visiting the church of San Damiano, the first home of St. Clare's nuns, Tolkien found it inspiring to read a plaque inscribed in Latin with the words of St. Francis's "Hymn to the Sun." He noted in his diary, "I felt the whole place more soaked with a sense of the personality of St Clare, and of St Francis, than of anywhere else in Assisi, even the tombs."[9]

Of the saints for whom he felt a personal regard, we saw in chapter 4 that St. Philip Neri, the founder of the Oratorians, was of special importance to Tolkien, so much so that he took 'Philip' as his confirmation name and wove the initial 'P' into his monogram. But Philip was not the only member of the communion of saints to have a significant place in his spiritual life. We turn now to consider three other saints who played a substantial role in Tolkien's faith.

St. John the Evangelist

Tolkien owned that he had a "special devotion" to St. John the Evangelist.[10] (See figure 46.) In fact, he considered John as his patron, alongside St. Philip, on account of having been born on the octave of that saint.[11] The feast day of St. John is December 27, which means that the octave day of that feast falls on Tolkien's birthday, January 3. He knew that his parents had not named him for the saint but rather given him 'John' as a family name (both his grandfathers had been Johns), a name he bequeathed in turn to his first-born son. However, the coincidence of the dates combined with his shared name would have increased his sense of a familial tie on the spiritual level.

His use of the phrase "special devotion" to the saint means that Tolkien would have regularly included St. John in his prayers as an intercessor and in general held him in high esteem as a model for the Christian life. John, the author of the fourth Gospel, is known as the 'beloved disciple,' the one who reclined on Jesus's bosom at the Last Supper (John 13:23–25) and who was the only member of the Twelve to stay with Jesus at his Crucifixion, standing with Mary at the foot of the cross. One of the last words of Jesus before his death was to say to John, "Behold, your mother," and to Mary, "Behold, your son." From that moment, John took Mary into his own home (John 19:26–27). Since Tolkien had a strong devotion to the Mother of God and evidently put store by the 'Words' from the cross (see chapter 10), these factors would have added to his reverence for John.

John's Gospel is the most poetically written of the four Gospels, and it has a particular emphasis on the divinity of Christ; it opens with a passage that connects the Incarnation with the Genesis account of creation: "In the beginning was the Word, and the Word was with God, and the Word was God . . ." In fact, this specific passage was the Scripture that Tolkien would have known better than any other, because during almost his entire life, the prologue of the Gospel of John (John 1:1–14) was read as the 'Last Gospel' at the end of every Mass. (See Appendix B.) John is considered the patron saint of writers—another point that would have been increasingly relevant to Tolkien as time went on. St. John's symbol is the eagle, which in legend has the ability to look into the sun without being blinded; the farsightedness of the eagle and its ability to soar into the heights makes it an apt emblem of the most literary of the Evangelists. And in Tolkien's own literary output, eagles acquire extraordinary importance. They provide help when all seems lost: whether rescuing Frodo and Sam from Mount Doom, plucking Bilbo from a tree surrounded by goblins and wargs, or turning the tide at the Battle of the Five Armies, there is always a eucatastrophic turn at hand when we hear the cry, "The Eagles! The Eagles are coming!"

St. Bernadette

Another saint who was important to Tolkien was St. Bernadette Soubirous (1844–79). Bernadette was a French peasant girl who, in 1858, saw a series of visions of the Virgin Mary in a grotto outside her hometown of Lourdes. (See figures 20 and 49.) The beautiful lady, as Bernadette described her, prayed with her, revealed the existence of a spring of water that became the source of miraculous healings, and asked for pilgrimages to be made and a chapel to be built there. Most importantly, this lady identified herself as 'the Immaculate Conception': she was Mary conceived without the stain of original sin, a truth of the faith that had been declared a dogma of the Catholic Church just four years earlier in 1854 (and which the illiterate Bernadette knew nothing about at the time). This Marian dogma was important to Tolkien—the Birmingham Oratory was, after all, the Church of the Immaculate Conception, and he was married at St. Mary Immaculate, Warwick—and indeed he said that he had "a special devotion"[12] to the Feast of the Immaculate Conception.

Bernadette's story was carefully examined by Church authorities, all the more as this was a time of increasing skepticism in France, and clergy were more than usually cautious about putting forward claims that might turn out to be a hoax. But in 1862, the apparitions were officially declared to be worthy of belief—which means that the faithful may believe them, not that they must do so. A chapel was built, and by the early 1900s, pilgrims came to Lourdes by the thousands, with many miracles of healing documented. Bernadette herself became a nun; she died of tuberculosis at the age of only 35.

Tolkien's veneration for St. Bernadette is well-attested. Warren Lewis recorded in his diary in 1947 that Tolkien wrote him a "most kind and sympathetic letter" while he was in the hospital recovering from illness, "saying that he had invoked the aid of 'that child of Grace who is nearest his heart,' St Bernadette, to assist his own feeble prayers for my recovery."[13] In a 1956 letter, Tolkien referred to her as "beloved Bernadette."[14] Priscilla recalled that her father was "particularly struck" by one detail from an account of the saint's life: "Bernadette's shuddering at being shown various devotional pictures and her evident horror at the gaudy and twee representations of Mary after the reality which she had known."[15] That Bernadette should have been offended by these kitschy caricatures would have resonated with Tolkien's deep devotion to Mary and her Immaculate Conception and with his own keen sense of aesthetic propriety.

Writing to Christopher, Tolkien related a report, which he had just heard in a sermon, of a miracle that occurred at the Lourdes shrine in 1927. A young boy with tuberculosis who had *not* been cured at Lourdes was being taken home by his parents, who were no doubt sad and disappointed that their prayers for his healing had not been answered. As the train passed by the Grotto—the exact place where the Virgin had appeared—the boy went to play with a little girl on the train who *had* been healed: "then he came back, and he said, 'I'm hungry now.' And they gave him cake and two bowls of chocolate and enormous potted meat sandwiches, and he ate them!" Tolkien pointed out that the account of the boy's healing had the "plain and matter of fact" quality of all (credible) miraculous accounts. He went on to say that he was "deeply moved" by this story, "with its apparent sad ending and then its sudden unhoped-for happy ending."[16] This emotion, he explained, was precisely that of 'eucatastrophe,' an idea that he had recently developed as part of his essay "On Fairy-stories." It is "a sudden and miraculous grace: never to be counted on to recur."[17]

Reflecting on the story of the little boy's healing, Tolkien added a further comment about its theological significance: a story such as that has its effect because "your whole nature chained in material cause and effect, the chain of death, feels a sudden relief as if a major limb out of joint had suddenly snapped back." As a result, we understand that reality is both natural and supernatural: "this is indeed how things really do work in the Great World for which our nature is made."[18]

St. Thomas More

Tolkien also had a great appreciation for the sixteenth-century English saint Thomas More.* (See figure 48.) One of the great humanist scholars of his day, More was a lawyer and judge, a member of Parliament, and a writer who penned the satiric fiction *Utopia* as well as poetry, history, and works of controversy over religious matters. He served King Henry VIII in various roles, eventually being made Lord Chancellor of England at a most inauspicious moment: in the midst of Henry's divorce from Catherine and marriage to Anne Boleyn, after which the king broke with Rome and established himself as the head of the Church of England. More did not publicly oppose Henry's actions, hoping that silence would be sufficient. It was not. He was viewed as a threat to Henry's government and was required to take an oath denying the supreme authority of the pope. This he refused to do and as a result was imprisoned in the Tower of London. A year later, he was beheaded, declaring on the scaffold that he was dying "in the faith and for the faith of the Catholic Church, the king's good servant but God's first."[19]

More is an interesting figure in English culture, as he has retained a high reputation, or at least level of interest, among non-Catholics as well as Catholics. He was beatified in 1886 and canonized in 1935.

Thomas More was one of the patrons of the Oxford University Newman Society, and after his canonization, the University's Catholic Association raised funds for his statue to be placed in the chapel. Tolkien was almost certainly involved with this project to some extent; not only did he have an ongoing connection with the Newman Society (see chapter 21), but in 1939, the year that the statue was installed, he served as secretary to the Catholic Association.[20]

---

* He even used "Oxymore" as a pen name in the late 1930s, which John Garth points out "is (besides other things) a portmanteau of 'Oxford' and 'More'" ("How J.R.R. Tolkien Came to Write the Stories of 'The Rings of Power'").

In 1935, Tolkien's Anglican friend R.W. Chambers wrote a biography of More that Tolkien read with great appreciation; in fact, he said that despite the busyness of the exam-grading season, he read it twice, "and shall read it often again," remarking that More himself "must approve with celestial pleasure." Tolkien evidently already knew More's life and writings well, for he praises Chambers by saying that at times the biography reads "like his own self translated to our times." Tolkien found the book to be "almost burningly topical"; he evidently felt that the issue of freedom of religious conscience against a coercive state was a distressingly relevant subject. Indeed, since Tolkien followed both national and international news, he may well have had in mind the rise of communism and fascism, not only in Europe, but also even in England where, for instance, Oswald Moseley's British Union of Fascists was gaining a following. And so, Tolkien valued greatly the spirit of Christian humanism embodied by More and remarked that it is "a great refreshment to observe the same spirit reviving amidst learning yet again—at such a necessary and unpropitious time."[21]

Yet the biography was not just of intellectual interest to Tolkien; he also found it "overwhelmingly moving."[22] This is a strong statement. What might account for it? No doubt there are many reasons, but three that are worth mentioning here are as follows.

First, More's loyalty to the Church would have deeply impressed Tolkien, who regarded his own mother as a kind of martyr to the Catholic faith. Chambers makes it clear—as later tellings of the story sometimes soft-pedal*—that More was not just a champion of the freedom of individual conscience, he "died for the Papacy, 'suffering death in and for the faith of the Holy Catholic Church.'"[23] It was one thing for Tolkien to say, as he did, that he was "convinced by the Petrine claims": it would be quite another to die for that conviction as Thomas More had done. The moral challenge of More's story to Tolkien, as to any English Catholic, was sharp in the extreme.

Secondly, More's magnanimity toward his accusers springs vividly out of the transcript of the remarks he made in his own defense at his trial in Westminster

* Notably, Robert Bolt's play, *A Man for All Seasons*, which became, in 1966, an Oscar-winning film. Bolt openly admitted that he was "treating Thomas More, a Christian saint, as a hero of selfhood" (Robert Bolt, *A Man for All Seasons* [London: Heinemann, 1996], xvii).

Hall. Knowing that he was to be condemned to death, More told the Commissioners of the Court that he had nothing further to add:

> but that like as the blessed apostle St. Paul, as we read in the Acts of the Apostles, was present, and consented to the death of St. Stephen, and kept their clothes that stoned him to death, and yet be they now both twain holy saints in Heaven, and shall continue there friends for ever, so I verily trust, and shall therefore right heartily pray, that though your Lordships have now here in earth been judges to my condemnation, we may yet hereafter in Heaven merrily all meet together, to our everlasting salvation.[24]

Finally, Chambers's own largeness of heart would surely have struck Tolkien, for Chambers was writing as an Anglican yet could find it in himself to say that More's blessing "belongs of right to those of the faith for which he died, and that the rest of us can only have such blessing as poor Esau claimed, who had lost his birthright: 'Hast thou but one blessing: bless me, even me also, oh my father [Genesis 27:38].'"[25] This irenic approach doubtless contributed to the warm and frank way Tolkien responded to Chambers, which we will examine more closely in chapter 31.

Angels

We should now consider the topic of angels, some of whom, such as St. Michael and St. Gabriel, are (somewhat confusingly) included in the Church calendar alongside saints. Saints are human beings who are now in the presence of God; they are at present separated from their bodies by death but will have glorified bodies in the general resurrection. Angels, on the other hand, are spiritual, non-corporeal beings.

Scripture makes frequent references to angels, naming three: Gabriel, Raphael, and Michael. Gabriel brought tidings to Mary (Luke 1:26–33) that she would be the mother of the savior (Tolkien himself acquired the nickname Gabriel for a while as a schoolboy, as we noted in chapter 6). Raphael appears in the Old Testament book of Tobit and announces himself as "one of the seven holy angels who present the prayers of the saints and enter into the presence of the glory of the Holy One"

(Tobit 12:15). Raphael is known as the healer, and it is interesting to note that Frodo wakes up in Rivendell on October 24, which was, during Tolkien's lifetime, the Feast of St. Raphael. Michael is the leader of the heavenly hosts of angels in the final apocalyptic battle with the forces of evil (Revelation 12:7). Of those angels who rebelled against God at the beginning of creation and consequently fell from heaven, the chief is Satan. Tolkien would have prayed to St. Michael for victory over Satan at the end of every Low Mass for most of his life.

Once again, we can discover Tolkien's views on angels by the way that he explains the Valar. They are, he says, "created spirits—of high angelic order we should say, with their attendant lesser angels—reverend, therefore, but not worshipful."[26] That is to say, angels are worthy of reverence and honor, but they are not to be worshiped; they are not divine themselves but are creations of the one God. Tolkien would have been well aware that the word 'angel' means 'messenger' and, specifically, a messenger of God.

Catholics also believe that every human being is assigned a guardian angel (Matthew 18:10; Acts 12:15) who has a unique protective and guiding relationship with that person. Most Catholic children are taught to pray to their guardian angel; unfortunately, this devotion often becomes stuck at a childish level, especially in popular art that can be (as Bernadette herself found) distressingly gaudy and twee.

Tolkien was well aware of the temptation to misunderstand what an angel is. Writing to his son Christopher, he declares, "Remember your guardian angel. Not a plump lady with swan-wings!"[27] Far from endorsing the piously sentimental picture from popular art, Tolkien had a theologically robust understanding of what an angel is. As he put it, the human soul can always turn toward God, but he is also always 'behind' us, that is, supporting and sustaining us as created beings. Our guardian angel, Tolkien says, is found at the "bright point of power" where we are connected to God, simultaneously facing us, and also turned "to God behind us in the direction we cannot see."[28]

On another occasion, while in Adoration of the Blessed Sacrament at St. Gregory's (see figure 38), Tolkien had a vision, or "apperception" of spiritual reality, that brought him profound joy:

> I perceived or thought of the Light of God and in it suspended one small mote (or millions of motes to only one of which was my small mind directed), glittering white because of the individual ray from the Light which both held and lit it. . . . And the ray was the Guardian Angel of the mote: not a thing interposed between God and the creature, but God's very attention itself, personalized.[29]

He realized, as part of this flash of vision, that "the shining poised mote was myself (or any other human person that I might think of with love)." Tentatively, he suggested a possible way of understanding what an angel is. Just as in the Christian understanding of the Trinity, the Holy Spirit proceeds from the Father and the Son, as being the love between them, "so the love and attention of the Light to the Mote is a person (that is both with us and in Heaven): finite but divine: i.e., angelic."[30]

One more glimpse of his view of guardian angels is provided by a brief reference in a 1958 letter. He remarks that "only one's guardian Angel, or indeed God Himself, could unravel the real relationship between personal facts and an author's works."[31] Here he is neither being ironic nor speaking metaphorically, but, rather, offering a reminder of the limits of biographical-literary analysis by noting that human beings lack complete understanding even of their own inner lives. If that is the case about even one's own life, how much more so must it be the case about one's knowledge of other people. This is a salutary caution to everybody, and especially to the biographer seeking to understand a long-dead writer's faith and the influence it may have had on his works . . .

23

Charity and Forgiveness

One day in the early 1930s, while grading papers, Tolkien was relieved to find a blank page on an exam script and scribbled down the line: "In a hole in the ground there lived a hobbit."[1] From this unlikely beginning arose the tale of Bilbo Baggins, who is called upon by the wizard Gandalf to serve as burglar for a party of dwarves aiming to recover treasure stolen by the dragon Smaug. It was published in 1937 as *The Hobbit* and soon acquired popularity and the status of something like a modern classic.

The Hobbit originated as a children's story, with abundant touches of humor and, at least in the first edition, only a slight connection to his larger world of Middle-earth.* But it also dealt with serious themes: greed, revenge, self-sacrifice—and forgiveness. Near the end of the story, there is a falling out between Bilbo and Thorin, the leader of the dwarves. Bilbo has double-crossed Thorin (for a good reason), but Thorin is mightily displeased and calls his erstwhile colleague a "descendant of rats." How they forgive each other is something we will return to at the end of this chapter. Our present concern is to examine what Tolkien believed about forgiveness and the part it played in his life of faith.

He said in his later years that he "first learned charity and forgiveness"[2] from his guardian, Fr. Francis Morgan—a statement that merits our full attention. To begin with, it may seem strange that he should include "charity"—that is, love—alongside forgiveness. How could he have "first" learned love from his guardian when he had loved and been loved by his mother, Mabel? We can understand this better when we consider his precise choice of terminology. Tolkien was a man of warm emotions, frequently using the word 'love' to speak of his personal regard

* The key link to *The Lord of the Rings*—that the magic ring Bilbo finds is "the One Ring"—was a later development, not part of the original tale. Tolkien re-wrote the "Riddles in the Dark" chapter of *The Hobbit* for the 1951 second edition to bring this part of the story in line with the Ring as it had come to be in *The Lord of the Rings*. (See Anderson, ed.,*The Annotated Hobbit* for more details.)

and closeness to his wife, children, and friends, including Fr. Francis. The word 'charity' appears much less often, so it is notable that he uses it twice with regard to his guardian, both in Francis teaching him "charity" and in describing Francis's "astonishing charity."[3]

Tolkien described charity as a "Christian virtue" and noted that "charity must cover a multitude of sins,"[4] a reference to 1 Peter 4:8. The word is an older English rendering of the Latin *caritas* and Greek *agape*, and though it is often rendered in modern translations as 'love,' it does not refer to romantic love or love in general. Rather, as the *Oxford English Dictionary* explains, it is specifically "the Christian love of one's fellow human beings; Christian benignity of disposition expressing itself in Christ-like conduct."[5] It is described in detail in St. Paul's First Letter to the Corinthians as the highest of all virtues: "And now there remain faith, hope, and charity, these three: but the greatest of these is charity" (1 Corinthians 13:13, Douay Version).

'Charity,' *caritas*, *agape*-love, is not just a warm feeling but is self-giving, Christ-like love of one's neighbor, and is a duty of every Christian: "If any one says, 'I love God,' and hates his brother, he is a liar; for he who does not love his brother whom he has seen, cannot love God whom he has not seen. And this commandment we have from him, that he who loves God should love his brother also" (1 John 4:20–21). Charity, in this sense, is not calculating or self-serving; it demands nothing from the other but quite a lot from oneself. And so, when Tolkien referred to "the sudden miraculous experience of Fr. Francis' love and care and humour,"[6] he was using 'miraculous' in a fairly literal way: to indicate that these gifts were possible only through the grace of God. It was in this sense that Tolkien had to *learn* charity: self-giving love, which he received as a boy with such generosity from his guardian.

And it was not only charity that he first learned from Fr. Francis but also forgiveness, which is a much harder task than excusing or forgetting. We have seen that, as a boy, Tolkien had much to forgive. His extended family had rejected his mother after she became a Catholic, and he felt that her early death came from "a disease hastened by persecution of her faith";[7] his aunt May was the only family member who came to his dying mother's side; and after her death, his aunt Beatrice Suffield, showed "no affection" to him and burned all his mother's letters.[8] Possibly,

Tolkien also had quite natural impulses of resentment toward his mother and toward the Church—for after all, if she had *not* become a Catholic, things would have been very different. He might also have needed to forgive himself, as it is not uncommon for children who lose their parents to blame themselves in some way.

For all these reasons, Fr. Francis would have felt that learning forgiveness was essential for his young ward's spiritual well-being. Feelings of grief, loneliness, anger, and hurt were not sins but rather wounds to be healed, but if those wounds were allowed to fester, they could lead to hardness of heart, bitterness, even hatred: a breakdown of the charity to which all Christians are called.

It is remarkable, given the circumstances, that Tolkien was able so rapidly to develop a genuinely close relationship with parts of his extended family. Fr. Francis would have been watchful that the family did not try to undermine the faith of the boys to whom he was guardian. It would have been simpler and easier for him to have isolated Tolkien from his relatives; easier perhaps, emotionally, for young John Ronald to have written them off himself. But instead, Fr. Francis ensured that Tolkien spent school holidays with relatives on both his father's and mother's sides, the Tolkien, Mitton, and Incledon families.[9] These interactions were an embodiment of "charity and forgiveness," a demonstration in action that Tolkien had forgiven (or was endeavoring to forgive) his relatives for the role that he believed they had played, or may have played, in his mother's suffering and death.

He had to learn to forgive others and to forgive himself—and he had one further, perhaps even more challenging lesson. He had to learn how to *accept* forgiveness as well.

As we saw in chapter 10, Tolkien's love for Edith had brought him into conflict with his guardian. If he leafed back through his diary, he would have seen the entry in 1910 about receiving "a dreadful letter from Fr. F saying I had been seen with a girl again, calling it evil and foolish. Threatening to cut short my University career if I did not stop."[10] Thinking back on his Exeter days, he would have had the uncomfortable recollection that he had spent beyond his means as a student, such that Fr. Francis had to continue to subsidize him, and that he had fallen away from the good habits of faithful observance he had formed in his boyhood. He was well aware that he had been a source of trouble and worry, perhaps even anger, to his "second father"; he was nervous about telling Fr. Francis of his engagement to

Edith and later about their wedding date. Tolkien tended toward scrupulosity. It is easy to see how these guilty feelings and anxieties could have led him to keep his former guardian at arm's length.

And indeed, Fr. Francis might well have stepped out of Tolkien's life once his ward had come of age and his official responsibilities were completed. It would have been a less demanding course of action than trying to heal a strained relationship with his now slightly wary spiritual son. But instead, he persisted in keeping up the connection, showing through word and deed that any breach between them was, at least from his point of view, healed.

Tolkien recounted one such occasion in 1914 when the priest visited him in Oxford: "As for Fr. Francis, he was very jolly, quite content to sit with his breviary or paper while I worked & full of his usual kindly 'scandal' and rumours."[11] This ordinary scene is an indication that the relationship is becoming one between equals, between two adult men who know the measure of each other and are prepared to rub along together. Tolkien continues with his work; he doesn't stop to play the attentive host. And in that thumbnail personality sketch ("his usual kindly 'scandal' and rumours"), Tolkien is effectively saying that Francis is a bit of an old gossip, yet softening the picture with the qualifier "kindly." We have a picture of the priest and the young man sitting comfortably enough together, but wise to each other's limitations.

Francis undoubtedly realized that his three-year separation of Tolkien and Edith would not be easily forgotten, so he made an effort to show his support for the young couple. On at least one occasion, he chaperoned Edith on the train so that she could see her fiancé. They made a stop at Banbury *en route*, and "Father Francis insisting on buying Banbury cakes—the local delicacy—which were very greasy. The grease got everywhere and caused considerable confusion."[12] Edith would later recount this to her children, as it was so characteristic of Fr. Francis. He seems to have made an effort to put her at her ease with his generosity, and then made St. Philip Neri-like fun out of it when it slightly backfired.

Francis had been, and continued to be, a father figure to Tolkien, yet their relationship was changing.* Francis was having to cope with the somewhat painful

* A small but notable sign of the full healing of their bruised relationship appears in Tolkien's 1917 Gnomish Lexicon, a word-list in which he was working out the beginnings of his Elvish languages. Tolkien gave Elvish names to various people in his family, and the meanings of

reality that Tolkien's marriage meant he would be leaving his oversight ("for this reason a man shall leave his father and mother and be joined to his wife": Matthew 19:5). Tolkien was having to shoulder the responsibilities that accompanied independence, while still remembering to "rise up before the hoary head, and honor the face of an old man" (Leviticus 19:32). In short, they went through a natural if awkward period of adjustment.

In the Douay translation of the Bible that Tolkien knew as a boy, the petition in the Lord's Prayer is rendered "forgive us our *debts*, as we also forgive our *debtors*" (Matthew 6:12). As a young man, wrestling with obeying Fr. Francis's stipulation about not seeing Edith, Tolkien had written in his diary, "I owe all to Fr. F."[13] He could easily have continued through life with an emotional and spiritual sense of an unbalanced ledger, but Fr. Francis made it clear, through his actions, that he *had* forgiven Tolkien for his youthful intemperance; the account was cleared; there were no arrears to feel scrupulous about. In learning to accept forgiveness as well as to confer it, Tolkien opened the way for an enduring adult relationship with his second father.

On June 11, 1935, Tolkien learned from the Birmingham Oratory that Francis Morgan had died.[14] He felt the grief of the loss keenly, observing to C.S. Lewis, "I feel like a lost survivor into a new alien world after the real world has passed away."[15] Priscilla, who was six years old at the time, preserved a vivid memory "of the time of his death and of the sadness I sensed in the house, and especially in my father, without my understanding at that time what this was about."[16] Tolkien was unable to attend the funeral, but sent his eldest son as the family representative.[17] The old priest was buried in the Rednal cemetery of the Birmingham Oratory Fathers. In his will, he bequeathed £1,000 each to Tolkien and his brother: an extremely generous sum, more than Tolkien's annual salary at that time. He also gave a personal bequest to Tolkien: a clock that was an heirloom of the Morgan family, which he had gone to considerable trouble to have brought over from Spain a few years earlier.[18]

---

these names usually contained significance; they weren't arbitrarily assigned. Tolkien bestowed on his former guardian the names of *Faidron* and *Faithron*, whose meaning is suggested by the surrounding entries in the lexicon, such as *faidwen* (freedom) and *faithir* (liberator, Savior). The invention of languages was a profoundly self-expressive, creative act for Tolkien. "He composed the name of his guardian using roots related to 'liberty' or 'liberator'" (*UC*, 92–93). It was no small compliment.

Food and cheer and song

Fr. Francis was seventy-eight years old, the same age, Tolkien noted, that his own father Arthur would have been had he lived.[19]

Tolkien could look back with gratitude and without bitterness because Fr. Francis had become a beloved friend of the whole family. He had traveled to Cheltenham to baptize Tolkien's firstborn son John Francis Reuel, whose middle name was given in his honor. In the 1920s, when Tolkien had taken up his teaching position at Leeds, Francis regularly came to visit. One occasion went into family legend:

> [Edith] told the story of going with Fr. Francis on the tram from the suburb where they lived into the city. Fr. Francis was anxious to buy a present and knew my father was particularly fond of camembert cheese, which was quite expensive in those days and so would be a special treat. It is a very strong smelling cheese and this one was extremely ripe, so my mother said the smell was quite dreadful, so bad that everybody else got off the tram and they rode all the way home having a whole tram to themselves.[20]

When the Tolkiens moved back to Oxford, Francis continued to be a regular visitor; Priscilla, then a very young girl, recalled that "in spite of the authority and powerful presence that he conveyed, he was charming to me as a little girl."[21]

An incident in the early 1930s that made its way into family history shows clearly the fatherly place that Francis had in the Tolkien house. He was a guest at 20 Northmoor Road, and at breakfast, he took his seat "at the head of the table." Edith asked him which cereal he would prefer:

> [Fr. Francis] Morgan chose a cereal called "Force," and he was helping himself from the packet when he discovered Priscilla, the youngest of the family, crying inconsolably. They were in fact tears of rage, because the priest had inadvertently chosen the girl's favourite cereal, and she regarded the packet as hers alone. Edith, her mother, was cross about this apparent rudeness; Morgan, realising the problem, stood up and bowed

> to Priscilla. Handing her the packet, he said: "Did I take the young lady's cereal? May I give it back to her and will she accept my apology?" By doing this, she was completely won over and her tears ceased.[22]

He even joined the family on vacation. John recalled one such holiday trip to Lyme Regis in 1928, at which Fr. Francis amused the children by "producing a pile of marshmallows on top of an ant-hill as if by magic."[23] Lyme Regis was the very place where Fr. Francis had taken Tolkien and his brother for a holiday every summer in the years after they had been orphaned, with the boys not much older than Tolkien's own sons at that moment. It was a picture of a family healed and a fatherly vocation fulfilled.

Francis Morgan died two years before *The Hobbit* was published, having taught Tolkien so much about love and forgiveness. Perhaps it is due in part to the guidance and example of his "second father" that Tolkien could write such a moving passage as the last scene between Bilbo Baggins and Thorin Oakenshield, Dwarven King under the Mountain. The context is very different, but we will perhaps not be far wrong in catching the echoes of filial and paternal love and grief, and the truth that Tolkien had learned from Francis about the healing effects of forgiveness. The Battle of the Five Armies has been won, but at great cost; Thorin is wounded unto death. He calls the little hobbit to his side:

> "Farewell, good thief," he said. "I go now to the halls of waiting to sit beside my fathers, until the world is renewed. Since I leave now all gold and silver, and go where it is of little worth, I wish to part in friendship from you. . . . If more of us valued food and cheer and song above hoarded gold, it would be a merrier world. But sad or merry, I must leave it now. Farewell!"
>
> Then Bilbo turned away, and he went by himself, and sat alone wrapped in a blanket, and, whether you believe it or not, he wept until his eyes were red and his voice was hoarse. He was a kindly little soul. Indeed it was long before he had the heart to make a joke again. "A mercy it is," he said at last to himself, "that I woke up when I did. I wish Thorin were living, but I am glad that we parted in kindness.[24]

24

Men of Valor

In the same year that Fr. Francis died, 1935, Sir Thomas More was canonized by Pope Pius XI. As we discussed in chapter 22, Tolkien was keenly interested in More and had been reading a new biography of him, which he found deeply moving. More had been Lord Chancellor under King Henry VIII and after resisting Henry's authority on a matter of conscience, paid for it with his life. Tolkien remarked that the subject of More's life "seems almost burningly topical"[1] at that moment.

What was it about More that made him so burningly topical in the mid-1930s? It would seem that Tolkien had in mind the international situation and the need for good people to stand up before tyrannical authority, whatever the cost. Just two years earlier, Adolf Hitler had come to power in Germany. In Italy, Benito Mussolini was well established at the head of a fascist government. In Spain, the political situation was about to erupt into civil war.

Of these extant or looming perils, the most serious was the growing crisis in Germany. Tolkien did not mince words in denouncing Hitler, calling him "a man inspired by a mad, whirlwind, devil" and declaring that he had a "demonic inspiration and impetus."[2] "Devil" and "demonic" are not mere figures of speech. Tolkien had a firm belief in the objective reality of both angelic and demonic forces. Just as angels were not sentimental ladies with feathery wings, demons were not cartoonish, red-suited trident-wielders: Tolkien would have based his belief on (among other biblical warrants) Ephesians 6:12: "We are not contending against flesh and blood, but against the principalities, against the powers, against the world rulers of this present darkness, against the spiritual hosts of wickedness in the heavenly places."

Tolkien, who followed the news closely, was well aware of the social and political injustices that Nazi ideology was beginning to inflict on many Germans.

Even someone like C.S. Lewis, who made a point of *not* following the news, was informed or perceptive enough to write (in 1933) about "the iniquity of Hitler's persecution of the Jews," calling the German leader "as contemptible for his stupidity as he is detestable for his cruelty."[3] Both Lewis and Tolkien also derided Hitler for distorting Norse and Germanic mythology into a racist Aryan ideal. Tolkien confessed that he harbored a "burning private grudge . . . against that ruddy little ignoramus Adolf Hitler" for "ruining, perverting, misapplying, and making for ever accursed, that noble northern spirit" found in the tales he had loved all his life.[4]* In lamenting Hitler's corrupting effect on "that noble northern spirit," Tolkien adds, "nowhere, incidentally, was it nobler than in England, nor more early sanctified and Christianized."[5] The northern spirit became noble, in his view, precisely as it had been *sanctified and Christianized*: a process that Hitler's neo-pagan Aryanism was now "perverting."

Against anti-Semitism

But this private grudge was far from the only black mark that Tolkien put against Hitler. Much worse was what, in 1938, he called the "wholly pernicious" quality of the Nazi views on race, an issue that he was still alert to nearly thirty years later when he corrected an interviewer's association of Middle-earth with "Nordic Europe": "Not *Nordic*, please! A word I personally dislike; it is associated, though of French origins, with racialist theories."[6]

Tolkien was forthright in rejecting anti-Semitism, an attitude that is particularly notable as it ran counter to a strain of opinion that, even in polite society, was considered acceptable. In mid-twentieth century England, negative Jewish stereotypes were mainstream in fiction and popular entertainment, and outright discrimination was commonplace. In his biography of Winston Churchill, William Manchester explains that the martyrdom of the Jews under Hitler

---

* The *Oxford English Dictionary* reminds us that 'ruddy' is a euphemism for 'bloody,' in this context meaning 'damned.' Tolkien was prescient in seeing that Hitler would have a lasting negative effect on perceptions of his field of study. Even the term 'Anglo-Saxon,' which in Tolkien's youth was a name for Old English that attempted to convey its Germanic cultural and linguistic connections, has become so strongly associated with Nazi-influenced racialist views and propagandistic misuse of early medieval English history that scholars in this field increasingly prefer to use 'Old English.'

> would strip anti-Semitism of its respectability, but it was a quite ordinary thing to see restaurants, hotels, clubs, beaches, and residential neighborhoods barred to people with what were delicately called "dietary requirements." As late as the 1950s the *Pocket Oxford Dictionary* defined *Jew* as "1. *n.* Person of the Hebrew race; (fig.) unscrupulous usurer or bargainer. 2. *v.t.* (colloq.) Cheat, overreach." Contempt for them was not considered bad form.[7]

In 1938, a year before Britain declared war on Germany, Prime Minister Neville Chamberlain's policy of appeasement toward Hitler was in full force. Many of Tolkien's contemporaries were ignorant of, indifferent about, or even in favor of Germany's prejudicial treatment of its Jewish citizens. Tolkien, however, recognized early on that all was not well. Not only did he take a strong interest in international news, but in this instance, he had received firsthand insight into the situation. His old friend from the Oratory, Fr. Vincent Reade, had recently traveled on the continent, and when visiting the Tolkiens at home shortly before the war began, he offered "an eyewitness account of the maltreatment of Jews in Germany."[8]

In the summer of 1938, Tolkien received a request from a German publisher who was producing a translation of *The Hobbit* to supply a declaration that he was 'arisch': that is, Aryan (not Jewish).

Tolkien was having none of it. He made it clear to his publisher that he was, himself, entirely willing to "let a German translation go hang" if need be: "I have many Jewish friends, and should regret giving any colour to the notion that I subscribed to the wholly pernicious and unscientific race-doctrine."[9] He drafted two responses for his publisher, recognizing that he couldn't cancel the translation project without Unwin's approval. In the reply sent to Germany, "Tolkien refused to make any declaration of 'arisch' origin."[10] In the alternate draft, which seems to have been the *less* heated of the two, he majestically squashes both the impudent German publisher and the entire concept of Aryanism:

> If I am to understand that you are enquiring whether I am of *Jewish* origin, I can only reply that I regret that I appear to have *no* ancestors of that gifted people. . . . I cannot, however, forbear to comment that if

> impertinent and irrelevant inquiries of this sort are to become the rule in matters of literature, then the time is not far distant when a German name will no longer be a source of pride.[11]

In 1944, while doing an overnight stint as an air warden, Tolkien had an encounter that he found personally moving. His fellow warden, Tolkien says, "was Cecil Roth (the learned Jew historian). I found him charming, full of gentleness (in every sense*); and we sat up till after 12 talking. He lent me his watch as there were no going clocks in the place:—and nonetheless himself came and called me at 10 to 7: so that I could go to Communion! It seemed like a fleeting glimpse of an unfallen world."[12] Tolkien adds, self-deprecatingly, that when Roth came to call him, he was already awake and "discovering a number of reasons" to skip Mass, but Roth's arrival, "and his sombre glance at my rosary by my bed, settled it. I was down at St Aloysius at 7.15 just in time to go to Confession before Mass."[13] Tolkien, it seems, appreciated the compliment that his Jewish companion was making by taking his faith seriously despite not sharing his belief.

A glimpse of *an unfallen world*: one in which a Jew and a Christian could enjoy companionship with mutual respect. Tolkien's sense of the rightness of such camaraderie suggests that he was already approaching the question of Jewish-Christian relations in the way that would be officially taught in the Second Vatican Council. According to the 1965 decree *Nostra Aetate*, the Church "cannot forget that she received the revelation of the Old Testament" through the Jewish people and that "the Church believes that by His cross Christ, Our Peace, reconciled Jews and Gentiles, making both one in Himself." Furthermore, "God holds the Jews most dear for the sake of their Fathers; He does not repent of the gifts He makes or of the calls He issues. . . . the Church awaits that day, known to God alone, on which all peoples will address the Lord in a single voice and 'serve him shoulder to shoulder' [Zephaniah 3:9]."[14]

The council's teaching confirmed Tolkien's already well-established philo-Semitic stance, which he reiterated in 1971 when he pointed out that his name "is not Jewish in origin, though I should consider it an honour if it were."[15] Why would Tolkien have considered it an honor? Partly it was because, as we have seen, he

* That is, not only the modern meaning of mildness and kindness, but the older meaning that encompasses courtesy, nobility, and refinement as well.

respected individual Jews whom he knew, and partly because, of course, Jesus was a Jew, as was his mother, Mary, and all the Apostles. The history of Christianity has, alas, involved anti-Semitism, but it would have been utterly repugnant to the Evangelists and to the author of the majority of the New Testament—namely, St. Paul, a self-described "Hebrew born of Hebrews" (Philippians 3:5), who was greatly concerned with the right relationship between Jews and Gentiles and how the dividing wall of hostility is broken down in Jesus (Ephesians 2:14; Galatians 3:28).

This view may help us to better understand a complex element in Tolkien's legendarium. His initial creation of the Dwarves had its main and earliest source in Germanic and Old Norse stories, but in later years, he drew a parallel between the Dwarves and the Jewish people. He commented in a letter, "I do think of the 'Dwarves' like Jews: at once native and alien in their habitations, speaking the languages of the country, but with an accent due to their own private tongue."[16] In another interview, the host asked, "Did you intend that certain races should embody certain principles: the Elves wisdom, the Dwarves craftsmanship . . . and so forth?" Tolkien replied, "I didn't intend it but when you've got these people on your hands you've got to make them different."[17] The initial intent may not have been present, but as the composition process unfolded, a clear purpose emerged. Regarding the Dwarves, Tolkien said, "Wouldn't you say that in many ways they remind you of the Jews? Their words are Semitic obviously, constructed to be Semitic."[18] He went on to add, "There's a tremendous love of the artefact, and of course the immense warlike capacity of the Jews, which we tend to forget nowadays."[19] The Dwarves, with their great ability for craftsmanship in metal and stone and their capacity for fighting, represent a set of human gifts writ large in one of the races of Middle-earth—and also characteristics that are celebrated in the Bible.

We should remember how thoroughly Tolkien knew the Hebrew Scriptures, called by Christians the Old Testament: the portion of the Bible that predates Christ and is thus held in common with Judaism, in which the Jewish people are revealed as God's chosen people. The characteristics that Tolkien points out as Semitic could, of course, have been influenced by popular stereotypes of his own day but are more probably drawn from the Old Testament. Here we find the Israelites repeatedly having the experience of being both "native and alien in their habitations": in Egypt, as slaves under Pharaoh, and, later, in the Babylonian Captivity. We see the "love of the artefact" in such details as the elaborate divine instructions for the construction and decoration of the ark of the covenant, and the temple at Jerusalem and all its fixtures. And we see their "warlike capacity" throughout the Old Testament, particularly celebrated in the figures of King David and, later, Judas Maccabeus.

This latter figure is particularly worth noting, since 1 and 2 Maccabees are not included in Protestant Bibles and are today often overlooked even by Catholics. These books recount the heroism and military achievements of Judas Maccabeus and his brothers in leading the Jewish war of resistance against Greek aggression in the second century BC. The books of Maccabees were more familiar to the average Christian in Tolkien's day than they are now. For instance, in the first speech that Winston Churchill made to the nation after becoming prime minister in 1940, he ended with a direct quote from 1 Maccabees, without explanation, assuming that his hearers would pick up the reference: "Arm yourselves, and be ye men of valor, and be in readiness for the conflict; for it is better for us to perish in battle than to look upon the outrage of our nation and our altar. As the Will of God is in Heaven, even so let it be" (1 Maccabees 3:58–60).

It is also worth noting that *The Lord of the Rings* is surprisingly forthright about the existence of Elvish racism against Dwarves; the dwarf Gimli experiences this firsthand from the Elves of Lothlórien. Gimli's friendship with the elf Legolas has become so much a staple of popular imagination that it is easy to miss the significance of their interactions. Writing in a time when overt racism and anti-Semitism were commonplace, Tolkien shows two characters of different races, whose cultures have a history of conflict, overcoming stereotyped assumptions and becoming the best of friends.

The concept of the Dwarves was remarkably fluid as Tolkien worked and reworked his legendarium. In his later years, he came to reshape their origin story in a way that is consistent with an awareness of the similarities between his Dwarves and the Jewish people, and a desire to handle the material appropriately. In the *Silmarillion*, we learn that "Aforetime it was held among the Elves in Middle-earth that dying the Dwarves returned to the earth and the stone of which they were made; yet that is not their own belief. For they say that Aulë the Maker, whom they call Mahal, cares for them, and gathers them to Mandos in halls set apart; and that he declared to their Fathers of old that Ilúvatar will hallow them and give them a place among the Children in the end."[20]

25

Darkness Visible

From 1939 to 1941, Britain stood almost entirely alone against the Nazi threat, her cities bombed repeatedly by German aircraft. London was hard hit, as were Bristol and Portsmouth. Priscilla recalled that one night when her father was working late, as was his habit, "he saw a light outside his window and went straight to bed because he had thought he had worked through to the dawn and was worried that he would be too tired to get up and lecture the next day." The next morning, however, Edith told him "that Coventry is burning and he knew that the light he had seen had not been the dawn, but fires from the saturation bombing of the city by the Luftwaffe."[1]

Oxford, mercifully, was spared aerial bombardment; some said it was because Hitler wanted it for his capital. Though escaping the attention of the Luftwaffe altogether, Tolkien's neighborhood did not go unscathed. In 1941, a Royal Air Force bomber crashed on a training exercise only a few hundred yards away from his house in Northmoor Road, killing the entire crew and one of Tolkien's neighbors. Christopher and Priscilla witnessed the accident, with Christopher observing the event through his telescope.[2]

Britain prepared for the expected invasion. German U-boats were attacking imports by sea, meaning that, along with bombs from the air, the British people faced a shortage of food on the ground—something that Tolkien would have all the more keenly felt, having lived through the 'starvation year' of 1917. Evacuees from the cities were sent into the countryside and smaller cities; two women were housed for a short time with the Tolkiens.[3]

And now two of his sons, Michael and Christopher, were serving in the war, something that put him in solidarity with worried fathers and mothers all over the country. In 1940, C.S. Lewis told him he was "sorry to hear" Christopher was trying to transfer from the army to the RAF—where the life expectancy for pilots was measured in weeks. Tolkien replied, "Everyone else who joins it is equally precious to someone."[4]

Too old to be in the army again himself, he put in his time in the Home Guard, wishing that he could do more active service against the menace of Hitler and the Axis powers.[5]

The problem of evil

As the threat of war turned into reality, the situation would have been nightmarishly familiar. The Great War, now increasingly referred to as the *First* World War, was supposed to have been 'the war to end all wars'—but now it was all happening again, with the horrors of the first fully mechanized war not only renewed but expanded. Civilians had suffered in the Great War; now they were deliberately targeted in bombardments or systematically exterminated in German concentration camps. Tolkien was dismayed at the news of the invention of the atomic bomb, writing to Christopher that its inventors had been "calmly plotting the destruction of the world!" The fact that the bomb was in the hands of the Allies did not reassure him: "Such explosives in men's hands, while their moral and intellectual status is declining, is about as useful as giving out firearms to all inmates of a gaol and then saying that you hope 'this will ensure peace.'"[6]

The Second World War once again raised the theological problem of evil and suffering. As Fr. Martin D'Arcy, a Jesuit priest and philosopher whom Tolkien knew in Oxford, put it a few years after the Great War: "Why does God permit suffering, mental and physical, and the moral evil of sin in this world which He has created and governs?"[7]

Tolkien knew that there were no simple answers. Writing to Michael, then an officer cadet, he was forthright that the Germans, as people, had genuine virtues of "obedience and patriotism," and whose "brave men are just about as brave as ours"; but in the mysterious workings of providence, they are now, "under the curse of God," led by Hitler, whom, as we have seen, he considered as being under a demonic inspiration.[8]

He resisted any attempt to avoid the problem of evil by suggesting that suffering was simply a matter of perspective. We can see this in his reaction to the views of E.R. Eddison, whose stories Tolkien greatly admired at a literary level, even as he deplored their implicit moral philosophy. Eddison, who was not a Christian, suggested that evil has "something less than reality" and that suffering could be treated as "the imagined ills of a tragic drama," such that the death of a loved one "would be but a deepening of experience for you, if you could believe and know . . . that there *is* no death, except of the body in this transient and unsatisfactory life."[9] Tolkien declared this view "an evil and indeed silly 'philosophy.'"[10] His belief in the immortality of the soul and the resurrection of the body did not lead him to view suffering in one's earthly life as unreal or insignificant. As he wrote in his poem "Mythopoeia," "pain is pain" and "Evil is."[11]

Evil is: but that does not mean that Tolkien held a 'dualistic' view in which good and evil are equal and opposite. As he once put it emphatically, "I don't believe in absolute evil but I do believe in absolute good."[12] In saying this, he was stating the traditional Christian metaphysical position that evil has no independent existence but is always a distortion or a deprivation of something good. God is absolute goodness: "God is light and in him is no darkness at all" (1 John 1:5); he is "the Father of lights" from whom comes "every good endowment and every perfect gift" (James 1:17). Furthermore, the world as God made it is good: in Genesis, after he has created the world, "God saw everything that he had made, and behold, it was very good" (Genesis 1:31). As Tolkien said firmly, drawing a moral analogy with his own subcreated world, "There are no genuine Uruks, that is folk made bad by the intention of their maker."[13]

Satan (the fallen angel Lucifer) is therefore not an equal and opposite force to God; he and the other fallen angels are created beings who were, like all created beings, originally good. As Tolkien put it, the fall of Satan was "a rebellion of created free-will at a higher level than Man."[14] Likewise, Tolkien explains that Sauron, the demonic character in *The Lord of the Rings*, was not originally evil: "He descends into evil but he was not evil to begin with." He is, he says, fallen like Lucifer, "but he's several stages down from Lucifer!"[15]

The Lucifer character is off-stage in *The Lord of the Rings* but is a major figure in the legendarium: Melkor (later known as Morgoth) is one of the Valar, the archangelic figures. In the creation account in *The Silmarillion*, Eru, also known as Ilúvatar (that is, God), invites the Valar to participate in the unfolding of a great musical theme, of which he eventually declares, "*Eä!*: Let these things Be!" bringing into existence Arda, the created world of Middle-earth.[16] During the unfolding of this theme, Melkor repeatedly introduces discord into the music, and each time, this discord is taken up into a richer and more intricate version of the theme and incorporated into its increasingly complex and poignant harmony.*

After the creation of Arda, Melkor persists in his desire for dominance, eventually warring with the other Valar, sowing lies and discord among the Elves that leads to internecine war, making the orcs and other monstrous creatures, and laying waste to Middle-earth. Woven through all of this is the mystery of free will. Melkor chooses to take his rebellious path; likewise, Feänor and his brothers, corrupted by possessiveness toward the holy jewels, the Silmarils, have opportunities to turn aside from their ruinous course of action but elect not to.

One of the objections to the idea of an all-powerful and all-good God is that, if he existed, he would prevent evil from occurring. Tolkien's Catholic view was that while God does not create or do evil, he permits it to be done by his creatures, because he created them with the ability to make meaningful moral choices. Without the ability to choose, there can be no love; we would be only automatons or tools, not children of God in free relationships with him and one another.

Tolkien was clear about the metaphysical status of Middle-earth. When asked, "who was the One God of Middle-earth?" he promptly replied, "*The* one, of course!"[17] Eru Ilúvatar *is* God as Tolkien understood him (albeit depicted only as fully as the fictional world requires), and therefore, the moral structure of Middle-earth is the same as our own world. As Aragorn puts it in *The Two Towers*, "Good and ill have not changed since yesteryear; nor are they one thing among Elves and Dwarves and another among Men."[18] With this fundamental moral structure established, Tolkien took the opportunity to imaginatively explore the problem of evil via the question of free will.

Whether it is a world war in reality or the War of the Jewels in fiction, conflict has, in Tolkien's understanding, the same poisonous roots: the misuse of free will to act in selfishness, pride, and violence rather than selfless love and charity. As he wearily remarked in 1945, everyone is "free not to rise again but to go to perdition

* "It is one of the mysteries of pain that it is, for the sufferer, an opportunity for good, a path of ascent however hard. But it remains an 'evil,' and it must dismay any conscience to have caused it carelessly, or in excess, let alone wilfully" (*Letters*, 126).

and carry out the Fall to its bitter bottom."[19] Writing to his son Christopher, who was serving in the RAF, he hoped they would meet again soon and added that he felt certain their bond would "last beyond this life—subject of course always to the mystery of free will, by which either of us could throw away 'salvation.'"[20] For Tolkien, hope and trust in God did not take the form of pious wishful thinking.

Yet Tolkien also affirmed the mystery of divine providence, which is deeper than human understanding. In this he echoes St. Paul's words in his Letter to the Philippians: "work out your own salvation with fear and trembling; for God is at work in you, both to will and to work for his good pleasure" (Philippians 2:12–13). We see this paradoxical collaboration in *The Lord of the Rings* at Mount Doom, where Frodo actually fails in the Quest, at the last moment claiming the Ring for himself, but the Quest is nevertheless completed as Gollum seizes the Ring and falls into the fire. Thus Middle-earth is saved—and Frodo himself is saved—not through the assertion of creaturely power, however heroic, but by divine action, a providential intervention made possible because Frodo had previously acted toward Gollum in mercy.

Absolute good

Here, we should turn again to Tolkien's affirmation that he did believe in "absolute good." He was emphatic that evil is not attractive or ultimately powerful; it is goodness that has the ultimate reality and strength. In a BBC interview, Tolkien declared that "There isn't such a thing as magnificence in badness. It's a delusion."* Tolkien elaborated about the character of Sauron: "You never see him. Everything you know about him is pretty caddish and low in the extreme—mean. It's your imagination of this great dark shadow that makes it seem magnificent." Satan, he says, is nothing more than a "toad."[21]

During the Second World War, he brooded on the strange way in which evil *seems* to be stronger than good. He felt "appalled" by the "anguish" of the world at the present day: "the millions parted, fretting, wasting in unprofitable days—quite apart from torture, pain, death, bereavement, injustice." But, he goes on to say, we cannot know what is in reality happening *sub specie aeternitatis*—that is, from the

* He added that Milton, in his all-too-compelling depiction of Satan in *Paradise Lost*, knew this but had "failed" to convey it in his poem.

perspective of eternity; "All we do know . . . is that evil labours with vast power and perpetual success—in vain: preparing always only the soil for unexpected good to sprout in."[22] In a similar vein, he conceded that despite "the everlasting mass and weight of human iniquity . . . one knows that there is always good much more hidden, much less clearly discerned." Mysteriously, this goodness is seldom apparent in "recognizable, visible, beauties of word or deed or face" even when holiness is truly present. But, he adds, this hidden, obscure sanctity is really "far greater than the visible advertised wickedness."[23] Hidden goodness: visible darkness. But the small and humble is, ultimately, stronger and more lasting than the superficially great.

"Not many of you were wise according to worldly standards, not many were powerful, not many were of noble birth"—so St. Paul writes to the Christians in Corinth. "But God chose what is foolish in the world to shame the wise, God chose what is weak in the world to shame the strong" (1 Corinthians 1:26–27). Likewise, in Middle-earth, Elrond declares, "This is the hour of the Shire-folk, when they arise from their quiet fields to shake the towers and counsels of the Great."[24]

PHOTO GALLERY

Figure 1. Arthur Tolkien (1857-1896). A devout Anglican, he died when John Ronald was only four years old.

Figure 2. Mabel Tolkien, née Suffield (1870-1904). Her elder son described her as "a gifted lady of great beauty and wit."

Figure 3. The Anglican Cathedral of St. Andrew and St. Michael, Bloemfontein, South Africa, one of a handful of major buildings in the young, fast-growing capital of the Orange Free State.

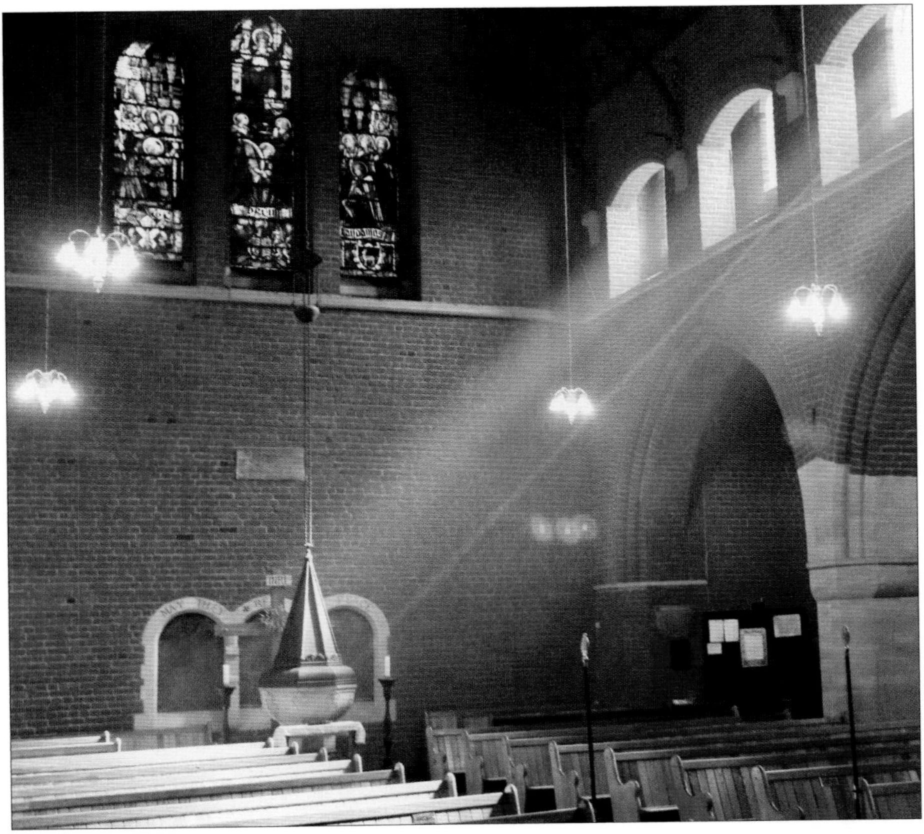

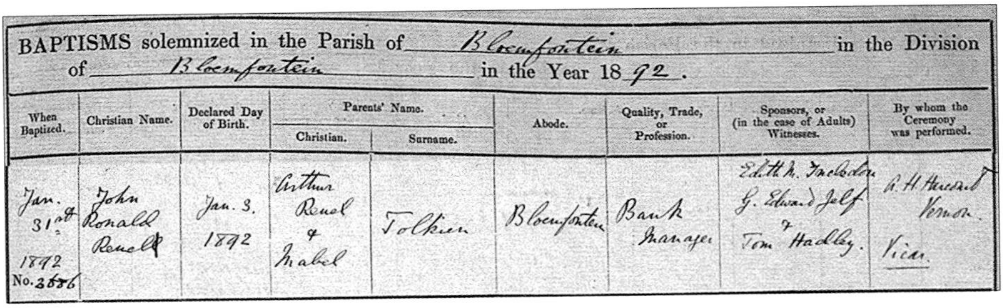

BAPTISMS solemnized in the Parish of Bloemfontein in the Division of Bloemfontein in the Year 1892.

When Baptized.	Christian Name.	Declared Day of Birth.	Parents' Name. Christian.	Parents' Name. Surname.	Abode.	Quality, Trade, or Profession.	Sponsors, or (in the case of Adults) Witnesses.	By whom the Ceremony was performed.
Jan. 31st 1892 No. [illegible]	John Ronald Reuel	Jan. 3. 1892	Arthur Reuel & Mabel	Tolkien	Bloemfontein	Bank Manager	Edith M. Incledon G. Edward Jelf & Tom Hadley.	R. H. [illegible] Vernon. Vicar.

Figure 4. The baptismal font in the Cathedral of St. Andrew and St. Michael, Bloemfontein, and the record of John Ronald Reuel's baptism there. His godfather G. Edward Jelf provided a strong link to the Oxford Movement.

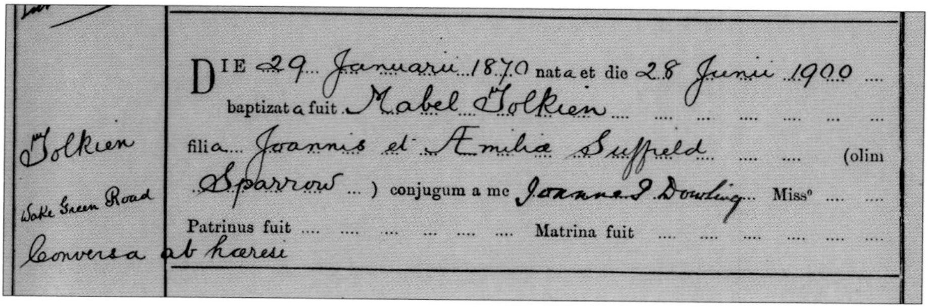
Tolkien
Wake Green Road
Conversa ab haeresi

DIE 29 Januarii 1870 nata et die 28 Junii 1900
baptizata fuit Mabel Tolkien
filia Joannis et Æmilia Suffield (olim
Sparrow) conjugum a me Joannes J. Dowling Miss°
Patrinus fuit .... Matrina fuit ....

Figure 5. The record of Mabel Tolkien's Catholic baptism, 28 June 1900, at St. Anne's Church, Birmingham. She is listed as *conversa ab haeresi* (converted from heresy), an indication that she was an adult entering into full communion with the Church from a non-Catholic background.

Figure 6. John Ronald and his younger brother Hilary. Tolkien never forgot the effort that his mother made "to hand on to us small boys the Faith," despite being "worn out with persecution, poverty, and, largely consequent, disease."

Figure 7. Tolkien lost his mother when he was twelve. Mabel died from diabetes, leaving her sons under the care of Fr. Francis Morgan, a priest of the Birmingham Oratory. It was he who chose her gravestone to be of the same design as that used for the Oratorian Fathers.

Figure 8. Fr. Francis Morgan. After their mother's death, the orphaned Tolkien boys had "the sudden miraculous experience of Fr. Francis' love and care and humour."

Figure 9. The Birmingham Oratory was founded in 1852, and there Tolkien came to know "many learned fathers." This 1878 photo shows the founder, Fr. John Henry Newman (front right) and, next to him, Fr. Austin Mills. Back row (right to left): Fr. Ignatius Ryder, Fr. John Norris, and Fr. Francis Morgan, who twenty-six years later would become Tolkien's guardian.

Figure 10. Shrine of St. Philip Neri in the Birmingham Oratory. Tolkien took the name Philip in his honor when he was confirmed in 1903.

The Latin inscription above the portrait reads *Exaltavit humiles*, 'He has exalted the humble,' words from the Magnificat, Mary's song of praise (Luke 1:46-55). Tolkien used these words in relation to hobbits, who, he said, were "subjects for 'ennoblement' and heroes more praiseworthy than professionals."

Figure 11. The Birmingham Oratory. Tolkien recalled that growing up here, he had the advantage "of a 'good Catholic home'—'in excelsis'": that is, a home 'in the highest.' (Photo: High Mass to celebrate Newman's canonization, 2019.)

Figure 12. Newman's memorial tablet in the Birmingham Oratory. The epitaph *Ex umbris et imaginibus in veritatem* ('from shadows and images into truth') finds an echo in Tolkien's 1913 work-diary at Oxford, where he wrote the phrase *Per Umbras Et Imagines* ('through shadows and images').

Figure 13. Edith Bratt, aged seventeen. Tolkien met her, a fellow orphan, in 1908 and, as he later put it, "we rescued one another" from "the dreadful sufferings of our childhoods." His story of Beren and Lúthien, whose love for each other endures despite great tribulation, reflects something of his relationship with Edith.

Figure 14. Tolkien, aged nineteen, during his final year at King Edward's School, Birmingham. Fr. Francis, concerned that Tolkien should gain a scholarship to Oxford and not be distracted while studying there, insisted that his ward give up all contact with Edith until he came of age. Their three-year separation began in 1910 and ended on Tolkien's twenty-first birthday when he wrote her a letter, resuming his courtship.

Figure 15. "Towery city": Oxford's skyline, showing the dome of the Radcliffe Camera, the spire of the University Church of St. Mary the Virgin, and the tower of Merton College, where Tolkien would become Professor of English Language and Literature. (From *Oxford Water-colours* by John Fulleylove, 1916.)

Figure 16. Tolkien began his studies at Exeter College in 1911. Of the men who matriculated alongside him, fifty-nine served, as he did, in the Great War and more than a third were killed. (Detail from a photograph of Exeter undergraduates, June 1914: Tolkien is holding on to the vine.)

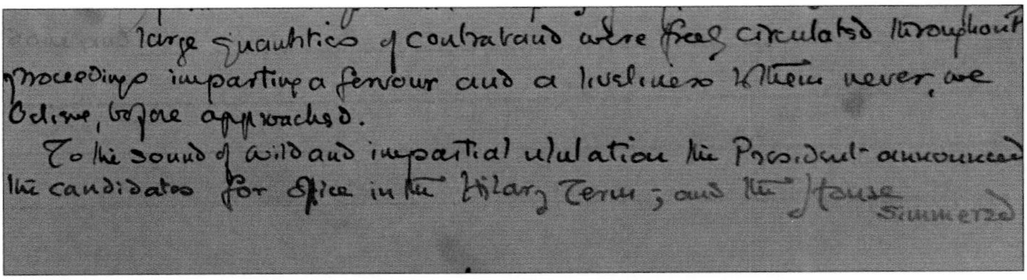

large quantities of contraband were freely circulated throughout proceedings imparting a fervour and a liveliness to them never, we believe, before approached.
To the sound of wild and impartial ululation the President announced the candidates for office in the Hilary Term; and the House simmered

Figure 17. As Secretary of Exeter's Stapeldon Society, Tolkien recorded a 1913 meeting in which "large quantities of contraband [i.e., "spiritous liquors"] were freely circulated throughout proceedings imparting a fervour and a liveliness to them never, we believe, before approached. / To the sound of wild and impartial ululation the President announced the candidates for office in the Hilary Term [Tolkien would be elected the new President]; and the House simmered . . ."

Figure 18. The chapel of the Catholic Chaplaincy at the University of Oxford (circa 1912), featuring a simple 'rood beam' upon which figures of the Virgin Mary and St. John stand either side of the crucified Christ. The unsettled state of the Chaplaincy during Tolkien's time at Exeter partly accounts for his admission that his first terms as an undergraduate included "none or very little practice of religion." After his 1913 reunion with Edith, however, he resumed the practice of his faith with vigor.

Figure 19. St. Aloysius's Church, Oxford; from Tolkien's student days onward, it was a recurring place of worship for him. Its reredos provides a visual reminder of the Communion of Saints. This photo shows the statues with candles alight at their feet in honor of All Saints' Day. Writing of the Valar, the angelic spirits in his fictional world, Tolkien remarked that the people of Middle-earth might call on their help "as a Catholic might on a saint."

Figure 20. "I am the Immaculate Conception": statue of the Virgin Mary, Lourdes, France. Tolkien had a devotion to the Feast of the Immaculate Conception and declared, "I attribute whatever there is of beauty and goodness in my work to the influence of the Holy Mother of God."

Figure 21. St. Mary Immaculate, Warwick, where Edith was received into the Catholic Church in 1914. To mark the occasion, Tolkien wrote a poem,"Magna Dei Gloria (Warwick)," and dedicated it to Edith. "Magna Dei Gloria" means 'to the great glory of God.'

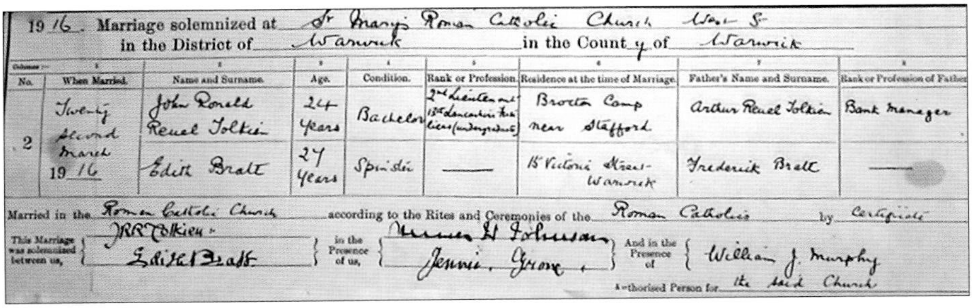

1916. Marriage solemnized at St Mary's Roman Catholic Church West St in the District of Warwick in the County of Warwick

No.	When Married.	Name and Surname.	Age.	Condition.	Rank or Profession.	Residence at the time of Marriage.	Father's Name and Surname.	Rank or Profession of Father.
2	Twenty second March 1916	John Ronald Reuel Tolkien	24 Years	Bachelor	2nd Lieutenant 13th Lancashire Fusiliers (unattached)	Brocton Camp near Stafford	Arthur Reuel Tolkien	Bank manager
		Edith Bratt	27 Years	Spinster	—	15 Victoria Street Warwick	Frederick Bratt	—

Married in the Roman Catholic Church according to the Rites and Ceremonies of the Roman Catholic by Certificate

This Marriage was solemnized between us, JRR Tolkien, Edith Bratt; in the Presence of us, [illegible], Jennie Grove; And in the Presence of William J. Murphy, Authorised Person for the said Church

Figure 22. The marriage certificate of J.R.R. Tolkien and Edith Bratt, whose wedding occurred at St. Mary Immaculate, Warwick, on March 22, 1916. As the date fell during the season of Lent, the service was a simple ceremony without a full Nuptial Mass.

Figure 23. St. John the Baptist, Great Haywood, where the new Mr. and Mrs. Tolkien had a belated Nuptial Blessing before he was deployed to France in June 1916. Edith would later describe with great amusement how the congregation thought that this meant they were a couple who had been living in sin and now the priest was making an honest woman of her. The pastor, Fr. Augustin Emery, would become the godfather of their second son, Michael.

❧ **Figure 24.** "The Last General Absolution of the Munsters at Rue du Bois" by Fortunino Matania (1916). It was difficult for Catholic soldiers to have access to the sacraments in the trenches; when it was not possible to hear individual confessions, the chaplain would offer a general absolution before battle.

❧ **Figure 25.** At King Edward's School, Tolkien and three friends formed the Tea Club, Barrovian Society; all four went on to serve in the Great War. They believed, as Tolkien later put it, "that the TCBS was destined to testify for God and Truth." Left to right: Geoffrey Smith, Rob Gilson, and Christopher Wiseman.

Figure 26. The Cross of Sacrifice in front of the Thiepval Memorial, Picardy, France, which commemorates the 72,337 missing British and South African servicemen who died during the Battles of the Somme.

Tolkien saw action on the front line near Thiepval. "By 1918," as he wrote years later, "all but one of my close friends were dead."

Figure 27. Lt. Tolkien, Signals Officer in the 11th Battalion Lancashire Fusiliers. He served on the Somme from July to November 1916, when he fell ill with trench fever. While on the front lines, he composed a poem in honor of the Virgin Mary, addressing her as "Consolatrix Afflictorum" (Consoler of the Afflicted), a title from the Litany of Loreto.

Figure 28. Exposition of the Blessed Sacrament at St. Aloysius's Church during the *Quarant'ore* (Forty Hours' Devotion). Tolkien considered the Eucharist to be "the one great thing to love on earth." He confessed "I fell in love with the Blessed Sacrament from the beginning—and by the mercy of God never have fallen out again."

Figure 29. In 1925, Tolkien was elected Rawlinson and Bosworth Professor of Anglo-Saxon at the University of Oxford. The move from Leeds back to Oxford came in the middle of a period when he "almost ceased" to practice his faith. Still, even then, he said he felt "the never-ceasing silent appeal" of Christ in the Sacrament and had a sense of "starving hunger."

Figure 30. C.S. Lewis, of whom Tolkien said, "But for his interest and unceasing eagerness for more I should never have brought *The L. of the R.* to a conclusion."

Figure 31. "The Life and Death of the Party": Hugo Dyson, a friend, colleague, fellow Inkling, and later something of an antagonist to Tolkien.

Figure 32. Addison's Walk, Magdalen College, where in 1931 Tolkien and Dyson had a conversation with Lewis that led to his Christian conversion and to Tolkien's poem "Mythopoeia." To the left is the New Building, where the Inklings would meet in Lewis's rooms to share their works-in-progress.

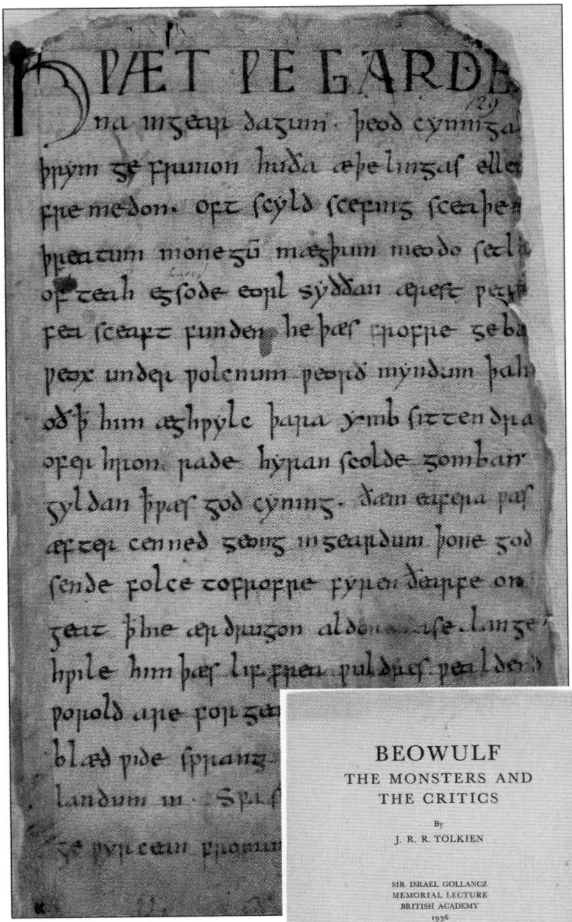

Figure 34. A sketch of Tolkien in the *Advocate*, the newspaper of the Catholic Archdiocese of Melbourne, accompanying a 1934 report (nine years after the fact!) on his appointment as Professor of Anglo-Saxon at Oxford. Not yet known as an author, it was his prominence as a Catholic academic at England's oldest university that was deemed worthy of comment in Australia.

Figure 33. The first page of the manuscript of the Old English poem *Beowulf*, which Tolkien translated in 1926.

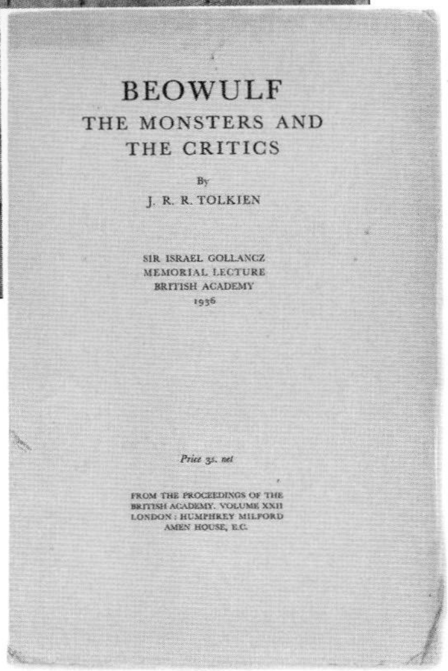

Figure 35. In 1936, Tolkien gave his lecture "Beowulf: The Monsters and the Critics," defending the literary value of the poem: "The significance of a myth is not easily to be pinned on paper by analytical reasoning. It is at its best when it is presented by a poet who feels rather than makes explicit what his theme portends; who presents it incarnate in the world of history and geography, as our poet has done."

Figure 36. Until Tolkien's appointment as Professor of Anglo-Saxon in 1925, there were only three Catholic professors at Oxford: (left to right) Francis de Zulueta, Regius Professor of Civil Law; John Fraser, Jesus Professor of Celtic; and Cesare Foligno, Serena Professor of Italian.

Figure 37. In 1934, Tolkien and his three fellow Catholic professors carried the baldachin in the first Corpus Christi procession in central Oxford since the Reformation. This photo shows just such a Eucharistic procession, emerging from St. Aloysius's Church (circa 1950).

Figure 38. St. Gregory and St. Augustine, Oxford, where Tolkien was a parishioner for over twenty years. It was here, during Adoration of the Blessed Sacrament, that he had a "sudden vision" or "apperception" of "the Light of God."

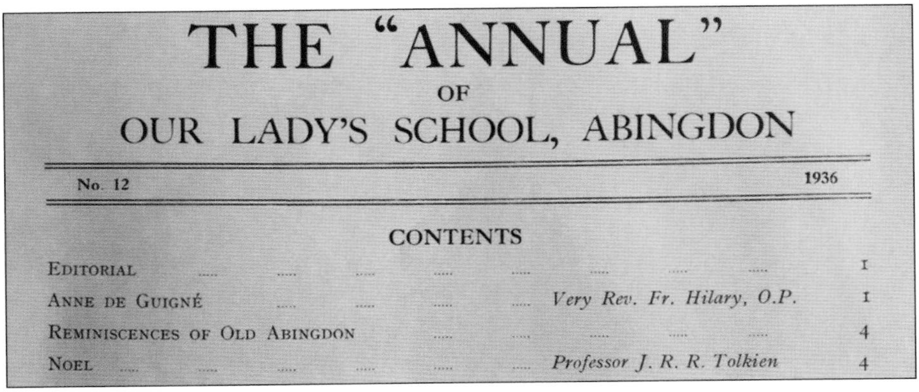

THE "ANNUAL"
OF
OUR LADY'S SCHOOL, ABINGDON

No. 12 1936

CONTENTS

Figure 39. Tolkien's poem "Noel," celebrating the birth of Christ, was published in the journal of Our Lady's School, Abingdon, in 1936.

Figure 40. Tolkien in his study. Regarding the act of literary creation, Tolkien wrote in his essay "On Fairy-stories" that "we make in our measure and in our derivative mode, because we are made: and not only made, but made in the image and likeness of a Maker."

Figure 41. Tolkien knew the prayers of the Rosary by heart and drew on them for his linguistic experiments, creating almost a full set of Rosary prayers in Elvish. This rosary belonged to G.K. Chesterton, a writer whose works Tolkien valued; he had a particular appreciation for *The Everlasting Man*, an essay in Christian apologetics, and "Lepanto," a poem about Our Lady of the Rosary.

Figure 42. Tolkien's illustration for the American first edition of *The Hobbit* (1938). Bilbo Baggins, employed as a burglar to a party of dwarves, becomes "A Thief in the Night" (according to the title of Chapter XVI). The story is no allegory, but this is an echo of the Biblical text, 1 Thessalonians 5:2: "The day of the Lord will come like a thief in the night."

Figure 43. Crucifix at St. Gregory's, Oxford, which Tolkien venerated annually on Good Friday during his time as a parishioner. It was given to the church in memory of Captain Basil Brooks, who died on the Somme during the Great War.

Figure 44. Tolkien gave a copy of *The Same Scourge* (1954), a historical novel about Christ's crucifixion, to his son Michael, pointing out for special note several passages that deal with Mary's sorrow at seeing Jesus put to death. The "scourging at the pillar" (John 19:1) is one of the Sorrowful Mysteries of the Rosary.

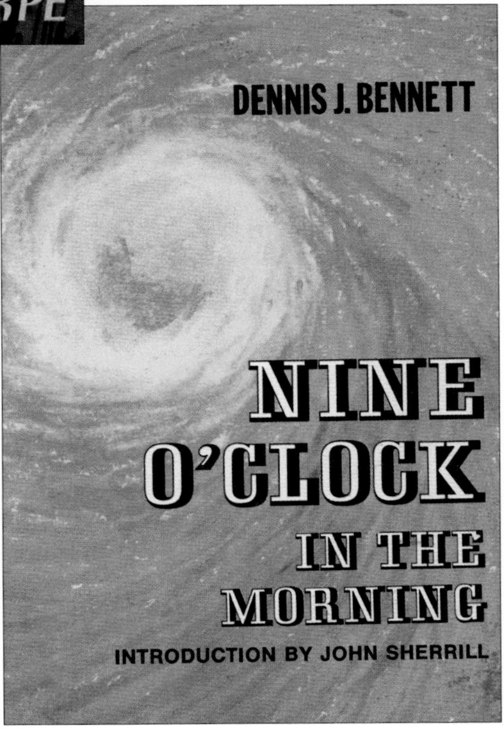

Figure 45. *Nine O'Clock in the Morning* (1970), an account of the Pentecostal movement in the Episcopal Church of the United States. Tolkien found it "very interesting both as a Christian and a lover of languages." Its title refers to the episode on the day of Pentecost when, after the disciples are inspired to spread the Gospel in other tongues and are accused of babbling drunkenly, St. Peter declares that they are not drunk, "for it is only nine o'clock in the morning" (Acts 2:15).

❧ **Figure 46.** St. John the Evangelist, by Vladimir Borovikovsky (circa 1809). Tolkien had a particular devotion to St. John. On learning this, C.S. Lewis remarked, "I can't imagine any two persons more dissimilar."

❧ **Figure 47.** St. Jerome, by Jacopo Bassano (1556). On his Italian holiday in 1955, Tolkien was "much moved" by seeing this portrait of the fourth-century translator of the Bible into Latin (the Vulgate).

Figure 48. St. Thomas More, by Hans Holbein the Younger (1527). Tolkien found the 1935 biography of More by R.W. Chambers to be "almost burningly topical" and "overwhelmingly moving." He told the author that he had read it more than once "and shall read it often again."

Figure 49. St. Bernadette Soubirous, the visionary of Lourdes, whom Tolkien called "that child of Grace who is nearest my heart." He invoked her aid "to assist his own feeble prayers" for the health of C.S. Lewis's brother, Warren.

Figure 50. Charles Williams, novelist, poet, and Anglican member of the Inklings. Tolkien referenced what he called "the wise words of Charles Williams, that it is our duty to tend the accredited and established altar, though the Holy Spirit may send the fire down somewhere else." In other words, Tolkien believed, as he put it, that "God cannot be limited (even by his own Foundations) . . . and may use any channel for His grace."

Figure 51. Blackfriars Priory, Oxford: the high altar. After the death of Charles Williams in 1945, Tolkien had a Mass said for him here, and served at it.

Figure 52. Warren Lewis, historian of France, older brother of C.S. Lewis, and, like him, a member of the Church of England.

On an Inklings' walking-tour in 1945, the group entered the Anglican parish church of Whelford where, according to Warren's diary, "we all felt that God dwells" and "there, to my surprise and pleasure, Tollers said a prayer."

Figure 53. R.W. Chambers, friend, colleague, and author of the biography of Thomas More that Tolkien found so moving. Tolkien was desirous that Chambers might be received into full communion with the Catholic Church and wrote to him saying, "I hope it is not an impertinence . . . these are doubtless matters on which trespassers are unwelcome . . . but the desire is so intense (that it may not wholly be suppressed) that those whom we love and reverence should share in that communion, which is no mere theological word."

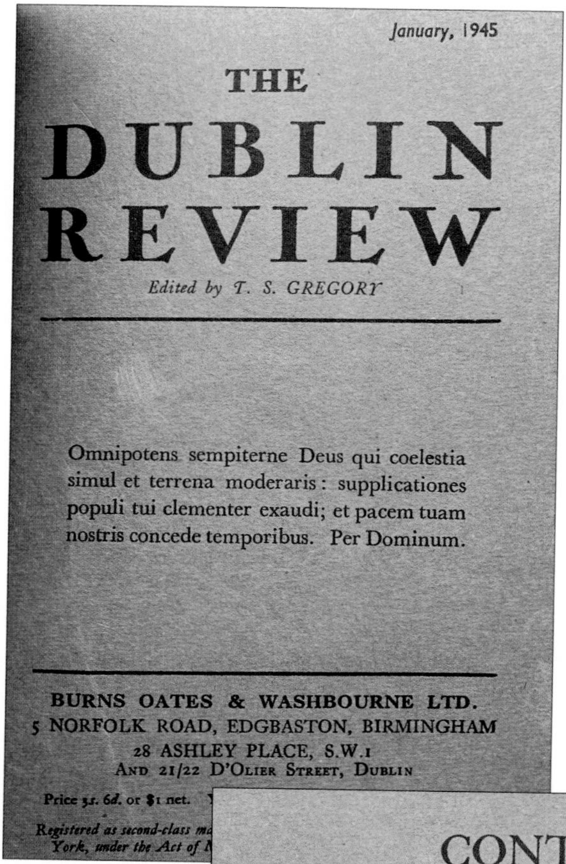
January, 1945

THE

DUBLIN

REVIEW

Edited by T. S. GREGORY

Omnipotens sempiterne Deus qui coelestia simul et terrena moderaris: supplicationes populi tui clementer exaudi; et pacem tuam nostris concede temporibus. Per Dominum.

BURNS OATES & WASHBOURNE LTD.
5 NORFOLK ROAD, EDGBASTON, BIRMINGHAM
28 ASHLEY PLACE, S.W.1
AND 21/22 D'OLIER STREET, DUBLIN

Price 5*s.* 6*d.* or $1 net.

Registered as second-class ma
York, under the Act of M

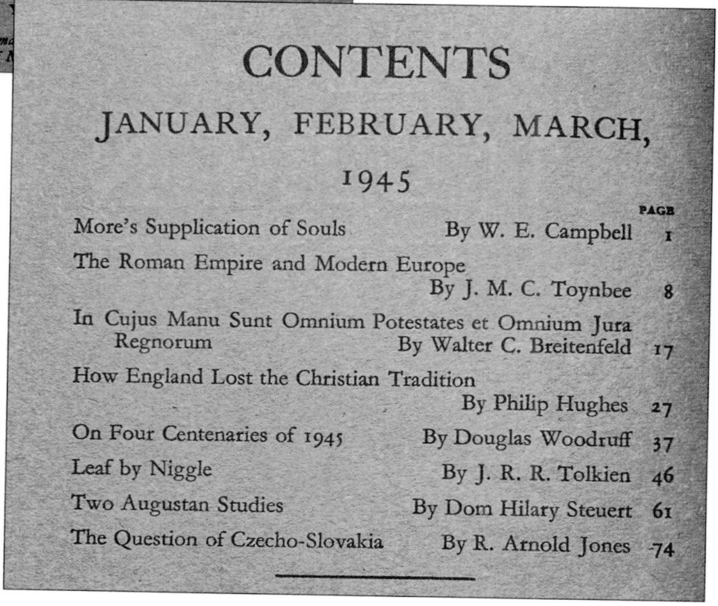
CONTENTS

JANUARY, FEBRUARY, MARCH,

1945

Figure 54. "My 'purgatorial' story," as Tolkien called "Leaf by Niggle," was published in *The Dublin Review*, the Catholic theological journal, in 1945.

It was written at a time when "I was anxious about my own internal tree, *The Lord of the Rings*." Unusually for Tolkien, the story "reached manuscript form, very swiftly, one day when I awoke with it already in mind."

Figure 55. Tolkien at Merton College, 1954, the year that *The Lord of the Rings* began to be published. In his view it was "a fundamentally religious and Catholic work . . . the religious element is absorbed into the story and the symbolism." He added: "It was written in my life-blood, such as that is, thick or thin, and I can no other."

Figure 56. The spine of his *magnum opus*, featuring his monogram of intertwined initials: J, R, P, R, T: John Ronald Philip Reuel Tolkien. The 'P' represents his continuing devotion to St. Philip Neri, whose name he had taken at his confirmation.

Figure 57. Statue of St. Peter by Arnolfo di Cambio, in St. Peter's Basilica, Rome. Tolkien stated: "I myself am convinced by the Petrine claims."

In Tolkien's day a replica of this statue was positioned near the door of St Aloysius's Church, Oxford, facing worshippers as they entered the building.

Figure 58. Pius X, who was Pope from 1903-1914. "The greatest reform of our time was that carried out by St Pius X," Tolkien wrote. "I wonder what state the Church would now be but for it."

Figure 59. Santa Fosca, Torcello, Italy, which Tolkien visited in 1955. Here, he said, "I first had the feeling . . . of having come to the heart of Christendom, an exile from the borders and far provinces returning home, or at least to the home of his fathers."

Figure 60. The Second Vatican Council (1962-1965) introduced liturgical changes that Tolkien struggled to accept. He wrote, "There is nothing to do but to pray, for the Church, the Vicar of Christ, and for ourselves; and meanwhile to exercise the virtue of loyalty, which indeed only becomes a virtue when one is under pressure to desert it."

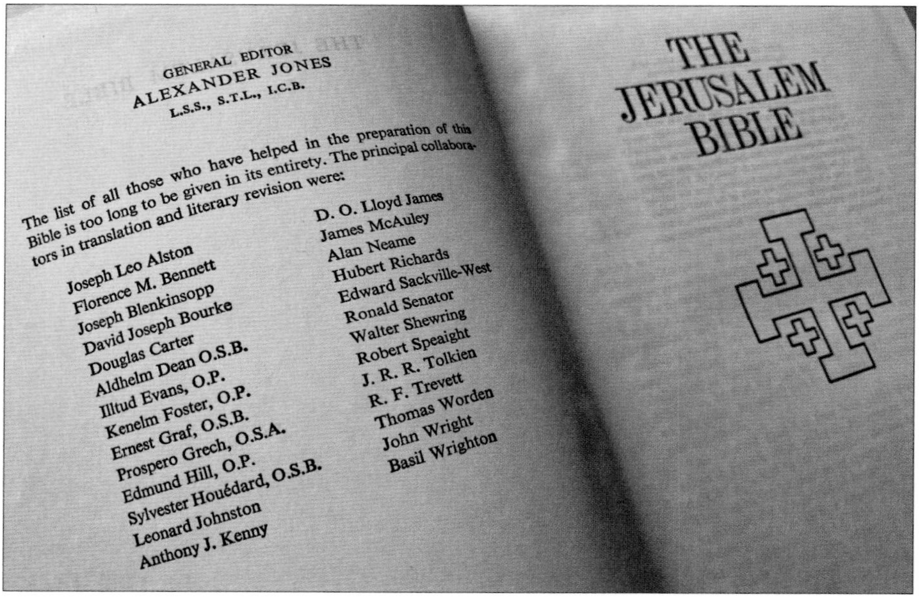

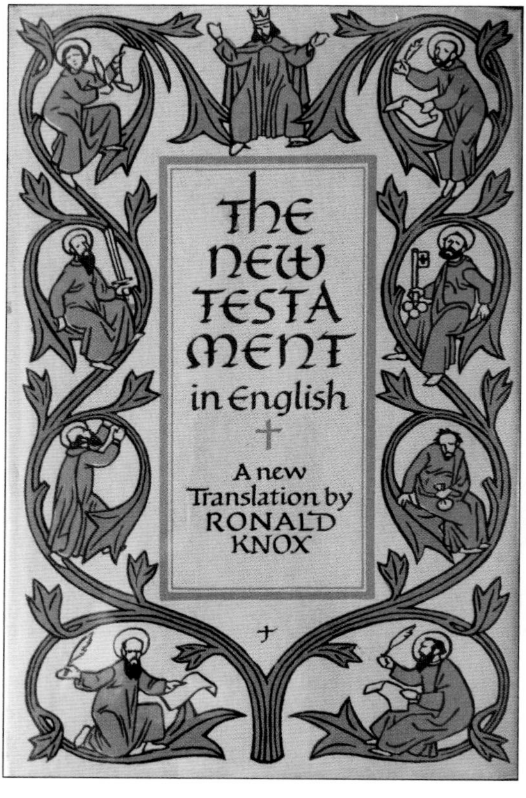

Figure 61. Tolkien translated the Book of Jonah for the Jerusalem Bible (1966). He remarked that the whale which swallows Jonah "is quite unimportant. The real point is that God is much more merciful than 'prophets,' is easily moved by penitence, and won't be dictated to even by high ecclesiastics whom he has himself appointed."

Figure 62. The New Testament translation by Ronald Knox (Catholic chaplain at Oxford, 1926–1939), whom Tolkien knew well; in 1954 they received honorary degrees alongside each other from the National University of Ireland. Tolkien disliked this translation, asserting that Knox "had written so much parody and pastiche that he had lost what little ear for prose he ever had."

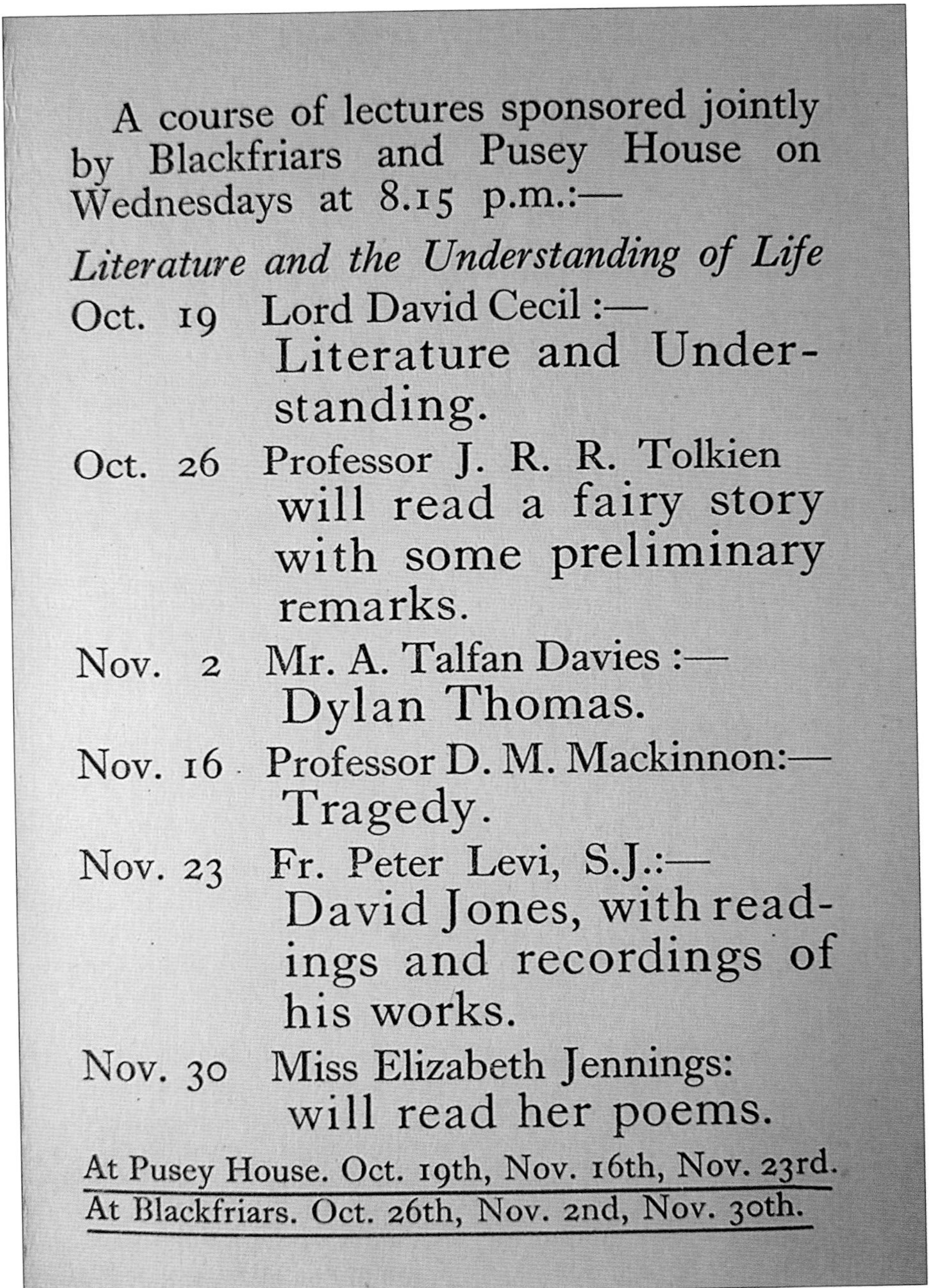

A course of lectures sponsored jointly by Blackfriars and Pusey House on Wednesdays at 8.15 p.m.:—

Literature and the Understanding of Life

Oct. 19	Lord David Cecil :— Literature and Understanding.
Oct. 26	Professor J. R. R. Tolkien will read a fairy story with some preliminary remarks.
Nov. 2	Mr. A. Talfan Davies :— Dylan Thomas.
Nov. 16	Professor D. M. Mackinnon:— Tragedy.
Nov. 23	Fr. Peter Levi, S.J.:— David Jones, with readings and recordings of his works.
Nov. 30	Miss Elizabeth Jennings: will read her poems.

At Pusey House. Oct. 19th, Nov. 16th, Nov. 23rd.

At Blackfriars. Oct. 26th, Nov. 2nd, Nov. 30th.

Figure 63. Blackfriars / Pusey House joint lecture series term-card (1966), showing Tolkien's contribution to this ecumenical endeavor: a reading of *Smith of Wootton Major.* Normal attendance at these lectures was about 150, but for Tolkien's event 700 people turned up.

Figure 64. The Church of Corpus Christi, Headington. Tolkien served as a lector at this parish after the 1964 reform of the liturgy allowed laymen to read Scripture lessons at Mass.

Figure 65. Our Lady of Częstochowa, the icon associated with Polish national identity. Tolkien felt a special affinity for Polish Catholics; in 1969, he disclosed that "Poland . . . is ever in my mind."

Our Lady of Częstochowa provided the subject of a poem by Hilaire Belloc, with the refrain, "This is the faith that I have held and hold, / And this is that in which I mean to die." In 1960, at the request of the former editor of the BBC's Polish news service, Tolkien made a copy of the poem in beautiful calligraphy. The following year it was taken to Poland and hung in the chapel of the Shrine of Our Lady of Częstochowa at Jasna Góra.

Figure 66. Two of the Stations of the Cross at St. Anthony of Padua, Headington (below). Tolkien helped fund the building of this church where he was a parishioner in his last years, and it was here that his funeral was held in 1973. So many flowers were sent from all over the world that they had to be piled up round the walls outside.

Figure 67. Przemysław Mroczkowski, the Polish academic and friend whom Tolkien helped financially, an idea that occurred to him as "an answer to prayer, for on the way from church on Sunday I had a sudden clear intuition that you were worried and in difficulties."

Figure 68. Fr. Louis Bouyer, French Catholic priest, theologian, and friend, who described Tolkien as someone who understood "how myths, even pre-Christian myths, could become the vehicle of Christian realities."

Figure 69. Clyde Kilby, an Evangelical American professor who helped Tolkien with *The Silmarillion*. Kilby recalled that "Every single day he would get on to scriptural things," and that Tolkien "spoke of his special regard for the Book of Luke because that writer included so much about women."

Figure 70. Tolkien and Edith in 1966. An interviewer recalled Tolkien's "sudden grin which would charm birds off trees," adding that he had "the most humorous eyes I've ever seen on mortal man."

Figure 71. The shared grave of "Luthien" and "Beren" in Wolvercote Cemetery, Oxford.

Figure 72. The last photograph of Tolkien (August 1973): in the Botanical Gardens, Oxford, by his favorite tree, a black pine. In "Leaf by Niggle," Tolkien described his protagonist's reaction to seeing, after death, the living Tree which he had labored all his life to paint. Niggle "gazed at the Tree, and slowly he lifted his arms and opened them wide. 'It's a gift!' he said. He was referring to his art, and also to the result; but he was using the word quite literally."

26

The Inklings

Tolkien was instrumental in helping his friend C.S. Lewis return to Christian faith in his early thirties. In chapter 20, we recorded how Tolkien, along with Hugo Dyson, talked into the small hours of one September night with the then non-Christian Lewis, convincing him to reconsider the story of Christ as a "true myth." As Lewis himself reported, this conversation "had a good deal to do" with his acceptance of Christianity.[1] Having played such a central part in Lewis's conversion, Tolkien now had all the more reason to invest in this friendship. The two men had known each other as colleagues in the English Faculty since 1926 and had discovered many common interests in the world of literature and language. Now that they were both Christians, they had a new and much more important bond.

After Tolkien's gesture of trust in asking Lewis to read the draft of "The Lay of Leithian" and Lewis's encouraging response, they began to meet frequently, and other friends and Oxford colleagues began to join them. Before long, these weekly gatherings took upon themselves a group identity. They called themselves "the Inklings" and met regularly from the early 1930s until Lewis's death in 1963. During its heyday, they met twice a week (at least during university term time): Tuesday mornings at The Eagle and Child pub and Thursday evenings in Lewis's Magdalen College rooms. Members had in common that they enjoyed one another's company (on the whole), that they were all scholars or writers or professionals, and that they were all Christians.* The group's name suggested both 'thoughts, notions' and 'those who dabble in ink.'†

---

* They were also all men; in those decades, sex-specific socializing was more common than it is today. However, the fact that the Inklings was a male-only group does not indicate that Tolkien never socialized with women on an equal footing. He was, in fact, a co-founder of 'The Cave,' a 1930s Oxford literary and social club that was open to both men and women and included among its members his English Faculty colleagues Dorothy Everett and Elaine Griffiths, both of whom Tolkien considered to be good friends (Priscilla Tolkien, "Memories of J.R.R. Tolkien," 12; *TCG:RG*, 1232–33; Collins, "The most expensive Tolkien book in the world").

† For a detailed study of the formation and functioning of the Inklings as a group, see Diana Glyer, *The Company They Keep*.

The Inklings were mostly Anglicans. At the core of the group was C.S. Lewis, who described himself (with hilarious understatement) as "a very ordinary layman of the Church of England."[2] His brother, Warren Lewis (see figure 52), was a frequent attendee, and it is from Warren's diaries that most of our information about the group comes. Warren, like C.S. Lewis, attended Holy Trinity Church, Headington Quarry, and even served as a churchwarden there for a period.* Alongside the Lewis brothers were their fellow Anglicans, Hugo Dyson, Lord David Cecil, Nevill Coghill, and Adam Fox, who was chaplain of Magdalen College. Two other Anglican members of the group pushed the envelope of orthodoxy: Owen Barfield, who, while still identifying as an anthroposophist,† was baptized in the Church of England in 1949; and Charles Williams, whose somewhat heterodox approach to Christianity included a not wholly suppressed interest in occultic rituals.[3] Despite differences in personal belief and practice, all of these men knew themselves to be under the large tent of the Church of England and using the same Book of Common Prayer. R.B. McCallum, the only Scot in the group, was (perhaps predictably) Presbyterian.‡ Certain other Inklings, such as C.L. Wrenn and John Wain, though Christians, appear to have had relatively loose denominational commitments.

Tolkien was not the only Catholic in the group. Other "papists," as C.S. Lewis somewhat provocatively called them, included the physician Robert Havard, the Dominican priest Gervase Mathew,§ Commander Jim Dundas-Grant, Colin Har-

---

* A 'churchwarden' in the Church of England is a layman who assists in maintaining order in church and looking after the church building and churchyard.

† Anthroposophy is an esoteric movement based on the thought of Rudolf Steiner. It was condemned by the Catholic Church in 1919 as incompatible with Christian faith.

‡ The Established Church in Scotland is Presbyterian, and the monarch, the Supreme Governor of the Church of England, nevertheless is bound by oath to maintain "the settlement of the true Protestant religion as established by the laws made in Scotland" as affirmed in the 1707 Act of Union between England and Scotland.

§ Tolkien had in fact met him as a boy when he visited the Mathews on a walking holiday with Fr. Vincent Reade in Cornwall (Grotta, *The Biography of J.R.R. Tolkien*, 30). Mathew read Modern History at Balliol College, Oxford, and after he became a Dominican in 1928 (taking the name Gervase at that time) lived at the Blackfriars Priory for the rest of his life. He lectured at Oxford in the faculties of Modern History, Theology, and English, and in 1947 was appointed University Lecturer in Byzantine studies (Hooper, *C.S. Lewis: A Companion and Guide*, 707–8).

die,* and J.A.W. Bennett,† who were both Fellows of Magdalen, like C.S. Lewis. The outspoken Hugo Dyson (see figure 31) once said (more or less jokingly) that he would resign his membership in the group if any more Catholics joined.[4] We will soon see that Dyson eventually became a source of real difficulty for the group's cohesion and especially a trial to Tolkien.

Despite Dyson's remark, the group was remarkably ecumenical. Because it had grown in large part out of the friendship between Lewis and Tolkien, there was never a sense that Catholics were merely tolerated. Though Lewis had his own difficulties with Catholicism that were occasionally uncomfortably evident, he was by and large exceptionally generous and friendly to Catholics, and his 'mere Christian' mindset made ecclesiological questions matters of secondary importance. Given that he effectively exercised chairmanship of the group—both because of his extroverted personality and because the Thursday evening gatherings took place in his college rooms—his attitude on such matters was decisive for the tone of the meetings. Sparks could and did fly between the Anglicans and Catholics, as we shall see, but Lewis would not allow disputes to destroy their collective understanding of themselves as being united in their adherence to the Christian faith, whatever their differences pertaining to the doctrine of the Church.

Lewis's generous attitude to Catholics was evident not just in his abiding friendship with Tolkien but in how he drew Havard and Dundas-Grant into the circle in the first place. Dundas-Grant was a Naval officer billeted during the war at Magdalen College, where he met Lewis, who generously gave him unofficial tutorial lessons in philosophy.[5]‡ Robert Havard, the doctor, was invited to the

* Hardie took a Double First in Classics from Balliol College, Oxford. He was made a Fellow of Magdalen in 1936 and became a Catholic in 1945. As Public Orator at the University of Oxford from 1967–73, he composed speeches in Latin to present those who were to receive honorary degrees. Most notably, he did so in 1972 when Tolkien was awarded the Doctorate of Letters. His speech referenced Tolkien's Middle-earth stories and "concluded with the hope 'that in such green leaf, as the Road goes ever on, he will produce from his store Silmarillion and scholarship'" (Hooper, *C.S. Lewis: A Companion and Guide*, 675).

† Bennett was a "devout" Catholic; according to Walter Hooper, he "devoted much energy and scholarship" to "the preservation of the old liturgy. His unofficial translation of the *Order of Mass* was published by the Association for the Latin Liturgy in 1974" (Hooper, *C.S. Lewis: A Companion and Guide*, 628).

‡ Dundas-Grant was educated at Eton before entering the Royal Navy. Hooper notes that "He was a devout Catholic and following his retirement, he and his wife leased a house in Iffley Road, Oxford, turning the garage into a chapel, and lodging in the property eight Catholic undergraduates" (Hooper, *C.S. Lewis: A Companion and Guide*, 650).

Inklings after he made a house call to see Lewis, suffering from the flu, and ended up having a lively discussion about philosophy.[6]

Robert Havard (nicknamed "Humphrey") is particularly notable, since he was one of the central Inklings—certainly more so than Owen Barfield, who despite being a close friend of Lewis, rarely attended meetings as he lived in London. Tolkien warmed to Havard quickly, once commenting, "Most doctors are either fools or mere 'doctors,' tinkerers with machinery. Havard at any rate is a Catholic who thinks of people as people, not as collections of 'works.'"[7] Havard had been raised an Anglican, his father being a vicar in the Church of England, and was received into the Catholic Church by Ronald Knox.* Tolkien would serve as godfather to Havard's youngest son, David, in 1943.[8]

"Fell enemies hurling deadly insults"

One might expect this diverse group of Christians to have kept the peace by a strict avoidance of any discussion of religion. Nothing could be further from the truth. C.S. Lewis's letters and Warren Lewis's diaries, as well as many recollections by those who attended, attest to the fact that 'hot-button' topics were part of the ordinary range of subjects.

Since Tolkien sedulously avoided engaging in public religious controversy, we might expect him to have kept an equally low profile among his friends, but in fact, he engaged in the dynamic, no-holds-barred conversations of the Inklings even on the topics closest to his heart and even when he was defending the minority position. The conversations that we know him to have entered into show his interest in matters of theology and practice outside his own communion. For instance, at a 1948 meeting that Tolkien hosted at Merton College, they discussed the different versions of the Bible and also of the 'Collects,'[9] short prayers that are used in both the Anglican liturgy (in English) and the Catholic liturgy (in Latin, at that time) but in different ways. At another meeting, Tolkien recalled having "some

* Havard took a First Class degree in Chemistry in 1921 at Keble College, Oxford. When he was received into the Catholic Church, he had to resign his membership of Keble, which had a ban against Catholics (finally lifted in the 1940s). He then became a member of Queen's College, Oxford, from which he later received his Doctorate in Medicine (Hooper, *C.S. Lewis: A Companion and Guide*, 679–80). He was also Ronald Knox's personal physician and friend; Knox dedicated his mystery novel *Still Dead* to him (Waugh, *Ronald Knox*, 330).

illuminating discussion of 'ghosts,' and of the special nature of Hymns."[10] On one occasion, Tolkien was part of a meeting that discussed the work of Bishop Ernest Barnes, an Anglican bishop who had just published his book *The Rise of Christianity* (1947), an attack on the doctrine of the virgin birth and bodily resurrection of Christ. At that gathering, topics also included "the extraordinary difficulty in interesting the uneducated indifferent in religion" and "how far pagan mythology was a substitute for theology."[11]

At another session, the Inklings discussed the objection to Christianity on the grounds that it is implausible that God would take any special interest in human beings on one tiny planet in the whole of the universe. C.S. Lewis recalled that, with regard to the argument based on the smallness of the Earth, "Tolkien said that the Earth might owe its importance in the eyes of God solely to the principle of the one lost sheep as against the ninety nine."[12] On another occasion, Warren recorded that the discussion addressed the difference between aesthetic distaste for and principled opposition to immoral conduct: "do we really hate the *sin* as we should do, or have we a mere disgust at the thought of the act?"[13]

Tolkien tended on the whole to be a quieter participant. Havard recalled that "Tollers' contributions were usually brief, but witty, and to the point, so far as they could be heard."[14] But Tolkien could hold his own in a fierce argument on a religious topic. On one occasion, Warren noted in his diary a meeting in which he and his brother were joined by Tolkien and Havard. They had a "long argument about the ethics of cannibalism. . . . Tollers very firm, though in a minority of one, that no circumstances—death or consent of the victim included—can justify it. Jack instanced the Communion rite without shaking him."[15] Without shaking him and, it seems, without offending him.*

It is interesting to note a recollection by Havard's son Mark of an Inklings session at which he was a visitor. C.S. Lewis launched a particularly heated discussion by declaring, "Will anyone here tell me what's so bad about suicide?" Lewis enlarged

---

* We don't know what Lewis's precise point was, but of course, "the Communion rite" is utterly distinct from cannibalism. Certainly, Catholics believe that in the Mass, the consecrated bread really, truly becomes the body of Christ, but 'substantially' rather than 'physically.' (To be more technical, Christ's body has its 'proper species' in heaven, where it is seen in a form that is physically the same as what the disciples said goodbye to at the Ascension. What is encountered in the Mass is his body's 'sacramental species.') Furthermore, the body that is consumed is alive, Christ's risen body. Cannibals, by contrast, feed on dead flesh.

upon the subject, producing "as strong an argument as he could for saying there's nothing wrong with suicide." Meanwhile, "Tolkien, who was a very orthodox Catholic, was fluttering in his corner" and soon engaged in "trying to shoot down Lewis's arguments." Mark realized that Lewis was simply playing devil's advocate to spark a lively discussion—and that he was also teasing Tolkien: "he was what they call in England 'taking the Mickey out of' Tolkien in particular."[16] It seems that Tolkien would reliably rise to the bait to defend the Catholic point of view, which is how Lewis knew he would be able to provoke him in this way.

Tolkien was not personally unsettled by the wide range of views of his fellow Inklings. With regard to Owen Barfield, he remarked in 1964, "I am not in the least alarmed by 'anthroposophy.' I have a friend who is an anthroposophist. . . . We have had many discussions."[17] But certainly, those discussions could get very animated—and loud (Dyson, in particular, was notorious for his noisy voice).* Tolkien described one meeting as "a most amusing and highly contentious evening, on which had an outsider dropped he would have thought it a meeting of fell enemies hurling deadly insults before drawing their guns."[18]

Sometimes the conversations touched on very serious points. In 1939, C.S. Lewis recalled a small gathering of himself, Tolkien, Williams, and C.L. Wrenn in which they tackled "the most distressing text in the Bible ('narrow is the way and few they be that find it') and whether one really could believe in a universe where the majority were damned and also in the goodness of God." By the end, they were in general agreement that "Our Lord's replies are never straight answers and never gratify curiosity, and that whatever this one meant its purpose was certainly not statistical,"[19] but Williams evidently generated quite a lot of conflict with his views. Lewis dryly remarked, "Wrenn almost seriously expressed a strong wish to burn Williams, or at least maintained that conversation with Williams enabled him to understand how inquisitors had felt it right to burn people. Tolkien and I agreed afterwards that we just knew what he meant: that as some people at school . . . are eminently kickable, so Williams is eminently combustible."[20]

Lewis recalled another occasion in which the group had "a furious argument about cremation." He went on to say:

---

* Dyson's continual bonhomie meant that he could be great company, but tiring. The noted Oxford wit, Maurice Bowra, on seeing him approach at a social function, once muttered, "Here comes Dyson, the Life and Death of the Party" (Wilson, *Confessions*, 9).

> I had never realised the violence of the Papist dislike of the practice, which they forbid. Neither Tolkien nor Havard, to my mind, produced a real argument against it, but only said 'you'd find in fact' that it was always supported by atheists; and that a human corpse was the temple of the Holy Ghost. I said 'but a vacated temple' and said it wd. be reasonable to blow up a Church to prevent it being defiled by Communists. They denied this, and said if you destroyed a chalice to prevent it being used for Black Mass you wd. be mortally guilty: for it was your business to reverence it and what the magicians did to it afterwards was theirs. I was surprised at the degree of passion the subject awoke in us all.[21]*

These lively and sometimes heated discussions were characteristic of all the Inklings' meetings, both the purely social meetings on Tuesday mornings at The Eagle and Child pub and the more focused literary meetings on Thursday evenings at Magdalen. It is those Thursday meetings where members read aloud from drafts of their works in progress, and to these and their particular features we now turn.

The men who met Thursday

As Warren Lewis explained, the routine was "unvarying." The Inklings would begin to arrive at his brother's Magdalen rooms around 9 p.m. When there was a quorum of half-a-dozen members, drinks would be poured, pipes would be lit, and C.S. Lewis would ask, "Well, has nobody got anything to read us?" At that point, "out would come a manuscript, and we would settle down to sit in judgment upon it."[22] This sharing of work among the Inklings was very important for Tolkien, who praised Lewis's talent for extemporaneous criticism.[23]

Tolkien's own work was read aloud here, first by Tolkien himself, and then in later years by his son Christopher, who had himself become a member of the group, as Christopher's reading voice was better than his father's. It was subject to the group's feedback, some of which, as we will see, could be not only "highly

* The Catholic Church's ban was based on respect for the body and as a counter to historically pagan practices of cremation. It was lifted in 1963, as at that point it no longer had an atheistic association and was recognized as more sanitary in areas with crowded cemeteries. The Church does still favor burial, and if a cremation takes place, requires that the ashes be buried, not scattered or kept as a personal possession.

contentious" but truly wounding. And Tolkien, in turn, offered feedback on his fellow writers' work, including on theological points, as when Charles Williams shared a piece discussing the phrase "give us this day our daily bread" from the Lord's Prayer. As Lewis noted, Tolkien "raised some philological questions" about the meaning of the Greek word for 'daily.'[24] Undoubtedly, Tolkien would have pointed out that the word 'daily' is what is known as a *dis legomenon* in the Bible, a word that occurs only twice.* The word used is *epiousion* (ἐπιούσιον in Greek script), formed of the prefix *epi-*, meaning 'around, above, about,' and *ousion*, which denotes being or substance. "Super-substantial" is how the Douay version renders it. The bread that Jesus taught his followers to pray for was, therefore, not just regular bread that one needs every day but exceptional bread, bread raised to a higher level of being—in other words, the Eucharist.†

Warren emphasized the unbiased nature of the discussion: "We were no mutual admiration society: praise for good work was unstinted, but censure for bad work—or even not-so-good work—was often brutally frank."[25] Robert Havard gave it the same assessment: the feedback was "frank but friendly . . . often profuse and detailed."[26]

Sometimes, to be sure, the "brutally frank" criticism could be hurtful. On at least one occasion, Tolkien found himself needing to bind up some wounds with Lewis after being overly critical of what Lewis had read to the group. He wrote a thoughtful letter of apology, saying, "I regret causing pain, even if and in so far as I had the right; and I am very sorry indeed still for having caused it quite excessively and unnecessarily."[27] Tolkien made a direct admission of his fault, which was that his frankness had not been balanced as it ought to have been by the friendliness characteristic of the Inklings' dynamic exchanges: "There may have been one or two of my comments that were just or valid, but I should have limited myself to them, and expressed them differently."[28]

Tolkien was firm, however, in saying that he had *no* objection to Lewis's forthright conversational style. Apparently, Hugo Dyson had been putting words into Tolkien's mouth, saying to Lewis that he, Tolkien, objected to Lewis's "loudness." This Tolkien denied: "Nay! That is largely a self-defensive rumour put about by

* In the parallel passages, Matthew 6:11 and Luke 11:3. In the Vulgate, Jerome rendered *epiousion* into Latin as "super-substantial" in Matthew 6:11 and "daily" in Luke 11:3.

† As the *Catechism of the Catholic Church* puts it: "Taken literally (*epi-ousious*: 'super-essential'), it refers directly to the Bread of Life, the Body of Christ, the 'medicine of immortality,' without which we have no life within us" (§ 2837).

Hugo." He went on to emphasize his confidence in Lewis's chairmanship of these gatherings: "We are safe in your presence and presidency from contention, ill will, detraction, or accusations without evidence."[29]

Victor Hugo?

This is the second time that we have encountered Hugo Dyson as a bit of an edgy figure among the Inklings—and he would arguably be a major factor in the ending of the Thursday gatherings, which faded out in 1949.[30]

Lewis and his brother, Warren, had certain issues with Catholicism, which at times were noticeable to the other Inklings. Havard's son Mark recalled that although C.S. Lewis was very generous-minded in his writings about Christianity, his upbringing in Northern Ireland meant that he "retained some of the suspicion of Catholics—not Tolkien or my father, but Catholics in general. 'You never really can trust a Catholic' was the sort of sentiment, and he let it slip every now and then, and that offended Tolkien and my father." But Mark Havard did not feel that it was intentional: it was a "sort of insensitivity on his part according to my father and Tolkien," and he makes the observation that, in turn, "Lewis would have said they were oversensitive and he was just being himself."[31]

Dyson, on the other hand, was increasingly anti-Catholic, an attitude that showed itself in more than occasional insensitivity in his choice of words. In 1946, Warren Lewis noted in his diary that he felt "dismay" at J.A.W. Bennett joining the Inklings, in part because he was worried about Dyson's reaction to another Catholic in the group.[32] As it happens, Bennett was not yet a Catholic at that point, but Warren had observed a genuine, and growing, problem.

Dyson disliked Tolkien's *magnum opus* and did not keep his views to himself. He took to exercising an effective veto on any reading of *The Lord of the Rings* whenever Tolkien brought any passages to share, often in an aggressive manner.[33] On at least one occasion, when Tolkien pulled out a manuscript chapter and prepared to read, Dyson, who had been lolling about on a nearby sofa, shouted, "Oh God, not another f-ing elf!"[34] This is not the brutally frank but helpful criticism that Warren described but a vulgar expression of scorn that was certain to wound. Tolkien took Dyson's opposition hard; Christopher later recalled vividly "my father's pain, his shyness" in the face of such antagonism. Lewis tried to intervene when he could, saying, "Shut up, Hugo. . . . Come on Tollers,"[35] but it was no use. Not only did Tolkien not begin reading if Dyson was there, if he had already begun and Dyson arrived late, he would simply stop and put the manuscript away.*

Curiously, although Warren Lewis remarked on how "unfair" it was, Dyson's 'veto' of Tolkien was allowed to continue. Dyson had at various times threatened to quit the Inklings if any more papists became members—but he did not quit; instead, he was victorious in silencing the most prominent Catholic in the group.†

Nor was the negative effect limited to Tolkien. Diana Glyer, in her study of the Inklings as creative collaborators, suggests that in "impeding the participation" of one of its members, Dyson was "attacking the raison d'être of the group . . . eroding its spirit."[36] The tension between Dyson and Tolkien certainly damaged the circle's *esprit de corps* and may have contributed to the ebbing away of the Thursday gatherings in late 1949. It is a particularly sad irony since it was Dyson and Tolkien together who had been instrumental in Lewis's conversion to Christianity and hence to the creation of the Inklings in the first place.

Whatever the internal tensions of the group, its fruitfulness and its long-term cultural impact cannot be denied, for it was only Lewis's endless encouragement of Tolkien, driven at times to the point of nagging, that convinced him there would be an audience for "the new Hobbit" (i.e., *The Lord of the Rings*). And since that epic work would go on to acquire a reputation as one of the greatest literary products of the twentieth century, the importance of the Inklings as a testing ground or incubator, and of Lewis in particular as a literary 'mid-wife,' can hardly be overestimated.

Let the last word go to a junior member of the Inklings, John Wain, who wrote in his memoir *Sprightly Running*:

---

* Still, at times Tolkien managed to give (almost) as good as he got. When Lewis read aloud draft chapters of what would become *The Great Divorce*, but which at that point was provisionally entitled *Who Goes Home?*, Tolkien landed a thwacking blow on the head of his tormentor. "Hugo was there: rather tired-looking, but reasonably noisy," Tolkien reported to Christopher; "[we heard] some excerpts from C.S.L.'s 'Who Goes Home?'—a book on Hell, which I suggested should be called rather 'Hugo's Home'" (*Letters*, 83).

† Philip and Carol Zaleski observe that Dyson "was continually irked by Tolkien's religion," and suggest, "It may be that his disdain for *The Lord of the Rings*, which grew pronounced as the years passed, originated in animosity (conscious or not) to its Catholic undercurrents" (*The Fellowship*, 342).

I can see the room so clearly now, the electric fire pumping heat into the dank air, the faded screen that broke some of the keener draughts, the enamel beer-jug on the table, the well-worn sofa and armchairs, and the men drifting in . . . leaving overcoats and hats in any corner and coming over to warm their hands before finding a chair. There was no fixed etiquette, but the rudimentary honours would be done partly by Lewis and partly by his brother. . . . Sometimes, when the less vital members of the circle were in a big majority the evening would fall flat; but the best of them were as good as anything I shall live to see. [37]

27

Praises

So far in this account of Tolkien's faith, we have considered his views on some dark and difficult topics: evil, sin, suffering, repentance. Now we turn to explore a happier theme: his adult practice of prayer and praise. We have seen, in chapters 5 and 16, certain key aspects of Tolkien's prayer life as a boy and a young man. But a healthy spirituality does not stay fixed on boyhood prayers, however meaningful and formative those are. Rather, it grows and develops, and in this chapter, we will survey some of those developments.

We get a glimpse of Tolkien's mature prayer life from Clyde Kilby, who spent the summer of 1966 helping him assemble the materials for the *Silmarillion*. Kilby recalls that Tolkien "told me that he had many times been given a story as an answer to prayer. Mrs. Tolkien joined him in remarking that one of their children had been cured, as they firmly believed, of a heart ailment, through prayer."[1]

Tolkien frequently assured correspondents, such as his son Christopher, of his prayers for them.[2] On the day of Charles Williams's death, he wrote to his widow, Michal: "of course I shall have you all in my prayers immediately and continually."[3] He was also grateful for other people's intercessions, thanking Katherine Farrer for her prayers and noting, late in life, how he is "benefitting from the prayers of others."[4] He took seriously the idea that his actions could be the answer to another's prayer, and in very practical mundane matters too, including money worries; for instance, he offered £30 in financial assistance to Przemysław Mroczkowski, a Polish academic and fellow Catholic whom Tolkien had befriended, and was glad to have it accepted, explaining that he believes it will be "an answer to prayer, for on the way from church on Sunday I had a sudden clear intuition that you were worried and in difficulties."[5]

Of course, we have no access to the private, informal, and extempore prayers that Tolkien uttered on innumerable occasions throughout his life. What we have to focus on is what he said about the prayers that appear in Scripture and that have developed in the Christian tradition. But we should not conclude from this that Tolkien's prayer life was always "by the book" and unspontaneous. Clyde Kilby recalled that Tolkien "commonly referred to Christ as 'our Lord' and was much upset when he heard others address God as though He were the Lord Mayor."[6] In other words, Tolkien believed that although God is 'the Lord' and to be approached with profound reverence, he is principally '*our* Lord.' We can and should have a loving confidence before God as our Father, and indeed Christ as our Brother. The relationship is familial, not just formal.

"Gloria in excelsis Deo"

A characteristic element of Tolkien's adult prayer life is his emphasis on what he calls the 'praises,' that is, prayers that offer praise and thanksgiving to God; he said to Christopher, "I use them much."[7] Indeed, he held that "the chief purpose of life, for any one of us, is to increase according to our capacity our knowledge of God by all the means we have, and to be moved by it to praise and thanks."[8] He recorded his own preference for using them in Latin; nonetheless, he readily quoted from some of these 'praises' in English to a young correspondent who would not have known Latin. The particular prayers that provided him with "words of joy" and as means to give "praise and thanks"[9] are likely to be unfamiliar to many readers, so it is worth considering each one. (See Appendix B.) One of these, the Glory Be, we have discussed in chapter 5. Now we turn to consider the others.

One of the prayers he singles out is the *Gloria in Excelsis Deo*. Often just called the *Gloria*, this is an ancient hymn to God as Father, Son, and Holy Spirit that is sung or said at every Sunday Mass except during the more somber seasons of Advent and Lent. It begins, "Glory be to God on high, and on earth peace to men of good will. We praise thee; we bless thee; we adore thee; we glorify thee." Tolkien made frequent use of portions of the Gloria as a text for his Elvish transliterations and did some work on translating the opening phrase of it into Quenya as well.[10]

He also appreciated the "Song of the Three Children"[11] from the Old Testament book of Daniel.* Daniel's three companions, Shadrach, Meshach, and Abednego, have been thrown into a fiery furnace because they refused to worship a golden image set up by King Nebuchadnezzar, but they are miraculously unharmed. As a result, the three men give praise and thanks to God. A portion of this prayer is used as a canticle (by definition a sung prayer, though it can be said) in the Daily Office (daily prayer) of the Catholic Church, so Tolkien would have been familiar with its use as a prayer of thanksgiving.

Tolkien gives special mention to three of the Psalms. He was "specially fond" of Psalm 113,[12] which is known as the *Laudate Pueri Dominum*. It begins, "Praise the Lord, ye children: praise ye the name of the Lord," and at only nine verses, is short enough to memorize easily, as he suggests. He also recommends for memorization Psalm 117, the *Laudate Dominum*, which is only two lines long, the shortest of all the Psalms: "O praise the Lord, all ye gentiles: praise him, all ye people. For his mercy is confirmed upon us: and the truth of the Lord endureth for ever."[13] Lastly, Psalm 148, *Laudate Dominum de caelis*, is a song of praise in which, so Tolkien explains, we "call on all created things to join in our chorus, speaking on their behalf."[14] As the Psalm has it:

> Praise the Lord from the earth, ye dragons, and all ye deeps:
> Fire, hail, snow, ice, stormy winds, which fulfil his word:
> Mountains and all hills: fruitful trees and all cedars:
> Beasts and all cattle: serpents and feathered fowls . . .[15]

In one letter, after quoting "PRAISE THE LORD" (he puts it all in capital letters) from this Psalm, Tolkien follows with his own evocative paraphrase, which includes an exhortation for praise from "all orchards and forests."[16] Tolkien's singling out of orchards and forests from the many invocations in this prayer, which calls on *all* of creation to praise God, reflects his lifelong love of trees.

---

* This song is omitted from Protestant editions of the Bible on account of the passage where it occurs not being included in the surviving Hebrew manuscripts, but as it appears in the Greek manuscripts (which had been translated from earlier, now lost Hebrew manuscripts), the Catholic Church recognizes it as canonical.

"My soul magnifies the Lord"

The Blessed Virgin Mary's important place in Tolkien's devotional life is illustrated by his inclusion of three Marian prayers among those he recommends learning by heart.[17] They are the Magnificat, the Litany of Loreto, and the *Sub tuum praesidium*. (See Appendix B.)

The Magnificat is Mary's song of praise (recorded in Luke 1:46–55) after she has conceived Jesus by the power of the Holy Spirit and has gone to visit her cousin Elizabeth. It is called the Magnificat from its opening words in the Latin translation: *Magnificat anima mea Dominum*, "My soul magnifies the Lord." This prayer is recited or sung daily in the Church's service of Vespers. Her statement that "all generations will call me blessed" is a reminder that all subsequent generations of believers will celebrate what God has done for her, in her, and with her. Mary is the archetypal disciple, for she cooperates willingly and definitively in the Incarnation: God does not command, but rather invites her to be the mother of Jesus, and she responds 'Yes' in her *Fiat*, 'let it be so.'

Tolkien's appreciation of the Magnificat comes through particularly in his 1936 poem "Noel," written for the school magazine of Our Lady of Abingdon. (See figure 39.) It is a recounting of the birth of Christ and envisions Mary singing out once again at the Nativity as she had done at the Visitation. The poem opens with a bleak, wintry scene into which breaks the song of Mary at the moment of the Savior's birth:

> And the tongue of many bells was stirred
> In Heaven's towers to ring
> When the voice of mortal maid was heard,
> That was mother of Heaven's King.[18]

The poem ends with bells ringing in both earth and heaven and with the singing of the *Gloria* for the arrival of "God on earth." The entire theme of the Magnificat is one that is close to Tolkien's heart. For what reason does Mary praise God in her song? Because God is merciful, and in his strength, he lifts up the weak: "He hath regarded the humility of his handmaid. . . . He hath scattered the proud in the imagination of their heart. He hath put down the mighty from their seat, and hath exalted the humble."[19] It is in almost exactly these terms that Tolkien explained one of the fundamental themes of *The Lord of the Rings*: it is, he wrote, "planned to be 'hobbito-centric,' that is, primarily a study of the ennoblement (or sanctification) of the humble."[20]

Elsewhere, his thoughts on this theme lead him to quote directly from the Magnificat. He remarks that he "saw the value of Hobbits, in putting earth under the feet of 'romance,' and in providing subjects for 'ennoblement' and heroes more praiseworthy than the professionals: *nolo heroizari* [I would not be a hero] is of course as good a start for a hero, as *nolo episcopari* [I would not be a bishop] for a bishop." Then, in the very next sentence, he adds, "we are all equal before the Great Author, *qui deposuit potentes de sede et exaltavit humiles* [who put down the mighty from their seat, and exalted the humble]."[21] It was evidently entirely natural for his mind to turn from the humility of the hobbits to the humility of Mary.

Tolkien greatly valued the Litany of Loreto, and he recommended for memorization both the Litany and its accompanying prayer *Sub tuum praesidium*. He also translated the latter into Quenya.[22] In English, it translates as: "We fly to thy patronage, O holy Mother of God, despise not our petitions in our necessities; but deliver us always from all dangers, O glorious and blessed Virgin." It is an indication that Tolkien appreciated both aspects of Mary: as a figure of profound humility and also—precisely because God lifts up the humble and meek—as a mighty figure, a protector, even a warrior against the forces of evil.

Tolkien's use of these Marian canticles in his own prayer life is perhaps reflected in the way that the characters in *The Lord of the Rings* on many occasions are heard singing in honor of Elbereth, Queen of the Valar, sometimes in Elvish and sometimes in English.* For instance, Frodo on the road from the Shire hears Elves singing, "Snow-white! Snow-white! O Lady clear! O Queen beyond the Western Seas!" At Rivendell, the Elves sing "*A Elbereth Gilthoniel . . .* " The Marian echoes cannot be missed by anyone acquainted with the regular habits of Tolkien's faith.

---

* In his battle with Shelob, Sam cries out a prayer to Elbereth in Elvish, in a kind of divine inspiration, a Middle-earth equivalent of 'speaking in tongues' (see 1 Corinthians 14), as he does not know the language.

"We praise Thee, O God"

He also seems to have had a fondness for the *Te Deum*, a canticle so named from its opening words, "*Te Deum laudamus: te Dominum confitemur*": "We praise thee, O God: we acknowledge thee to be the Lord." When he wanted to practice his Elvish script, Tolkien turned to the *Te Deum*, frequently excerpting phrases from this lengthy song of worship.[23]

He would have encountered nearly all of the prayers and praises discussed in this chapter in the liturgy of the Mass or other services, such as Vespers. Some of them, such as the Our Father, the Hail Mary, and the Glory Be, which we discussed in chapter 5, are so frequently used that all Catholics typically know them by heart; others, like the Magnificat and the *Sub tuum praesidium*, are very widely, if not universally, known. But Tolkien's suggestions of prayers to learn by heart ranged far beyond these relatively short passages. He had an exceptionally powerful capacity for recall and was therefore able to retain in memory many prayers and scriptural texts such as these and bring them readily to mind when the occasion suited.* He even recommended memorizing the entire Canon of the Mass (as we saw in chapter 16). In this way, Tolkien shows his ability to bridge the formal and the extemporaneous in his life of faith. He did not isolate these prayers in formal church settings or view them as just words in a book. Rather, he wished to have these prayers available at all times and in all places so that he could pray them whenever he wanted to or needed to, thus bringing the resources of Catholic devotional tradition to bear on his day-to-day life.

It is also notable that Tolkien singles out prayers of *praise* as especially worth knowing by heart, since this is a category distinctive of his own spirituality. Devotional handbooks of the time, such as *The Garden of the Soul*, typically included a section of 'penitential psalms' (that is, of lament and repentance) but no corresponding category of 'psalms of praise.'[24] In providing a more balanced

* For example, he could recite G.K. Chesterton's "Lepanto," which is nearly 150 lines long. The poem tells of the Christian defense of the West against an invasion by the Ottoman Turks in 1571, when the Holy League, assembled by Pope Pius V, achieved an unlikely victory at Lepanto in the Gulf of Patras. The outcome was attributed to the Virgin's intercession, and the day of the battle, October 7, became dedicated to Mary as Our Lady of Victory (soon thereafter renamed the Feast of Our Lady of the Rosary). Priscilla recalled that her father enjoyed declaiming it (Foster, "'That Most Unselfish Man,'" 23).

taxonomy, Tolkien manifests something of the long-lasting influence on his faith of Oratorian spirituality, with its emphasis on joy (which is not the same thing as happiness; one can be joyful even without anything external to be happy about). St. Philip Neri believed that "the true way to advance in holy virtues, is to persevere in a holy cheerfulness," and he exhorted his brethren: "Let us learn here below to give God the confession of praise which we ought to hope to give Him in heaven above."[25]

28

Tolkien's Parish

The Hobbit had been a huge hit. Published in 1937, it soon achieved such critical acclaim and such commercial success that the publisher, Stanley Unwin, urged Tolkien to produce a sequel of some kind to capitalize on its popularity. In response, Tolkien began to work on a story that was initially known simply as 'the new Hobbit.' It started small but grew and grew, eventually becoming the massive epic that we now know as *The Lord of Rings*, released in the mid-1950s.

It is testimony to the gigantic scale of *The Lord of the Rings* that its very process of composition yielded another important work—namely, "Leaf by Niggle." Though much shorter and simpler than Tolkien's masterpiece, "Leaf by Niggle" is effectively a kind of commentary on its production. This tale, which Tolkien called his "'purgatorial' story,"[1] concerns a busy perfectionist, distracted and harried in every direction, who yet hopes to produce worthwhile art and who only discovers in the afterlife the true nature of his achievement. Priscilla Tolkien says of "Leaf by Niggle" that it was "written with an exquisite sense of religious consolation"[2] and the story indeed tells us a lot about her father's faith. The main character is a painter called Niggle, who is trying to complete a painting of a tree and who continually has to deal with interruptions from his very unartistic neighbor, a man called Parish.

Tolkien's names are never happenstance. To "niggle," as the *Oxford English Dictionary* defines it, is to do something "in a painstaking, finicky, fussy, or ineffective manner; to trifle, fiddle; to waste effort or time on petty details."[3] "Niggling" precisely describes the habits of the story's protagonist but also points to Tolkien's clear-eyed awareness of these faults in himself. And though Tolkien disclaimed any deliberate intention in choosing the name "Parish," noting only that it "proved convenient"[4] for the play on words at the end, it is much too perfect to be accidental, even if it was generated at the level of intuition rather than conscious choice. A parish is, of course, a church district, a subdivision of a diocese. By giving the name of Mr. Parish to Niggle's difficult neighbor (who becomes, in the end, his collaborator in sub-creation), Tolkien is saying something about the responsibility that Niggle has to respect and sustain his relationship with the wider community of faith.

Before we turn our attention to "Leaf by Niggle," we would do well to spend most of this chapter detailing what we know of Tolkien's parish life, especially during the years when he was laboring to complete his masterpiece. Regular church membership, week in and week out, is usually a fairly humdrum affair, and Tolkien's experience was little different from the average Christian's. Yet it is vital that we try to gain a sense of the sheer ordinariness of his life in this regard, not least in order to understand the backdrop against which "Leaf by Niggle" was written, that story which was itself but an off-shoot of *The Lord of the Rings*.

Parish life

'Parish' is the ecclesiastical term for a particular territory that has its own church, serving as the central focus of day-to-day Christian life: Sunday services, marriages, baptisms, funerals, and so on. Every Catholic is normally a member of a particular parish and formally transfers from one to another if they move to a different location. The territorial parish system has become less apparent since automobiles have extended the range of possible churchgoing, but during Tolkien's lifetime, one's parish church was usually whichever church was within walking distance.*

The sense of belonging to a local parish is balanced by the fact that Catholics are free to attend any Catholic church, since each church is equally part of the one Church. One might go to a different parish for a change of pace, convenience of Mass times, while visiting friends, or for a special event. For example, in 1959,

* The Catholic parish system of Tolkien's day was a mix of historic and new. After the Reformation, all the formerly Catholic churches were appropriated for Anglican use; during the worst of the penal times, Catholics met secretly for Mass in houses or private chapels of landed Catholic families. Until 1791, Catholics were forbidden to build places of worship. It was only after the restoration of the English hierarchy in 1850 that parishes began to be re-established and grouped into dioceses under the care of a bishop with the new system finally codified in 1918 (Sweeney, 116–24). This entailed the building of (or designation of existing churches as) cathedrals—the cathedral being the seat of the bishop, the 'mother church' of the diocese—since the pre-Reformation Catholic cathedrals (such as Canterbury, York, Durham, and Winchester) were now in use by Anglicans.

while a parishioner at Corpus Christi in Headington, Tolkien served at Robert Murray's first Mass as a newly ordained priest at St. Aloysius's Church near the center of Oxford.[5]

Since the Sunday obligation to attend Mass is constant, Catholics on holiday typically go to whichever Catholic church is most conveniently located, even if they don't speak the language; the liturgy itself would, at that time, have been in Latin, but the homily and any announcements would have been in the vernacular. So, for instance, Tolkien went to Mass in Paris in 1913 when he was supervising two Spanish boys on their travels, and when he and Priscilla took a holiday to Italy, they attended Mass there. (See figure 59.) Visiting Ireland with Edith and Priscilla in 1951, they took a taxi five miles to get to church. A few years later, Tolkien attended Mass on Palm Sunday in Amsterdam, where he was a guest of honor at a publisher's dinner.[6]

As for his parish attendance while at home in England, Tolkien's longest uninterrupted association was with the Oxford church of St. Gregory and St. Augustine, familiarly known as St. Gregory's or St. Greg's.* From 1926 to 1947, the family lived on Northmoor Road, which falls within its parish boundaries. For over twenty years, then, this was Tolkien's parish, and the long association of his family with the church is marked by a plaque in the narthex.[7] It is this parish that we will now consider in some detail.

The church of St. Gregory and St. Augustine was built in 1911 in the Arts and Crafts style. It is a simple structure with no pillars and no stained glass; the nave is small, with two rows of pews and a central aisle, and a central tabernacle. (See figure 38.) It was while praying here during a service of Adoration that Tolkien had the special moment of spiritual insight that we discussed in chapter 22. He usually sat in the front pew on the right as you face the altar. Large, painted statues of Mary holding the Christ child and of St. Joseph, the foster father of Jesus,† comprised most of the religious adornments of the building in Tolkien's day.[8]

---

* The Tolkiens moved house in 1947 to 3 Manor Road and then in 1950 to 99 Holywell Street. These houses are near the center of Oxford and it would have been more convenient for him to attend St. Aloysius, than St. Gregory's, though we don't know the specific church he usually attended at this time. In 1953, Tolkien and Edith moved to 76 Sandfield Road in Headington, where they became parishioners first at Corpus Christi and then at St. Anthony of Padua. We will return to these churches in chapter 37.

† Tolkien referred to this statue of St. Joseph in a letter of 1944: "On the porch of St Gregory's . . . I saw the most touching sight. . . . Leaning against the wall as we came out of

The patrons of the parish, Pope St. Gregory I and St. Augustine of Canterbury, were especially celebrated on their respective feast days (March 12 and May 26).* The statue of Mary with the Christ-child in her arms was decked with flowers and given a lace mantilla on her special feasts and during the month of May, Mary's month. In Tolkien's day, the church also had a substantial outdoor altar, built in a small open-fronted booth to protect it from the weather, which made it possible to have larger crowds of worshipers, as in June, for the feast of Corpus Christi, when it hosted the Deanery Eucharistic procession, a major event involving several parishes from the local area of the diocese.[9] Ronald Knox and Vernon Johnson, another priest who was a convert from Anglicanism and a highly regarded author of apologetics and devotional books, both preached at these events in the 1940s.[10]

When the family first arrived at St. Gregory's in 1926, the pastor was the Rev. William Smith, who served until 1938. He was succeeded by the Rev. Douglas Carter, who came into his ministry under the shadow of war.[11] Priscilla recalled that on September 3, 1939, while at Mass with her father, the announcement came through that Britain had declared war on Germany. The priest invited anyone who wanted to stay to listen to the news on his wireless, but her father, "visibly upset to be at war," opted to return home immediately.[12]

During the years of conflict, Fr. Carter provided pastoral care for Italian prisoners of war in the Oxfordshire area and was so impressed by their piety that he castigated his congregation at St. Gregory's for not being as devout. He remained at St. Gregory's until 1950 and developed a lasting friendship with Tolkien;[13] the two were still actively corresponding till the year before Tolkien's death, when they discussed the Entwives.[14] They had much in common. Fr. Carter, a classicist and linguist, was, like Tolkien, one of the translators of the Jerusalem Bible. They also shared an interest in John Henry Newman: in 1957, Carter was the narrator for a film about Newman, for which Tolkien's son John wrote the script.[15] He had an eye for beauty, doing the flower arrangements for the altar himself, and the

---

church was an old tramp in rags, something like sandals tied on his feet with string . . . and in his other hand a rough staff. He had a brown beard, and a curiously 'clean' face. . . . I could not resist the impulse of offering him a small alms, and he took it with grave kindliness. . . . Just for once I rather took Fr. C[arter] aback by saying to him that I thought the old man looked a great deal more like St Joseph than the statue in the church" (*Letters*, 101).

* These dates are according to the calendar in use during Tolkien's time at St. Gregory's; in later calendrical reforms, they were moved to September 3 and May 27, respectively ("Kalendar of the Universal Church," *Roman Missal*, 1935).

experience of chronic ailment, as he suffered from an ingrown beard, which was both disfiguring and painful.[16]

A convert from Anglicanism, Carter took a charitable approach toward his former coreligionists; he remarked that the Anglican church "was a good stepmother to me years ago, and much of what I believe as a Catholic I first learnt from her," and in 1957, he preached at Westminster Cathedral, London, as part of the Octave for Christian Unity.[17] Carter made a point of recognizing the presence of "abundant graces" in Anglican ministry, noting that these are "uncovenanted graces" (that is, ones that are not tied to any specific sacrament, except perhaps baptism).[18] This approach was very much in line with, and perhaps helped to support, Tolkien's approach to ecumenical relationships.

Preaching

Tolkien thought well of Fr. Carter's preaching; Robert Murray recalled that he "had a high ideal of what a good sermon should be" and "recognised this gift in his parish priest, Douglas Carter."[19] Since one of the basic features of Tolkien's week-by-week spiritual life was the hearing of sermons, it is worth considering what Tolkien thought on the subject.

Tolkien observed to Christopher that competent preaching is a form of rhetoric and, as such, requires both "native talent" and "learning and practice." But preaching, he says, is more than public speaking: it requires "truth and sincerity" without anything that shows the preacher's personal flaws. A good sermon, he concludes, needs to have "some art, some virtue, some knowledge"; on a few occasions, there is also some "special grace" of the Holy Spirit that raises the sermon up to a higher level.[20]

Tolkien's appreciation of good preaching was undoubtedly shaped at an early age by his experiences at the Birmingham Oratory, where the Fathers took it in turn to preach at the Sunday Mass and weekday Benediction.[21] Their approach, as taught by St. Philip Neri, was to have "a plain and familiar style of preaching, avoiding all elaboration not only in thought but also in diction." There was no flowery wording or attempts to work up an emotional atmosphere. Fr. Ignatius Ryder's sermons were, by the Birmingham Fathers' own account, typical. He had "the happy knack or gift of illustration and apt analogy" and "drew upon his wide reading" to make his points to his audience.[22] The level of education and culture among the Fathers was high, and their vocation was precisely to preach to the more educated in Birmingham; Tolkien began his spiritual life having imbibed a high standard for sermons.

These high standards meant that he was usually disappointed; in fact, he remarked that most sermons are simply "bad."[23] However, he found a way to make even a bad homily into a personal devotional exercise—much as he did for a badly handled Mass. He explained that the "critical faculty," though it need not be suppressed, "should be kept in order by a constant endeavour to apply the truth (if any), even in cliché form, to oneself exclusively!"[24] In this point, he expresses a view articulated by Fr. Ignatius Ryder, who in preaching on Christ as the Eternal Word, explained that "a sermon, which is not at all original, which ministers no fresh food for thought to anyone, need not on that account be inefficacious. It is part of a great institution [i.e., the Church] for conveying to us the word of God, which is no dead thing, but a living embodied grace."[25]

Creeping to the Cross

The mainstay of parish life, however, is not the parish priest or his sermons but the regular liturgical rhythm of worship: day by day, week by week, month by month, year by year. The most important period of the entire year was Holy Week and especially the Triduum: Maundy Thursday, Good Friday, and Holy Saturday, culminating in the Vigil of Easter. One of the devotional elements of the Good Friday liturgy is the veneration of the cross, which at St. Gregory's may have taken on a special significance for Tolkien, given his experiences during the First World War.

In this solemn ceremony, a crucifix is brought forward and unveiled (all other crucifixes, images, and statues being covered in purple cloth at this latter part of Lent). First, the priest and all his assistants take it in turn to genuflect before the crucifix and kiss it; then all the people in the congregation came up, in turn, one by one, to do the same.[26] In the Middle Ages, it was a rite known as 'the creeping to the Cross,' a humble approach of love and reverence for the crucified Savior who "bore our sins in his body on the tree" (1 Peter 2:24) and whose death opened up the way to eternal life.

Year after year, when Tolkien knelt to kiss the crucifix at St. Gregory's on Good Friday, he would have seen the brass plate affixed to its base: "In loving memory of Capt. B. Brooks, Killed in Action, July 23 1916." (See figure 43.) It honors Basil Brooks, a young Oxford man who was killed on the Somme during the Great War. Like Tolkien at that time, Brooks had been an officer; like Tolkien, he was newly married. He was killed going 'over the top' on an attack that took place the day before Tolkien entered the trenches at Auchonvillers.[27] Brooks's grieving young widow, Gertrude, gave the crucifix to St. Gregory's in his memory.[28]

Tolkien knew well the medieval phrase *Media vita in morte sumus*, 'In midst of life we are in death.' Creeping to the cross on Good Friday was a vivid reminder of that truth. And yet, the context of the liturgy meant that this remembrance of death was inextricably intertwined with the Resurrection. Good Friday led to the tomb, but to a tomb that was then found to be empty on the first Easter morning. The silence and darkness of the Good Friday liturgy was followed by the exultant music, candles, bells, and rejoicing of Easter. The Basil Brooks crucifix was a deeply personal reminder of death: the death of nearly all his close friends in the war, the fact that he might well have been killed on the front line as Brooks was; it might have been Edith and not Gertrude who had a memorial put up for him. But it was also a reminder, conversely, that 'in midst of death we are in life.' As St. Paul wrote in the first letter to the Corinthians, "Death is swallowed up in victory. O death, where is thy victory? O death, where is thy sting?" (1 Corinthians 15:54–55). The pains of death and the cleansing pangs of purgatory are what bring the faithful soul to the beatific vision.

"The Tree, his Tree"

This brings us back to "Leaf by Niggle." It was written around 1938–39, when, as Tolkien recalled, "*The Lord of the Rings* was beginning to unroll itself and to unfold prospects of labour and exploration in yet unknown country as daunting to me as to the hobbits." It was published in 1945 in the Catholic theological journal *The*

Dublin Review. (See figure 54.) Most unusually for Tolkien, "it reached manuscript form, very swiftly, one day when I awoke with it already in mind."[29]

This is quite unlike Tolkien's usual habit of composition and repeated revision and also somewhat ironic, given the theme of the story, which has to do with painstaking labor and slow progress. The character Niggle, who is very much a self-portrait of Tolkien, has the ambition to one day paint a great Tree, but he manages only to finish a few leaves, due mostly to his own inefficiency but also because of interruptions to attend to the needs of his ordinary and rather annoying neighbor, Mr. Parish. Niggle is suddenly called away on a train journey (signifying his death), after which he wakes up in the Workhouse Infirmary (signifying purgatory). After a stretch of hard work and bitter medicine, he begins to be more internally restful, and finally he is judged ready for gentler treatment. For this next stage of his healing, he is taken to a beautiful garden country, where he makes a startling discovery:

> Before him stood the Tree, his Tree, finished. . . . All the leaves he had ever laboured at were there, as he had imagined them rather than as he had made them; and there were others that had only budded in his mind, and many that might have budded, if only he had had time.[30]

He realizes that some of the most beautiful of the Tree's leaves, and also "the most characteristic, the most perfect examples of the Niggle style—were seen to have been produced in collaboration with Mr Parish." Soon he realizes that to shape the landscape as it should be, he needs Parish—who then arrives, to complete his own healing by working alongside Niggle. When, in due time, Niggle is ready, a shepherd comes down to guide him onward and upward into the mountains: "Beyond that I cannot guess what became of him. Even little Niggle in his old home could glimpse the Mountains far away, and they got into the borders of his picture; but what they are really like, and what lies beyond them only those can say who have climbed them." The story ends with the discovery that the garden country he helped to shape is now called, with poignant aptness, "Niggle's Parish."[31]

The story presents Tolkien's imagined conception of what purgatory is like—a process of healing, sometimes painful but always oriented toward heaven—and, as he explains in his introductory note, the story also depicts the process of artistic creativity, what he calls 'sub-creation.'[32] It is a deeply autobiographical piece; he told his aunt, Jane Neave, that when he was writing the story, "I was anxious about my own internal Tree, *The Lord of the Rings*.* It was growing out of hand, and revealing endless new vistas—and I wanted to finish it, but the world was threatening."[33]

"Leaf by Niggle" is a kind of artistic prophecy; it foretells the completion of the major work to which it is merely a sideshow. Yet how beautifully it does so. Niggle "gazed at the Tree, and slowly he lifted his arms and opened them wide. 'It's a gift!' he said. He was referring to his art, and also to the result; but he was using the word quite literally."[34]

---

* It is also a highly theological story. In 1954, ruminating on the relationship between free will and artistic subcreation, Tolkien wrote that "I tried to show allegorically how that might come to be taken up into Creation in some plane in my 'purgatorial' story Leaf by Niggle . . . to make visible and physical the effects of Sin or misused Free Will by men" (*Letters*, 195).

END: 1952–1973

29

"I have exposed my heart to be shot at"

The Tree was finished—but only in "Leaf by Niggle." Tolkien's "internal Tree," as he called *The Lord of the Rings*, was effectively ready for release by 1949, but as the calendar flicked over into a new decade, it remained unpublished. Tolkien was standing in his own way by insisting that his epic be issued alongside another huge and unusual work (still incomplete), *The Silmarillion*. Naturally, publishers were not sanguine about taking on such a massive financial risk. And so, 1950 became 1951, and 1951 became 1952; and still he had nothing to show for his labors.

In February 1952, King George VI died unexpectedly in his sleep at the age of just fifty-six, and his daughter, the twenty-five-year-old Elizabeth, was now the sovereign. A new era was beginning for the nation and Commonwealth, and Tolkien decided it was time to embark on a new era for himself as well. That summer, he finally conceded to his publisher, Rayner Unwin, "Better something than nothing!" adding "Years are becoming precious. . . . Can anything be done . . . to unlock gates I slammed myself?"[1]

Unwin wrote back, saying, "We do *want* to publish for you—it's only ways and means that have held us up."[2] But these "ways and means," coupled with Tolkien's own distractibility and perfectionism, continued to be obstacles in the path. The protracted birth pangs distressed him ("Uncertainty is a great weight on the heart"). Persistent money worries concerned him (he sent one whole letter typed on the red strip of his typewriter ribbon for the sake of "economy").[3] The need to split the whole work into three volumes caused further complications. Eventually, a title was settled on for the first part—*The Fellowship of the Ring*—and a date agreed upon for its release: July 29, 1954. *The Two Towers* followed later that year; *The Return of the King* came out in 1955.

As the date of release drew near, Tolkien wrote to his friend Robert Murray, "I am dreading the publication, for it will be impossible not to mind what is said. I have exposed my heart to be shot at."[4]

"I have exposed my heart to be shot at"

Tolkien was sixty-two years old when *The Fellowship of the Ring* made its way into readers' hands. He was, of course, already a published author and a moderately famous one to boot, with the success of *The Hobbit* behind him. But *The Lord of the Rings* was different. It was complex, more substantial, more deeply fed by the well-springs of his imagination and indeed of his faith. It had cost him more than a decade of literary effort; its publication had almost foundered on the rocks of his own stubbornness. All of these things doubtless contributed to his having a feeling of special personal vulnerability as the publication date approached. But we should also consider the context of Tolkien's admission.

Robert Murray was a fellow Catholic, one who had come into the Church in large part because of Tolkien's influence and example; he was studying for the priesthood when Tolkien confessed how exposed his heart had become. Having been asked to read and comment upon *The Lord of the Rings* pre-publication, Murray remarked on the way "the work is bathed in an atmosphere suggesting the order of grace," adding that "the female characters each in their way seem like reflections of Our Lady."[5]

Tolkien was greatly encouraged: "you are more perceptive, especially in some directions, than any one else, and have even revealed to me more clearly some things about my work." The exchange is telling. Murray comments on the "atmosphere" bathing the work and Tolkien admits that it is imbued with his faith at such a deep level that certain aspects he hasn't recognized himself until they are pointed out to him. He goes on to say, "I think I know exactly what you mean by the order of Grace; and of course by your references to Our Lady, upon which all my own small perception of beauty both in majesty and simplicity is founded." Galadriel and the other women in the tale are not direct representations of Mary but are, as Murray put it, "reflections" of her—for the author's Marian piety naturally came into play when he was envisioning certain characters. Tolkien then goes on to make the famous pronouncement that we quoted in the opening chapter:

> *The Lord of the Rings* is of course a fundamentally religious and Catholic work; unconsciously so at first, but consciously in the revision. That is why I have not put in, or have cut out, practically all references to anything like 'religion,' to cults or practices, in the imaginary world. For the religious element is absorbed into the story and the symbolism.[6]

We are now better equipped to understand what he meant by these words. He does *not* mean that the book is some sort of Christian allegory, a suggestion he vehemently rejected.* He was emphatic that he had no "message" in the sense "of preaching, or of delivering myself of a vision of truth specially revealed to me!" Rather, he says, he was writing the sort of story he enjoyed—but, he says, "in such a process inevitably one's own taste, ideas, and beliefs get taken up."

His ideas and beliefs, as we have seen, were deeply rooted in the Christian faith; and so "inevitably," by a sort of imaginative osmosis, they have been absorbed into, and become part of the foundations of, his fictional world. One way that this occurs is in the religion that Middle-earth itself is explicitly shown to have. The other way is implicit, through the deep embedding of Tolkien's own faith in the whole tone, shape, and—to use Murray's word again—atmosphere of the story. Let us consider each way in turn.

The faith of Middle-earth

Tolkien was annoyed when a critic claimed that *The Lord of the Rings* "contained no religion." On the contrary, he asserted, Middle-earth "is a monotheistic world of 'natural theology.'" True, he acknowledges that there is no organized religion,

---

* Murray himself emphasized this point in later years when responding to queries from a graduate student writing about the Catholic element in *The Lord of the Rings* who had, it seems, interpreted Tolkien's remarks in over-simplistic terms. Murray is clear that the story does not contain direct "theological statements"; nor does the Christian element exclude other sources of influence. Tolkien was, in Murray's view, "a very complex and depressed man," and he felt that *The Lord of the Rings* reflected this "as much as it reflects his Catholic faith" (West, "Letter from Father Murray," 135).

no churches or religious ceremonies, but this is, he says, because Middle-earth was a pre-Christian world.[7] Even so, he points out that its religious practices, though undeveloped, were not altogether missing:

> As a matter of fact, there are references to God, either direct, in which he is called 'the One' in one place, or by implication, as in the conversation between Gandalf and Bilbo and Frodo and what it was that was directing the finding of the Ring, or in the Númenórean Grace, which is said by Faramir. But, of course, if you mean religious practices, you don't get much, except perhaps, say, the Elvish hymn to Elbereth.[8]

Tolkien explained that because it is a pre-Christian world, he has not put in an "'embodiment' of the Creator" into his story. In other words, there is no equivalent to the Christ-like Aslan in Lewis's Narnia Chronicles, no single character who represents the divine, although figures such as Gandalf allow the reader to be, as Tolkien said, "reminded of the Gospels."

Gandalf provides a useful illustration of the way in which Tolkien integrates a Christian theme into the story. In his fight with the Balrog, Gandalf the Grey falls into the chasm beneath the Bridge of Khazad-dûm. Later, he reappears as Gandalf the White, having been "sent back." This story element is coherent and compelling in its own right and requires no recognition of any Gospel element for its imaginative effect. But a reader with even limited biblical knowledge will be reminded of the death and Resurrection of Jesus Christ, and greater familiarity with the Scriptures will allow for other resonances to be perceived. The scene in Fangorn Forest where Aragorn, Gimli, and Legolas encounter Gandalf the White, but at first fail to recognize him, has echoes of the Emmaus Road encounter in which two of the down-hearted disciples, leaving Jerusalem after the Crucifixion, meet the risen Jesus on the road—and even speak with him—but do not realize whom they have met: "their eyes were kept from recognizing him." Jesus explains to them the meaning of the events they have witnessed and then, at their request, stays with them for a meal; at the breaking of the bread, "their eyes were opened and they recognized him; and he vanished out of their sight. They said to each other, "Did not our hearts burn within us while he talked to us on the road, while he opened to us the scriptures?" (Luke 24:13–35)

Even so, Gandalf is a reminder or echo only, not a portrayal of Christ. The pattern of Gandalf's story, like that of the Old Testament prophet Jonah who descends into the belly of the whale and is then vomited forth three days later—and like the pagan stories of dying and rising gods that meant so much to the pre-Christian Lewis—prefigures or foreshadows the narrative trajectory of Christ but does not represent it. Tolkien's reticence in portraying the Incarnate God sprang not only from the fact that the 'Third Age' is a pre-Christian age but also from a deep sense of humility at this central Christian mystery: "The Incarnation of God is an *infinitely* greater thing than anything I would dare to write."[9]

Tolkien's faith embedded in Middle-earth

But though he dared not ascend the Mount Everest of the Incarnation, Tolkien did imaginatively tackle lower religious summits—by implicit means. He remarked in one letter, "There is, in fact, quite a lot of theology included in *The Lord of the Rings*."[10] He noted that its conflict is not directly about "freedom" but is rather "about God, and His sole right to divine honour."[11] In other words, Tolkien is exploring matters that pertain to his Christian faith by embedding them in the whole warp and woof of his text, not by painting them onto it.

Hence he wrote, on several occasions, that the theme of *The Lord of the Rings* is in fact "Death and the desire for deathlessness." The abuse of power was a major element in the story, he explained, but not at its heart: "The real theme for me is about something much more permanent and difficult: Death and Immortality."[12]

Tolkien had been meditating for years on the significance of death as a theme in fantasy literature. It is a point that he makes in "On Fairy-stories," which is essentially his manifesto for the writing of fantasy, and one that he also labored over for years: he delivered it as a lecture at St. Andrews in 1939, revised it for inclusion in the memorial volume to Charles Williams in 1945, and finally published it in *Tree and Leaf* in 1963. It contains his mature and developed thought on the subject, worked out during the very years in which he was writing *The Lord of the Rings*.

In this essay, he argues for the value of escape (as distinct from escapism), noting that people have always desired to flee from "hunger, thirst, poverty, pain, sorrow, injustice, death," of which, he says, "the oldest and deepest desire" is "the Great Escape: the Escape from Death." From there, he moves to a consideration of the "consolation" that a fantasy story provides—most fully, the "Consolation of the Happy Ending," for which he coins the word *eucatastrophe*. He argues that this is the "highest function" of a fantasy: it "does not deny the existence of *dyscatastrophe*, of sorrow and failure: the possibility of these is necessary to the joy of deliverance; it denies (in the face of much evidence, if you will) universal final defeat." In this way, he says, the happy ending of a fantasy is a form of "evangelium."[13]

"Evangelium" is a word worth noticing. It means—as the *Oxford English Dictionary* explains succinctly—"a proclamation of the 'glad tidings' of the Gospel."[14] Tolkien deliberately uses an archaic word that will be slightly unfamiliar to most of his readers; it introduces the concept of the Christian Gospels without immediately triggering conventional associations. We saw in chapter 20 that Tolkien was emphatic about the importance of an integrated, holistic view of reality, the meaning of which was inherent in it, not abstracted from it; here we see him applying this concept to the functioning of a fantasy story.

In the epilogue to "On Fairy-stories," Tolkien directly draws a link between faith and fantastic fiction. The Gospels, he says, "contain a fairy-story, or a story of a larger kind which embraces all the essence of fairy-stories," with the difference that *this* story, the story of Christ, has "entered History." He goes on to say that when we feel joy at the happy ending of a fantasy, this joy "has the very taste of primary truth"—that is, of reality—because it echoes "the Great Eucatastrophe." And this is precisely what is narrated in the Gospels: as Tolkien put it, "The Birth of Christ is the eucatastrophe of Man's history. The Resurrection is the eucatastrophe of the story of the Incarnation." The story in the Gospels, he says, "is supreme; and it is true. Art has been verified. God is the Lord, of angels, and of men—and of elves. Legend and History have met and fused."[15]

And what is true in the primary world can be rendered in fiction, not through allegory in which story elements explicitly represent Gospel elements, but through an artistic imagining of a whole subcreated reality with its own inner consistency. Thus, it is the mark of a good fairy story, Tolkien says, that when the "turn" comes, it causes "a catch of the breath, a beat and lifting of the heart, near to (or indeed accompanied by) tears."[16]

Eucatastrophe

It was in *The Hobbit* that Tolkien first tried his hand at creating a eucatastrophic climax. The arrival of the Eagles at the Battle of the Five Armies turns the tide so that the Elves, Dwarves, and Men can defeat the Goblins and Wargs. The Eagles themselves, of course, evoke a very appropriate resonance of the Gospel, being the symbol of St. John the Evangelist, but more importantly, they arrive when victory appears lost and indeed *is* lost. The peculiar quality of the eucatastrophic "turn" depends upon its being unexpected. In other words, the eagles are not an objective correlative of the hope of an optimist, but rather the hope of the hopeless. A certain despair has to set in before there can be any real joy at deliverance.

Having produced a sort of prototype of eucatastrophe in *The Hobbit* and having articulated the Christian meaning of the happy ending in "On Fairy-stories," Tolkien was well prepared to present a eucatastrophic moment on a much larger canvas in *The Lord of the Rings*. After the Ring has gone into the fires of Mount Doom, Frodo accepts that he has come "to the end of all things." As he tells Sam, "Hopes fail. An end comes. We have only a little time to wait now. We are lost in ruin and downfall, and there is no escape." Sam replies, "What a tale we have been in. . . . I wonder how it will go on after our part." They fall to the ground, "worn out, or choked with fumes and heat, or stricken down by despair at last, hiding their eyes from death."[17]

It is at this extremity of hopelessness that help comes. Without knowing it, they are plucked from death, and after a sleep lasting fourteen days, they find themselves awake in Ithilien, on the Field of Cormallen.[18] They rise, dress, and are taken to a feast in which their accomplishments are praised by a minstrel of Gondor, singing the lay of Frodo of the Nine Fingers.

> And when Sam heard that he laughed aloud for sheer delight, and he stood up and cried: "O great glory and splendour! And all my wishes have come true!" And then he wept.

> And all the host laughed and wept, and in the midst of their merriment and tears the clear voice of the minstrel rose like silver and gold, and all men were hushed. And he sang to them, now in the Elven-tongue, now in the speech of the West, until their hearts, wounded with sweet words, overflowed, and their joy was like swords, and they passed in thought out to regions where pain and delight flow together and tears are the very wine of blessedness.[19]

It is not just the characters in the story who weep: Tolkien blotted the page with his own tears as he wrote.[20] He called this moment the "peak" of the whole epic, and its bittersweet poignancy is so piercing that for a moment it "passes outside the frame, rends indeed the very web of story, and lets a gleam come through."[21] The gleam comes from his belief that the whole human story is moving toward—and indeed is already participating in—a destiny with a similar sense of loss and gain, of pain and delight, of wounds and joy. The final destiny is the hope of heaven, where Christ, the "first fruits" of the dead (1 Corinthians 15:23), rises to new life while bearing still the wounds he won on earth (John 20:19–29). And the present participation is the Eucharist, for the Blessed Sacrament is "the divine paradox, that which ends life, and demands the surrender of all, and yet . . . which every man's heart desires."[22]

In this light, we can see something of what Tolkien meant when he said that *The Lord of the Rings* is "fundamentally religious and Catholic": its narrative form and the poignant joy of its ending mirror the Gospel account of Christ's Incarnation and Resurrection—and not only mirror that account but receive validation from it. Having declared that the Gospel is the "supreme" story, he goes on to explain that there is still abundant scope for human artists—and that their work is all the more meaningful as a result: "The Evangelium has not abrogated legends; it has hallowed them." The Christian writer must still work, but now can do so with the awareness that he has a purpose; and, Tolkien adds, "So great is the bounty with which he has been treated that he may now, perhaps, fairly dare to guess that in Fantasy he may actually assist in the effoliation and multiple enrichment of creation."[23] To take up the work of writing stories as a Christian artist is a serious endeavor, but that does not squash creativity; rather, in Tolkien's view, it blesses and encourages it.

30

The Accredited Altar

At this point in our story, we are well prepared to engage with one of the core questions related to Tolkien's faith. As a devout Catholic, Tolkien held religious views that are shared by only a fraction of his total readership—perhaps a very small fraction, considering how wide the reach of *The Lord of the Rings* has become. He produced a world best-seller, appearing, at present count, in more than fifty languages, including Afrikaans, Arabic, Chinese, Greek, Hebrew, Japanese, Korean, Finnish, Persian, Russian, Thai, Turkish, Vietnamese, and Yiddish. Peter Jackson's cinematic version is hugely popular with a whole demographic of enthusiasts who have never read the book. This epic tale is profoundly meaningful and personally compelling for readers of all faiths and none.

In short, a deeply religious man has produced an imaginative work that is fantastically popular with the secular world. This oddity is perhaps one reason why non-Christian readers of Tolkien, and even non-Catholic Christian readers of Tolkien, are sometimes reluctant to explore his faith or even acknowledge it. Not unreasonably, they may fear disappointment: perhaps the author of the work they so admire will turn out to be narrow-minded, even bigoted against those outside his own faith community. What did he really think of non-Catholics?

A good starting point for consideration of this issue is the exchange between Gandalf and Frodo that we quoted in an earlier chapter, when the wizard tells the hobbit, "Do not be too eager to deal out death in judgement." Tolkien, though he was firm about where his own spiritual loyalties lay, did not draw hard and fast negative conclusions about the moral status, let alone the eternal destiny, of others: "For even the very wise cannot see all ends." Mercy and pity were key qualities of the moral ecology he presented in Middle-earth, qualities that he believed could be discovered and acted upon in the real world too. Tolkien's faith was in the light he believed he had been granted, a light he found personified in Jesus Christ, the light of the world (John 8:12). His concern was to follow that light and to encourage others, as appropriate, to follow it with him; he would leave it to "the only Wise" (as he names God in the poem "Mythopoeia") to determine other people's fates. He need not have an opinion on that subject. In effect, he asked himself the same question that St. Paul asked the Christians in Rome, "Who are you to pass judgment on the servant of another?" (Romans 14:4).

The Petrine claims

Tolkien's own belief was clear: "I myself am convinced by the Petrine claims." These "Petrine claims" would require a whole book to unpack thoroughly, but they boil down to two essential tenets: that St. Peter was given authority by Jesus himself to govern the Church as his vicar or representative, and that that authority is inherited by his successors.[1] These claims stem principally from the account of Jesus naming Peter "the rock" on which he would build his Church (Matthew 16:18) and from the practice of apostolic succession (Acts 1:15–26). Jesus equips Peter with "the keys of the kingdom" (Matthew 16:19; cf. Isaiah 22:22), thereby appointing him as steward of the household of faith. (See figure 57.) Jesus promised that he would pray for Peter that his faith would not fail and that he would "strengthen [his] brethren" (Luke 22:32). Jesus commanded Peter three times to pastor his flock (John 21:15–17). Peter is named more often in the pages of the New Testament than all the other disciples put together and is always named first, indicating his headship of the apostolic college. It is Peter, standing up "with the Eleven" on the day of Pentecost, who announces Christ's Resurrection (Acts 2:14–41).

While Tolkien undoubtedly accepted these and other scriptural arguments for Petrine authority (as well as those deriving from history and tradition that we do not have space to explore), interestingly, he prefers to focus on the Eucharist. The most important marker of the Church's authority and its identity as the "True Church" is, in his view, its enduring defense and honor of the Blessed Sacrament, putting it "(as Christ plainly intended) in the prime place."[2] The Body of Christ understood ecclesiologically is made known by its reverence for the Body of Christ understood Eucharistically. Yet again, we see the centrality of the Blessed Sacrament in his life of faith.

In declaring his acceptance of the Petrine claims, was Tolkien implicitly damning those who did not accept them? Not at all. He was a member of a Church that had declared "*extra ecclesiam nulla salus*"—there is no salvation outside the Church—but, as Pope Pius X in his 1908 Catechism had taught, if a person "is outside the Church through no fault of his" and if that person "sincerely seeks the truth and does God's will as best he can," then "such a man is indeed separated from the body of the Church, but is united to the soul of the Church and consequently is on the way of salvation."[3]

In 1963, in a long theological letter to his son Michael, Tolkien articulated an understanding of the Church as "the temple of the Spirit dying but living, corrupt but holy, self-reforming and rearising." His frank realism about the imperfections of the Church helps explain his own frequent recourse to the sacrament of Reconciliation. He knew the Church to be not the home of the already sanctified but the place where sinners can, by the grace of God, grow in sanctity.

He goes on to note, in a similarly humble manner, "the wise words of Charles Williams, that it is our duty to tend the accredited and established altar, though the Holy Spirit may send the fire down somewhere else."[4] (See figure 50.)

This is a statement worth pausing over—not least because Tolkien intensely disliked the novels in which the Anglican Williams embodied much of his theology (he called them "dreadful").[5] That he should praise Williams's "wise words" about "the accredited and established altar" points to Tolkien's ability to separate what he regarded as the wheat from the chaff in someone's thought as well as his ability to differentiate between human duty and divine freedom. Williams's original words were, "Usually the way must be made ready for heaven, and then it will come by some other; the sacrifice must be made ready, and the fire will strike on another altar."[6] As is typical of Williams, he does not name God directly but connotes him by means of the image of fire, a common biblical sign of divine action and the presence of the Holy Spirit (1 Kings 18:16–39; Acts 2:3).

Tolkien's willingness to make use of Williams's idea sheds interesting light on his attitude to those outside the Catholic Church. In Tolkien's view, the Catholic Church is not just any altar but the "accredited and established altar," which it is his "duty" to attend. Therefore, his admission that God may send his Holy Spirit "somewhere else" is quite a strong affirmation of the Spirit's presence among those who are *not* members of that communion. Tolkien's phrasing, in fact, echoes the language of a Catholic prayer that he would have known well, one commonly used for personal devotions: "Come, O Holy Ghost, fill the hearts of thy faithful, and kindle in them the fire of thy love. Send forth thy Spirit, and they shall be created, and thou shalt renew the face of the earth."[7] This, he is indicating, is an experience of grace that is not the exclusive preserve of Catholics.

As Tolkien goes on to explain, "God cannot be limited (even by his own Foundations) . . . and may use any channel for His grace."[8] Or, as he wrote on another occasion, musing upon the book of Jonah, God "won't be dictated to even by high ecclesiastics whom he has himself appointed."[9] That is, he affirms that the Church is divinely established, such that Catholics can be certain of the objective reality of the sacraments and of the way to salvation; but also that God is not restricted by his establishment of the Church and can work through the power of the Holy Spirit outside the boundaries of the visible Church. In saying this, Tolkien was echoing the teaching of Pope Pius IX in 1854: that the Church is "the ark of salvation" but ignorance of this fact, "if that ignorance be invincible, is not a fault in the eyes of God." It would be arrogant for anyone to assume they can "mark the limits of such an ignorance, holding in account the various conditions of peoples, of countries, of minds, and of the infinite multiplicity of human things." Only after death, when we "shall see God as He is" will anyone be able to "comprehend perfectly by what admirable and indissoluble bond the divine mercy and the divine justice are united."[10]

Seeing the light

Tolkien believed that all people, whether Catholic or not, have been made in the "image" and "likeness" of God (Genesis 1:26) and that God is "the Father of lights" (James 1:17), the "true light" who enlightens everyone (John 1:9), imparting the common grace of conscience to all humanity (Romans 2:14–15). Tolkien was sadly aware that not everyone responds to the promptings of their conscience: "I am afraid, whatever our beliefs, we have to face the fact that there are persons who yield to temptation, reject their chances of nobility or salvation, and appear to be 'damnable.'" But he adds, "we who are all 'in the same boat' must not usurp the

Judge."[11] It was not for him, Tolkien, to know the extent to which other people's souls were illuminated by that divine light; the only soul he was finally responsible for was his own, making the best of what he had been given (Luke 12:48). He could rest in the assurance that God wants all people "to be saved and to come to the knowledge of the truth" (1 Timothy 2:4).

And if people outside the Church altogether might receive divine illumination, would this not apply even more to those who already enjoy the grace of Christian baptism but who are not in communion with the Catholic Church? These non-Catholic Christian groups also receive real light, Tolkien believed: "Besides the Sun there may be moonlight (even bright enough to read by)."[12] As he put it, "Even to love Our Lord, and certainly to call him Lord, and God, is a grace, and may bring more grace."[13] It is this view that allowed him to have a deep spiritual friendship, as well as a warm social connection, with non-Catholics like Lewis and Williams and many others. For instance, he recalled that Frederick Wiseman, the father of his friend Christopher and the president of the Wesleyan Methodist Conference, was "one of the most delightful Christian men I have met."[14]

Tolkien effectively held, and expressed, and indeed lived out, the teaching of *Unitatis Redintegratio*, the 1964 Decree on Ecumenism, long before it was promulgated. In that decree, the bishops of the Second Vatican Council stated that "Christ the Lord founded one Church and one Church only" and that those who "believe in Christ and have been truly baptized are in communion with the Catholic Church even though this communion is imperfect." All the baptized "are members of Christ's body, and have a right to be called Christian, and so are correctly accepted as brothers by the children of the Catholic Church." To be sure, they are "separated brethren," lacking the unity Christ desires for his Church and unable to "benefit fully from the means of salvation" through the other sacraments. However, even so, the council taught that "some and even very many of the significant elements and endowments which together go to build up and give life to the Church itself, can exist outside the visible boundaries of the Catholic Church: the written word of God; the life of grace; faith, hope and charity, with the other interior gifts of the Holy Spirit, and visible elements too."[15]

When, in 1935, Tolkien wrote to his Anglican friend R.W. Chambers that there is a "spirit" that binds together "kindred men" even if it is "not complete" without their common union, their communion, in the Catholic Church,[16] he articulated an ecclesiological understanding that followed in the vein of Newman and that anticipated by thirty years the pronouncements of the Second Vatican Council.[17] Tolkien was keen to have as much fellowship as he could with other Christians, consistent with honesty about genuine differences. Baptism gave a strong ground for such fellowship, even as disagreements about other matters made for impaired unity. As the Decree on Ecumenism puts it:

> Catholics must gladly acknowledge and esteem the truly Christian endowments from our common heritage which are to be found among our separated brethren. It is right and salutary to recognize the riches of Christ and virtuous works in the lives of others who are bearing witness to Christ, sometimes even to the shedding of their blood. For God is always wonderful in His works and worthy of all praise. Nor should we forget that anything wrought by the grace of the Holy Spirit in the hearts of our separated brethren can be a help to our own edification. Whatever is truly Christian is never contrary to what genuinely belongs to the faith; indeed, it can always bring a deeper realization of the mystery of Christ and the Church.[18]

"Peace and unity"

In 1967, Tolkien observed, with a certain humor, that "We have prayed endlessly for Christian re-union,"[19] and 'endlessly' was only a minor exaggeration: it had been a theme in his prayer for most of his life. The "Octave of Prayer for Christian Unity" was approved in 1909 and was encouraged by various English cardinals and bishops; in 1916, it was made an observance for the Church worldwide and continued to be an important feature of English Catholic prayer through the following decades. Tolkien's friend and pastor at St. Gregory's, Fr. Douglas Carter, was a keen supporter of this endeavor as well. Each day of the Octave, participants were to pray (as helpfully printed in *The Tablet*):

Antiphon: That they may all be One, as Thou, Father, in Me and I in Thee, that they also may be one in Us; that the world may believe that Thou hast sent me.

V. I say unto thee, that thou art Peter;

R. And upon this Rock I will build my Church.

Let us pray.

O Lord Christ, who saidst unto Thine Apostles: Peace I leave with you, My Peace I give unto you; regard not our sins, but the faith of Thy Church, and grant unto her that Peace and Unity which are agreeable to Thy Will Who livest and reignest God for ever and ever. Amen.[20]*

"Peace and unity"—that was what Tolkien prayed for "endlessly." And he didn't just pray for it, but actively befriended non-Catholic Christians in an attempt to help bring it about, extending his religious life to intersect with theirs in various ways. In the next chapter, we will look at how he shared his faith explicitly with a number of friends and family members; in the remainder of this chapter, we will consider a few examples from his prayer life.

On a walking tour in 1945, for instance, he and some of his fellow Inklings visited the little hamlet of Whelford, which had, according to Warren Lewis, "a simple little Church where we all felt that God dwells; nothing to 'see' in it. There, to my surprise and pleasure, Tollers said a prayer."[21] Presumably, he knelt at the altar rail and prayed silently; anything more obvious and he might have felt he deserved a boot thrown at his head. We have no knowledge what he prayed for, of course, but the very act of praying in an Anglican church in such a fashion was significant and evidently touched Warren.

Tolkien considered it important to pray for the souls of those who had died, and he made no distinctions among his friends in this regard. He attended the funerals of non-Catholic family and friends, such as his aunt Mabel Mitton (his

---

* How did Tolkien envisage this oneness transpiring? The answer would appear to be either through freely chosen reunion with the Catholic Church (as has now occurred in the twenty-first century, for example, by means of the various Ordinariates) or through expiration of the separated ecclesial communities. "Speaking institutionally and not of individual souls the channel [of faith] must eventually run back into the ordained course [i.e., the Catholic Church], or run into the sands and perish" (*Letters*, 339n).

father's sister), in 1937, and R.F.W. Fletcher, a colleague in the Oxford English Faculty and an Anglican clergyman, at St-Peter-in-the-East, Oxford, an Anglican church, in 1950.[22]

For his closer friends among the Inklings, he went further. When Charles Williams died in 1945, Tolkien went to the funeral at St. Cross Church, along with Fr. Gervase Mathew—and then, when Mathew offered a Mass for Williams the next day at Blackfriars, Tolkien served at the altar (assisting the priest by providing vessels of wine and water and helping afterward with the ablutions).[23] (See figure 51.) Likewise, when C.S. Lewis died in 1963, Tolkien attended his funeral at Holy Trinity Headington Quarry, had a Mass said for him, and, again, served at it.[24] To have Mass offered for the repose of their souls suggests he believed that they were now in the same state as any faithful Catholic who had died—that is, that they were *en route* to heaven via that condition of the soul known as purgatory, and the prayers of the Mass would help them in their process of final sanctification before they came finally to enjoy the beatific vision.

In addition to these prayerful attempts to bring about the longed-for peace and unity, there are two other little things we should note among Tolkien's efforts to encourage an irenic and ecumenical spirit: one was expressed in practical action, the other implied in his fiction. In 1944, Tolkien joined "a combined Christian Council of all denominations" that Frank Pakenham (later Lord Longford) was establishing in Oxford.[25] Ten years later, when *The Fellowship of the Ring* was published, Tolkien put into the mouth of Haldir, an elf of Lothlórien, words that could encapsulate his entire attitude to this topic: "In nothing is the power of the Dark Lord more clearly shown than in the estrangement that divides all those who still oppose him."[26]

31

Bearing Witness

At the end of every Mass, Tolkien heard the priest say the words "*Ite, missa est*": "Go forth, the Mass is ended," to which the congregation replies, "*Deo Gratias*": "thanks be to God." This is not merely a dismissal at the end of the service but a reminder of the 'Great Commission' given by Jesus to his Apostles: "Go therefore and make disciples of all nations, baptizing them in the name of the Father and of the Son and of the Holy Spirit, teaching them to observe all that I have commanded you" (Matthew 28:19–20). To be a serious Christian, as Tolkien was, meant coming to grips with Christ's command to bear witness to his faith. How did he go about this?

We saw in chapter 20 that his preference was to take a mythopoeic approach when writing about matters of religion; he felt that "theological disquisition" was a mode for which he was "not fitted."[1] Furthermore, with the wariness about the spiritual effects of praise that he had learned from the Oratorians, he considered that public recognition as a defender of the faith, gratifying though it might be, could place one in a false position. He felt, for instance, that C.S. Lewis's wartime BBC broadcasts were getting him "too much publicity for his or any of our tastes." The main problem was that enthusiastic reporters were portraying him as a sort of idealized Christian: Tolkien remarked that Lewis had received "the doubtful honour of a peculiarly misrepresentative and asinine paragraph in the *Daily Telegraph* of Tuesday last. It began 'Ascetic Mr. Lewis——'!!! I ask you! He put away three pints in a very short session this morning, and said he was 'going short for Lent.'"[2*]

---

* Tolkien seems to have been less of a drinker than Lewis. Though he remarked that he was "very fond of beer," he added, "I dislike the sensation of being inebriated intensely. I mean the actual sensation, quite apart from a hangover" (Lee, "Tolkien in Oxford," 149). Of his own Lenten observances, the only one that has come down to us was that one year, according to his diary, he "gave up smoking for Lent" (Charles Noad with Jessica Kemball-Cook, "AGM & Dinner, 21 February 1976," *Amon Hen* 19 [May 1976]: 5).

Sharing the faith in private interactions between individuals also had its potential pitfalls. It was one thing to be known and tolerated as a Catholic, and another entirely to be seen as someone who was trying to convert others. Even Ronald Knox, the Catholic chaplain to the university, had exercised caution, writing in 1939 that although he had three dinner parties a week for students throughout the year, "I have never been in the habit of asking non-Catholic undergraduates to dine, because it has seemed to me that my own immediate job was enough, without encouraging the dons to look on the Old Palace [the chaplaincy] as a centre of propagandism."[3] Tolkien pointed out to George Sayer that the hatred Catholics had historically experienced in Britain "still goes on. I have a friend who walked in procession in the Eucharistic Congress held in Edinburgh, and who reached the end with a face drenched with the spittle of the populace which lined the road and were only restrained by mounted police from tearing the garments and faces of the Catholics."[4] He was referring to the Morningside Riot of June 25, 1935, and was not exaggerating. Thousands of Catholics had gathered for the first Eucharistic Congress held in Scotland since the Reformation and were met by an equal number of 'No Popery' demonstrators. Newspaper reports of the day, even from papers aiming to downplay the events, indicate that protestors shouted verbal abuse and threw stones at Catholics; the police had to resort to the use of batons to control the crowd.[5]

Paradoxically, Tolkien's personal ease with non-Catholics may also have discouraged him from anything that might be perceived as evangelizing, for fear of upsetting a collegial dynamic or a personal friendship. If a conversation about religion went badly, Tolkien might still have to interact with that person over dinner at high table, in faculty committee meetings, or at informal gatherings. Indeed, anti-Catholic prejudice sometimes turned up out of the blue in ordinary social intercourse. For instance, in 1944, Tolkien brought a guest to dine with him at Pembroke. The conversation turned to university politics and the recent election of the new Rector of Lincoln College. As Tolkien recalled, "Sitting next to me, the Master [of Pembroke] in a loud voice said: 'Thank heaven they did not elect a Roman Catholic to the Rectorship anyway: disastrous, disastrous for the college.' 'Yes, indeed,' echoed Dr Ramsden, 'disastrous.' My guest looked at me and smiled and whispered, 'models of tact and courtesy!'"[6]

With these reasons to tread cautiously, it is all the more worthwhile to consider the ways in which Tolkien did, in fact, bear witness to his faith on an individual level.

Robert Murray: Seeker

We can begin with one person who acknowledged Tolkien's influence as being significant in his becoming a Catholic. Robert Murray was the grandson of Sir James Murray, the founding editor of the *Oxford English Dictionary*. As an undergraduate at Corpus Christi, he was introduced to the Tolkiens by his aunt Rosfrith, a family friend.[7]

Murray explained that "it was the attraction unconsciously exercised by Ronald Tolkien and his family which, under God, did most to draw me to the Catholic Church in 1946." But it was more than a silent witness: Murray also noted that "From many conversations I know the depth of Ronald's faith and of the spiritual suffering through which it sustained him."[8] Tolkien evidently talked about his faith with him and was willing to share his own experiences of "spiritual suffering," perhaps those which we have discussed in chapter 18.

Tolkien also actively helped his young friend to meet others in the Catholic community. Murray later recalled that, early in his friendship with the Tolkiens, "when they realised that I was being drawn to share their faith, they introduced me to Father Carter, which led to a lasting friendship with that wonderful man and preacher."[9] As we saw in chapter 28, Fr. Douglas Carter, the parish priest of St. Gregory's, was himself a convert, a deeply learned man who had a charitable approach for ecumenical relations with Anglicans and yet was also ready to speak his mind and engage in debate; it was an ideal connection for Murray, who not only became a Catholic but was later ordained a priest. He recalled that Tolkien "was proud to serve my first mass in 1959 (in full academic dress, excitement making him clumsy as a small boy)."[10]

Warren Lewis: Protestant

An exchange of letters with Warren Lewis (figure 52), C.S. Lewis's brother, shows Tolkien's willingness to discuss his faith on a personal level with a friend who held a position of active disagreement with and even dislike of the Catholic Church.

In June 1947, while on holiday in Ireland, Warren Lewis had a dangerous bout of alcohol abuse (something that he struggled with throughout his adult life) and checked himself into the Convent Hospital of Our Lady of Lourdes in Drogheda, a Catholic institution run by the Sisters of the Medical Missionaries of Mary. In his diary, Warren admitted his previous negative impression of Catholicism: "To the Protestant—or at any rate to me—there has always been something sinister, a little repulsive, almost ogreish, about the practice of the R.C. religion. So far as I had any idea of a convent, it was of something grey and secret, with sad faced women gliding about noiselessly; rarely speaking and never smiling, spying and spied upon." However, his stay at the convent under the care of the Sisters effected a change in his views, such that he continued, "There could be nothing more preposterously unlike the truth: the first thing that strikes you is the radiant happiness of these holy and very loveable women. . . . I shall not soon or easily forget this little fortress of happy, valiant Christianity."[11]

While he was at Drogheda, Warren wrote in his diary that he had received from Tolkien "A most kind and sympathetic letter . . . saying that he had invoked the aid of 'that child of Grace who is nearest his heart,' St. Bernadette, to assist his own feeble prayers for my recovery."[12] In saying not only that he would pray for Warren but that he would ask for the intercession of a saint on his behalf, Tolkien was frankly exposing his own spiritual habits—after all, he was pained all the way to the end of his life by a dismissive comment that C.S. Lewis had made about his devotion to St. John—which speaks to the strength of their friendship and maybe also to the serious condition that Warren found himself in.

Not only was Bernadette a favorite saint of Tolkien's, but choosing her as an intercessor in this case also shows his attention to a detail of the situation: Warren was recovering at the convent of Our Lady of Lourdes. The grotto at Lourdes is the site at which Mary, in her apparition to Bernadette in 1858, identified herself as 'the

Immaculate Conception.' (See figure 20.) With Lourdes a major pilgrimage site for the sick, Our Lady of Lourdes was an appropriate patron for the convent hospital.

When Warren replied to Tolkien's letter, he seems to have indicated something of his more positive view about Catholics, as they evidently began to discuss more substantial topics. Warren wrote, about a week later, that he had spent the afternoon "in answering Tollers' theological letter—a difficult task."[13]

One of the topics under consideration was what Warren described in his diary as "the R.C. attitude to the B.V.M. [Blessed Virgin Mary],"[14] and in particular, her Immaculate Conception. As we have seen, Tolkien upheld this view, noting that Mary was "the only *unfallen* person."[15] As part of his "general objection" to the Catholic view of Mary, Warren cited what he had just heard at a service in the convent, that "the Virgin was endowed with full reason *from the moment of her birth*," which he felt was "a *pointless* miracle. For how did her coming high destiny in any way make it necessary? And why should this be done for her when her Son '*grew* in stature and in *wisdom*'?"[16] We do not know how Tolkien responded; he might have pointed out that these specific ideas about Mary are not in fact part of the dogma of the Immaculate Conception, but rather a way in which it was sometimes interpreted on the popular level. What is relevant for our discussion is that Warren felt able to put his objections into his response to Tolkien—and made an effort to be respectful even as he argued the point; as he wrote in his diary, "I put it however a little less bluntly than this."

Tolkien may not have changed Warren's mind on Mary, but his letters and Warren's experience at the convent hospital did have an effect. Tolkien had put forward "his contention that most of the talk about conventual corruption was nonsense." Warren noted in his diary that he was able to conclude his reply to Tolkien "by heartily endorsing" this point of view.[17]

Michael Tolkien: Doubting Catholic

In 1963, Michael had written to his father in a discouraged state of mind, his faith evidently shaken by the shortcomings he observed among his fellow teachers and the clergy at Ampleforth College, a Catholic school in Yorkshire. Tolkien's reply gives us one of the few examples of a more direct approach to apologetics (defense of the faith) in his letters.

In his reply, Tolkien made a candid declaration of his own Catholic faith, affirming that "We must . . . either believe in [Jesus] and in what he said and take the consequences; or reject him and take the consequences." But he does not *begin* his response to Michael's doubts in this way. Rather, he straightforwardly acknowledges that it is reasonable for Michael to be "scandalized" by the failings he observes and admits that both the ideal of devotion to learning, and religious devotion in general, is "generally degraded and smirched," most noticeably by the "professionals" (whether professional teachers or religious such as the Benedictine monks at Ampleforth). From there, he cautions against self-righteousness, pointing out that "*all* professing Christians" fall short of proper devotion to religion. Most significantly, he says that as he grows older, "I find I become less cynical rather than more—remembering my own sins and follies; and realize that men's hearts are seldom as bad as their words." He gently reminds his son that the danger of paying too much attention to scandal is that "it tends to turn our eyes away from ourselves and our own faults."[18]

Tolkien's characteristic hyperbole is completely absent, a sign that he is at his most serious and thoughtful, as he advises his son in the spirit of Matthew chapter 7: "Judge not, that ye may not be judged: for with what judgment ye judge, ye shall be judged: and with what measure ye measure, it shall be measured unto you. Why seest thou the mote in thy brother's eye, and perceivest not the beam in thine own eye?" (Matthew 7:1–3, Westminster).[19]

In counseling his son specifically with regard to his "sagging faith," Tolkien again takes a realistic tone. He explains that faith is "an act of will, inspired by love," and must be continually repeated; it is not something that is achieved once and for all. We have already observed the importance he attached to "feeding the will." That the will should be "inspired by love" is also worth noting. Love is the underpinning of the whole enterprise, for, as St. Paul taught, even having faith that can move mountains means nothing without love (1 Corinthians 13:2).

Tolkien then sketches out a brief argument for the reality of Jesus and the significance of his teachings. His first defense is of the historicity of Jesus: he notes that the New Testament is not legendary, but rather consists of historical documents that are "virtually contemporary" with the events they record.[20] His second point is psychological, arguing that the teachings of Jesus, identifying himself with God the Father and declaring that 'he who eats my flesh and drinks my blood has eternal life,' were too shocking to have been invented by the people of the day. His third move is logical, noting that if Christ's claims to be one with God are untrue, then the "only alternative" is that the Gospels feature the "garbled accounts of a demented megalomaniac."[21]* Having outlined a few apologetics points, he goes on in a more directly pastoral vein.

We have already discussed, in chapter 13, how Tolkien advised his son that a badly done Mass can be spiritually helpful, a reminder of the principle of *ex opere operato*, that the grace of the sacrament comes from the sacrament itself, and not from the aesthetic experience of the liturgy or the virtues of the priest. But Tolkien went further in his counterintuitive advice by also advising that his son attend a Mass alongside "the usual bourgeois crowd," badly behaved children, "open necked and dirty youths," and "women in trousers and often with hair both unkempt and uncovered." Tolkien is not merely taking potshots at what he perceives as inappropriate attire (for both men and women). Being disheveled and badly dressed are not moral issues per se, but they are things that—as Tolkien put it—will "affront" his son's "taste":[22] his sense of what is socially and aesthetically appropriate.

But he also includes behavior that will *scandalize* his son, in the sense of being offensive to his religious sensibilities. Students from Catholic schools know how they ought to behave, but instead "the moment the tabernacle is opened [they] sit back and yawn." With regard to the women who lack hats or veils, we should note that at that time, it was still a requirement of Church discipline that women cover their heads at Mass and men be bareheaded; it was not until the 1970s that the Congregation for the Doctrine of the Faith declared that it was optional for women to veil (the requirement for men still holds). So, in 1963, a woman who went to Mass with her hair "uncovered" was either ignorant of the Church's rule on the matter, indifferent to it, or actively disobedient.

* This is, in essence, C.S. Lewis's "liar, lunatic, Lord" trilemma from *Mere Christianity*. Lewis's lunatic, "the man who says he is a poached egg," derives from "the man [who] is free to think himself a poached egg" in chapter 2 of Chesterton's *Orthodoxy*, a book that Tolkien appreciated.

The point of the matter comes in what Tolkien says next: "Go to Communion *with* them" (Tolkien's emphasis)—that is, he instructs his son to consciously perceive himself as being part of the Body of Christ with them, not as separate or superior—"and pray for them."[23] It is practical advice on how to perform an act of spiritual charity, pushing back against personal feelings of annoyance.

The point here is not that Tolkien doesn't care about beauty or reverence—it's clear that he does. But his advice to Michael is addressed to the specific issues that he is struggling with: fading faith (which needs to be bolstered by a keener awareness of the reality of Christ in the Blessed Sacrament) and a tendency to be irritated by others that could easily become bitterness or a Pharisaical holier-than-thou attitude. The letter shows Tolkien leveraging the Philippine quality of humility as he helps a younger Catholic navigate both the reality of scandal in the Church and the spiritual dangers that come from self-righteousness.

Simonne d'Ardenne: Lapsed Catholic

This awareness of the difficulties of faith is also shown in Tolkien's mentoring of Simonne d'Ardenne, his former student and a family friend. Writing to R.W. Chambers, he remarks that he is giving to d'Ardenne a copy of Chambers's new book *Thomas More*, evidently as a way of encouraging her in her faith. He describes her as "a Catholic in origin," which is a gentle way of saying that she is a lapsed, or non-practicing, Catholic. Since d'Ardenne lived with the Tolkien family for a time in the early 1930s while she was completing her thesis, Tolkien had the opportunity, through observation and conversation, to understand what her difficulties were. She was "confused," he says, "by the misery of the war [the Great War] and the rancours of our days."[24] Tolkien had himself come through his immediate wartime experiences with his faith intact, though the next decade had been difficult; he knew from experience that the life of faith cannot be taken for granted but has to be struggled with and worked at.

D'Ardenne already knew and valued Chambers's work in the field of Anglo-Saxon language and literature. The gift of his new book would therefore be appreciated in itself and also provide her with material for reflection on the

Catholic faith as lived out by Thomas More, who himself had to struggle with staying faithful in very difficult times, as we saw in chapter 22.

In her reminiscences on Tolkien for his memorial volume, d'Ardenne noted that she had difficulty choosing which aspect of Tolkien's complex personality to focus on. Even once she settled on his "humanity," she found that "so many aspects of him were revealed that I was left still more perplexed: should it be the Christian, or the friend, the artist or the humanist, the father or the teacher?"[25] It is notable that after forty years of friendship, "Christian" should be the first word that she used in attempting to sum up his personality—an indication that he did indeed bear witness to his faith over the years.

R.W. Chambers: Anglo-Catholic

And this brings us to perhaps the most significant of Tolkien's evangelizing encounters, with his friend Raymond Chambers, the Quain Professor of English at University College London, who was a fellow medievalist and an authority on Thomas More. (See figure 53.) Chambers considered himself an 'Anglo-Catholic': that is, a member of the Church of England who was to all intents and purposes Catholic, despite not being in communion with the pope. It was in many respects an awkward position to occupy because the Catholic Church could not recognize Anglo-Catholics as Catholics (since they denied the visible unity of the Church—the *oneness* of the 'one, holy, Catholic, and apostolic Church' described in the Creed), while many in the Church of England, especially its more Evangelical wing, looked askance at these 'ritualist' Anglicans and even forbade some of their practices. With this in mind, Chambers humorously described his religious views in this way: "I am not a papist myself, but an anglo-cat—that is to say, an animal like a hippopotamus, which partakes of the nature of a fish and of a beast, and therefore cannot live on land and dies in the water."[26]

Tolkien was keenly desirous of Chambers taking the final step into the Catholic Church.* He expresses himself most fully in a 1935 letter to Chambers praising his new biography, *Thomas More*:

* Chambers never did become a Catholic, but their friendship continued unimpaired until his death in 1942. In gratitude for the 1935 More biography, Tolkien sent Chambers a copy of *The Hobbit* when it was published two years later.

> I hope it is not an impertinence to conclude that I pray ever for your repose in the bosom of magna mater ecclesia [great Mother Church]—the solution of her puzzles is inside not out. But I am speaking in ignorance, and these are doubtless matters on which trespassers are unwelcome. But you would be of greater benefit than I to the ever-losing cause. Forgive this epilogue—but the desire is so intense (that it may not wholly be suppressed) that those whom we love and reverence should share in that communion, which is no mere theological word. Without it the closeness of spirit which kindred men may feel across centuries, or across contemporary barriers, is—but a spirit: not incarnate, and therefore, for such is Humanity, not complete. But I speak as a child.[27]

He signed it "yours affectionately, Ronald Tolkien"—underscoring the personal and relational aspect of his appeal to Chambers.

We should note that Tolkien's understanding of being a Catholic is more than simply assenting to certain doctrines. As an 'Anglo-Catholic,' Chambers would in fact have agreed with Tolkien on nearly every point except those relating to ecclesiology (that is, the nature of the Church itself). It is for that reason that Tolkien can assume a shared commitment on Chambers's part to "the ever-losing cause": that is, the life and teachings of the Catholic Church, which perpetually appears to be on the brink of fading away as an irrelevance in the modern world and yet still remains because the Lord is with it "always" (Matthew 28:20). But, Tolkien believes, this agreement on doctrines is insufficient. However much Chambers agrees with various doctrinal points, he is outside the Church, and Tolkien longs to welcome him inside.

Being part of the Catholic Church is, in his view, a sacramental reality, not just an intellectual consensus; it can only be fully understood by experiencing it from "inside." The full communion of the Church is, he says, "no mere theological word" but rather an "incarnate" reality. Here Tolkien expresses in his own words one of the central distinguishing beliefs of Catholicism: that the Church is the Mystical Body of Christ, such that all the believers are part of a spiritual organism that extends across time and space. In desiring that Chambers would "share in that communion," he is inviting him not merely to agree with him but, in effect, to join his spiritual family.

In noting that there is a "spirit" that binds together "kindred men" even if it is "not complete" without their common union in the Catholic Church, Tolkien is expressing an ecclesiological understanding that, as we have seen, anticipates the Second Vatican Council's teachings.

Tolkien's honesty is also worth noting here. He admits that the Church has "puzzles": there's no arrogant assumption that the mysteries of the Catholic Church are perfectly clear. Here, perhaps, we glimpse some of the fruits of Tolkien's own season of spiritual difficulty. He does not merely wish for his friend to become a Catholic, he prays constantly for it. And although he is aware that he is taking a risk in saying so—that it might be perceived as an "impertinence" or "unwelcome"—he feels compelled to speak. It is a "desire" (not just a wish) that is "so intense" that it "may not wholly be suppressed." These are heartfelt words, expressing a longing that "those whom we love and reverence" should share in a "communion" that is no mere abstract concept, but "incarnate." The Church, according to Tolkien's understanding, is the continuation of Christ's incarnation in time and space, upon whose bosom one can repose as St. John at the Last Supper (John 13:23) reposed on the bosom of the Lord.

32

In the Beginning Was the Word

In addition to reading Chambers's biography of Thomas More, Tolkien read many other works on religious, theological, and spiritual topics. He was familiar with the Catholic historian Christopher Dawson's *Progress and Religion.*[1] He read Dennis Bennett's *Nine O'Clock in the Morning* (1970), an account of the Pentecostal movement in the Episcopal Church of the United States, and found it "very interesting both as a Christian and a lover of languages."[2] (See figure 45.) He had a great appreciation for the apologetics writings of G.K. Chesterton, including *The Everlasting Man, Heretics,* and *Orthodoxy.*[3] His library included Fr. Martin D'Arcy's *The Nature of Belief* (1931) and a seven-volume set of Thomas Aquinas's *Summa Theologica.*[4] His appreciation of literature on religious themes included, of course, the great Christian literature of the Middle Ages, such as the poems *Pearl* and *Sir Gawain and the Green Knight,* both of which he translated; he declared that Dante was a "supreme poet" despite not having much of a personal liking for *The Divine Comedy.*[5] His interest extended to modern works by Catholics such as Elizabeth Jennings and Anglicans such as Dorothy L. Sayers, whose *The Man Born to Be King* he admired.[6] He also readily engaged with the fiction of writers whose philosophy and ethics were at odds with his own. For instance, he praised the science fiction writer H.G. Wells (an atheist whose *An Outline of History* rejects the divinity of Christ), and enjoyed, at least to some extent, the novels of authors such as Olaf Stapledon and David Lindsay, who wrote from a non- or even anti-Christian viewpoint.[7] His reading, as well as his friendships, was not limited by sectarian boundaries.

The one book that meant the most to Tolkien, however, was the Bible—though of course he would correctly point out that 'the Bible' is better described as the Holy Scriptures, in the plural, containing seventy-three separate writings in a range of genres.* It is to this book, this Book of books, that we now turn to explore its deep, indeed central, significance in his life.

As Simonne d'Ardenne, a friend and colleague of Tolkien's for over forty years, recalled, "Tolkien belonged to that very rare class of linguists, now becoming extinct, who . . . could understand and recapture the glamour of 'the word.' 'In the beginning was the Word, and the Word was with God, and the word was God.'" She goes on to say that "This love of the Word led him to study languages wherever he could find them, with the result that his knowledge of languages other than his native English was amazing, and filled his students with wonder mingled with awe: he was so learned."[8]

"In the beginning was the Word"

"In the beginning was the Word, and the Word was with God, and the Word was God": these words that d'Ardenne quoted come from the Prologue to the Gospel of John (John 1:1–14)—the single passage of Scripture that he heard more often during his lifetime than any other. Before the liturgical reforms of the 1960s, it comprised the 'Last Gospel,' which was read (in Latin) at the end of the Mass. (See Appendix B.) In it, St. John writes of Christ's role in Creation and of his Incarnation into the world that God the Father had spoken into being through him; its themes of light shining in the darkness and the creative power of language echo throughout Tolkien's writings.

Tolkien's expertise in philology (literally, 'love of words,' i.e., languages and the study of their history) was, d'Ardenne believed, rooted in his love of 'the Word.' In chapter 13, we saw Tolkien's devotion to the Incarnate Word as present in the Blessed Sacrament; he also had a deep knowledge and love of the written Word of God, Sacred Scripture. Clyde Kilby, who spent a summer helping the elderly Tolkien with the *Silmarillion*, recalled that in their conversations, "Every single day he would get on to scriptural things."[9]

* The Catholic edition of the Bible contains seven books omitted from Protestant editions, all from the Old Testament: Tobit, Judith, Wisdom, Sirach, Baruch, and 1 and 2 Maccabees. The Catholic books of Esther and Daniel also contain additional material not included in Protestant Bibles.

His knowledge of the Bible in its original languages, as well as his careful attention to the meaning of the text, is evident in the notes that he made on his copy of the Westminster Version of the New Testament.[10] For instance, John 21, in which the risen Jesus gives Peter the threefold charge to "feed my sheep," is heavily marked with annotations in Greek and comments comparing the text both to the Latin Vulgate and to the Revised Standard Version English translation. This passage is an important one for the Catholic understanding of Peter's primacy; here we see Tolkien looking carefully at the scriptural evidence.*

Tolkien also had a great appreciation for the sheer literary power of John's Gospel. One of his military-cadet students during the Second World War recalled that at the beginning of their class, Tolkien "handed round some sample passages of medieval English he had had typed out. One of them was an English translation of the first verses of the Gospel According to John. 'You see,' he said triumphantly, 'English was a language that could move easily in abstract concepts when French was still a vulgar Norman patois.'"[11]

Kilby recalled that Tolkien also "spoke of his special regard for the Book of Luke"—and for a specific reason: "because that writer included so much about women."[12] It is only Luke who presents the story of the Annunciation, who records Mary's Magnificat, and who describes the Blessed Mother's reaction to finding her son in the temple after losing track of him for three days: "Son, why have you treated us so? Behold, your father and I have been looking for you anxiously" (Luke 2:48). It is only Luke who tells of Mary's cousin Elizabeth, the prophetess Anna, Joanna, Susanna, and numerous other female figures, a total of thirteen women who do not appear in Matthew, Mark, or John, including two who feature in parables. The fact that Tolkien was alive to this distinctive aspect of Luke's Gospel and valued it for that reason speaks to his awareness of the importance of the feminine perspective in the Scriptures, something we will explore further below.

---

* Elsewhere he provides cross-references among the Gospels for the narrative of the Passion and comments on the Annunciation. He also seems to have objected to the awkward translation of a phrase in the Lord's Prayer, "And forgive us our debts, as ourselves have forgiven our debtors" (Matthew 6:12).

Trials of translations

Tolkien's knowledge of languages meant that he could read the New Testament in Greek (he had indeed studied it in that language as a pupil at King Edward's School) and could read the Bible in its officially approved Latin Vulgate version translated by St. Jerome.* But he also kept abreast of new English translations. The most widely used Catholic version in Tolkien's youth was Challoner's eighteenth-century revision of the Douay-Rheims translation; there were many versions of the Douay Bible in the late 1800s, but an edition published by Washbourne in 1900 became for many years "the standard Douay Bible in England."[13] The Westminster Version of the New Testament was published in 1948; it was this edition that Tolkien owned, commented upon, and quoted from in his long letter to Michael in 1963.[14] It was intended not for liturgical use but primarily "for the devotional reading of the faithful."[15] That Tolkien spent a great deal of time poring over this edition is attested to both by the marginal notes in his copy and by the tobacco ash spilled from his pipe among its pages.

Tolkien had a long-standing interest in matters of Scriptural translation. In 1936, he corresponded with Adrien Morey, a Benedictine monk who had written to him regarding an Anglo-Saxon version of the Our Father.[16] Tolkien later recalled that this had prompted him "lightheartedly" to explore the topic of the history of the *Pater Noster* in English, touching on matters of syntax (such as 'Our Father *which* art in heaven' vs. 'Our Father *who* art in heaven'), and "the variants used for temptation and trespass(es)."[17] As we saw discussed in chapter 5, Tolkien drew a connection between this passage and Frodo's failure to give up the Ring—and Gollum's providential seizing of it—at Mount Doom.

One notable new version of the Bible that Tolkien knew well was translated by Ronald Knox, who had taken on this monumental task after he left the Oxford chaplaincy. Knox's New Testament was published in 1945, and the Old Testament five years later. (See figure 62.) Authorized by the Catholic hierarchy, it was intended to promote the knowledge of Scripture by offering "freshness of approach," "lively language," and ease of reading.[18] Tolkien, however, was not impressed and tore it "in pieces" (metaphorically) at a meeting of the Inklings. Tolkien knew Knox

* This may partly be why, as we noted in chapter 22, Tolkien was particularly struck by a painting of St. Jerome that he saw in Italy.

personally, well enough to call him 'Ronnie,' as did all his friends. Ronnie, he thought, "had written so much parody and pastiche that he had lost what little ear for prose he ever had."[19]*

Tolkien's point seems to be that because Knox had done so much imitation of archaic styles for humorous or satiric effect, he could no longer write naturally when it came to translating something that needed to be done seriously. Knox's biographer Evelyn Waugh observed that "All his life he found it easiest to express his thoughts in parody and needed special exertion and discipline to write *in propria persona*."[20] One can see something of Tolkien's point in considering, for instance, Knox's rendition of the opening of the Gospel of John: "At the beginning of time the Word already was; and God had the Word abiding with him, and the Word was God. He abode, at the beginning of time, with God." Tolkien's dim view was not, however, shared by all his friends; C.S. Lewis thought the translation as a whole "particularly good" and recommended it in private correspondence.[21] Perhaps Tolkien's dissatisfaction with Knox's work helped spark his interest in trying his own hand at Bible translation—a topic we will turn to in our next chapter.

Echoes of the Word

We discussed in chapter 29 the way that the events of Jesus's Incarnation and Resurrection, narrated in the Gospels, were fundamental to Tolkien's understanding of the eucatastrophic structure of fantasy and, specifically, the kind of fantasy story that he himself was creating in *The Lord of the Rings*. As we consider Tolkien's lifelong immersion in the words of Scripture, we can also recognize the way that certain characters, images, and phrases made their way from the Bible into his tales of Middle-earth.

We find one such instance in *The Hobbit*, with Bilbo's unlikely appointment as a burglar to a party of dwarves. Though their quest is to recover treasure stolen from them by the dragon Smaug, it is not a morally straightforward endeavor: greed takes hold of Thorin to the point that he is ready to make war rather than give any

* Knox's parodies include *Absolute and Abitofhell* (1913), modeled on John Dryden's "Absalom and Achitophel"; *Reunion All Round* (1914), in the manner of Jonathan Swift; and *Barchester Pilgrimage* (1935), a sequel to Anthony Trollope's Barchester Chronicles, written in Trollopian style.

of it up. Bilbo, however, by pocketing the Arkenstone and then renouncing his own share in the treasure, brings about peace and reconciliation. The chapter in which this happens is entitled "A Thief in the Night," a deliberate echo of St. Paul's words in 1 Thessalonians 5:2: "The day of the Lord will come like a thief in the night." Bilbo has not suddenly become a Christ-character (the story is no allegory), but if we miss the scriptural allusion, we miss how Tolkien is subtly pointing up the moral seriousness of Bilbo's action.*

Galadriel is also worth noting in this regard. In *The Lord of the Rings*, when the Fellowship is leaving Lothlórien, Galadriel takes a cup of mead and says, "Now it is time to drink the cup of farewell. . . . And let not your heart be sad, though night must follow noon, and already our evening draweth nigh."[22] The phrase *let not your heart be sad* has a strong echo of Jesus's words to the disciples: "Let not your hearts be troubled" (John 14:1). The allusion is all the clearer if we consider that these words are spoken during the Last Supper when Jesus himself takes a cup and bids farewell to his disciples.

The fact that Galadriel speaks a line echoing Jesus's words to his disciples is a reminder that the Christian resonances of *The Lord of the Rings* are subtle and unpredictable. Galadriel is more obviously Marian than Christlike. Yet here, Tolkien gives her a line that evokes Mary's Son, not Mary herself. It indicates how he saw Mary as the perfect disciple. If readers know the Scriptures, they can note this unexpected allusion, but it does not intrude into the story.

And here, we can also benefit from considering Tolkien's engagement with certain books of the Bible that are less familiar than the Gospel of John. His familiarity with the book of Judith, for instance, is shown in a letter he wrote about references to elves in Old English literature: he was struck by "the occurrence of *aelfsciene* 'elven-fair' applied to Sarah and Judith!"[23]† That well-placed exclamation point—Tolkien's own—calls attention to the heroic figure of Judith, a widow who saves Israel from the invading Assyrians by infiltrating the enemy camp, decapitating their general Holofernes, and bringing his head back to her people in a bag. The book of Judith celebrates her bravery and includes her song of praise to God in

* The image of Christ coming as the thief in the night also appears in in Matthew 24:42–51 and 2 Peter 3:10. For more on Tolkien's use of this imagery, see Michael Ward, "A Thief in the Night: The Christian Ethic at the Heart of *The Hobbit*."

† Sarah, the wife of Abraham, miraculously bears a son Isaac in her old age (Genesis 18:9–15, 21:1–3).

which she gives thanks that the Lord has defeated the invaders "by the hand of a woman" (Judith 16:6).

One would not normally think it characteristic of an "elven-fair" lady to chop someone's head off, but Tolkien would have seen Judith, along with another Old Testament heroine, Jael (who put a tent peg through the head of Sisera, another oppressor, in the book of Judges), as a prefiguration of the Virgin Mary. This association of the fierce Jael and Judith with the Virgin Mary may seem surprising, but in the Catholic devotional tradition, Mary is a powerful figure with certain warrior characteristics. She is often depicted in art as treading on a serpent, a representation of the way that, by being the mother of the Savior, she helps to bring about the downfall of Satan. This is underscored by the way that Genesis 3:15 appears in the Latin Vulgate and thus in the Douay translation: God declares to the serpent, "I will put enmities between thee and the woman, and thy seed and her seed: she shall crush thy head, and thou shalt lie in wait for her heel."*

Galadriel is not sinless like Mary: in one letter, Tolkien remarks that she is "a penitent" since she had participated in the rebellion against the Valar, though he clarifies that she "had committed no evil deeds."[24] Her preeminent Marian quality seems to be her combination of beauty with strength. In *The Silmarillion*, she appears at the time of Fëanor's oath as "tall and valiant among the contending princes" and later as "the mightiest and fairest of all the Elves that remained in Middle-earth."[25] In *The Lord of the Rings*, Sam notes her apparent contradictions, adding, "perhaps you could call her perilous, because she's so strong in herself."[26]

Recognizing the warrior side of the Catholic understanding of Mary is particularly helpful in allowing us to see a wider range of prototypes for Éowyn, the shield maiden of Rohan. Confronting the Lord of the Nazgûl, who boasts that "No living man may hinder me," she declares, "no living man am I! You look upon a woman." Tolkien's description of her at this moment is evocative of Mary: a "maiden . . . slender but as a steel-blade, fair yet terrible." It is worth noting here that she does not stab but rather decapitates the Witch-King's hideous flying steed: "The outstretched neck she clove asunder, and the hewn head fell like a stone."[27]

---

* The Greek Septuagint renders the passage as "*He* shall crush thy head," as Tolkien would have been aware; but either way, it provided the Church with a potent image of Mary contributing to the defeat of Satan. As one of the Doctors of the Church put it, "either the Son by means of the Mother, or the Mother by means of the Son, has overcome Lucifer" (Alphonsus de' Liguori, *The Glories of Mary* [London: Burns, Oates & Washbourne, 1852], 111).

Like Judith beheading Holofernes, like Jael crushing the temples of Sisera, and like Mary treading on the serpent's head, Éowyn has decapitated a figure of evil. Tolkien even adds a suggestive detail: as she strikes the beast of the Nazgûl, "A light fell about her, and her hair shone in the sunrise"[28]—just as Mary shines in, and by virtue of, the light of her risen Son.

But we should not suppose that Tolkien's engagement with the Scriptures was conducted purely on a theological or literary level. It was also deeply personal. He learned portions of the Bible by heart to use as prayers (see chapter 27) and assimilated it into his way of thinking about what was most important to him. In the 1930s, he wrote a list (in Elvish script) of all the names of his family, adding the phrase "like branches of olive trees" at the end both in Latin and Old English,[29] an allusion to Psalm 128:3. The Psalm opens as follows:

> Blessed are all they that fear the Lord: that walk in his ways.
> For thou shalt eat the labours of thy hands: blessed art thou, and it shall
> be well with thee.
> Thy wife as a fruitful vine, on the sides of thy house.
> Thy children as olive plants, round about thy table.[30]

The way that Tolkien connects this Psalm of blessing with the names of his family gives us a sense of his hopes for himself, his wife, and his children. The vine and the olive would naturally have appealed to him, given his lifelong love for all things arboreal. But we should not overlook the biblical source of the arboreal image, for he also had a lifelong love for, interest in, and knowledge about all things scriptural.

33

Jonah

As a Christian academic, Tolkien was both personally and professionally interested in one of the challenges for the Church in his lifetime: how to respond to modern developments in textual criticism as applied to biblical scholarship. New methods of critical analysis had been adopted, affecting how people—both in the academy and in the pew—approached the Bible. These methods provided insight into historical context and authorship, showing, for instance, parallels between scriptural texts and other ancient Near Eastern literature and providing evidence that Moses was not the sole author of the Pentateuch, the first five books of the Old Testament. These new approaches allowed for better editions of the Bible, but they were also taken up in the general cultural shift toward theological modernism; there was an increasing perception that science had disproved the inspiration and accuracy of the Bible, and that only the credulous and uneducated could continue to believe it as the Church had traditionally taught it.

"The Eden 'myth'"

Tolkien observed this shift in attitudes with regard to the Genesis account of the Garden of Eden, remarking in 1945 that some Christians had rejected the whole story "as soon as modern taste began to sneer" and that even among those who had not abandoned it entirely, many came to consider it "as not very fashionable furniture, a bit ashamed to have it about the house, don't you know, when the bright clever young people called."[1] If the Bible was nothing more than an ancient myth, it could not be an authoritative sacred text. However, if affirming the divine inspiration of the Bible meant rejecting the mythic dimension entirely and reading it on a flatly literalistic level, much was lost.

Tolkien had evidently wrestled with this very issue, for he noted, "I do not now feel either ashamed or dubious on the Eden 'myth.'" Not *now*—but at some earlier point he *had* been among those who felt "a bit ashamed" of it and had consequently "forgotten the beauty of the matter even 'as a story.'"[2]

How had he come to terms with the Garden of Eden? Tolkien explained that while the New Testament contains "virtually contemporary documents," the book of Genesis "is separated by we do not know how many sad exiled generations from the Fall." But, he adds, "certainly there was an Eden on this very unhappy earth,"* which the human spirit somehow recalls: "As far as we can go back the nobler part of the human mind is filled with the thoughts of *sibb*, peace and goodwill, and with the thought of its *loss*."[3]

Tolkien identified three influences that shaped his deeper appreciation of the Genesis account. The first was his own literary and linguistic work, which, as we saw in chapter 20, helped him to convince the not-yet-Christian Lewis that a myth can also be *true*. The second was an essay written by the now-converted Lewis that made a defense of the "story-value" of Christianity. The essay in question, probably "Myth Became Fact,"[4] was much indebted to the insights that Lewis had received from Tolkien and Dyson in their nighttime conversation in Addison's Walk. Lewis, returning the favor, now enabled Tolkien to see more clearly that although a story's beauty was "not necessarily a guarantee of its truth," it was "a concomitant of it," and the faithful are "meant to draw nourishment from the beauty as well as the truth."[5] This seems to have helped Tolkien adopt a new and deeper reading of the story of Eden.

The third influence that Tolkien names is "the firm guiding hand of Alma Mater Ecclesia"[6]—that is, Our Mother, the Church. One of the firm teachings Tolkien presumably had in mind was the encyclical *Providentissimus Deus* (1893), which had rejected theological modernism and affirmed the inerrancy and divine inspiration of the Scriptures, while also approving the use of historical-critical methods. Another teaching, and probably one nearer the forefront of his mind (given the 1945 date of this letter), was the more recent encyclical *Divino Afflante Spiritu*, on the reading and study of Holy Scripture.

---

* In saying "certainly there was an Eden," he is not committing himself to a literal belief in a historical talking snake but affirming the truth of the Genesis myth from an etiological and theological point of view.

In this encyclical, Pope Pius XII remarked upon the improved methodologies of biblical scholarship and the discoveries of more ancient manuscripts, and declared that Catholics should produce new editions of the Scriptures that "unite the greatest reverence for the sacred text with an exact observance of all the rules of criticism."[7] The pope observed that "the literal sense of a passage is not always as obvious in the speeches and writings of the ancient authors of the East, as it is in the works of our time." He explained that the human authors of Scripture, like other ancient authors, used "certain definite idioms . . . and certain hyperbolical modes of expression, nay, at times, even paradoxical, which even help to impress the ideas more deeply on the mind." It is crucial, therefore, to identify the "literary mode" of a given text as well as to understand the "customary modes of expression and narration peculiar to the ancients."[8]

Divino Afflante Spiritu includes an exhortation that Tolkien would have found relevant as a teacher of language and literature. The pope explains that it is important "to make better known the mentality of the ancient writers, as well as their manner and art of reasoning, narrating and writing." Therefore, "Catholic laymen . . . will render a conspicuous service to the Christian cause if they devote themselves with all due diligence and application to the exploration and investigation of the monuments of antiquity and contribute, according to their abilities, to the solution of questions hitherto obscure."[9]

Tolkien's academic expertise in philology was certainly relevant to this issue; he had solved with great skill various textual difficulties in Old English manuscripts caused by scribal errors, dialect variations, and so on—and, more to the point perhaps, he had spent his career teaching students how to do the same. These skills and attitudes are transferable: when one can enter into the point of view of a medieval writer of Old English and understand the way the scribal process works, one is better equipped to encounter the Scriptures on their own terms, without projecting modern assumptions onto them. Tolkien always used his literary and philological skills with respect for the genre of old texts and with attention to their original meaning; indeed, his 1936 lecture "Beowulf: The Monsters and the Critics" was his manifesto for the importance of doing so. *Divino Afflante Spiritu* was, in a way, an affirmation of the indirect value of his academic work for the Church.

Translating Jonah

But Tolkien also had a hand in a project that was much more directly a response to *Divino Afflante Spiritu*: he helped to translate the Bible.

Pius XII's encouragement of new and better editions of the Bible resulted in the publication, between 1948 and 1953, of *La Bible de Jérusalem*, a highly acclaimed French translation from the original Hebrew, Greek, and Aramaic sources, with extensive notes.[10] The Jerusalem Bible in English was the brainchild of Alexander Jones, who set out to assemble a team of translators for an English version, working from the French text.*

Tolkien was one of the first people Jones recruited for his team of translators. Jones so greatly admired *The Lord of the Rings* that he wrote to Tolkien in 1957 explaining that it "made me long to have an English Bible translation from such a hand."[11] Recognizing the impossibility of such a large project as that, Jones was eager to have Tolkien as one of his contributors—and Tolkien responded positively from the outset.

Appropriately for a writer of fantasy, the scriptural text that Tolkien translated is one of the most fantastic of all biblical stories: the book of Jonah, firmly established in the cultural imagination of even non-Bible-readers as the account of a man swallowed by a whale.† It is also (fittingly for Tolkien's personality) a story with a touch of humor.

This book begins with the word of the Lord coming to Jonah: he is to go to Nineveh and tell the people there to repent of their sins. Jonah's response is to head in the opposite direction: as Tolkien translates it, "He came down to Joppa and found a ship bound for Tarshish; and he paid the fare and went on board, to go with them to Tarshish, away from Yahweh."‡ God causes a storm that threatens all on

* Although it may seem odd to translate from the French rather than from the Hebrew and Greek originals, the decision was based on the practical recognition that there were very few Catholics able to do such work, and that the preparation of a translation from Hebrew would require an immense amount of time and effort. The New Testament version that Tolkien used, the Westminster, did in fact go back to the original Greek. However, as Jones pointed out to Tolkien, "the Westminster Version from the originals is not nearly half-done (and never will be finished) after thirty years!" (Wolfe, "Tolkien's Jonah," 16).

† This was Jones's choice; he also hoped for Tolkien to translate more of the historical books of the Old Testament, though in the end he did not do so (Wolfe, "Tolkien's Jonah," 19).

‡ All quotations from Jonah in this chapter come from Tolkien's original translation, which was slightly revised by the editors for the final version that appears in the Jerusalem Bible. The

board, so Jonah—realizing that this is all his fault—allows the crew to throw him overboard. He is swallowed by a great fish and after three days and three nights is vomited up on land. At this point, he is told a second time, "Arise, go to Nineveh, the great city, and say to them what I tell you to say." This time, he obeys. Jonah declares to the Ninevites that in forty days, the city will be destroyed; hearing this, all the people repent in sackcloth and ashes, and God declares that he will not destroy them. At this, Jonah is *angry* that God has had mercy on the Ninevites, and he goes off to the desert to sulk. God then causes a plant to grow up over Jonah's head to shade him from the sun—which he appreciates—but the next day, the plant withers and dies. Jonah, now feeling faint from the sun, declares that he is angry enough to die. God says to him, "You grieve for this colocynth, which cost you no labour, and which you did not make grow, which sprouted in a night, and in a night has perished. And I forsooth should not grieve for Nineveh, the great city, in which there are more than a hundred and twenty thousand people who cannot tell their right hand from their left, and many cattle as well!"[12] On that exasperated note—which Tolkien makes into an exclamation from God rather than a question, as in most translations—the book of Jonah ends.

Tolkien's translation, begun in 1957, was completed by 1961. (See figure 61.) He worked from the French text of the *Bible de Jérusalem*, but he did learn some basic Hebrew, the study of which allowed him to make some revisions to the draft of his translation.[13] The final version as published in the Jerusalem Bible (1966) incorporates various editorial revisions, but Tolkien was consulted on these and "the printed text represents his work."[14] But as the quotations above show, one charming aspect of Tolkien's translation that unfortunately didn't make it into the final version was his name for the plant that provides shade for Jonah. In other translations, this has been rendered as "ivy" (Douay Version), "gourd" (KJV), or simply "a plant" (RSV). The botanically minded Tolkien took great pains over researching this name and exchanging notes with Jones on the subject; he ultimately opted for "colocynth." However, the final version used "castor oil plant."[15]

---

choice of "Yahweh" for what is usually rendered "the Lord" was Alexander Jones's editorial decision (Tolkien, "The Book of Jonah").

The value of the vernacular

Before we consider Tolkien's approach to translating the Bible, it is worth noting the significance of his accepting the invitation in the first place.

Although he could and sometimes did read the Bible in Latin, a language in which he was completely fluent, we have seen that he also used an English translation for his personal devotions and study. Furthermore, he not only accepted but warmly approved of the Bible being translated into vernacular languages. Robert Murray recalled how, shortly before Tolkien's death, he declared that it had been a historical disaster that the Gothic people of Europe had embraced the Arian heresy; if that had not happened, Tolkien said, their languages "would have been enriched not only with a great bible version but also, on Byzantine principles, with a vernacular liturgy, which would have served as a model for all the Germanic peoples and would have given them a native Catholicism which would never break apart. And with that he rose and in splendidly sonorous tones declaimed the Our Father in Gothic."[16]

Another interesting point is that translating the Bible meant entering into work that had hitherto been done almost exclusively by men in ordained ministry. The other examples he had of Catholic versions of the Bible were all done by those in Holy Orders: the Westminster Version by a team of priests; whatever the deficits of Knox's translation, he was at least a priest; the translators of the *Bible de Jérusalem* were Dominicans; Alexander Jones, the head of the Jerusalem Bible project, was a priest. Would a layman like Tolkien feel that it was appropriate to venture into clerical territory in this way? But as we saw in chapter 21, for a number of years, Tolkien was a member of the Catenians, a group that was established on the premise that Catholic laymen should be encouraged to be involved in the life of the Church and not leave everything to the clergy; by this time, he had decades of active engagement in the life of Catholic Oxford. When Jones invited him to be part of the team, he did not defer the task to specialists in biblical studies, nor to the clergy; he mulled it over and said yes.[17]

As a translator, Tolkien made some choices that are slightly unexpected. For one thing, he favored a slightly modernizing approach in the language. In working on the Jerusalem Bible, he offered advice regarding the translation as a whole as well as contributing his own piece. One of the questions under consideration was whether to use the modern pronoun 'you' or the more archaic forms of 'thee,' 'thou,' and 'ye.' Tolkien personally appreciated the older forms, and was adept in using them, but was in favor of using 'you.' Jones thanked him for his "support for the 'you' policy; without it I should have been most uneasy, having no great confidence in my own decisions; like you I regret the passing of 'thou' etc."[18] It is interesting to note that as Jones was on the fence about whether to use the modern form, Tolkien probably could have convinced him to stick with 'thee' and 'thou' if he had made a case for it.

The other interesting choice is his use of a plain style. Brendan Wolfe notes that although Tolkien framed Jonah 2:3–10 as a poem, he "did not attempt any poetic embellishment. . . . Indeed, there is nothing especially distinctive about the translation as a whole, and one would be hard pressed to link it to the author of *The Lord of the Rings* or the verse translator of *Sir Gawain and the Green Knight*."[19] Tolkien had translated the first chapter of the book of Isaiah as a sample of his approach before starting on Jonah,[20] and this passage is also revealing. He began "with stark alliteration, the poetic form dearest to him, but afterwards quickly grows more prosaic, perhaps out of respect for the sacred text."[21]

The plainness of Tolkien's style in Jonah was the result of a deliberate decision. On the one hand, he was profoundly committed to the beauty of language and literary style; he once remarked disparagingly on the "flattening, Bible-in-basic-English attitude"* which he felt led to young people having limited vocabularies and no love of language.[22] But as we have seen, he also criticized Knox's version for its flavor of pastiche, suggesting that he was skeptical of attempts to recapture in English a supposed 'biblical style.' What he aimed for, it seems, in his own translation of the Bible was a simplicity that kept the focus on the text, not drawing attention to the stylistic panache of the translator. This simplicity still allowed for the scriptural text to be presented in beautiful, resonant language—and indeed, his Jonah translation has some striking passages, such as in his rendering of Jonah's prayer to God from the belly of the fish:

* Devised by C.K. Ogden and I.A. Richards, who advocated its use in *The Meaning of Meaning* (1923), Basic English was a simplified form of English, reduced to 850 words in order to make it easier to teach as a second language.

> The waters were all about me even to my throat, the abyss encompassed me.
> The seaweed was wrapped about my head at the roots of the mountains.
> I went down into the countries beneath the earth, unto the peoples of the past.
> (Jonah 2:6–7)

Intriguingly, the phrase "the roots of the mountains" appears in *The Hobbit*, where we are told that Gollum dwells "down at the very roots of the mountains."[23] Tolkien used the phrase again repeatedly in *The Lord of the Rings* to refer to the location of Gollum's home. It is an unusual choice of words (we usually speak of the foot of a mountain, not its roots), but it was one that Tolkien had encountered long before in a novel by one of his favorite authors, William Morris: its very title was *The Roots of the Mountains* (1889). He assimilated the term, like other Morrisean vocabulary and stylistic features, into his Middle-earth writings. And so, when he came to translate Jonah for the Jerusalem Bible, Tolkien chose not the Douay phrasing ("the lowest parts of the mountains") nor the direct translation of the French *A la racine des montagnes* ('at the root [singular] of the mountains') but the plural "roots." Thus, we can now trace a link between Jonah and *The Lord of the Rings*!

Translating the book of Jonah meant that Tolkien approached the text in much the same way that he would have done any other literary work for translation. However, he retained his basic orientation toward the text as inspired and authoritative (2 Timothy 3:16)—something with direct relevance to him as a Christian. As he wrote to his grandson Michael George after finishing his initial draft, "the 'whale'—it's not really said to be a whale but a big fish—is quite unimportant. The real point is that God is much more merciful than 'prophets,' is easily moved by penitence, and won't be dictated to even by high ecclesiastics whom he has himself appointed."[24]

Mercy and repentance: these are themes that continue to resonate with Tolkien in his later years as much as they did in youth and middle age.

34

"An axe-blow near the roots"

Through all the years of Tolkien's professorial work in Oxford, one constant was his friendship with C.S. Lewis. Fellow Inklings, academics, and Christians, the two men are sometimes blurred together as a sort of composite Oxonian fantasy writer, but they were very different personalities. And it was a complex friendship, one that was deep-rooted and enduring despite many differences between them—professionally, temperamentally, spiritually.

Their friendship took root in 1929, when Tolkien showed Lewis his poem "The Lay of Leithian." Throughout the 1930s and 1940s, they met frequently, at Inklings meetings and just to socialize, going on the occasional walking tour together, and encouraging each other in fiction writing. So spiritually helpful did Tolkien find these interactions that he became alert to the surprising number of obstacles that seemed to arise when they were planned; jokingly, he surmised that a "minor imp of Slubgob's brood . . . specially attends to preventing C.S.L. and myself from meeting."[1]

Though they were close and deep friends, they weren't always on the same wavelength. Tolkien didn't care much for the Narnia Chronicles. When Lewis read to him the first few draft chapters of *The Lion, the Witch and the Wardrobe*, he was unimpressed, and in the Chronicles overall, he disliked what he perceived as a hodgepodge of unrelated mythologies (though in fact, Lewis's stories have a hidden imaginative structure that Tolkien might well have appreciated, if he had recognized it).[2] Further, Lewis's less oblique way of putting Christian elements into his stories went against the grain of his own approach. Nevertheless, in later years he wrote to a correspondent, "I am glad that you have discovered Narnia. These stories are deservedly very popular"; although he personally does not like them, this is simply a "difference of taste" with Lewis.[3] And Tolkien admitted that it went both ways: he remarked that he and his friend had, over the years, greatly enjoyed reading each other's work, but "Naturally neither of us liked all that we found in the other's fiction."[4]

After Lewis died, in 1963, Tolkien commented to his son Michael that he and Lewis had ceased to be "intimates" about ten years earlier.[5] Sometimes this is taken as an indication of a rift between the two men, or even a dramatic falling-out, but this was not the view of those who knew them both. John Tolkien declared that it was "nonsense" to say that Tolkien's friendship with Lewis ended. Priscilla noted that, in the late 1950s and into the 1960s, they experienced "a loosening of the bonds, and a loss of what my father would call the communion between them." But, she says, "the affection remained." Christopher concurred, noting that "it was no more than a drifting apart."[6] We should recognize, for one thing, that by the mid-1950s, Lewis was working in Cambridge during the week and so the opportunities for meetings were reduced;* also, Tolkien now had two grandchildren, who provided fresh distractions. It is not surprising that they simply found less time to spend with each other than in earlier years.

There were some real strains, as could be expected. A friendship of thirty years' standing is, like a marriage, certain to provide opportunities for discord as well as delight. And as the issues that tested this bond—as well as Tolkien's response—touch on matters of importance in the spiritual life, it will be worth looking in some detail at the last years of their friendship.

* In 1954, Lewis was offered the new Chair in Medieval and Renaissance English at the University of Cambridge. He initially declined, thinking he would have to dissolve his Oxford household, which for his brother's sake he was unwilling to do. Tolkien, who was one of the eight electors for the position, went to see Lewis and explained he could commute weekly and not move house. He reported to the appointment committee: "Whatever may be strictly correct in an elector, it was clear to me that without some such talk the offer to Lewis would be a mere gesture. . . . I felt able to urge the case for Cambridge sincerely, since I do think that, besides being the precise man for the job, Lewis would probably be happy there, and actually be reinvigorated by a change of air. Oxford, has not, I think, treated him very well, and though he is incapable of 'dudgeon,' or of showing resentment, he has been a little dispirited. After our talk he said he would accept!" (Barbour, "Lewis and Cambridge," 463). Tolkien understood Lewis's personality and his needs. He did not stand on his dignity as an elector to an important professorial chair but went privately to his friend to convince him to change his mind. And he rejoiced in Lewis's acceptance, knowing that it would do him good, despite the fact that it would mean seeing less of his friend.

Joy and sorrow

Tolkien was of the view that Lewis's "great generosity and capacity for friendship"[7] led at times to his being hasty in forming new attachments; indeed, he remarked that Lewis was "too impressionable."[8] With Lewis's openness of heart came the danger of being taken advantage of, something that may well have been of concern to Tolkien (as it was to some others of Lewis's friends*) when Lewis met the woman who would become his wife.

In 1950, Lewis began replying to letters from Joy Davidman Gresham: a married American woman with two children, she was a convert from atheism to Christianity who had benefited greatly from Lewis's writings. In 1952, she came to England and became friends with Lewis in person. A year later, with her marriage in difficulty and divorce an on-again, off-again possibility, she returned, this time with her two sons, Douglas and David (her husband would eventually file for divorce on the grounds of desertion). At that time, Lewis's feeling for her was entirely platonic but, unbeknownst to him, on her side it was romantic.[9] In 1956, she was faced with difficulties with renewing her visa, and so, Lewis entered into what was a pure formality to enable her stay in the UK: he married her in a civil ceremony, but they did not live together as husband and wife, and the arrangement was kept secret from almost everybody. Tolkien later wrote plaintively, "he never even told me; I learned of it long after the event."[10]

As Mark Havard recalled, Lewis had talked it over with his father, Robert Havard, arguing that it wasn't really a marriage, just a "charitable way" of solving Joy's problem:

> Although my father was a pretty orthodox Catholic, he felt that this argument was fine with him, because this was just an arrangement. Lewis did not talk about it to Tolkien because he was sure (and I think rightly sure) that Tolkien was much more strictly orthodox Catholic than my father, and would have said, "Marrying not in front of a priest in whatever form is always wrong." And Tolkien would have been very shocked.[11]

* Robert Havard thought that she was "making an obvious pass at Lewis," and George Sayer recalled, "We thought she had designs on Lewis and we didn't know her well enough to trust her" (Santamaria, *Joy*, 279).

Knowing that the devoutly Catholic Tolkien would certainly have disapproved of the proceedings, Lewis understandably avoided the issue. Although the two of them had in the past debated issues of the highest importance ("true myth," the Incarnation and Resurrection of Christ, and so on), it was another thing altogether for Lewis to invite an opinion from his friend that would be sure to cause pain to them both.

Joy was shortly thereafter diagnosed with bone cancer, by all evidences terminal. Lewis realized that he loved her and wanted to marry her in a Christian ceremony while there was still time. Now the issue was much more serious, since Joy had previously been married. In Tolkien's understanding of marriage, the fact that Joy was divorced indicated only her legal status, not the moral and spiritual reality of her situation. If Lewis were to make the 'legal arrangement' with Joy into a real, consummated marriage, this would, in Tolkien's understanding of the matter, mean committing the grave sin of adultery. And in fact, Lewis himself originally thought that a real marriage to Joy would be "from my point of view, adultery and therefore mustn't happen."[12]

As it happens, Joy's first husband, Bill Gresham, had himself previously been married and divorced, thus arguably rendering invalid his marriage to Joy. Lewis put precisely this argument to the Anglican bishop of Oxford when he sought a Christian marriage with Joy. The bishop, however, said no. In the Church of England at that time, remarriage after divorce was not allowed; and, unlike the Catholic Church, it has no process to distinguish valid from invalid marriages. Lewis then convinced a clergyman friend of his, Peter Bide, an Anglican parish priest from the south coast of England, to conduct the wedding anyway, and in March 1957, they were married at Joy's hospital bed.* Everyone expected Joy to die soon thereafter, but she experienced what by all accounts was a miraculous recovery, and they enjoyed three years of married life together until her death in July 1960.

Tolkien was very worried about his friend. If Lewis were in fact in an adulterous relationship, it would certainly have a negative effect on his spiritual well-being, and it was disturbing that he had circumvented the authority of his own bishop in

* When asked by Lewis to conduct the marriage, Bide was troubled: "The fact that there were church laws by the dozen which forbade me to do anything of the sort really worried me. . . . I wasn't in my own parish, I wasn't in my own diocese. What right had I to go charging into a situation like this which everybody else had refused to have anything to do with?" (Bide, "Marrying C.S. Lewis," 190).

order to achieve the end he had in view. Tolkien didn't avoid Lewis or give him the cold shoulder, but he was troubled. On one occasion in 1958, Tolkien had dinner with Lewis, George Sayer, and Robert Havard. Sayer recounts that

> While Jack was paying the bill after a hilarious dinner, we talked a little about his health. Tolkien was gloomy about the terrible strains and anxieties Jack was suffering. . . . It turned out that what worried him most was that [Joy] was a divorcee. He did not accept my argument that she could not have been divorced, since as a Christian she had never been married.[13]

Sayer's argument was that since Joy had not become a Christian until after her first marriage, which was therefore only a civil procedure, she was not really married at all. But Tolkien did not accept this distinction between 'civil' and 'Christian' marriage and had objected to Lewis suggesting such a thing in his book *Christian Behaviour*. (We will return to this point in chapter 38.) If he did eventually learn the real grounds upon which Joy's first marriage could have been adjudged invalid, he would no doubt have been much relieved.

Tolkien was hurt by being kept in the dark about Lewis's first, civil marriage to Joy and kept at arm's length when it came to their second, Christian marriage. But he presumably also realized that Lewis's reluctance to be open with him was to be expected, a natural result of his, Tolkien's, holding to a Catholic understanding of indissolubility. This was part of the cost of faith: he could not *both* keep the witness to what he believed, in its fullness, *and* always be in harmony with what his friends believed and did.

Lewis's "very strange marriage,"[14] as Tolkien described it, certainly introduced tensions into their friendship, but it did not produce a break. To be sure, they saw less of each other in these years. Some of this was undoubtedly produced by a certain relational discomfort. Some of it was Lewis's natural shifting of focus to his new wife and stepsons. And we should also keep in mind that during these years, Tolkien had many things on his mind that drew his attention away from his old friend: he was finishing up his teaching at Oxford and entering into retirement, and Edith had recurring, serious health issues. Ironically, Edith Tolkien got to know Joy Davidman when they were both patients in the Acland Nursing Home and liked her "very much." Though Lewis's marriage had caused a problem for Tolkien, strangely the two men were now united by the fact that they were both caring for "invalid wives."[15]

The distance that had formed between the two men didn't disappear instantly, but efforts came from both sides. In 1962, Lewis wrote a cheerful note to Tolkien, closing with "I wish we could ever meet." Later that winter, Tolkien went with his son Christopher to visit Lewis at his home, The Kilns, a meeting that, from Christopher's recollection, was apparently rather awkward and conversation lagged.[16] (It probably did not help that the weather was icy cold, and The Kilns is not the warmest of houses.) But in any case, it is not surprising that the first stages of renewal of a friendship should be a little difficult.

John recalled that in the last autumn of Lewis's life, he drove his father for another visit to The Kilns, "for what turned out to be a very excellent time together for about an hour. I remember the conversation was very much about the *Morte d'Arthur* and whether trees died."[17] A warm and friendly conversation between old friends—which neither of them realized would be their last meeting.

In June 1963, Lewis became seriously ill and went into a coma. Tolkien went to his friend's side, attending what he believed to be his deathbed.[18] Lewis recovered, but only for a few months: on November 22, 1963, he died, suddenly and unexpectedly. He was sixty-four years old.

Tolkien was devastated. He turned down an invitation to write an obituary for Lewis, saying that "I feel his loss so deeply that I have since his death refused to write or speak about him."[19] Priscilla, realizing how much Lewis meant to her father, sent a letter of sympathy immediately upon hearing the news. He was deeply grateful for the gesture and stated bluntly that Lewis's death "feels like an axe-blow near the roots."[20]

On November 26, Tolkien had a Mass said for Lewis and served at it.[21] Later that day, he attended Lewis's funeral at the Anglican church of Holy Trinity, Headington Quarry. It was a quiet occasion, and it caught his attention that Lewis's grave was beneath a larch tree.[22]

Walter Hooper, Lewis's friend and literary executor, visited Tolkien soon after Lewis's death. Hooper recalled that one of the points Tolkien made "was that Lewis 'had not made enough time for me' and I explained that Lewis's view was that Tolkien had not made enough time for him. I think he felt then that it was a pity that they had both claimed to be very busy, which they doubtless were, but you just don't really believe your friends will die."[23]

"A distressing and in parts horrifying work"

We come now to an issue that had troubled Tolkien to some extent during his friend's life and presented itself all-too-vividly after his death: the question of Lewis's attitudes toward Catholicism.

Tolkien had occasionally noticed what he considered anti-Catholic tendencies in Lewis, as on the occasion, in 1944, when the Catholic poet Roy Campbell joined them at an Inklings gathering. Campbell had firsthand accounts of the atrocities perpetrated in the Spanish Civil War by the Communists against Catholic loyalists. Tolkien felt that Lewis was strangely willing to believe Communist propaganda on these points: "if a Lutheran is put in jail he is up in arms; but if Catholic priests are slaughtered—he disbelieves it (and I daresay really thinks they asked for it)."[24] But as we saw in chapter 26, he also knew firsthand that Lewis had a warm and genuinely welcoming attitude toward Catholics and counted many among his friends.

The year after Lewis's death, his final book appeared in print. *Letters to Malcolm: Chiefly on Prayer* is structured around the conceit of a series of letters to "Malcolm," who is a fictional character invented precisely to allow Lewis to discuss his topic in an informal, colloquial manner. It is relaxed in tone and filled with remarks about ordinary life, such that one could easily take it as a genuine correspondence. It is, on the whole, a wise and insightful book, containing quite a lot that Tolkien could and undoubtedly did approve of and agree with.

Yet when Tolkien read it, he was also dismayed; he wrote to a Catholic correspondent that "I personally found *Letters to Malcolm* a distressing and in parts horrifying work. I began a commentary on it, but if finished it would not be publishable."[25]

This unfinished commentary, popularly known as 'The Ulsterior Motive,' has acquired a sort of malign importance, probably because, like the majority of Tolkien's letters and private papers, it has not been published or made readily available to scholars. Usefully, Humphrey Carpenter quoted from it in his group biography of the Inklings,[26] but these passages are too often quoted out of context, as if they represented Tolkien's settled views about Lewis rather than his personal and highly emotional response to a particular work that he read while still grieving Lewis's death.

What distressed him about Lewis's book, and what were the parts that horrified him?

There are various small points scattered throughout *Letters to Malcolm* that might have proved to be irritants, such as Lewis's extravagant claim that John Henry Newman "makes my blood run cold" by his comparison of heaven to a church; he has, Lewis claims, "substituted *religion* for God."[27] The idea that Newman would have endorsed religiosity in place of a real relationship with God is ludicrous to anyone who is familiar with his sermons. True, Newman's phrasing is a bit awkward and it touched Lewis on a sensitive point that he was forever keen to emphasize—namely, not putting second things first.* Religiosity is a real problem, but Tolkien knew that Newman was not an example of it and also knew that if Lewis had been reading Newman with his normal attentiveness, he would have recognized it too.†

Tolkien might also have objected to a passage in which Lewis criticizes the view on purgatory held by Catholics in the sixteenth century as a "degradation" from that seen in Dante's *Purgatorio*, and claims that Thomas More and John Fisher (two of the Catholic martyrs of that era) present a view of purgatory that is "disgusting and unhallowed."[28] Lewis's inflammatory phrasing is probably strategic; he is actually arguing for the existence and value of purgatory, which is not a doctrine normally held by Anglicans, and he may have, in effect, thrown More and Fisher 'under the bus' in order to gain a hearing from readers who were skeptical of such 'popish' doctrines. In fact, Lewis's articulation of purgatory as a healing and cleansing state is not so different from Tolkien's own in "Leaf by Niggle." But Tolkien, who had a high regard for Thomas More, might well have taken exception to the rhetorical moves by which Lewis arrived at his presentation.

---

* In the opening chapter of *Letters to Malcolm*, Lewis remarks: "The perfect church service would be one we were almost unaware of; our attention would have been on God." See also his essay "First and Second Things."

† Newman writes that heaven is like a church insofar as in both places, there is no attention given to "how to strengthen our worldly interests, extend our influence, or establish our credit." Rather, we attend to God: "We praise Him, worship Him, sing to Him, thank Him, confess to Him. . . . And *therefore*, a church is like heaven; viz. because both in the one and the other, there is one single sovereign subject—religion—brought before us" (*Parochial and Plain Sermons* [London: Rivingtons, 1875], 1:5).

However, these are minor points. The portion of *Letters to Malcolm* that would certainly have distressed Tolkien at a deep level was Lewis's extended discussion of transubstantiation: that is, the Catholic doctrine that the bread and wine of the altar become, when consecrated, the Body and Blood of Christ.

Lewis begins by saying that it is "almost impossible to state the negative effect which certain doctrines have on me—my failure to be nourished by them—without seeming to mount an attack against them." He said that he does not wish to "unsettle" the concepts by which a fellow Christian "finds it profitable to represent to himself what is happening when he receives the bread and wine."[29] But then he goes on to do that very thing, in a passage that is remarkable in how uncharacteristic it is:

> I do not know and can't imagine what the disciples understood Our Lord to mean when, His body still unbroken and His blood unshed, He handed them the bread and wine, saying they were His body and blood. I can find within the forms of my human understanding no connection between eating a man—and it is as Man that the Lord has flesh—and entering into any spiritual oneness or community or κοινωνία with him. And I find "substance" (in Aristotle's sense), when stripped of its own accidents and endowed with the accidents of some other subject, an object I cannot think. My effort to do so produces mere nursery-thinking—a picture of something like very rarefied plasticine.[30]

He goes on to say that the question "'What is this?'*—this wafer, this sip of wine . . . has a dreadful effect on me. It invites me to take 'this' out of its holy context and regard it as an object among objects, indeed as part of nature. It is like taking a red coal out of the fire to examine it: it becomes a dead coal."[31]

Lewis had an extraordinarily powerful, supple, and disciplined imagination. Regardless of whether he accepted the doctrine or not, it is hard to believe that he "cannot think" the concept of transubstantiation with regard to the Blessed Sacrament. He himself uses the word 'transubstantiate' in his sermon "Transposition," where he

* The irony of Lewis's remark here should not be missed. "What is this?" is the very question that the ancient Israelites asked about the manna (Exodus 16:15), the Old Testament prefiguration of the Eucharist (John 6:49–50). Indeed, the word *manna* derives from the question "What is it?"! (Matthew Black and H.H. Rowley, eds., *Peake's Commentary on the Bible* [London: Thomas Nelson, 1962], 224–25).

makes a sophisticated argument for the way that we can understand the 'higher' or spiritual life in relation to the 'lower' natural life—using, for instance, the analogy of a two-dimensional drawing on paper to represent three-dimensional reality. Writing of how we experience emotions in terms of bodily sensations, he notes that "The emotion descends bodily, as it were, into the sensation and digests, transforms, transubstantiates it, so that the same thrill along the nerves *is* delight or *is* agony"; the sensation, he says, "becomes what it signifies."[32]

To Tolkien, for whom the Blessed Sacrament was "the one great thing to love on earth," Lewis's treatment of this topic would indeed have been horrifying, a dismissive handling of the central mystery of his faith. And it would have been distressing, as well, on another level. Lewis concludes the passage about his difficulties with transubstantiation with the disclaimer that "All this is autobiography, not theology."[33] Yet in other writings, he had shown a very high view of the Eucharist,* and Tolkien had himself observed that Lewis "reveres the Blessed Sacrament."[34]

An Ulsterior motive?

With this in mind, we can better understand why Tolkien's 'commentary' on *Letters to Malcolm* quickly shifted into a consideration of Lewis himself and what Tolkien suggested was his "Ulsterior Motive" (as opposed to his ulterior motive) for rejecting certain Catholic doctrines. Lewis had been raised in Ulster, in the north of Ireland, and had been indelibly affected, so Tolkien thought, by the anti-Catholicism of his upbringing there.

Calling to mind the first book Lewis published after his Christian conversion, *The Pilgrim's Regress*, Tolkien remarked, "It was not for some time that I realized that there was more in the title *Pilgrim's Regress* than I had understood (or the author either, maybe). Lewis would regress. He would not re-enter Christianity by a new door, but by the old one: at least in the sense that in taking it up again he would also take up, or reawaken, the prejudices so sedulously planted in boyhood. He would become again a Northern Ireland protestant."[35]†

* For instance, in his sermon "The Weight of Glory."

† This is Tolkien feeling rather than thinking, or an example of the hyperbole to which he was sometimes susceptible. If he really thought that Lewis became "a Northern Ireland protestant," he clearly hadn't met many such folk! How many Northern Ireland protestants use the term 'Blessed Sacrament,' receive Holy Communion every week, hold a high view of the (male-only)

Tolkien recalled an incident from many years earlier when he had unguardedly shared his particular devotion to St. John the Evangelist and been hurt by Lewis's response: "he said in the brusque harsh tones which I was later to hear him use again when dismissing something he disapproved of: 'I can't imagine any two persons more dissimilar.'" What saddened Tolkien was the feeling that he could never share with Lewis what the communion of saints meant to him.[36]

In 1944, appraising Lewis's reactions to Roy Campbell and the issues of the Spanish Civil War, Tolkien had remarked, "There is a good deal of Ulster still left in C.S.L. if hidden from himself."[37]

Interestingly, Lewis was himself remarkably aware (and self-critical) of his 'Ulsterior' tendencies. George Sayer recalled a conversation with Lewis in which Havard had asked him, "Jack, most of your friends seem to be Catholic. Why don't you join us? Aren't you tempted?" Lewis said that he felt it relatively unimportant which branch of the Church one joined and that he was not tempted by what he called Catholic "heresies." Havard exclaimed, "Heresies! What heresies, Jack?" Lewis replied, "Well, here are two—the position you give to the Virgin Mary and the doctrine of papal infallibility."* But, Sayer recalls, "he refused to discuss them. He attributed his prejudice against the Roman church to his upbringing in Northern Ireland."[38]

Another of Lewis's Catholic friends, the Jesuit priest Fr. Guy Brinkworth, recalled that Lewis asked him for "prayers that the prejudices instilled in me by an

---

priesthood, have a deep respect for natural theology, fast on Fridays, go to auricular confession, entertain serious doubts about the morality of contraception, believe in purgatory, and pray for the dead? All these things are true of C.S. Lewis. And indeed, when Tolkien was writing more dispassionately, he could recognize that Lewis was actually surprisingly warm to Catholicism, warmer (at least in one respect) even than he was: "I discovered [that the Shroud of Turin] had made a profound impression on C.S. Lewis. But I am instinctively more 'protestant' than even he is with regard to relics. I am inclined to feel that Providence rightly removed . . . most of those that seem certainly to have existed" (Sotheby's *English Literature and History 18 July 1991*, Lot 362, 224).

* In *Mere Christianity*, Lewis omitted any discussion of Mary beyond what was involved in asserting the virgin birth of Christ. He was of the opinion that to say any more than this would transgress the bounds of 'mere' Christianity, despite the fact that the Virgin's role in the New Testament involves more than her being Christ's mother. Lewis even goes so far as to state (in "Priestesses in the Church?") that Mary was "absent . . . from the descent of the Spirit at Pentecost," which is not clear from the Book of Acts (see Acts 1:14; 2:1). This downplaying of the Blessed Virgin's part in the life of Christ and the Church would have dismayed Tolkien, for whom Mary was the archetypal disciple (Luke 1:38), a spiritual mother (John 19:27), and the unerring guide to her Son (John 2:5).

Ulster nurse might be overcome."[39] There is no evidence that Lewis ever seriously considered becoming a Catholic,* but he certainly strove against his own prejudices to achieve a charitable attitude to his fellow Christians in the Church of Rome.†

And, in fact, Tolkien understood this. For one thing, the ventings of grief and anger in his commentary do not comprise the whole of his reaction to *Letters to Malcolm*. In the margins of his copy, he made a pithy analysis of the strengths and weaknesses of the book, pointing out that it is not really about prayer

> but about Lewis praying. The book is in fact entirely *egocentric*, by which I do not mean that C.S.L. worshipped himself or was a proud or vain man, overesteeming his worth or wisdom. But I do mean that as must be the case with anyone who essays autobiography, under any form, he found C.S.L. an absorbing topic.[40]

Then Tolkien added an affectionate note:

> But the whole book is *always interesting*. Why? Because it is about Jack, by Jack, and that is a topic that no one who knew him well could fail to find interesting, even when exasperating.[41]

It is this more measured tone that we find a few months later in Tolkien's comments on an article about Lewis. He observed that Lewis "of course had some oddities and could sometimes be irritating. He was after all and remained an Irishman of Ulster."

* Christopher Derrick noted that "My own impression—and one's impressions, in such a matter, can only be extremely subjective and unreliable—is that insofar as Lewis was ever likely to become a Catholic, the likelihood was at its greatest around the year 1950" (*C.S. Lewis and the Church of Rome*, 215). George Sayer observed that "There is no evidence that he ever seriously considered becoming a Roman Catholic. . . . All the time I knew him, Jack was about as nonsectarian as it is possible for a devout Christian to be. I agree with Derrick that Lewis was nearest to becoming a Roman Catholic in about 1950" (*Jack*, 135, 422). One might more safely put it the other way round and say that in 1950 his becoming a Catholic was least unlikely.

† For instance, in his magnum opus, *English Literature in the Sixteenth Century Excluding Drama*, Lewis writes: "It will not be easy to [discuss the English Reformation] without giving offence: I ask my readers to believe that I have at least intended to be impartial. Unfortunately the very names we have to use in describing this controversy are themselves controversial. To call the one party Catholics implicitly grants their claim; to call them Roman Catholics implicitly denies it. I shall therefore call them Papists: the word I believe, is not now used dyslogistically except in Ulster, and it is certainly not so intended here" (157).

But, Tolkien said, he "was generous-minded, on guard against all prejudices, though a few were too deep-rooted in his native background to be observed by him."[42]

Lewis wrote in his autobiography, *Surprised by Joy*, that "At my first coming into the world I had been (implicitly) warned never to trust a Papist, and at my first coming into the English Faculty (explicitly) never to trust a philologist. Tolkien was both." And in that way, he said, friendship with Tolkien "marked the breakdown of two old prejudices."[43] The prejudice may never have altogether disappeared, but the wall had come down to a remarkable extent.

Tolkien knew that Lewis was a faithful Christian. Perhaps the greatest compliment that he paid his friend in this regard—albeit one that Lewis might not have appreciated at the time—was an element woven into *The Lord of the Rings*. After Lewis died, Tolkien envisioned his being reconciled with the Virgin Mary in heaven, noting that, "According to my fashion and in a remote way this is an ingredient in the meeting of Gimli and Galadriel."[44]

35

"The Tree is the thing"

Tolkien retired from his professorship at Merton in 1959. He was sixty-seven years old and had worked in academia for thirty-nine years, first at Leeds and then, for most of his career, at Oxford. *The Lord of the Rings* had been published only a few years earlier; it proved such an immediate and thoroughgoing success that, in short order, Tolkien acquired international fame and a degree of wealth that was as unexpected as it was welcome. His newfound status, coupled with retirement, meant that he faced two major life changes more or less simultaneously. At least he could rely on continuity in his religious life as he moved toward his threescore years and ten.

Or so one might have supposed. However, it was not to be. The last two decades of Tolkien's life were ones of increasing tumult in both the wider culture and in the Church. In 1967, he spoke frankly of his distress at the "strife and change" in the Church; he observed that "the Church which once felt like a refuge, now often feels like a trap."[1]

England in the second half of the twentieth century was undergoing massive cultural turmoil. The country, which had been brought to its knees by the Second World War, was dependent on the U.S. Marshall Plan for financial survival, and foodstuffs as basic as sugar and meat continued to be rationed until the mid-1950s. That sort of economic and social pressure might be considered enough to cope with on its own, but the zeitgeist for change and modernization made for even more turbulence as the 'Swinging Sixties' got underway. Legal changes on matters such as contraception, prostitution, abortion, and public obscenity led to the widespread use of the term 'the Permissive Society' to describe contemporary culture. Anglican confirmations per head dropped by a third and ordinations by a quarter.[2] The very appearance of the country changed with the construction of the first motorways and the erection of massive tower blocks to address the housing shortage caused by the Blitz. Even Oxford, which had not been bombed during the war, was not immune, with the medieval neighborhood of St. Ebbe's totally destroyed in the 1960s as part of a new road layout.[3]

Nor were Catholics immune to these winds of change. Starting in the 1950s, Catholic churches saw sweeping alterations that in some cases amounted to nearly as much 'stripping of the altars' as had been done in the Reformation era. St. Aloysius's Church in Oxford suffered greatly in this regard. In 1954, the Jesuits did a wholesale renovation: "Nearly all the statues and pictures disappeared . . . and the whole building was painted battleship-grey, obliterating all the brilliant colouring of the internal decorations." Later, an extensive collection of relics and historic vestments was dispersed: the relics were burned and the vestments, including pieces that had belonged to Pope Pius IX, were "given away to amateur actors."[4] Tolkien's son John recalled the reaction of Ronald Knox on visiting the 'updated' church: seeing the carved saints' heads in their round openings above the altar, everything now painted gray, Knox remarked, "It looks as if the cardinals are being sick out of their portholes."[5]

"The ways of life of modern Christians"

The years leading up to the Second Vatican Council* saw several reforms in Church practice. In 1953, Pope Pius XII eased the fasting requirements for receiving communion. Until then, the Eucharistic fast began at midnight and prohibited water as well as food. Pius XII observed that his predecessor's encouragement for daily communion had resulted in more people wishing to partake of the Eucharist. However, he considered that in the modern day, many people had schedules and responsibilities that made it impossible for them to fast during the evening, and that wartime conditions had weakened the health of many people. The pope decreed

* The Catholic Church has held numerous ecumenical councils in the course of its history to adjudicate disputed matters and define the parameters of orthodoxy. The first of these was the Council of Jerusalem, as recounted in the fifteenth chapter of the Acts of the Apostles, assembled to settle questions about the relationship between Jews and Gentiles. Other famous conciliar gatherings include the Council of Chalcedon (in the year 451), which defined how Christ's divine and human natures were related, and the Council of Trent, held in the sixteenth century to respond to the Protestant Reformation. The First Vatican Council (1869–70) was convened to address, among other things, the extent of papal authority; Tolkien was born twelve years after its end. The only council he lived through was its successor, the Second Vatican Council (1962–65).

a number of changes to the fasting rules: that water does not break the fast and that the sick and infirm could also have medicine and non-alcoholic beverages. Four years later, he reduced the length of the fast to three hours.[6] We don't know Tolkien's views about these changes, but he probably benefited from the relaxation of the fasting rules for the sick and infirm when he was in the hospital for a broken leg in 1968. The chaplain to the Nuffield Orthopaedic Hospital noted that "he had Holy Communion most mornings, about four or five times during the week."[7]

A more visible change took place with the 1955 reform of the Holy Week liturgies. The details are too complicated to get into, but broadly speaking, the liturgy and the schedule of the Holy Week services were simplified, and the observance of Maundy Thursday, Good Friday, and the Easter Vigil was moved from the morning to the evening of their respective days. One effect of the change of times meant that the Easter Vigil's imagery of light in the darkness made more sense. Another was that a far greater number of Catholics could attend these major liturgical events now that they took place after the end of the workday.[8]

In 1962, Evelyn Waugh (whom, as we have noted, Tolkien knew from Oxford) expressed his vehement dislike for the new Holy Week arrangements. Waugh lamented the loss of certain "devotions which were dear to the laity" and regretted that the simplified Holy Week now had many "blank" hours without any scheduled liturgical activity. Ironically, his complaint unintentionally highlighted some of the problems that the reforms were intended to address. Waugh admitted that "Not all Catholics were able to avail themselves of the services," (i.e., on the pre-1955 schedule),"but hundreds did, going to live in or near the monastic houses and making an annual retreat which began with *Tenebrae* on Wednesday afternoon and ended about midday on Saturday with the anticipated Easter Mass."[9] Even with Catholics a minority in England, "hundreds" is a small number, and Waugh seems not to be concerned that most working people could not arrange (or could not afford) to spend several days away from home in the run-up to Easter.

What did Tolkien think of these changes? In 1956, just before Holy Week, he wrote to his friend Patricia Kirke that "one feels a little dislocated and even a little sad at my age to know that the ceremonies and modes so long familiar and deeply associated with the season will never be heard again!"[10] It is not at all surprising that he should feel "sad" to know that the liturgies that he knew so well were gone forever. What is striking, however, is that he also explains that he approves "in the abstract of the reform of the liturgy" and for a significant reason: the revised Holy Week is, he says, "more suitable to the ways of life of modern Christians."[11] As an academic, he would have had the flexibility of schedule to attend most or all of the old Holy Week liturgy, but he was well aware that for most Catholics, the revised and simplified schedule meant that more people could participate. He appreciated the beauties of the past but recognized that a living liturgy (not a museum piece) needed to adapt to changes in the lives of contemporary believers.

It is a nuanced response, one that balances emotion and rational judgment, and coming down on the side of acceptance regarding a highly controversial reform that infuriated some of his coreligionists. This qualified statement of approval is specific to the revisions of Holy Week, the liturgy of which continued to be in Latin, and does not refer to the changes that would later come from the Second Vatican Council. But it is highly valuable in underscoring the fact that Tolkien's views were complex and sometimes unexpected; with this in mind, we are better prepared to ask, what did Tolkien make of the council and of changes in the Church broadly speaking?*

"I am not a reformer nor an 'embalmer'!"

As the 1960s wore on, Tolkien was disturbed by many things going on in the Church. Irene Tolkien Cook, the first wife of his grandson Michael, recalled that he "was in constant debate with family and friends about his growing alarm and sense of betrayal by Rome, especially at the time of the Second Vatican Council, when he sadly lamented the loss of the Latin Mass, and all that that implied."[12] George Sayer recalled that Tolkien felt the reforms to be "misguided and unnecessary."[13] John Tolkien said that his father "didn't like the changes in the Church post-war" and "opposed" them.[14] Tolkien had found the Church to be "a solace and a 'pax' in times of temporal trouble,"[15] and—very naturally and understandably—he found

* This point is worth emphasizing because Vatican II and the changes in the liturgy of the Mass that happened in the 1960s and 1970s continue to be a source of much debate and division for Catholics today. Many assume that, were Tolkien alive today, his view would of course be one that rejected the Novus Ordo and supported the Traditional Latin Mass—whether that be considered commendable or reprehensible on Tolkien's part. But such retroactive projection of twenty-first-century debates tends to flatten out his actual, complex views.

change in the Church to be inherently unsettling. But Tolkien could be surprisingly analytical about separating his own preferences and emotional reactions from his reasoned judgment.

For Tolkien, the experience of traumatic change began early, with the death of his parents, and was followed by the catastrophe of the Great War. As Giuseppe Pezzini has observed, a negative attitude toward change reflected "his wounded sensitivity as a man who lived through moments of great crisis and loss, but, crucially, it is not the only [attitude]."[16] Conservatism, desiring to preserve the past in aspic, is, as Pezzini explains, "for Tolkien an understandable and yet 'wrong,' 'partial' attitude; this of course should not lead anyone to affiliate Tolkien with the opposite party."[17]

Tolkien himself declared, "I am not a reformer nor an 'embalmer'! I am not a 'reformer' (by exercise of power) since it seems doomed to Sarumanism. But 'embalming' has its own punishments."[18] What these "punishments" are can be seen in his explanation of the fault of the Elves. In one letter, he explained that their obsession with preserving Middle-earth unchanged meant that they "became sad, and their art (shall we say) antiquarian, and their efforts all really a kind of embalming"; he reiterates the point in another letter, saying that the Elves were "embalmers," trying in Middle-earth "to stop its change and history, stop its growth" and as a result, suffering "sadness and nostalgic regret."[19]

Tolkien famously described himself as "a *hobbit* (in all but size),"[20] but his self-identification was not uncritical. As he explained, the hobbits are "not a Utopian vision, or recommended as an ideal in their own or any age. They, as all peoples and their situations, are an historical accident . . . and an impermanent one in the long view."[21] Although the hobbits' Shire is an embodiment of a pre-industrial, culturally stable, 'conservative' society, this comes with a cost and cannot be maintained indefinitely. As Aragorn points out, an ordinary hobbit "lives within a day's march of foes that would freeze his heart, or lay his little town in ruin, if he were not guarded ceaselessly. Yet we would not have it otherwise. If simple folk are free from care and fear, simple they will be. . . . But now the world is changing once again. A new hour comes. Isildur's Bane is found. Battle is at hand. The Sword shall be reforged."[22]

Like John Henry Newman, Tolkien viewed change (however painful) as inevitable, something that must be faced and accepted. As Newman wrote: "Wrap not yourself round in the associations of years past, nor determine that to be truth which you wish to be so, nor make an idol of cherished anticipations."[23] Tolkien recalled what a Catholic professor had said to him when, aged twenty-one, he had "bemoaned the collapse of all my world": that it was "'Back to normal'—political and Christian predicaments."[24] Political and religious turmoil was the rule, not the exception, in history. Absolute fixity was not a feature of this world for, as the Letter to the Hebrews has it, "Here we have no lasting city, but we seek the city which is to come" (Hebrews 13:14).

Tolkien specifies that he is not a reformer "by exercise of power," as this leads to pride and a desire for control: Saruman's great failings. But it is not reform *per se* that he rejects. For instance, as we discussed in chapter 13, he was of the view that the promotion of daily communion by Pius X (before the Great War), which was highly controversial at the time, was "the greatest reform of our time. . . . I wonder what state the Church would now be but for it."[25] Furthermore, Tolkien's life up to this point provides valuable context for his rejection of "embalming": his attendance at King Edward's School and Oxford University, his courtship of a non-Catholic woman to be his wife, and the extent of his social and religious interactions with non-Catholics all ran counter to the more 'traditionalist' wing of the Church during his own lifetime.

In a letter of 1963, commenting to his son Michael about the opening of the Second Vatican Council, Tolkien describes the Church as "dying but living, corrupt but holy, self-reforming and rearising."[26] With his historical perspective, he was perhaps not surprised—though personally distressed—to find himself in a time when the Church was going through a period of "self-reforming."

He was keenly aware that fallible human beings can implement things very badly and that good and bad motives can be muddled together in people's behavior, whether inside or outside the Church. In the 1967 letter in which he expresses his feelings about the disquieting condition of the Church, he also offers a judicious verdict on another aspect of modern society that he found personally disagreeable, the beginnings of the 'hippie' era. The anti-social behavior of "modern youth" he ascribes partly to drugs and idleness ("fainéance") but also partly to "admirable motives such as anti-regimentation, and anti-drabness."[27] Even with aspects of contemporary secular culture that discomfited him, he was making an effort to understand and not merely to reject or dismiss.

The Council

It was in this context of massive cultural change that Pope John XXIII, in his opening address to the Second Vatican Council, declared, "it is necessary first of all that the Church should never depart from the sacred patrimony of truth received from the Fathers; but at the same time she must ever look to the present, to new conditions and new forms of life introduced into the modern world, which have opened new avenues to the Catholic apostolate."[28]*

The most visible change that came from the Second Vatican Council was the revision of the liturgy of the Mass, which unfolded in stages over a number of years; we will consider Tolkien's views on this topic in the next chapter. But the liturgy was only one aspect of the council's work, which was expressed in a number of documents issued during its session. With his deep devotion to the Blessed Sacrament, Tolkien surely approved of the description in *Sacrosanctum Concilium* of the Eucharist as "the summit toward which the activity of the Church is directed; at the same time it is the font from which all her power flows."[29]

Vatican II was the only council that occurred in the course of Tolkien's life, and naturally, he paid thoughtful attention to its proceedings. It was of course covered in detail by the Catholic press; *The Tablet*, for instance, not only provided commentary but also English translations of the relevant documents. As an avid reader of newspapers, Tolkien followed the events closely. His friendship with Fr. Louis Bouyer (to which we will return in chapter 37), who served as a consultant for the council, also gave him the opportunity to get more first-hand insight into the process and to consider the strengths and weaknesses of those arguing for or

* Over the course of its history, the Church has continually been taking cognizance of "new conditions and new forms of life." It has clarified its teaching about Church membership (e.g., opening the door fully to Gentiles, see Acts 15); adjusted its internal structures (e.g., establishing an order of deacons, see Acts 6); learned how to deal with recalcitrant members (see, e.g., 1 Corinthians 5); and so on. To attempt to recreate an unchanging "Scriptural Church" would be impossible, for the Church described in the Scriptures was itself continually undergoing change. The Church, Tolkien writes, "was not intended by Our Lord to be static" (*Letters*, 394).

against changes on various fronts. To simplify matters so they become manageable within the limits of this chapter, we might describe the council as a debate between the principles of *aggiornamento* and primitivism.

'*Aggiornamento*,' the Italian word for 'updating' or 'bringing up to date,' was a term used by Pope John XXIII in his discussion of the aims of the council; his successor, Paul VI, declared that it was the council's "guiding principle."[30] Tolkien was skeptical, and cautioned that "*aggiornamento*: bringing up to date . . . has its own grave dangers, as has been apparent throughout history."[31] *Aggiornamento* soon became a kind of buzzword, applied not to specific targeted matters but adopted as a general umbrella term for numerous sweeping changes and modernizing moves—what would end up being called 'the spirit of Vatican II.'

But Tolkien was also skeptical about primitivism and in fact spends considerably more time discussing what he calls the "search backwards for 'simplicity' and directness," the attempt to find "primitive Christianity." This approach aims to return to the forms practiced by the earliest Christians or to the basic elements deduced from Scripture, bypassing the ecclesiastical, liturgical, and theological developments of later centuries. Tolkien recognizes that this approach has "some good or at least intelligible motives" but declares that overall it is both "mistaken" and unattainable. For one thing, he says, even if we could manage to determine exactly what constituted the earliest form of Christian worship, "'primitiveness' is no guarantee of value"—pointing out that "grave abuses" in liturgical behavior were present from the beginning of the Church, as evidenced by St. Paul's letters to the Corinthians, which are full of corrections to the worship habits of those early believers.[32] But more significant in his view is that such an attempt runs counter to the organic life of the Church.

Tolkien's deliberations here issue in a profound meditation on the nature of the Church, which, he says,

> was not intended by Our Lord to . . . remain in perpetual childhood; but to be a living organism (likened to a plant), which develops and changes in externals by the interaction of its bequeathed divine life and history. . . . There is no resemblance between the 'mustardseed' and the full-grown tree.[33]

That Tolkien chose a tree for his example of a living organism is not surprising, given his lifelong fascination with all things arboreal. The fact that he specifies a mustard tree rather than a more familiar English tree, such as an oak, indicates a scriptural allusion. He is alluding to the parable of the mustard seed, found in all three synoptic Gospels. Jesus said, "The kingdom of heaven is like a grain of mustard seed which a man took and sowed in his field; it is the smallest of all seeds, but when it has grown it is the greatest of shrubs and becomes a tree, so that the birds of the air come and make nests in its branches" (Matthew 13:31–32).

In his great study of the nature of ecclesial life and growth, *An Essay on the Development of Christian Doctrine*, Newman also focused on the image of the mustard seed: "In one of our Lord's parables 'the Kingdom of Heaven' is even compared to 'a grain of mustard-seed.'. . . Here an internal element of life, whether principle or doctrine, is spoken of rather than any mere external manifestation; and it is observable that the spontaneous, as well as the gradual, character of the growth is intimated."[34]

Tolkien's view of the Church as a living organism that may be pruned but must be approached with care and respect for its intrinsic nature reflects the conclusion that Newman reached. Growing up as he did at Newman's Oratory—and with his guardian, role models, and later friends coming from among Newman's own disciples—it is certain that this understanding of the Church would have been familiar to him. It is therefore worth considering this idea in more detail.

Newman's overall argument is vividly expressed in this passage, in which he challenges the premise of primitivism:

> It is indeed sometimes said that the stream is clearest near the spring. Whatever use may fairly be made of this image, it does not apply to the history of a philosophy or belief, which on the contrary is more equable, and purer, and stronger, when its bed has become deep, and broad, and full. . . . Its beginnings are no measure of its capabilities, nor of its scope. At first no one knows what it is, or what it is worth. It remains perhaps for a time quiescent; it tries, as it were, its limbs, and proves the ground under it, and feels its way. From time to time it makes essays which fail, and are in consequence abandoned. It seems in suspense which way to

> go; it wavers, and at length strikes out in one definite direction. In time it enters upon strange territory; points of controversy alter their bearing; parties rise and fall around it; dangers and hopes appear in new relations; and old principles reappear under new forms. It changes with them in order to remain the same. In a higher world it is otherwise, but here below to live is to change, and to be perfect is to have changed often.[35]

Tolkien makes exactly this argument as he expands his own arboreal analogy, explaining that for those living "in the days of its branching growth the Tree is the thing": it must be taken as it is, as a whole, because as a living organism its history "is part of its life, and the history of a divine thing is sacred." The seed from which it began "no longer exists, and the virtue and powers that it had now reside in the Tree." If the keepers of this Tree fixate on the idea that they can return the Tree to its condition as a seedling "when it was (as they imagine) pretty and unafflicted by evils," then they will in fact do great harm, for a mature living creature cannot be made immature once again.[36]

He is not arguing for acceptance of the modern life and liturgical practice of the Church *in toto*, as if every aspect of it were divinely inspired. Again, in line with Newman, who distinguished between development and corruption, Tolkien says that those who seek the health of the tree must "look after it, according to such wisdom as they possess, prune it, remove cankers, rid it of parasites, and so forth."[37] As a "living organism" that must mature or die, the Church changes in order to remain essentially unchanged.

Tolkien advises "the authorities, the keepers of the Tree" to exercise their surgery "with trepidation, knowing how little their knowledge of growth is!"[38] Pruning is a delicate art. Trim a branch too severely or in the wrong season, and the tree may take a while to recover. And even if the keepers make no mistakes, pruning may cause other problems, may require certain birds to rebuild their nests in different branches if they are to remain living in the tree. This was Tolkien's painful experience, as we will see in the next chapter.

36

Loyalty

Some of the changes of the 1960s (inside the Church or outside) Tolkien could assess on an intellectual or aesthetic level, without too much personal involvement. But in 1963, one change struck close to home. The Second Vatican Council issued the constitution *Sacrosanctum Concilium*, which allowed the various regional ecclesiastical authorities to determine to what extent the Mass would be celebrated in the vernacular rather than only in Latin.[1] It was a permission, not a requirement, but it was immediately put into effect with such decisiveness that it took on the appearance of a requirement. In England, the First Sunday of Advent, November 1964, became 'Vernacular Sunday' and the liturgy began its shift into English.*

This was a severe blow. Tolkien had, by his own account, "a particular love for the Latin language" as well as complete fluency in it, and he disapproved entirely of its abandonment in the liturgy.[2]

As we consider how he reacted to the changes in the liturgy, our understanding will be aided if we take into account the fact that Tolkien could be hot-headed and

---

* It is important to note that what Tolkien experienced in 1964 was not the 'Novus Ordo,' the significantly revised liturgy that most Catholics today encounter when they hear a Mass in English. To begin with, only part of the Mass was initially in English. In June 1964, the Bishops of England and Wales issued a decree that "the whole of the Mass known as the Liturgy of the Word and also the Communion of the People and the concluding prayers at the end of Mass are to be in English"; this was to be done in two stages, with first "the *Gloria*, all scripture readings, and the Creed to be recited in English" ("English in the Liturgy: What the Bishops Have Decided," *The Tablet*, 27 June 1964, 732). Second, it was an essentially line-for-line translation of the Mass that he had known all his life. Some of the changes trialed in the Holy Week reforms of 1955, such as the omission of the Last Gospel, were evident, but overall, this initial version of the Mass in the vernacular would have been recognizably what is today called 'the Traditional Latin Mass,' albeit in English. The Missal of 1966, for the use of the priest, makes this visible: it is in two columns, with the original Latin on the left and the new English translation on the right. This point is significant because it helps us to resist directly equating Tolkien's views of the *language* change with his reaction to the *liturgical* reforms. (I am indebted to Fr. Hugh Somerville Knapman, OSB, for details about the 1966 Missal and the introduction of the Mass in the vernacular.)

intemperate, especially when he was privately venting anger or frustration. We explored this in some detail in chapter 34 in terms of his 'blow-up' over C.S. Lewis's *Letters to Malcolm*, but it was characteristic of him throughout his life. As far back as the 1920s, Owen Barfield recalled meeting Tolkien, who was "in a ridiculously combative mood and seemed to me to contradict nearly everything I said."[3]

Tolkien also had a habit of expressing himself hyperbolically, which many of his friends noticed and remarked upon. Lewis said, "Tolkien's lively mind sometimes leads him (with perfectly innocent intentions) to overstate things."[4] In his writings, it is not uncommon to find him rejecting or condemning something with apparent finality, only to then nuance his point or backtrack entirely, with the result that he may seem self-contradictory. It seems to have been a rhetorical technique to preemptively clear out any simplistic views or assumptions on the topic so as to allow for his more subtle point to be understood properly.[5] Therefore, in considering his reaction to the change in the liturgy—something that brought out quite an emotional response—we will do well to look at as many different points of evidence as we can in order to get a three-dimensional view. Typically, his dramatic reaction served to indicate the strength of his feeling on a subject; the calmer follow-up showed how he worked through that feeling to a more settled intellectual view; his actions show how he exercised his will.

No rose-colored glasses

Tolkien was professionally a medievalist; he valued many aspects of pre-industrial life and criticized sharply many of the excesses of the modern era. However, he did not look at what we now consider the 'preconciliar' Mass (the Mass before the council) through rose-colored glasses.[6] In his 1963 letter of advice to his son Michael (discussed in chapters 13 and 31), he remarked that it is "all too easy" to find a Mass that was badly celebrated by the priest and heard by an inattentive and disrespectful congregation. He wrote this at a time when the liturgy was still the 'Traditional Latin Mass' as it is called today.

Indeed, comments from English Catholics in the 1920s and 1930s suggest that Mass was often rather chaotic, to an extent that would seem indecorous and irreverent to many people today. One widespread practice before Vatican II was that of distributing communion at the beginning of Mass (or even at multiple points through the Mass) rather than at a single moment near the end of the Mass after the priest has consecrated the elements and taken communion himself.[7] In 1936, a reader of the *Catholic Herald* lamented that "the practice of giving Communion at the beginning of Mass is the rule instead of the exception in so many of our churches" and pointed out some of the problems that came from it, including "one case of a child who had arrived in time for Mass but late for the Communion at its start being found in tears after the service because he had missed his Communion."[8] In 1927, Ronald Knox attempted to put a positive spin on the typical behavior of Catholics in church, with regard to the attitude of "reverence":

> For good or for evil, the ordinary, easy-going Catholic pays far less tribute to this sentiment than a Protestant, or even an agnostic brought up in the atmosphere of Protestantism. No traveller fails to be struck, and perhaps shocked, by the 'irreverence' or 'naturalness' (call it which you will) that marks the behaviour of Catholic children wandering about in church. Even grown-up Catholics will usually talk in church, if anything needs to be said, while Protestants will usually whisper.[9]

But these problems were insignificant compared to failures on the part of the clergy. Tolkien recalled that he had "suffered grievously in my life from stupid, tired, dimmed, and even bad priests." He remarked in another letter that over the course of his life, he had met "snuffy, stupid, undutiful, conceited, ignorant, hypocritical, lazy, tipsy, hardhearted, cynical, mean, grasping, vulgar, snobbish, and even (at a guess) immoral priests"—one can imagine him running through a sort of rogues' gallery in his memory.[10] The point of this remark was to emphasize in contrast the virtues of his guardian ("for me one Fr. Francis outweighs them all"), but for our purposes, it is useful to note that all of these examples were men who had been ordained and were exercising their ministry *before* the Second Vatican Council. Tolkien held the Church in high esteem but was well aware that its ministers had, like other men, feet of clay.

"He spoke Latin"

The main objection that Tolkien voiced to the 1960s reform of the liturgy concerned the shift from Latin to the vernacular. As his son John recalled in 1992, Tolkien "very strongly couldn't see any point in abandoning Latin, because he spoke Latin."[11]

Tolkien *spoke Latin*. This is the essential point. He had total command over the language in a way that was probably distinctive even in his youth, but by his old age was exceptional. Not only did he understand enough Latin to follow the recurring parts of the liturgy, as altar servers readily learn, he understood *all* of the Latin used, even the Latin of the Scripture readings and the collects that change from day to day, and he did so with a linguist's and an artist's appreciation of the language. Most priests would not have had the command of Latin that Tolkien enjoyed.

His attachment to Latin was not in any way an affectation, a merely nostalgic, antiquarian preference, but a love for Latin as—for him at least—a still living language. For Tolkien, to whom languages were an abiding passion, the foundation for all his creative as well as academic work, this loss must have cut very deep indeed, in a way that probably no one can ever fully understand.

If his primary objection was to the loss of Latin, his secondary objection was to the awkward English that replaced it. George Sayer recalled that Tolkien "frequently complained about the new English translations of the Latin texts used in Catholic services, because they were inaccurate or in bad or clumsy English."[12] Tolkien was a gifted prose stylist and would have been keenly aware of any faults to be found in the renderings of the Latin. The fact that the translation selected for the Psalms was Knox's[13]—a version that Tolkien disliked—could not have helped matters much.

When the Mass shifted into English, the seventy-two-year-old Tolkien expressed his views in an idiosyncratic way: by attempting to ignore the change entirely. His granddaughter Joanna noted that "In the early '60s when the Liturgy changed to the vernacular, he continued to answer the responses in Latin."[14] Likewise, his grandson Simon recalled "I vividly remember going to church with him in Bournemouth. . . . it was soon after the Church had changed the liturgy from Latin to English. My Grandfather obviously didn't agree with this and made all the responses very loudly in Latin while the rest of the congregation answered in English."[15] Joanna was unbothered by this habit, commenting that "Anything that Grandfather did was all right with me, and I had no problems joining him."[16] However, Simon, then only nine years old, was embarrassed: "I found the whole experience quite excruciating, but my Grandfather was oblivious. He simply had to do what he believed to be right."[17] (It is not unlikely that the loudness of his responses was an unintentional result of the fact that he was by that time, as Rayner Unwin recalled, "rather deaf."[18])

A valuable insight into Tolkien's attitude about the English liturgy is provided by the young chaplain, Fr. Gerard Hanlon, who attended Tolkien during his hospital stay in 1968:

> I started the service, as we could in those days, in English, to give him Holy Communion and he automatically responded in Latin. So I stopped halfway through and said, "Excuse me, professor, are you the Emeritus Professor of English?"
>
> "I am, I am father, yes," he said.
>
> So I asked, "Well why are you speaking Latin?"
>
> "Because I like to pray to God in Latin," he replied.[19]

The encounter was evidently a relaxed one: Hanlon liked Tolkien immensely and recalled this particular incident as "one of the most amusing things in my life." His responses in Latin may have begun at least in part as a protest, but they also came from a lifetime of using Latin in the Mass and in his private prayers.

Bowing the knee

One thing that he clearly regretted, apart from the shift into Latin, was the simplification of the rituals of the Mass, for instance the reduction in the number of times that the priest offered a genuflection (a reverent bow on one knee). In fact, it seems to have been the occasion for a memorable loss of temper. Clyde Kilby wrote in his recollections of Tolkien:

> An anecdote I have heard involved his attendance at mass not long after Vatican II. An expert in Latin, he had reluctantly composed himself to its abolishment in favor of English. But when he arrived next time at services and seated himself in the middle of a bench, he began to notice other changes than the language, one a diminution of genuflection. His disappointment was such that he rose up and made his way awkwardly to the aisle and there made three very low bows, then stomped out of the church.[20]

We should not place too much weight on this anecdote, which is at best secondhand: Kilby does not identify from whom he heard the story, so we don't know if his source saw this himself or heard it from yet another person, and we can't judge how much the story might have grown in the telling. We also don't know if the account included relevant details that Kilby, who was not a Catholic, missed; as it is, we can see his non-Catholic perspective in his word choice: "bench" instead of pew, "services" instead of Mass.

But it is not unreasonable to accept that some such incident occurred. It would be in character for Tolkien to lose his temper in this way—and subsequently to calm down and express a more nuanced view. And for that part of the equation, we have Tolkien's own words.

In a 1968 interview, when he was asked about his liking for "ritual, ceremonial," he replied, "Love it, oh yes. I think most of the objection to it is because people know so little about language. Of course it's very current in my Church at the present time." He goes on to explain that the modern "objection" to ritual stems from the way that that people are "quite ignorant" of the way that verbal speech is "only one form of language. You can attach meanings to other actions than wagging your tongue." He disagrees in general terms with the idea that symbolic actions lose meaning by repetition (a common criticism of the preconciliar Mass), noting that "For instance, to genuflect is much terser, sometimes much more expressive, than a word expressing homage. It's no good telling me that you can get used to genuflecting, you can get used to saying 'Milord' or 'I honour you' just as well." But despite having the opportunity to be as vehemently critical as he wished on this point, he was instead calmly reflective. He had, it seems, come to view the abandonment of an aspect of the liturgy that he found deeply meaningful as primarily an indication of the profound ignorance of Catholics in the 1960s: troubling, but a source of regret rather than anger. And he concluded his comments on a positive note, giving an example of a ritual practice that was still common: "To light a candle becomes a beautiful thing, to light a candle and then go away and leave it as a model of your aspiration."[21]

No comment

Tolkien readily identified himself as a Christian and as a Catholic in many public interviews, but never did he publicly talk or write about changes in the liturgy. Here it is interesting to compare Tolkien with his contemporary and fellow layman Evelyn Waugh. Best known today as the author of *Brideshead Revisited*, Waugh had taken his degree at Oxford in the 1920s and made a career as a writer; he converted to Catholicism as an adult and became an ardent defender of the traditional forms of the liturgy. Waugh deplored the Holy Week changes of Pope Pius XII and abhorred the shift to the vernacular that began in the early 1960s. In their preference for Mass in Latin, Waugh and Tolkien were in agreement; however, Waugh differed in that he publicly voiced opposition to the changes, writing letters to the editor of *The Tablet* and the *Catholic Herald* to argue against them.

Tolkien's fame in the 1960s was such that if he had chosen to speak about the liturgy, he would certainly have had an audience. The majority of his readers (or at least of his most enthusiastic ones) were in America, but they, too, were experiencing the change in the liturgy.

And he was, in fact, willing to write letters to the editor. We know of at least three examples: one to *The Times* concerning religious freedom,* one to the *Daily Telegraph* about trees,[22] and one to the *Catholic Herald* about the origin of the place-name 'Coventry.'† Since he was willing to publicly speak up on these matters,

* In 1949, he co-signed the Newman Association's letter to *The Times* about religious freedom (we will return to this in chapter 37).

† A reader, with more piety than precision, suggested it was "in keeping with Catholic tradition" to say that the name Coventry came from "convent." Tolkien squashed this, declaring, "I am at a loss to know how the etymology of any place-name can be pursued 'in keeping with Catholic tradition,' except by seeking the truth without bias, whether one ends up in a convent or not." He goes on to explain the actual derivation of "Coventry" and to direct readers' attention to various scholarly resources on the topic (Tolkien, "The Name Coventry," 2).

in both the secular and Catholic press, it would not have been out of character for him to speak up as a private citizen and layman about his concerns regarding the liturgy. However, this he did not do.

It is interesting to note, as well, that Tolkien was *not* among the signatories of the so-called 'Agatha Christie indult,' the 1971 petition to preserve the older form of the Mass after the Novus Ordo had come into effect.* This "Petition to Pope Paul VI by Distinguished Writers, Scholars, Artists, and Historians Living in England to Spare the Traditional Latin Mass" was an attempt to sidestep theological questions by framing the request not in terms of "religious or spiritual experience" but rather in aesthetic terms. The signatories sought the preservation of a "magnificent Latin text" that has "inspired a host of priceless achievements in the arts" and "belongs to universal culture as well as to churchmen and formal Christians."[23] Furthermore, the request was described as "entirely ecumenical and nonpolitical," because many of the signatories were non-Catholics, including Agatha Christie (one of Tolkien's favorite authors) and Iris Murdoch (a novelist with whom Tolkien corresponded and whose 'fan letter' he cherished). Most notably, the list also included fellow Inklings Colin Hardie and Nevill Coghill.[24] But it did not include Tolkien. Why not?

In 1971, he was elderly and living in Bournemouth, not Oxford, but he was still an active correspondent and would not have been difficult to reach. We do not know whether he was approached and declined to sign or was not asked at all. He may well simply have decided to continue his consistent policy of refraining from public comment about the changes in the liturgy.

* The *Novus Ordo Missae* or 'new order of the Mass' was promulgated by Pope Paul VI in 1969, codifying some changes from 1964–68 and introducing others. It simplified and reordered the structure of the Mass (e.g., removing the reading of the 'Last Gospel' after the dismissal); other changes included three new options for a Eucharistic Prayer; the Our Father said by the whole congregation rather than just the priest; the removal of many instances of genuflections, bows, and signs of the cross; a wider selection of Scripture readings in a three-year cycle; and permission for priests to celebrate Mass facing the congregation (rather than both priest and congregation facing the altar). The *Novus Ordo* is now the 'Ordinary Form' of the Roman Rite; the earlier form is generally called the 'Extraordinary Form.' Other authorized Catholic rites exist, including the Byzantine Rite and the Anglican Use of the Roman Rite (the Divine Worship liturgy used in the Ordinariates).

"The virtue of loyalty"

In his retirement years in Headington, one of the churches that Tolkien attended was Corpus Christi, where he also served as an acolyte at Mass and—surprisingly—as a reader.[25] (See figure 64.) An acolyte assists the priest in the celebration of the Mass; a reader, or 'lector,' reads the Scripture lessons aloud to the congregation from a lectern in the sanctuary as part of the Mass. Tolkien had served as an acolyte since he was a boy, but not as a reader, because until 1964, when the Mass was brought into the vernacular, the Scripture lessons could only be read by a priest, deacon, or subdeacon.[26] Having a layman read the Scripture lessons was an innovation, and furthermore one that was directly related to the shift from Latin into English. We don't know how often Tolkien served in this capacity at Corpus Christi, but the fact that he did so at all is highly relevant for gauging his measured response to the change in the liturgy.

Perhaps it was a deliberate act of obedience or humility. Perhaps it indicated that, despite his personal distress at the loss of Latin for the liturgy, he accepted the need for Scripture to be read in English in this new era in which Latin was no longer taught as a second language in the schools, as it had been for so many centuries.* In any case, it indicates that Tolkien managed to move beyond mere toleration of the changed, and changing, liturgy, such that he was willing to participate in it actively. The branch where he had built his nest had been lopped off, but he was prepared to settle elsewhere in the tree.

Tolkien's death in 1973 meant that he saw only the first instances of the massive cultural shift in the Catholic Church in the 1970s, often described as 'the spirit of Vatican II' (over against the actual conciliar texts, which are in fact much less radical than many of the changes that were made in their name†), but it was still very difficult for him. For instance, it must have been painful when the Canon of the Mass—which he knew by heart, as we saw in chapter 16—became variable, so that it no longer had a singular form; the priest could choose one of four different Eucharistic prayers. Irene Tolkien Cook recalled that during this time, "he had long

* In fact, even before this point, it was not uncommon for the Scripture lessons, though read in Latin in the context of the liturgy, to be read again by the priest in English immediately before the homily.

† For more on this, see Fr. Blake Britton, *Reclaiming Vatican II* (Notre Dame, IN: Ave Maria, 2021).

telephone debates with [his grandson] Michael about the changes in the liturgy, which he found most disturbing." But, crucially, she goes on to say, "As he had an enquiring mind, he agonised over his personal beliefs, but kept the Faith."[27] Joanna Tolkien elaborates on what seems to be a key point in Tolkien's relationship to the council and the changes it brought about, directly or indirectly: "I think it fortunate that Grandfather was not alive for these [further] changes, because I think he may have had difficulty in accommodating them. But no doubt his strong belief in the sacramental system of the Catholic Church would have enabled him to overcome all problems."[28]

Joanna's assessment is in accord with Tolkien's actions in the last year and a half of his life. Now living at Merton College, each week he attended the 11 a.m. Mass at the Church of St. Anthony of Padua in Headington, an ordinary suburban parish church. (See figure 66; we will return to St. Anthony's in chapter 37.) At this point, in 1972, the Novus Ordo had come into effect. He could have made his age and chronic health issues an excuse to stop going to Mass, but he did not: every Sunday, he went, whatever he might have thought about the liturgy.

For all the discomfiture caused by the changes brought about to the Church in his lifetime, he never considered leaving the barque of St. Peter and retreating into a private spirituality. "There is nowhere else to go!" as he exclaimed to his son Michael, echoing the words of St. Peter: "Lord, to whom shall we go? You have the words of eternal life" (John 6:68). Choppy waters are a common feature of marine travel, and only a landlubber would consider them unacceptable. Tolkien, the now fairly ancient mariner, accepted them, retaining his faithful adherence to the Church he had been a member of since the age of eight. "I think there is nothing to do but to pray, for the Church, the Vicar of Christ, and for ourselves; and meanwhile to exercise the virtue of loyalty, which indeed only becomes a virtue when one is under pressure to desert it."[29]

And his experiences of the Novus Ordo at St. Anthony's were not merely exercises in dry duty but part of his continuingly heartfelt spiritual life. His biographer Humphrey Carpenter sums it up thus: "even during an English mass in the bare modern church in Headington that he attended during his retirement, where he was sometimes irritated by the singing of the children's choir and the wailing of babies, he would, when receiving communion, experience a profound spiritual joy, a state of contentment that he could reach in no other way."[30]

37

New Friends, New Horizons

As we noted in chapter 29, the mid-1950s marked the beginning of a new era for Tolkien. The success of *The Lord of the Rings* brought newfound wealth but also the necessity to deal with innumerable problems, from printing errors and American pirate editions to bad translators and worse ideas for film treatments. It also brought great masses of correspondence. Tolkien eventually gained the assistance of Joy Hill, from his publisher Allen and Unwin, to assist with handling his correspondence. On one occasion, she recalled, fans had sent so many gifts that in order for her to carry them, "the packers in the warehouse tied the parcels with great loops of twine and hung them on my arms under my cape," prompting Tolkien to remark that Unwin had sent him a walking Christmas tree.[1*]

Tolkien also spent an enormous amount of time responding in detail to readers who had queries about his invented languages, his world of Middle-earth, and the story of *The Lord of the Rings*. Although it must have been at times a tiring burden, it was also a welcome discovery that the legendarium at which he had labored all of his adult life really did resonate with readers when they caught even a glimpse of it in the story of the *Rings*.

With all this attention on Middle-earth, it would have been easy for Tolkien to turn inward and focus exclusively on his literary world, especially since many of his other ties had been lost through the passage of time.† By the mid-1950s, C.S. Lewis was working in Cambridge and would soon be married. And with the changes in the liturgy beginning in 1955, as we have seen, it would also have been

* The energetic Joy was not just a much-valued and dedicated assistant but came to be considered a member of the family. Rayner Unwin recalled that "both Tolkien and his wife came to regard her almost as a daughter" (*George Allen & Unwin: A Remembrancer*, 122).

† That he resisted the temptation to identify himself with his legendarium is evident in a remark he made in a 1969 letter: "As for an 'Elvish' name: I could of course invent one. But I do not really belong inside my invented history; and do not wish to!" (*Letters*, 398). This is particularly notable since in the earliest days of his legendarium, he had invented Elvish names for himself and those closest to him (*UC*, 93), a habit that evidently faded as he matured.

understandable if he had withdrawn into a more private sphere and a more individualistic spirituality. However, that was not the case. Though not so energetic and adaptable as he had been in his younger years, Tolkien continued to look outward.* In this chapter, we will survey some of the most important new relationships and the new prospects that opened before Tolkien in the last two decades or so of his life.

A new home in Headington

In 1953, he and Edith moved to 76 Sandfield Road, Headington, on the east side of Oxford, where they would live for the next fifteen years. This meant transferring from St. Gregory's, their parish of twenty years' standing, and getting used to a new church, with a congregation that was more working-class than had been the case in wealthy, professional, donnish North Oxford.

The new place of worship was the Church of Corpus Christi, St. Alfonsus, and St. Margaret—an unwieldy name, usually abbreviated to Corpus Christi. (See figure 64.) The history of the church reflected the poorer economic situation of the Headington area; it began in 1936 as just a parish hall where Mass could be celebrated, and, owing to limited funds, the church building itself was not finished until 1953, and other elements such as the stained glass were added in later years.[2] As we saw in chapter 36, Tolkien was active as a parishioner, even serving as a lector at Mass after it shifted into English.†

In 1960, the plain, modern church of St. Anthony of Padua was built not far from Tolkien's Sandfield Road home, making it a more convenient option than Corpus Christi (Tolkien did not own a car at this stage of his life), and so he became a member of this brand-new parish.[3] (See figure 66.) Tolkien gave "a substantial sum" to the church when he began to be wealthy from the success of *The Lord of*

* In 1967, when Tolkien was seventy-five years old, an interviewer commented that many of his readers "tend to view the real world with a certain amount of dismay. They try to get away from it when they can"—clearly expecting a sympathetic response. Tolkien responded firmly, "No, I'm not one of those chaps. No. Neither am I obsessed by my own work. I read newspapers . . . I take a strong interest in what is going on, both in the university and in the country and in the world" (Resnik, "An Interview with Tolkien," 39).

† Tolkien's presence at Corpus Christi helps to explain an interesting later development in the church's devotional art. Very unusually, the parish has, in addition to the traditional Stations of the Cross, a second set of Stations that presents fourteen episodes from the scriptural accounts of Holy Week. This set, installed in 1988, is an original design by Tolkien's daughter-in-law Faith Tolkien ("The Stations of the Cross," Corpus Christi, Headington).

the Rings.[4] Since he was later remembered at St. Anthony's as "a great benefactor of our Parish," it seems probable that he contributed funds to the building of the new church.[5] When Tolkien returned to Oxford after Edith's death and settled into his rooms at Merton College, it was at St. Anthony's that he attended Sunday Mass each week in the last year of his life.[6]

One of the new friends that he made at this time was Monsignor Wilfred Doran (1909–1991), who became the parish priest at St. Anthony's in 1967. The Cambridge-educated Doran had been headmaster of a Catholic boys' boarding school before coming to Oxford and was known for the special depth of his "ecumenical understanding"; this was something that gave him a shared interest with Tolkien.[7]

Tolkien also stayed in touch with the educational scene even after his retirement. In 1962, he was a prize-giver at the Catholic boys' school of St. Joseph's in Stoke-on-Trent.[8] And closer to home, Roger Highfield, one of his Merton colleagues, recalled that Tolkien was very interested in "the Catholic chaplains of the university" and he "took a great interest" when the Spanish Catholic organization Opus Dei purchased Grandpont House in Oxford.[9]

And in 1966, he participated in an initiative motivated by the Decree on Ecumenism: he gave a public reading of the as-yet-unpublished *Smith of Wootton Major* at Blackfriars. This reading was not a one-off event; rather, it was part of a Michaelmas Term lecture series, jointly mounted by Blackfriars and Pusey House, an Anglican theological house of studies, with events hosted alternately at the two locations. Pusey House is named for Edward Bouverie Pusey, who was John Henry Newman's ally in the original Oxford Movement; Pusey stayed in the Church of England while Newman became a Catholic, but they remained friends. Pusey House was opened in 1884,* Blackfriars Priory in 1921. The two institutions are next-door neighbors and in fact are physically joined together in the same block on St. Giles' in Oxford, so it is just as well that they have good ecumenical relations.

Tolkien was invited to participate by Fr. Bede Bailey, the prior of Blackfriars.[10] Bailey was deeply interested in ecumenism, and this joint lecture series was a prime example of his efforts in this line during his time as prior.[11]† The topic was "Lit-

* October 9, 1884, to be exact. It is a striking coincidence that October 9 was the date of Newman's reception, in 1845, into the Catholic Church; it is now the feast day of St. John Henry Newman.

† On the literary-critical side, Lord David Cecil (one of the Inklings and an Anglican) gave the opening lecture on "Literature and Understanding"; there was also a lecture on tragedy

erature and the Understanding of Life" and featured both literary-critical lectures and literary readings; Catholic and non-Catholic speakers were equally represented.

The event was advertised in the most low-key of ways, on the Pusey House Term Card (see figure 63), the printed list of lectures and other events being held that term; Blackfriars seems not to have promoted it "apart perhaps from a piece of paper at the church door,"[12] as the prior recalled years later. Nevertheless, news of Tolkien's scheduled talk spread rapidly by word of mouth, such that the hall was filled to overflowing. The normal attendance at lectures was about 150, but for Tolkien, as the Pusey House principal noted, "700 people turned up."[13]

International interests

The busloads of people who filled Blackfriars to hear Tolkien (or at least to see him) betokened his growing fame, a fame that was not limited to Oxford or even to England or the United Kingdom; it was increasingly international. And the interest went both ways: Tolkien's own taste for international affairs can be traced to his enduring interest in South Africa, the land of his birth, and in Spain, because of Fr. Francis's Spanish heritage; as he matured, his horizons of interest steadily broadened. In 1949, as part of his involvement with the national Newman Association, he cosigned a letter to *The Times* protesting the Hungarian government's arrest of Cardinal Mindszenty.* The letter is a strong protest against "the ever-extending violation of freedom in countries under Soviet domination or Soviet influence." The letter goes on to declare that "it must be made clear, without diplomatic equivocation, that the conscience of the civilized world is shocked by the denial of religious

---

and another on the poet Dylan Thomas. On the literary side, the penultimate lecture was on the Catholic poet of the Great War, David Jones, "with readings and recordings of his works," while the closing session featured the Catholic poet Elizabeth Jennings—a friend of Tolkien and of his daughter, Priscilla—reading her own poetry. In this context, we can see that Tolkien's session, in which he was scheduled to read "a fairy story with some preliminary remarks," fits in perfectly with the approach of the series overall (Woodward, "Notes from the Library," 6).

* Cardinal József Mindszenty was an uncompromising opponent of fascism and communism. After his arrest, he was tortured, given a show trial, and sentenced to life imprisonment for alleged treason, remaining in prison until he was freed during the Hungarian Revolution of 1956. When the Soviet Union invaded Hungary later that year, Mindszenty was granted asylum at the US embassy in Budapest, where he remained for the next fifteen years. He died in exile in Vienna in 1975. He was given the title Servant of God in 1993, and, in 2019, Pope Francis gave him the title of Venerable on account of his display of "heroic virtue."

liberty in Hungary and other areas of eastern and central Europe" and that the Hungarian government had "made a mockery" of movements "for the promotion of peace based on justice and freedom."[14]

Here we see Tolkien's lasting interest in events on the international level and his concern about injustice. He made a similar, if more subtle, gesture in 1959 in his "Valedictory Address" to the University of Oxford upon his retirement, which was a major occasion that featured a full house and reportage by the local papers. In this lecture, he declared, with reference to South Africa, "I have the hatred of *apartheid* in my bones"[15]—a remarkable statement at the time, when apartheid had been in effect for only ten years and before the formation of the British Anti-Apartheid Movement.* He deftly ties it into the subject of his lecture by remarking that he also detests "the segregation or separation of Language and Literature," but he reinforces his point with the sharp comment, "I do not care which of them [Lang. or Lit.] you think White."[16] Tolkien understood university politics and knew very well that his audience would take note of his repudiation of the racist South African regime.

International friendships

Not only did Tolkien take an interest in international events from a Christian perspective, but he also formed, in his later years, a number of international friendships with devout men of faith.

Ireland

One of these was Fr. Thomas Patrick Dunning. Born in Tipperary and educated at University College Dublin,† he was ordained a priest in 1939 and became a member of the Congregation of the Mission, a religious order founded by St. Vincent de Paul with the purpose of evangelizing the poor and helping the clergy in their formation.[17] Dunning came to Oxford in 1953 for doctoral studies on

* Tolkien delivered his address on June 5, 1959; the British Anti-Apartheid Movement was founded later that same month. International public opinion began to turn against apartheid in 1960 with the Sharpeville massacre.

† Dunning was from the Republic of Ireland, as distinct from Northern Ireland, which is part of the United Kingdom.

early English homilies. Tolkien was his supervisor for only one term, after which J.A.W. Bennett, a fellow Inkling, took over the responsibility, but the friendship between Dunning and Tolkien endured, and they continued to correspond. Tolkien gave Dunning a first edition set of *The Lord of the Rings*, inscribing each volume with lines from that book: "Now who shall fill my cup for me?" (in Quenya), "Come back to me and say my land is fair," and "Sing, be glad all ye children of the West / for your King shall come again"—personalized inscriptions that speak to the friendship between the two men.[18] In turn, Dunning contributed an essay to the 1962 festschrift *English and Medieval Studies Presented to J.R.R. Tolkien on the Occasion of his Seventieth Birthday*. When Dunning died in 1973, his brother (also a priest of the Congregation of the Mission) gave his breviary to Tolkien as a remembrance, inscribing it "To Professor Tolkien in memory of dear Tom."[19]

America

A new friend in the 1960s was the American Evangelical Protestant Clyde Kilby. (See figure 69.) A professor of English literature at Wheaton College, Illinois, and a great admirer of *The Lord of the Rings*, Kilby visited Tolkien at his home in Headington in 1964, in part with the hopes of getting some of Tolkien's manuscripts for the college.* Their initial meeting burgeoned into a warm friendship, and in 1966 Kilby spent the summer in Oxford assisting Tolkien with his work on preparing the texts of the *Silmarillion* for publication. Tolkien felt at ease with Kilby, speaking with him about his Christian faith. Perhaps because Kilby was himself a literary critic and experienced teacher, Tolkien also felt able to discuss the Christian themes in his writing—confident that Kilby would appreciate the nuances of his approach. For instance, Kilby reported that "Professor Tolkien talked to me at some length about the use of the word 'holy' in *The Silmarillion*. Very specifically he told me that the 'Secret Fire sent to burn at the heart of the World' in the beginning was the Holy Spirit."[20]

---

* Kilby would go on to establish the Marion E. Wade Center, which is now one of the major research centers for scholarship on Tolkien.

Poland

Tolkien had a long-standing interest in Poland and the situation of Polish Catholics; in 1969, he observed to a Polish friend that "Poland for its own sake, but especially since it is your country, is ever in my mind."[21]

He was concerned about Poland as early as 1944, when he corresponded with a Polish army officer who wanted some assistance with technical vocabulary. Tolkien, who was learning Polish at that time and finding it "rather sticky," remarked to Christopher that it would be a long time before he would be able to help and that the vocabulary "will just happen along anyway"—adding grimly, "if there are any Poles and Poland left."[22]

His interest continued after the war, when he paid particular attention to the fate of Poland's Catholics under the Communist regime. Zbigniew Pełczyński, a Polish academic who met Tolkien in 1955, recalled that in their conversations, "academic topics connected with Tolkien's linguistic and literary work were virtually never mentioned. . . . Instead, he seemed to be very interested in Poland and my wartime experiences under German occupation but most of all in the situation of the Polish Roman Catholic Church."[23]

Tolkien would later become good friends with another Pole, the Catholic academic Przemysław Mroczkowski (see figure 67), whose scholarly interests included medieval literature and the writings of G.K. Chesterton (a favorite author of Tolkien's). After finishing his doctoral work in 1947, Mroczkowski became a professor at the Catholic University of Lublin, where he and his colleagues suffered continual harassment under the Communist regime.* He was regularly visited by the Secret Service, especially "during the years of Stalinist repressions (1948–56), when the Polish scholar was often subject to all-night questioning."[24]

Tolkien first corresponded with Mroczkowski in 1946 when the younger man wrote for advice about studying in Oxford. Tolkien attempted to help him secure a place, including discussing it with C.S. Lewis, but in the end, he advised Mroczkowski to study at the University of Notre Dame instead, which he did. Then, in 1957, Mroczkowski obtained a scholarship for a year's study at Oxford

* From 1944 until the late 1980s, the university staff "was under continuous vigilance from the State Security Service" because of "its independence—limited, but independence nonetheless—from the communist authorities" (Neubauer, "The 'Polish Inkling,'" 151).

and arrived with his wife and three children. He immediately sought out Tolkien, meeting him at the British Council office with the dramatic exclamation, "I come from Mordor"—an instance of 'applicability' of *The Lord of the Rings* to the distressing political situation in Poland that Tolkien evidently appreciated.[25] Mroczkowski attended some of Tolkien's lectures that year, and the two men quickly established a friendship that lasted for the rest of Tolkien's life. Even when, in a 1969 letter, Tolkien admitted to tardiness on his side of the correspondence, he affirmed that the whole family remained in his thoughts.[26]

That their friendship was grounded in part in their shared faith is suggested by a 1958 letter in which Tolkien offered a gift of £30 to Mroczkowski (a generous sum and a real help: it was more than a month's salary in Poland at that time).[27] A suggestion like this could easily cause offense, and Tolkien approached it carefully, explaining that the gift would help express his love for his fellow Catholics in Poland.[28] He was delighted when the offer was accepted, and considered it (as we saw in chapter 27) "an answer to prayer."[29] It was a realization of St. Paul's charge to "bear one another's burdens, and so fulfil the law of Christ" (Galatians 6:2).

A further indication of Tolkien's close bond with Polish Catholics appears in the intriguing story of his connection to Our Lady of Częstochowa. Marian devotion is a particularly strong component of Polish Catholic devotional life; in 1908, Pope Pius X gave permission for the Marian title "Queen of Poland" to be included in the Litany of Loreto in Poland. "Our Lady of Częstochowa" is a famous Byzantine icon of Mary as the Immaculate Conception, which since the fourteenth century, has been deeply associated with Polish national identity; it was probably made around the sixth century, although one legend has it that it was painted by St. Luke the Evangelist himself.[30] It is kept at the monastery of Jasna Góra.

The icon of Our Lady of Częstochowa played a significant role in Catholic resistance to the Communist regime after the Second World War. Though Catholics were officially tolerated, the Communists attempted to undermine and restrict their practice of the faith, for instance by refusing to allow any new churches to be built.[31] In 1957, Cardinal Stefan Wyszyński declared a "Great Novena," a nine-year cycle of prayer ahead of the thousandth anniversary of the arrival of Christianity in Poland. It began with a pilgrimage of over a million Poles to the shrine of Our Lady of Częstochowa at Jasna Góra, and concluded in 1966 with a consecration of Poland to Mary, Mother of the Church.[32] After the millennial celebration, a copy of the icon of Our Lady of Częstochowa began to be taken to parishes throughout the country, bringing great crowds of Catholics together for prayer; this so disturbed the Communist authorities that they 'arrested' the image and forbade it from being taken from Jasna Góra. In response, for the next six years, the empty frame of the icon was taken from parish to parish instead.[33]

The difficulties faced by the Church in Poland were reported in the English Catholic press. Our Lady of Częstochowa would have interested Tolkien both because of his Marian piety and because he was deeply concerned about the dangers of Communism and violations of religious freedom. Both of these points help to explain his own contribution to this Polish Catholic devotion, a contribution that involves his old sparring partner Hilaire Belloc.

Long before the Second World War, Belloc had written a poem entitled "The Ballade to Our Lady of Częstochowa" and made a pilgrimage to Jasna Góra where a framed copy of the poem was hung on the chapel wall.[34] However, at some point during the war, Belloc's poem disappeared. In 1960, Tolkien was contacted by Gregory Macdonald, the former wartime editor of the BBC's Polish news service. Macdonald wanted to replace Belloc's missing "Ballade" at the Jasna Góra chapel and asked Tolkien, known for his beautiful calligraphy, to make a copy. (Belloc had died in 1953.) Tolkien agreed, approving of the devotional act, although he "had misgivings about the literary merit of Belloc's poem."[35] He sent the final version to Macdonald, who reported in November 1961 that it had arrived at Jasna Góra, where it was hung, once again, in the chapel. Such a gesture would have been newsworthy, given Tolkien's international status, but, as Gregory Macdonald recalled, "a general discretion was observed."[36] (See figure 65.)

France

As we saw in chapter 35, Tolkien was well informed about the proceedings of Vatican II. Much of his knowledge of the council came from newspapers, but he also had the opportunity to get at least some insight from a more direct source—a French theologian who became a good friend and regular correspondent, was on a preparatory commission for the council, served as an advisor when the council began, and was involved in some of the work related to the revision of the liturgy and to ecumenical relations.[37]

This intriguing figure is Fr. Louis Bouyer (1913–2004), one of the leading Catholic theologians of the second half of the twentieth century. (See figure 68.) A former Lutheran pastor, Bouyer converted to Catholicism in 1944 and became a member of the Congregation of the French Oratory, which is closely related to the Oratory of St. Philip Neri. Bouyer wrote an insightful biography of Newman which was translated into English in the same year that his short biography *St. Philip Neri: A Portrait* was published in both French and English. That year was 1958—notable because it was also the year in which Bouyer, having discovered with delight *The Lord of the Rings*, composed a long, thoughtful, and deeply appreciative review, "*Le Seigneur des Anneaux:* Une nouvelle épopée [a new epic]?" in the journal *La Tour Saint-Jacques*.[38]

At some point in the 1960s, Bouyer began to correspond with Tolkien,[39] and they soon became good friends—a friendship, Michaël Devaux notes, that Bouyer repeatedly mentions but that has "escaped all the biographers,"[40] perhaps because Bouyer's memoir, though written in the 1980s, was not published until 2014,[41] and the earlier works in which he discusses his friendship with Tolkien have never been translated into English.

Bouyer visited Tolkien in Oxford on several occasions. On one such visit in 1967, Tolkien gave him a copy of C.S. Lewis's *Poems*, a posthumous collection that had come out the year before. He also visited Tolkien and Edith in 1969, at which point they were living in Bournemouth[42]—an indication of the genuine friendship between them, as this would have been much more out of the way for Bouyer, and one of Tolkien's reasons for the move to Bournemouth was to avoid annoying visitors.

In his memoir, Bouyer described his relationship with Tolkien as one of his two "most prized friendships": he named T.S. Eliot first but then went on to say, "I would enter into an even greater intimacy with John Ronald Reuel Tolkien." Bouyer recalled that he had been the first in France to discover and write about *The Lord of the Rings*, but his regard for Tolkien grew even more when he met him in person: "this exquisite old man's good nature, knowledge, and very simple yet very profound poetic and Christian view on life could only be truly appreciated in an informal tête-a-tête."[43] Elsewhere Bouyer spoke very warmly of Tolkien, calling him "prodigiously learned," an "excellent and charming man" with whom he "had the privilege" of carrying on "endless conversations."[44]

What did they talk about? They certainly had many interests in common. Bouyer had not only written a biography of Newman, but he had spent months living at the Birmingham Oratory, working in Newman's own study with the Cardinal's unpublished papers, and had become friends with several of the now-elderly Oratorians whom Tolkien had known in his youth, including Fr. Denis Sheil.[45] Although Bouyer also visited the London Oratory, he admitted that he preferred "the smaller, but more simply beautiful, Birmingham church"[46]—which would undoubtedly have pleased Tolkien. Bouyer was also a teacher, and his ecclesiastical interests included both ecumenism and the liturgical movement.[47]

It is not surprising that their friendship blossomed quickly, given the many values and experiences they had in common. Furthermore, Bouyer had a genuine enthusiasm for Tolkien's imaginative world and characters, which he frequently references in his writings, and the two of them also shared an interest in "the question of the relationship of myth to the Christian spirit."[48] All of this gave Tolkien, in his old age, a conversational partner who must have helped assuage some of the sense of loneliness and isolation that he felt after the death of Lewis, the one friend who had best understood and shared his mythopoeic ideas.

And indeed, this was no superficial interest. Bouyer refers to Tolkien's belief, expressed in "On Fairy-stories," that the Christian writer "may actually assist in the effoliation and multiple enrichment of creation,"[49] and then goes a step further to make an explicitly evangelistic connection. Bouyer suggests that the Christian writer might be able to "not only enrich creation, but also express the Creator":

> Not perhaps for a direct expression of Christianity, which requires a total recasting of the myth such as only the Word of God could do, but on the level of the journey of the pre-Christian towards Christianity, of the human being who is necessarily religious insofar as he is human.[50]

Bouyer had a deep interest in the Arthurian legends and would go on to write a book about the Grail. Tolkien evidently encouraged him in this line of thought;

in fact, in the introduction to his book *Les lieux magiques de la légende du Graal*, Bouyer remarks that the entire work is really "a simple continuation" of his conversations with Tolkien.[51] Indeed, Bouyer recalled that he talked with Tolkien "a lot" about these ideas: about "the Grail and more generally about how myths, even pre-Christian myths could become the vehicle of Christian realities," conversations that Bouyer greatly valued because Tolkien was "one of the rare modern authors to have himself created a new myth and a myth imbued with a Christian spirit."[52]

But it was not a conversation about mythopoeia, nor about the Grail, nor even about Tolkien's legendarium that Bouyer later recalled as their "best conversation," one that "filled a beautiful autumn afternoon in his Headington study." The "inexhaustible subject" of this conversation was a volume written by American scholars who had, it seemed, sent a questionnaire to Tolkien that supplied some of their material. Unfortunately, we don't know the title of the work or what the questionnaire was about, only that Tolkien evidently found it preposterous and decided to play a joke on them by sending them "farcical answers." But in a brilliant exhibition of American misunderstanding of dry English humor, these "grave university scholars from across the pond . . . were totally fooled" by Tolkien's replies. Bouyer remembered reading the book together with Tolkien that afternoon, adding, "I don't think I have ever seen the pseudo-scholarship of so many modern studies of that ilk go down in flames so magnificently, and I don't mean only American ones!"[53] Fellow sons of St. Philip Neri, indeed!

38

"Companions in shipwreck"

Retiring from his university position in 1959 meant letting go of active involvement in a professional environment that, whatever its frustrations, had been the focus of many of Tolkien's relationships for decades. C.S. Lewis died in 1963, and with his death, the Inklings' social meetings in Oxford pubs had come to an end. Tolkien's four children were now mature adults themselves, with their own busy lives. Despite the new friendships and the new horizons that opened before Tolkien in the last two decades of his life, there was less keeping him in Oxford than before.

Tolkien and Edith began to make regular visits to Bournemouth, a resort town on the south coast of England, staying at the Hotel Miramar; Edith loved it and made friends locally, which is why Tolkien eventually bought a bungalow there for them to move to in 1968. It was a sacrifice for her sake and one that he found difficult at times, as he missed his familiar Oxford environs. And so, it is not surprising that—especially with frequent bouts of ill-health—he experienced times of loneliness, even depression. He would have had to face these challenges in any case, as the inevitable consequence of growing older and outliving many of his friends.

Mortality was on Tolkien's mind as the 1960s shifted into the 1970s. Edith was suffering from severe arthritis that limited her mobility; his own health, too, was often bad. Perhaps it was this increasing awareness of physical fragility that led him into new philosophical writings for his legendarium, even though he knew he was supposed to be systematizing the stories he had already written. Christopher noted that his father had declared that "the fundamental underpinning concern of all his work was death." He was fascinated by the metaphysical implications of the fact that Elves, in his legendarium, "were not in their nature destined to die, whereas Men are of their nature destined to spend only a short while in the world."[1]

Tolkien and Edith lived in their "admirable and commodious bungalow"[2] in Bournemouth for three and a half years. They attended the nearby Church of the Sacred Heart, where they became friends with Denis Tolhurst and his wife, Jocelyn; Denis became their physician as well.[3]* This beautiful English Gothic church is now, appropriately enough, the Bournemouth Oratory.[4]

Then, in November 1971, Edith fell ill and was taken to the hospital. Ten days later, on November 29, she died. She was eighty-two years old, and they had been married for fifty-five years.

That day, Tolkien wrote, "I am utterly bereaved, and cannot yet lift up heart."[5] Here, with his grief freshly fallen upon him, he nevertheless struck a distant note of hope ("cannot *yet*") that came from his deep Christian faith. It was right and proper to feel profound sorrow—Christ wept at the death of Lazarus (John 11:35); St. Paul enjoins Christians to "weep with those who weep" (Romans 12:15)—and though he was currently unable to lift up his heart, his faith in the Resurrection meant that, again in the words of Paul, he did "not grieve as others do who have no hope" (1 Thessalonians 4:13). His words echo an exchange in the liturgy of the Mass that he had heard so many times over the course of his life: the versicle *Sursum corda*, "Lift up your hearts," and the response, *Habemus ad Dominum*, "We lift them up to the Lord."

A Requiem Mass was celebrated for Edith at the Church of the Sacred Heart;[6] then her body was laid to rest in Wolvercote Cemetery, Oxford.

Parting from Edith in 1916, when he went off to war in France, had felt "like a death."[7] Fifty-five years later, it was Edith who had gone before him. In the story of Beren and Lúthien, whose names appear on their shared gravestone, it was Beren who died first and Lúthien who went to plead for him in the Halls of Mandos. But now, Tolkien lamented, the story had "gone crooked" and he was the one left.[8]

The summer after Edith's death, Tolkien reflected to Christopher that ever since their three years' enforced separation had come to an end (when he turned 21), "we had shared all joys and griefs, and all opinions (in agreement or otherwise), so that I still often find myself thinking 'I must tell E. about this'—and then suddenly I

---

* A charming glimpse of their friendship appears in an inscription that Tolkien wrote on a birthday card to Denis Tolhurst: "If one would live 'tis often best / to treat one's doctor as a jest / but if he clothes advice with wit / then wiser 'tis to follow it / quoth Gandalf" (*TCG:RG*, 1297).

feel like a castaway left on a barren island under a heedless sky after the loss of a great ship."[9]

A castaway after the loss of a great ship: it is a striking image, and all the more so if we realize its resonance. Thirty years earlier, he had written to his son Michael with advice about marriage, cautioning him that the tradition of chivalry—which idealizes the man as a knight in shining armor, serving his perfect lady love—is good insofar as it encourages "fidelity . . . self-denial . . . courtesy, honour, and courage," but it has a serious weakness, in that even a Christianized chivalry "is not perfectly 'theocentric.'" Without being centered on God, a man tends to make the beloved "a kind of guiding star or divinity" rather than seeing that she is "another fallen human-being with a soul in peril." Women, he says, are "companions in shipwreck not guiding stars."[10]

His courtship of Edith and their early married life had been highly dramatic, as we saw in chapters 10 and 14. The Catholic/Protestant divide gave their early courtship a certain resonance with the Montagues and Capulets of *Romeo and Juliet*. Their enforced three-year separation and Edith's engagement to another man, which Tolkien successfully defeated, brought their romance to a new level of intensity, almost like something out of a fairy tale. Looking back on those days long afterward, Tolkien remembered:

> my first kiss to you and your first kiss to me (which was almost accidental)—and our goodnights when sometimes you were in your little white nightgown, and our absurd long window talks; and how we watched the sun come up over town through the mist . . . and the moths almost used to frighten you away—and our whistle-call—and our cycle-rides—and the fire talks—and the three great kisses.[11]

The subsequent decades were more ordinary, though not necessarily easier. In their marriage, they dealt with the challenges inherent in raising four children, the privations of two world wars, living in places that one or the other (or both!) of them found uncongenial, disagreements about the practice of their faith, differences in personality and interests, health issues, and financial strain. But as the couple reached middle age, they settled into a comfortable routine. C.S. Lewis, then a bachelor, once exclaimed in some exasperation that Tolkien was "the most married man he knew."[12] Their marriage, despite its many difficulties, endured; it did not fail. They kept the vows they had made to each other before God.

And so, it is fitting, at this point in our story, to consider Tolkien's understanding of his vocation to married life and how that understanding developed and matured.

He recalled, later in life, his "romantic upbringing"[13] coming into play in his early love of Edith, and his biographer Humphrey Carpenter describes Tolkien's letters to Edith after their engagement as expressing real love, but often full of "amatory cliché."[14] This is a common enough foible in adolescence and perhaps all the more excusable in this case, given that Tolkien had lost the mother who might have been able to keep his feet on the ground. It probably didn't help matters much that in his Oxford student years the chaplaincy was in disarray, and there were fewer opportunities for him to be guided by a wise and reliable chaplain to understand the nature of marriage as a vocation and the self-sacrifice it entails.

Tolkien advised his son Michael that however much a man loves his wife, he cannot be faithful to her "without deliberate conscious exercise of the *will*, without self-denial. Too few are told that—even those brought up 'in the Church.'"[15] Tolkien could certainly have concluded by observation that "too few are told that," but it seems probable that he speaks from his own experience as well.

In his own case, he had made a full, Catholic commitment in his marriage to Edith, but he had to mature into a fuller understanding of the meaning of that commitment.

Thinking with the Church

We can see this development in a draft letter he wrote in 1943, criticizing C.S. Lewis's views on Christian marriage. In his book *Christian Behaviour* (which later became part of *Mere Christianity*), Lewis argues for a two-tier system of marriage in which Christian marriage was recognized as being permanent but in which Christians tolerated the practice of civil divorce. Tolkien regarded this as an incoherent position, because if permanent, faithful, monogamous marriage is, as Lewis suggests, the best way for human beings to handle the sexual impulse, then divorce is harmful to everyone, whether they are practicing Christians or not. Tolkien says that although it may be a losing fight, he considers that those who oppose the legalization of divorce are in the right.

More significant, for our purposes, is a remark he makes along the way, that "Sentire cum ecclesia" is here, as often, "a true guide."[16] *Sentire cum ecclesia* is a Latin phrase coined by Ignatius of Loyola in his *Spiritual Exercises*; it means "thinking with the Church." St. Ignatius explains that to be in the right frame of mind as a Catholic, "We must put aside all judgment of our own, and keep the mind ever ready and prompt to obey in all things the true Spouse of Christ our Lord, our holy Mother, the hierarchical Church."[17] Since the Catholic Church has always consistently taught that a validly contracted marriage is permanent (Matthew 19:6), to 'think with the Church' in this regard would guide a person to regard such a union as indissoluble.

After he affirms that 'thinking with the Church' is a "true guide," Tolkien adds, "I say this all the more cheerfully, because on this point I myself *dissented* in feeling (not expressly because I am under saving obedience). But I was then still under the delusion that Christian marriage was just a bit of special behaviour of my 'sect or order.'"[18] Here it is necessary to explain more fully what Tolkien means, as he uses some Catholic terminology in a shorthand manner.

He emphasizes that he "dissented" (that is, he did not agree with the Church's teaching) but clarifies that he did so "in feeling" and "not expressly." This distinction indicates that although he did not personally agree with the Church on this matter, he did not express that dissent vocally or in action. Why not? Because he was "under saving obedience." By this he means that, as a Catholic, he was committed to accepting (and abiding by) what the Church declared as its teachings, whether or not he privately found it congenial; this is, after all, the test of obedience, since it is hardly obedience to accept things that you already agree with. It is "saving" obedience because it keeps a person within the bounds of the Church, where he can be sure of his salvation.

Tolkien points to his experience as an example of 'thinking with the Church' precisely because he had to learn to do so. He had begun by *obeying* the Church's teachings on marriage and divorce, but without fully understanding and accepting those teachings.

What, precisely, was the point of disagreement? Tolkien's next comment makes this clear: "I was then still under the delusion that Christian marriage was just a bit of special behaviour of my 'sect or order.'" This is a subtle but important point: it shows Tolkien's developing understanding of ecclesiology—that is, Catholicism's doctrine of the Church, its self-understanding. The Catholic Church's position is that it is the one, holy, catholic (that is, universal), and apostolic Church, and therefore what it teaches is true for everyone, everywhere, whether those people are aware of it or not. So, with regard to the specific point on which he disagreed with Lewis, Tolkien explains that when he was younger, he thought that what the Church taught about marriage was simply a set of rules that Christians had to follow as Christians, rather than universal principles. He wouldn't then have had any major problem with Lewis's suggestion of two kinds of marriage, one Christian and one purely civic, with different standards of permanence. But now, as a mature man, he has come to understand what the Church actually teaches: that faithful, monogamous, permanent marriage is the best way for all human beings to behave with regard to a sexual relationship, Christian or not, and Catholic or not.

A mature view

This mature view led Tolkien to adopt a sacramental view of valid marriage: marriage meant a faithful, lifelong commitment that was, by its very nature, indissoluble.* It included openness to children, welcoming them into the world even when it would have been more convenient or less costly to avoid having them. And, far from being a continued 'romance' in the sentimental sense, it involved the hard virtue of self-denial.

Writing to his son Michael, Tolkien is perfectly frank about the fact that marriage to one's beloved will not remove all temptations. Men are not instinctively monogamous, he says; the ideal of Christian marriage is a truth of revelation: "Each of us could healthily beget, in our 30 odd years of full manhood, a few hundred children, and enjoy the process. . . . It is a fallen world, and there is no consonance between our bodies, minds, and souls." Marriage may help "to sanctify & direct

* Separation and divorce are not always and in every case immoral acts, according to Catholic teaching (see paragraphs 2383 and 2386 of the *Catechism*). Annulment allows for the recognition that a given marriage was never valid in the first place (see §1629).

to its proper object [a man's] sexual desires; its grace may help him in the struggle; but the struggle remains." There is no hint that Tolkien considers it shameful to have to struggle; it is not a sin to be tempted, only to consent to the temptation. (And if temptation is consented to, so that sin is committed, even then, when that failure is honestly repented, the grace of the sacrament of Confession is available to heal a wounded relationship.) He emphasizes very strongly to Michael that it takes "deliberate conscious exercise of the *will*" and "self-denial" to be faithful to one's wife "in mind and body."[19] In that last phrase, we can see Tolkien's holistic understanding of fidelity, as expressed in Jesus's teaching, "You have heard that it was said, 'You shall not commit adultery.' But I say to you that every one who looks at a woman lustfully has already committed adultery with her in his heart" (Matthew 5:27–28).

Marriage, for Tolkien, was a reality that goes much deeper than the feeling of being 'in love'—and since he had been such a romantic himself as a young man, it is probable that he speaks from personal experience when he counsels his son, "When the glamour wears off, or merely works a bit thin, [men] think they have made a mistake, and that the real soul-mate is still to find"—and that is precisely what leads to the divorce court. But, he says drily, "the 'real soul-mate' is the one you are actually married to."[20]

Tolkien's realism about marriage is as bracing as his passion is stirring. In another letter to his son, he speaks frankly of "the dreadful sufferings of our childhoods, from which we rescued one another, but could not wholly heal wounds that later often proved disabling." But these "lapses and darknesses . . . never touched our depths nor dimmed the memories of our youthful love. For ever (especially when alone) we still met in the woodland glade and went hand in hand many times to escape the shadow of imminent death before our last parting."[21]

Beren and Lúthien

The story of Beren and Lúthien in *The Silmarillion* offers us an important insight into Tolkien's understanding of marriage. Those two names are engraved on their shared tombstone in Wolvercote Cemetery. (See figure 71.) "I never called Edith

'Lúthien,'" he told Christopher after Edith's death, "but she was the source of the story. . . . she was (and knew she was) my Lúthien."[22]

Lúthien is an Elvish princess and Beren is a mortal man. They fall in love, but her father, King Thingol, disapproves and wishes to forbid their marriage. Finally, he sets a seemingly impossible condition: that Beren bring him one of the great jewels known as the Silmarils, now held by the evil Morgoth in his impregnable fortress of Angband. Beren attempts it—and fails; he is captured and held prisoner. Lúthien finds and rescues him, and it is by her efforts that they recover one of the Silmarils from Morgoth's crown. But as they escape, Morgoth's wolf Carcharoth bites off Beren's hand, holding the Silmaril, and flees with the sacred jewel burning in its stomach. Beren, then, is able, truly enough, to declare to Thingol that "a Silmaril is in my hand"; recognizing his bravery, Thingol consents to their marriage. The wolf is hunted down and killed, and Beren's incorrupt hand is found inside its stomach, still grasping the Silmaril. Beren, however, is wounded in the fight and dies; grief-stricken, Lúthien also dies. But in the Halls of Mandos where their spirits are gathered, she sings so beautifully that she moves the heart of Mandos himself, the archangelic guardian of the dead. She is allowed to become mortal, accepting the lot of humans rather than that of elves, and Mandos returns her and Beren to life in Middle-earth, where they have a son, Dior, and live until they die of old age.

It is certainly a story of great and persistent love, but we should not miss the fact that it is also a story of great tribulation. Both Beren and Lúthien must repeatedly display precisely those characteristics that Tolkien said to his son are guides to marriage in a fallen world: "prudence, wisdom . . . a clean heart, and fidelity of *will*."[23] Beren and Lúthien, not unlike Tolkien and Edith, had many opportunities and temptations to give up on each other, and they endured much suffering—physical, mental, spiritual—but it is precisely this endurance, this determination to persist in love despite everything, that makes their story, like that of their real-life counterparts, beautiful.

39

Reuel

In the spring of 1972, after Edith's death, Tolkien returned to Oxford, where Merton College had made him an Emeritus Fellow and provided a furnished flat for him, with meals included. He was sometimes lonely, a condition which was exacerbated by the need to take precautions against overenthusiastic fans (and less well-intentioned people too: his rooms were burglarized at one point). But despite his very natural times of sadness and frustration, he was grateful for his new environment and maintained a surprisingly engaged social life for a man of eighty years. He kept up his correspondence, including with Fr. Douglas Carter, his former parish priest from St. Gregory's, and enjoyed visits from his children, his cousin Marjorie Incledon, and friends including Christopher Wiseman, his old companion in the TCBS.

And every Sunday, he took a taxi to attend Mass at St. Anthony's,[1] the unpretentious modern church that he had attended with Edith when they lived in Headington, which he himself had helped fund.

In late August 1973, he traveled back to Bournemouth for a visit with the Tolhursts. It was just as well he was staying with his doctor, because he was taken ill. He had to be hospitalized. The problem was a bleeding gastric ulcer, soon complicated by a chest infection. Priscilla and John were able to come to his side; Michael and Christopher, who were abroad, did not get there in time, and on September 2, 1973, he died.

Four days later, a Requiem Mass was held for him at St. Anthony's. It was a notable occasion in the history of this parish: "So many flowers were sent from all over the world for this funeral that they had to be piled up all round the outside of the church."[2]

The Mass was celebrated by his son Fr. John, with the assistance of Fr. Robert Murray and Monsignor Wilfred Doran, the parish priest, both old friends of Tolkien.

There was no sermon and no reference to his writings,[3] which was as he would have wanted it: the focus was on praying for the repose of his soul. His grandson Michael George described the funeral in a poem, "His Last Party," recalling the "dark flock of academics perched out of reach" behind the family's seats, and, beyond them, "a crowd blurred with a million motives," all under the watchful eyes of

> The carved modern Lady gracious over
> Empty candle sockets,
> And places where he'd kneel.[4]

From the church, family and close friends followed the hearse to Wolvercote Cemetery, where Tolkien was buried in the same plot as Edith: Beren reunited with Lúthien. (See figure 71.)

Among the bequests that he made in his will was a gift of £1,000 to the Birmingham Oratory in memory of Fr. Francis Morgan.*

In the following Michaelmas Term, Merton held a memorial service in the college chapel. Appropriately, given Tolkien's perennial witness to friendship in charity with Christians outside the communion of the Catholic Church, this Anglican service was an ecumenical occasion. The college chaplain officiated; the Scripture lessons were read by Fr. John Tolkien and Nevill Coghill, sometime an Inkling, who had been Tolkien's colleague as Merton Professor of English Literature. There were representatives from across the University, including Exeter College, where he'd been an undergraduate, and Pembroke, where he began his professorial life at Oxford. The English Faculty and the Early English Text Society were represented, as were the Catholic Chaplaincy and the Newman Trustees.[5]

The closing hymn was one of John Henry Newman's, taken from *The Dream of Gerontius*: "Praise to the Holiest in the Height."[6] This was particularly fitting for Tolkien, whose spirituality had been so deeply formed by the English Oratory that Newman founded. And the Newmanian connection had continued even after Tolkien left Birmingham: he was involved with the Newman Society and the Newman Association, forwarding the cardinal's vision of Catholic education and eventually receiving an honorary doctorate from the University in Ireland that Newman founded.[7]

* It was his largest single bequest to an institution: he also gave £500 to Trinity College, £300 to Exeter, and £200 to Pembroke (*TCG:C*, 815).

Tolkien's family, in a manner of speaking, was grafted onto Newman's spiritual family when the cardinal's great-niece became godmother to Tolkien's youngest son. Given that Fr. Francis, Tolkien's guardian and "second father," was one of Newman's spiritual sons at the Birmingham Oratory, we might even venture to entertain the beguiling notion that Tolkien was the grandson Newman never had.

Tolkien's own grandson, Michael George, looking back on the extraordinary life and work of his grandfather, remarked, "Normality is, of course, by definition indefinable. But Tolkien for me was if anything aggressively and hugely normal and human even if he had his annoying and loveable eccentricities."[8] His biographer Humphrey Carpenter found this very quality of normality, which Michael George delighted in, unaccountable. Observing that Tolkien lived "the ordinary unremarkable life led by countless other scholars" and had "an ordinary suburban life bringing up his children and tending his garden," Carpenter wondered whether it is a paradox that such a life could produce such extraordinary successes as *The Hobbit* and *The Lord of the Rings*. Then he asks, "Is not the opposite precisely true? Should we not wonder instead at the fact that a mind of such brilliance and imagination should be happy to be contained in the petty routine of academic and domestic life"?[9]

But we need not choose between seeing Tolkien *either* as an ordinary man capable of astonishing brilliance *or* as a world-shaking genius content with humdrum routine; Rayner Unwin gives us a glimpse of a more integrated personality. Thinking back on twenty years of friendship and (sometimes tumultuous) collaboration over the publication of *The Lord of the Rings*, he describes Tolkien as "an author of unwavering integrity, who was never tarnished by the fame that ultimately engulphed him, courteous even in exasperation, joyous in good company, wracked by private despairs and sustained by faith."[10]

Sustained by faith: here we are at the heart of the matter. And here—as befits the complexity and depth of Tolkien's character—we will approach it in a slightly oblique manner: by considering Tolkien's name.

Friend of God

To Tolkien, far more than the average person, names were of the highest importance. And so, it is worth noting that his third given name, Reuel, was particularly significant to him. He shared it with his brother, Hilary, and he gave it to all four of his children—his daughter as well as his three sons—and he pointed out in 1969 that all of his grandchildren and great-grandchildren bore the name as well.[11]*

'Reuel' is an unusual name; Tolkien believed that his father (Arthur Reuel) had been given the name in honor of a friend of his grandfather and that the family thought it French in origin, which he doubted, noting that it appears in the Old Testament as the name of Moses's father-in-law (Exodus 2:17–19; Numbers 10:29). In Hebrew, it appears to mean "friend of God."[12]†

To what extent was Tolkien a friend of God? This is a work of biography, not hagiography; as Priscilla Tolkien herself observed, nobody who had read all of her father's published letters, let alone the unpublished ones, would take away a picture of him as "almost saint-like."[13] Nonetheless, the purpose of this biographical account has been to record his path of faith, and the whole point of the Christian life, as he saw it, was to grow in virtue and eventually achieve sainthood. He was preparing himself to enjoy the beatific vision, which ultimately could be attained only by someone who had become a perfect friend of God. That was the path Tolkien was attempting to tread, in imitation of those men and women of faith who had gone before him. The venerable name of Abraham naturally occurs in this context, for, as the epistle of St. James puts it, "faith was active along with his works, and faith was completed by works . . . 'and it was reckoned to him as righteousness'; and he was called the friend of God" (James 2:22–23). Tolkien's faith likewise issued in works, not because he felt he had to earn his salvation, but because he knew that "faith apart from works is dead" (James 2:26). If he were to become truly a Reuel,

---

* "He sometimes said that he did not feel [Ronald] to be his real name" (*Biography*, 21), even though that he was how he was generally known. He gave the name 'Ronald' to none of his sons; he gave 'John' to two of them; but 'Reuel' he gave to all four of his children.

† 'Reuel' can be rendered in English as 'friend of El' or 'El-friend,' which is so suggestive of 'elf-friend' that one might well wonder if there is some kind of link—be it subliminal or deliberate, playful or serious—to his creation of friends of *elves*. The name 'Ælfwine' (Old English for Elf-friend) became, in Tolkien's typically complicated way, an element connecting *The Book of Lost Tales* (written circa 1920) to real medieval history. Years later, in "The Lost Road," Tolkien created a frame-story that involves a sequence of father-son pairs with repeating etymologically connected names, in which the son's name is some version of Elf-friend. Verlyn Flieger observes that "These figures have widely different characteristics and fulfill a variety of different plot functions in the stories in which they appear, but the important position they all share is that of the link, the connector or mediator between the 'real' or natural world and the world of Faërie—the supernatural world of myth and the imagination" ("The Footsteps of Ælfwine," 185).

a friend of God, he would have to *do* something. "You are my friends if you do what I command you," Jesus said (John 15:14).

If you do what I command you. What did that entail?

"Take, eat" was one command that Tolkien fulfilled most actively, receiving his Eucharistic Lord regularly, frequently, devoutly.

Another was the command to "Bless those who curse you and pray for those who persecute you": he exercised forgiveness, not without effort, and not without help from Fr. Francis.

He also prayed and read the sacred Scriptures (in many tongues). He was faithful to his wife, his "companion in shipwreck." He was a loyal and present father, if an imperfect one by his own reckoning. He obeyed and respected his spiritual elders in the Church, even when deeply pained by changes they brought about.

He gave alms, for instance to a homeless man at the door of St. Greg's, and also provided for his elderly aunt Jane Neave and others in need, such as his Polish friend Mroczkowski. He donated the desk at which he wrote his celebrated fiction to be auctioned on behalf of charity.[14] At the age of seventy, when he began to receive a national pension, he gave away all of it.[15]

He showed no partiality. "He liked to strike up a conversation with a Central European refugee on a train, a waiter in a favourite restaurant, or a hall porter in a hotel."[16] This talent for enjoying human company from every walk of life is something he learned when he got to know regular English soldiers, "the privates and batmen I knew in the 1914 war, and recognized as so far superior to myself" and of whom Sam Gamgee was, he said, "a reflexion."[17]* In the last year of his life, he enjoyed both the company of his old friend Anthony Giffard, the third Earl of Halsbury, a scientist and active member of the House of Lords,[18] and also of Charlie Carr and his wife, who lived in the basement of his flat and served as caretaker and housekeeper. In fact, he once caused Joy Hill a certain amount of alarm for not answering his telephone, because he had been enjoying himself watching the tennis at Wimbledon with the Carrs![19]

He fulfilled the spiritual works of mercy, to comfort the bereaved, and especially to give aid to widows and orphans. The day Charles Williams died, he wrote to his

* Priscilla and John also recall their father's "warm relations with the college's domestic staff. He was their champion, often arguing that they should enjoy better working conditions" (*TFA*, 79).

widow, Michal, assuring her of his prayers and adding, "if you find that there is anything in which I might be of service to you and your son, please tell me."[20] On another occasion, in 1948, Lewis phoned to say that Charlie Blagrove, landlord of The Eagle and Child pub, had died suddenly. Tolkien immediately walked to the 'Bird & Baby' (so he told Priscilla) "and paid my respects to Mrs. Blagrove and did what I could to sympathise."[21] When Lewis himself was hospitalized in 1963—his wife, Joy, having died three years earlier—his stepson Douglas Gresham recalls that Tolkien crossed paths with him outside the ward. "He was on his way in to visit Jack, and before we parted, he said, 'If I can ever be of any help to you, if you ever need a place to stay, please don't hesitate to let me know.' I thanked him, and he went in to see Jack."[22]

He lived out his vocation as a Catholic academic and author, which entailed being present and visible as a role model and public figure. He accepted awards with gratitude and enjoyment but was not above replying to letters written to him by schoolchildren. His old friend and colleague Nevill Coghill remarked that he "gave unstinted help to all who asked for it. I have known him plan a set of lectures for another don who was a beginner."[23] Other colleagues noted that he gave assistance freely to younger scholars, content to remain in the background without a co-author credit.[24]

Christ's most challenging command, of course, is "Love another as I have loved you. Greater love has no man than this, that a man lay down his life for his friends" (John 15:12–13). Few people are called upon literally to lay down their lives, but Tolkien came close to doing so during the Great War,* and it is fair to point out the countless small sacrifices he made over the years that enacted the same principle on a smaller scale: attending to his academic and familial responsibilities first and his own creative work second, writing late into the night after the household was asleep. He was a "dilatory and unmethodical man," to be sure, as Lewis remarked with affectionate exasperation;[25] but he also chose to put others' needs above his own. Rayner Unwin admitted that while he lacked the ability to curb his "perfectionist tendencies," he "lacked, too, the arrogance that allows busy men to chart their own course through the pressures that surround him. He wanted to oblige everyone."[26] Michael

* During his active service in 1916, Tolkien spoke to a captured German officer who had been wounded, offering him a drink of water, very much in the spirit of Christ's command to give "a cup of cold water" to one who needs it (Matthew 10:42) and to "love your enemies" (Matthew 5:44). The officer corrected Tolkien's German pronunciation (*Biography*, 92).

George Tolkien reflected of his grandfather, "I'm often asked if he was the archetypal absent-minded professor. . . . Had he been, his life would have been easier and his art less rich."[27] We can get a sense of his habitual attention to others' well-being in a thank-you note he wrote to Unwin, who had hosted a dinner for him after he had received from Queen Elizabeth II the honor of a C.B.E. (Commander of the British Empire) for services to English literature: "I enjoyed the party immensely, not least because as I looked round everyone else seemed to be doing so too."[28]

He certainly had his faults. Scrupulosity was one of them, as we have seen. Another was a contrarian and pedantic streak, which could tip over into curmudgeonliness. He could be hypersensitive to perceived slights and, what is more, keep a record of them, as with his pained recollection decades later of what he took to be Lewis's dismissal of his devotion to St. John. This hypersensitivity occasionally resulted in what John Lawlor called an "absolutely volcanic upheaval" of "his habitually mild and benevolently quizzical temper." Lawlor remembered the time when C.L. Wrenn, having organized a conference at Magdalen, invited attendees who had been especially helpful to dine at High Table before gathering for postprandial drinks:

> Comfortably seated and contentedly gathered around Wrenn, the participants heard the door thrown open and a wild-eyed Tolkien—veritably 'tollkühn,' the foolhardy one—burst in, to harangue Wrenn for his unseemly action in so using Magdalen's High Table, to the neglect, it seemed, of his fellow-Professors in Oxford. . . . Speechless at last, stammering as he subsided, Tolkien glared in outrage at the astonished company. Was this the time or the place?, Wrenn murmured. Tolkien flung out and came no more to any Conference proceeding.[29]

He was a flawed man and knew it, lamenting, for instance, the personal weaknesses that marred his marriage. His frequent recourse to the sacrament of Confession speaks to his self-awareness on this score. How fitting, then, that the Newman hymn at his memorial service should come from *Gerontius*, that poem which concludes with Gerontius (literally, "old man") entering not directly into heaven but first into the cleansing process of purgatory, where

> Angels, to whom the willing task is given,
> Shall tend, and nurse, and lull thee, as thou liest;
> And Masses on the earth, and prayers in heaven,
> Shall aid thee at the Throne of the Most Highest.[30]

Tolkien believed in purgatory and fully expected his soul, at death, to be in a condition that would need further healing and purifying (hence Niggle's time in the "Infirmary"). Only then could he enter heaven and stand before the throne (Revelation 21:27). And standing there, he would finally have become a saint, an unequivocal friend of God, participating in the Resurrection life of which Jesus Christ was the firstfruits.

Tolkien didn't write a great deal about the Resurrection, but there is no doubt he believed it to be a reality, one that he hoped and expected—by God's grace—to experience some day. In a letter to Christopher, he declares his conviction that the Resurrection gives rise to "that essential emotion: Christian joy" and that this joy is qualitatively like sorrow "because it comes from those places where Joy and Sorrow are at one, reconciled."* He goes on to say:

> in the Primary Miracle (the Resurrection) and the lesser Christian miracles too though less, you have not only that sudden glimpse of the truth behind the apparent Anankê [necessity, constraint] of our world, but a glimpse that is actually a ray of light through the very chinks of the

---

* It may be asked whether Tolkien assigns too high a place to sorrow in his conception of the resurrection life. After all, St. John's vision in the book of Revelation is of heavenly beatitude so complete that God "will wipe away every tear from their eyes . . . neither shall there be mourning nor crying nor pain any more" (Revelation 21:4). The question is worth asking but is too large a topic to consider properly in a biographical work. A short answer would point to Tolkien's use of the word "reconciled." Sorrow is *reconciled* with joy in the resurrection: it is overcome and healed, not simply cancelled or eradicated from memory. That Christ's wounds are still visible after his Resurrection and provoke worshipful adoration, not grief or disgust (John 20:27–28), is surely the chief biblical template for Tolkien's understanding. The seventh-century work of St. John Climacus, *The Ladder of Divine Ascent*, coins the word 'charmolypi' (joy-sorrow) to express something of this paradox. The Field of Cormallen scene at the end of *The Lord of the Rings* is the most intensely charmolypic moment in Tolkien's fiction: "their hearts, wounded with sweet words, overflowed, and their joy was like swords, and they passed in thought out to regions where pain and delight flow together and tears are the very wine of blessedness." For an exploration of this theme in the writings of C.S. Lewis, which touches at times on Tolkien's work, see Jahdiel Perez, "'Love is Tears': The Charmolypic Theological Vision of C.S. Lewis" (D.Phil, University of Oxford, 2023).

> universe about us. I was riding along on a bicycle one day, not so long ago, past the Radcliffe Infirmary, when I had one of those sudden clarities which sometimes come in dreams (even anaesthetic-produced ones). I remember saying aloud with absolute conviction: 'But of course! Of course that's how things really do work.'[31]

The sudden glimpse of a transformative ray of light from beyond the universe may fairly bring to mind Frodo's closing vision in the final chapter of *The Return of the King*:

> And the ship went out into the High Sea and passed on into the West, until at last on a night of rain Frodo smelled a fragrance on the air and heard the sound of singing that came over the water. And then it seemed to him that as in his dream in the house of Bombadil, the grey rain-curtain turned all to silver glass and was rolled back, and he beheld white shores and beyond them a far green country under a swift sunrise.[32]

The End

At the Merton memorial service, there were two Scripture readings, one from the Old Testament and one from the New.

The Old Testament passage was taken from the book of Wisdom. It recounts King Solomon's love of wisdom, personified as a gracious lady:

> She knows the things of old, and infers the things to come;
> she understands turns of speech and the solutions of riddles. . . .
>
> Therefore I determined to take her to live with me,
> knowing that she would give me good counsel
> and encouragement in cares and grief.
>
> Because of her I shall have immortality,
> and leave an everlasting remembrance to those who come after me.[33]

The New Testament reading was 1 John 4:7–21, the great meditation on divine love in which St. John repeatedly states the Christian's ground for believing that God is well-disposed to the world he has made:

> In this was manifested the love of God toward us, because that God sent his only begotten Son into the world. . . .
>
> Herein is love, not that we loved God, but that he loved us, and sent his Son to be the propitiation for our sins. . . .
>
> We have seen and do testify that the Father sent the Son to be the Saviour of the world.

Tolkien believed this divine mission to be a reality: this was the root of his faith. To reject the "Christian story," as he called it, "leads either to sadness or to wrath." He did not reject it; he accepted it, built his life upon it, upon this in-breaking of "a sudden and miraculous grace." He coined his own word for it—eucatastrophe, the *good* catastrophe. Such eucatastrophic grace could even be expressed in a story told by a mere man, such as himself. And it could be expressed in fiction precisely because human beings are subcreators, made in the image and likeness of a Creator. And not only made in that likeness, but remade in it too. It had long been his "joyous feeling," he said, that God redeemed men in a way fitting to this aspect of their nature. Since they are story-makers, God makes their redemption happen in a story:

> The Gospels contain a fairy-story . . . which embraces all the essence of fairy-stories. . . . But this story has entered History and the primary world. . . . The Birth of Christ is the eucatastrophe of Man's history. The Resurrection is the eucatastrophe of the story of the Incarnation. This story begins and ends in joy. . . . There is no tale ever told that men would rather find was true, and none which so many sceptical men have accepted as true on its own merits.[34]

Eucatastrophe, he clarifies, does not deny the existence of tragedy, of sorrow, failure, darkness, and death, the long defeat of this mortal life: it is only because these sad things are possible that the deliverance of grace, when it comes, can lift up the heart, cause a catching of the breath, bring tears to the eyes. What eucatastrophe does deny, in the face of strong, almost overwhelming evidence to the contrary, is "universal final defeat." It is therefore *evangelium*, good news, the best possible news, giving those who receive it "a glimpse of Joy, Joy beyond the walls of the world, poignant as grief."

John Ronald Philip Reuel Tolkien (1892–1973)

APPENDIX A: Timeline of Tolkien's Life

Restoration of Catholic hierarchy in England	1850	
Oxford University removes requirement that students assent to the Anglican Thirty-Nine Articles, allowing Catholics to matriculate Proclamation of the dogma of the Immaculate Conception	1854	
	1857	Francis Morgan born Arthur Tolkien born
	1870	Mabel Suffield born
Universities Tests Act removes remaining barriers to Catholics earning degrees and holding academic positions at Oxford	1871	
	1883	Francis Morgan ordained priest
	1889	Edith Bratt born
John Henry Cardinal Newman dies	1890	
	1891	Arthur Tolkien and Mabel Suffield marry, Anglican Cathedral of St. George, Cape Town, South Africa
	1892	January 3: John Ronald Reuel Tolkien born, Bloemfontein, South Africa January 31: baptized, Anglican Cathedral of St. Andrew and St. Michael
	1894	Tolkien's brother Hilary born
Hierarchy allows Catholics to attend Oxford without requiring special permission from their bishop; Catholic Chaplaincy established	1895	
	1896	Arthur Tolkien dies, Bloemfontein; Mabel and her sons settle in Birmingham, England

World / Church Events	Year	Tolkien's Life
	1900	Mabel Tolkien enters the Catholic Church; financial support cut off by her family John Ronald begins studies at King Edward's School
Queen Victoria dies, succeeded by Edward VII; at his coronation he is required to repudiate doctrine of transubstantiation	1901	
	1902	Mabel and her sons become members of the parish of the Birmingham Oratory
Pope Leo XIII dies, succeeded by Pius X	1903	John Ronald receives First Holy Communion and Confirmation in the Catholic Church; takes the name 'Philip' after St. Philip Neri
Work begins on Birmingham Oratory's Cardinal Newman Memorial Church	1904	November 14: Mabel dies; Fr. Francis Morgan becomes guardian of John Ronald and Hilary
Sacra Tridentina: on frequent and daily reception of Holy Communion	1905	John Ronald and Hilary lodge with their Aunt Beatrice Suffield, where they are unhappy
	1908	Fr. Francis finds new lodgings for the boys at 37 Duchess Road, where John Ronald meets Edith Bratt; they become friends and fall in love
Birmingham Oratory's Newman Memorial Church officially opened	1909	Tolkien fails first scholarship examination for Oxford
King Edward VII dies, succeeded by George V; Coronation Oath no longer disavows transubstantiation *Quam Singulari*: on children receiving the Eucharist	1910	Fr. Francis forbids Tolkien to see or write to Edith until he comes of age Tolkien takes scholarship examination a second time; wins Open Classical Exhibition for Exeter College
	1911	Matriculates at Exeter College, Oxford
	1913	Turns twenty-one; renews relationship with Edith
Pope Pius X dies, succeeded by Benedict XV August 4: Great Britain declares war on Germany United Kingdom establishes provisional diplomatic relations with the Holy See	1914	Tolkien and Edith formally engaged Tolkien joins Officers' Training Corps at Oxford

	1915	Completes Oxford studies, earning First Class Honours degree in English Language and Literature. Enters army; trains as signals officer
July-November: Battle of the Somme	1916	March 22: Tolkien and Edith marry, Church of St. Mary Immaculate, Warwick June 4: Tolkien departs for Western Front, serving in Lancashire Fusiliers October: contracts trench fever; invalided back to England for convalescence
Royal family changes surname to Windsor	1917	Tolkien writes *The Fall of Gondolin* John Francis Reuel Tolkien born
November 11: Great War ends	1918	After repeated relapses of trench fever, Tolkien declared 100% disabled by Army Medical Board
	1919	Tolkien demobilized; begins work as assistant lexicographer for the *Oxford English Dictionary*
	1920	Michael Hilary Reuel Tolkien born Tolkien begins teaching at Leeds University as Reader in English Language Starts writing annual *Father Christmas Letters* for his children
Pope Benedict XV dies, succeeded by Pius XI	1922	
U.K. establishes legation level diplomatic relations with the Holy See	1923	
	1924	Christopher John Reuel Tolkien born Tolkien promoted to Professor of English Language at Leeds
	1925	Elected to the Rawlinson and Bosworth Chair of Anglo-Saxon at Oxford
Roman Catholic Relief Act removes last of the penal laws Fr. Ronald Knox becomes Chaplain at Oxford University	1926	Tolkien family moves to 22 Northmoor Road, Oxford; he becomes member of parish church of St. Gregory and St. Augustine Tolkien meets C.S. Lewis at English Faculty meeting

World events	Year	Tolkien's life
	1929	Priscilla Anne Reuel Tolkien born Tolkien shows Lewis draft of "The Lay of Leithian"
	1930	Tolkien family moves to 20 Northmoor Road Early in the 1930s, the Inklings start to meet; Tolkien begins story that will become *The Hobbit*
	1931	Tolkien, Lewis, and Hugo Dyson converse in Addison's Walk, leading to Lewis's Christian conversion and Tolkien's poem "Mythopoeia"
Edinburgh Eucharistic Congress held, triggering anti-Catholic Morningside Riot Sir Thomas More canonized	1935	Fr. Francis Morgan dies
King George V dies, succeeded by Edward VIII, who abdicates; George VI accedes to the throne	1936	Tolkien gives "Beowulf: The Monsters and the Critics" as Gollancz Memorial Lecture to the British Academy
	1937	*The Hobbit* published
Pius XI dies, succeeded by Pius XII Britain declares war on Germany after invasion of Poland	1939	Tolkien delivers "On Fairy-stories" as the Andrew Lang Lecture at the University of St. Andrews
Food rationing begins in Britain	1940	
Divino Afflante Spiritu: on promoting biblical studies and vernacular translations	1943	Writes last of the *Father Christmas Letters* Becomes founding vice-president of Oxford Circle of the Catenians; remains a member until 1956
Second World War ends	1945	Elected to the Merton Chair in English Language and Literature at Oxford "Leaf by Niggle" published in *The Dublin Review* Charles Williams dies; Tolkien has a Requiem Mass said for him and serves at it
	1947	Tolkien begins to serve as honorary vice-president for the Newman Association. Family moves to 3 Manor Road, Oxford

Establishment of the State of Israel	1948	
	1949	The Inklings' Thursday gatherings end; social meetings continue until Lewis's death in 1963
Proclamation of the dogma of the Assumption of Mary	1950	Tolkiens move to 99 Holywell Street, Oxford
King George VI dies, succeeded by Elizabeth II	1952	Allen & Unwin agree to publish *The Lord of the Rings*
Queen Elizabeth II's coronation in Westminster Abbey	1953	Tolkien and Edith move to 76 Sandfield Road, Headington; he attends parish church of Corpus Christi
Canonization of Pope Pius X Food rationing ends in England	1954	*The Fellowship of the Ring* and *The Two Towers* published Tolkien receives honorary doctorate from National University of Ireland
Pope Pius XII institutes reforms to the liturgies of Holy Week	1955	*The Return of the King* published
Pius XII dies, succeeded by John XXIII	1958	
	1959	Tolkien delivers his "Valedictory Address to the University of Oxford" and retires
	1960	Church of St. Anthony of Padua built, with contributions from Tolkien; he becomes a member of the parish
Queen Elizabeth II meets Pope John XXIII in Rome, first official visit of a British monarch to the Vatican since the Reformation	1961	Translates book of Jonah for the Jerusalem Bible
Second Vatican Council begins	1962	
Pope John XXIII dies, succeeded by Paul VI *Sacrosanctum Concilium* permits vernacular to be used in the liturgy	1963	November 22: C.S. Lewis dies; Tolkien has a Requiem Mass said for him and serves at it; attends his funeral at Holy Trinity, Headington Quarry

Church events	Year	Tolkien's life
Liturgy of the Mass begins shift into English *Unitatis Redintegratio*: the Decree on Ecumenism	1964	Tolkien comments on C.S. Lewis's posthumously published *Letters to Malcolm: Chiefly on Prayer*
Nostra Aetate: on relations between the Church and non-Christian religions Second Vatican Council concludes	1965	
	1966	Tolkien reads *Smith of Wootton Major* at ecumenical lecture series hosted by Blackfriars and Pusey House Works with Clyde Kilby to assemble materials for *The Silmarillion* Jerusalem Bible published
	1968	Tolkien and Edith move to Bournemouth
Pope Paul VI promulgates *Novus Ordo Missae* (new order of the Mass)	1969	
	1971	November 29: Edith dies; Requiem Mass held at Church of the Sacred Heart, Bournemouth; her body laid to rest in Wolvercote Cemetery, Oxford
	1972	Tolkien returns to Oxford; made Emeritus Fellow of Merton College; honored by Queen Elizabeth II for services to English literature; receives Honorary Doctorate of Letters from Oxford
	1973	September 2: Tolkien dies; Requiem Mass at St. Anthony of Padua, Oxford; his body laid to rest alongside Edith at Wolvercote Cemetery Memorial Service at Merton College, Oxford

APPENDIX B:
Prayers and Liturgical Extracts

The Latin texts are reproduced here without accent marks (which were included for the purpose of reading aloud) but are otherwise exactly as in the original source material, including variant approaches to the use of ae / æ.

***Pater Noster* / Our Father** (see chapter 5)

Latin text and English translation from *The Roman Missal Adapted to the Use of the Laity from the Missale Romanum* (1913)

Pater noster, qui es in cælis, sanctificetur nomen tuum; adveniat regnum tuum: fiat voluntas tua, sicut in cælo et in terra. Panem nostrum quotidianum da nobis hodie. Et dimitte nobis debita nostra, sicut et nos dimittimus debitoribus nostris. Et ne nos inducas in tentationem: sed libera nos a malo. Amen.

Our Father, who art in heaven, hallowed be Thy name: Thy kingdom come: Thy will be done on earth as it is in heaven. Give us this day our daily bread. And forgive us our trespasses, as we forgive them that trespass against us. And lead us not into temptation. But deliver us from evil.
Amen.

***Ave Maria* / Hail Mary** (see chapter 5)

Latin text and English translation from *The Catholic's Vade Mecum* (1851)

Ave, Maria, gratia plena; Dominus tecum: benedicta tu in mulieribus, et benedictus fructus ventris tui, Jesus. Sancta Maria, Mater Dei, ora pro nobis peccatoribus, nunc et in hora mortis nostrae. Amen.

Hail, Mary, full of grace; the Lord is with thee: blessed art thou among women, and blessed is the fruit of thy womb, Jesus. Holy Mary, Mother of God, pray for us sinners, now and at the hour of our death. Amen.

***Gloria Patria* / Glory Be** (see chapter 5)

Latin text and English translation from *The Catholic's Vade Mecum* (1851)

Gloria Patri, et Filio, et Spiritui Sancto. Sicut erat in principio, et nunc, et semper, et in saecula saeculorum. Amen.

Glory be to the Father, and to the Son, and to the Holy Ghost. As it was in the beginning, is now, and ever shall be, world without end. Amen.

The Canon of the Mass (see chapter 16)

Latin text and English translation from *The Order and Canon of the Mass in Latin and English* (1916)

Preconciliar missals agreed on the beginning of the Canon at "Te igitur" but varied as to its extent: some marked the end of the Canon at the "Pater noster," while others included as part of the Canon various prayers that followed. This extract is from the "Te igitur" to the "Pater noster" and therefore represents the material that we can be certain Tolkien considered as part of the "Canon of the Mass."

Te igitur, clementissime Pater, per Jesum Christum Filium tuum Dominum nostrum, supplices rogamus, ac petimus, uti accepta habeas, et benedicas, hæc dona, hæc munera, hæc sancta sacrifícia illibata, in primis, quæ tibi offerimus pro Ecclesia tua sancta catholica: quam pacificare, custodire, adunare, et regere digneris toto orbe terrarum: una cum famulo tuo Papa nostro *N.* et Antistite nostro *N.*, et omnibus orthodoxis, atque catholicæ, et apostolicae fídei cultoribus.	Thee, therefore, O most merciful Father, we humbly pray and beseech through Jesus Christ, thy Son, our Lord, that thou wouldest be pleased to accept and bless these gifts, these offerings, these holy and unspotted sacrifices which we offer unto thee in the first place for thy holy catholic church, that thou wouldest be pleased to keep her in peace under thy protection, to bring her to unity, and guide her throughout the world; together with thy servant *N.* our pope, and *N.* our bishop, and all orthodox promoters of the catholic and apostolic faith.
Memento, Domine, famulorum famularumque tuarum *N.* et *N.*,	Remember, O Lord, thy servants and handmaids, *N.* and *N.*,
et omnium circumstantium, quorum tibi fides cognita est, et nota devotio, pro quibus tibi offerimus, vel qui tibi offerunt hoc sacrificium laudis, pro se suisque omnibus, pro redemptione animarum suarum, pro spe salutis, et incolumitatis suæ: tibique reddunt vota sua æterno Deo, vivo et vero. Communicantes, et memoriam venerantes, in primis gloriosæ semper Vírginis Mariæ, Genetricis Dei et Domini nostri Jesu Christi: sed et beatorum Apostolorum ac Martyrum tuorum, Petri et Pauli, Andreæ, Jacobi, Joannis, Thomæ, Jacobi, Philippi,	and all here present whose faith thou knowest and whose devotion thou beholdest; for whom we offer, or who themselves do offer unto thee, this sacrifice of praise for themselves and all theirs; for the redemption of their souls; for their hope of safety and salvation: and who pay their vows unto thee, the eternal, living and true God. Being in communion with, and venerating the memory of first the glorious Mary, ever a virgin, mother of God and of our Lord Jesus Christ; and also of thy blessed apostles and martyrs, Peter and Paul, Andrew, James, John,

Bartholomæi, Matthæi, Simonis et Thaddæi: Lini, Cleti, Clementis, Xysti, Cornelii, Cypriani, Laurentii, Chrysogoni, Joannis et Pauli, Cosmæ et Damiani, et omnium Sanctorum tuorum: quorum meritis precibusque concedas, ut in omnibus protectionis tuæ muniamur auxilio. Per eundem Christum Dominum nostrum. Amen.

Thomas, James, Philip, Bartholomew, Matthew, Simon and Thaddæus; of Linus, Cletus, Clement, Sixtus, Cornelius, Cyprian, Lawrence, Chrysogonus, John and Paul, Cosmas and Damian, and of all thy saints; by whose good deeds and prayers do thou grant that in all things we may be guarded by the help of thy protection. Through the same Christ our Lord. Amen.

Hanc igitur oblationem servitutis nostræ, sed et cunctae familiæ tuæ, quæsumus Domine, ut placatus accipias: diesque nostros in tua pace disponas, atque ab æterna damnatione nos eripi, et in electorum tuorum jubeas grege numerari. Per Christum Dominum nostrum. Amen.

We therefore pray thee, O Lord, graciously to accept this oblation of our bounden duty and service and that of all thy family: and do thou order our days in thy peace, and bid us to be delivered from eternal damnation and to be numbered in the flock of thine elect. Through Christ our Lord. Amen.

Quam oblationem tu, Deus, in omnibus, quæsumus, benedictam, adscriptam, ratam, rationabilem, acceptabilemque facere digneris: ut nobis Corpus et Sanguis fiat dilectissimi Filii tui Domini nostri Jesu Christi.

This our offering, do thou, O God, vouchsafe in all things to make blessed, consecrated, approved, reasonable, and acceptable: that it may become for us the body and blood of thy most dearly beloved Son, our Lord Jesus Christ.

Qui pridie quam pateretur, accepit panem in sanctas, ac venerabiles manus suas et elevatis oculis in cælum ad te Deum Patrem suum omnipotentem, tibi gratias agens, benedixit, fregit, deditque discipulis suis, dicens: Accipite, et manducate ex hoc omnes.

Who the day before he suffered took bread into his holy and venerable hands and with his eyes lifted up towards heaven unto thee, God, his almighty Father, giving thanks to thee, he blessed, brake, and gave to his disciples, saying: Take and eat ye all of this.

HOC EST ENIM CORPUS MEUM.

FOR THIS IS MY BODY.

Simili modo postquam cœnatum est, accipiens et hunc præclarum Calicem in sanctas, ac venerabiles manus suas: item tibi gratias agens, benedixit, deditque discipulis suis, dicens: Accipite, et bibite ex eo omnes.

Likewise after he had supped, taking also this glorious chalice into his holy and venerable hands and presently giving thanks to thee, he blessed and gave to his disciples, saying: Take and drink ye all of this.

HIC EST ENIM CALIX SANGUINIS MEI, NOVI ET ÆTERNI TESTAMENTI: MYSTERIUM FIDEI: QUI PRO VOBIS ET PRO MULTIS EFFUNDETUR IN REMISSIONEM PECCATORUM.

FOR THIS IS THE CHALICE OF MY BLOOD, OF THE NEW AND ETERNAL TESTAMENT: THE MYSTERY OF FAITH, WHICH SHALL BE SHED FOR YOU AND FOR MANY UNTO TO THE REMISSION OF SINS.

Hæc quotiescumque feceritis, in mei memoriam facietis.

As often as you shall do these things, you shall do them in memory of me.

Unde et memores, Domine, nos servi tui, sed et plebs tua sancta, ejusdem Christi Filii tui Domini nostri tam beatæ passionis, nec non et ab inferis resurrectionis, sed et in cælos gloriosæ ascensionis: offerimus præclaræ majestati tuæ de tuis donis, ac datis, hostiam puram, hostiam sanctam, hostiam immaculatam: Panem sanctum vitæ æternæ, et Calicem salutis perpetuæ.

Wherefore, O Lord, we thy servants, together with all thy holy people, mindful of the blessed passion of the same Christ, thy Son, our Lord, also his rising up from hell and his glorious ascension into heaven, do offer unto thy most excellent majesty of thine own gifts, albeit given unto us, a victim pure, a victim holy, a victim immaculate: the holy bread of eternal life, and the chalice of everlasting salvation.

Supra quæ propitio ac sereno vultu respicere digneris: et accepta habere, sicuti accepta habere dignatus es munera pueri tui justi Abel, et sacrifícium Patriarchæ nostri Abrahæ: et quod tibi obtulit summus sacerdos tuus Melchisedech, sanctum sacrifícium, immaculatam Hostiam.

Upon which vouchsafe to look with a favourable and gracious countenance, and to accept them, as thou wast pleased to accept the gifts of thy just servant Abel, and the sacrifice of our father Abraham, and that which Melchisedech thy high priest offered unto thee, even a holy sacrifice, a spotless victim.

Supplices te rogamus, omnipotens Deus: jube hæc perferri per manus sancti Angeli tui in sublime altare tuum, in conspectu divinæ majestatis tuæ: ut quotquot ex hac altaris participatione sacrosanctum Filii tui, Corpus, et Sanguinem sumpserimus, omni benedictione cælesti et gratia repleamur. Per eumdem Christum Dominum nostrum. Amen.

We most humbly beseech thee, almighty God, to command that these sacrifices be borne in the hands of thy holy angel to thine altar on high, before the sight of thy divine majesty, that so many as are partakers at the altar of the precious body and blood of thy Son may be filled with all heavenly benediction and grace. Through the same Christ our Lord. Amen.

Memento etiam, Domine, famulorum, famularumque tuarum *N.* et *N.*, qui nos præcesserunt cum signo fidei, et dormiunt in somno pacis.

Remember, likewise, O Lord, thy servants and handmaids *N.* and *N.*, who are gone hence before us with the sign of faith, and sleep the sleep of peace.

Ipsis, Domine, et omnibus in Christo quiescentibus, locum refrigerii, lucis et pacis, ut indulgeas, deprecamur. Per eumdem Christum Dominum nostrum. Amen.

To these, O Lord, and to all that rest in Christ, we pray thee grant a place of refreshment, light and peace. Through the same Christ our Lord. Amen.

Nobis quoque peccatoribus famulis tuis, de multitudine miserationum tuarum sperantibus, partem aliquam et societatem donare digneris, cum tuis sanctis apostolis et martyribus: cum Joanne, Stephano, Mathia, Barnaba, Ignatio, Alexandro, Marcellino, Petro, Felicitate, Perpetua, Agatha, Lucia, Agnete, Cæcilia, Anastasia, et omnibus sanctis tuis: intra quorum nos consortium, non æstimator meriti, sed veniæ, quæsumus, largitor admitte. Per Christum Dominum nostrum.

To us also, thy sinful servants, hoping in the multitude of thy mercies, vouchsafe to grant some lot and fellowship with thy holy apostles and martyrs; with John, Stephen, Matthias, Barnabas, Ignatius, Alexander, Marcellinus, Peter, Felicitas, Perpetua, Agatha, Lucy, Agnes, Cecily, Anastasia, and all thy saints; into whose company, we pray thee of thy mercy admit us, not weighing our merits but pardoning our offences. Through Christ our Lord.

Per quem hæc omnia, Domine, semper bona creas, sanctificas, vivificas, benedicis, et præstas nobis. Per ipsum, et cum ipso, et in ipso, est tibi Deo Patri omnipotenti, in unitate Spiritus Sancti, omnis honor et gloria. Per omnia sæcula sæculorum. Amen.

By whom, O Lord, thou ever dost create, hallow, quicken, bless and bestow upon us all these good things. Through him, and with him, and in him, is unto thee, God the Father almighty, in the unity of the Holy Ghost, all honour and glory. For ever and ever. Amen.

The Litany of Loreto (see chapters 16 and 27)

Latin text and English translation from *The Roman Missal Adapted to the Use of the Laity from the Missale Romanum* (1913)

The Litany of Loreto is also called the Litany of the Blessed Virgin Mary. This text is of the Litany as it was in 1913; further Marian titles have been added in subsequent years, including, in Tolkien's lifetime, "Queen of peace" (1916) and "Queen assumed into heaven" (1950).

Kyrie, eleison.		Lord, have mercy on us.	
Christe, eleison.		Christ, have mercy on us.	
Kyrie, eleison.		Lord, have mercy on us.	
Christe, audi nos.		Christ, hear us.	
Christe, exaudi nos.		Christ, graciously hear us.	
Pater de caelis Deus,	*Misere nobis.*	God, the Father of heaven,	*Have mercy on us.*
Fili, Redemptor mundi Deus,		God the Son, Redeemer of the world,	
Spiritus Sancte Deus,		God the Holy Ghost,	
Sancta Trinitas unus Deus,		Holy Trinity, one God,	

Sancta Maria,	*Ora pro nobis.*	Holy Mary,	*Pray for us.*
Sancta Dei Genetrix,		Holy Mother of God,	
Sancta Virgo virginum,		Holy Virgin of Virgins,	
Mater Christi,		Mother of Christ,	
Mater divinae gratiae,		Mother of Divine Grace,	
Mater purissima,		Mother most pure,	
Mater castissima,		Mother most chaste,	
Mater inviolata,		Mother inviolate,	
Mater intemerata,		Mother undefiled,	
Mater amabilis,		Mother most amiable,	
Mater admirabilis,		Mother most admirable,	
Mater Boni Consilii,		Mother of Good Counsel,	
Mater Creatoris,		Mother of our Creator	
Mater Salvatoris,		Mother of our Redeemer,	
Virgo prudentissima,		Virgin most prudent,	
Virgo veneranda,		Virgin most venerable,	
Virgo praedicanda,		Virgin most renowned,	
Virgo potens,		Virgin most powerful,	
Virgo clemens,		Virgin most merciful,	
Virgo fidelis,		Virgin most faithful,	
Speculum justitiae,		Mirror of Justice,	
Sedes sapientiae,		Seat of Wisdom,	
Causa nostrae laetitiae,		Cause of our joy,	
Vas spirituale,		Spiritual Vessel,	
Vas honorabile,		Vessel of honour,	

Vas insigne devotionis,
Rosa mystica,
Turris Davidica,
Turris eburnea,
Domus aurea,
Foederis arca,
Janua caeli,
Stella matutina,
Salus infirmorum,
Refugium peccatorum,
Consolatrix afflictorum,
Auxilium Christianorum,
Regina Angelorum,
Regina Patriarcharum,
Regina Prophetarum,
Regina Apostolorum,
Regina Martyrum,
Regina Confessorum,
Regina Virginum,
Regina Sanctorum omnium,
Regina sine labe originali concepta,
Regina sacratissimi Rosarii,

Ora pro nobis.

Agnus Dei, qui tollis peccata mundi: Parce nobis, Domine.
Agnus Dei, qui tollis peccata mundi: Exaudi nobis, Domine.
Agnus Dei, qui tollis peccata mundi: Miserere nobis.

V. Ora pro nobis, Sancta Dei Genetrix.
R. Ut digni efficiamur promissionibus Christi.

Singular Vessel of devotion,
Mystical Rose,
Tower of David,
Tower of ivory,
House of gold,
Ark of the Covenant,
Gate of heaven,
Morning Star,
Health of the weak,
Refuge of sinners,
Comforter of the afflicted,
Help of Christians,
Queen of Angels,
Queen of Patriarchs,
Queen of Prophets,
Queen of Apostles,
Queen of Martyrs,
Queen of Confessors,
Queen of Virgins,
Queen of all Saints,
Queen conceived without original sin,
Queen of the most holy Rosary,

Pray for us.

Lamb of God, who takest away the sins of the world, spare us, O Lord.
Lamb of God, who takest away the sins of the world, graciously hear us O Lord.
Lamb of God, who takest away the sins of the world, have mercy on us.

V. Pray for us, O holy Mother of God.
R. That we may be made worthy of the promises of Christ.

Gloria in Excelsis Deo / **The Gloria** (see chapter 27)

Latin text and English translation from *The Order and Canon of the Mass in Latin and English* (1916)

Gloria in excelsis Deo. Et in terra pax hominibus bonae voluntatis. Laudamus te. Benedicimus te. Adoramus te. Glorificamus te. Gratias agimus tibi propter magnam gloriam tuam. Domine Deus, Rex cælestis, Deus Pater omnipotens. Domine Fili unigenite Jesu Christe. Domine Deus, Agnus Dei, Filius Patris. Qui tollis peccata mundi, suscipe deprecationem nostram. Qui sedes ad dexteram Patris, miserere nobis. Quoniam tu solus sanctus. Tu solus Dominus. Tu solus altissimus, Jesu Christe. Cum Sancto Spiritu, in gloria Dei Patris. Amen

Glory to God in the highest, and on earth peace to men of good will. We praise thee, we bless thee, we adore thee, we glorify thee. We give thee thanks for thy great glory. O Lord God, heavenly King, God the Father almighty. O Lord Jesus Christ, the only-begotten Son. O Lord God, Lamb of God, Son of the Father, who takest away the sins of the world, receive our prayer. Who sittest at the right hand of the Father, have mercy upon us. For thou only art holy. Thou only art Lord. Thou only, O Jesus Christ, art most high, together with the Holy Ghost, in the glory of God the Father. Amen.

Psalms of Praise (see chapter 27)

Latin texts are from the Vulgate; English translations are from the Douay Version of the Bible, Catholic Truth Society edition (1955). Certain Psalms are numbered differently in the Vulgate and in editions based on the Vulgate, such as the Douay; these numbers are given in brackets.

Laudate Pueri Dominum

Laudate, pueri, Dominum: laudate nomen Domini.

Sit nomen Domini benedictum: ex hoc nunc et usque in saeculum.

A solis ortu usque ad occasum: laudabile nomen Domini.

Excelsus super omnes gentes Dominus: et super cælos gloria ejus.

Quis sicut Dominus Deus noster, qui in altis habitat: et humilia respicit in cælo et in terra?

Psalm 113 [112]

Praise the Lord, ye children: praise ye the name of the Lord.

Blessed be the name of the Lord, from henceforth now and for ever.

From the rising of the sun unto the going down of the same, the name of the Lord is worthy of praise.

The Lord is high above all nations; and his glory above the heavens.

Who is as the Lord our God, who dwelleth on high: and looketh down on the low things in heaven and in earth?

Suscitans a terra inopem: et de stercore erigens pauperem:

Ut collocet eum cum principibus: cum principibus populi sui.

Qui habitare facit sterilem in domo: matrem filiorum lætantem.

Raising up the needy from the earth, and lifting up the poor out of the dunghill:

That he may place him with princes, with the princes of his people.

Who maketh a barren woman to dwell in a house, the joyful mother of children

Laudate Dominum

Laudate Dominum, omnes gentes: laudate eum, omnes populi:

Quoniam confirmata est super nos, misericordia ejus: et veritas Domini manet in æternum.

Psalm 117 [116]

O Praise the Lord, all ye nations: praise him, all ye people.

For his mercy is confirmed upon us: and the truth of the Lord remaineth for ever.

Laudate Dominum de cælis

Alleluja. Laudate Dominum de cælis; laudate eum in excelsis.

Laudate eum, omnes angeli ejus; laudate eum, omnes virtutes ejus.

Laudate eum, sol et luna; laudate eum, omnes stellæ et lumen.

Laudate eum, cæli cælorum; et aquæ omnes quæ super cælos sunt, laudent nomen Domini.

Quia ipse dixit, et facta sunt; ipse mandavit, et creata sunt.

Statuit ea in æternum, et in sæculum sæculi; præceptum posuit, et non præteribit.

Laudate Dominum de terra, dracones et omnes abyssi;

ignis, grando, nix, glacies, spiritus procellarum, quæ faciunt verbum ejus;

montes, et omnes colles; ligna fructifera, et omnes cedri;

bestiæ, et universa pecora; serpentes, et volucres pennatæ;

reges terræ et omnes populi, principes et omnes judices terræ;

juvenes et virgines, senes cum junioribus laudent nomen Domini, quia exaltatum est nomen ejus solius.

Psalm 148

Alleluia. Praise ye the Lord from the heavens: praise ye him in the high places.

Praise ye him, all his angels: praise ye him, all his hosts.

Praise ye him, O sun and moon: praise him, all ye stars and light.

Praise him, ye heavens of heavens: and let all the waters that are above the heavens praise the name of the Lord.

For he spoke, and they were made: he commanded, and they were created.

He hath established them for ever, and for ages of ages: he hath made a decree, and it shall not pass away.

Praise the Lord from the earth, ye dragons, and all ye deeps:

Fire, hail, snow, ice, stormy winds, which fulfil his word:

Mountains and all hills: fruitful trees and all cedars:

Beasts and all cattle: serpents and feathered fowls:

Kings of the earth and all people: princes and all judges of the earth:

Young men and maidens: let the old with the younger, praise the name of the Lord: for his name alone is exalted.

Confessio ejus super cælum et terram; et exaltavit cornu populi sui.

Hymnus omnibus sanctis ejus; filiis Isræl, populo appropinquanti sibi. Alleluja.

The praise of him is above heaven and earth: and he hath exalted the horn of his people.

A hymn to all his saints: to the children of Israel, a people approaching to him. Alleluia.

Magnificat (See chapter 27)

Latin text and English translation from *The Roman Missal Adapted to the Use of the Laity from the Missale Romanum* (1913)

Magnificat: anima mea Dominum:
Et exultavit spiritus meus: in Deo salutari meo.
Quia respexit humilitatem ancillae suae: ecce enim ex hoc beatam me dicent omnes generationes.

Quia fecit mihi magna qui potens est: et sanctum Nomen ejus,
Et misericordia ejus a progenie in progenies: timentibus eum.
Fecit potentiam in brachio suo: dispersit superbos mente cordis sui.

Deposuit potentes de sede: et exaltavit humiles.
Esurientes implevit bonis: et divites dimisit inanes.

Suscepit Israel puerum suum: recordatus misericordiae suae.
Sicut locutus est ad patres nostros: Abraham et semini ejus in saecula.

My soul doth magnify the Lord:
And my spirit hath rejoiced in God my Saviour.
For he hath regarded the lowliness of his His handmaid; for behold, from henceforth, all generations shall call me blessed.
For He that is mighty, hath done great things to me: and holy is His Name.
And His mercy is from generation to generations: to them that fear Him.
He hath shown might in His arm: He hath scattered the proud in the conceit of their hearts.
He hath put down the mighty from their seat: and hath exalted the humble.
He hath filled the hungry with good things: and the rich He hath sent empty away.
He hath holpen Israel His servant: being mindful of His mercy.
As he spoke to our fathers: to Abraham and to his seed for ever.

Sub tuum praesidium (see chapter 27)

Latin text and English translation from *The Catholic's Vade Mecum* (1851)

Sub tuum præsidium confugimus, sancta Dei Genitrix, nostras deprecationes ne despicias in necessitatibus nostris; sed a periculis cunctis libera nos semper,Virgo gloriosa et benedicta.	We fly to thy patronage, O holy Mother of God, despise not our petitions in our necessities; but deliver us always from all dangers, O glorious and blessed Virgin.

Te Deum (see chapter 27)

Latin text and English translation from *The Catholic's Vade Mecum* (1851)

Te Deum laudamus: te Dominum confitemur.	We praise thee, O God: we acknowledge thee to be the Lord.
Te æternum Patrem omnis terra veneratur.	All the earth doth worship thee: the Father everlasting.
Tibi omnes Angeli; tibi cæli et universae potestates:	To thee all angels cry aloud: the heavens and all the powers therein:
Tibi Cherubim et Seraphim incessabili voce proclamant:	To thee cherubim and seraphim: continually do cry:
Sanctus, Sanctus, Sanctus, Dominus Deus Sabaoth:	Holy, holy, holy: Lord God of Sabaoth.
Pleni sunt cæli et terra majestatis gloriæ tuæ.	Heaven and earth are full: of the majesty of thy glory.
Te gloriosus Apostolorum chorus.	The glorious choir of the Apostles: praise thee.
Te Prophetarum laudabilis numerus.	The admirable company of the Prophets: praise thee.
Te Martyrum candidatus laudat exercitus.	The white-robed army of Martyrs: praise thee.
Te per orbem terrarum sancta confitetur Ecclesia.	The Holy Church throughout all the world: doth acknowledge thee.
Patrem immensæ majestatis.	The Father: of an infinite majesty.
Venerandum tuum verum et unicum Filium.	Thy adorable, true: and only Son.
Sanctum quoque Paraclitum Spiritum.	Also the Holy Ghost: the Comforter.
Tu Rex gloriæ, Christe.	Thou art the King of Glory: O Christ.
Tu Patris sempiternus es Filius.	Thou art the everlasting Son: of the Father.
Tu ad liberandum suscepturus hominem, non horruisti Virginis uterum.	When thou tookest upon thee to deliver man: thou didst not abhor the Virgin's womb.

Tu devicto mortis aculeo, aperuisti credentibus regna cælorum.

Tu ad dexteram Dei sedes, in gloria Patris.

Judex crederis esse venturus.

Te ergo quæsumus, tuis famulis subveni, quos pretioso sanguine redemisti.

Æterna fac cum Sanctis tuis in gloria numerari.

Salvum fac populum tuum, Domine, et benedic hæreditati tuæ.

Et rege eos, et extolle illos usque in æternum.

Per singulos dies benedicimus te.

Et laudamus nomen tuum in sæculum, et in sæculum sæculi.

Dignare, Domine, die isto, sine peccato nos custodire.

Miserere nostri, Domine, miserere nostri.

Fiat misericordia tua, Domine, super nos, quemadmodum speravimus in te.

In te, Domine, speravi: non confundar in æternum.

When thou hadst overcome the sting of death: thou didst open the kingdom of heaven to all believers.

Thou sittest at the right hand of God: in the glory of the Father.

We believe that thou shalt come: to be our Judge.

We pray thee, therefore, help thy servants: whom thou hast redeemed with thy precious blood.

Make them to be numbered with thy Saints: in glory everlasting.

O Lord, save thy people: and bless thine inheritance.

Govern them: and lift them up for ever.

Day by day: we magnify thee.

And we praise thy name for ever: yea, for ever and ever.

Vouchsafe, O Lord, this day: to keep us without sin.

O Lord, have mercy upon us: have mercy upon us.

O Lord, let thy mercy be shewed upon us: as we have hoped in thee.

O Lord, in thee have I hoped: let me not be confounded for ever.

The Last Gospel: John 1:1–14 (see chapters 22 and 32)

Latin text and English translation from *The Roman Missal Adapted to the Use of the Laity from the Missale Romanum* (1913)

The "John" named in the text is John the Baptist, forerunner of Christ (see Matthew 3; Luke 1; John 1:19-34).

In principio erat Verbum, et Verbum erat apud Deum; et Deus erat Verbum: hoc erat in principio apud Deum. Omnia per ipsum facta sunt, et sine ipso factum est nihil quod factum est: in ipso vita erat, et vita erat lux hominum; et lux in tenebris lucet, et tenebræ eam non comprehenderunt. Fuit homo missus a Deo, cui nomen erat Joannes. Hic venit in testimonium, ut testimonium perhiberet de lumine, ut omnes crederent per illum. Non erat ille lux; sed ut testimonium perhiberet de lumine. Erat lux vera quæ illuminat omnem hominem venientem in hunc mundum. In mundo erat, et mundus per ipsum factus est, et mundus eum non cognovit. In propria venit, et sui eum non receperunt. Quotquot autem receperunt eum, dedit eis potestatem filios Dei fieri: his qui credunt in nomine ejus, qui non ex sanguinibus, neque ex voluntate carnis, neque ex voluntate viri, sed ex Deo nati sunt. ET VERBUM CARO FACTUM EST, et habitavit in nobis; et vidimus gloriam ejus, gloriam quasi Unigeniti a Patre, plenum gratiæ et veritatis.

In the beginning was the Word, and the Word was with God, and the Word was God: the Same was in the beginning with God. All things were made by Him: and without Him was made nothing that was made. In Him was life; and the life was the light of men; and the light shineth in darkness, and the darkness did not comprehend it. There was a man sent from God, whose name was John. This man came for a witness, to bear witness of the light, that all might believe through him. He was not the light, but was to bear witness of the light. That was the true light, which enlighteneth every man that cometh into this world. He was in the world, and the world was made by Him: and the world knew Him not. He came unto His own; and His own received Him not. But as many as received Him, to them gave He power to be made the sons of God: to them that believe in His Name; who are born, not of blood, nor of the will of the flesh, nor of the will of man, but of God. And THE WORD WAS MADE FLESH, and dwelt among us; and we saw His glory, the glory as it were of the Only-begotten of the Father, full of grace and truth.

GLOSSARY

Cross-references are indicated by the symbol °

Absolution: The act by which a priest,° acting *in persona Christi* (in the person of Christ), conveys God's forgiveness of sins to a person who has made a confession.° See John 20:21–23. In extraordinary circumstances (e.g., imminent death), a priest may grant a general absolution to a group of people without hearing individual confessions.

Acolyte: One who assists a priest° or deacon° at Mass° or other liturgies by handling vessels, ringing bells, lighting candles, and so on.

Adoration: A devotional practice in which the Blessed Sacrament° is brought out of the tabernacle° and displayed publicly on the altar inside a monstrance° as a focus for prayer and worship.°

Advent: The liturgical season, with a partially penitential character, beginning four Sundays before Christmas and concluding with Christmas Eve.

Aggiornamento: Italian for 'updating' or 'bringing up to date.' The guiding principle of reforms introduced during the Second Vatican Council.°

All Saints' Day: Solemnity° occurring on November 1, collectively honoring all saints.°

All Souls' Day: The Commemoration of All the Faithful Departed, on November 2, during which the faithful pray for the repose of the souls of all who have died.

Angel: From the Greek for 'messenger.' A spiritual being created by God, acting as his messenger or agent. Catholic teaching holds that every human being has a guardian angel. See Genesis 28:11–22; Matthew 1:20, 18:10; Luke 2:9–14.

Anglican: Member of the Church of England° or of a church in communion° with it.

Anglo-Catholic: Member of the Church of England° who views Anglicanism as a branch of the Catholic Church° but does not accept the authority of the pope.° Characterized by 'high church' liturgical practices such as using bells, incense, and candles.

Annunciation: The announcement by the Archangel° Gabriel to Mary that she had been chosen to be the Mother of God°; upon her acceptance, she conceived Christ° by the power of the Holy Spirit.° See Luke 1:26–38. Celebrated in the Catholic liturgical calendar on March 25. The date of the Annunciation is traditionally held also to be the date of Christ's Crucifixion.

Apostolate: From the Greek for 'sent.' Work of evangelization,° especially that done by the laity,° either as an individual with a personal sense of mission or as part of an organized group with a joint focus. See Matthew 28:18–20.

Archangel: A chief or lead angel.° The Catholic tradition recognizes three by name: Gabriel (Luke 1:26–38), Michael (Revelation 12:7–9), and Raphael (Tobit 12).

Ark of the Covenant: In the Old Testament,° the wooden chest, covered in gold, constructed to hold the stone tablets of the Ten Commandments and an urn containing manna. Understood in Catholic theology to be a type or foreshadowing of the Blessed Virgin Mary. See Exodus 25 and 37; Hebrews 9:3-5; Revelation 11:19.

Ascension: Christ's bodily ascent into heaven,° forty days after the Resurrection,° marking the end of his earthly ministry. See Mark 16:19–20; Acts 1:6–12.

Assumption: The Catholic dogma° that Mary, at the end of her earthly life, was taken up body and soul into heaven.° It was declared in 1950 by Pope Pius XII. The Bible records that Enoch and Eljiah were also assumed into heaven. See Genesis 5:24; 2 Kings 2:11.

Baptism: The first of the seven sacraments,° which removes original and actual sin° and incorporates a person into the Body of Christ by means of water (immersion, pouring, or sprinkling) and the Trinitarian formula, "I baptize you in the name of the Father, and of the Son, and of the Holy Spirit." See Matthew 28:19; 1 Peter 3:21–22.

Baptists: A Protestant denomination distinguished by their practice of administering baptism° only to adult believers.

Beatification: Official recognition by the Catholic Church° that a deceased member of the faithful is now in heaven,° having lived a life of heroic virtue or been martyred° for their faith; usually warranted by evidence of a miracle that occurred after their intercession was invoked. The person is given the title of 'Blessed' and may be publicly venerated° at the local level. Beatification is sometimes followed by canonization.°

Beatific Vision: The direct knowledge and presence of God experienced by the angels° and the saints° in heaven.° See 1 Corinthians 13:12.

Benediction: A Catholic service of worship, consisting of Adoration° and including the singing of hymns and Psalms.° At its conclusion, the priest blesses the congregation by making the sign of the cross with the monstrance° containing the Blessed Sacrament.°

Bishop: From the Greek for 'overseer.' The clergyman responsible for the spiritual and pastoral care of a diocese,° ranking above priests.° See 1 Timothy 3:1–7.

Blessed: Title given to those who have been beatified.°

Blessed Sacrament: Alternative name for the Host° that has been consecrated° in the liturgy of the Mass;° the Eucharistic Body of Christ.

Breviary: A Catholic prayer book containing the Divine Office, which comprises prayers, Psalms,° and Scripture readings for particular hours of the day. All priests are obligated to pray the Divine Office daily.

Canon (clergyman): A clerical title, usually denoting a priest° with an official connection to a cathedral.

Canon (of the Mass): In the liturgy of the Mass,° the section between the *Sanctus* and the *Pater Noster* or, in English, between the acclamation that begins "Holy, holy, holy, Lord God of hosts" and the Lord's Prayer.

Canon (of Scripture): Writings regarded as authoritative parts of the Christian Bible. The New Testament° canon is identical for Protestants and Catholics, but Catholics regard as canonical certain Old Testament° writings that are not included in Protestant Bibles—namely, the books of Tobit, Judith, Wisdom, Sirach (or Ecclesiasticus), Baruch, 1 and 2 Maccabees, and portions of Esther and Daniel.

Canon law: The rules and laws by which an ecclesiastical body is governed.

Canonization: Official recognition by the Catholic Church° that a deceased member of the faithful is now in heaven,° having lived a life of heroic virtue or been martyred° for their faith; usually on the grounds of a miracle occurring after beatification.° The person receives the title of 'Saint.' Having being 'raised to the full honors of the altar,' a saint is approved for veneration° worldwide.

Canticle: A sacred song typically derived from Scripture, such as the Magnificat (see Appendix B).

Cardinal: A member of the Sacred College, the body responsible for electing the pope.° Known for a distinctive red hat ('biretta') and cassock, denoting the cardinal's willingness to give his life for the faith.

Catechesis: The process of instructing someone in the principles of the Christian faith.

Catechumen: One who receives catechesis,° as preparation for baptism° or entering into full communion° with the Catholic Church.°

Catenians: An association founded in Manchester, England, in 1908 to promote brotherhood and mutual assistance amongst Catholic laymen.°

Catholic Church: 'Catholic' from the Greek for 'universal.' (1) The whole body of the Christian faithful, especially before the Great Schism of 1054 between the Eastern and Western Church; (2) that Church which acknowledges the pope° to be the Vicar of Christ, the visible head of the universal Church.

Cause (for canonization°): Process by which a deceased Catholic is presented as a candidate for official recognition as a saint,° involving a careful examination of that person's life and character.

Celebrant: The priest° who officiates at the liturgy of the Mass.°

Charism: From the Greek for 'gift.' A grace° given by God to a member of the faithful, or to a religious community or organization, for the benefit of the whole Church. See John 16:7; Ephesians 4:11–12.

Christ: Greek for 'anointed one.' The title, used as a proper name, given to Jesus of Nazareth as the Messiah, the fulfillment of Old Testament° prophecies.

Church of England: The established state church in England, originating in the 1534 Act of Supremacy designating King Henry VIII, rather than the pope,° as its head.

Clergy: Those who have received Holy Orders,° as distinct from members of the laity°; namely, deacons,° priests,° and bishops.°

CofE: Abbreviation for Church of England.°

Communion (ecclesiological): Body of Christian believers who submit to the same authority and adhere in principle to the same doctrine.°

Communion (sacramental): Reception of the Blessed Sacrament°; also referred to as 'Holy Communion.'°

Communion of saints: The whole body of the faithful, both the living on earth and the dead in purgatory° or heaven.° See Hebrews 12:1, 12:23.

Confession: Also called the sacrament of Reconciliation or the sacrament of Penance. The act of telling one's sins° to a priest,° so as to receive absolution.° The priest assigns a penance° and may offer counsel. Catholics are required to go to confession at least once a year, and to do so before receiving the Eucharist° if they have any grave sins° on their conscience. See John 20:21–23; James 5:16.

Congregation (assembly of the people): Those gathered together to participate in a Mass° or act of public worship.°

Congregation (of the Oratory): Way of religious life instituted by St. Philip Neri. It is a 'congregation' and not an 'order' because members are not bound by vows.

Confirmation: A sacrament° of initiation, in which a member of the faithful is anointed by a bishop or his delegate, confirming the grace° of Baptism° and increasing the gifts of the Holy Spirit° to equip that person for full participation in the life of the Church. See Acts 8:14–17; Ephesians 4:30.

Consecration: An action during the liturgy of the Mass° in which the priest's prayer over the bread and wine effects their change into the Body and Blood of Christ.

Corpus Christi: Latin for 'body of Christ.' In the Catholic liturgical calendar, the Solemnity° of the Most Holy Body and Blood of Christ, celebrated on the Thursday following Trinity Sunday. Many churches are named 'Corpus Christi,' as is one of the colleges of Oxford University, founded 1517.

Council: Meeting of bishops° to decide matters of doctrine° and discipline within the Catholic Church.° A worldwide gathering, usually called by the pope,° is known as an ecumenical council. There have been twenty-one ecumenical councils in history, the most recent being the Second Vatican Council.°

Cradle Catholic: A person who has been born and baptized in a Catholic family and raised in the practice of the faith.

Crossing the Tiber: Colloquial phrase for converting to the Catholic faith. The Tiber is the river that runs through Rome.

Curate: A priest° or deacon° who serves as an assistant to the pastor of a parish.°

Deacon: A man who has been ordained to the third rank of Holy Orders° (after bishop° and priest°). Deacons focus on pastoral ministry and service and assist the priest at Mass.° See Acts 6:1–6.

Devotion: A spiritual practice or habit of prayer with a particular focus, such as the Eucharist,° the Sacred Heart,° or Mary the Mother of God.°

Diocese: A region under the pastoral administration of a bishop,° comprised of multiple parishes.°

Dispensation: An official Church exemption from a normal discipline or observance. For instance, the sick are automatically dispensed from the Sunday obligation to attend Mass.°

Dissenter: See *Nonconformist.*

Doctrine: The teachings of the Church on matters of faith and morals. Doctrine cannot essentially change, as it is derived from the deposit of faith, the body of truth revealed in Scripture and Sacred Tradition, but it can develop more fully over time (as with the doctrine of the Trinity°).

Dogma: Those doctrines that the Magisterium° has formally declared as being necessary for the faithful to believe, consisting of truths contained in divine Revelation or having a necessary connection with them.

Dominican: Member of the religious order dedicated to study and preaching, founded by St. Dominic in 1216. Known as the 'Order of Preachers.'

Easter: The Solemnity° of the Resurrection° of Christ, the culmination of Holy Week.° In Catholic liturgical practice, the main celebration of Easter is the Easter Vigil, which takes place on the eve of Easter Sunday.

Ecclesiastical: Relating to the institutional structure of the Church.

Ecclesiological: Related to the theology and doctrine of the nature of the Church; its self-understanding.

Ecumenism: The promotion of, and efforts toward, the restoration of unity among all Christians.

Eden: In the biblical account of creation, the perfect garden in which God placed Adam and Eve, and from which they were expelled after their act of disobedience known as the fall.° See Genesis 1–3.

Elevation: Moment of the Mass,° immediately following the Consecration,° when the priest° raises up the Blessed Sacrament.°

Encyclical: A letter written by the pope,° distributed across the entire Catholic Church,° to express Church teaching on a particular matter.

Erastianism: The political view that the church should be subordinate to the state. Named after the Calvinist theologian Thomas Erastus (1524–83).

Eucharist: From the Greek for 'thanksgiving.' (1) The Eucharistic Sacrifice instituted at the Last Supper°; (2) the bread that is consecrated during the Eucharistic Prayer of the Mass° and that the congregation receives. See Luke 22:19–20; John 6:35.

Evangelism/evangelization: From the Greek for 'good news.' The preaching or sharing of the Gospel.° See Matthew 28:18–20.

Extreme Unction: Sacrament° given to the sick and dying. A priest° applies oil to the forehead of the sick and prays over him or her. Also called 'Anointing of the Sick' and 'last rites.' See James 5:14–15.

Fall: The act of deliberate disobedience to God by Adam and Eve that constituted the first sin.° In Catholic teaching, the effect of the fall is that all human beings are born into the condition of alienation from God that is called original sin,° from which rescue is only possible through Christ. See Genesis 3; Romans 5:12–21.

Feast: Liturgical celebration marked by special prayers and readings from Scripture that commemorates a particular saint° or aspect of salvation history.

First Holy Communion: A Catholic's first reception of the Eucharist,° usually in childhood, after a period of basic catechesis.°

Fr.: Abbreviation of 'Father.' Title given to priests,° a practice derived from the example of the Apostles. See, e.g., 1 Corinthians 4:15; Philippians 2:22; Philemon 10.

Franciscan: Member of the order founded by St. Francis of Assisi in 1209, emphasizing poverty and simplicity in pursuit of a life according to the Gospel.°

Genuflect: To bow on one knee as an act of reverence, for instance when entering or leaving a church that contains the Blessed Sacrament° or by the priest° at particular moments during the liturgy of the Mass.°

Good Friday: Part of Holy Week°; the Friday before Easter,° commemorating the Crucifixion and death of Christ.

Gospel: From the Old English for 'good news.' (1) The teachings of Christ and his Apostles; (2) one of the four books in the New Testament° that recount the life and teaching of Christ: Matthew, Mark, Luke, and John.

Grace: From the Greek for 'favor.' The undeserved gifts of God freely given to individuals, especially with regard to redemption and sanctification. See John 1:16; Ephesians 2:8–9; Romans 3:23–25.

Hagiography: Writings that depict a saint's life with an emphasis on its positive aspects.

Heaven: (1) The condition of eternal life with God; (2) the spiritual realm in which the angels° and saints° enjoy the direct presence of God while awaiting the general resurrection.° See 2 Corinthians 5:1; Wisdom 3:1–9.

Hell: (1) The condition of self-exclusion from heaven°; the freely chosen rejection of God and refusal to renounce sin°; (2) the spiritual realm of Satan, the rebel angels, and the souls of those who died in deliberate rejection of God. See Matthew 5:29–30, 13:47–50; 2 Peter 2:4.

Hierarchy: The organizational and jurisdictional structure of the Catholic Church:° priests,° bishops,° archbishops, cardinals,° and the pope.° See 1 Timothy 3.

Holy Communion: The reception of the Eucharist° by an individual. Though this is usually done during Mass,° it can occur in other contexts, as when the Blessed Sacrament° is brought to the sick or housebound.

Holy Day of Obligation: Important feast° day on which Catholics are required to attend Mass.° Every Sunday is a day of obligation, along with certain solemnities° including All Saints' Day° and Christmas.

Holy Orders: In the Catholic Church,° the sacrament° in which the laying on of hands by a bishop° confers upon a man the grace° of ordination to the diaconate, priesthood, or episcopate. See 1 Timothy 4:14; 2 Timothy 1:6.

Holy Saturday: The day in Holy Week° following Good Friday° and preceding Easter° Sunday, commemorating the time in which Jesus's body lay in the tomb. Before 1955, the Easter Vigil was held in the morning of Holy Saturday rather than the evening as it is now.

Holy Spirit (Holy Ghost): The third person of the Trinity,° who proceeds from the Father and the Son; sometimes named according to his particular functions in the life of the believer (e.g., Sanctifier, Advocate, Consoler). Appeared as a dove at Christ's baptism and as tongues of fire at Pentecost. See Matthew 3:13–17; Acts 2:2–4.

Holy Water: Water that has been blessed by a man in Holy Orders° and is used to baptize and to bless. Often used devotionally as a reminder of one's baptism.°

Holy Week: In the Church calendar, the week before Easter,° beginning on Palm Sunday; it moves liturgically° through Christ's entrance into Jerusalem, his Last Supper,° Passion,° Crucifixion, death, and descent into hell.

Host: A wafer of bread made from wheaten flour, typically circular in shape, that is consecrated° during the celebration of the Eucharist.°

Immaculate Conception: The Catholic dogma° that by the action of God's grace,° the Blessed Virgin Mary was conceived without original sin.° Officially declared in 1854 by Pope Pius IX.

Incarnation: The Christian doctrine° that God the Son, the second person of the Trinity,° took on a human nature, being conceived by the Holy Spirit° in Mary's womb, in order to redeem fallen humankind. Christ is therefore fully divine and fully human. See Luke 1:26–38.

Indissolubility: Belief that a validly contracted marriage (entered into freely and with full understanding and agreement) is permanent and cannot be dissolved; the theological basis for the Catholic rejection of remarriage after divorce. See Matthew 19:1–12.

Indult: Special permission from the pope° authorizing a practice that is otherwise not permitted in the law of the Church.

Jesuits: Members of the Society of Jesus, a religious order founded by St. Ignatius of Loyola in 1534, dedicated to education, charity, and missionary works.

Last rites: See *Extreme Unction.*

Last Supper: The meal Christ shared with his disciples on the night before his Crucifixion, when he instituted the Sacrament° of the Eucharist.° See Matthew 26:17–30; Mark 14:12–26; Luke 22:7–39; John 13:1–17:26.

Laity: The main body of the faithful; those who have not received Holy Orders° or entered into religious life.

Layman: A member of the laity.°

Lent: The penitential liturgical season lasting from Ash Wednesday to Holy Saturday,° with an emphasis on prayer, fasting, and almsgiving. The forty days of Lent do not count Sundays, which are always celebrated as feasts of the Resurrection.°

Litany: A form of prayer consisting of numerous petitions. A litany typically involves an invocation uttered by the officiant, followed by a supplication uttered by the other people present. Examples include the Litany of Loreto (see Appendix B).

Liturgy: The public worship of the Church, following established forms, as opposed to private prayers and devotions.

Magisterium: The teaching authority of the Catholic Church,° with the task to preserve and interpret divine revelation.

Manna: The supernatural bread provided for the ancient Israelites while wandering in the desert. See Exodus 16. Understood by Christians as a precursor to the Eucharist.° See John 6:22–58.

Marian: Relating to Mary,° the Mother of God.°

Martyr: From the Greek for 'witness.' One who accepts death rather than reject the Christian faith.

Mass: The central liturgy ° of the Catholic Church,° which comprises a penitential rite, followed by the 'Liturgy of the Word' (readings from the Bible) and the 'Liturgy of the Eucharist.'° A 'Low Mass' has a spoken liturgy and a limited amount of ceremonial action; a 'High Mass' has portions of the liturgy chanted or sung and features the full ceremonial action.

Maundy Thursday (Holy Thursday): The Thursday in Holy Week° that commemorates the Last Supper° and the institution of the Eucharist.°

Methodism: A movement originating in the eighteenth century in the Church of England° and eventually forming its own Protestant denomination. Founded by John Wesley, it emphasized sanctification and personal transformation through faith and took its name from the "methodical" approach to devotion and study that its members exhibited.

Missal: A book containing the text of the liturgy of the Mass.°

Modernism (theological): In the late nineteenth and twentieth centuries, a movement toward modifying traditional theology and doctrines ° in response to modern philosophy and biblical criticism; often associated with a rejection or downplaying of the authority or accuracy of the Bible.

Monsignor: A title of honor given by the pope° to distinguished members of the clergy.°

Monstrance: a metal stand (usually ornately decorated) in the shape of a cross or sunburst in which the consecrated Host° is placed to be visible behind a glass circle at the center.

Mother of God: Title given to Mary for her unique status as the mother of Jesus, who is both God and man. See Luke 1:41–45.

Mystery: From the Greek for 'secret.' A divinely revealed truth that cannot be fully comprehended by the finite human mind. A theological mystery is intelligible to reason, and can be studied and reasoned about, but its meaning is inexhaustible.

Narthex: The entryway or antechamber of a church.

New Testament: The second of the two major sections of the Christian Bible, originally written in Greek, comprised of the Gospels,° the Acts of the Apostles, the Epistles, and the book of Revelation. It is called the New Testament because these Scriptures attest to the "new covenant" or "new testament" in Christ's sacrificial blood (Matthew 26:28; Luke 22:20).

Nonconformists: Protestant dissenters from the Church of England,° including Baptists° and Methodists.° Until the nineteenth century, their civil rights were restricted, but to a lesser extent than those of Catholic recusants.° The 1688 Toleration Act allowed freedom of worship to Nonconformists who took the oaths of allegiance and supremacy and who rejected the doctrine of transubstantiation.°

Novus Ordo: Latin for 'new order'; the name given to the Mass of Paul VI, corresponding to the liturgical reforms that followed the Second Vatican Council.° Sometimes called the 'Ordinary Form.'

Octave: A period of eight days of liturgical celebration attached to a solemnity,° beginning with the date of the solemnity itself; also the name of the eighth day in that period.

Old Testament: Name given by Christians to the Jewish Scriptures, the first of the two major sections of the Christian Bible, written in Hebrew, Aramaic, and Greek, comprised of the Pentateuch, historical books, wisdom literature, and the major and minor prophets.

Opus Dei: Latin for 'work of God,' a Catholic apostolate° founded by St. Josemaría Escrivá to help the laity° cultivate personal holiness that they can share in their workplaces and the culture at large.

Oratorians: Members of the Congregation of the Oratory of St. Philip Neri.°

Oratory: The church of a particular Congregation of the Oratory,° such as the Birmingham Oratory or Oxford Oratory.

Ordinariate: A Catholic ecclesiastical structure, equivalent to a diocese,° established in 2011 by Pope Benedict XVI as a means for former Anglicans to enter into full communion° with the Catholic Church° while retaining elements of the liturgical and spiritual heritage of the Anglican tradition.

Original sin: The result of the fall,° which deprived the human race of its original holiness; the condition of alienation from God resulting in the human experience of sin° and death, from which state Christ provides redemption. See Romans 5:12-19; 1 Corinthians 15:21-22.

Our Lady of . . .: Referring to the Blessed Virgin Mary under a particular title that reflects an aspect of her character or mission (e.g., Our Lady of Mercy), a place where she is reported to have appeared in visions (e.g., Our Lady of Lourdes), or a place where she is honored (e.g., Our Lady of Częstochowa).

Oxford Movement: A Catholicizing movement within Anglicanism in the nineteenth century, led by Oxford scholars John Keble, Edward Pusey, and John Henry Newman (who later became a Catholic). Also called Tractarians because of their publication of *Tracts for the Times*.

Palm Sunday: The beginning of Holy Week,° commemorating Jesus's triumphal entry into Jerusalem on a donkey as crowds worshipfully greeted him with palm branches. See Luke 19:28–40.

Papist: A Catholic; usually derogatory.

Parish: A local church and its associated territory, under the supervision of a priest° who serves as the pastor; multiple parishes comprise a diocese.° Also refers collectively to the people who are members of that parish.

Passion (of Christ): From the Latin for 'to suffer.' The final days of Jesus's life, including his arrest, trial, scourging, and Crucifixion. See Matthew 26–27; Luke 22–23.

Penal laws: Laws enacted after the Reformation° in England, restricting the civil rights of Catholics and criminalizing their religious practices.

Penance: An act of self-discipline taken on to express repentance and contrition; for instance, after confession° or during Lent.° See Daniel 9:3; 1 Corinthians 9:25–27.

Pentecost: The solemnity° celebrating the descent of the Holy Spirit° upon the disciples of Jesus fifty days after Easter;° the Holy Spirit appeared in the form of flames upon their heads, and they gained the ability to speak in the languages of the many travelers to Jerusalem. See Acts 2:1–42.

Pope: From the Latin for 'father.' As the bishop° of Rome, the pope, or Holy Father, is held by Catholics to be the successor of St. Peter, to whom Christ granted authority to govern the Church on his behalf; hence the pope's title 'Vicar of Christ.' See Matthew 16:18–19.

Preconciliar/postconciliar: Before/after the Second Vatican Council.°

Priest: From the Greek for 'presbyter, elder.' A man who has been ordained by a bishop° in the apostolic succession, thereby receiving authority to celebrate the Mass,° hear confessions,° celebrate the other sacraments, and to preach. See Romans 15:15–16; 1 Peter 5:1–3.

Primitivism: Efforts to return Christian practice to that of the first-century Church, removing the ecclesiastical, liturgical, and theological developments of later centuries.

Protestantism: A sixteenth-century protest movement against certain aspects of Catholic doctrine,° and implicitly against Catholic authority, which led to the Reformation° in Europe and the establishment of a variety of separate Christian denominations that reject the primacy of the pope.°

Providence: The protective care and guidance of God, often understood to be operating in unfathomable ways.

Psalm: One of the poems in the Old Testament° book of Psalms. These are extensively used in Catholic liturgy° and devotions.

Purgatory: In Catholic doctrine, the spiritual condition in which the souls of the faithful departed are cleansed of the effects of sin° incurred during their lives before entering into heaven.° See Matthew 5:25–26; 1 Corinthians 3:11–15.

Quarant'ore: Also called the Forty Hours' Devotion. A Eucharistic devotion in which the Blessed Sacrament° is placed in view of the congregation for veneration° for forty continuous hours.

Real Presence: The doctrine that Christ is really, truly, and substantially present in the consecrated bread and wine of the Eucharist,° without specifying the way in which this occurs.

Reconciliation: See *Confession.*

Rector: Clerical title used to denote the pastor of certain parish° churches, Catholic or Anglican. It is also the title used for the head of Exeter College and Lincoln College, Oxford.

Recusant: A person who refused to comply with the state requirement to attend Anglican services following the 1558 Act of Uniformity. Recusants could include Nonconformists,° but Catholics were specifically targeted by the 1592 Act Against Popish Recusants. Steep fines were enacted for recusancy; these penalties continued until the Second Relief Act of 1791.

Reformation: The theological upheaval initiated by Martin Luther in the sixteenth century that led to the creation of various Protestant churches as separate from the Catholic Church.°

Resurrection (of Christ): The Christian belief that Christ, having died on the cross and been buried in the tomb, was bodily raised to life on the third day; considered to be the precursor or 'firstfruits' of the general resurrection° of all the faithful on the last day. See Matthew 28:1–10; Mark 16; Luke 24:1–12; John 20; 1 Corinthians 15; Colossians 1:18.

Resurrection (general): The Christian belief that on the last day, the souls of the dead will be reunited with new, immortal bodies; "those who have done good, to the resurrection of the just, and those who have done evil, to the resurrection of judgment" (John 5:29). See John 11:25; Acts 24:14–16; 1 Corinthians 15; Romans 6:5.

Roman: Of or related to the Catholic Church.°

Romish: Of or related to the Catholic Church.° Usually derogatory.

Rosary: A Catholic devotional practice of meditating on various mysteries° (events of spiritual significance) in the life of Mary, Christ, and the Church; the string of beads used to keep track of the prayers said.

Sacrament: A outward and physical sign effecting an inward and spiritual grace.° The Catholic Church recognizes seven: Baptism,° Confirmation,° the Eucharist,° Confession,° Marriage, Holy Orders,° and Extreme Unction.°

Sacred Heart: Devotion° to the heart of Jesus, representing both his humanity in the Incarnation° and his sacrificial love for humankind.

Sanctuary: Section of a church containing the main altar for the celebration of the Eucharist,° often elevated and separated from the body of the church by a railing.

Saint: (1) A deceased member of the faithful who has been formally canonized° by the Catholic Church; (2) one of the persons who are now in heaven,° whether or not they have been canonized; (3) all Christian believers. See Hebrews 12:1, 12:23.

Scrupulosity: The persistent tendency to consider things to be sins° that, in fact, are not, and to be fearful or troubled by these scruples.

Second Vatican Council: The twenty-first ecumenical council° of the Church, called by Pope John XXIII; focused on the relationship of the Catholic Church° to the modern world. Important documents of the Council include *Nostra Aetate* (Declaration of the Relationship of the Church to Non-Christian Religions); *Sacrosanctum Concilum* (Constitution on the Sacred Liturgy), which allowed for the vernacular° to be used in the liturgy of the Mass°; and *Unitatis Redintegratio* (Decree on Ecumenism°).

Secular: Pertaining to "the world," as distinct from "the Church"; denotes that which is non-religious and possibly anti-religious.

Sin: A personal act (of commission or omission) contrary to the moral law. Catholic teaching distinguishes between grave sins and venial sins. Grave sins are those of serious matter; when done with full knowledge and consent, they destroy the divine life in the soul. Venial sins consist in failing to keep the moral law with regard to a less serious matter or committing a serious sin without full knowledge or consent; these damage or diminish the divine life in the soul and if unchecked can lead to habitual vices and grave sins. See 1 John 5:16–17; Mark 10:17–19; Galatians 5:19–21.

SJ: Abbreviation for 'Society of Jesus,' the Jesuits.°

Solemnity: In the Catholic liturgical calendar, a feast° day of the highest rank. These include Easter,° Pentecost,° the Annunciation,° Corpus Christi,° All Saints' Day,° the Immaculate Conception,° and the Nativity (Christmas).

Spiritual communion: Interior act of desire to receive Holy Communion° and the graces° it brings, often because physical reception of the sacrament is not possible.

St.: abbreviation for 'Saint,' as a title given to persons who have been formally canonized.°

Stations of the Cross: A devotional practice of meditating on fourteen 'stations' or stages of Jesus's Passion,° beginning with his condemnation to death and ending with his burial in the tomb.

Sunday obligation: Rule that Catholics must attend Sunday Mass° each week if it is possible to do so.

Tabernacle: The box, usually of metal and ornately decorated, in which the Blessed Sacrament° is reserved in a Catholic church.

Tenebrae: Latin for 'darkness.' A liturgical service of Holy Week,° including readings from the Old Testament° book of Lamentations.

Thirty-Nine Articles: The official doctrinal statement of the Church of England,° drawn up in the sixteenth century and included in the Anglican Book of Common Prayer.

Tractarian Movement: See *Oxford Movement.*

Traditional Latin Mass: Name commonly used to denote the preconciliar° form of the Mass, as distinct from the Novus Ordo.° Also referred to as the 'Tridentine Mass' or the 'Extraordinary Form.'

Transubstantiation: Catholic doctrine related to the Real Presence° of Christ in the Blessed Sacrament,° stating that at the consecration,° the entire substance of the bread and wine is changed into the Body, Blood, Soul, and Divinity of Christ, although the 'accidents' or appearances of bread and wine remain.

Trinity: The doctrine that God, though one, is three coequal Persons: Father, Son, and Holy Spirit.° See Matthew 28:18–20.

Trinitarian: Belief in or pertaining to the doctrine of the Trinity.°

Unitarianism: Belief in God as one divine Person, rejecting the Trinitarian doctrine of God as one God in three coequal Persons: Father, Son, and Holy Spirit.°

Vatican II: See *Second Vatican Council.*

Veneration: Act of reverence. Often used for a saint° or relic.

Vernacular: The use of the common spoken language for liturgy° and translations, as opposed to the use of Latin as a universal language.

Vespers: The evening prayer of the Divine Office (see *Breviary*).

Viaticum: Latin for 'food for the journey'; the final Holy Communion° given to a dying person.

Vicar of Christ: See *Pope.*

Vulgate: Latin translation of the Bible by St. Jerome, completed in 405.

Worship: In Christian theology, the reverence given to God alone; to participate in acts of public worship. Distinct from the veneration or honor given to Mary and the saints.

LIST OF BIBLIOGRAPHICAL ABBREVIATIONS

Biography: *J.R.R. Tolkien: A Biography*, by Humphrey Carpenter

BF: *Brothers and Friends: The Diaries of Major Warren Hamilton Lewis*, by Warren Lewis

CLI: *Collected Letters of C.S. Lewis*, vol. 1, ed. Walter Hooper

CLII: *Collected Letters of C.S. Lewis*, vol. 2, ed. Walter Hooper

CLIII: *Collected Letters of C.S. Lewis*, vol. 3, ed. Walter Hooper

Inklings: *The Inklings: C.S. Lewis, J.R.R. Tolkien, Charles Williams, and Their Friends*, by Humphrey Carpenter

Letters: *The Letters of J.R.R. Tolkien*, by J.R.R. Tolkien, ed. Humphrey Carpenter

LOTR: *The Lord of the Rings*: 50th Anniversary One-Volume Edition, by J.R.R. Tolkien

MME: *Tolkien: Maker of Middle-earth*, ed. Catherine McIlwaine

OED: *Oxford English Dictionary*, online edition

OFS: *Tolkien On Fairy-stories*, by J.R.R. Tolkien, ed. Verlyn Flieger and Douglas A. Anderson

TCG:C: *The J.R.R. Tolkien Companion and Guide: Chronology*, revised and expanded edition, by Christina Scull and Wayne G. Hammond

TCG:RG: *The J.R.R. Tolkien Companion and Guide: Reader's Guide*, revised and expanded edition, by Christina Scull and Wayne G. Hammond

TEC: *Tolkien at Exeter College*, 2nd edition, by John Garth

TGW: *Tolkien and the Great War*, by John Garth

TFA: *The Tolkien Family Album*, ed. John and Priscilla Tolkien

UC: *"Uncle Curro": J.R.R. Tolkien's Spanish Connection*, by José Manuel Ferrández Bru

A note on Scripture versions: The Revised Standard Version: Catholic Edition is used unless otherwise indicated. Other translations used include the Douay, Jerusalem, and Westminster, all of which Tolkien knew.

ENDNOTES

Notes to Chapter 1: "I am in any case myself a Christian"

1. *Letters*, 172.
2. J.R.R. Tolkien, Letter to L.M. Cutts, October 26, 1956, in Sotheby's *English Literature, History, Fine Bindings, Private Press Books, Children's Books, Illustrated Books and Drawings, 10 July 2003*, Lot 474, 297.
3. *Letters*, 255; 220; 288.
4. *Letters*, 220; 414.
5. Of the major biographers, John Garth, in *Tolkien and the Great War*, makes note of Tolkien's faith but (quite reasonably) does not say much about it given the focus of his study. Raymond Edwards relegates all mention of religion to an appendix. Humphrey Carpenter recognizes the "total" importance of Tolkien's faith but nonetheless presents it as largely a private conviction borne out of love for his mother and does not go into detail. Philip and Carol Zaleski, in their group biography of the Inklings, mention Tolkien's faith but lack space to discuss it in depth. Bradley Birzer and Joseph Pearce include elements of biography in their studies but are more focused on the themes of his writings.
6. Denis Gueroult, "An Interview with J.R.R. Tolkien," 7.
7. Priscilla Tolkien, "An Evening with P. Tolkien," 26; Priscilla Tolkien, "Talk Given at the Church House Westminster."
8. *J.R.R.T.: A Film Portrait.*
9. Julian Tolkien, "Related to Tolkien."
10. Simon Tolkien, "My Grandfather J.R.R. Tolkien"; Joanna Tolkien, "Joanna Tolkien speaks," 32; Michael George Tolkien, "Autobiographical Essay on My Grandfather."
11. Robert Havard, "Tolkien: A Personal Memoir," 61.
12. Daniel Helen and Morgan Thomsen, "A recollection of Tolkien: Canon Gerard Hanlon," 41.
13. Martin D'Arcy, *Laughter and the Love of Friends*, 112.
14. Deborah Webster Rogers and Ivor A. Rogers, *J.R.R. Tolkien*, 125–26.
15. Charlotte and Denis Plimmer, "The Man Who Understands Hobbits," 35.
16. Tolkien, letter to Joyce Biddell, October 24, 1955, in Sotheby's *English Literature, History, Children's Books and Illustrations, London, 12 July 2016*, 148.
17. *Letters*, 194.
18. C.S. Lewis, *Letters to Malcolm*, 30.
19. Havard, "Tolkien: A Personal Memoir," 6.
20. Helen and Thomsen, "A recollection of Tolkien," 41.
21. Clyde Kilby, *Tolkien and the Silmarillion*, 53; Kilby, "Dr. Clyde S. Kilby Recalls The Inklings," 4–5.
22. *TCG:C*, 491.
23. *OFS*, 66.
24. Clyde Kilby, "Meeting Professor Tolkien."
25. Some of the better works to explore Tolkien's faith as expressed in his fiction are Stratford Caldecott, *The Power of the Ring*; Bradley Birzer, *J.R.R. Tolkien's Sanctifying Myth*; Ralph C. Wood, *The Gospel According to Tolkien*; Paul E. Kerry, ed., *The Ring and the Cross*; and Claudio A. Testi, *Pagan Saints in Middle-earth.*
26. Priscilla Tolkien, "The Letters of J.R.R. Tolkien."
27. Priscilla Tolkien, "The Letters of J.R.R. Tolkien."

Notes to Chapter 2: Two Worlds

1. The Bloemfontein Cathedral register gives the date as January 31 (Ryszard Derdziński, "Tolkien's Baptism Act!").
2. *TCG:RG*, 1300.
3. *Biography*, 31.
4. Ryszard Derdziński, "Arthur Tolkien (1857–96) as a devoted Anglican."
5. Ryszard Derdziński, "Mabel Tolkien (Suffield) baptized in . . . 1891!"
6. *TCG:C*, 2. George Edward Jelf was born in 1865 and earned his BA at Oriel College in 1887. Newman, Pusey, and Keble had all been Fellows there (L.S. Milford, ed., *Haileybury Register, 1862–1891*, 177).
7. *George Edward Jelf: A Memoir by his Wife* (London: Skeffington & Son, 1909), 9. His books include *The Secret Trials of the Christian Life* (1873) and *The Consolations of the Christian Seasons* (1880).
8. *MME*, 122.
9. "Death of Mr. Tolkien," in *TFA*, 19.
10. *Biography*, 31.
11. See in particular the Corporation Act of 1661 and the Test Acts of 1673 and 1678. Edwin Burton, Edward D'Alton, and Jarvis Kelley, "Penal Laws."
12. John Gerard and Edward D'Alton, "Roman Catholic Relief Bill."
13. Herbert Thurston, "The Royal Declaration."
14. The Succession to the Crown Act (2013).
15. Edward Norman, *The English Catholic Church in the Nineteenth Century*, 15–16.
16. Pauline Adams, *English Catholic Converts and the Oxford Movement in Mid 19th Century Britain: The Cost of Conversion*, 143–44.
17. Adams, 52.
18. Jonathan Wood, "Wilfred Rowland Mary Childe," 18.
19. Penelope Fitzgerald, *The Knox Brothers* (London: Macmillan, 1977), 261.
20. *Letters*, 354.
21. Norman, *The English Catholic Church in the Nineteenth Century*, 21.
22. St. Anne's Catholic Church, "Parish History."

Notes to Chapter 3: Mabel's Choice

1. Pauline Adams, *English Catholic Converts and the Oxford Movement in Mid 19th Century Britain: The Cost of Conversion*, 47.
2. Adams, 29. The archivist of the Birmingham Oratory confirmed this was Catholic practice in Birmingham in 1900 (Daniel Joyce, personal communication, November 2019).
3. Adams, *English Catholic Converts*, 52.
4. St. Anne's Catholic Church, "Parish History." Fr. Dowling (1828–1904) served at St. Anne's from 1859 until his death in 1904.
5. St. Anne's Catholic Church, "Parish History."
6. William Dargue, "The Irish Quarter" and "Digbeth," in *A History of Birmingham Places and Placenames*.
7. See Ian Ker, *John Henry Newman*, 350.
8. St. Anne's Catholic Church, "Parish History."
9. The 'penny catechism' was officially approved by the Bishops of England and Wales and appeared in many editions in almost identical forms. Mabel might well have used *A Catechism of Christian Doctrine Approved by Cardinal Vaughan and the Bishops of England.*

10. Mabel was received on Thursday, June 28, 1900; May had been received separately, exactly one week earlier. (Birmingham Archdiocesan Archives, Baptisms section, archive reference P4/1/7, 151).
11. At that time, conditional baptism ("if you have not been previously baptized, I baptize you . . .") was part of the standard process for receiving converts into the Church. (Adams, *English Catholic Converts*, 30).
12. Ben Quash, prologue to *Heresies and How to Avoid Them*, 1–2.
13. John Sutherland, *Mrs Humphry Ward*, 9.
14. Adams, *English Catholic Converts*, 49.
15. *Biography*, 32.
16. *Biography*, 32.

Notes to Chapter 4: J.R.R.R.T.

1. Pauline Adams, *English Catholic Converts and the Oxford Movement in Mid 19th Century Britain: The Cost of Conversion,* 167.
2. John Henry Newman, *Letters and Diaries* (London: Thomas Nelson, 1962), 12:277.
3. *The Catholic Directory* (1900), 12, 14–15.
4. *TFA*, 23.
5. *Biography*, 34; *The Catholic Directory* (1900), 12, 14–15.
6. "Religious History: Missions and churches founded since 1786," in W.B. Stephens, ed., *A History of the County of Warwick*, 7:405–10.
7. It was destroyed by German bombs on Good Friday, 1941, and later replaced by the current brick building. No photographs survive of its exterior ("Religious History: Missions and churches founded since 1786," in W.B. Stephens, ed.).
8. *Biography*, 34.
9. Adams, *English Catholic Converts,* 181.
10. "A Short History of St. Dunstan's Church," St. Dunstan and St. Jude.
11. "The History of St. Chad's," St. Chad's Cathedral.
12. Henry Tristram, *Cardinal Newman and the Church of the Birmingham Oratory: A History and Guide*, 31.
13. Tristram, 33.
14. *Biography*, 32.
15. *Biography*, 40.
16. Adams, *English Catholic Converts*, 62–63, 64.
17. Adams, 152, 154.
18. *Biography*, 35.
19. *Biography*, 34.
20. For Philip's life, see Louis Bouyer, *St. Philip Neri: A Portrait* and Paul Türks, *Philip Neri: The Fire of Joy*; for more on his life and influence from the perspective of English Oratorians, see *St. Philip Neri and the Oratory* by Jerome Bertram and *The Legacy of St. Philip* by the Oxford Oratorians.
21. *Biography*, 36.
22. *Letters*, 340.
23. *Letters*, 354.
24. Personal communication with Priscilla Tolkien, October 2, 2020.
25. Tolkien, "The Qenya Alphabet," 76–78.
26. Tolkien, "English and Welsh," 170.

27. For a detailed analysis of the monogram's evolution, see Gabriele Bonomelli, "Il monogramma di Tolkien tra storia e letteratura." No equivalent study appears in English. My thanks to Sebastiano Tassarini for bringing this scholarship to my attention and for assisting me in translating it. Due to its fragile condition, *The Book of Ishness* is not available for general scholarly reference, but at Bonomelli's request, Catherine McIlwaine, the Tolkien Archivist, confirmed that the monogram appears as it does in the published version (Bonomelli, 30), except that it is a mirror-image (Tolkien, *J.R.R. Tolkien: Artist and Illustrator*, 43). I suspect that this testifies to Tolkien's interest in mirror-writing; for instance, his 1930s notes include various instances of mirrored writing in Elvish script (see *Parma Eldalamberon* 20).
28. *TCG:C*, 10; Tolkien, letter to Patricia Kirke, December 24, 1956, The Superior Galleries May 9th, 1992 *Auction of Autographs, Manuscripts & Select Books*; *Biography*, 36.

Notes to Chapter 5: Learning to Pray

1. *Letters*, 354.
2. *Letters*, 340.
3. *A Catechism of Christian Doctrine*, 23.
4. Jerome Savonarola, *The Lord's Prayer and the Angelical Salutation*, 8.
5. Tolkien, "'Words of Joy,'" part 1; Tolkien, "*Ae Adar Nín*: The Lord's Prayer in Sindarin."
6. *Letters*, 233, 244. Tolkien explores this topic in Letters 181, 191, 192, and 246.
7. *Letters*, 233; 252; 326; 326n1.
8. George Sayer, "Recollections," 23.
9. Clyde Kilby, "Dr. Clyde S. Kilby Recalls The Inklings," 4.
10. Tolkien, "The Qenya Alphabet," 42–43, 87; Tolkien, "'Words of Joy,'" part 1, 26–28.
11. Tolkien, "'Words of Joy,'" part 1, 28.
12. Tolkien, "'Words of Joy,'" part 1, 36.
13. *TCG:C*, 495; 494.
14. *Letters*, 67.

Notes to Chapter 6: Formation

1. Maggie Burns, "John Ronald's Schooldays," 28; *Biography*, 32. It was possibly his godfather, Tom Hadley. Unfortunately, he would die relatively young, in 1911, at the age of 49.
2. Dominic Jacob, "Blessed John Henry Newman the Musician," 95.
3. See Paul Shrimpton, *A Catholic Eton? Newman's Oratory School*, 209.
4. King Edward's School cost £12 per year; St. Philip's Grammar School fees were 2–3 guineas per term, amounting to £6–10 annually ("Oratorians," in "Religious History: Religious Houses: Oratorians," in Stephens, ed., *A History of the County of Warwick*). The net financial effect may well have been about the same, since it is doubtful that the uncle's generosity would have extended to paying his nephew's tuition at a school run by Catholic priests.
5. *Letters*, 395.
6. *TCG:C*, 9.
7. Burns, "John Ronald's Schooldays," 29.
8. *Letters*, 395.
9. *TGW*, 18.
10. *Letters*, 10.
11. *TGW*, 19.
12. *TCG:RG*, 1286.
13. "Round the Parish Pump," *The Oratory Parish Magazine*, May 1909, 4.

14. "Round the Parish Pump," 4.
15. Jacob, "Blessed John Henry Newman the Musician," 95.
16. *Biography*, 36.
17. Robert Eaton, *A Book of Oratorios*.
18. Guy Nicholls, *Unearthly Beauty: The Aesthetic of St. John Henry Newman*, 193; John Ainslie, "English Liturgical Music before Vatican II," 47–49. The Oratory hymn book had various editions. One of these was *A Collection of Hymns in Use at the Oratory of St. Philip Neri, at Birmingham*.
19. Priscilla Tolkien, "Talk Given at the Church House Westminster," 5
20. Stuart D. Lee, "A Milestone in BBC History?" 147. See also Letter to William Galbraith, March 8, 1956, Wade JRRT L-Galbraith 2.
21. Tristram gives the date as "Friday, March 25, 1903," and subsequent accounts repeat this, but it was in fact 1904 (See "The Cardinal Newman Memorial Church: Laying of the Foundation," *The Tablet*, April 2, 1904, 530–31).
22. Bryan Little, *Catholic Churches Since 1623*, 159.
23. Henry Tristram, *Cardinal Newman and the Church of the Birmingham Oratory: A History and a Guide*, 35.
24. Nothing is known about this St. Valentine except that he was a martyr buried in the Roman catacombs; and in fact, his body is entombed beneath the altar, a gift of Pope Pius IX to Newman in honor of the Oratory's establishment (Tristram, 58).
25. This was converted into a chapel honoring St. John Henry Newman after his canonization in 2019.

Notes to Chapter 7: Death in a Cottage

1. *Biography*, 36–37.
2. See, for instance, diabetes.org.uk, diabetes.co.uk, and mayoclinic.org.
3. *Letters*, 354.
4. *Biography*, 37–38.
5. John Newbold, "History," *St Peter's Catholic Church, Bromsgrove*.
6. "Bromsgrove—St Peter," *Taking Stock: Catholic Churches of England & Wales*.
7. *Letters*, 54.
8. *Biography*, 38.
9. *Letters*, 354.
10. *Letters*, 354.
11. Adrian Fortescue, *Ceremonies of the Roman Rite Described*, 413–14.
12. Fortescue, 414–15.
13. *Letters*, 340.
14. *Biography*, 39.

Notes to Chapter 8: A Home in the Highest

1. Adrian Fortescue, *Ceremonies of the Roman Rite Described*, 253.
2. *A Collection of Hymns in Use at the Oratory of St. Philip Neri, at Birmingham*, 7–8.
3. Canon Norman Power, "Ring of Doom."
4. *Biography*, 39.
5. *Letters*, 340.
6. *Letters*, 416.
7. *Letters*, 395.

8. Birmingham Oratory. I am grateful to Br. Zachariah Heritage of the Birmingham Oratory for details about the Fathers at the Oratory during Tolkien's time there. Some, but not all, have biographies on the Birmingham Oratory website.
9. *UC*, 77n2.
10. "F. Charles Heurtley," Birmingham Oratory.
11. "F. Basil Lynch," Birmingham Oratory.
12. David Haden, *Tree and Star: Tolkien and the Quest for Earendel,* 358–59.
13. "F. Vincent Reade," Birmingham Oratory.
14. *Biography*, 78–79.
15. John Garth, *The Worlds of J.R.R. Tolkien*, 62.
16. *TCG:C*, 60; see *Biography*, 70–71, Tolkien, *J.R.R. Tolkien: Artist and Illustrator*, figures 20, 21, and Garth, *The Worlds of J.R.R. Tolkien*, 63.
17. *Letters*, 78.
18. *MME*, 153.
19. *TCG:RG*, 1052.
20. "F. Vincent Reade," Birmingham Oratory.
21. Daphne Castell, "Talking to a Maker of Modern Myths."
22. *O.S. Lives*, 76.
23. Robert Eaton, *The Divine Refreshment*, 86.
24. "F. Denis Sheil," Birmingham Oratory.
25. "Fr. Denis Sheil." Obituary, *O.S. Lives*, 14–15.
26. "F. Denis Sheil," Birmingham Oratory.
27. "F. Denis Sheil," Birmingham Oratory.
28. *Biography*, 37; Tolkien, "Rebus Letter," 1.
29. See *Letters and Diaries of John Henry Newman*, vols. 29 and 30.
30. "F. Francis Morgan," Birmingham Oratory; *UC*, 57–58.
31. "F. Francis Morgan," Birmingham Oratory.
32. Obituary, *The Oratory School Magazine*, in *UC*, 79.
33. Birmingham Oratory Archives.
34. "F. Francis Morgan," Birmingham Oratory; Birmingham Oratory Archives.
35. Obituary, *The Oratory School Magazine*, in *UC*, 79.
36. *Letters*, 354.
37. "F. Francis Morgan," Birmingham Oratory.
38. *TFA*, 61.
39. *Letters*, 416.
40. Obituary of Michael Tolkien, *O.S. Lives*, 209.
41. *Letters*, 395.

Notes to Chapter 9: Horsemaster

1. *Letters*, 395.
2. *Biography*, 134.
3. William Cater, "The Filial Duty of Christopher Tolkien," 61; Cater, "More and More Readers Are Getting the J.R.R. Tolkien Habit," 14.
4. *LOTR*, 2.
5. Deborah Webster Rogers and Ivor A. Rogers, *J.R.R. Tolkien*, 126.
6. *LOTR*, 6.
7. Priscilla Tolkien, "Religion and Morality in Tolkien."
8. F.W. Faber, ed., *The School of St. Philip Neri*, 149.

9. Tolkien, "W.P. Ker Memorial Lecture on *Sir Gawain*," 146.
10. George Sayer, "Recollections," 24.
11. Sayer, 23.
12. *Letters*, 110.
13. Gerard Tracey, "Tolkien and the Oratory."
14. Tolkien, "The Notion Club Papers," 246.
15. John Garth, "JRR Tolkien: Academic, Philologist—and Prankster Extraordinaire."
16. *TCG:RG*, 233. John Lawlor recounts another ursine anecdote that one snowy night, as Tolkien and his colleague C.L. Wrenn were walking home from a party in North Oxford, the two men—wearing fur hats—pretended to be Russian bears (Lawlor, *C.S. Lewis: Memories and Reflections*, 32). These bear-impersonating incidents seem to have been conflated to create the widely circulated but inaccurate claim that Tolkien and C.S. Lewis once went to a non-costume party dressed as bears. This error seems to have its origin in Neil Heims' 2004 biography *J.R.R. Tolkien*, in which Heims adds the spurious C.S. Lewis element to a paraphrased version of Carpenter's genuine quote that "At a New Year's Eve party in the nineteen-thirties he would don an Icelandic sheepskin hearthrug and paint his face white to impersonate a polar bear" (*Biography*, 134).
17. Sayer, "Recollections," 16.
18. Norman Power, "Recollections," 10.
19. *Biography*, 134.
20. *Biography*, 134.
21. F.W. Faber, ed., *If God Be With Us: The Maxims of St Philip Neri*, 41.
22. Andrew H. Morton and John Hayes, *Tolkien's Gedling 1914*, 48–49
23. Faber, ed., *The School of St. Philip*, 111.
24. Faber, ed., *If God Be With Us*, 44.
25. *Letters*, 98.
26. *Letters*, 265.
27. *Letters*, 418.

Notes to Chapter 10: Love's Labors

1. *TCG:C*, 12.
2. *Biography*, 41.
3. "Religious History: Religious Houses: Oratorians," in W.B. Stephens, ed., *A History of the County of Warwick*; "F. Edmund Hodgson," Birmingham Oratory.
4. Tolkien, "Rebus Letter," 1.
5. *TFA*, 26; *TCG:C*, 15.
6. Norman Power, "Ring of Doom."
7. *Letters*, 421.
8. *Biography*, 47.
9. *Biography*, 49.
10. *A Catechism of Christian Doctrine* (1900), 37.
11. *Biography*, 50.
12. *Biography*, 51.
13. *Biography*, 51.
14. *TGW*, 144.
15. *Letters*, 53.
16. *Letters*, 52–53.
17. *Letters*, 52.

18. *Letters*, 52.
19. *Letters*, 51.
20. *Letters*, 52.
21. *Biography*, 51.
22. Scull and Hammond call this 'Easter Saturday,' which is ambiguous. 'Easter Saturday' is technically the Saturday that follows Easter Day, within what is called the Easter Octave, that is, the eight days from Easter Day to the following Sunday (now called 'Divine Mercy Sunday'), counting inclusively. The day before Easter Day, falling as it does in Holy Week, is therefore called Holy Saturday, even though at that time, confusingly, the Vigil of Easter was celebrated on Saturday morning rather than in the evening.
23. Anthony Kenny, *A Path from Rome*, 32–33.
24. *TCG:C*, 23.
25. John Henry Newman, *Stations of the Cross*, 86.
26. Daniel Joyce, Birmingham Oratory Archivist, personal communication, 2019.
27. It was almost certainly titled "The Seven Words on [not *of*] the Cross." Two versions of this are included in Ryder's *Sermons and Notes of Sermons* (100–117). Oronzo Cilli suggests that the booklet was *The Seven Words from the Cross* (1895) by William Robertson Nicoll (*Tolkien's Library*, 257), but as Nicoll was a Nonconformist, this identification is unlikely.
28. Ryder, *Sermons and Notes of Sermons*, 117.

Notes to Chapter 11: Towery City

1. *Letters*, 52.
2. *Letters*, 52.
3. The Oxford University Act of 1854 removed the religious test for BA degrees; the Universities Tests Act of 1871 abolished all religious tests (except for divinity degrees) at Oxford, Cambridge, and Durham. See "Opening Oxford: 1871–2021," University of Oxford, https://www.ox.ac.uk/news/2021-06-16-opening-oxford-1871-2021.
4. *TCG:C*, 76.
5. University of Oxford, "Organisation."
6. C.B. Dawson, *The Mirror of Oxford*, 245. Today there are more than 12,000 undergraduates.
7. "University Notes—Oxford," *The Tablet*, October 28, 1911, 686–87.
8. Exeter College, "History of the Chapel."
9. Oswald Hunter-Blair, "University of Oxford," This was fortuitous; the scholarship that Tolkien won was specific to Exeter College. (My thanks to John Garth for clarifying this point.)
10. *TEC*, 13.
11. *TEC*, 19.
12. Walter Drumm, *The Old Palace*, 52.
13. Drumm, 56.
14. This purchase was a rare example of Catholic pushback against the tide of post-Reformation Anglican hegemony in Oxford, since the bishopric had been established under Henry VIII after his break with Rome.
15. "University Notes," *The Tablet*, June 8, 1912, 886.
16. Drumm, *The Old Palace*, 53.
17. "University Notes," *The Tablet*, November 22, 1913, 804; Drumm, *The Old Palace*, 54.
18. To his credit, Lang went on to be a success as a parish priest in Surrey; he seems simply not to have been a good fit for the pastoral care of college students (Drumm, *The Old Palace*, 55).
19. "University Notes," *The Tablet*, November 22, 1913, 804.
20. *Letters*, 53.

21. *TEC*, 22.
22. *TEC*, 22.
23. *TEC*, 23, 56.
24. *Biography*, 62.
25. *TEC*, 13.
26. *TEC*, 14.
27. *TFA*, 32.
28. Oxford Union Library archive for May 18, 1912 (Wade Center Archives JRRT MS-6).
29. *TFA*, 32.
30. *Biography*, 66, 73
31. *Biography*, 66.
32. *TCG:RG*, 1284.
33. *Biography*, 68.
34. *TFA*, 30, 34.
35. *TFA*, 34.
36. *Biography*, 70.
37. *TFA*, 34.

Notes to Chapter 12: A Second Wind

1. *Biography*, 66.
2. *Letters*, 52.
3. *TCG:RG*, 1284.
4. *TCG:RG*, 1284.
5. *TFA*, 35.
6. *MME*, 153.
7. *MME*, 149.
8. *J.R.R. Tolkien: Life and Legend*, 27; these can be seen in *MME*, 149.
9. *J.R.R. Tolkien: Life and Legend*, 27.
10. Jerome Bertram, *St Aloysius' Parish*, 45.
11. *MME*, 149.
12. Henry Tristram, *Cardinal Newman and the Church of the Birmingham Oratory*, 11.
13. Walter Drumm, *The Old Palace*, 56.
14. Drumm, 55.
15. Robert Eaton, *Book of Oratorios*.
16. Maisie Ward, *Father Maturin*, 5–6.
17. *TEC*, 14.
18. Maisie Ward, *Father Maturin*, 26–27.
19. Maisie Ward, 6.
20. Drumm, *The Old Palace*, 57.
21. "Urquhart, Francis Fortescue, of Urquhart [*nicknamed* Sligger]," *Oxford Dictionary of National Biography*, 2004, https://doi.org/10.1093/ref:odnb/38480.
22. *TCG:C*, 163; *TCG:C*, 187.
23. *The Catholic Encyclopedia and Its Makers*, v.
24. Obituary for Mr. F.F. Urquhart, *The Guardian*, September 19, 1934, 16.
25. Jo Grimond, in *My Oxford*, 111.

Notes to Chapter 13: "The one great thing to love on earth"

1. *Letters*, 54, 340.
2. *Catechism of the Catholic Church* §1376.
3. *Letters*, 274.
4. John 6:35–69.
5. *Letters*, 338–39.
6. Joanna Tolkien, "Joanna Tolkien speaks," 35.
7. *Letters*, 337–38.
8. *Letters*, 339.
9. Pius X, *Sacra Tridentina* 19.
10. *Letters*, 337–38.
11. Pius X, *Sacra Tridentina* 19, 2, 3.
12. *Letters*, 339.
13. *Letters*, 223.
14. *TCG:C*, 489.
15. *TCG:C*, 494.
16. These usually include the Latin "O Salutaris Hostia" and "Tantum Ergo." In an English-speaking country, it might also feature English hymns such as "Jesus, my Lord, my God, my all" (composed by the Oratorian Fr. Frederick Faber) and "Sweet Sacrament Divine" (Adrian Fortescue, *Ceremonies of the Roman Rite Described*, 243). For more on the history and practice of Benediction among English Catholics, see Mary Heimann, *Catholic Devotion in Victorian England*, 45–58.
17. Fortescue, *Ceremonies of the Roman Rite Described*, 242–46.
18. *Letters*, 99.
19. *Letters*, 53–54.
20. Deborah Webster Rogers and Ivor A. Rogers, *J.R.R. Tolkien*, 126.
21. *OED*, waybread, n.1; Peter Gilliver, Jeremy Marshall, and Edmund Weiner, *Ring of Words*, 208. This is confirmed by a Google Ngram analysis of 'waybread.'
22. *Letters*, 275.
23. *OED*, waybread, n.2

Notes to Chapter 14: "With this ring I thee wed"

1. *UC*, 26.
2. Ethelred Taunton, *The Law of the Church*, 439.
3. Taunton, 440.
4. *Biography*, 73.
5. Taunton, *The Law of the Church*, 440.
6. Obituary of Father Denis Sheil, *O.S. Lives*, 15.
7. *Letters*, 73.
8. *Biography*, 73.
9. *Gloucestershire Echo*, May 2, 1913, 3. I am grateful to Peter Gilliver and John Garth for bringing this detail to my attention.
10. *TFA*, 36; *TCG:C*, 42.
11. *Biography*, 76.
12. *TFA*, 30. St. Mary's was the parish church of Cheltenham, so it is probable that Edith was a parishioner here, but we do not know for certain. It is now known as Cheltenham Minster.
13. *Biography*, 76.

14. *Biography*, 73.
15. It was published in the *Lyra Apostolica* (1836), a collection of hymns and poems for the Church of England with contributions from Newman, John Keble, and others.
16. *Biography*, 73.
17. *Biography*, 74.
18. *TCG:C*, 56.
19. Adrian Fortescue, *Ceremonies of the Roman Rite Described*, 406.
20. *TCG:C*, 84.
21. *Biography*, 86.
22. *TCG:C*, 86.
23. Fortescue, *Ceremonies of the Roman Rite Described*, 407.
24. Tolkien, *The Book of Lost Tales*, part one, 71–72.
25. *TFA*, 36.
26. *TCG:C*, 86.
27. Priscilla Tolkien, "J.R.R. Tolkien and Edith Tolkien's Stay in Staffordshire," 5.
28. William Cater, "We Talked of Love, Death, and Fairy Tales," 23.

Notes to Chapter 15: Into Battle

1. A.J.P. Taylor, *English History 1914–1945*, 20.
2. *Letters*, 53.
3. *TCG:RG*, 1399.
4. James Hagerty, *Priests in Uniform*, 7–8.
5. J.M. Winter, "Oxford and the First World War," 5–6, 16.
6. Gavin Thompson et al, "The Fallen: Military strength and deaths in combat," in *Olympic Britain: Social and economic change since the 1908 and 1948 Olympic Games*, 155; *Encyclopedia Britannica*, "World War I," https://www.britannica.com/event/World-War-I/Killed-wounded-and-missing.
7. *TGW*, 211.
8. Tolkien, foreword to the second edition of *LOTR*, xxiv.
9. Robert Graves, *Goodbye to All That*, 157–58.
10. Leo Baker, "Near the Beginning," in *Remembering C.S. Lewis*, ed. James T. Como, 69.
11. John Terraine, *The Road to Passchendaele: The Flanders Offensive 1917, A Study in Inevitability* (London: Leo Cooper, 1977), xx.
12. Hagerty, *Priests in Uniform*, 12.
13. Hagerty, 258–60.
14. Charles Plater, ed., *Catholic Soldiers*, 48.
15. Hagerty, *Priests in Uniform*, 35.
16. Hagerty, 363.
17. *Westminster Cathedral Chronicle*, February 1915, quoted in *Stories of the Great War* by Eileen Boland, 49–50.
18. *TGW*, 173.
19. *TGW*, 157.
20. Plater, ed., *Catholic Soldiers*, 52, 64, 55, 53.
21. *TCG:C*, 830.
22. *TGW*, 69
23. B. Gordon Blackwood, "Lancashire Catholics, Protestants and Jacobites During the 1715 Rebellion," *Recusant History* 22, no. 1 (1994): 41–59; F.J. Singleton, *Mowbreck Hall and the*

Willows: A History of the Catholic Community in the Kirkham District of Lancashire (Kirkham, UK: St. John the Evangelist, 1983), 44.
24. Plater, ed., *Catholic Soldiers*, 79.
25. *TGW*, 157.
26. I am indebted to John Garth for sharing with me his research notes identifying the chaplains who ministered to Tolkien's battalion.
27. Hagerty, *Priests in Uniform*, 135.
28. Hagerty, 98.
29. Plater, ed., *Catholic Soldiers*, 42.
30. Plater ed., 47.
31. *The Army and Religion*, 99.
32. *The Army and Religion*, 124, 82, 21.
33. Plater, ed., *Catholic Soldiers*, 11, 146, 56.
34. Plater, ed., 10.
35. Hagerty, *Priests in Uniform*, 67.
36. Hagerty, 346.
37. Hagerty, 11.
38. Hagerty, 362.
39. Graves, *Goodbye to All That*, 158.
40. Alan Wilkinson, *The Church of England and the First World War*, 111.
41. Evelyn Waugh, *Ronald Knox*, 240–41.
42. For more on this, see Michael Snape, "Church of England Army Chaplains in the First World War: Goodbye to 'Goodbye to All That,'" *The Journal of Ecclesiastical History* 62, no. 2 (2011): 318–45.
43. *TCG:C*, 101–4.
44. *TCG:C*, 101–12, 112–13.
45. R.L. Atenstaedt, "Trench fever: the British medical response in the Great War," 564–68.
46. His publisher, Rayner Unwin, later reflected, "Probably the most insidious and saddest distraction that overwhelmed Tolkien throughout his later life was his constant battle with ill-health" (*George Allen & Unwin: A Remembrancer*, 115).
47. Plater, ed., *Catholic Soldiers*, 146.

Notes to Chapter 16: Stella Vespertina

1. *Letters*, 10.
2. *Letters*, 66.
3. For most of Tolkien's life, there was no standard English translation of the liturgy, but bilingual missals and devotional manuals were widely used and commonly available. The English quotations from the Canon of the Mass in this chapter and in Appendix B are taken from the 1916 *The Order and Canon of the Mass in Latin and English*, an edition approved by the Vicar General of the Diocese of Westminster (London).
4. Joseph Pearce, *C.S. Lewis and the Catholic Church*, 156.
5. *Letters*, 172.
6. Clyde Kilby, "Meeting Professor Tolkien."
7. Clyde Kilby, *Tolkien and the Silmarillion*, 53.
8. Oronzo Cilli, *Tolkien's Library: An Annotated Checklist*, 107.
9. John Goldthorpe, *The Same Scourge* (London: Longmans, Green, 1954), 308, 353.

10. Tolkien, letter to Patricia Kirke, December 24, 1956, in Sotheby's *English Literature and History 18 July 1991*, Lot 362; see also The Superior Galleries May 9th, 1992, *Auction of Autographs, Manuscripts & Select Books.*
11. Henry Tristram, *Cardinal Newman and the Church of the Birmingham Oratory*, 35.
12. Pius IX, *Ineffabilis Deus.*
13. *Letters*, 286n.
14. *Letters*, 286n.
15. *TCG:C*, 97.
16. *Letters*, 66.
17. Tolkien, "'Words of Joy,'" part 2, 11–20.
18. Paul Fussell, *The Great War and Modern Memory*, 55–56.
19. *LOTR*, 975.
20. *LOTR*, 972.
21. *TCG:C*, 97.
22. *LOTR*, 922.

Notes to Chapter 17: Demobilization

1. Paul Fussell, *The Great War and Modern Memory*, 69–74.
2. Fussell, 70.
3. Martin Gilbert, "What Tolkien taught me about the Battle of the Somme."
4. *TFA*, 40.
5. Tom Shippey, *J.R.R. Tolkien: Author of the Century*, xxx.
6. Foreword to the second edition of *LOTR*, xxiv.
7. *Letters*, 70.
8. John Garth, "'As under a Green Sea,'" 20.
9. *TCG:RG*, 454.
10. *TGW*, 118–19.
11. *Letters*, 128.
12. Gerard Manley Hopkins, *The Correspondence of Gerard Manley Hopkins and Richard Watson Dixon*, ed. Claude Colleer Abbott (London: Oxford University Press, 1935), 8.
13. *Letters*, 110.
14. *LOTR*, 59
15. *Letters*, 111.
16. *OED*, "bowels," n. 3a.
17. *OED*, "pity," n. 1.
18. *LOTR*, 59.

Notes to Chapter 18: "I almost ceased to practise my religion"

1. *TCG:C*, 124.
2. *Biography*, 113; *TCG:C*, 134.
3. *Biography*, 112.
4. *TFA*, 45.
5. *Biography*, 111.
6. In the *Letters*, Humphrey Carpenter has included only three from this ten-year period, and two of those are formal letters relating to his leaving Leeds to take up his chair at Pembroke.
7. *Letters*, 421.
8. Charles Plater, ed., *Catholic Soldiers*, 148–49.

9. *Letters*, 340.
10. *MME*, 150
11. Thomas Aquinas, *Summa theologica* 2-2.35.1, trans. Laurence Shapcote (New York: Benzinger, 1947–48).
12. *The Catholic's Vade Mecum*, 166.
13. Joseph Delaney, "Sloth."
14. *Letters*, 340.
15. L.L.H. Thompson, "Report on J.R.R. Tolkien's paper on Catholic poet Francis Thompson (4 March 1914)," in Andrew S. Higgins, *The Genesis of Tolkien's Mythology*, 288–89. For more on Francis Thompson's influence on Tolkien's writings, see my *Tolkien's Modern Reading*, 230–34.
16. *Letters*, 66.
17. *The Catholic's Vade Mecum*, 11.
18. Philippians 2:12–13, Douay Version.
19. *Letters*, 66.

Notes to Chapter 19: The Domestic Church

1. *TFA*, 68; S.T.R.O. d'Ardenne, "The Man and the Scholar," 34.
2. Michael Tolkien, "Wizard Father," 3, 4.
3. *A Catechism of Christian Doctrine*, 34.
4. *Letters*, 340.
5. Andrea Monda and Wu Ming, "Tolkien the Catholic Philosopher?" 86; Oronzo Cilli, *Tolkien's Library*, 93. As another example, in 1945, he gave Michael two books by Hilaire Belloc, *Characters of the Reformation* (1936) and *The Crisis of Civilization* (1937) (*TCG:C*, 313).
6. Priscilla Tolkien, "The Letters of J.R.R. Tolkien."
7. *Biography*, 160.
8. Adrian Fortescue, *Ceremonies of the Roman Rite Described*, 392.
9. *Biography*, 104.
10. *TCG:C*, 110.
11. *TCG:C*, 110.
12. Fortescue, *Ceremonies of the Roman Rite Described*, 393.
13. *TCG:RG*, 568.
14. Priscilla Tolkien, "J.R.R. Tolkien and Edith Tolkien's Stay in Staffordshire," 5.
15. *TFA*, 62.
16. *TCG:RG*, 777.
17. James Hagerty, *Priests in Uniform*, 270–71.
18. John Rateliff, "The Missing Women," 51.
19. Phil Mathison, *Tolkien in East Yorkshire*, 23. Sister Mary Michael (Mary McLaughlin) entered the Sisters of Mercy in 1885, making the first profession of her vows in 1889. She later became Mother Mary Michael (*TCG:RG*, 777).
20. *TCG:RG*, 777; Rateliff, "The Missing Women," 51.
21. Bradley Buck, "An Inspired Alias? J.R.R. Tolkien's Frodo Baggins 'Underhill' and Fr Gerard Albert Plunket 'Underhill,' O.P. (1744–1814)," 197n53.
22. *TFA*, 44. John and Priscilla Tolkien later wrote the name as 'Moseley' in *The Tolkien Family Album*, undoubtedly from the fact that it sounds the same, and 'Moseley' was the name of one of the places their father had lived as a child. However, my archival research indicates that it is certainly 'Mozley.'

23. The National Archives of the UK, *Census Returns of England and Wales, 1891*; The National Archives of the UK, *Census Returns of England and Wales, 1901*; The Wellcome Trust; London, England; The Midwives Roll, 1904–1959, Ancestry.co.uk.
24. The 1921 census shows that the Tolkiens had 5 Holly Bank to themselves; the 1926 Midwives Roll lists Eleanor Mozley as resident at 1 Holly Bank (The National Archives of the UK, *Census Returns of England and Wales, 1921*).
25. *The Daily Mail*, Hull, Wednesday, January 22, 1930, 1.
26. *TCG:C*, 124, 125.
27. Paolo Petrocelli, *The Resonance of a Small Voice: William Walton and the Violin Concerto in England Between 1900 and 1940* (Newcastle upon Tyne, UK: Cambridge Scholars Publishing, 2010), 75; Joy Porter, *Trauma, Primitivism and the First World War: The Making of Frank Prewett* (London: Bloomsbury, 2021), 246.
28. *TCG:RG*, 229.
29. He was baptized as Wilfred Rowland and is listed as such in the UK census rolls, but later, as a Catholic poet, his name often appears as 'Wilfred Rowland Mary Childe,' as in *The Oxford Book of Mystical Verse* (1917).
30. Tolkien, Letter to Selby, September 19, 1944 (Wade JRRT L-Selby W); *Biography*, 114, 119.
31. *TCG:C*, 159.
32. *TCG:RG*, 297–98.
33. *TCG:C*, 163.
34. Inscription by Priscilla Tolkien in *The English Poets*, author's private collection.
35. *TCG:RG*, 203.
36. Tolkien, *Letters from Father Christmas*, 9.
37. Tolkien, *Letters from Father Christmas*, 74; 84, 142, 179; 117.
38. Hilary Tolkien, *Black and White Ogre Country*, 71.
39. *Letters*, 76, 55.

Notes to Chapter 20: Fellow Pilgrim

1. C.S. Lewis, *All My Road Before Me*, 393.
2. *Letters*, 362.
3. C.S. Lewis, *Surprised by Joy*, 216.
4. *Letters*, 341.
5. *CLI*, 701.
6. Tolkien, *The Lays of Beleriand*, 184.
7. Tolkien, 374.
8. See Diana Glyer, *The Company They Keep*, 110–16 for a detailed account of this exchange.
9. Michael Ward, *After Humanity: A Guide to C.S. Lewis's "The Abolition of Man"* (Park Ridge, IL: Word on Fire Academic, 2021), 24–36.
10. *CLI*, 838.
11. *CLI*, 970, 974.
12. *CLI*, 976–77.
13. *CLI*, 977.
14. *OFS*, 77–78.
15. Tolkien, "Mythopoeia," 85, 87, 89.
16. Tolkien, 87, 88, 90.
17. *CLI*, 974.
18. *CLII*, 501.
19. G.K. Chesterton, *The Everlasting Man* (New York: Dodd, Mead, and Company, 1925), 310.

20. Tolkien, "Mythopoeia," 87–88.
21. *Letters*, 339.
22. *CLI*, 969.
23. E.L. Edmonds, "C.S. Lewis the Teacher," in *In Search of C.S. Lewis*, ed. Stephen Schofield, 45.
24. *Inklings*, 52.

Notes to Chapter 21: An Academic Vocation

1. Tolkien's appointment as Professor of Anglo-Saxon at Oxford began in October 1925, but to provide the required six months' notice for vacating his Chair at Leeds, he continued to teach there until December 1925. During this autumn term he commuted to Oxford every other week for lectures on Friday and Saturday. The family moved to Oxford in January of 1926.
2. Tolkien, "Beowulf: The Monsters and the Critics," 8.
3. Tolkien, 15.
4. Outram Evennett, "The Vocation of a Catholic Don," *Catholic Herald*, September 16, 1949, 3.
5. "Catholics and the Universities," *Catholic Herald*, July 3, 1936, 7.
6. "Oxford University Association," *Catholic Herald*, February 26, 1937, 14.
7. "Universities Catholic Education Board," *The Tablet*, July 1, 1933, 11.
8. "Social and Personal," *The Tablet*, May 11, 1935, 612.
9. Caroline Chabot, "Raymond Wilson Chambers, continued," 86.
10. "University Notes—Oxford," *The Tablet*, April 7, 1928, 467.
11. "News and Notes," *The Tablet*, June 30, 1928, 864.
12. "The Pax Romana Congress, by the President of P.R.," *The Tablet*, September 1, 1928, 279. Pax Romana is still in existence but no longer with a focus specifically on student life. Under the name of the International Catholic Movement for Intellectual and Cultural Affairs (ICMICA-Pax Romana), it is recognized as an International Association of the Faithful by the Vatican.
13. Ramon Sugranyes de Franch, *Pax Romana: 1921–1961* (Fribourg, CH: 1961), 7–8.
14. *TCG:C*, 156.
15. "The Pax Romana Congress, by the President of P.R.," *The Tablet*, September 1, 1928, 280.
16. Walter Drumm, *The Old Palace*, 73–74.
17. Drumm, 74.
18. Martin D'Arcy, *Laughter and the Love of Friends*, 112–13.
19. "The New Franciscan Friary at Oxford," *The Tablet*, October 10, 1931, 478. Tolkien is erroneously identified as "the Censor of St. Catherine's Society" (i.e., the supervisor of the Oxford University students not attached to a particular college). The Censor was at that time Rev. V.J.K. Brook, and Tolkien seems to have had no involvement with the Society ("An Information Paper Concerning St. Catherine's Society, University of Oxford," Oxford: St Catherine's Society, February 1937).
20. "Blessed Agnellus," *Catholic Herald*, May 22, 1936, 11.
21. "Catholics and Oxford: The Meaning of Campion Hall," *Catholic Herald*, July 3, 1936.
22. "Oxford's Farewell to Mgr. Knox," *The Tablet*, June 17, 1939, 790.
23. Constitution of the Newman Association, Palace Green Archives, Newman Association, D1/C/1/4.
24. No individual AGM reports survive from 1942–46. Extant AGM reports show that he was elected in 1947 and in 1949 through 1955. His signature to the *Times* as Honorary VP in January 1949, before the April elections, shows that he served in 1948 (Newman Association

Report 1942–47; Minutes of the Newman Association, 1949–54. Palace Green Archives, Newman Association, D1/J/1/1/1).

25. 1953 Report, Palace Green Archives, Newman Association, D1/J/1/1/1. Among his fellow Honorary VPs in the 1950s were a number of notable Catholic academics, including Monsignor Ronald Knox, Christopher Dawson, Francis de Zulueta, Fr. C.C. Martindale, and Fr. Martin D'Arcy (Palace Green Archives, Newman Association, Minutes of the Newman Association, 1949–54, D1/J/1/1/1).
26. Annual Report 1955–56, 18. Palace Green Archives, Newman Association, D1/J/1/1/5.
27. James Hagerty, *The Catenian Association*, 88; *TCG:RG*, 1232.
28. This limitation was in fact imposed by Bishop Casartelli, who was involved in founding the Association. Peter Lane, *The Catenian Association 1908–1983*, 20.
29. Hagerty, *The Catenian Association*, 1–2.
30. *Catholic Herald*, November 12, 1943, 5. The inaugural meeting was on October 31, 1943, and was held at the Randolph Hotel (Catenian Association, "Short History of the Oxford Circle").
31. Lane, *The Catenian Association 1908–1983*, 21.
32. *TCG:RG*, 1232.
33. Lane, *The Catenian Association 1908–1983*, 153, 160.
34. *Letters*, 395.
35. Sister M. Madeleva, *My First Seventy Years*, 96–97.

Notes to Chapter 22: Saints and Angels

1. Clyde Kilby, *Tolkien and the Silmarillion*, 54.
2. Tolkien, *Pearl* stanza 32, in *Sir Gawain and the Green Knight, Pearl, and Sir Orfeo*, 183. The original reads: "Bot crystes mersy & mary & Ion, / Þise arn þe grounde of alle my blysse."
3. *Inklings*, 52.
4. *Letters*, 193n.
5. *Letters*, 339.
6. Tolkien, "Imram," 1561.
7. *TCG:C*, 491.
8. *TCG:C*, 495.
9. *TCG:C*, 496.
10. *Inklings*, 51.
11. *Letters*, 397.
12. Tolkien, Letter to Patricia Kirke, December 24, 1956, in Sotheby's *English Literature and History 18 July 1991*, Lot 362. See also The Superior Galleries *May 9th, 1992 Auction of Autographs, Manuscripts & Select Books.*
13. *BF*, 203.
14. Tolkien, Letter to Patricia Kirke, December 24, 1956, in Sotheby's *English Literature and History 18 July 1991*, Lot 362. See also The Superior Galleries *May 9th, 1992 Auction of Autographs, Manuscripts & Select Books.*
15. Priscilla Tolkien, "Religion and Morality in Tolkien."
16. *Letters*, 100.
17. *OFS*, 75.
18. *Letters*, 100.
19. R.W. Chambers, *Thomas More*, 349.
20. "Plans for Oxford Chaplaincy; Catholic Association's Annual Report," *Catholic Herald*, March 24, 1939, 15.

21. Caroline Chabot, "Raymond Wilson Chambers, continued," 85.
22. Chabot, 85.
23. Chambers, *Thomas More*, 374.
24. Chambers, 342.
25. Chambers, 374.
26. *Letters*, 193.
27. *Letters*, 66.
28. *Letters*, 66.
29. *Letters*, 99.
30. *Letters*, 99.
31. Deborah Webster Rogers and Ivor A. Rogers, *J.R.R. Tolkien*, 125.

Notes to Chapter 23: Charity and Forgiveness

1. This page is now lost, but Tolkien recounted the experience in *Letters*, 215 and various interviews. Cf. John Rateliff, *The History of The Hobbit*, xi–xiii. Tolkien himself placed the origins of *The Hobbit* to the early 1930s (see, for instance, *Letters*, 215), but some scholars suggest an earlier date. For more on the chronology of composition, see Rateliff, *The History of The Hobbit*, xi–xx and *TCG:RG*, 511ff.
2. *Letters*, 354.
3. *Letters*, 340.
4. *Letters*, 61; 395.
5. *OED*, "Charity, n." sense 1 and 1c.
6. *Letters*, 417.
7. *Letters*, 54.
8. *TFA*, 25.
9. *TCG:C*, 12.
10. *Biography*, 51.
11. *MME*, 155.
12. *TFA*, 35.
13. *Biography*, 51.
14. *TCG:C*, 190.
15. *Letters*, 416.
16. *UC*, 101.
17. *UC*, 106.
18. It became in turn a feature of the Tolkien household: the family "called it the 'flip-flap' clock, because it told the time by flipping the figures over as though they were the pages of a book" (*UC*, 106, 106n7).
19. *Letters*, 416n.
20. *UC*, 99.
21. *UC*, 99.
22. *UC*, 100–101.
23. *TFA*, 61.
24. Tolkien, *The Hobbit*, 262–63.

Notes to Chapter 24: Men of Valor

1. Caroline Chabot, "Raymond Wilson Chambers," 85.
2. *Letters*, 55.

3. *CLII*, 128.
4. *Letters*, 55. For similar thoughts from C.S. Lewis, see his essay "First and Second Things."
5. *Letters*, 55.
6. *Letters*, 37; 375.
7. William Manchester, *The Last Lion*, 2:100.
8. *TCG:RG*, 1052.
9. *Letters*, 37; *Letters*, 37.
10. Prefatory note to Letter 30, *Letters*, 37.
11. *Letters*, 37.
12. *Letters*, 67.
13. *Letters*, 67.
14. Vatican Council II, *Nostra Aetate* 4.
15. *Letters*, 410n.
16. *Letters*, 229. For more on this, see Renée Vink, "'Jewish' Dwarves: Tolkien and Anti-Semitic Stereotyping."
17. Denis Gueroult, "An Interview with J.R.R. Tolkien," 5.
18. Denis Gueroult, interview with Tolkien for BBC radio, "Now Read On."
19. Zak Cramer, "Jewish influences in Middle-earth," 10.
20. Tolkien, *The Silmarillion*, 32.

Notes to Chapter 25: Darkness Visible

1. Simon Tolkien, "Remarks by Simon Tolkien." Oxford is approximately fifty miles from Coventry—and the fires were so intense that they were visible up to one hundred miles away.
2. Priscilla Tolkien, "A Personal Memory," 48, 210n2.
3. *Letters*, 46.
4. Caroline Chabot, "Raymond Wilson Chambers, continued," 94.
5. *Letters*, 55.
6. *Letters*, 116.
7. Martin D'Arcy, *The Problem of Evil*, 11.
8. *Letters*, 55.
9. E.R. Eddison, "A Letter of Introduction," in *Zimiamvia: A Trilogy* (New York: Dell, 1992), 320–21.
10. *Letters*, 258.
11. Tolkien, "Mythopoeia," 88.
12. John Bowen, "Bookstand."
13. *Letters*, 90.
14. *Letters*, 286–87.
15. Bowen, "Bookstand."
16. Tolkien, *The Silmarillion*, 8.
17. Charlotte and Denis Plimmer, "The Man Who Understands Hobbits," 35.
18. *LOTR*, 438.
19. *Letters*, 110.
20. *Letters*, 76.
21. Stuart Lee, "Tolkien in Oxford," 164.
22. *Letters*, 76.
23. *Letters*, 80.
24. *LOTR*, 270.

Notes to Chapter 26: The Inklings

1. *CLI*, 974.
2. C.S. Lewis, preface to *Mere Christianity*, viii.
3. See Grevel Lindop, *Charles Williams: The Third Inkling*.
4. *BF*, 193. Dyson seems to have been relatively camera-shy during his Inklings years. One of the few extant images of him appears in figure 31. Julian Reid, archivist of Merton College, confirmed Dyson's identity in this 1951 Merton College photo and clarified that the man seated next to Tolkien in a widely reproduced photo at Merton College is not, in fact, Dyson.
5. Philip Zaleski and Carol Zaleski, *The Fellowship*, 342–43.
6. Walter Hooper, *C.S. Lewis: A Companion and Guide*, 680.
7. *Inklings*, 130.
8. *TCG:C*, 275.
9. *TCG:C*, 347.
10. *Inklings*, 178.
11. *BF*, 216.
12. *CLII*, 431–32.
13. *BF*, 212.
14. Robert Havard, "Tolkien: A Personal Memoir," 61.
15. *BF*, 212.
16. Mark 'Colin' Havard, "The Inklings Remembered," 35–36. Robert Havard's second son, Mark Emlyn Havard, used a variety of pseudonyms throughout his life.
17. Tolkien, letter to James Heaf, February 28, 1964. Christie's *Autograph Letters and Printed Books*, 7 October 1997.
18. *Inklings*, 177.
19. *CLII*, 283.
20. *CLII*, 283.
21. *CLII*, 358.
22. Diana Glyer, *The Company They Keep*, 17.
23. *Letters*, 388.
24. Glyer, *The Company They Keep*, 109.
25. Warren Lewis, "Memoir of C.S. Lewis," 13.
26. Glyer, *The Company They Keep*, 18.
27. *Letters*, 126.
28. *Letters*, 126.
29. *Letters*, 128.
30. Glyer, *The Company They Keep*, 88.
31. Colin Havard, "The Inklings Remembered," 42.
32. *BF*, 193.
33. *BF*, 200.
34. A.N. Wilson, *C.S. Lewis: A Biography*, 217. There is debate in the scholarship over the exact language used. On the one hand, Wilson claimed that he got the story directly from Christopher ("Tolkien was not a writer," *The Telegraph*, November 24, 2001). On the other hand, Christopher rendered it more politely as "Oh God, no more Elves" in *J.R.R. Tolkien: A Film Portrait*; but for a public presentation, it is possible that he rephrased it so as not to give offense. As Dyson appears to have made this objection repeatedly, he may have been ruder on some occasions than others.
35. Glyer, *The Company They Keep*, 88.
36. Glyer, 88.
37. John Wain, *Sprightly Running*, 184.

Notes to Chapter 27: Praises

1. Clyde Kilby, "Meeting Professor Tolkien."
2. *Letters*, 80
3. *Letters*, 115.
4. *Letters*, 130; 401.
5. *TCG:C*, 547.
6. Kilby, "Meeting Professor Tolkien."
7. *Letters*, 66.
8. *Letters*, 400.
9. *Letters*, 66, 400.
10. Tolkien, "The Qenya Alphabet," 42–43, 71–72, 98, 100, 102, 104; Tolkien, *"Alcar mi Tarmenel na Erun,"* 31.
11. *Letters*, 400. Tolkien mistakenly cites it as Daniel chapter 2, not 3.
12. *Letters*, 66. The Bible translation used by Catholics at that time (Bishop Challoner's revision of the Douay Bible) was based on the Latin Vulgate text, which has slightly different numbering of some Psalms. Therefore, the Psalms now numbered 113 and 117 were known to Tolkien as 112 and 116, respectively.
13. *Letters*, 66.
14. *Letters*, 400.
15. Psalm 148:7–10, Douay Version.
16. *Letters*, 400.
17. *Letters*, 66.
18. Tolkien, "Noel," 4.
19. *The Catholic's Vade Mecum*, 103–4.
20. *Letters*, 237.
21. *Letters*, 215.
22. *Letters*, 66; Tolkien, "'Words of Joy,'" part 2, 11.
23. Tolkien, "The Qenya Alphabet," 82, 90, 92, 158.
24. Richard Challoner, *The Garden of the Soul*. What is customarily listed as 'The Divine Praises' is a specific prayer, often used publicly after Benediction, that runs "Blessed be God; blessed be his holy name," and so on. Tolkien would have known this prayer, but he doesn't include it among his recommended 'praises,' perhaps because he felt it to be so obvious as not to need mentioning.
25. F.W. Faber, ed., *If God Be With Us: The Maxims of St Philip Neri*, 30, 59.

Notes to Chapter 28: Tolkien's Parish

1. *Letters*, 195.
2. Priscilla Tolkien, "Religion and Morality in Tolkien."
3. *OED*, niggle, v., 2.
4. *Letters*, 321.
5. Robert Murray, "A Tribute to Tolkien," 880.
6. *TCG:C*, 51; 493ff; 398; *TCG:C*, 552.
7. Two of Tolkien's children had their funerals at St. Gregory's: John (d. 2003) and Priscilla (d. 2022).
8. St. Gregory and St. Augustine, "History of the Parish." More recently, a painted reredos has been installed featuring Mary and the Christ child above the tabernacle, with large depictions

of St. Gregory and St. Augustine to either side. To the left and right of the altar, ten other saints are depicted.

9. North and central Oxford are in the Birmingham diocese; south Oxford is in the Portsmouth diocese.
10. John Saward, John Morrill, and Michael Tomko, eds., *Firmly I Believe and Truly: The Spiritual Tradition of Catholic England, 1483–1999*, ii. Johnson was the author of *One Lord, One Faith* (1929) among other titles, and served as the Oxford University chaplain from 1941–47.
11. *The Official Catholic Directory*, 1925, 1938, 1939, and 1940. *The Catholic Directory* lists two interim pastors between Smith and Carter: the Rev. B. Singleton, MA, in 1938 and the Rev. J. Ryan in 1939, before Douglas Carter is listed as the pastor in the 1940 directory. However, the parish records at St. Gregory's indicate that Carter began in 1938. It is important to disambiguate this Douglas Carter from an Anglican cleric of the same name (author of *Many Mighty Works* [1958]), also based in Oxford.
12. *TCG:C*, 246.
13. Personal communication, Fr. John Saward (pastor of St. Gregory and St. Augustine), August 24, 2022.
14. *Letters*, 419.
15. Carter was responsible for the book of Maccabees and the Acts of the Apostles. Anne Crowther, "The Jerusalem Bible and the role of the Newman Association," 12; "A Film on Newman," *The Tablet*, June 22, 1957, 587.
16. Personal communication, Fr. John Saward, pastor of St. Gregory and St. Augustine, August 24, 2022.
17. Douglas Carter, letter to the editor, *The Tablet*, August 3, 1968, 774; *The Tablet*, January 19, 1957, 71.
18. Carter, letter to the editor, *The Tablet*, July 20, 1968, 726.
19. Robert Murray, "Sermon at Thanksgiving Service," 17.
20. *Letters*, 75.
21. The schedule of Masses given in Tristram's 1934 history would be characteristic of the offerings in the preceding decades as well.
22. Introduction to Ignatius Ryder, *Sermons and Notes of Sermons*, vi–vii.
23. *Letters*, 75.
24. *Letters*, 75.
25. Ignatius Ryder, "Sixth Sunday after Epiphany: The Voice of God," in *Sermons and Notes of Sermons*, 48.
26. Adrian Fortescue, *Ceremonies of the Roman Rite Described*, 306.
27. *TGW*, 172.
28. The crucifix was used for decades in the Good Friday liturgy; it is now in place as the main crucifix at the high altar (Personal communication, Fr. John Saward, August 24 and August 31, 2022; see also Patrick Taylor, "Germaine and Basil," https://patricktaylor.com/germaine-and-basil).
29. Tolkien, in Christopher Tolkien, Preface to *Tree and Leaf*, vi. Tolkien said that it was published in 1947, but he misremembered. It appeared in the January 1945 issue.
30. Tolkien, "Leaf by Niggle," 109–10.
31. Tolkien, "Leaf by Niggle," 110, 115–16, 118.
32. Tolkien, in Christopher Tolkien, Preface to *Tree and Leaf*, vi.
33. *Letters*, 321.
34. Tolkien, "Leaf by Niggle," 110.

Notes to Chapter 29: "I have exposed my heart to be shot at"

1. *Letters*, 163.
2. Rayner Unwin, *George Allen & Unwin: A Remembrancer*, 97. Cf Introductory note to Letter 134, *Letters*, 163–64.
3. *Letters*, 165, 171.
4. *Letters*, 172.
5. Richard West, "Letter from Father Murray," 135.
6. *Letters*, 172.
7. *Letters*, 220.
8. Stuart Lee, "Tolkien in Oxford," 151.
9. *Letters*, 237. Emphasis in original.
10. Tolkien, Letter to G.S. Rigby Jr, December 6, 1965, in Sotheby's *Books & Manuscripts, 11 June 2013*, Lot 227.
11. *Letters*, 234.
12. *Letters*, 262, 246.
13. *OFS*, 75.
14. *OED*, "evangelium," n.
15. *OFS*, 78.
16. *OFS*, 75.
17. *LOTR*, 950–51
18. See Michael Ward, "Peak Middle-earth."
19. *LOTR*, 954
20. *J.R.R. Tolkien: The Art of the Manuscript*, 94: it reproduces the tear-stained page.
21. Wayne G. Hammond and Christina Scull, *The Lord of the Rings: A Reader's Companion*, 748; *OFS*, 76.
22. *Letters*, 53–54.
23. *OFS*, 78–79.

Notes to Chapter 30: The Accredited Altar

1. *Letters*, 339.
2. *Letters*, 339.
3. *Catechism of Pius X*, "The Communion of Saints," Q10 (*Saint Pius X Collection* [London: Aeterna, 2016], 41); "The Ninth Article of the Creed," Q29 (*Collection*, 33).
4. *Letters*, 339.
5. See Holly Ordway, *Tolkien's Modern Reading*, 215–19, for more detail on Tolkien's view of Williams's writing.
6. Charles Williams, *He Came Down from Heaven* (Berkeley, CA: Apocryphile, 2005; first published 1938), 25.
7. *The Catholic's Vade Mecum*, 19.
8. *Letters*, 339. The *Catechism of the Catholic Church* puts it thus: "God has bound salvation to the sacrament of Baptism, but he himself is not bound by his sacraments" (§1257).
9. Michael George Tolkien, "Lecture on J.R.R. Tolkien."
10. Pius IX, *Singulari Quadam Perfusi*.
11. *Letters*, 234.
12. *Letters*, 339n.
13. *Letters*, 339.
14. *Letters*, 395.

15. Vatican II, *Unitatis Redintegratio*, 1.3.
16. Caroline Chabot, "Raymond Wilson Chambers, continued," 86.
17. See, e.g., Newman on "invincible ignorance" (Ian Ker, *John Henry Newman*, 681).
18. *Unitatis Redintegratio*, 1.4.
19. *Letters*, 394.
20. "The Reunion of Christendom: The Church Unity Octave of Prayer," *The Tablet*, January 15, 1921, 90. See also Benedict XVI, "General Audience: Week of Prayer for Christian Unity," January 23, 2008. The octave began with the Feast of the Chair of St. Peter (then January 18) and ended with the Feast of the Conversion of St. Paul (January 25).
21. *BF*, 185.
22. *TCG:C*, 220; 390.
23. Grevel Lindop, *Charles Williams: The Third Inkling*, 423–24.
24. *Letters*, 341.
25. *Letters*, 73.
26. *LOTR*, 348

Notes to Chapter 31: Bearing Witness

1. *Letters*, 284.
2. *Inklings*, 185.
3. Ronald Knox, "The Whole Art of Chaplaincraft," in Walter Drumm, *The Old Palace*, 75.
4. George Sayer, "Recollections," 24.
5. "Batons Drawn: Exciting Scenes in Edinburgh: Catholic Congress Ends," *The Scotsman*, June 26, 1935. Cf. Tom Gallagher, *Edinburgh Divided: John Cormack and No Popery in the 1930s*.
6. *Letters*, 84.
7. *TCG:C*, 281.
8. Robert Murray, "A Tribute to Tolkien," 880.
9. Robert Murray, "Sermon at Thanksgiving Service," 17.
10. Murray, "A Tribute to Tolkien," 880.
11. *BF*, 202.
12. *BF*, 203.
13. *BF*, 205.
14. *BF*, 205.
15. *Letters*, 286n.
16. *BF*, 205. Emphasis in original.
17. *BF*, 205.
18. *Letters*, 337–38.
19. At this point in his life, Tolkien frequently used the Westminster Version.
20. *Letters*, 109.
21. *Letters*, 338.
22. *Letters*, 339.
23. *Letters*, 339.
24. Caroline Chabot, "Raymond Wilson Chambers, continued," 86.
25. S.T.R.O. d'Ardenne, "The Man and the Scholar," 33.
26. Chabot, "Raymond Wilson Chambers," 81.
27. Chabot, "Raymond Wilson Chambers, continued," 86.

Notes to Chapter 32: In the Beginning Was the Word

1. *OFS*, 44n1, 72n1.
2. Naomi Collyer, "Recollections of Professor J.R.R. Tolkien," 2.
3. Humphrey Carpenter et al., "A Dialogue," 21; *TCG:C*, 16.
4. Oronzo Cilli, *Tolkien's Library*, 72, 300.
5. *Letters*, 377; Charlotte and Denis Plimmer, "The Man Who Understands Hobbits," 35. He was a member of the Oxford University Dante Society from 1945–55, alongside Cesare Foligno, Fr. Martin D'Arcy, C.S. Lewis, and (briefly) Charles Williams. (Appendix to Oxford University Dante Society, *Centenary Essays on Dante*, 146–47).
6. Holly Ordway, *Tolkien's Modern Reading*, 262; *Inklings*, 189.
7. Ordway, *Tolkien's Modern Reading*, 207–13.
8. S.T.R.O. d'Ardenne, "The Man and the Scholar," 35.
9. Clyde Kilby, "Dr. Clyde S. Kilby Recalls The Inklings," 4.
10. This analysis is based on the annotated pages shown in the sales listing of this volume; presumably there are further annotations as well. Tolkien, attentive as always to detail, corrected errors in the footnotes as well (*The New Testament in the Westminster Version of the Sacred Scriptures*, published by Sands in 1947, previously owned by J.R.R. Tolkien, sales listing: http://www.tolkienlibrary.com/tolkien-book-store/001343.htm).
11. Anthony Curtis, "Remembering Tolkien and Lewis," 429.
12. Clyde Kilby, "Meeting Professor Tolkien."
13. Hugh Pope, *English Versions of the Bible* (London: B. Herder, 1952), 483.
14. Pope, *English Versions of the Bible*, 500. The translation Tolkien used is identifiable by his rendition of John 8:58 as "before Abraham came to be *I am*," a phrasing that was found at that time in the Westminster Version. The Douay Version has "before Abraham was made, I AM"; the Revised Standard Version has "before Abraham was, I am."
15. Preface, *The Westminster Version*, i.
16. *TCG:C*, 197.
17. *TCG:C*, 197. However, it turned out to be too complex a matter for him to address, as there were differences "between the use as a prayer and the translations of the Gospels," as well as "difficulties in the Greek and Latin texts" and "a very large number of divergent versions in English."
18. Bernard Cardinal Griffith, Preface to *The Holy Bible*, trans. Ronald Knox (New York: Sheed & Ward, 1956), vii.
19. *BF*, 242.
20. Evelyn Waugh, *Ronald Knox*, 165.
21. C.S. Lewis, "Modern Translations of the Bible," an essay that was originally published as an introduction to J.B. Phillips's *Letters to Young Churches: A Translation of the New Testament Epistles* (London: Macmillan, 1947). See also *CLII*, 941.
22. *LOTR*, 374.
23. *Letters*, 314.
24. *Letters*, 407, 431.
25. Tolkien, *The Silmarillion*, 70, 276.
26. *LOTR*, 680. In having Faramir describe her as "perilously fair" and Sam remarking that "you could dash yourself to pieces on her, like a ship on a rock; or drownd yourself, like a hobbit in a river," Tolkien may also be alluding to Protestant difficulties with Mary.
27. *LOTR*, 841.
28. *LOTR*, 842.
29. Tolkien, "The Qenya Alphabet," 78.

30. Psalm 127 (Vulgate numbering), Douay Version. Certain Psalms are numbered differently in the Vulgate translation and in editions based on the Vulgate, such as the Douay.

Notes to Chapter 33: Jonah

1. *Letters*, 109.
2. *Letters*, 109.
3. *Letters*, 110.
4. Tolkien does not provide the name of this piece, which he evidently read in manuscript form. "Myth Became Fact" is the likeliest candidate, but alternative possibilities are "The Grand Miracle" and "Is Theology Poetry?" as these touch on similar points and fit the date.
5. *Letters*, 109.
6. *Letters*, 109.
7. Pius XII, *Divino Afflante Spiritu* 19.
8. Pius XII, *Divino Afflante Spiritu* 34, 35, 38.
9. Pius XII, *Divino Afflante Spiritu* 40.
10. Joseph A. Fitzmyer, review of La Bible de Jérusalem: La Sainte Bible traduite en français sous la direction de l'Ecole Biblique de Jérusalem, *Journal of Biblical Literature* 95, no. 4 (December 1976): 640–41.
11. Brendan Wolfe, "Tolkien's Jonah," 16.
12. Tolkien, "The Book of Jonah," 5, 7, 9.
13. Wolfe, "Tolkien's Jonah," 15.
14. Wolfe, 20.
15. Wolfe, 21.
16. Robert Murray, "A Tribute to Tolkien," 880.
17. Wolfe, "Tolkien's Jonah," 16.
18. Wolfe, 19.
19. Wolfe, 21.
20. Wolfe, 19.
21. Wolfe, 19.
22. *Letters*, 310.
23. Tolkien, *The Hobbit*, 68.
24. Michael George Tolkien, "Lecture on J.R.R. Tolkien."

Notes to Chapter 34: "An axe-blow near the roots"

1. *Letters*, 108. Slubgob is one of Lewis's devils in *The Screwtape Letters* (1942).
2. For more on this, see Michael Ward, *Planet Narnia: The Seven Heavens in the Imagination of C.S. Lewis*.
3. Josh Long, "Disparaging Narnia," 39. For more on Tolkien's reaction to Narnia, see my *Tolkien's Modern Reading*, 75–81.
4. *Letters*, 378.
5. *Letters*, 341
6. John Tolkien, "Reminiscences of Tolkien and Lewis"; *J.R.R.T.: A Film Portrait; J.R.R.T.: A Film Portrait*.
7. *Letters*, 362.
8. *Letters*, 349.
9. For full details of Joy's life and relationship with Lewis, see Abigail Santamaria, *Joy: Poet, Seeker, and the Woman Who Captivated C.S. Lewis*.

10. *Letters*, 341.
11. Colin Havard, "The Inklings Remembered," 40–41.
12. *CLIII*, 669.
13. George Sayer, *Jack: A Life of C.S. Lewis*, 375.
14. *Letters*, 349.
15. John Tolkien, "Reminiscences of Tolkien and Lewis."
16. A.N. Wilson, *C.S. Lewis: A Biography*, 294.
17. Roger Green and Walter Hooper, *C.S. Lewis: A Biography*, 430.
18. Tolkien, Letter to Przemysław Mroczkowski, January 20–26, 1964, in Christie's *Fine Printed Books and Manuscripts 1 June 2009.*
19. *TCG:C*, 625.
20. *Letters*, 241.
21. *Letters*, 341.
22. *Letters*, 241.
23. Walter Hooper, "Tolkien and C.S. Lewis," 191.
24. *Letters*, 95–96.
25. *Letters*, 352.
26. Carpenter does not identify these in-text but does in the Appendix: Sources of Quotations.
27. C.S. Lewis, *Letters to Malcolm*, 30.
28. Lewis, 108, 109.
29. Lewis, 101.
30. Lewis, 102.
31. Lewis, 104–5.
32. C.S. Lewis, "Transposition," 272.
33. Lewis, *Letters to Malcolm*, 105.
34. *Letters*, 95.
35. *Inklings*, 50.
36. *Inklings*, 51–52.
37. *Letters*, 95–96.
38. Sayer, *Jack*, 422.
39. Guy Brinkworth, letter to the Editor, *The Tablet*, December 7, 1963, 1317.
40. Wilson, *C.S. Lewis*, xvii.
41. Wilson, xvii.
42. *Letters*, 350. He read *Letters to Malcolm* in January of 1964, having been sent a pre-publication copy (*TCG:C*, 648).
43. C.S. Lewis, *Surprised by Joy*, 216.
44. Tolkien, Letter to George Sayer, November 28, 1963, in Christie's *20th Century Books and Manuscripts*, Lot 20, November 16, 2001.

Notes to Chapter 35: "The Tree is the thing"

1. *Letters*, 393.
2. Callum G. Brown, "What was the Religious Crisis of the 1960s?" *Journal of Religious History* 34, no. 4 (December 2010): 471.
3. James Stephen Curl, *The Erosion of Oxford*, 107–31.
4. Jerome Bertram, *St Aloysius' Parish*, 32, 34.
5. Bertram, *St Aloysius' Parish*, 33.
6. In his apostolic constitution *Christus Dominus*. In 1964, Pope Paul VI shortened the fast to its current length of one hour before receiving Communion (Madeleine Grace, "Eucharistic

Fasting: A Review of Its Practice and Evaluation of Its Benefit," *Antiphon: A Journal for Liturgical Renewal* 17, no. 3 [2013]).
7. Daniel Helen and Morgan Thomsen, "A recollection of Tolkien: Canon Gerard Hanlon," 41.
8. Gregory DiPippo, "Compendium of the 1955 Holy Week Revisions of Pius XII, Part 5: Tenebrae and the Divine Office of the Triduum" and "Part 8: The Hours of the Celebration of the Holy Week Liturgies."
9. Evelyn Waugh, in Alcuin Reid, ed., *A Bitter Trial*, 37.
10. *TCG:RG*, 1073.
11. *TCG:RG*, 1073, *TCG:C*, 515.
12. Irene Tolkien Cook, letter to the editor of *Amon Hen*, 24.
13. George Sayer, "Recollections," 24.
14. *J.R.R.T.: A Film Portrait.*
15. *Letters*, 393.
16. Giuseppe Pezzini, "Tolkien and Newman."
17. Pezzini, "Tolkien and Newman."
18. *Letters*, 197.
19. *Letters*, 151, 197.
20. Deborah Webster Rogers and Ivor A. Rogers, *J.R.R. Tolkien*, 126.
21. *Letters*, 197.
22. *LOTR*, 248.
23. John Henry Newman, *An Essay on the Development of Christian Doctrine*, 445.
24. *Letters*, 393.
25. *Letters*, 339.
26. *Letters*, 339.
27. *Letters*, 393.
28. John XXIII, "The Council's Aims: The Full Text of Pope John's Opening Speech," *The Tablet*, October 20, 1962, 998. The full text of this opening address, in a different translation, can be found in *The Word on Fire Vatican II Collection*, ed. Matthew Levering.
29. Vatican II, *Sacrosanctum Concilium* 10.
30. Paul VI, *Ecclesiam Suam* 50.
31. *Letters*, 393.
32. *Letters*, 394.
33. *Letters*, 394.
34. Newman, *An Essay on the Development of Christian Doctrine*, 73. I have not unearthed decisive evidence that Tolkien read *The Development of Doctrine*, but I find it impossible to believe that he was unfamiliar with its basic contentions.
35. Newman, *An Essay on the Development of Christian Doctrine*, 40.
36. *Letters*, 394.
37. *Letters*, 393.
38. *Letters*, 394.

Notes to Chapter 36: Loyalty

1. The Office of the Liturgical Celebrations of the Sovereign Pontiff, "The Use of the Latin Language," https://www.vatican.va The relevant portion of *Sacrosanctum Concilium* reads: "But since the use of the mother tongue, whether in the Mass, the administration of the sacraments, or other parts of the liturgy, frequently may be of great advantage to the people, the limits of its employment may be extended. . . . it is for the competent territorial ecclesiastical authority

mentioned in Art. 22, 2, to decide whether, and to what extent, the vernacular language is to be used" (Article 36).

2. *Letters*, 376; Irene Tolkien Cook, letter to the editor of *Amon Hen*, 24.
3. Owen Barfield, "Foreword," 9.
4. *CLIII*, 476.
5. For more on this and how it relates specifically to Tolkien's Englishness, see my *Tolkien's Modern Reading*, 284–86.
6. George Sayer thought that Tolkien "found little or nothing wrong with the pre-Vatican II Church" but this was his personal impression formed in the context specifically of Tolkien's criticism of the reforms of the 1960s ("Recollections," 24). In that context, Tolkien would naturally focus on the positive aspects of his experience of the Church rather than its faults. As a generalization, it is not backed up by Tolkien's letters.
7. Mark R. Francis, "Church Life in the First Half of the Twentieth Century," in *The Cambridge Companion to Vatican II*, ed. Richard R. Gaillardetz, 12–13.
8. Roger Kynaston, letter to the editor, *Catholic Herald*, August 21, 1936, 6.
9. Ronald Knox, *The Belief of Catholics*, 180–81.
10. *Letters*, 338; 354.
11. *J.R.R.T.: A Film Portrait.*
12. Sayer, "Recollections," 24–25.
13. Lancelot Sheppard, "The Changing Liturgy," *The Tablet*, July 4, 1964, 743.
14. Joanna Tolkien, "Joanna Tolkien speaks," 35 .
15. Simon Tolkien, "My Grandfather J.R.R. Tolkien."
16. Joanna Tolkien, "Joanna Tolkien speaks," 35. She would have been in her early twenties at this time.
17. Simon Tolkien, "My Grandfather J.R.R. Tolkien."
18. *TCG:RG*, 1369.
19. Daniel Helen and Morgan Thomsen, "A recollection of Tolkien: Canon Gerard Hanlon," 41.
20. Clyde Kilby, "Woodland Prisoner," 55
21. Stuart Lee, "Tolkien in Oxford," 149.
22. Tolkien, letter to the editor, *Daily Telegraph*.
23. The 1971 Petition, in Alcuin Reid, ed., *A Bitter Trial: Evelyn Waugh and John Carmel Cardinal Heenan on the Liturgical Changes*, 121.
24. Reid, ed., 121–23.
25. Report on the Golden Jubilee of Corpus Christi, Headington, *Catholic Herald*, June 26, 1987, 8; "About Corpus Christi," Corpus Christi Headington.
26. J.B. O'Connell, "Liturgical Changes from 1964, Roman Rite of Mass," 2–3.
27. Irene Tolkien Cook, letter to the editor, *Amon Hen*, 24.
28. Joanna Tolkien, "Joanna Tolkien speaks," 35.
29. *Letters*, 393.
30. *Biography*, 133.

Notes to Chapter 37: New Friends, New Horizons

1. *TCG:RG*, 489.
2. Canon Mervyn Tower, "History of the Parish."
3. "Solemn Consecration of the Church of St Anthony of Padua," 17.
4. *Biography*, 246.
5. St. Anthony of Padua, Headington Hill, "A Brief History of Our Parish."
6. *TCG:C*, 798.

7. "The Parish of St Anthony of Padua," in "St Anthony of Padua: Solemn Consecration," June 13, 2000, 17; "Mgr Wilfred Doran," obituary, *Oxford Times*, June 21, 1991; St Anthony of Padua, Headington Hill, "A Brief History of Our Parish."
8. *Catholic Herald*, June 1, 1962, 5.
9. Marco di Noia, "Best wishes from Thorin and Company!" 22–23.
10. Verlyn Flieger, afterword to Tolkien, *Smith of Wootton Major*, 76.
11. Richard Conrad, "Sermon for the Funeral of Fr. Bede Bailey OP."
12. Flieger, afterword to Tolkien, *Smith of Wootton Major*, 76.
13. Jessica Woodward, "Notes from the Library: The Tolkien Connection," 6.
14. Newman Association letter to the editor, *The Times*, January 28, 1949.
15. "Valedictory Address," 238.
16. "Valedictory Address," 238.
17. The Congregation of the Mission, https://cmglobal.org/en/the-congregation-of-mission/.
18. Bloomsbury Auctions, *Important Books & Manuscripts, 30 May 2013*, Lot 390.
19. The inscribed volume was the first of four parts of the breviary; it is now owned by Susan Griffith. Personal communication, Haley Stewart and Susan Griffith, June 28 and July 1, 2022.
20. Clyde Kilby, *Tolkien and the Silmarillion*, 59.
21. Łukasz Neubauer, "The 'Polish Inkling,'" 165.
22. *Letters*, 68. Neubauer notes that it is misspelled in the *Letters* as "Poptawski" but should read "Popławski."
23. Zbigniew Pełczyński, "My J.R.R. Tolkien Memories," 12.
24. Neubauer, "The 'Polish Inkling,'" 152.
25. Neubauer, 154–55.
26. Letters of J.R.R. Tolkien to Prof. Przemysław Mroczkowski, transcription by Ryszard Derdziński with the help of Carl F. Hostetter. I am indebted to Ryszard Derdziński for his kind sharing of this material with me.
27. Neubauer, "The 'Polish Inkling,'" 163n64.
28. Letters of J.R.R. Tolkien to Prof. Przemysław Mroczkowski, transcription by Ryszard Derdziński with the help of Carl F. Hostetter.
29. *TCG:C*, 547.
30. Michael Duricy, "Black Madonnas: Our Lady of Czestochowa."
31. "News, Notes & Texts: Poland," *The Tablet*, June 14, 1958, 564.
32. "Church in Poland Begins 4th Year of 'Great Novena,'" *The Catholic Standard and Times*, June 3, 1960, 16.
33. Pawel Szylak, "Our Lady of Częstochowa, Queen of Poland."
34. Introduction to Hilaire Belloc, "The Ballade of Our Lady of Czestochowa," *The Chesterton Review* 32, no. 1/2 (Spring/Summer 2006): 29.
35. *J.R.R. Tolkien: The Art of the Manuscript*, 174.
36. Gregory Macdonald, notes for the provenance of a copy of Tolkien's calligraphic "The Ballade to Our Lady of Czestochowa," Macdonald family heritage site, http://woolleymacdonaldtopping.com/wp-content/uploads/2018/11/Ballade-to-Our-Lady-of-Czestochowa.pdf.
37. Louis Bouyer, *Memoirs*, chapter 12.
38. Michaël Devaux, "Louis Bouyer et J.R.R. Tolkien: une amité d'écrivains," 86.
39. Devaux places their correspondence as beginning by the late 1950s or early 1960s. Hammond and Scull record that Bouyer corresponded with Tolkien in 1966 (Addenda to the *TCG:C*).
40. Devaux, "Louis Bouyer et J.R.R. Tolkien," 87.
41. John Pepino, Preface to Bouyer, *Memoirs*, 7.
42. Addenda to the *TCG:C*.
43. Bouyer, *Memoirs*, 179–80.

44. Louis Bouyer, *Les lieux magiques de la légende du Graal*, quoted in Devaux, "Louis Bouyer et J.R.R. Tolkien," 88 (my translation).
45. Bouyer, *Memoirs*, 168–70.
46. Bouyer, 170.
47. Pepino, Preface to Bouyer, *Memoirs*, 9.
48. Devaux, "Louis Bouyer et J.R.R. Tolkien," 89 (my translation).
49. *OFS*, 79.
50. Louis Bouyer, *Le métier de théologien. Entretiens avec Georges Daix*, in Devaux, "Louis Bouyer et J.R.R. Tolkien," 127 (my translation).
51. Devaux, "Louis Bouyer et J.R.R. Tolkien," 88.
52. Bouyer, *Le métier de théologien*, 126 (my translation).
53. Bouyer, *Memoirs*, 180.

Notes to Chapter 38: "Companions in shipwreck"

1. *J.R.R.T.: A Film Portrait*. Many of the writings he produced on this topic appear in *The Nature of Middle-earth*, ed. Carl F. Hostetter.
2. *TCG:C*, 760.
3. *TCG:RG*, 1297.
4. To be precise, the Bournemouth Oratory in formation. https://www.bournemouthoratory.org.uk.
5. *Letters*, 415.
6. *TCG:C*, 796.
7. William Cater, "We Talked of Love, Death, and Fairy Tales," 23.
8. *Letters*, 420.
9. *Letters*, 416.
10. *Letters*, 49.
11. *Biography*, 48.
12. George Sayer, "Recollections," 14.
13. *Letters*, 52.
14. *Biography*, 75.
15. *Letters*, 51.
16. *Letters*, 62.
17. Ignatius of Loyola, *The Spiritual Exercises of St. Ignatius*, trans. and ed. Louis J. Puhl, in *Ignatian Collection* (Park Ridge, IL: Word on Fire Classics, 2020), 120.
18. *Letters*, 62. The emphasis is in the original.
19. *Letters*, 51.
20. *Letters*, 51.
21. *Letters*, 421.
22. *Letters*, 420.
23. *Letters*, 52.

Notes to Chapter 39: Reuel

1. Charlie Carr, "The Ringmaker in Oxford," part 4. Oxfordshire History Centre Archives.
2. "The Parish of St Anthony of Padua," in "Solemn Consecration of the Church of Saint Anthony of Padua," 17.
3. *Biography*, 260.
4. Michael George Tolkien, "Lecture on J.R.R. Tolkien."

5. "Memorial service," *The Times*, November 19, 1973, 17.
6. All details of the content of the memorial service are from the Order of Service, "John Ronald Reuel Tolkien," Merton College Chapel, November 17, 1973 (Oxford: Oxford University Press). Marquette University Archives, JRRT_S7B1F7.
7. In 1954, Tolkien received an honorary doctorate of literature from the National University of Ireland (as did Ronald Knox on the same occasion) at University College Dublin, which since 1909 had been a component part of the NUI. University College Dublin had its origins in the Catholic University of Ireland, established in 1854, with John Henry Newman as rector until 1857 (National University of Ireland, "Honorary Degrees Awarded," http://www.nui.ie/college/Honorary_Degree_Recipients.asp).
8. Michael George Tolkien, "Lecture on J.R.R. Tolkien."
9. *Biography*, 118.
10. Rayner Unwin, "Tributes to J.R.R. Tolkien," 32.
11. *Letters*, 398.
12. *Letters*, 398; *Abarim Publications Theological Dictionary of the Old Testament*, https://www.abarim-publications.com/Meaning/Reuel.html. Another possible meaning is 'shepherd of God,' but the *Brown-Driver-Briggs Hebrew and English Lexicon of the Old Testament* indicates that 'friend of God' is the most likely etymology.
13. Priscilla Tolkien, "The Letters of J.R.R. Tolkien."
14. The charity was Help the Aged. (Note accompanying desk, July 27, 1972. Marquette Archives, JRRT Series 7, Box 1, Folder 9.) The desk is now at the Wade Center, Wheaton College.
15. *Letters*, 316.
16. *Biography*, 132.
17. *Biography*, 89.
18. See Lord Halsbury, obituary in *The Guardian*, January 31, 2000.
19. *TCG:C*, 812.
20. *Letters*, 115.
21. Priscilla Tolkien, "The Letters of J.R.R. Tolkien."
22. Douglas Gresham, *Lenten Lands*, 152.
23. Penny Radford, "Professor Tolkien Leaves an Unpublished Book," 1.
24. For example, in 1966, Alan Bliss realized to his dismay that it was "impossible" to publish a paper he had written because "nearly all my conclusions had been anticipated" in lectures by Tolkien; he explained the situation to Tolkien, who "wrote to me offering, with characteristic generosity, to hand over to me all his material on the story of Finn and Hengest, to make what use of it I wished" (Preface to *Finn and Hengest* by J.R.R. Tolkien, v). Cf. *TCG:G*, 291, and Douglas Gray, *A Marriage of Mercury and Philology*, 21.
25. *CLIII*, 6.
26. Rayner Unwin, *George Allen & Unwin: A Remembrancer*, 113.
27. Michael George Tolkien, "Lecture on J.R.R. Tolkien."
28. *Letters*, 417.
29. John Lawlor, *C.S. Lewis: Memories and Reflections*, 33–34.
30. John Henry Newman, *The Dream of Gerontius*, 71.
31. *Letters*, 101.
32. *LOTR*, 1030
33. Wisdom 8:8–9, 8:13.
34. *OFS*, 78.

BIBLIOGRAPHY

Works by J.R.R. Tolkien

The Adventures of Tom Bombadil. Edited by Christina Scull and Wayne G. Hammond. London: HarperCollins, 2014.

"*Ae Adar Nín*: The Lord's Prayer in Sindarin." Edited with notes and analysis by Bill Welden. *Vinyar Tengwar* 44 (June 2002): 21–30.

"*Alcar mi Tarmenel na Erun*: The *Gloria in Excelsis Deo* in Quenya." Edited with notes and analysis by Arden R. Smith. *Vinyar Tengwar* 44 (June 2002): 31–38.

The Art of "The Hobbit." Edited by Wayne G. Hammond and Christina Scull. Boston: Houghton Mifflin Harcourt, 2012.

The Art of "The Lord of the Rings." Edited by Wayne G. Hammond and Christina Scull. Boston: Houghton Mifflin Harcourt, 2015.

Beowulf and the Critics. Edited by Michael D.C. Drout. Rev. ed. Tempe, AZ: Arizona Center for Medieval and Renaissance Studies, 2011.

Beowulf: A Translation and Commentary, Together with Sellic Spell. Edited by Christopher Tolkien. Boston: Houghton Mifflin, 2014.

"Beowulf: The Monsters and the Critics." In *The Monsters and the Critics and Other Essays*, 5–48.

"The Book of Jonah" (translation). *Journal of Inklings Studies* 4, no. 2 (October 2014): 5–9.

The Book of Lost Tales, part 1. Vol. 1 of The History of Middle-earth, edited by Christopher Tolkien. London: George Allen & Unwin, 1984.

"English and Welsh." In *The Monsters and the Critics and Other Essays*, 162–98.

Finn and Hengest: The Fragment and the Episode. Edited by Alan Bliss. London: HarperCollins, 2006.

"'Genesis of the story': Tolkien's Note to Clyde Kilby." In *Smith of Wootton Major*, edited by Verlyn Flieger, 85–87.

The History of Middle-earth. Three-volume ed. Edited by Christopher Tolkien. London: HarperCollins, 2017.

The Hobbit. 75th anniversary ed. Boston: Houghton Mifflin, 2007. First published 1937.

"Imram." In *Time and Tide* 36, no. 3 (December 3, 1955): 1561.

J.R.R. Tolkien: Artist and Illustrator. Edited by Wayne G. Hammond and Christina Scull. Boston: Houghton Mifflin, 1995.

"The Last Ship." In *The Adventures of Tom Bombadil*, 109–14.

The Lays of Beleriand. Vol. 3 of The History of Middle-earth, edited by Christopher Tolkien. London: George Allen & Unwin, 1985.

"Leaf by Niggle." In *Tree and Leaf*, 91–118.

Letter to the editor. *Daily Telegraph*, July 4, 1972.

Letters from Father Christmas. Deluxe ed. Edited by Baillie Tolkien. London: HarperCollins, 2019.

The Letters of J.R.R. Tolkien. Edited by Humphrey Carpenter. London: George Allen & Unwin, 1981.

The Lord of the Rings: 50th Anniversary One-Volume Edition. Boston: Houghton Mifflin, 2004.

The Monsters and the Critics and Other Essays. Edited by Christopher Tolkien. London: HarperCollins, 2006.

"Mythopoeia." In *Tree and Leaf*, 83–90.

"The Name Coventry." *Catholic Herald*, February 23, 1945, 2.

The Nature of Middle-earth. Edited by Carl F. Hostetter. Boston: Houghton Mifflin Harcourt, 2021.

"Noel." In *The "Annual" of Our Lady's School, Abingdon*, no. 12, 1936, 4.

Nomenclature of "The Lord of the Rings." In *"The Lord of the Rings": A Reader's Companion*, edited by Wayne G. Hammond and Christina Scull, 750–82.

"The Notion Club Papers." In *Sauron Defeated*. The History of Middle-earth, edited by Christopher Tolkien, 9:145–327. London: George Allen & Unwin, 1996.

"Of Lembas." In *The Peoples of Middle-earth*. The History of Middle-earth, edited by Christopher Tolkien, 12:403–5. London: George Allen & Unwin, 1996.

"On Fairy-stories." In *Tolkien On Fairy-stories*, edited by Verlyn Flieger and Douglas A. Anderson. London: HarperCollins, 2014. First published 1947 in *Essays Presented to Charles Williams*, edited by C.S. Lewis.

"The Qenya Alphabet." Edited with introduction and commentary by Arden R. Smith. In *Parma Eldalamberon* 20. Revised second printing. Mountain View, CA: The Tolkien Trust, 2019.

"Rebus letter," decoded by Carl F. Hostetter. In Denis Bridoux, "Tolkien's Rebus Letter: Decryption and Comments." *Beyond Bree* (November 2020): 1–2, 11–12.

The Silmarillion. 2nd ed. Edited by Christopher Tolkien. London: HarperCollins, 2006.

Sir Gawain and the Green Knight, Pearl, and Sir Orfeo. Edited by Christopher Tolkien. London: HarperCollins, 2020. First published 1975.

Smith of Wootton Major. Extended ed. Edited by Verlyn Flieger. London: HarperCollins, 2005.

Tree and Leaf: Including Mythopoeia. London: HarperCollins, 2001. First published 1964.

"Valedictory Address." In *The Monsters and the Critics and Other Essays*, 224–40.

"'Words of Joy': Five Catholic Prayers in Quenya," part 1. Edited with notes and analysis by Patrick Wynne, Arden R. Smith, and Carl F. Hostetter. *Vinyar Tengwar* 43 (January 2002): 5–38.

"'Words of Joy': Five Catholic Prayers in Quenya," part 2. Edited with notes and analysis by Patrick Wynne, Arden R. Smith, and Carl F. Hostetter. *Vinyar Tengwar* 44 (June 2002): 5–20.

"W.P. Ker Memorial Lecture on *Sir Gawain*." In *Sir Gawain and the Green Knight, Pearl, and Sir Orfeo*, 109–57.

Tolkien, J.R.R., with Donald Swann. *The Road Goes Ever On: A Song Cycle*. 2nd ed. Music by Donald Swann, poems by J.R.R. Tolkien. London: George Allen & Unwin, 1978. First published 1968.

Primary and Secondary Sources on Tolkien and the Inklings

Anderson, Douglas A., ed. *The Annotated Hobbit.* J.R.R. Tolkien. Revised and expanded ed. Boston: Houghton Mifflin, 2002.

———. "Tolkien and the Newman Association." *Tolkien and Fantasy*, November 22, 2011. http://tolkienandfantasy.blogspot.com.

Arduini, Roberto, and Claudio A. Testi, eds. *Tolkien and Philosophy.* Zurich: Walking Tree, 2014.

Barbour, Brian. "Lewis and Cambridge." *Modern Philology* 96, no. 4 (May, 1999): 439–84.

Barfield, Owen. Foreword. *VII (Seven): An Anglo-American Literary Review* 1 (1980): 9.

Bernthal, Craig. *Tolkien's Sacramental Vision: Discerning the Holy in Middle Earth.* Kettering, OH: Second Spring, 2014.

Bide, Peter. "Marrying C.S. Lewis." In *C.S. Lewis and His Circle: Essays and Memoirs from the Oxford C.S. Lewis Society*, edited by Roger White, Judith Wolfe, and Brendan Wolfe, 187–91. Oxford: Oxford University Press, 2015.

Birzer, Bradley J. *J.R.R. Tolkien's Sanctifying Myth: Understanding Middle-earth.* Wilmington, DE: ISI Books, 2003.

———. "Sir Martin Gilbert and the Inklings." *The Imaginative Conservative*, January 21, 2015. https://www.theimaginativeconservative.org.

Blackham, Robert S. *The Roots of Tolkien's Middle Earth.* Stroud, UK: Tempus, 2006.

Bonomelli, Gabriele. "Il monogramma di Tolkien tra storia e letteratura: percorsi evolutivi e ipotesi di utilizzo." *Minas Tirith: Rivista della Società Tolkieniana Italiana* 24 (September 2021).

Bouyer, Louis. *The Memoirs of Louis Bouyer: From Youth and Conversion to Vatican II, the Liturgical Reform, and After.* Translated and with a Preface by John Pepino. Kettering, OH: Angelico, 2015.

Bowen, John. "Bookstand." BBC radio interview with Tolkien. December 12, 1962.

Bratman, David. "Hugo Dyson: Inkling, Teacher, *Bon Vivant.*" *Mythlore* 21, no. 4 (Winter 1997): 19–34.

Bridoux, Denis. "Tolkien's Rebus Letter: Decryption and Comments," including "Rebus letter," decoded by Carl Hostetter. *Beyond Bree* (November 2020): 1–2, 11–12.

Buck, Bradley. "An Inspired Alias? J.R.R. Tolkien's Frodo Baggins 'Underhill' and Fr Gerard Albert Plunket 'Underhill,' O.P. (1744–1814)." *Journal of Inklings Studies* 12, no. 2 (2022): 187–209.

Bunting, Nancy. "Tolkien and the Boy Scouts." In *Lembas Extra 2015: Unexplored Aspects of Tolkien and Arda*, edited by Cécile van Zon and Reneé Vink, 75–87. Soest, NL: Boekscout, 2015.

Bunting, Nancy, and Seamus Hamill-Keays. *The Gallant Edith Bratt: J.R.R. Tolkien's Inspiration*. Zurich: Walking Tree, 2021.

Burns, Maggie. "John Ronald's Schooldays." *Mallorn* 45 (Spring 2008): 27–31.

Caldecott, Stratford. *The Power of the Ring: The Spiritual Vision Behind "The Lord of the Rings" and "The Hobbit."* 2nd ed. New York: Crossroad, 2012.

Carpenter, Humphrey. *The Inklings: C.S. Lewis, J.R.R. Tolkien, Charles Williams, and Their Friends.* London: HarperCollins, 1997. First published 1978.

———. *J.R.R. Tolkien: A Biography.* Boston: Houghton Mifflin, 2000. First published by George Allen & Unwin, 1977.

Carpenter, Humphrey, George Sayer, and Clyde S. Kilby. "A Dialogue." *Minas Tirith Evening-Star* 13, no. 1 (January–February 1984): 20–24.

Castell, Daphne. "The Realms of Tolkien." *New Worlds SF* 50, no. 168 (November 1966): 143–54.

———. "Talking to a Maker of Modern Myths." *The Glasgow Herald*, August 6, 1966.

Cater, William. "The Filial Duty of Christopher Tolkien." *Sunday Times Magazine*, September 25, 1977.

———. "More and More Readers Are Getting the J.R.R. Tolkien Habit." *Los Angeles Times* "Calendar," April 9, 1972, 14.

———. "We Talked of Love, Death, and Fairy Tales." *London Daily Telegraph*, November 29, 2001, 23.

Chabot, Caroline. "Raymond Wilson Chambers (1874–1942)." *Moreana* 24, no. 93 (February 1987): 69–82.

———. "Raymond Wilson Chambers (1874–1942), continued." *Moreana* 24, no. 94 (June 1987): 83–96.

Chambers, R.W. *Thomas More.* Ann Arbor, MI: University of Michigan Press, 1973. First published 1935.

Chance, Jane, ed. *Tolkien and the Invention of Myth: A Reader.* Lexington, KY: The University Press of Kentucky, 2004.

Cilli, Oronzo. *Tolkien's Library: An Annotated Checklist.* 2nd ed., revised and expanded. Edinburgh: Luna, 2023.

Collier, Pieter. "The most expensive Tolkien book in the world." *Tolkien Library,* December 18, 2008. https://www.tolkienlibrary.com.

Collyer, Naomi. "Recollections of Professor J.R.R. Tolkien." *Arda* 5 (1985): 1–3.

Como, James T., ed. *Remembering C.S. Lewis: Recollections of Those Who Knew Him.* 3rd ed. San Francisco: Ignatius, 2005.

Cook, Irene Tolkien. Letter to the editor. *Amon Hen* 162 (March 2000): 24–25.

Coutras, Lisa. *Tolkien's Theology of Beauty: Majesty, Splendor, and Transcendence in Middle-earth.* New York: Palgrave Macmillan, 2016.

Cramer, Zak. "Jewish influences in Middle-earth." *Mallorn* 44 (August 2006): 9–16.

Croft, Janet Brennan, and Leslie A. Donovan, eds. *Perilous and Fair: Women in the Works and Life of J.R.R. Tolkien.* Altadena, CA: Mythopoeic Press, 2015.

Curtis, Anthony. "Remembering Tolkien and Lewis." *British Book News* (June 1977): 429–30.

D'Ardenne, S.T.R.O. "The Man and the Scholar." In *J.R.R. Tolkien: Scholar and Storyteller,* edited by Mary Salu and Robert T. Farrell, 33–37.

Derdziński, Ryszard. "Arthur Tolkien (1857–1896) as a devoted Anglican." *Tolknięty,* May 4, 2018. http://www.tolkniety.blogspot.com.

———. "Mabel Tolkien (Suffield) baptized in . . . 1891!" *Tolknięty,* January 5, 2018. http://www.tolkniety.blogspot.com.

———. "Scout Ronald Tolkien." *Tolknięty,* June 11, 2020. http://www.tolkniety.blogspot.com.

———. "J.R.R. Tolkien's Baptism Act!" *Tolknięty,* April 4, 2017. http://www.tolkniety.blogspot.com.

Derrick, Christopher. *C.S. Lewis and the Church of Rome.* San Francisco: Ignatius, 1981.

Devaux, Michaël. "Louis Bouyer et J.R.R. Tolkien: une amité d'écrivains." *Cahiers d'études tolkiniennes* 2 (2003): 85–146.

Di Noia, Marco. "Best wishes from Thorin and Company!—Following Tolkien's trails in Oxford." *Amon Hen* 212 (2008): 18–23.

Drout, Michael D.C., ed. *J.R.R. Tolkien Encyclopedia: Scholarship and Critical Assessment*. New York: Routledge, 2007.

DuPlessis, Nicole M. "On the Shoulders of Humphrey Carpenter: Reconsidering Biographical Representation and Scholarly Perception of Edith Tolkien." *Mythlore* 37, no. 2 (134) (Spring 2019): 39–74.

Edwards, Raymond. *Tolkien*. London: Robert Hale, 2014.

Ferrández Bru, José Manuel. *"Uncle Curro": J.R.R. Tolkien's Spanish Connection*. Edinburgh: Luna, 2018.

———. "'Wingless fluttering': Some Personal Connections in Tolkien's Formative Years." *Tolkien Studies* 8 (2011): 51–65.

Fimi, Dimitra. *Tolkien, Race and Cultural History: From Fairies to Hobbits*. New York: Palgrave Macmillan, 2009.

Fisher, Jason, ed. *Tolkien and the Study of His Sources: Critical Essays*. Jefferson, NC: McFarland, 2011.

Flieger, Verlyn. "The Footsteps of Ælfwine." In *Tolkien's Legendarium*, edited by Verlyn Flieger and Carl F. Hostetter, 183–98.

Flieger, Verlyn, and Carl F. Hostetter, eds. *Tolkien's Legendarium: Essays on The History of Middle-earth*. Westport, CT: Greenwood, 2000.

Flieger, Verlyn, and Douglas A. Anderson. Introduction, commentary, and notes to *Tolkien On Fairy-stories* by J.R.R. Tolkien. Edited by Verlyn Flieger and Douglas A. Anderson. London: HarperCollins, 2014.

Foster, Mike. "'That Most Unselfish Man': George Sayer, 1914–2005: Pupil, Biographer, and Friend of Inklings." *Mythlore* 26, no. 3/4 (101/102) (Spring/Summer 2008): 5–26.

Freeman, Austin M. *Tolkien Dogmatics: Theology through Mythology with the Maker of Middle-earth*. Bellingham, WA: Lexham, 2022.

Garbowski, Christopher. "Tolkien's Philosophy and Theology of Death." In *Tolkien and Philosophy*, edited by Roberto Arduini and Claudio A. Testi, 125–44.

Garth, John. "'As under a Green Sea': Visions of War in the Dead Marshes." In *The Ring Goes Ever On*, edited by Sarah Wells, 1:9–21.

———. "How J.R.R. Tolkien Came to Write the Stories of 'The Rings of Power.'" *Smithsonian Magazine*, October 2022.

Garth, John. "JRR Tolkien: Academic, Philologist—and Prankster Extraordinaire." *The Telegraph*, August 16, 2022.

———. *Tolkien and the Great War: The Threshold of Middle-earth*. Boston: Houghton Mifflin, 2003.

———. *Tolkien at Exeter College: How an Oxford Undergraduate Created Middle-earth*. Rev. 2nd ed. Oxford: Exeter College, 2022.

———. *The Worlds of J.R.R. Tolkien: The Places that Inspired Middle-earth*. Princeton, NJ: Princeton University Press, 2020.

Gilbert, Martin. "What Tolkien Taught Me About the Battle of the Somme." *FT Magazine*, July 29/30, 2006.

Gilliver, Peter, Jeremy Marshall, and Edmund Weiner. *Ring of Words: Tolkien and the Oxford English Dictionary*. Oxford: Oxford University Press, 2006.

Glyer, Diana. *The Company They Keep: C.S. Lewis and J.R.R. Tolkien as Writers in Community*. Kent, OH: Kent State University Press, 2007.

Gray, Douglas. *A Marriage of Mercury and Philology: An Inaugural Lecture Delivered Before the University of Oxford on 21 May 1981*. Oxford: Clarendon, 1982.

Green, Roger Lanceyln, and Walter Hooper. *C.S. Lewis: A Biography*. Rev. ed. San Diego: Harcourt, Brace, and Co., 1994. First published 1974.

Gresham, Douglas. *Lenten Lands: My Childhood with Joy Davidman and C.S. Lewis*. San Francisco: HarperCollins, 1988.

Grotta, Daniel. *The Biography of J.R.R. Tolkien: Architect of Middle-earth*. Philadelphia: Running Press, 1978.

Gueroult, Denis. "An Interview with J.R.R. Tolkien." *Minas Tirith Evening-Star* 8, no. 2 (1984): 3–7. Partial transcript of interview for BBC radio, "Now Read On."

———. Interview with Tolkien for BBC radio, "Now Read On" (full recording, not aired). The Randolph Hotel, Oxford, January 20, 1964 [1965]. On *Basil Bunting and J.R.R. Tolkien (Author Speaks)*. Cassette tape. Audio-Forum. Guilford, CT: 1980. [Portions of this interview, transcribed, appear in *Minas Tirith Evening-Star* 13, no. 1 (January–Feburary 1984); previously printed in *News from Bree* 13 (November 1974) and *Minas Tirith Evening-Star* 4, no. 3 (June 1975); in these, the interviewer's name is incorrectly given as David Gerrolt.]

Haden, David. *Tree and Star: Tolkien and the Quest for Earendel*. N.p., 2022.

Halsall, Michael John. *Creation and Beauty in Tolkien's Catholic Vision: A Study in the Influence of Neoplatonism in J. R. R. Tolkien's Philosophy of Life as 'Being and Gift'*. Eugene, OR: Pickwick, 2020.

Hammond, Wayne G., ed. *The J.R.R. Tolkien Centenary Conference Souvenir Book*. Williamstown, MA: McClelland Press, 1992.

Hammond, Wayne G., and Christina Scull. *The Lord of the Rings: A Reader's Companion*. Rev. ed. London: HarperCollins, 2014.

Hampson, Martin. *Images of England: Edgbaston*. Stroud, UK: Tempus, 1999.

Havard, Mark ("Colin"). "The Inklings Remembered: A Conversation with Colin Havard," by Justin T. Noetzel and Matthew R. Bardowell. *Mythlore* 31, no. 1/2 (119/120) (Fall/Winter 2012): 26–46.

Havard, Robert (R.E.). "Professor J.R.R. Tolkien: A Personal Memoir." *Mythlore* 17, no. 2 (64) (Winter 1990): 61.

Heck, Joel. *No Ordinary People: 21 Friendships of C.S. Lewis*. Hamden, CT: Winged Lion, 2021.

Helen, Daniel and Morgan Thomsen. "A recollection of Tolkien: Canon Gerard Hanlon." *Mallorn* 54 (Spring 2013): 40–42.

Higgins, Andrew S. *The Genesis of J.R.R. Tolkien's Mythology*. PhD thesis, School of Education, Cardiff Metropolitan University, 2015.

Hooper, Walter. *C.S. Lewis: A Companion and Guide*. London: HarperCollins, 2005.

———. "Tolkien and C.S. Lewis: An Interview with Walter Hooper." In *Tolkien: A Celebration*, edited by Joseph Pearce. 190–98.

Hostetter, Carl F. "Appendix I: Metaphysical and Theological Themes." In *The Nature of Middle-earth* by J.R.R. Tolkien, edited by Carl F. Hostetter, 401–12.

———. "Over Middle-earth Sent Unto Men: On the Philological Origins of Tolkien's Eärendel Myth." *Mythlore* 17, no. 3 (65) (Spring 1991): 5–10.

Jakupcak, Sister Maria Frassati. "'A Particular Cast of Fancy': Addison's Walk with Tolkien and Lewis." *Tolkien Studies* 11 (2014): 45–66.

J.R.R.T: A Film Portrait of J.R.R. Tolkien. [Also called *J.R.R. Tolkien: A Portrait* or *J.R.R. Tolkien: An Authorized Film Portrait*]. Directed by Derek Bailey. Narrated by Judi Dench. Landseer, 1996.

J.R.R. Tolkien: Life and Legend. An Exhibition to Commemorate the Centenary of the Birth of J.R.R. Tolkien (1892–1973). Oxford: Bodleian Library, 1992.

J.R.R. Tolkien: The Art of the Manuscript. Hagerty Museum of Art, Marquette University, 2022.

Kerry, Paul E., ed. *The Ring and the Cross: Christianity and The Lord of the Rings*. Madison, WI: Fairleigh Dickinson University Press, 2011.

Kerry, Paul E., and Sandra Miesel, *Light Beyond All Shadow: Religious Experience in Tolkien's Work*. Madison, WI: Fairleigh Dickinson University Press, 2011.

Kilby, Clyde. "Dr. Clyde S. Kilby Recalls J.R.R. Tolkien and C.S. Lewis, 1980." Interview notes collected by Annette Brown, Michael Foster, and Sue Storts, Wheaton College, October 10, 1980. Wade Center Oral History Archive.

———. "Dr. Clyde S. Kilby Recalls The Inklings." Notes from an interview with Michael Foster, October 10, 1980. Marquette University Department of Special Collections and University Archives.

———. "I'd Like to Have You Come." [Recollections of Tolkien.] *Minas Tirith Evening-Star* 9, no. 2 (January 1980): 17–19.

———. "Many Meetings with Tolkien (transcripts of talks by Dr. C.S. Kilby and Dick Plotz)." *Niekas* 18 (December 1968): 39–40.

———. "Meeting Professor Tolkien." *Christian History* 22, no. 2 (May 2003): 8–9.

———. *Tolkien and the Silmarillion*. Berhamstead, UK: Lion, 1976.

———. "Woodland Prisoner." *VII (Seven): An Anglo-American Literary Review* 27 (2010): 48–60.

King, Don W. *Inkling, Historian, Soldier, and Brother: A Life of Warren Hamilton Lewis*. Kent, OH: Kent State University Press, 2023.

Koslowski, Philip, John Tuttle, and Joseph Tuttle, eds. *Tolkien & Faith: Essays on Christian Truth in Middle-Earth*. Monee, IL: Voyage Comics, 2021.

Lawlor, John. *C.S. Lewis: Memories and Reflections*. Dallas: Spence, 1998.

Lee, Stuart D., ed. *A Companion to J.R.R. Tolkien*. Chichester, West Sussex, UK: John Wiley & Sons, 2014.

———. "A Milestone in BBC History? The 1955–56 Radio Dramatization of *The Lord of the Rings*." In Richard Ovenden and Catherine McIlwaine, *The Great Tales Never End*. 145–165.

———. "'Tolkien in Oxford' (BBC, 1968): A Reconstruction." *Tolkien Studies* 15 (2018): 115–76.

Lewis, C.S. *All My Road Before Me: The Diary of C.S. Lewis 1922–1927*. San Diego: Harvest, 1991.

———. *The Collected Letters of C.S. Lewis*, vol. 1, *Family Letters, 1905–1931*. New York: HarperCollins, 2000.

———. *The Collected Letters of C.S. Lewis*, vol. 2, *Books, Broadcasts, and the War, 1931–1949*. Edited by Walter Hooper. New York: HarperCollins, 2004.

———. *The Collected Letters of C.S. Lewis*, vol. 3, *Narnia, Cambridge, and Joy, 1950–1963*. Edited by Walter Hooper. New York: HarperCollins, 2007.

———. *C.S. Lewis Essay Collection and Other Short Pieces*. Edited by Lesley Walmsley. London: HarperCollins, 2000.

———. *English Literature in the Sixteenth Century, Excluding Drama*. Oxford: Oxford University Press, 1954.

———. *Letters to Malcolm: Chiefly on Prayer*. San Diego: Harcourt, 1964.

———. *Mere Christianity*. New York: HarperCollins, 1952.

———. "Modern Translations of the Bible." In *C.S. Lewis Essay Collection and Other Short Pieces*, 472–75.

———. *Surprised by Joy: The Shape of My Early Life*. Orlando: Harcourt, 1955.

———. "Transposition." In *C.S. Lewis Essay Collection and Other Short Pieces*, 267–78.

Lewis, Warren. *Brothers and Friends: The Diaries of Major Warren Hamilton Lewis*. Edited by Clyde S. Kilby and Marjorie Lamp Mead. San Francisco: Harper & Row, 1982.

———. "Memoir of C.S. Lewis." In *Letters of C.S. Lewis*, edited by W.H. Lewis, 1–26. New York: Harcourt, Brace & World, 1966.

Lindop, Grevel. *Charles Williams: The Third Inkling*. Oxford: Oxford University Press, 2015.

Long, Josh. "Disparaging Narnia: Reconsidering Tolkien's View of *The Lion, the Witch, and the Wardrobe*." *Mythlore* 31, no. 3/4 (121/122) (Spring/Summer 2013): 31–46.

Lovell, Joel. "The Late, Great Stephen Colbert." *GQ*, August 17, 2015. https://www.gq.com.

Mathison, Phil. *Tolkien in East Yorkshire 1917–1918: An Illustrated Tour*. Newport, East Yorkshire: Dead Good Productions, 2012.

McBride, Sam. *Tolkien's Cosmology: Divine Beings and Middle-earth*. Kent, OH: Kent State University Press, 2020.

McIlwaine, Catherine, ed. *Tolkien: Maker of Middle-earth*. Oxford: Bodleian Library, 2018.

McIntosh, Jonathan S. *The Flame Imperishable: Tolkien, St. Thomas, and the Metaphysics of Faërie*. Kettering, OH: Angelico, 2017.

Monda, Andrea, and Wu Ming. "Tolkien the Catholic Philosopher?" In *Tolkien and Philosophy*, edited by Roberto Arduini and Claudio A. Testi, 85–124.

Morton, Andrew H., and John Hayes. *Tolkien's Gedling 1914: The Birth of a Legend*. Warwickshire: Brewin Books, 2008.

Murray, Robert, "Sermon at Thanksgiving Service, Keble College Chapel, 23rd August 1992." *Mythlore* 21, no. 2 (80) (Winter 1996):17–20.

———. "A Tribute to Tolkien." *The Tablet*, September 15, 1973, 879–80.

Neubauer, Łukasz. "The 'Polish Inkling': Professor Przemyslaw Mroczkowski as J.R.R. Tolkien's Friend and Scholar." *Mythlore* 39, no. 1 (137) (Fall/Winter 2020): 149–76.

———, ed. *Middle-earth, or There and Back Again*. Zurich: Walking Tree, 2020.

"Obituary of John Ronald Reuel Tolkien." *The Times*, September 3, 1973.

Ordway, Holly. *Tolkien's Modern Reading: Middle-earth Beyond the Middle Ages*. Park Ridge, IL: Word on Fire Academic, 2021.

Ovenden, Richard, and Catherine McIlwaine, eds. *The Great Tales Never End: Essays in Memory of Christopher Tolkien*. Oxford: Bodleian Library, 2022.

Oxfordshire History Centre Archives. "The Ringmaker in Oxford." Sound recording. OXOHA/MT/677.

Oxford University Dante Society, *Centenary Essays on Dante*. Oxford: Oxford University Press, 1965.

Pearce, Joseph. *C.S. Lewis and the Catholic Church*. Charlotte, NC: Saint Benedict, 2013.

———, ed. *Tolkien: A Celebration: Collected Writings on a Literary Legacy*. San Francisco: Ignatius, 1999.

———. *Tolkien: Man and Myth*. London: HarperCollins, 1998.

Pełczyński, Zbigniew. "My J.R.R. Tolkien Memories." *Simbelmynë* 2, no. 31 (2019): 11–13. http://www.elendilion.pl/wp-content/uploads/2019/01/Sn_31_English.pdf.

Pezzini, Giuseppe. "'A Fundamentally Religious and Catholic Work': Symbolic Veiling and Creative Freedom in Tolkien." Address given at the Oxford C.S. Lewis Society, Oxford, England, May 2, 2022.

Pezzini, Giuseppe. "Tolkien and Newman." Address given at "Tolkien Among the Theologians" symposium, Houston Christian University, Houston, Texas, October 22, 2022.

Plimmer, Charlotte and Denis. "The Man Who Understands Hobbits." *Daily Telegraph Magazine* (London), March 22, 1968, 31–32, 35.

Power, Canon N. (Norman) S. "Recollections." In *The J.R.R. Tolkien Centenary Conference Souvenir Book*, edited by Wayne G. Hammond, 9–10.

———. "Ring of Doom." *The Tablet*, December 20/27, 1975, 1247–48.

Radford, Penny. "Professor Tolkien Leaves an Unpublished Book." *The Times* (London), September 3, 1973, 1.

Rateliff, John D. *The History of The Hobbit*. Revised and expanded one-volume ed. London: HarperCollins, 2013.

———. "The Missing Women: J.R.R. Tolkien's Lifelong Support for Women's Higher Education." In *Perilous and Fair*, edited by Janet Brennan Croft and Leslie A. Donovan, 41–69.

Resnik, Henry. "An Interview with Tolkien." March 2, 1966. *Niekas* 18 (Spring 1967): 37–43.

Rogers, Deborah Webster, and Ivor A. Rogers, *J.R.R. Tolkien*. Boston: Twayne, 1980.

Ryken, Philip. *The Messiah Comes to Middle-earth: Images of Christ's Threefold Office in The Lord of the Rings*. Downers Grove, IL: IVP Academic, 2017.

Salu, Mary, and Robert T. Farrell, eds. *J.R.R. Tolkien: Scholar and Storyteller. Essays in Memoriam*. Ithaca, NY: Cornell University Press, 1979.

Santamaria, Abigail. *Joy: Poet, Seeker, and the Woman Who Captivated C.S. Lewis*. Boston: Houghton Mifflin Harcourt, 2015.

Sayer, George. *Jack: A Life of C.S. Lewis*. 2nd ed. Wheaton, IL: Crossway Books, 1994.

———. "Recollections of J.R.R. Tolkien." In *Tolkien: A Celebration*, edited by Joseph Pearce, 1–16.

Schofield, Stephen, ed. *In Search of C.S. Lewis*. South Plainfield, NJ: Bridge, 1983.

Schweicher, Eric. *J.R.R. Tolkien: The Lyf So Short, the Craft So Long to Lerne*. Liège: University of Liège, 1992. Exhibition Catalogue.

Scott, Nan C.L. "A Visit with Tolkien." *The Living Church*, February 5, 1978, 11–12.

Scull, Christina, and Wayne G. Hammond. *Addenda & Corrigenda for The J.R.R. Tolkien Companion and Guide*. Revised and expanded ed. http://www.hammondandscull.com/addenda/chronology2.html.

———. Introduction and commentary on *The Adventures of Tom Bombadil* by J.R.R. Tolkien.

———. *The J.R.R. Tolkien Companion and Guide: Chronology*. Revised and expanded ed. Boston: Houghton Mifflin, 2017.

———. *The J.R.R. Tolkien Companion and Guide: Reader's Guide*. Revised and expanded ed. Boston: Houghton Mifflin, 2017.

Shippey, Tom. *J.R.R. Tolkien: Author of the Century*. Boston: Houghton Mifflin, 2000.

Smith, Peter. *C.S. Lewis, J.R.R. Tolkien & George Sayer in Malvern: A Memoir*. Malvern, Worcestershire: Aspect Design, 2022.

Tabb, David. "Bloemfontein: On the trail of Tolkien." *Picking up the Tabb*, August 13, 2017. https://pickingupthetabb.wordpress.com.

Testi, Claudio A. *Pagan Saints in Middle-earth*. Zurich: Walking Tree, 2018.

Thompson, L.L.H. "Report on J.R.R. Tolkien's Paper on Catholic Poet Francis Thompson (4 March 1914)." In Andrew S. Higgins, *The Genesis of J.R.R. Tolkien's Mythology*, appendix 5, 288–90.

Tolkien, Hilary. *Black & White Ogre Country: The Lost Tales of Hilary Tolkien*. Edited by Angela Gardner. Moreton-in-Marsh, UK: ADC, 2009.

Tolkien, Joan. "Origins of a Tolkien tale." Letter to *The Sunday Times*, October 10, 1982, 25.

Tolkien, Joanna. "Joanna Tolkien speaks at the Tolkien Society Annual Dinner, Shrewsbury, April 16, 1994." In *Digging Potatoes, Growing Trees*, vol. 2, edited by Helen Armstrong, 31–36. Telford, UK: The Tolkien Society, 1998.

Tolkien, John. "Reminiscences of Tolkien and Lewis." Talk given at the Oxford C.S. Lewis Society, February 23, 1988.

Tolkien, John, and Priscilla Tolkien. *The Tolkien Family Album*. London: HarperCollins, 1992.

Tolkien, Julian. "Related to Tolkien." Interview by Sandra Carter. *This Is Local London*, December 14, 2001. https://www.thisislocallondon.co.uk.

Tolkien, Michael George. "Autobiographical Essay on My Grandfather, J.R.R. Tolkien." http://www.michaeltolkien.com.

Tolkien, Michael George. "Lecture on J.R.R. Tolkien Given to the University of St Andrews Science Fiction and Fantasy Society, 2nd May, 1989." http://www.michaeltolkien.com.

Tolkien, Michael (Hilary). "An Interview with Michael Hilary Reuel Tolkien." Transcribed by Gary Hunnewell with help from Sylvia Hunnewell from a radio program, "Radio Blackburn." Interviewer Derek Mills. *Minas Tirith Evening-Star* 18, no. 1 (Spring, 1989): 5–9. Joint issue with *Ravenhill.*

———. "The Wizard Father." *Mythprint* 11 no. 1 (January 1975): 3-4. First published in *Sunday Telegraph*, September 7, 1973.

Tolkien, Priscilla. "An Evening with P. Tolkien" by Anne Etkin. *Minas Tirith Evening-Star* 13, no. 1 (1984): 25–27.

———. "J.R.R. Tolkien and Edith Tolkien's Stay in Staffordshire 1916, 1917 and 1918." *Angerthas in English* 3 (July 1997): 5–7.

———. "The Letters of J.R.R. Tolkien." Talk given to the Oxford C.S. Lewis Society, April 30, 1991.

———. "Memories of J.R.R. Tolkien in his Centenary Year." *The Brown Book*, Lady Margaret Hall, Oxford, December 1992, 12–14.

———. "A Personal Memory." In *The Great Tales Never End*, edited by Richard Ovenden and Catherine McIlwaine,46–52.

———. "Religion and Morality in Tolkien." Talk given to the Oxford University C.S. Lewis Society, May 20, 1986.

———. "Talk Given at the Church House Westminster on 16.9.77." *Amon Hen* 29 (1977): 4–7.

Tolkien, Simon. "My Grandfather J.R.R. Tolkien." First published by *The Mail On Sunday*, 2003. http://simontolkien.com/mygrandfather.

———. "Remarks by Simon Tolkien for the Marquette University exhibition *J.R.R. Tolkien: The Art of the Manuscript*." Marquette University Haggerty Museum of Art. August 11, 2022. https://www.marquette.edu/haggerty-museum/tolkien.php.

Tracey, Gerard. "Tolkien and the Oratory." *The Oratory, Birmingham*. Archived version. December 24, 2011.

Unwin, Rayner. *George Allen & Unwin: A Remembrancer.* Privately printed for the Author by Merlin Unwin Books. Ludlow: Merlin Unwin Books, 1999.

Unwin, Rayner. "Tributes to J.R.R. Tolkien." Special J.R.R. Tolkien Centenary Issue. *Mythlore* 18, no. 3 (69) (Summer 1992): 32.

Vink, Renée. "'Jewish' Dwarves: Tolkien and Anti-Semitic Stereotyping." *Tolkien Studies* 10 (2013): 123–45.

Wain, John. *Sprightly Running* (London: Macmillan, 1962).

Ward, Michael. "Peak Middle-earth: Why Mount Doom is not the Climax of *The Lord of the Rings*." *An Unexpected Journal* 4, no. 4 (Advent 2021): 39–86.

———. *Planet Narnia: The Seven Heavens in the Imagination of C.S. Lewis*. Oxford: Oxford University Press, 2008.

———. "A Thief in the Night: The Christian Ethic at the Heart of *The Hobbit*." *Christian Research Journal* 35. no. 6 (2012): 26–36.

Wells, Sarah, ed. *The Ring Goes Ever On: Proceedings of the Tolkien 2005 Conference: 50 Years of "The Lord of the Rings."* 2 vols. Coventry, UK: The Tolkien Society, 2008.

West, Richard. "A Letter from Father Murray." *Tolkien Studies* 16 (2019): 133–39.

Wilson, A.N. *Confessions: A Life of Failed Promises*. London: Bloomsbury, 2022.

———. *C.S. Lewis: A Biography*. London: Collins, 1990.

Wolfe, Brendan. "Tolkien's Jonah." *Journal of Inklings Studies* 4, no. 2 (October 2014): 11–26.

Wood, Jonathan. "Wilfred Rowland Mary Childe." *Wormwood: Literature of the Fantastic, Supernatural and Decadent* 15 (Autumn 2010): 11–34.

Wood, Ralph C. *The Gospel According to Tolkien: Visions of the Kingdom in Middle-earth*. Louisville, KY: Westminster John Knox, 2003.

Woodward, Jessica. "Notes from the Library: The Tolkien Connection." *Pusey House Journal*, Michaelmas 2020: 6.

Zaleski, Philip, and Carol Zaleski. *The Fellowship: The Literary Lives of the Inklings: J.R.R. Tolkien, C.S. Lewis, Owen Barfield, Charles Williams*. New York: Farrar, Straus and Giroux, 2015.

Historical, Cultural, and Ecclesiological Context

Adams, Pauline. *English Catholic Converts and the Oxford Movement in Mid 19th Century Britain: The Cost of Conversion*. Bethesda, MD: Academica, 2010.

Ainslie, John. "English Liturgical Music before Vatican II." In *English Catholic Worship: Liturgical Renewal in England since 1900*, edited by J.D. Crichton, H.E. Winstone, and J.R. Ainslie, 47–59.

The Army and Religion: An Enquiry and Its Bearing upon the Religious Life of the Nation. London: Macmillan, 1919.

Atenstaedt, R.L. "Trench fever: the British medical response in the Great War." *Journal of the Royal Society of Medicine* 99, no. 11 (2006): 564–68.

Austin, M.S. "Sisters of Mercy." In *The Catholic Encyclopedia*, vol. 10 (1911). http://www.newadvent.org/cathen/10199a.htm.

Baden-Powell, Robert. *Scouting for Boys: A Handbook for Instruction in Good Citizenship; the Original 1909 Edition*. Edited with an Introduction and Notes by Elleke Boehmer. Oxford: Oxford University Press, 2004.

Bailey, Cyril. *Francis Fortescue Urquhart: A Memoir*. London: Macmillan, 1936.

Battersby, W.J. "Secondary Education for Boys." In *The English Catholics*, edited by George Andrew Beck, 322–36.

Beck, George Andrew, ed. *The English Catholics, 1850–1950: Essays to Commemorate the Centenary of the Restoration of the Hierarchy of England and Wales*. London: Burns & Oates, 1950.

Bertram, Jerome. *Newman and the Oxford Oratory*. Oxford: Lulu, 2012.

———. *St Aloysius' Parish: The Third English Oratory: A Brief History and Guide, 1793–2000*. New ed. Oxford: Oxuniprint, 2000.

———. *St Philip Neri and the Oratory*. Oxford: The Oxford Oratory, 2015.

Birmingham Oratory. "Fathers and Brothers." https://www.birminghamoratory.org.uk/fathers-and-brothers/.

Bischoff, D. Anthony. *St. Aloysius: The First Eighty Years, 1875–1955*. Oxford: Oxford University Press, 1955.

Boland, Eileen. *Stories of the Great War*, comprising *Stories of the War* and *More Stories of the War*. London: Catholic Truth Society, 2017. First published 1915.

Bouyer, Louis. *Newman: His Life and Spirituality.* Translated by J. Lewis May. San Francisco: Ignatius, 2011. First published in 1952 as *Newman: Sa vie, sa spiritualité.*

———. *St. Philip Neri: A Portrait.* Herefordshire, UK: Gracewing, 1995. First published 1958.

Brown, Francis, Samuel Rolles Driver, and Charles Augustus Briggs. *The Brown-Driver-Briggs Hebrew and English Lexicon of the Old Testament.* Peabody, MA: Hendrickson Academic, 1994.

Bruce, Steve. *No Pope of Rome: Anti-Catholicism in Modern Scotland.* Edinburgh: Mainstream, 1985.

Burton, Edwin, Edward D'Alton, and Jarvis Kelley. "Penal Laws." In *The Catholic Encyclopedia*, vol. 11 (1911). http://www.newadvent.org/cathen/11611c.htm.

Campion Hall, Oxford. "A Short History of Campion Hall." https://www.campion.ox.ac.uk/history-campion-hall.

A Catechism of Christian Doctrine: Approved by Cardinal Vaughan and the Bishops of England. London: Catholic Truth Society, 1900.

Catenian Association: Oxford Circle. "Short History of the Oxford Circle." https://www.oxfordshire-catenians.uk/the-catenians/.

The Catholic Directory, Almanac and Clergy List for the Year of Our Lord 1900: Containing Complete Reports of all Dioceses in the United States, Canada and Newfoundland, Great Britain and Ireland. Vol. 15. No. 1. Milwaukee, WI: M.H. Wiltzius, 1900.

The Catholic Directory, Almanac and Clergy List for the Year of Our Lord 1905: Containing Complete Reports of all Dioceses in the United States, Canada and Newfoundland, Great Britain and Ireland. Vol. 19. No. 1. Milwaukee, WI: M.H. Wiltzius, 1905.

Catholic Emancipation 1829–1929: Essays by Various Writers. Essay Index Reprint Series. Freeport, NY: Books for Libraries, 1966. First published 1929.

The Catholic Encyclopedia. New York: Robert Appleton, 1911–12. https://www.newadvent.org/cathen/.

The Catholic Encyclopedia and Its Makers. New York: Encyclopedia Press, 1917. https://www.archive.org.

The Catholic's Vade Mecum: A Select Manual of Prayers for Daily Use. London: Burns & Lambert, 1851.

Chadwick, Owen. *The Victorian Church*, part 2, *1860–1901.* London: SCM, 1987.

Challoner, Richard. *The Catholic Christian Instructed.* Derby, UK: Richardson & Son, 1843.

———. *The Garden of the Soul: A Manual of Spiritual Exercises.* London: Washbourne, 1872.

Chavasse, Paul. *The Birmingham Oratory Church: A History and Guide.* Birmingham: Clarkeprint, n.d.

A Collection of Hymns in Use at the Oratory of St. Philip Neri, at Birmingham. Birmingham: Lander, Powell, 1850.

Conrad, Richard. "Sermon for the Funeral of Fr Bede Bailey OP, 19th August 2014." *Godzdogz: The Blog of the Dominican Friars of Scotland, England & Wales.* https://www.english.op.org.

Corpus Christi, Headington. "About Corpus Christi." https://www.corpuschristiheadington.co.uk/about-corpus-christi/.

———. "The Stations of the Cross." https://www.corpuschristiheadington.co.uk/the-stations-of-the-cross/.

Courtship for Girls: And Practical Instructions for Those About to be Married. In *Courtship: Some Practical Advice*, by Hubert McEvoy, Tony Kirwin, and Malcolm Brennan. London: Catholic Truth Society, 2017. First published 1936.

Crichton, J.D. "1920–1940: The Dawn of a Liturgical Movement." In *English Catholic Worship: Liturgical Renewal in England since 1900*, edited by J.D. Crichton, H.E. Winstone, and J.R. Ainslie, 17–46.

Crichton, J.D., H.E. Winstone, and J.R. Ainslie, eds. *English Catholic Worship: Liturgical Renewal in England since 1900.* London: Geoffrey Chapman, 1979.

Crowther, Anne. "The Jerusalem Bible and the role of the Newman Association." *The Newman Association*, June 6, 2013. https://www.newman.org.uk.

Curl, James Stephen. *The Erosion of Oxford.* Oxford: Oxford Illustrated Press, 1977.

D'Arcy, Martin. *Laughter and the Love of Friends: Reminiscences of the Distinguished Priest and Philosopher Martin Cyril D'Arcy, S.J.* Edited by William S. Abell. Westminster, MD: Christian Classics, 1991.

———. *The Problem of Evil.* London: Catholic Truth Society, 2017. First published 1929.

Dargue, William. *A History of Birmingham Places and Placenames from A to Y.* 2008–12. billdargue.jimdofree.com.

Dawson, C.B. *The Mirror of Oxford.* London: Sands & Co., 1912.

Delaney, Joseph. "Sloth." In *The Catholic Encyclopedia*, vol. 14 (1912). http://www.newadvent.org/cathen/14057c.htm.

DiPippo, Gregory. "Compendium of the 1955 Holy Week Revisions of Pius XII: Part 5–Tenebrae and the Divine Office of the Triduum." *New Liturgical Movement*, April 7, 2009. https://www.newliturgicalmovement.org.

———. "Compendium of the 1955 Holy Week Revisions of Pius XII: Part 8–The Hours of the Celebration of the Holy Week Liturgies." *New Liturgical Movement*, May 3, 2009. https://www.newliturgicalmovement.org.

The Douay Bible. Translated from the Latin Vulgate. London: Catholic Truth Society, 1955.

Drumm, Walter. *The Old Palace: A History of the Oxford University Catholic Chaplaincy*. Dublin: Veritas, 1991.

Duffy, Eamon. *A People's Tragedy: Studies in Reformation*. London: Bloomsbury Continuum, 2020.

———. *The Stripping of the Altars: Traditional Religion in England, 1400–1580*. New ed. New Haven, CT: Yale University Press, 2022.

Duricy, Michael. "Black Madonnas: Our Lady of Czestochowa." University of Dayton International Marian Research Institute. https://www.udayton.edu.

Eaton, Robert. *A Book of Oratorios*. London: Catholic Truth Society, 1902.

———. *The Divine Refreshment*. London: Sands & Co., 1927.

Ensor, R.C.K. *England: 1870–1914*. Oxford: Oxford University Press, 1936.

Evennett, H.O. "Catholics and the Universities." In *The English Catholics*, edited by George Andrew Beck, 291–21.

Exeter College. "History of the Chapel." https://www.exeter.ox.ac.uk/about/chapel/history/.

Faber, F.W., ed. *If God Be With Us: The Maxims of St Philip Neri*. Leominster, UK: Gracewing, 1994.

———, ed. *The School of St. Philip Neri*. Translated by F.W. Faber. London: Burns & Lambert, 1850.

Finnigan, Robert E., and George T. Bradley, eds. *Catholicism in Leeds: A Community of Faith, 1794–1994*. Leeds, UK: Leeds Diocesan Archives, 1994.

Fitzalan, Viscount. "Catholics in Public Life." In *Catholic Emancipation 1829–1929: Essays by Various Writers*, 141–58.

Fortescue, Adrian. *The Ceremonies of the Roman Rite Described.* London: Burnes, Oates, & Washbourne: 1917.

Francis, Mark R. "Church Life in the First Half of the Twentieth Century." In *The Cambridge Companion to Vatican II,* edited by Richard R. Gaillardetz, 3–18.

Fussell, Paul. *The Great War and Modern Memory.* Oxford: Oxford University Press. First published 1975. 2nd ed. with a new afterword, 2013.

Gaillardetz, Richard R., ed. *The Cambridge Companion to Vatican II.* Cambridge: Cambridge University Press, 2020.

Gallagher, Tom. *Edinburgh Divided: John Cormack and No Popery in the 1930s.* Edinburgh: Polygon, 1987.

Gallonio, Antonio. *The Life of Saint Philip Neri.* Translated by Jerome Bertram of the Oxford Oratory. Oxford: Family Publications, 2005.

Gard, Robin. "Catholic Lay Societies in England and Wales, 1870–1970: A Preliminary List." *Catholic Archives: The Journal of the Catholic Archives Society* 10 (1990): 48–57.

Gerard, John, and Edward D'Alton, "Roman Catholic Relief Bill." In *The Catholic Encyclopedia*, vol. 13 (1912). http://www.newadvent.org/cathen/13123a.htm.

Gilbert, John. "The Catholic Church and Education." In *Catholic Emancipation 1829–1929: Essays by Various Writers*, 45–76.

Gilley, Sheridan. "The Years of Equipoise, 1892–1943." In *From Without the Flaminian Gate: 150 Years of Roman Catholicism in England and Wales 1850–2000*, edited by V. Alan McClelland and Michael Hodgetts, 21–61.

Goodier, Alban. *Sermon Preached at the Opening of the Priory of the Holy Ghost, Blackfriars, Oxford.* May 21, 1929. Oxford: Basil Blackwell, 1929.

Graves, Robert. *Goodbye to All That.* London: Penguin Classics, 2000. First published 1929.

Green, V.H.H. *Religion at Oxford and Cambridge.* London: SCM, 1964.

Griffin, Penny, ed. *St Hugh's: One Hundred Years of Women's Education in Oxford.* Basingstoke, UK: Macmillan, 1986.

Grimond, Jo. Entry in *My Oxford*, edited by Ann Thwaite. London: Robson Books, 1977. 111–24.

Hagerty, James. *The Catenian Association: A Centenary History.* Dalton Mills, UK: Catenian Association, 2007.

Hagerty, James. *Priests in Uniform: Catholic Chaplains to the British Forces in the First World War*. Leominster, UK: Gracewing, 2017.

Harrison, Brian, ed. *The History of the University of Oxford*. Vol. 8, *The Twentieth Century*. Oxford: Clarendon, 1994.

Heimann, Mary. *Catholic Devotion in Victorian England*. Oxford: Clarendon, 1995.

Historic England, "19th- and 20th-Century Roman Catholic Churches: Introductions to Heritage Assets." September 29, 2017. https://www.historicengland.org.uk.

Hodgetts, Michael. "The Iron Form: Catholics and Philosophy Between the Councils." In *From Without the Flaminian Gate: 150 Years of Roman Catholicism in England and Wales 1850–2000*, edited by V. Alan McClelland and Michael Hodgetts, 84–107.

Hollis, Crispian. *Catholic Oxford*. London: Catholic Truth Society, 1974.

Hunter-Blair, Oswald. "University of Oxford." In *The Catholic Encyclopedia*, vol. 11 (1911). http://www.newadvent.org/cathen/11365c.htm.

Jacob, Dominic. "Blessed John Henry Newman the Musician." In the Oxford Oratory, *The Legacy of St Philip*, 87–103.

Jelf, Katherine [Mrs. George Edward Jelf] *George Edward Jelf: A Memoir by his Wife*. London: Skeffington & Son, 1909.

The Jerusalem Bible. Edited by Alexander Jones. London: Darton, Longman, and Todd, 1966.

Kenny, Anthony. *A Path from Rome: An Autobiography*. Oxford: Oxford University Press, 1986.

Ker, Ian. *John Henry Newman*. Oxford: Oxford University Press, 1988. Rev. ed. 2019.

Kiernan, R.H. *The Story of the Archdiocese of Birmingham*. Birmingham, UK: S.J. Wones, 1951.

Knox, Ronald. *The Belief of Catholics*. London: Ernest Benn, 1927.

———, trans. *The Holy Bible: A Translation from the Latin Vulgate in the Light of the Hebrew and Greek originals*. London: Burns and Oates, 1959.

Lane, Peter. *The Catenian Association 1908–1983: A Microcosm of the Development of the Catholic Middle Class*. London: Catenian Association, 1982.

Levering, Matthew, ed. *The Word on Fire Vatican II Collection*. Park Ridge, IL: Word on Fire Institute, 2021.

———, ed. *The Word on Fire Vatican II Collection: Declarations and Decrees*. Park Ridge, IL: Word on Fire Institute, 2023.

Little, Bryan. *Catholic Churches Since 1623: A Study of Roman Catholic Churches in England and Wales from Penal Times to the Present Decade*. London: Robert Hale, 1966.

Madeleva, Sister M. *My First Seventy Years*. New York: Macmillan, 1959.

Malpass, Robert. *Exeter College Oxford: Roll of Honour, 1914–1919*. 2009.

Manchester, William. *The Last Lion*. Vol. 1, *Winston Spencer Churchill: Visions of Glory, 1874–1932*. New York: Bantam, 1983.

———. *The Last Lion*. Vol. 2, *Winston Spencer Churchill: Alone, 1932–1940*. New York: Bantam, 1988.

Marthaler, Berard L. *The Catechism Yesterday and Today: The Evolution of a Genre*. Collegeville, MN: Liturgical Press, 1995.

Martindale, C.C. *Catholics in Oxford*. Oxford: Basil Blackwell, 1925.

Mathew, David. *Catholicism in England. The Portrait of a Minority: Its Culture and Tradition*. London: Eyre & Spottiswoode, 1955.

McClelland, Vincent Alan. *English Roman Catholics and Higher Education 1830–1903*. Oxford: Oxford University Press, 1973.

McClelland, V. Alan, and Michael Hodgetts, eds. *From Without the Flaminian Gate: 150 Years of Roman Catholicism in England and Wales 1850–2000*. London: Darton, Longman, and Todd, 1999.

McNicholas, John. "Quam singulari." In *The Catholic Encyclopedia*, vol. 12 (1911). http://www.newadvent.org/cathen/12590b.htm.

Milford, L.S., ed. *Haileybury Register, 1862–1891*. 2nd ed. Hertford, UK: Stephen Austin & Sons, 1891.

Neill, Stephen. *Anglicanism*. New York: Oxford University Press, 1958.

Newbold, John. "History." St. Peter's Catholic Church, Bromsgrove. https://www.stpetersbromsgrove.co.uk/history.html.

Newman, John Henry. *The Dream of Gerontius*. Oxford: Family Publications, 2001.

———. *An Essay on the Development of Christian Doctrine*. London: Longmans, Green, 1909.

———. *The Letters and Diaries of John Henry Newman*. Vol. 28, *Fellow of Trinity, January 1876–1878*, edited by Charles Stephen Dessain and Thomas Gornall. Oxford: Clarendon, 1975.

Newman, John Henry. *The Letters and Diaries of John Henry Newman*. Vol. 29, *The Cardinalate, January 1879 to September 1881*, edited by Charles Stephen Dessain and Thomas Gornall. Oxford: Clarendon, 1976.

———. *The Letters and Diaries of John Henry Newman*. Vol. 30, *A Cardinal's Apostolate, October 1881 to December 1884*, edited by Charles Stephen Dessain and Thomas Gornall. Oxford: Clarendon, 1976.

———. *Stations of the Cross: Meditations and Devotions,* part 2. London: Longmans, Green, 1908.

The New Testament: In the Westminster Version of the Sacred Scriptures. Translated by Cuthbert Lattey. New York: Longmans, Green, 1948.

Nicholls, Guy. *Unearthly Beauty: The Aesthetic of St John Henry Newman*. Leominster, UK: Gracewing, 2019.

Norman, Edward. *The English Catholic Church in the Nineteenth Century*. Oxford: Oxford University Press, 1984.

O'Connell, J.B. *The Celebration of Mass: A Study of the Rubrics of the Roman Missal*. 4th ed. Milwaukee, WI: Bruce, 1964.

———. "Liturgical Changes from 1964, Roman Rite of Mass." Supplement to *The Celebration of Mass* (1964) by J.B. O'Connell.

The Official Catholic Directory, 1925. New York: P.J. Kenedy & Sons, 1925.

The Official Catholic Directory, 1938. New York: P.J. Kenedy & Sons, 1938.

The Official Catholic Directory, 1939. New York: P.J. Kenedy & Sons, 1939.

The Official Catholic Directory, 1940. New York: P.J. Kenedy & Sons, 1940.

The Order and Canon of the Mass in Latin and English. With a historical introduction by the Right Reverend the Lord Abbot of Farnborough Abbey. London: Burns, Oates and Washbourne, 1916.

O.S. Lives: Obituaries from The Oratory School Magazine, 1962–1992. Exeter, Devon: The Oratory School Society, 1999.

Owen, John. "A Parish Priest: Hinksey Catholic Churches." *Oxford Mail*, December 3, 1965.

Oxford English Dictionary. Online edition. Oxford University Press. https://www.oed.com.

Oxford Oratory. "Corpus Christi Processions from the Archive." June 22, 2022. https://www.youtube.com/watch?v=Q5TDK2QyEw0.

Oxford Oratory. *The Legacy of St Philip*. Oxford: The Oratory, 2016.

Paul VI. *Ecclesiam Suam*. Encyclical letter. August 6, 1964. https://www. vatican.va.

———. *Missale Romanum*. April 3, 1969. https://www.papalencyclicals.net.

Penrith, Mary Caroline. "A Historical and Critical Account of the Teaching of English Language and Literature in English-medium Universities in South Africa, with Particular Reference to the University of Cape Town and the South African College." Thesis presented for the degree of Master of Arts in the University of Cape Town, 1972. https://www.open.uct.ac.za/bitstream/handle/11427/15807/thesis_hum_1972_penrith_mary_caroline.pdf.

Periero, James. "'Who are the laity?'" In *From Without the Flaminian Gate: 150 Years of Roman Catholicism in England and Wales 1850–2000*, edited by V. Alan McClelland and Michael Hodgetts, 167–91.

Pius IX. *Ineffabilis Deus*. Apostolic constitution. December 8, 1854. https://www.papalencyclicals.net.

———. *Singulari Quadam Perfusi*. Allocution. December 9, 1854. https://catholicheritage.blogspot.com/2013/12/the-immaculate-conception-iv-singulari.html.

Pius X. *Quam Singulari*. Decree. 1910. https://www.papalencyclicals.net.

———. "*Sacra Tridentina*: On Frequent and Daily Reception of Holy Communion." December 20, 1905. In Juan B. Ferreres, *The Decree on Daily Communion: A Historical Sketch and Commentary*, trans. H. Jimenez, 24–33. London: Sands & Co., 1910.

Pius XII. *Divino Afflante Spiritu*. Encyclical letter. September 30, 1943. https://www.papalencyclicals.net.

Plater, Charles, ed. *Catholic Soldiers: By Sixty Chaplains and Many Others*. London: Longmans, Green, 1919.

Pusey House, Oxford. "What is Pusey House?" http://www.puseyhouse.org.uk/what-is-pusey-house.html.

Quash, Ben, and Michael Ward, eds. *Heresies and How to Avoid Them: Why It Matters What Christians Believe*. London: SPCK, 2007.

Reid, Alcuin, ed. *A Bitter Trial: Evelyn Waugh and John Carmel Cardinal Heenan on the Liturgical Changes*. Expanded ed. San Francisco: Ignatius, 2011.

———. *The Organic Development of the Liturgy*. San Francisco: Ignatius, 2005.

Reynolds, E.E. *The Roman Catholic Church in England and Wales: A Short History.* Hertfordshire: Anthony Clarke Books, 1973.

Richards, Michael. "Prelude: 1890s to 1920." In *English Catholic Worship: Liturgical Renewal in England since 1900*, edited by J.D. Crichton, H.E. Winstone, and J.R. Ainslie, 1–15.

Rickaby, Joseph. *Oxford and Cambridge Conferences, 1897–1899*. London: Burns & Oates, 1899.

Robinson, Jonathan of the Oratory. *In No Strange Land: The Embodied Mysticism of Saint Philip Neri*. Kettering, OH: Angelico, 2015.

The Roman Missal. 9th ed. London: 1935.

The Roman Missal Adapted to the Use of the Laity from the Missale Romanum. 21st ed. W.E. Blake & Sons, 1913.

Ryder, Henry Ignatius Dudley. *Essays*. Edited by Francis Bacchus of the Oratory, Birmingham. London: Longmans, Green, 1911.

———. *Sermons and Notes of Sermons*. London: Sands & Co., 1920.

Savonarola, Jerome. *The Lord's Prayer and the Angelical Salutation*. London: Catholic Truth Society, 1899.

Saward, John, John Morrill, and Michael Tomko, eds. *Firmly I Believe and Truly: The Spiritual Tradition of Catholic England, 1483–1999*. Oxford: Oxford University Press, 2011.

Second Vatican Council. *Nostra Aetate* (Declaration on the Relation of the Church to Non-Christian Religions). October 28, 1965. In *The Word on Fire Vatican II Collection: Declarations and Decrees*, edited by Matthew Levering, 43–58.

———. *Sacrosanctum Concilium* (Constitution on the Sacred Liturgy). December 4, 1963. In *The Word on Fire Vatican II Collection*, edited by Matthew Levering, 155–209.

———. *Unitatis Redintegratio* (Decree on Ecumenism). November 21, 1964. In *The Word on Fire Vatican II Collection: Declarations and Decrees*, edited by Matthew Levering, 133–67.

Shepherd, Margaret. "King's Heath in the 20th and 21st Centuries." *History of King's Heath*, King's Heath Local History Society. http://www.kingsheathhistory.co.uk/history4.htm.

Short, Edward. *Newman and His Family*. London: Bloomsbury, 2013.

Shrimpton, Paul. *A Catholic Eton? Newman's Oratory School.* Herefordshire, UK: Gracewing, 2005.

Sire, H.J.A. *Father Martin D'Arcy: Philosopher of Christian Love.* Herefordshire, UK: Gracewing, 1997.

"Solemn Consecration of the Church of St Anthony of Padua, Headley Way, Oxford." June 13, 2000. Oxford: De La Salle, 2000.

St. Anne's Catholic Church. "Parish History." http://www.stannesbirmingham.com/parish-history.html.

St. Anthony of Padua, Headington Hill. "A Brief History of Our Parish." Parish Guide, 2018. http://www.stanthonyofpadua.org.uk.

St. Benet's Hall, Oxford. "History of St Benet's Hall." https://www.st-benets.ox.ac.uk/history, archived December 7, 2021.

St. Chad's Cathedral. "The History of St. Chad's." https://www.stchadscathedral.org.uk/cathedral/history/.

St. Dunstan and St. Jude. "A Short History of St Dunstan's Church." https://www.stdunstanandstjude.co.uk/st-dunstan-s.

St. Gregory and St. Augustine. Parish Chronicle: "The History of the Parish" and "Fr Richard's Centenary Sermon." https://www.ssgregoryandaugustine.org/.

St. John, Ambrose. *The Raccolta; or, Collection of Indulgenced Prayers.* 5th ed. London: Burns, Oates, 1880.

Stephens, W.B., ed. *A History of the County of Warwick.* Vol. 7, *The City of Birmingham.* London: Victoria County History, 1964. *British History Online.* https://www.british-history.ac.uk/vch/warks/vol7.

Sutcliffe, Peter. *The Oxford University Press: An Informal History.* Oxford: Oxford University Press, 1978.

Sutherland, John. *Mrs Humphry Ward: Eminent Victorian, Pre-Eminent Edwardian.* Oxford: Oxford University Press, 1990.

Sweeney, Morgan V. "Diocesan Organisation and Administration." In *The English Catholics*, edited by George Andrew Beck, 116–50.

Szylak, Pawel. "Our Lady of Częstochowa, Queen of Poland." *Godzdogz: The blog of the Dominican Friars of Scotland, England & Wales.* May 2, 2014. https://www.english.op.org/.

Taking Stock: Catholic Churches of England & Wales. "Bromsgrove—St Peter." https://www.taking-stock.org.uk/building/bromsgrove-st-peter/.

Tallett, Frank, and Nicholas Atkin, eds. *Catholicism in Britain and France Since 1789.* London: Hambledon, 1996.

Taunton, Ethelred. *The Law of the Church: A Cyclopædia of Canon Law for English-Speaking Countries.* London: Kegan Paul, Trench, Trübner & Co., 1906.

Taylor, A.J.P. *English History 1914–1945.* Vol. 15 of *The Oxford History of England*, edited by Sir George Clark. Oxford: Oxford University Press, 1965.

Thompson, Gavin, Oliver Hawkins, Aliyah Dar, Mark Taylor, et al. *Olympic Britain: Social and economic change since the 1908 and 1948 London Games.* London: House of Commons Library, 2012.

Thurston, Herbert. "The Royal Declaration." In *The Catholic Encyclopedia*, vol. 13 (1912). http://www.newadvent.org/cathen/13213a.htm.

Thwaite, Ann, ed. *My Oxford.* London: Robson Books, 1977.

Tower, Canon Mervyn. "History of the Church." Corpus Christi, Headington. https://www.corpuschristiheadington.co.uk/church-history/.

Tristram, Henry. *Cardinal Newman and the Church of the Birmingham Oratory: A History and a Guide.* Gloucester: The British Publishing Company, 1934.

Türks, Paul. *Philip Neri: The Fire of Joy.* Translated by Daniel Utrecht of the Oratory. New York: Alba House, 1995.

Turner, F.M. "Religion." In *The History of the University of Oxford*, vol. 8, *The Twentieth Century*, edited by Brian Harrison, 293–316.

University of Oxford. "Facts and figures." https://www.ox.ac.uk/about/facts-and-figures.

———. "Organisation." https://www.ox.ac.uk/about/organisation.

Ward, Maisie. *Father Maturin: A Memoir with Selected Letters.* London: Longmans, Green, 1920.

Ward-Penny, Christine. *Images of England: Catholics in Birmingham.* Stroud, UK: Tempus, 2004.

Waugh, Evelyn. *Ronald Knox.* In *Two Lives.* London: Continuum, 2001. First published 1959.

Wilkinson, Alan. *The Church of England and the First World War.* London: SPCK, 1978.

Winter, J.M. "Oxford and the First World War." In *The History of the University of Oxford*, vol. 8, *The Twentieth Century*, edited by Brian Harrison, 3–25.

BIBLICAL INDEX

New Testament

GENERAL INDEX

Works by J.R.R. Tolkien appear in bold type